Handbook of Research on User Experience in Web 2.0 Technologies and Its Impact on Universities and Businesses

Jean-Éric Pelet
ESCE International Business School, INSEEC U Research Center, Paris, France

A volume in the Advances in Business Information
Systems and Analytics (ABISA) Book Series

Published in the United States of America by
IGI Global
Business Science Reference (an imprint of IGI Global)
701 E. Chocolate Avenue
Hershey PA, USA 17033
Tel: 717-533-8845
Fax: 717-533-8661
E-mail: cust@igi-global.com
Web site: http://www.igi-global.com

Library of Congress Cataloging-in-Publication Data

Names: Pelet, Jean-Éric, 1976- editor.
Title: Handbook of research on user experience in web 2.0 technologies and its
    impact on universities and businesses / Jean-Éric Pelet, editor.
Description: Hershey, PA : Business Science Reference, [2020] | Includes
    bibliographical references and index. | Summary: "This book explores the
    role of user experience in e-commerce, e-learning, and web 2.0
    technologies. It also examines their impact on businesses and
    universities"-- Provided by publisher.
Identifiers: LCCN 2019058368 (print) | LCCN 2019058369 (ebook) | ISBN
    9781799837565 (hardcover) | ISBN 9781799837589 (ebook)
Subjects: LCSH: Human-computer interaction. | User-centered system design.
    | Web 2.0. | Electronic commerce. | Internet in higher education.
Classification: LCC QA76.9.H85 U84 2020 (print) | LCC QA76.9.H85 (ebook)
    | DDC 004.01/9--dc23
LC record available at https://lccn.loc.gov/2019058368
LC ebook record available at https://lccn.loc.gov/2019058369

This book is published in the IGI Global book series Advances in Business Information Systems and Analytics (ABISA) (ISSN: 2327-3275; eISSN: 2327-3283)

British Cataloguing in Publication Data
A Cataloguing in Publication record for this book is available from the British Library.

All work contributed to this book is new, previously-unpublished material. The views expressed in this book are those of the authors, but not necessarily of the publisher.

For electronic access to this publication, please contact: eresources@igi-global.com.

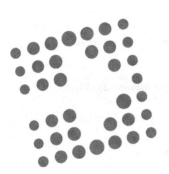

Advances in Business Information Systems and Analytics (ABISA) Book Series

Madjid Tavana
La Salle University, USA

ISSN:2327-3275
EISSN:2327-3283

MISSION

The successful development and management of information systems and business analytics is crucial to the success of an organization. New technological developments and methods for data analysis have allowed organizations to not only improve their processes and allow for greater productivity, but have also provided businesses with a venue through which to cut costs, plan for the future, and maintain competitive advantage in the information age.

The **Advances in Business Information Systems and Analytics (ABISA) Book Series** aims to present diverse and timely research in the development, deployment, and management of business information systems and business analytics for continued organizational development and improved business value.

COVERAGE

- Business Models
- Geo-BIS
- Data Strategy
- Management Information Systems
- Big Data
- Statistics
- Data Analytics
- Business Information Security
- Data Management
- Business Intelligence

IGI Global is currently accepting manuscripts for publication within this series. To submit a proposal for a volume in this series, please contact our Acquisition Editors at Acquisitions@igi-global.com or visit: http://www.igi-global.com/publish/.

Titles in this Series

For a list of additional titles in this series, please visit:
https://www.igi-global.com/book-series/advances-business-information-systems-analytics/37155

Achieving Organizational Agility, Intelligence, and Resilience Through Information Systems
Hakikur Rahman (Institute of Computer Management and Science, Bangladesh)
Business Science Reference • © 2021 • 300pp • H/C (ISBN: 9781799847991) • US $195.00

Empowering Businesses With Collaborative Enterprise Architecture Frameworks
Tiko Iyamu (Cape Peninsula University of Technology, South Africa)
Business Science Reference • © 2021 • 309pp • H/C (ISBN: 9781522582298) • US $195.00

Natural Language Processing for Global and Local Business
Fatih Pinarbasi (Istanbul Medipol University, Turkey) and M. Nurdan Taskiran (Istanbul Medipol University, Turkey)
Business Science Reference • © 2021 • 452pp • H/C (ISBN: 9781799842408) • US $225.00

Applications of Big Data and Business Analytics in Management
Sneha Kumari (Vaikunth Mehta National Institute of Cooperative Management, India) K. K. Tripathy (Vaikunth Mehta National Institute of Cooperative Management, India) and Vidya Kumbhar (Symbiosis International University (Deemed), India)
Business Science Reference • © 2020 • 300pp • H/C (ISBN: 9781799832614) • US $225.00

Handbook of Research on Integrating Industry 4.0 in Business and Manufacturing
Isak Karabegović (Academy of Sciences and Arts of Bosnia and Herzegovina, Bosnia and Herzegovina) Ahmed Kovačević (City, University London, UK) Lejla Banjanović-Mehmedović (University of Tuzla, Bosnia and Herzegovina) and Predrag Dašić (High Technical Mechanical School of Professional Studies in Trstenik, Serbia)
Business Science Reference • © 2020 • 661pp • H/C (ISBN: 9781799827252) • US $265.00

Internet of Things (IoT) Applications for Enterprise Productivity
Erdinç Koç (Bingol University, Turkey)
Business Science Reference • © 2020 • 357pp • H/C (ISBN: 9781799831754) • US $215.00

Trends and Issues in International Planning for Businesses
Babayemi Adekunle (Arden University, UK) Husam Helmi Alharahsheh (University of Wales Trinity Saint David, UK) and Abraham Pius (Arden University, UK)
Business Science Reference • © 2020 • 225pp • H/C (ISBN: 9781799825470) • US $225.00

701 East Chocolate Avenue, Hershey, PA 17033, USA
Tel: 717-533-8845 x100 • Fax: 717-533-8661
E-Mail: cust@igi-global.com • www.igi-global.com

List of Contributors

Table of Contents

Detailed Table of Contents

Chapter 1

Jean-Éric Pelet, ESCE International Business School, INSEEC U Research Center, Paris, France

The design of interfaces has become an essential dimension of companies' digital strategies, aiming at enhancing user experiences through User Experience goals, alternatively named UX. From user tests to front-end development, UX now affects all areas of digital production. This book presents relevant and recent studies conducted in various fields, from Marketing to Information Systems over Human Resource Management to Strategic Management. Its objective is to provide up-to-date results in relation to UX concerns, which exist in both e-learning and e-commerce. It is composed of 20 chapters and contains the most recent findings in research, as well as case studies and relevant works conducted by experts in User Experience, from the field of e-learning to e-commerce. 40 authors from Australia, China, France, Germany, Italy, Japan, Nigeria, Portugal, Romania, Spain, Switzerland, Tunisia, Turkey and the United Kingdom present their case studies, practical experiences, and studies on User Experience and its impact on universities and businesses.

Chapter 2

Anabela Mesquita, Instituto Superior de Contabilidade e Administracao do Porto,
Polytechnic of Porto, Portugal
Paulino Silva, Polytechnic of Porto, Portugal

One of the key factors to be successful in the job market is to detain the right and needed knowledge and competences, being these hard or transversals (e.g., communication, negotiation, leadership, creativity, proactivity, responsibility, just to name a few). Experiential learning, problem-based learning, and game-based learning are pedagogical methods that allow students to consolidate the technical competences but also to develop the necessary soft skills in order to be employable in the Society 4.0. Among the solution offered is the business simulation that can be defined as an instrument that transforms the real business world in a simplified model enabling students to make decisions and simulate activities as if they were in a real business environment, without any risks. In this chapter, the authors describe a business simulation used in a higher education institution in Portugal. They analyze this simulation in terms of experiential learning and problem-based learning and draw some reflections about the results as this might be inspiring for other teachers/trainers.

Chapter 3

Anabela Mesquita, Polytechnic of Porto, Portugal & Algoritmi RC, Portugal

Luciana Oliveira, CEOS.PP ISCAP, Polytechnic of Porto, Portugal

Adriana Oliveira, CEOS.PP ISCAP, Polytechnic of Porto, Portugal

Arminda Sequeira, CEOS.PP ISCAP, Polytechnic of Porto, Portugal

Paulino Silva, CEOS.PP ISCAP, Polytechnic of Porto, Portugal

Changes brought by the 4th Industrial Revolution and digitalization impact directly in the way we live, shape the organizations, and change the way we work. These changes imply some challenges in the preparation of youngsters to work in such an environment due to their characteristics. All over Europe, and in order to anticipate the scope and depth of the impacts that current and emerging technologies are imposing, some projects and initiatives are being carried out. The aim of this chapter is to subsidize a reflection about this complex environment by discussing the possible changes brought by the technologies and present some of these initiatives aiming to prepare students to thrive in this world of work.

Chapter 4

Liudmila Bredikhina, Geneva University, Switzerland

The impact of fonts on user experience and brand perception has been widely discussed by a variety of specialists. In 2016 a new technology called variable fonts came out with a promise of lighter font files, responsiveness, variability, and adaptability on the web across devices. This chapter reminds users of parameters that should be taken into account when choosing a font and discuss ways in which brands can implement variable fonts to increase their performance. Unique perspective on variable fonts from specialist in different domains related to variable fonts and their implementation will be proposed in this chapter as it aims to focus on providing unique insider knowledge on currently developing projects that implement this new technology as well as on ideas and possibilities that might interest future e-learning and e-business brands.

Chapter 5

Reinaldo Padilha França, State University of Campinas (UNICAMP), Brazil

Ana Carolina Borges Monteiro, State University of Campinas (UNICAMP), Brazil

Rangel Arthur, Faculty of Technology (FT), State University of Campinas (UNICAMP), Brazil

Yuzo Iano, State University of Campinas (UNICAMP), Brazil

Web 2.0 is the evolution of the web. Seen as a new and second movement of access to information through the world wide web, Web 2.0 brings interactivity and collaboration as the main keys to its functioning. It is now possible and simpler and faster to send information at any time, by any user connected to the internet. The ease of uploading information, images, and videos on the Web 2.0 is due to the expansion of resources and codes, allowing anyone to be able to act naturally and take their own content to the internet. As the data and information shared daily is almost infinite, the search engines act even more intuitively and bring only results tailored to each user. Therefore, this chapter aims to provide an updated review and overview of Web 2.0, addressing its evolution and fundamental concepts, showing its relationship, as well as approaching its success with a concise bibliographic background, categorizing and synthesizing the potential of technology.

Chapter 6

Jialei Li, Dongbei University of Finance and Economics, China
Tao Meng, Dongbei University of Finance and Economics, China
Chunying Li, Dongbei University of Finance and Economics, China

The sharing economy has developed very quickly. However, organizations like Airbnb and Uber have encountered crisis of trust. Academia still does not know what is the type of trust in sharing economy organizations. Therefore, the authors designed two studies, used data from Airbnb, to test 2 hypotheses: (1) the level of inter-organizational trust in sharing economy organizations is relatively positive to the level of participation, and (2) the price of the product or service being shared is relatively negative to the level of participation. The results find out that consumers are more willing to choose non-shared renting methods in China, yet the opposite in America. Under both conditions, price is an important moderator. This shows that the role of trust in China is mainly inter-organizational trust, but interpersonal in America. The theoretical contribution is to reveal the type of trust in the sharing economy organizations, collaborative relations and studies of Airbnb.

Chapter 7

Coralie Haller, EM Strasbourg Business School, University of Strasbourg, France
Benjamin Louis, Région Grand Est, France

Wine regions constantly question their visibility on the internet to fully be able to embrace the 3.0 digitalization. Recent controversy of the geographic domain name ".vin" and ".wine" has raised awareness of the need to be proactive in Internet naming. The objective of the chapter is to understand how wine regions could develop a digital territory strategy to increase their competitive advantage by using specific geographic domain name. The chapter provides an overview of origin, role, and functioning of stakeholders involved in the internet naming industry. The specific case of Alsace wine region has been investigated with a specific focus on the digital wine territory strategy based on the development of the "wine.alsace."

Chapter 8

Anabela Mesquita, Polytechnic of Porto, Portugal & Algoritmi RC, Portugal
Luciana Oliveira, CEOS.PP ISCAP, Polytechnic of Porto, Portugal
Arminda Sa Sequeira, CEOS.PP ISCAP, Polytechnic of Porto, Portugal

People and organizations have been witnessing tremendous changes taking place in the job market. Technologies (ex. AI, machine learning, IoT) are pushing individuals away from their comfort zone and forcing them to adapt, to develop new skills and to reinvent their job positions. Reports on the changes in the workplace and on the workforce have been raising concerns about the potential of AI to replace humans in job positions. The current challenges, brought by the 4th IR, have been providing countless opportunities for business growth, optimization and internationalization; however, tremendous concerns are currently raised regarding the sustainability of the human resources which are currently on the market and of those who are being trained to enter it. In this chapter, the authors focus on administrative job positions, which have been pointed out as one of the most prone to be taken over by AI and identify the already available technologies that can perform the job description tasks, as a current diagnose of the profession.

Wine consumption becomes more informed, smart, and connected. A website is a vitrine for wineries providing better visibility and higher attractiveness toward visitors, buyers, and business partners. Due to the increasing competition on the wine market, it is important to assess the digital development of wineries. Yet, there is no common instrument to evaluate website development of wineries. This research aims to create an evaluation grid adapted for European wineries website based on the extended Model of Internet Commerce Adoption (eMICA) and the model of Davidson. The grid comprises 108 attributes organized under eleven dimensions. A quantitative methodology based on a questionnaire was developed to evaluate user-experience of wineries websites of 255 consumers. This approach allowed to validate a grid that might be used to analyze and benchmark the digital advancement within the specific context of the French wine industry.

The use of technological devices has become natural, which is why technology seems to become a natural learning environment. Many studies show that technologically-rich learning environments improve learning outcomes. It has been shown that technological integration helps to create more authentic learning environments, in which students are more motivated to participate. Digital world has greater opportunities for communication, collaboration, and problem-solving and have more opportunities to expand and even amplify thinking, thus changing the role of students by building knowledge rather than reproducing information. Given the possible disadvantages of using digital devices permanently, it is important to find a good balance between constructively using digital technology and keeping it to avoid distraction and concentration. However, some research shows that electronic learning does not differ in effectiveness or efficiency from traditional learning. This chapter presents an in-depth and reasoned analysis of cognitive learning of university students using Web 2.0 tools.

Chapter 11

The impact of increasing advancement in digital technologies is driving massive changes in contemporary business enterprises affecting every dimension of society, especially the way individuals buy, research, and interact with one another and with leading brands. This chapter explores case studies of specific leading brands to illustrate this principle with the purpose of better understanding how end-to-end customer experiences (CXs) can be maintained and improved. It begins with a detailed example of the cost of not adapting to the evolving changes in consumer behaviour, specifically the expectations of new generations of "digital natives" with a focus on the user experience (UX). This is followed by an analysis of six customer experience (CX) principles that deliver value, relevance, and superior CXs. Finally, this chapter highlights the importance of embracing a holistic customer-centric culture and offers valuable considerations for businesses seeking to make customer experience their new competitive advantage.

Chapter 12

The end of the 20th century was marked by the advent of the internet along with the transformation of the consumer behavior into an information behavior. As a matter of fact, our daily life becomes centered on a multitude of informational exhibitions through which brands have invested this cutting-edge information technology, tending for delivering the perfect service by adopting the multichannel communication strategies. The advent of interactive marketing has brought new features to the web, allowing online companies to configure websites and manage smarter, more social, and more personalized interactions and communications. Accordingly, this chapter aims to make a synthetic study of the concept of online interactivity and to present a review of the literature, and to better explain the concept and to how to achieve the role of Web 3.0.

Chapter 13

There are 1,518,207,412 websites in the world as of January 2019. These websites can be a personal, commercial, government, or non-profit organisation website. Websites are typically dedicated to a particular topic or purpose, ranging from entertainment and social networking to providing news and education. Blogs are another form of website and they have been in use for years, but it is more recently that teachers are including them as a learning tool in the classroom – as it provides many positive aspects to their students. When speaking about blogging in the classroom, we are running away from the academic writing and practising informal writing, which in many occasions takes off pressure and gives a voice to our students in a 'safe environment'. This does not mean that it may be also used to publish assignments and essays, which do contribute to share and educate in particular topics and to practice writing.

The reasons for introducing Web 2.0 tools into the business area are multiple, from efficiency to better time management. The provision of online services by companies develops the computer skills of team members, and the materials provided through Web tools 2.0 can be accessed by a larger number of end users and their quality can be permanently evaluated. This chapter proposes to investigate the motivational factors of the usage of Web tools 2.0 by companies' team members. In particular, the research is focused on e-learning based on Web 2.0 tools for training sessions organized by companies in Romania. The in-depth analysis revealed that this generally positive perception of using the e-learning course is founded on a series of objective aspects, identified in a multiple linear regression model, ranging from the perception of the benefit of professional development to the subjective character given by user experience (UX).

User experience (UX) measurement has become a powerful component in determining the usability success or failure of products or services that are marketed via e-business channels. Succcess in the e-business does not only depend on building stellar software interfaces but also on competitive receptiveness to customers experience or feedback. Only e-businesses that can effectively measure the UX to forecast and understand the future are able to stay afloat and not get drown in the highly competitive market. The development of various UX metrics and measurement techniques have helped to quantify user feedack but most of these rely on different contextual assumptions. As a result, choosing appropriate UX techniques that match a particular business need becomes difficult for most e-business concerns. This chapter provides an overview of recent UX measurement techniques that are relevant to the e-business settings in the Web 2.0 era. The objective is to elaborate on what tools that have been employed in literature to measure UX and possibly how these can be employed in practice.

Although the sharing economy's commercial practice is booming, the study on the formation mechanism is fragmented. This chapter captures a whole picture of sharing economy's research and gives suggestions for future interesting studies. Based on the method of the Prisma protocol for systematic literature review, with the help of CiteSpace software, the authors map out the structure of existing literature. Current research found out that sharing economy as a new organization model is the current developing trend, sharing economy could be a strong method in the organization's management area. The definition of sharing economy can be included as a new economic phenomenon based on the internet, including peer-to-peer-based activities of obtaining, giving, or sharing the access to goods and services to maximize the utilization. This chapter concluded the connotation of sharing economy, based on the resource view, property right view, and technique view, and several future research plans are generated.

Web 2.0 technologies refer to useful and modern tools to motivate students for actively engaging in learning activities. However, there are difficulties to Web 2.0 technologies adoption among university students. Understanding users' motivation could enhance the adoption of Web 2.0 technologies. The aim of this chapter was to use the multivariate methods to quantitative describe the student's user experience (UX) regarding the acceptance of Web 2.0 technologies in higher education. An excellent validity of the structural model for testing the intention to use Web 2.0 technologies by university students was revealed. The data indicate that the intrinsic motivation was composed by users' expectations and educational aspirations. Moreover, the findings revealed that the extrinsic motivation can influence the intention to use Web 2.0 educational tools. This study completed the current knowledge on behavioral intention to use digital tools across university students and released new opportunities for UX investigations.

E-commerce is expected to see considerable growth in the next years anywhere all over the world. A trend that has been accelerated by the COVID-19. To succeed in this increasingly global and increasingly competitive landscape, e-commerce companies need to attract more and more traffic, the condition for getting clients. The questions "How important is UX for increasing the e-commerce sales?" and "Do geography and culture impact the UX performance?" are therefore essential. This chapter on the one hand analyzes the specific e-commerce UX elements and dimensions, and on the other hand compares strengths and weaknesses in Europe, Asia, Africa, North and South America to find UX international best practices. Keywords: Ecommerce, Online Sales, Cross-Border, International, Marketplaces, Geo-Cultural Adaptation, Ux Elements, Ux Dimensions, Worldwide, Global

Non-profit organizations are becoming aware of the resourcefulness of Web 2.0 in terms of user engagement, communication, collaboration, and fundraising. Nonetheless, within the context of these organizations, the full potential of Web 2.0 technologies remains unrealized. This chapter explores the aspects that contribute to the successful implementation of Web 2.0 in non-profit organizations by using a case study of an international non-profit entity. The case study is based on an online questionnaire that was distributed among the members of the organization. The findings place an emphasis on the importance of the user-friendliness of the application, the participation of the users, on the availability of relevant content, and on the existence of features to create/exchange content in a multiplicity of formats.

Preface

The Importance of User Experience Feedback in Design

Design is a process of thinking, involves both creativity and an interdisciplinary conception that makes propositions and conducts experiments. Moreover, design applies a methodological approach, employs practical tools, is critical and reflexive, makes assumptions, and tries to find solutions to problems that surround us (Design & Digital Lab, 2019). Irrespective of the project, it articulates relationships with the world in search for meaning of different systems: human, societal, and environmental. It offers macro and micro visions of the project. The creative field in which design takes place questions evolving scientific approaches and emerging professional fields, in relation to socio-cultural, economic, technological and industrial changes. These changes make the designer conceive and give meaning to new uses between spaces, products, interactions, information, images, experiences, and services. It thus defines the way in which people, products and services interact in a specific context. The approaches and methodologies applied vary, according to the context of the project. The Design Thinking (Buchanan, 1992) is based on practical experiences, basic knowledge, and an observation of the uses and (potential) users, a diagnosis of the encountered problems.

Design studies give shape to our daily lives, determine the qualities and values of our interactions with the world and thus shape current or future uses of interfaces. In shaping our daily lives and the scenario in which products or services are used, aesthetics is mobilized in the creation of sensitive and graphic universes: it conveys a semantic language, which makes it possible to identify the values of an experience, a service, or a brand.

Design modifies and animates new industries and systems of production from a digital perspective. It offers new services, new ways of interacting and consuming, and new business models.

UI and UX

The UX (User Experience) design aims to make the experience of interaction as pleasant as possible by thinking about the experience before creating the product (Lallemand, 2016: 1). UX design finds its sources in the User Centered Design (Norman and Draper, 1986) and is particularly interested in the usability, the analysis of activities, and the assessment of user needs The development of Human Machine Interactions (HMI) or People - System Interfaces (PSI has contributed to the need for research on ergonomic usability criteria (Bastien and Scapin, Nielson 1993). Initially, "paper prototypes" tried to focus on the appreciation of interactive environments on computers or mobile phones. Now UX Design is applied to the process of designing and developing usable interfaces more extensively. The integration of this process essentially leads to designs which generate, promote, and improve user experience. It is about identifying and promoting the product's sensation of its grip, its cognitive ergonomics, the feeling during its use, and the fulfillment of user goals. This takes into consideration the quality of interactions in a context of global use (Alben, 1996).

Hassenzahl and Tractinsky (2006) define UX as "a consequence of the internal state of a user (predisposition, expectations, needs, motivation, mood, etc.), characteristics of the system designed (complexity, purpose, usability, functionality, etc..) and the context (or environment) in which the interaction takes place (organizational / social framework, sense of activity, willingness to use, etc.)" (p. 95).

The project in UX design then mobilizes a multidisciplinary approach and involves ergonomics, psychology, engineering, design, sociology, ethnography, etc. in an iterative design process. The back and forth between the phases of exploration, ideation, evaluation and generation of prototypes makes it possible to explore and evaluate the needs of potential users as closely as possible. UX is applicable to any design project starting at its planning phase. The development of the product and service integrates the users throughout the different design stages, according to various evaluations, which essentially stem from the understanding of the contexts of use and the user requirements. The whole experiences are taken into account; they relate to the performance and functionality of the system, where users are considered in accordance with their habits, personalities and skills. Hassenzahl's model shows different perspectives in the design of an interface, with respect to the individual and the situation in which they are in. Indeed, while the designer is more interested in product characteristics (content, presentation, functionality, interaction), users are more interested in the consequences of use in a specific situation. They are attached to the pragmatic and hedonic values involved: attractiveness, pleasure and satisfaction of use. Finally, the more pleasant and easy the access to the content, the more the user is satisfied: it saves his/her time and moves him/her within the content in a pleasant way. These precepts of use, aesthetics, functionality, and ergonomics are applicable in any type of field. The eXperience user (UX) is intrinsically linked to the UI (User Interface = IU). UX depends on the composition of the interface: harmony of space, hierarchy of information, aesthetic choices, visual qualities, cognitive ergonomics, fluidity of movement, etc. Thus, facilitated access to a product or a service via an application partly determines purchases. For example, we can notice a different use of the SNCF website from its application. One offers access to the train ticket in more than 5 clicks, whereas the mobile apps lead to the train ticket in no more than 3 clicks. It represents both a significant comfort for the user in a hurry, but also a gain in clarity. Let us take another example, i.e. the experience with Airbnb. The application offers customers to book a house, apartment or room with a local. The service is characterized by valuing the experience of the resident who rents their property and offers travelers the benefit of exploring a city or town from the angle of a local. The user benefits from the provision of addresses of restaurants, sights, and local residents' activities. The act of sharing is crucial, which personalizes the stay. The added value is both human and experiential; exchanges and tips are transmitted with great care, because the user enters into the habits of their host, neighborhood, bars, grocery store, places to be visited. The trip has a vernacular aspect and is adorned with a very singular flavor. Airbnb explores here the usage paths and uses all the feedback from residents as well as that of travelers who rate and leave their opinion on their experiences. The host is in an abyss, and, at the same time, subject to the pleasure of their guests. The host may change their home or decoration of their apartment, according to the customers' wishes.

UX and Learning

In the field of learning, digital technology brings about major transformations on two levels: access to educational content and student perception. The web offers ample access to knowledge; its formatting and its access remain fundamental in the transmission of knowledge. Online courses adopt rich formats (videos, articles, books, animations, videos), and are not always suitable for access optimization. We find 2-hour lectures filmed in university amphitheaters, content selections for courses in the form of literature reviews on scoop.it, interviews, PDF or online Powerpoint and lecture formats of MOOC types (Massive Open Online Courses). Participating in the implementation of MOOC on a ministerial platform as FUN (note: https://www.fun-mooc.fr/) captures the difficulty of staging and the adaptability of content for formats specific to online videos. However, these systems show a lack of accessibility for people with disabilities, especially people with cognitive disorders. Scientists from INRIA Bordeaux, experts in cognitive disability and accessibility (team Potïoc), have co-designed with cognitively deficient students, a prototype reader named MOOC entitled Aïana[1]. With the dissemination of a MOOC on the national FUN platform, the team tested the reader and evaluated its effectiveness with a fairly large sample of participants (N = 1087, 150 of whom declared a handicap). The reader is subject to design criteria determined with the help of students with special needs. In this context, efficiency refers to learning performance, the cognitive load, self-determination, usability, and efficiency of interactions "person system". The results confirm the good usability of the reader, a positive impact on learning and support for self-determination for people with disabilities, especially those with cognitive impairments. The reader thus reinforces the relevance of the design principles implemented (Cinquin, 2019).

In education, the analysis of student feedback regarding their use of digital tools integrated into the course is necessary in order to measure their impact. The objective consists essentially in evaluating the pedagogical usefulness of these tools and the user experience. This is the case for digital tablets or opendatas (Lehmans, Cardoso, 2017). With the LID[2] New Aquitaine Region research program [2] (Laboratory of Innovative Design Practices, Cardoso & al. 2016-2020), we have built "student's experience feedback" through interview guides and questionnaires established on the AttrakDiff model (Hassenzahl, Burmester, & Koller, 2003). This study was supplemented by an anthropological analysis of the video recordings of the courses (Fig. 1); its aim was to complete the quantitative data.

The LID represents experimental research in design applied to pedagogy. The LID team is composed of researchers (ICS, Information and Communication Science, Education Science, Design) and designers who have co-designed educational scenarios with teachers and students of the preceding promotion in using unpublished immersive digital tools: an immersive 3D dome (Fig. 2), a touch screen table and screen (Fig. 3). One of the objectives was to verify if there is a correlation between the screenwriting of an optimal experience (Csíkszentmihályi, 1996) and the design of educational scenarios focusing on the student and on improved learning conditions.

Overall, the results of the program show a good appreciation of digital tools and a very favorable student-teacher collaboration. It remains difficult to distinguish between these data and the role played by the teacher (mediator, accompanist, absent), the pedagogical scenario designed to engage students in acquiring skills as well as methodological or theoretical content, the collaboration between groups of students, the group atmosphere, the motivation and pleasure of learning (for each individual and for the group).

Figure 1. Practical Master Course and Engineering in Lecturing, ESPE Aquitaine. Extract from the LID uses catalog, anthropological analyzes.

Figure 2. First pedagogical experiments within LID (Laboratory of Innovative Design Practices) - (HYVE 3D, Hybridlab Inc, Canada), teachers in the Bachelor program of Contemporary History, Bordeaux Montaigne University, MSHA, 2016

Design is positioned at the heart of the LID "research-action" project as a space of mediation, because it offers a tangible space for dialogue that links scientific approaches in ICS (Information and Communication Sciences), Education and Cognitive Psychology, in particular. The experiences of learners enrich the results and improve the reception of courses. Our team has translated these experiences in the form of storyboards (Fig. 3) and graphics statements. Here, UX feedback is all the more important that it includes teachers and students in the co-creation of knowledge and its assimilation. Hence, it involves satisfaction in education and learning.

Figure 3. Same as Fig. 2 / Touch screen table and screen (Société Immersion, Bordeaux), Master design students: innovation, interaction, service, Bordeaux Montaigne University, MSHA, 2017

Figure 4. An extract from a storyboard produced for the needs of the program as part of a Master in Archeology.

This preface pointed out some of the challenges of UX design, relating to e-commerce on websites and apps, as well as different forms of digital learning. These are topics that we will find in the following chapters. Interest in the consequences of using an environment, a service, or a product, requires the ability to (re) work on its design. UX therefore requires agility and regular reviews of user needs. This approach encompasses the consideration of changes and evolutions in social and societal practices. The powers of UX design are substantial; they attract, captivate and enchant users around products or services. UX makes us think and design in accordance with user needs. In this sense, one should realize that the designer is subject to the measurement of feedbacks from the latter. This profoundly changes the ways of designing products and services.

Stéphanie Cardoso
EA MICA Laboratory, Bordeaux-Montaigne University, France

REFERENCES

Alben, L. (1996). Quality of experience: Defining the criteria for effective interaction design. *Interaction, 3*(3), 11–15. doi:10.1145/235008.235010

Bastien, J. M. C., & Scapin, D. (1993). *Ergonomic Criteria for the Evaluation of Human-Computer interfaces*. National Institute for Research in Computer Science and Automation.

Cinquin, P.-A. (2019). *Design, integration and validation of digital education systems accessible to people with cognitive disabilities* (Doctoral thesis). INRIA, University of Bordeaux, Bordeaux.

Csíkszentmihályi, M. (1996). *Creativity: flow and the Psychology of Discovery and Invention*. Harper Perennial.

Hassenzahl, M., Burmester, M., & Koller, F. (2003). AttrakDiff: Ein Fragebogen zur mes- sung wahrgenommener hedonischer und pragma5scher Qualität. In J. Ziegler & G. Szwillus (Eds.), *Mensch & Computer 2003. Interaktion in Bewegung* (pp. 187–196). BG Teubner. doi:10.1007/978-3-322-80058-9_19

Hassenzahl, M., & Tractinsky, N. (2006). User experience research. A research agenda. Behavor and Information Technology, 25(2).

Lallemand, C., & Grenier, G. (2006). *UX design methods*. Eyrolles.

Lallemand, C., Koenig, V., Gronier, G., & Marion, R. (2015). Creation and validation of a version of French 's questionnaire AttrakDiff for the evaluation of the experience user systems interfaces, review. *European Psychology Applied*.

Lehmans, A., & Cardoso, S. (2017). Datvisualization of open data and educational design in knowledge formats. In *Proceedings of the conference Digital in the era of designs, hypertext, hyper-experience H2PTM'17*. ISTE Editions.

ENDNOTES

[1]   https://www.aiana.fr
[2]   https://lab-design-pedagogie.com

Chapter 1
Introduction to the Book:
User Experience in Web 2.0 Technologies and Its Impact on Universities and Businesses

Jean-Éric Pelet

https://orcid.org/0000-0001-7069-8131

ESCE International Business School, INSEEC U Research Center, Paris, France

ABSTRACT

The design of interfaces has become an essential dimension of companies' digital strategies, aiming at enhancing user experiences through User Experience goals, alternatively named UX. From user tests to front-end development, UX now affects all areas of digital production. This book presents relevant and recent studies conducted in various fields, from Marketing to Information Systems over Human Resource Management to Strategic Management. Its objective is to provide up-to-date results in relation to UX concerns, which exist in both e-learning and e-commerce. It is composed of 20 chapters and contains the most recent findings in research, as well as case studies and relevant works conducted by experts in User Experience, from the field of e-learning to e-commerce. 40 authors from Australia, China, France, Germany, Italy, Japan, Nigeria, Portugal, Romania, Spain, Switzerland, Tunisia, Turkey and the United Kingdom present their case studies, practical experiences, and studies on User Experience and its impact on universities and businesses.

INTRODUCTION

The design of interfaces has become an essential dimension of companies' digital strategies, aiming at enhancing user experiences through User Experience goals, alternatively named UX. How has UX evolved, what are the current developments and what will be the future changes? How to implement it and why put the user at the center of its concerns? From user tests to front-end development, UX now affects all areas of digital production.

DOI: 10.4018/978-1-7998-3756-5.ch001

This book presents relevant and recent studies conducted in various fields, from Marketing to Information Systems over Human Resource Management to Strategic Management. Its objective is to provide up-to-date results in relation to UX concerns, which exist in both e-learning and e-commerce.

There is a slight difference between UX and ergonomics. The UX design approach is user-centered, while the ergonomic approach is anthropocentric. In both cases, practitioners will try to achieve common goals, such as anticipating user needs, defining services and functionalities, gaining knowledge in cognitive, human, and social sciences as well as creating a toolbox to observe and analyze consumers' expectations and usages (in using A/B tests, for example). Practitioners will also design interfaces and, from a multidisciplinary perspective, will draw upon different actors from different fields, like engineers, managers, designers, entrepreneurs, and artists. They make proposals to render the usage of these interfaces more efficient and, hence, increase the performance of the company.

Ergonomics no longer concerns only the professional world. UX could also be considered for software, such as office suits for people working on computers. Web ergonomics consists of optimizing the interaction between the site interface and its users, visitors and administrators, according to Usabilis (2020). To be ergonomic, a website, or an app, must present a utility, that is, serve the activity of the user, have a meaning in relation to its objectives and usability, which encompasses everything that allows users to use it easily, quickly, and effectively, without any error. This concept is based on three parameters which are efficacy, efficiency and satisfaction. **Mesquita and Silva (2020)** argue in their chapter **"Are we ready for the job market? The role of business simulation in the preparation of youngsters"** that one of the key factors to be successful in the job market is to be prepared to face the challenges equipped with the appropriate and required knowledge and competences, whether hard or transversal. Traditionally, education was focused on the acquisition of knowledge or technical skills, but over the last few decades, teachers and trainers have realized that students will be better prepared if they also develop transversal skills. The reason is that their work environment is becoming increasingly challenging and is changing at a very fast pace.

Experiential learning is a pedagogical approach that allows students to consolidate technical competences, while developing the necessary soft ones. Among the solutions offered by such softwares there is business simulation, which is defined as an instrument transforming the real business world into a simplified model and, therefore, enabling students to make decisions and simulate activities as if they were in a real business environment, without assuming any risks. **Mesquita and Silva (2020)** describe a business simulation used in a higher education institution in Portugal. They analyze this simulation based on the underlying theory and confirm that it meets the requirements of the pedagogical approaches used. They also show how such a simulation can contribute to the development of students' essential skills.

The user performs the desired action on the site in a simple way. They do it quickly, without complicated learning processes or mistakes that cannot be corrected. They will be satisfied with having successfully completed the task. The challenge is both human - the website satisfies the Internet user for which it is intended - and economic. Indeed, an effective, efficient and satisfying website, or a progressive web app or app, makes visitors want to stay and come back, making them a loyal customer or learner. This is important in the human resources field. **Mesquita, Oliveira and Sequeira (2020)** argue in their chapter **"Digital Transformation Work 4.0 and the preparation of youngsters for the job market"** that the 4th Industrial Revolution and digitalization has changed organizations and the way they work. The changes are reflected in the business models they use, their forms of communication and collaboration, the relationships between work and private life, the structure and organizational hierarchies, and the employment itself. These changes imply some challenges in the preparation of youngsters to work in such

Table 1. Chapter 2: Are we ready for the job market?: The role of business simulation in the preparation of youngsters

Market: Accounting	
Core question:	How can we use business simulations to develop the necessary competences to be employable and competitive in the job market?
Objective:	We present a case on the use of business simulators and also refer to other already existing cases, in particular in Portugal, in higher education.
How does it build upon and add value to the existing literature?	
We present a case on the use of business simulators and also refer to other already existing cases, in particular in Portugal, in higher education	
Beyond the business school, which other disciplines would you expect to be interested in the chapter:	Human Resources Development, Education

an environment. All over Europe and to anticipate the scope and depth of the impacts that current and emerging technologies exert, some projects and initiatives are being carried out. This chapter provides an analysis of this complex environment in discussing potential changes brought about by such technologies and presents some of these initiatives aiming at preparing students to thrive in the future world of work.

Ergonomic rules and principles allow the ergonomics of website interfaces to be successful. The action performed by the user on the interface relates, in particular, to the clarity of the home page with regard to the information sought by visitors, as well as the legibility of texts: fonts, bulleted list, content breakdown, etc. From this perspective, **Bredikhina (2020)** contends in her chapter entitled **"Variable fonts from pioneers' perspectives"** that the impact of fonts on user experience and brand perception has been widely discussed by a variety of specialists. In 2016 a new technology, named 'variable fonts', occurred, ensuring lighter font files, responsiveness, variability and adaptability on the web across devices. This chapter reminds users of parameters that should be considered when choosing a font and discusses ways in which brands can implement variable fonts to increase their performance. A unique perspective on variable fonts from specialists in different domains, related to variable fonts and their implementation, are proposed in this chapter. Moreover, it provides important knowledge of current projects that implement this new technology as well as ideas and opportunities that are of interest to future e-learning and e-business brands.

Table 2. Chapter 3: Digital Transformation Work 4.0 and the preparation of youngsters for the job market

Market: Human Resource Management	
Core message:	The chapter presents a reflection about the possible changes brought by the 4th Industrial Revolution, digitalization, the technologies.
Statement of Aims:	The chapter presents some projects and initiatives to prepare the youngsters for the job market.
How does it build upon and add value to the existing literature?	
The fourth Industrial Revolution and the digital transformation have had a huge impact on the way we live, socialize and work. Therefore, it is necessary to distinguish between the tasks that may be carried out by the applications/software/robots available and those that can (still) only be performed by humans. In this context, organizations and humans need to prepare to thrive in the Fourth Industrial Revolution and the digital transformation. In this context, sets and projects emerged to mitigate this problem.	
Beyond the business school, which other disciplines would you expect to be interested in the chapter:	Education

Table 3. Chapter 4: Variable fonts from pioneers' perspectives

Market: Marketing	
Core message:	Proposal of ideas and implementations of variable fonts by professionals.
Statement of Aims:	As discussed in the previous chapters, professionals in the field of variable fonts have innovative and creative solutions that can be of interest to those who are involved in e-business and e-learning.
How does it build upon and add value to the existing literature?	
It argues that the existing literature is usually considered, according to the type of designers and developers, hence, providing no specific value. This chapter proposes a unique and creative approach to the use of fonts based on interviews with professionals in this field, who describe their projects and views on technology.	
Beyond the business school, which other disciplines would you expect to be interested in the chapter:	Type design, Web design, Branding, Visual Identity

Both the accessibility of the menu and the simplicity of the tree structure for easier navigation is of great importance. The same holds true for the optimization of images and speed of display, because the user is normally impatient. The compatibility or consideration of different supports (responsive website) associated with the correct use of hypertext links (useful, clear, without being intrusive) is also of paramount importance, as well as the care taken in designing web forms.

The users' profiles must also be considered, because their expectations, their mental model, their digital maturity, etc. differ among users. The ergonomist should preferably intervene from the design of the website. The concept of usability has led to the development of specific criteria and recommendations. They are used either to carry out a usability assessment or to design ergonomic interfaces. **França, Borges, Monteiro, Arthur and Iano (2020)** claim in their chapter **"An Overview of Web 2.0 and its Technologies and their Impact in the Modern Era"**, that Web 2.0 is the evolution of the web, and can be seen as a new and second movement enabling access to information through the world wide web. Web 2.0 involves interactivity and collaboration as the main keys to its functioning. In the introduction phase the Web 2.0 did not offer many functionalities. If previously the content was produced by a few people and made available to millions, today it is millions of users who create content daily for themselves and others. However, any user connected to the internet is now able to send information in a simpler and faster way at any time. The ease of uploading information, images, and videos on the web 2.0 derives from the expansion of resources and codes, allowing anyone to act naturally and take their own content to the internet, even if they do not master HTML codes. As the data and information shared daily is almost infinite, search engines act even more intuitively and generate only results tailored to each user. Therefore, this chapter provides an updated review and overview of Web 2.0. Furthermore, it addresses the evolution and fundamental concepts of Web 2.0 and shows its relationship as well its success, with a concise bibliographic background, categorization, and synthesis of the potential of this technology.

Mobile ergonomics aims at making mobile devices - applications on smartphones, tablets, watches etc. - useful and usable. Currently, people mainly use mobile phones to make calls, but also to browse the Internet, find information, study, meet their soul mate, or find a shop. Whether for leisure or professional activities, these tools are mobile. However, many applications are deleted shortly after being downloaded, due to a lack of ergonomics. Therefore, it highlights that ergonomics is crucial for the success of a mobile application. **Li, Meng and Li (2020)** point out in their chapter **"Cross-cultural Study of Trust Types in Sharing Economy Organizations: Evidence from Airbnb"** that the sharing economy has developed very quickly. However, organizations, like Airbnb and Uber, have encountered a crisis of trust. Scholars

Table 4. Chapter 5: An Overview of Web 2.0 and its Technologies and their Impact in the Modern Era

Market: Operations & Information Management	
Core message:	This chapter aims at providing an updated review and overview of Web 2.0, addressing its evolution and fundamental concepts, showing its relationship with UX as well as its success.
Statement of Aims:	Readers will gain a scientific technical background on Web 2.0 that categorizes and synthesizes the potential of this technology
How does it build upon and add value to the existing literature?	
The chapter is an updated overview that was built on a concise bibliographic background, which summarizes the potential of this technology.	
Beyond the business school, which other disciplines would you expect to be interested in the chapter:	Academic research, mainly in the field of engineering and computing

still have not determined the particular type of trust which is recognized by users in sharing economy organizations. Therefore, the authors designed two studies in using data from Airbnb to test 2 hypotheses: (1) The level of inter-organizational trust in sharing economy organizations is positively correlated to the level of participation. (2) The price of the shared product or service is negatively connected to the level of participation. The results reveal that consumers are more willing to choose non-shared renting methods to borrow something or pay for a service in China. Yet the opposite holds true in the America where users are now used to such services. Under both conditions, price is an important moderator. This shows that whereas the role of trust in China is mainly an inter-organizational trust, in America it is rather interpersonal. The theoretical contribution consists of the detection of the type of trust which plays a role in sharing economy organizations, collaborative relations, and studies of Airbnb.

Table 5. Chapter 6: Cross-cultural Study of Trust Types in Sharing Economy Organizations: Evidence from Airbnb

Market: Marketing	
Core message:	This chapter argues that the role of trust in Chinese sharing economy organizations is mainly of an inter-organizational nature, rather than based on initial interpersonal trust, like peer to peer, from individuals to individuals, which is different from America.
Statement of Aims:	First, the type of trust in sharing economy organizations is one type of inter-organizational trust, not an organization to organization trust, but one person to a group of people (the organization). Second, the transaction costs are one significant impact on users' participation. Third, inter-organizational trust appears to be culture-bound. Chinese Airbnb participants are more willing to trust the platform itself, whereas, American Airbnb participants are more willing to build interpersonal trust.
How does it build upon and add value to the existing literature?	
First, this work adds to the small, but growing, body of research which considers sharing economy organizations. Second, the present work extends previous research on trust in collaborative relations. Third, it contributes to the ongoing conversation regarding Airbnb.	
Beyond the business school, which other disciplines would you expect to be interested in the chapter:	Economics

The appropriate ergonomic advice for a website does not necessarily apply to a mobile application. Indeed, it is also necessary to consider the tactile gesture and the context of use. In order to understand what mobile users want and how they act user tests need to be conducted. This is exactly what has been done by **Haller and Louis (2020)** in their chapter **"Development of a digital territory strategy: Case of the "wine.alsace" domaine name"**. They ascertain that the global wine sector is changing with the emergence of mass marketing and the changes in consumption patterns, which, in turn, are linked to the development of the Internet. The relationship to wine consumption has become more informed, intelligent, community-based and connected. Information and communication technologies (ICT) open up tremendous opportunities for wine companies in the promotion and marketing of their products and services as well as in the development of their distribution channels. There is a trend towards disintermediation, i.e. shortening wine distribution channels, which leads to an increase in online sales via virtual stores (ProWine, 2019). In France, online wine sales experienced an average annual growth of more than 30% between 2008 and 2015 and stabilized at 6.9% in 2020 (France Agrimer, 2020). From this perspective, wine regions have to analyze their visibility on the Internet to be fully able to embrace the 3.0 digitalization. There are approximately 362 million domain names registered "worldwide.Com" managed by the American multinational Verisign, which represents the first extension with around 145 million domains registered (Verisign Domain Name Industry, 2019). However, a study shows that one in two companies in France has no visibility on the web compared with other European companies (McKinsey, 2014). One needs to investigate how wine regions may develop a digital territory strategy to increase their competitive advantage by selecting specific geographic domain names.

Table 6. Chapter 7: Development of a digital territory strategy: Case of the "wine.alsace" domaine name

Market: Marketing	
Core message:	Website evaluations should be adjusted to different industries and regions. We propose a framework to evaluate European wine websites to evaluate user experience and estimate website maturity.
Statement of Aims:	Following this framework, you will understand the main elements important to a website in the wine industry and you will be able to evaluate the digital development of a wine website or a wine region..
How does it build upon and add value to the existing literature?	
Our framework is based on the core models applied to website evaluations, namely the eMICA model and the stage model of website development. We adjust the framework to account for the European wine market.	
Beyond the business school, which other disciplines would you expect to be interested in the chapter:	Besides in academia, this chapter will be an interesting reading to anyone working in the wine industry and seeks to benchmark one's company and understand consumers' expectations.

When it comes to designing mobile interfaces, certain ergonomic criteria have been established, which refer to navigation and prevent the user from getting lost.

Highlighting the interactivity of buttons and icons, which are less noticeable on mobile devices, should be considered during the conception phase. The role of Artificial Intelligence can become very important here. **Mesquita, Oliveira and Sequeira (2020)** point out in their chapter entitled **"Did AI kill my job? Impacts of the 4th Industrial Revolution in administrative job positions in Portugal"** that people and organizations have been witnessing tremendous changes taking place in the job market. Technologies, such as artificial intelligence (AI), machine learning, 3D printing, Internet of Things, among others, are pushing individuals away from their comfort zone and forcing them to adapt, change, or to develop new technology skills and, in some cases, to reinvent their job positions, given the profound alterations that AI and automation have been causing. This chapter presents evidence on the current state

Table 7. Chapter 8: Did AI kill my job? Impacts of the 4ᵗʰ Industrial Revolution in administrative job positions in Portugal

Market: Human Resource Management	
Core message:	This chapter presents evidence on the current state of the administrative job positions in Portugal, in using the core international attributions for the profession framed in a skills comprehensive diagnose framework.
Statement of Aims:	This chapter presents evidence on the current state of the administrative job positions in Portugal, using the core international attributions for the profession framed in a skills comprehensive diagnose framework.
How does it build upon and add value to the existing literature?	
A climate of instability and uncertainty for the current and future workforce (Workforce 4.0) has been installed. Thus, it is crucial to gather evidence on the impacts of AI in distinct job positions, analyze the extension of those impacts, analyze where human capital is still most valued, and develop educational and entrepreneurial strategies to aid professionals in striving during the current era. The administrative job occupations have been, for decades, an underprivileged subject of research, mainly because they are not considered as a specific domain of specialized knowledge, and, in fact, it consists of a highly technical profession, clerical for the majority, and with a level of specialization that occurs at the multi-domain of personal and technological skills, trained to assist most of the existing specialized professions.	
Beyond the business school, which other disciplines would you expect to be interested in the chapter:	Education

of the administrative job positions in Portugal using the core international attributions for the profession framed in a skills comprehensive diagnosis framework.

It is important to reinforce the intuitiveness of interactions, because the user only uses their fingers to interact. It is therefore necessary to go to the basics in order to help users quickly find what they are looking for. If possible, the best option is to find out about user usage. User tests are decisive in this respect, like the A/B test. **Haller and Plotkina (2020)** mention in their chapter **"Analysis of user-experience evaluation of French wineries websites"** that it is commonly known that possessing a good website is of crucial importance to any business in our digitized age. However, the criteria of website evaluation and consumer expectations are different for every industry and for every country. In this chapter they focus on the wine industry in Europe and, particularly, in France. Building upon their extensive literature review they carry out both a qualitative and quantitative study to create and validate a theoretical framework to be used for the evaluation of wine websites. Their evaluation approach allows accounting

Table 8. Chapter 9: Analysis of user-experience evaluation of French wineries' websites

Market: Marketing	
Core message:	Website evaluation should be adjusted to every industry and region. We propose a framework to evaluate European wine websites and, user experience, and to estimate website maturity.
Statement of Aims:	Following this framework, you will understand the main elements which are important to websites in the wine industry and you will be able to evaluate the digital development of a wine website or a wine region.
How does it build upon and add value to the existing literature?	
Our framework is based on the core models of website evaluation, namely the eMICA model and stage model of website development. They adjust the framework to account for the European wine market.	
Beyond the business school, which other disciplines would you expect to be interested in the chapter:	Beyond the business school that will be an interesting reading to anyone working in wine industry to bench mark one's company and to understand the expectations of the consumers.

for the optimal user experience and evaluating website advancements, according to the main existing models of website maturity.

The aim of software ergonomics is to make software easy and simple to use. The user must be able to reach their goal and to complete their tasks in a short period of time. The features of the interface should match their needs and run easily. It is all about cognition. **Ursu, Pânişoară and Chirca (2020)** stress **"The changes brought by digital technology to cognitive learning"**. Given that the current generation is being raised in an age of digital saturation, it is different from previous generations. Web 2.0 technology and tools have a major impact on both people's lives and education, giving students an unprecedented way to access, socialize, edit, categorize, collaborate, promote and create their path. These developments also bring about changes in learning, this is why it is necessary to create learning environments that support the development of students' higher-level thinking skills, by up-dating higher education programs so that the graduates' competences are in line with current requirements in our society.

Most studies show that technologically rich learning environments improve learning outcomes and considerably enhance learning achievements. In contrast, rich learning environments have a number of benefits. Indeed, research shows that e-learning does not differ from the effectiveness, or efficiency, of traditional learning; excessive exposure to digital devices can also have major disadvantages. In this chapter they present studies and specialists' opinions on the advantages and disadvantages involved. Moreover, they carry out an in-depth analysis of how Web 2.0 applications could influence the cognitive learning of university students. Moreover, they present different solutions to find a balance between the constructive use of technology and its use as a means of distraction.

Table 9. Chapter 10: The changes brought about by digital technology to cognitive learning

Market: Technology & Innovation Management	
Core message:	Web 2.0 applications positively influence the cognitive learning of university students.
Statement of Aims:	Readers will learn about the need to use web 2.0 technology and applications in education to develop the skills needed by future graduates in the labor market. Especially, their research results on the influence of Web 2.0 applications and technology on student learning shows the benefits of using them in the classroom, possible dangers, solutions to prevent negative aspects, and possible strategies for teachers to incorporate some of these Web 2.0 technologies into the students' learning experience.
How does it build upon and add value to the existing literature?	
This chapter contributes to the literature in the field by analyzing the influence of Web 2.0 applications and technology, with respect to students' cognitive learning.	
Beyond the business school, which other disciplines would you expect to be interested in the chapter:	The psychology of learning

Ergonomists, therefore, play an important role in the software field, especially when it comes to business applications. There is indeed a discrepancy between the software intended for individual consumers and professionals. **Vidili (2020)** highlights in her chapter entitled **"Customer Experience: The new competitive advantage for companies that want their customers at the center of their business"** that today's digital era allows companies to use interfaces that are smarter than ever before. There is a lot of interest and excitement around many of these new technologies. Yet, companies often forget that the focus should always be on the customer. It is thrilling to think about the advantages which new technologies have provided to companies and individuals. However, these advantages come at a price.

Digital technologies are driving massive changes in affecting every dimension of society, especially the way individuals buy, research, and interact with one another and with leading brands. With so much disruption happening in every industry how can a company maintain its competitive advantage? The brands that have succeeded are those that offer both exceptional customer experiences and added value to their customers in ways that go beyond the simple provision of products and services. This chapter explores the impact of digital technologies on businesses and consumer behavior. It analyses the failure of a photography company as a result of the mutation in the digital arena. It focuses on the six principles that create the perfect blend for a strong customer-first digital strategy: empathy, integrity, just-in-time delivery, data, seamless processes, and trust. Trust is the foundation on which customer experience strategies are built upon. In spite of the historical leadership position in the market of many global brands, trust has diminished, especially among the new generation of consumers. Consumers' trust in brands facilitates their decision-making process, reduces customers' purchase risk and reduces costs of information gathering (Rajavi et al: 651, 2019). The author analyses the implementation of the circle of trust adopted by an e-commerce firm to improve its customer experiences. Finally, this chapter highlights the importance of enhancing customer experiences, embracing a customer-driven culture and enabling consumers to feel part of a brand.

Table 10. Chapter 11: Customer Experience: The new competitive advantage for companies that want their customers to be at the center of their business

Market: Strategic Management	
Core message:	The importance of enhancing customer experiences, embracing a customer-driven culture and enabling consumers to feel part of a brand.
Statement of Aims:	The reader will understand the impacts that digital technologies have had on businesses and consumers. They will acknowledge why enhancing a company's customer experience is important in today's world, where products and services are similar in every industry and competitive advantages are fading as more agile companies emerge.
How does it build upon and add value to the existing literature?	
Digital technologies are impacting not only businesses but mostly consumer behavior in their decision-making processes. The user experience is a critical aspect for the delivery of a superior customer experience, therefore, UX and CX should go hand in hand when implementing a CX strategy.	
Beyond the business school, which other disciplines would you expect to be interested in the chapter:	Organization management

Very often, business applications lack ergonomics and waste time for employees. The software must absolutely meet user needs - personal or professional. When an employee does not use professional software as they would like to do, the entire company loses. To ensure the creation of a software solution that meets users' expectations, performing an ergonomic audit is recommended as well as explaining the basics of all these technologies. To this end, **Hrichi (2020)** has written a chapter on **"Online inter@ ctivity via web 3.0"**, which shows that the end of the twentieth century was marked by the advent of Internet media, and alongside, the transformation of consumer behavior into information behavior. Indeed, our daily life constantly revolves around a multitude of information, which is conveyed by brands to make them occur ubiquitously, in using multichannel communication strategies. We are now living in a time when customer expectations are changing very fast and retailers that cannot keep up get left behind. A consumer who enjoys the online shopping experience at an e-store automatically begins to expect the same level of service from every virtual point of sale. Thus, the expectation loop has been born, and the only thing retailers are required to do is to get ahead of the curve; to innovate in creating new shortcuts, new functions, etc. (Popov, 2019). Interactivity refers to responsiveness and the communication between consumers and manufacturers as well as between consumers and advertisers (Park & Yoo, 2020). The advent of interactive marketing has led to new features of the web, allowing online companies to configure websites and manage interactions and communications that are smarter, more social, and more personalized. In fact, this chapter investigates the concept of online interactivity and gives a comprehensive outline of the role of the Web 3.0.

Table 11. Chapter 12: Online inter@ctivity via web 3.0

Market: Marketing	
Core message:	This chapter seeks to investigate the concept of online interactivity by presenting a review of the literature explaining the concept better and invoking the role of web 3.0.
Statement of Aims:	The readers will have an overview of artificial intelligence
How does it build upon and add value to the existing literature?	
This chapter makes an important contribution to the literature through the presentation of the changes to web 3.0 on three different levels: semantic web, mobile web, and web applications.	
Beyond the business school, which other disciplines would you expect to be interested in the chapter:	Technology & Innovation Marketing

Therefore, one needs to make sure that the usability criteria are met. Many ergonomic tools and methods make it possible to involve the user from the design stage onwards in order to know what the user expects from the product. It is an investment that the designer, or the company, pays for itself quickly. In contrast, non-ergonomic software may not be used, or be sabotaged by users. The risk is, therefore, much greater for the company. This is why it might sometimes be interesting to explain through a blog how things work; creating a blog can be very relevant. **Relojo (2020)** explores in his chapter entitled **"Incorporating Classroom Blogs in Teaching"** the role which blog psychology can play within education. As an emerging field, blog psychology deals with the application and principles of blogging. This chapter offers strategies for the creation of an effective classroom blog. Furthermore, it points out some of the insights that blogging can generate in the field of education and pedagogy. For instance, a number of studies have demonstrated that blogs allow students to articulate their views. Moreover, students consider blogs to be more engaging than simply reading a textbook and it increases extroverts' satisfaction in the classroom. Finally, this chapter addresses one of the biggest challenges of blogging in the classroom, which is that many educators are not sure what a blog is, how to set it up, and how to use it in the classroom. More importantly, a large range of insights and pieces of advice relating to user experience have been incorporated throughout this chapter.

An ergonomist is generally distinguished by their knowledge in human and social sciences, and, more precisely, in cognitive sciences. This is how they are able to involve users and understand their real needs. Their multidisciplinary expertise represents an added value and allows for proposing effective methods and new solutions. In fact, e-learning can prove very precious, like during the COVID-19 pan-

Table 12. Chapter 13: Incorporating Classroom Blogs in Teaching

Market: Education	
Core message:	This chapter explores the role that blog psychology can play within education. As an emerging field, blog psychology deals with the application and principles of blogging. The chapter offers strategies for creating an effective classroom blog. Also, it will point out some of the benefits that blogging can contribute within the field of education and pedagogy. For instance, a number of studies have demonstrated that blogs allow students to articulate their views. Moreover, students consider blogs to be more engaging than simply reading a textbook and it increases extroverts' satisfaction in the classroom. Finally, the chapter will address one of the biggest challenges of blogging in the classroom. One of which is that many educators are not sure what a blog is, how to set it up, and how to use it in the classroom. More importantly, a range of insights and advice relating to user experience has been incorporated all throughout the chapter.
Statement of Aims:	This chapter examines the role that blog psychology can play in education. As an emerging field, blog psychology deals with the application and principles of blogging.
How does it build upon and add value to the existing literature?	
This chapter offers strategies for creating an effective classroom blog. Also, it will point out some of the benefits that blogging can contribute within the field of education and pedagogy.	
Beyond the business school, which other disciplines would you expect to be interested in the chapter:	Technology & Innovation Management

demic, where students had to rely on e-learning platforms. **Malureanu, Malureanu and Lazar (2020)** have written a chapter on **"Motivational Factors of the Usage of Web 2.0 Tools for e-Learning in Business"**. She believes that the reasons for introducing Web 2.0 tools into the business area are varied, from the improvement of efficiency to better time management. The provision of online services by companies develops the computer skills of team members. The materials provided through Web tools 2.0 can be accessed by a larger number of end users and their quality can be permanently evaluated. This chapter proposes investigating the motivational factors of the usage of Web tools 2.0 by companies' team members. In particular, her research is focused on e-learning based on Web 2.0 tools for training sessions organized by companies in Romania. Her in-depth analysis has revealed that the, generally, positive perception of using an e-learning course derives from a series of objective aspects, identified in a multiple linear regression model.

Table 13. Chapter 14: Motivational Factors of the Usage of Web 2.0 Tools for e-Learning in Business

Market: Human Resource Management	
Core message:	This chapter presents some motivational factors of the usage of Web 2.0 tools for e-learning in business, based on an experience of more than 13 years in the e-learning industry and as it emerged from a study conducted by questioning participants in an e-learning course.
Statement of Aims:	Readers will learn more about the e-Learning market: issues, opportunities, dimensions, solutions.
How does it build upon and add value to the existing literature?	
Beyond the synthetic presentation of current problems and possible solutions in the e-learning industry, this chapter also shows the results of a study on users' motivational factors in online training courses.	
Beyond the business school, which other disciplines would you expect to be interested in the chapter:	Education, human resources

Therefore, UX designers should share certain skills with the ergonomist, such as understanding cognitive functions and the human factor involved in order to really understand users. This represents an essential step in UX research. UX may also comprises sufficient notions to conduct an ethnographic survey in order to know how to analyze user activity in the field, through survey techniques for obtaining qualitative and quantitative data, through semi-direct interviews or online surveys. It is also important to understand the ability to consider the different exchanges between the client and server and especially the actual usages that occur in between them Therefore, the knowledge of the principles of human-machine interfaces (HMI) and ergonomics (web and/or software) remains essential. But ethics must be considered, too.

The ergonomist of HMI is a professional in the design of interfaces, especially web and software. Each of us interacts with systems every day. However, we do not all manage to exploit machines - computers, digital products, systems in general - as we would hope. The goal of an HMI ergonomist is to allow us to use the interfaces as we wish. The main idea is to put the machine at the service of the person who needs to use it. The improvement of HMI ergonomics normally results in user satisfaction. In a professional context, it is also a means of increasing the performance of the company. All this (ergonomics, performance of the company, etc.) must be effectively measured. **Akputu and Attai (2020)** present the UX measurement technique in their chapter entitled **"User Experience Measurement: Recent Practice of E-Businesses"**, where they mention that the e-business era has offered much convenience in the collection of data on customer experience in relation to the usage of products or services. Most e-businesses are more concerned about how to exploit this data, make sense of it, or precisely tailor product or service offerings, according to user recommendations. Hence, the "user experience (UX)" concept has emerged. The UX concept is the successor to "usability"- a widely accepted measure of the quality of most products and services in the information system domains. Most e-business outlets today have succeeded partly due to their offering of stellar UX. Others have, however, failed due to negative UX reports. Therefore, measuring the UX can be a powerful tool for improving usability and potentially enhancing the market share of an e-business. Not only will the business HMI improve its offerings, but effectively measuring the UX also helps forecast and understand the future to stay afloat. In practice, however, finding appropriate UX techniques that match a particular business need can be difficult for UX practitioners. Consequently, this chapter provides a systematic overview of recent UX measurement techniques that are relevant to the e-business setting. The objective is to elaborate on what tools have been employed by scholars to measure UX and how they can be employed in practice. E-business start-ups or first movers will find this chapter as a rich head start resource. E-business experts, on the other hand, can also use this chapter as a fundamental reference to the UX measurement concept. A key concern of most e-businesses is no longer the question of whether User Experience (UX) impacts the return-on-investment and to which extent, but rather the questions of how to reliably measure the UX and make sense of the data to attain a better customer loyalty score. This chapter is a rich head start to user measurement.

Concretely, an ergonomist uses their knowledge in cognitive sciences and relies on user-centered approaches. This is what allows them to design efficient, accessible and intuitive interfaces. The result will be user satisfaction - consumers, customers, employees - and an increase in revenues for the company that offers the digital product. The chapter relates to the organization and the sharing economy, where the economic situation obliges companies to think differently and to consider the application of UX. In their chapter **"Sharing Economy as a New Organization Model: Visualization Map Analysis and Future Research"**, **Li, Meng and Nawaz (2020)** emphasize that, although the sharing economy's com-

Table 14. Chapter 15: User Experience Measurement: Recent Practice of E-Businesses

Market: Operations & Information Management	
Core message:	This chapter gives a head start overview on how user experience measurement (UX) could be exploited to improve usability, UX and possibly, the return on investment (ROI) of a product or service.
Statement of Aims:	The objective of this chapter is to provide a systematic overview of recent UX measurement approaches that are relevant to the e-business setting. The chapter aims to elaborate on what tools that have been employed in the literature to measure UX and how these are employed in practice. The e-business start-ups or new comers will find this chapter as a rich head start resource. Besides, the e-business expert can also find this chapter as a rudimentary reference to UX measurement concept.
How does it build upon and add value to the existing literature?	
Recently, user experience (UX) measurement has become a central focus in product or service design as well as evaluation studies. For the UX measurement, in particular, several techniques exist, but a clear overview of the recent useful UX measurement methods is missing. This is partly due to a lack of agreement on the essential characteristics of UX in particular contexts including the e-business sector. In this chapter, we create insight from the existing literature to present the results of a multi-year effort of UX evaluation or measurement methods. From academia to the industry leaders, we use different sources, such a literature review in journal articles, workshops, conferences and reportable on online sources to build our data. Nevertheless, the authors contend that most organizations, or groups of companies, occasionally face challenges in their work with UX and in the integration of UX practices into existing development processes. Therefore, a better understanding of these challenges, based on a concise overview of the recent useful UX measurement methods can help researchers and practitioners to better address such challenges in the future.	
Beyond the business school, which other disciplines would you expect to be interested in the chapter:	Computer Science, Software Engineering

mercial practice is booming, studies on the formation mechanism are fragmented. This chapter captures a whole picture of research in the sharing economy and gives suggestions for future research. In using the method of Prisma protocol for a systematic literature review and with the help of CiteSpace software, the authors map out the structure of the existing literature. Recent research has found that the sharing economy, as a new organization model, is a current trend; the sharing economy could be a strong type of economy in organizational management. The 'sharing economy', as a new economic phenomenon, is based on the Internet and includes peer-to-peer-based activities of obtaining, giving, or sharing the access to goods and services to maximize the utilization of this organization model. This chapter con-

Table 15. Chapter 16: Sharing Economy as a New Organization Model: Visualization Map Analysis and Future Research

Market: Marketing	
Core message:	This chapter maps out the structure of existing studies and concludes that the sharing economy represents a new organization model and will be one potential trend in the future.
Statement of Aims:	This chapter captures a whole picture of sharing economy's research. And concludes the connotation of sharing economy. Furthermore, future research directions from the nature, model, and governance mechanism of sharing economy organizations are generated.
How does it build upon and add value to the existing literature?	
First, it puts the concept of 'sharing economy' into a new conceptual framework: resource-based view, property right view, and technology view. Second, it reveals that the sharing economy, as a new organization model, is a potential developing trend in the coming future.	
Beyond the business school, which other disciplines would you expect to be interested in the chapter:	Economics

cludes with a definition of the sharing economy, based on the resources, property rights, and techniques involved; several plans for future research are presented.

In HMI ergonomics, the users' profiles are considered, together with standards and techniques that are available to design appropriate interfaces. In view of the multitude of digital products, the quality of HMI is an essential issue. However, this requires the design of a successful human-machine interface for users and, therefore, a highly qualitative UX. Students have their view and must accept what is chosen by their professor or by the school at which they are studying. The chapter by **Lazar (2020)** entitled **"Academic Motivation of University Students' Towards the Usage of Web 2.0 Technologies"** ascertains that motivation is composed of internal and external factors that influence the behavior of students in universities. The main purpose of this study was to identify motivational factors that influence the intention to use Web 2.0 technologies across university students. Four latent variables were investigated (two internal motivational factors, an external motivational factor and a factor that measures the intention to use). The validated research model facilitated the explanation of motivational factors, which directly and indirectly influenced university students' intentions to use Web 2.0 technologies. The order of the presentation of Web 2.0 tools, corresponding to their decreasing importance, was the following: Web 2.0 educational tools (e.g. Microsoft Photo Story 3), Web 2.0 applications (e.g. Google Docs), social networking sites (Facebook) and online Web 2.0 services, like video hosting sites (e.g. YouTube). This preliminary investigation contributes to the current knowledge of behavioral intentions, with respect to the use of Web 2.0 technologies.

Table 16. Chapter 17: Academic Motivation of University Students' Towards the Usage of Web 2.0 Technologies

Market: Research Methods	
Core message:	There is a strong link between university students' motivation and intention to use Web 2.0 technologies.
Statement of Aims:	The main aim of this chapter was to demonstrate the total effect of extrinsic and intrinsic motivation on university students' intentions to use Web 2.0 educational tools.
How does it build upon and add value to the existing literature?	
The collection of the experimental data was important in adding value to the scientific literature on technology acceptance models.	
Beyond the business school, which other disciplines would you expect to be interested in the chapter:	Psychology

Ergonomics and UX are two recent disciplines, which have similar objectives and apply similar methodologies. In digital environments, the term 'UX designer' tends to replace that of 'ergonomist'. The question arises whether this is because ergonomics is still perceived as the analysis of physical work situations. However, ergonomists help design interfaces for websites, video games, etc. Moreover, the quality of user experience depends on parameters that are ergonomic, such as useful features compared to user needs, and an easy-to-use interface. Therefore, UX means that interfaces must enable an easy use by the target population, be desirable, and represent a pleasant user interface (UI), which is navigable (Internet users or users must find the information they look for), accessible and credible, consistent with the message the brand sends to its customers. It is extremely important to consider the user's culture in the conception phase. **Carter**'s chapter focuses on this particular aspect **(2020)**. In her contribution, **"UX**

and e-commerce - comparing the best practices in Europe, Asia, North.America, South America and Africa", Carter explains that e-commerce is expected to see a huge growth in the following years anywhere in the world, especially during and after the COVID-19 pandemic. To exploit this trend, e-commerce owners will need to fight hard for attracting relevant traffic. Two issues are analyzed in this chapter: 1) Is UX the most important factor for an e-commerce company to increase sales? 2) How do geography and culture impact the UX performance? The word UX, coined by Norman (2007), has spread widely. According to Garrett, it is formed by many layers: Visual Design, Interface Design, Information Architecture, etc. Hence, the chapter explains that the answer to the first question is positive as the UX includes all the strategic factors that impact e-commerce sales. For the second question, as cross-border trade is encouraging companies to sell more through global online business, the e-commerce UX must be orchestrated internationally, but, unfortunately, this is rarely the case. This chapter analyzes the e-commerce UX in Europe, Asia, Africa, North and South America, comparing its strengths and weaknesses to determine UX international best practices.

Table 17. Chapter 18: UX and e-commerce - comparing the best practices in Europe, Asia, North America, South America and Africa

Market: International Business	
Core message:	UX and e-commerce - comparing the best practices in Europe, Asia, North America, South America and Africa to determine the key drivers to grow sales internationally
Statement of Aims:	The importance of UX for online business The importance of geography and culture, for the effective use of e-commerce UX in cross-border trade
How does it build upon and add value to the existing literature?	
It adds value to the existing literature in pointing out the importance of UX for e-commerce as well as in giving numerous comparative examples, which cover the most important macro-regions in the world.	
Beyond the business school, which other disciplines would you expect to be interested in the chapter:	Entrepreneurship & Small Business Management

Pífano's, Isaias' and Miranda's (2020) chapter **"Successful implementation of web 2.0 in non-profit organizations: a case study"** presents a case-study on an international non-profit entity. The case study is based on an online questionnaire that was distributed among the members of the organization. The findings place emphasis on the significance of the user-friendliness of the application, the users' participation, the availability of relevant content, and the existence of features to create/exchange content in a multitude of formats. The most significant contribution of this chapter is the outline of guiding strategies for the implementation of Web 2.0 applications, which can assist non-profit organizations in using Web 2.0 in a more proficient manner and in accordance with their individual strategies.

The design market has gone through a lot of developments in recent years; changes in practice and concentrations of players have emerged. According to Drouillat (2019), a designer, "the design situation is paradoxical in France". Today, it is common practice, i.e. widespread within companies, and sometimes it even presents a strategic issue. But few companies have the capacity to give it meaning. We may never have had so many designers, but so little design in France: Jean-Louis Frechin's book, Le Design des choses numeriques (FYP, 2019) sums up this paradox well: with the very rapid spread of UX, we have followed an approach that does not allow innovation. As a matter of fact, this situation

Table 18. Chapter 19: Successful implementation of web 2.0 in non-profit organizations: a case study

Market: Public & Non-profit Management	
Core message:	The full potential of Web 2.0 technologies remains unrealized within the context of non-profit entities.
Statement of Aims:	Non-profit organizations are becoming growingly aware of the resourcefulness of Web 2.0 in terms of user engagement, communication, collaboration and fundraising. Nonetheless, within the context of these organizations, the full potential of Web 2.0 technologies remains unrealized. This paper explores the aspects that contribute to the successful implementation of Web 2.0 in non-profit organizations.
How does it build upon and add value to the existing literature?	
The most significant contribution of this chapter is the outline of guiding strategies for the implementation of Web 2.0 applications and the emphasis that it places on the user's role in determining their success.	
Beyond the business school, which other disciplines would you expect to be interested in the chapter:	Communication, Media Studies, Marketing

provides *"an endogenous and self-centered response to the world and the culture that proposed it"* (in the United States). He goes even further by affirming that *"design methods centered on users are suited for unimaginative organizations that cannot listen and have an aversion to risks"*.

According to Drouillat (2019), UX only disseminated "automatic methodologies" to speed up the use of interfaces, but did not answer the question of innovation or the more fundamental question of creation. For us, it offers standardized responses that ignore culture, values and meaning. Design stays on the surface. For example, symptomatically, UX skills have been dissociated from UI skills, as if it was a question of only designating experiences, the rest being only an ornamental question says Drouillat (2019). With the downgrading of interface design and interaction design, as practices, we have put aside the real creative dimension of projects. Fortunately, some designers maintain a more poetic vision of digital design. Readers of this book will make their own conclusion.

Based on interviews with various researchers and practitioners from diverse cultures, this book seeks to respond to the questions of UX, its effective use, as well as its conception and implementation around the world. It also presents practices and other disciplines that go with it.

REFERENCES

Akputu, K., & Attai, F. (2020). User Experience Measurement: Recent Practice of E-Businesses. In J.-É. Pelet (Ed.), *User Experience in Web 2.0 Technologies and Its Impact on Universities and Businesses.* IGI Global. doi:10.4018/978-1-7998-3756-5

Bredikhina, L. (2020). Variable fonts from pioneers' perspectives. In J.-É. Pelet (Ed.), *User Experience in Web 2.0 Technologies and Its Impact on Universities and Businesses.* IGI Global. doi:10.4018/978-1-7998-3756-5

Carter, S. (2020). UX and e-commerce - comparing the best practices in Europe, Asia, North America, South America and Africa. In J.-É. Pelet (Ed.), *User Experience in Web 2.0 Technologies and Its Impact on Universities and Businesses.* IGI Global. doi:10.4018/978-1-7998-3756-5

Drouillat, B. (2019). *Comment l'UX a tué le design.* Published 4 décembre 2019 retrieved the 16th of June 2020 from https://blog.fastandfresh.fr/benoit-drouillat-pourquoi-lux-tue-le-design/

França, R. B., Monteiro, A.-C., Arthur, R., & Iano, Y. (2020). An Overview of Web 2.0 and its Technologies and their Impact in the Modern Era. In User Experience in Web 2.0 Technologies and Its Impact on Universities and Businesses. IGI Global. DOI: doi:10.4018/978-1-7998-3756-5

Haller, C., & Louis, B. (2020). Development of a digital territory strategy: Case of the "wine.alsace" domaine name. In J.-É. Pelet (Ed.), *User Experience in Web 2.0 Technologies and Its Impact on Universities and Businesses*. IGI Global. doi:10.4018/978-1-7998-3756-5

Haller, C., & Plotkina, D. (2020). Analysis of user-experience evaluation of French wineries websites. In J.-É. Pelet (Ed.), *User Experience in Web 2.0 Technologies and Its Impact on Universities and Businesses*. IGI Global. doi:10.4018/978-1-7998-3756-5

Hrichi, A. (2020). Online inter@ctivity via web 3.0. In J.-É. Pelet (Ed.), *User Experience in Web 2.0 Technologies and Its Impact on Universities and Businesses*. IGI Global. doi:10.4018/978-1-7998-3756-5

Lazar, I. (2020). Academic Motivation of University Students' Towards the Usage of Web 2.0 Technologies. In J.-É. Pelet (Ed.), *User Experience in Web 2.0 Technologies and Its Impact on Universities and Businesses*. IGI Global. doi:10.4018/978-1-7998-3756-5

Li, J., Meng, T., & Li, C. (2020). Cross-cultural Study of Trust Types in Sharing Economy Organizations: Evidence from Airbnb. In J.-É. Pelet (Ed.), *User Experience in Web 2.0 Technologies and Its Impact on Universities and Businesses*. IGI Global. doi:10.4018/978-1-7998-3756-5

Li, J., Meng, T., & Nawaz, M. (2020). Sharing Economy as a New Organization Model: Visualization Map Analysis and Future Research. In J.-É. Pelet (Ed.), *User Experience in Web 2.0 Technologies and Its Impact on Universities and Businesses*. IGI Global. doi:10.4018/978-1-7998-3756-5

Malureanu, C., Malureanu, A., & Lazar, G. (2020). Motivational Factors of the Usage of Web 2.0 Tools for e-Learning in Business. In J.-É. Pelet (Ed.), *User Experience in Web 2.0 Technologies and Its Impact on Universities and Businesses*. IGI Global. doi:10.4018/978-1-7998-3756-5

Mesquita, A., Oliveira, L., Oliveira, A., Sequeira, A., & Silva, P. (2020). Digital Transformation Work 4.0 and the preparation of youngsters for the job market. In J.-É. Pelet (Ed.), *User Experience in Web 2.0 Technologies and Its Impact on Universities and Businesses*. IGI Global. doi:10.4018/978-1-7998-3756-5

Mesquita, A., & Silva, P. (2020). Are we ready for the job market?: The role of business simulation in the preparation of youngsters. In J.-É. Pelet (Ed.), *User Experience in Web 2.0 Technologies and Its Impact on Universities and Businesses*. IGI Global. doi:10.4018/978-1-7998-3756-5

Mesquita, Oliveira, & Sequeira. (2020). Did AI kill my job? Impacts of the 4th Industrial Revolution in administrative job positions in Portugal. In *User Experience in Web 2.0 Technologies and Its Impact on Universities and Businesses*. IGI Global. DOI: doi:10.4018/978-1-7998-3756-5

Pífano, S., Isaias, P., & Miranda, P. (2020). Successful implementation of web 2.0 in non-profit organizations: a case study. In J.-É. Pelet (Ed.), *User Experience in Web 2.0 Technologies and Its Impact on Universities and Businesses*. IGI Global. doi:10.4018/978-1-7998-3756-5

Relojo, D. (2020). Incorporating Classroom Blogs in Teaching. In J.-É. Pelet (Ed.), *User Experience in Web 2.0 Technologies and Its Impact on Universities and Businesses*. IGI Global. doi:10.4018/978-1-7998-3756-5

Ursu, A.-S., Pânişoară, I., & Chirca, R. (2020). The changes brought by digital technology to cognitive learning. In J.-É. Pelet (Ed.), *User Experience in Web 2.0 Technologies and Its Impact on Universities and Businesses*. IGI Global. doi:10.4018/978-1-7998-3756-5

Usabilis. (2020). *Qu'est-ce que l'ergonomie?* Retrieved 15/06/2020 from https://www.usabilis.com/qu-est-ce-que-l-ergonomie/

Vidili, I. (2020). Customer Experience: The new competitive advantage for companies that want their customers at the center of their business. In J.-É. Pelet (Ed.), *User Experience in Web 2.0 Technologies and Its Impact on Universities and Businesses*. IGI Global. doi:10.4018/978-1-7998-3756-5

Chapter 2
Are We Ready for the Job Market?
The Role of Business Simulation in the Preparation of Youngsters

Anabela Mesquita

https://orcid.org/0000-0001-8564-4582

Instituto Superior de Contabilidade e Administracao do Porto, Polytechnic of Porto, Portugal

Paulino Silva

https://orcid.org/0000-0003-1443-4961

Polytechnic of Porto, Portugal

ABSTRACT

One of the key factors to be successful in the job market is to detain the right and needed knowledge and competences, being these hard or transversals (e.g., communication, negotiation, leadership, creativity, proactivity, responsibility, just to name a few). Experiential learning, problem-based learning, and game-based learning are pedagogical methods that allow students to consolidate the technical competences but also to develop the necessary soft skills in order to be employable in the Society 4.0. Among the solution offered is the business simulation that can be defined as an instrument that transforms the real business world in a simplified model enabling students to make decisions and simulate activities as if they were in a real business environment, without any risks. In this chapter, the authors describe a business simulation used in a higher education institution in Portugal. They analyze this simulation in terms of experiential learning and problem-based learning and draw some reflections about the results as this might be inspiring for other teachers/trainers.

DOI: 10.4018/978-1-7998-3756-5.ch002

INTRODUCTION

The 4th Industrial Revolution, the digitalization, the changes enacted by demography and the economy, are transforming the society, namely, the way we live, socialize and work. The increased complexity of the working environment with all its challenges and demands are forcing youngsters to acquire technical skills and develop transversal (or essential) competencies (Warren, 2019). The job market is no longer looking for theory-knowledgeable potential workers but people that have the experience, and know how to do. And when we refer to the youngster, the best way to develop this knowledge is learning by doing. One of the pedagogical approaches that can be used to achieve the desired goals is experiential learning, based on the constructivist theory. This approach allows the student to consolidate technical competences while developing the necessary soft skills needed to be employable and competitive in society 4.0.

Experiential learning can take several formats being the business simulation one of them. It consists of a series of activities that imitates a real business environment. In this risk-free environment, the student experiences what is life in a real company. He performs the tasks that he is supposed to do in a real situation and applies the technical competences while developing soft skills such as communication, negotiation, leadership, problem-solving, among others.

Moreover, it is necessary to make sure that the motivation, engagement, involvement, and interest of the student remains the same, throughout the semester and in each class, as these are the requisites for successful learning according to the Flow Theory. Business simulators, as they contain a component of enjoyment, allow the student to be fully involved with the environment and the activities proposed, increasing the possibility of positive learning.

It is possible to find in the market different solutions and examples of business simulations. In Portugal, in higher education, in particular, in the Polytechnic Schools, this kind of enhanced learning environment already exists. ISCAP, the Porto Accounting and Business School of the Polytechnic of Porto has introduced a Business Simulation in the Accounting program of studies in 2003, to meet the requirement of the Portuguese Order of Certified Accountants. Although the results are positive, it is necessary to understand how this solution addresses the experiential learning characteristics and the enjoyment of the Flow theory. As such, in this paper, we will describe and identify the main characteristics of some theories that are contributing to the pedagogical approaches being used with business simulations – Constructivism, Experiential Learning, and Flow Theory. After the clarification of the differences between games and business simulations, we present and analyze the Business Simulation of ISCAP taking into consideration the theoretical framework presented before. Results will allow us to identify areas for improvement and contribute to the reflection and discussion concerning the development and introduction of these solutions in the classroom.

Background

There are several educational / learning theories that contribute to the development and use of simulations in the classroom. In this chapter, we will focus on Constructivism and Experiential Learning. Besides that, we will also present another theory that can be applied to education and to the use of simulations - the Flow theory. After a brief description of each, we relate them with the use of simulations.

Constructivist Theory

Constructivism is a theory that holds that people actively construct or make their own knowledge and that reality is determined by the experiences of the learner (Elliott et al., 2000, p. 256). This means that learning is a personal construction of meaning by the learner through experience and that meaning is influenced by the interaction of prior knowledge and new events. And of course, this prior knowledge influences what new or modified knowledge an individual will construct from new learning experiences (Philips, 1995). Another important idea is that learning is an active process. Learners construct meaning only through active engagement with the world (such as experiments, project-based learning, among others). And understanding cannot be passively received as it must come from making meaningful connections between prior knowledge, new knowledge and the process involved in learning. Moreover, one must consider that learning is a social activity, representing something people do together, in interaction (Dewey, 1938). Additionally, we need to consider that all knowledge is personal. As a matter of fact, each individual learner has a personal point of view based on his / her knowledge, experience and values. This explains why the same pedagogical approach or activity can result in different learning outputs as each person's interpretation differs.

The role of the teacher in the constructivist classroom is to create a collaborative environment (problem or project solving environment), where students become active participants in their own learning. Here, the role of the teacher is thus, a facilitator rather than an instructor. The teacher makes sure the student understands the pre-existing conceptions and guides the activities (Oliver, 2000).

The most important features of a constructivist classroom are:

1) Knowledge will be shared between teachers and students.
2) Teachers and students will share authority.
3) The teacher's role is one of a facilitator or guide.
4) Learning groups will consist of small numbers of heterogeneous students.

Honebein (1996), summarizes the seven pedagogical goals of constructivist learning environments:

1) To provide experience with the knowledge construction process (students determine how they will learn).
2) To provide experience in and appreciation for multiple perspectives (evaluation of alternative solutions).
3) To embed learning in realistic contexts (authentic tasks).
4) To encourage ownership and a voice in the learning process (student-centered learning).
5) To embed learning in social experience (collaboration).
6) To encourage the use of multiple modes of representation, (video, audio text, etc.)
7) To encourage awareness of the knowledge construction process (reflection, metacognition).

The most important limitation of the constructivist theory is its lack of structure as some students might require more structured learning environments in order to reach their potential. It also places more value on students evaluating their own progress, which may lead to some students falling behind (McLeod, 2019).

Experiential Learning

Experiential learning is a theory proposed by David Kolb who defends that learning involves experience. As Kolb explains, it is the "process whereby knowledge is created through the transformation of experience. Knowledge results from the combination of grasping and transforming the experience" (Kolb, 1999, p. 2). Lewis and Williams (1994, p. 5), define experiential learning as "learning from experience or learning by doing. Experiential education first immerses learners in an experience and then encourages reflection about the experience to develop new skills, new attitudes, or new ways of thinking".

The importance of experiential learning lies in the fact that it tries to reflect the real world where everything is connected. Moreover, experiential learning is based on the constructivist theory of learning as a result of the learning process that may vary from one student to the other (Wurdinger, 2005). The way one student decides to solve a problem may differ from another one, as well as the experience each one takes away from the learning process.

Experiential learning can take several formats - apprenticeship, clinical experiences, fellowship, fieldwork, internships, practicums, service learning, simulations, and gaming/role-playing, student teaching, study abroad, undergraduate research, volunteering, to name a few. Schwartz (2012) organizes experiential learning in two main categories: learning based on field experiences (includes internships) and learning based in classroom experiences (includes different formats such as case studies, role-playing, games, presentations, group work, and simulations).

A learning activity, in order to be classified as experiential learning, needs to comprise the following characteristics (Chapman, McPhee, & Proudman, 1995): 1. A mixture of content and processes (there must be a balance between the experiential activities and the underlying content or theory); 2. Absence of excessive judgment (the trainer must create a safe space for students to work through their own process of self-discovery); 3. Engagement in purposeful endeavors (the activities must be relevant to the student); 4. Encouraging the big picture perspective (students need to make connections between the learning they are doing and the world); 5. The role of reflection (activities should build in students the ability to see relationships in complex systems and find a way to work within them); 6. Creating emotional investment (students must be fully immersed in the experience, not merely doing what they feel it is required of them; 7. The re-examination of values (by working within a space that has been made safe for self- exploration, students can begin to analyze and even alter their own values); 8. The presence of meaningful relationships (one part of getting students to see their learning in the context of the whole world is to start by showing the relationships between "learner to self, learner to teacher, and learner to a learning environment"); 9. Learning outside one's perceived comfort zones (learning occurs when the student is challenged both in his physical and social environment. This could mean, for instance, "being accountable for one's actions and owning the consequences".

In an experiential learning approach, students can live real-life scenarios, experiment reactions and get feedback, in a risk-free environment. Moreover, teachers should enable the "pattern of inquiry" as this method helps the student to think, not only after the experience but "throughout the experience" (Wurdinger, 2005). In fact, this methodology encourages the student to inquire about a problem, to develop a plan to address the problem, test it against reality and then apply what he has learned to create a solution. Wurdinger (2005) gives some advice in the preparation of the classroom activities using experiential learning - First, students need to feel they can make mistakes; Secondly, activities must be relevant; Then, students need to understand why they are doing something; Activities need to match students; At the end, students need to reflect about the experience; and finally, the teachers need to delegate authority to the students.

In an experiential approach, the role of the teacher/instructor is different from the role of a teacher in a traditional classroom. Here, the teacher becomes a guide, a coach, a resource and support as students need to take control of their own learning. As Warren (1995) says, the role of the teacher should include establishing a vision, setting the rules and providing the tools.

As for the assessment, it should encompass the opportunity to reflect on the learning that occurred, as well as covering the goals reached and the process, the activities that lead to that result. In a simplified way, Qualters (2010) recommends Alexander Astin's I-E-O (Input-Environment-Output) Model: 1. Input (assess students' knowledge, skills, and attitudes prior to a learning experience); 2. Environment (assess students during the experience); and 3. Output (assess the success after the experience). As for the development of the activities, and the assessment, these should be student-centered. This means that students need to be involved in their own assessment (Wurdinger, 2005). This can be possible by letting them define how their work will be judged, for instance, by choosing the criteria that will be used to assess their work; by allowing students to keep track of their work which could be done using portfolios showing their progress over time; and finally, by allowing students to present their learning to an audience.

When it comes to the particular field of business or management, researchers argue that schools should focus more on creating ways of allowing students to see and deal with the world (Starkey & Tempest, 2009) and to learn by integrating experience and practice based on classroom instruction. As it is difficult to expose students to real situations, the solution might be to create experiences in a safe environment by adding activities that allow them to reach conclusions with other colleagues. Simulated environments can also provide experiences that increase engagement, critical thinking, and learning, essential competencies in order to be competitive and employable (Burch et al, 2017).

The Flow theory

As Aristotle concluded 2300 years ago, "people seek personal happiness and pleasure" (Chen, 2007). The implication of this statement for almost all-user-oriented designs today is to provide the opportunity and the means to provoke positive user feelings in all areas, including games and learning. In order to achieve this goal, it is first, necessary to understand what happiness is. And it is here that the concept of Flow enters. Flow represents the feeling of complete and energized focus in an activity, with a high level of enjoyment and fulfillment (Debold, 2002 in Chen, 2007).

As the Psychologist Mihaly Csikszentmihalyi describes it, the Flow is the "optimal experience" or, "a particular kind of experience that is so engrossing and enjoyable that it becomes... worth doing for its own sake even though it may have no consequence outside itself" (Csikszentmihalyi 1990, p. 4). And enjoyment means to have a sense of achievement, rather than only a pleasurable experience (op. cit, p. 46).

The most important aspect related to the flow experience is that when a user has such an experience, he loses track of time and worries, the level of focus maximizes his performance in and the pleasurable feelings from the activities. And this will promote intrinsic motivation, a necessary element to foster learning. Csikszentmihalyi identified eight components of flow (Csikszentmihalyi 1993, p. 178-9):

- A balance between the level of challenge and the necessary skills
- A merging of action and awareness
- Clear goals and feedback

- Concentration on the task at hand
- A sense of control
- A loss of self-consciousness
- An altered sense of time
- Autotelic or self-rewarding experience

Examples of being in flow situations are the football player in the ultimate goal, or a teacher talking about the topic during a full class of interested students.

Games vs Simulations

Experiential learning is very often connected to simulations and exposure to real situations and environments. And although simulations might have a gamification component, they are not synonyms. A game can be described as "an activity that has an explicit goal or challenge, rules that guide the achievement of the goal, interactivity with either other players or the game environment (or both), and feedback mechanisms that give clear cues as to how well or poorly" the player is performing. It results in a quantifiable outcome and usually generates an emotional reaction in the players (Boller, 2014).

Simulations can be designed to be games, but they don't have to be. A simulation is a re-creation of a situation that the player/student can encounter in real life, requiring the player to solve and make decisions that mimic what the person would have to do in the real world. Examples of simulations that might not have the gamification component are the flight simulators. Or simulators where patients need to learn to respond to common troubleshooting alarms when doing hemodialysis and then safely resolve the alarm. Or simply the simulation of managing a firm with the purpose of doing it better, learning with the process, and not having punctuation at the end, as it happens with a game.

The simulations that have gamification components can, for instance (Boller, 2014):

- Have levels of difficulty just like games do
- Be graphically rich
- Provide a lot of feedback regarding how the player is doing
- Present as a challenge that the player has to resolve
- Generate a lot of emotion within the participant

Simulations can be used in different domains. In the area of quality, Robinson (2002) developed a model of simulation quality to promote an understanding of the quality concept. In the agricultural area, Dörschner & Musshoff (2015) used a business simulation game to examine how action and result-oriented agricultural measures affect the species protection initiatives of agricultural managers. To evaluate the results of teams of masters' students competing in a production simulation game, Koltai et al. (2017) applied the data envelopment analysis (DEA). Papenhausen (2010) developed a model of the influence of managerial dispositional optimism on the propensity to search using a business simulation exercise.

As specific tools for education, some studies presented business simulation methodologies as very effective. The history of business simulations and their use in education and research is provided by a study of Larréché (1987). In this study, the author discusses the potential of using a realistic environment for education purposes. Robben et al. (1990) proved business simulation to be an effective tool when examined the role of decision frames as an opportunity in tax evasion using an experiment with students' set of decisions. Newbery et al (2018) explored how entrepreneurial micro-entity takes form in business undergraduates during an initial entrepreneurial experience, provided by a business simulation game. Their research helps to understand the impact of the cognitive dissonance on the salience of the emerging identity and the influence of key existing identities (Newbery, Lean, Moizer, & Haddoud, 2018). Ben-Zvi, T. (2010) suggest that business simulation games are also an effective way to engage students in Decision Support Systems (DSS).

Business Simulations in Portugal

Business Simulation courses were included in some Portuguese undergraduate programs since the end of the 1990s. Among the pioneers, there is the Instituto Superior de Contabilidade e Administração de Aveiro (ISCAA). The main objectives of this course were to provide an interactive environment, the consolidation, and integration of knowledge previously acquired in the first years of the program, especially in the areas of Accounting, Fiscal Law, Law, Management and Informatics; to provide a first contact of the student with the business world; to promote Ethics when performing the accountant job; to promote group work; and to promote the experience of working under pressure (Machado, Inácio, Fortes, & Sousa, 1999). More recently, a study conducted at ISCAA revealed that problem-based learning methodologies, included in the Business Simulation course, contribute to the development of soft skills, especially at the level of the use of resources and the building of knowledge (Pinheiro, Sarrico, & Santiago, 2011).

The Polytechnic of Setúbal also implemented a Business Simulation course in its graduation of Accounting and Finance, based in a partnership with ISCAA (Aleixo, Teixeira, & Silva, 2012). For this institution the main objective was to put in practice some knowledge acquired in other courses of the graduation and build a bridge between the academic and the business world, putting the student at the center of the learning system (Aleixo et al., 2012; Teixeira, Aleixo, & Silva, 2012).

The implementation of Business Simulation courses also took place at the Polytechnic Institute of Bragança (IPB). In a study conducted by IPB, researchers figured out that students were very motivated to attend BS courses, as they have realized they strengthened their knowledge, especially concerning imitative capabilities (Alves, Moutinho, Pires & Ribeiro, 2013). In another study, Rocha (2016) found that former students from Business Simulation courses from IPB considered the methodologies used in BS courses as very important to increase the approval rate of the exam to have access to the profession of certified accountant.

The Polytechnic Institute of Cávado and Ave (IPCA – Instituto Politécnico do Cávado e Ave) also implemented Business Simulation courses, which were similar to the ones in place in other higher education institutions. Recently, researchers concluded that the course was very important for students' development of professional and personal skills (Silva, Martins, & Jesus, 2018).

Today, more and more Portuguese higher education institutions are using similar courses of business simulation in order to prepare their students for a more demanding job market. The Porto Accounting and Business School (*ISCAP*) from the Polytechnic of Porto was one of the most important institutions to implement this type of education methodology. First, because *ISCAP* is the higher education institution with the highest number of students in the graduation of accountability. Second, because the methodology used was based in a very complex system, such as an ERP (Entreprise Resource Planning) and a powerful document management system. Third, because students valued the experience of the business simulation environment. Studies were done about the experience at *ISCAP*, especially in terms of the feedback from students about the acquisition of some important skills during the courses (see, for example, Silva & Bertuzi, 2015, 2017, 2019; Silva & Mesquita, 2018; Silva, Santos, & Vieira, 2014).

The Case Under Study

In this section, we present the Business Simulation offered at the Porto Accounting and Business School, (ISCAP) one of the schools of the Polytechnic of Porto (Portugal). We describe, first the background of this simulation. This is followed by the objectives, the resources used, the environment and the assessment. The description is based on the experiential learning approach, addressed in section 2 of this paper.

Context of the Case

The Polytechnic Institute of Porto is one of the biggest higher education institutions in Portugal. ISCAP, also known as Porto Accounting and Business School, which is one of the schools of the Polytechnic Institute of Porto, has approximately 4500 students, 250 teachers, and 50 non-teacher staff. There are nine different graduations, all related to business areas, but most of the students are enrolled in the Accounting and Administration undergraduate program. The case presented here is an experiential learning experience within the courses of Business Simulation (BS). This experience has its origins during the year 2002 when some old paradigms were questioned, and new ways of education were planned to be implemented in the following year for future accountants and managers. BS courses started being offered in February 2003, in the second semester of the academic year 2003/03. Concerning the study program of the Accounting and Administration, the BS courses are offered in the two last semesters of the three-year undergraduation course. Each BS class has a duration of three hours and students have classes twice a week. This leads to 90 face-to-face hours each semester. The introduction of BS courses has in its genesis the need to solve some problems and to change the paradigm of educating future accountants and managers. One of the most important causes of the change was the pressure of the Portuguese Order of Certified Accountants (OCC – Ordem dos Contabilistas Certificados) to have candidates with some professional experience. This also happens in other professional orders, which normally leads candidates to do an internship before being admitted as full members of the Order. Regarding the Order of Certifies Accountants, it was defined as compulsory for candidates to do an internship or take a course, or courses with very practical characteristics. The way BS courses were thought and planned should meet these requirements. Another question was the recognition that the way accounting education was being provided was not in line with a valued accounting professional of today. Too much of basic and technical skills and almost nothing of soft and transversal skills. It was also recognized that some old-fashion accounting practices were outdated and almost did not have practical use anymore. As so, ISCAP decided to implement BS courses in its main undergraduation program. This idea was followed by several other higher education institutions, because in the following years BS courses at ISCAP were recognized as best practices, not only in Portugal but also internationally. For example, the same approach was introduced in ISCAL, the School of Accounting of the Lisbon Polytechnic Institute and also in ISCAM, the School of Accounting and Auditing of Mozambique.

Objectives of BS Courses

The main objective of BS courses is to give students adequate preparation for working as professionals in a very competitive business world. One of the ways to achieve this goal is to eliminate the shortcomings of traditional education, which is normally considered as too theoretical and that does not connect the theory to the practice. Therefore, BS courses intend to give students the opportunity to be as they were in a real business life situation. This means they could prepare themselves in an action-based learning environment, which is in line with other studies (Adler & Milne, 1997; Fiet, 2001). BS courses also intend that students apply to practice some previous knowledge acquired in other courses. This means that courses like financial accounting, management accounting, tax law, commercial law, labor law, financial management, strategy management, entrepreneurship, marketing, logistics, just to mention a few, have their topics applied in the BS courses. However, this diversity, very important to students, is very demanding for BS teachers, as they are not supposed to master all these areas. Overcoming the difficulties with extra work and with the help of colleagues from other areas, BS teachers try to provide a very similar experience to students as if they were in their real life. In this simulated environment, students dominate both the theoretical and practical sides of the materials. Additionally, it is important to refer that the help of a powerful information system is fundamental to enable students to work in the top companies of the market (ISCAP, 2005).

Resources of BS Courses

In the beginning, there was a need for a high value of the investment, especially concerning the hardware and software. For the implementation of the BS course two big classrooms were totally equipped and an administrative room as well. Almost a hundred computers were bought, also printers, scanners, telephones, and of course, the servers to run the software, composed by the ERP – Enterprise Resource Planning and complementary software for managing digital documents and for education purposes. Besides material investment, also human resources were needed to start the project. This includes administrative, technical and pedagogical staff. In the first years, more than 15 teachers and assistant monitors were hired, since the number of students per semester was very high. There were lots of students waiting to apply to BS courses, as they could avoid doing an internship as a requirement to access the Order of Certified Accountants. And for students having classes in the same institution they were doing other courses was much more convenient than finding and moving to a company to do the internship. In the following years, the number of students started to decrease and stabilize, which led to a minor need for teachers. BS teachers have mainly a background in accounting and management areas, but regularly request the support of teachers from other areas, especially in areas that changed a lot. One of the most common examples is fiscal law, which changes every year. The main function of BS teachers is to explain in a general way the activities students need to perform and help them during the process, like coaches. The guides for each class are created with at least one week in advance, giving the opportunity to students to plan the activities and organize the work among themselves. The activities students perform during the classes and all the environment needed are prepared by teachers and assistant monitors long in advance. Some examples of activities are to set up a company, make a financial report, calculate the interests to pay to banks, prepare a factoring contract, ask for financing, paying royalties, implement a production process, analysis of financial statements, calculation of the value-added tax, payroll. The main software used is an ERP, adapted to be used for educational purposes. However, there is also other complementary software to help the management of digital documents and helping support activities. In addition, to have the function of helping assistant monitors and teachers with the preparation of classes, the administrative room is also a place that students can use to train and to test their knowledge. Over the last years, the possibility to access the system remotely was provided. This enabled students to practice and prepare classes with flexibility in terms of time and space (ISCAP, 2005).

The Environment of BS Courses

Nowadays we often hear that it is very easy to access information, especially since technology allows it. However, we have a big challenge, which is choosing the relevant information for making our decisions. This is fundamental for accountants and managers, that needed to be very selective in a world flooded with information. To help professionals in this task, management information systems perform a fundamental role, that is aggregating relevant information and enabling users to select the most adequate to make decisions. Furthermore, accountants are becoming more and more decisive in the decision-making process of any organization. This happens mainly especially in SME, because accountants have a transversal perspective of the organization, understanding all its particularities.

BS courses considered all these developments, therefore stimulates students through the analysis of texts and news in different languages and the writing about them in Portuguese or in English. It is believed that these types of activities enable students to improve their argumentation and also practicing their native and non-native language. The application in practice of previous knowledge learned in other courses is evidenced, for example, when students need to set up their own company. The different legal and accounting issues considered in this activity were taught previously in other courses. However, a fundamental point is to consider that all these activities are performed in a risk-free environment, giving the students a safe feeling that they are not penalized professionally for any mistake they make (ISCAP, 2005).

The BS Model

The model encompasses different entities. The most important ones are the students' companies that can be seen at the center of figure 1 in the Portugal Continental quadrant. Students' companies are groups of three or four elements, which is particularly important to emphasize teamwork. The creation of groups and the learning process in this context is very important for students, as most of them will perform their professional work as a member of a team (Pritchard et al, 2006). Each students' company has a different commercial or industrial activity which contributes in a complementary way to the whole market. This enables students' companies to sell and buy a diversified range of products and services to each other, such as food and drinks, furniture, office supplies, computers, just to mention a few. The BS model underlies a real calendar, which means that students need to meet the real deadlines, for example, for social security, salaries payment, and other tax payment, to deliver tax documents. Public institutions, such as social security can be seen at the center of figure 1 in the Portugal Continental quadrant. Additionally, the model includes wholesalers and retailers, national and internationally, that can be found in figure 1 in the quadrants of Continental Portugal (for domestic trade) and in the quadrants Rest of the World and European Union (for international trade). All external entities are controlled and managed by teachers and assistant monitors. This happens, because these entities have specific roles within the market and can be business associations, insurance companies, banks, leasing and factoring companies, governmental agencies, such as taxes or social security. The inclusion of these entities enables the simulation model to be more representative of the business reality (ISCAP, 2005). Nevertheless, students' companies are the most important, since they provide the business activities to students perform during the semester. The amount of data produced by students during each semester is so large, that only with an integrated management information system is it possible to process data and extract useful information for making decisions. If it is true that some decisions are limited to students to avoid too much complexity in the system, there are activities in which students have the autonomy to decide.

Figure 1. The Business Simulation Model.
Source: Business Simulation: Support Book, ISCAP (2005)

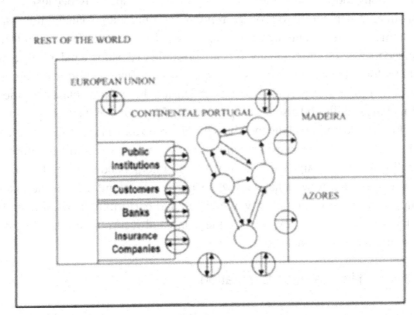

Another important activity students need to perform during the semester is making activity reports, one of them is in the middle of the semester and the other one at the end of it. These reports should include, not only an economic and financial analysis but also other relevant activities that the company has developed. The final report is one of the most important items for the assessment process, as it has to be delivered in writing and presented orally. Figure 1 presents the BS model in which we can observe the entities managed by students (simulated companies) and the other entities managed by teachers and assistant monitors in a national and international context (ISCAP, 2005).

Business Simulation as an Experiential Learning Opportunity and Enjoyment

When it comes to simulating the business environment, we need to simplify a lot of events, and even assume that it is not possible to include all the complexity of the real business world. So, we produce a model that tries to represent an important and more relevant part of reality.

During the classes, we provide students with an environment that is as much similar as possible with the one they will find in their professional life. As they are supposed to be accountants and managers, they need to know how to use an ERP – Enterprise Resource Planning software - in order to provide information for someone to make decisions. They need to know how to apply different and diversified law concepts, for example, learned during the law courses, beforehand. They need to know how to deal with the finances of their own company, as they have to pay to their providers and subcontractors and they have to receive from their customers. All these activities, that are provided during classes of three hours each, twice a week are just a basis for them to consolidate knowledge and also to develop their soft skills, such as teamwork and leadership. Outside the classes, students need to continue their work, especially because there are other stakeholders that need to have information about what is happening in each company. Among those stakeholders, we have the state, especially because of taxes, investors and banks. In this line, students need to produce reports, not only with financial information, which is fundamental for them as future accountants or managers but also with non-financial information, giving a wider and balanced idea about the company. It is not possible to develop a balanced scorecard in all its perspectives and in a formal way, but students are aware that the financial information of a company is not the only important information they need to master. During these out-of-class activities, students can consolidate their technical skills and also develop their soft skills. One of the examples the planning and the organization of the work among all the members of the group and its presentation as a result of a real workgroup. For business simulation, some students do not have the opportunity to know beforehand the colleagues that will form each group. This means they will interact and work with some people for the first time, which is very similar to what happens when a professional initiates his job in a new company. Managing a company with all the complexity associated and performing a set of activities with other people enables students to be more flexible, to understand and incorporate others' opinions in a final decision, just to mention a few examples of the benefits.

Experiential Learning in Business Simulation

Business simulation is a form of experiential learning. It happens in a controlled environment, in which students have the opportunity to learn by doing. Even if they make big mistakes during the simulation, they do not risk their jobs. Following the classification of Schwartz (2012), who divides experiential learning into two main categories (learning based on field experiences or in classroom experiences), the BS of ISCAP represents an example of the classroom experience. The reasons to consider BS as experiential learning are the following: First, the activities provided during business simulation are based on previous content students learned in other courses and applied to practical terms. Second, the BS represents a safe environment for students as they will not be fired if they make big mistakes. However, they know that their mistakes and also the right decisions made are always opportunities to learn. Third, activities are relevant to students, as most of the time they take notice for the first time how some contents can be applied in a real situation. Fourth, students realize they are doing activities as they were in a real company, since they use professional information systems and real online applications, for example from the state. Students can also interact with each other on a business-to-business basis. They have the opportunity to understand the big picture of the simulation. Fifth, students execute activities, especially as homework, when they reflect on their performance. One of these examples is the development of the report about the situation of the company during the semester. With this type of activity, students have the opportunity to understand that eventual mistakes can be solved. Sixth, sometimes students are so committed to doing their activities they lose the notion of time. Although classes last for three hours, there are students willing to stay longer. Seventh, when students have to work with others, to listen to their opinions, to discuss in a constructive way, they understand how important it is to have this experience. In a real context of work, students do not have the opportunity to learn with the experience, since they have strict deadlines to accomplish or other stressful targets to achieve. Eighth, students have a close relationship with their colleagues and with the teacher in the business simulation. This enables them to question, to learn not only for themselves but acting as educators for their colleagues. The environment enhances a sharing space, in which students and teachers have the opportunity to learn. Ninth, students learn in a very uncomfortable way since they are not just passive learners as it happens in lecturing sessions. They need to be active; they need to learn by doing, which is far away from their comfort zone. In summary, business simulation provides students an experiential learning environment, different from an internship for example, but much more effective than some of them.

Being in Flow During Business Simulation

A three-hour class with no break seems to be too long if we think in pedagogical terms. We can say that it can be seen as very demanding as well. What happens during the three hours is completely different from these assumptions. Sometimes, as referred, students want to stay longer. And this happens due to the enjoyment they feel when performing the activities, which is explained by the Flow theory. Most of the time, students are in flow, they are committed to performing all the activities they were suggested to. In that way, they sometimes lose the notion of time and are willing to continue their work. Of course, for this to happen we need to give students very clear and challenging activities and they need to have some skills to perform them. Students also need to be focused on the activities and are important to give them feedback about their performance, which are in line with the eight characteristics of flow described by Csikszentmihalyi (1990). However, the creation and organization of those activities are very challenging for all the teachers. First, one must consider that there are students that have different levels of mastering some topics. This happens because they do not need to conclude other courses that are being applied in business simulation. Second, because each student has a different way of thinking. Some are more motivated to be accountant professionals or managers, but others are completing graduation just because their parents make it compulsory for them. Third, because there are limitations in terms of resources. This applies, not only to teachers, that cannot master all the subjects that are applied in a business simulation but also to technical resources, that are fundamental when we try to simulate the real business world. With limitations in terms of software and hardware, the system is more difficult to implement.

FUTURE RESEARCH DIRECTIONS

This chapter established the ground to use business simulation as a pedagogic approach as it is based on some educational theories. It was demonstrated that Flow theory can be taken into account not only to make business simulations or serious games curriculum but also when developing the curriculum of other programs of studies. One of the fundamental aspects of any learning process is to allow students to enjoy what they are doing. And with the application of the Flow theory, in particular in business simulations, this might be possible. Moreover, it was also demonstrated that experiential learning and simulations can be used and applied in other domains of education, such as law, engineering, architecture. Finally, when thinking about graduation programs, the use of business simulations allow bringing together all the concepts taught. In a risk-free environment, students are invited to solve problems and make decisions and analyze and discuss the results of their decisions. This constitutes an opportunity to reflect on the decisions made and the results obtained, which is not possible with lectures or seminars. As such, we recommend that lectures should be complemented with learning by doing approaches, simulations, or other practical methodologies.

CONCLUSION

Provided the results presented in this chapter, it is possible to conclude that business simulations are nurtured by the constructivist theory, the experiential learning approach, and the flow theory. Additionally, one may say that face to face learning does not substitute online learning. Experiential learning examples revealed that students need to be present in the classroom and interact with each other. The development of some competences, especially the transversal / soft ones is much more effective in these situations. Moreover, business simulations are very popular regarding the practical application of more theoretical concepts from other courses, especially among jobs that require a more practical approach, such as accountants or managers. Moreover, learning by doing is an important teaching-learning approach, when the job is very practical. And the provision of safe environments such as those created by the use of business simulations is becoming more and more important in the higher education institutions. Finally, engaging students is fundamental for better performance. And in this situation, the flow theory is a very effective tool to demonstrate that.

REFERENCES

Adler, R. W., & Milne, M. J. (1997). Improving the quality of accounting students' learning through action-oriented learning tasks. *Accounting Education*, 6(3), 191–215. doi:10.1080/096392897331442

Aleixo, M. da C., Teixeira, A. B., & Silva, S. (2012). *Simulação empresarial: Um caso de sucesso*. XXII Jornadas Luso-Espanholas de Gestão Científica.

Alves, J., Moutinho, N., Pires, A., & Ribeiro, N. (2013). A motivação dos alunos em simulação empresarial: Análise de um ano lectivo. *XIV Congresso Internacional de Contabilidade e Auditoria*.

Barzilai & Blau. (2014). Scaffolding game-based learning: Impact on learning achievements, perceived learning, and game experiences. *Computers & Education*, 70(1), 65–79.

Ben-Zvi, T. (2010). The efficacy of business simulation games in creating Decision Support Systems: An experimental investigation. *Decision Support Systems*, 49(1), 61–69. doi:10.1016/j.dss.2010.01.002

Boller, S. (2014). Games vs Simulations: Choosing the Right Approach for Learning. *The Knowledge Guru*. Retrieved from http://www.theknowledgeguru.com/games-vs-simulations-choosing-right-approach/

Burch, G., Giambatista, R. C., Batchelor, J., Hoover, J. D., Burch, J., Heller, N., & Shaw, J. (2017, November 30). (2017). Do Experiential Learning Pedagogies Effect Student Learning? A Meta-Analysis of 40 Years of Research. *Academy of Management Journal*. Advance online publication. doi:10.5465/ambpp.2016.127

Chapman, S., McPhee, P., & Proudman, B. (1995). What is Experiential Education? In K. Warren (Ed.), *The Theory of Experiential Education* (pp. 235–248). Kendall/Hunt Publishing Company.

Chen, J. (2007). Flow in Games (and Everything Else). *Communications of the ACM, 50*(4), 31–34. doi:10.1145/1232743.1232769

Csikszentmihalyi, M. (1990). *Flow: The Psychology of Optimal Experience*. Harper & Row.

Csikszentmihalyi, M. (1993). *The Evolving Self: A Psychology for the Third Millennium*. Harper Collins.

Debold, E. (2002). Flow with soul: An interview with Dr. Mihaly Csikszentmihalyi. *What Is Enlightenment Magazine*. Retrieved from http://www.wie.org/j21/cziksz.asp

Dewey, J. (1938). *Experience and Education*. Collier Books.

Dogramaci, A., & Nabil, R. A. (1979). Applications of simulations. In R. A. Nabil & A. Dogramaci (Eds.), *Current Issues in Computer Simulation* (pp. 101–109). Academic Press. doi:10.1016/B978-0-12-044120-4.50012-X

Dörschner, T., & Musshoff, O. (2015). How do incentive-based environmental policies affect environment protection initiatives of farmers? An experimental economic analysis using the example of species richness. *Ecological Economics, 114*, 90–103. doi:10.1016/j.ecolecon.2015.03.013

dos Santos W. O., Bittencourt, I. I., Dermeval, D., Isotani, S., Marques, L. B., & Silveira, I. F. (2018). Flow Theory to Promote Learning in Educational Systems: Isit Really Relevant? *Brazilian Journal of Computers in Education (Revista Brasileira de Informática na Educação -RBIE), 26*(2), 29-59.

Elliott, S. N., Kratochwill, T. R., Littlefield Cook, J., & Travers, J. (2000). *Educational psychology: Effective teaching, effective learning* (3rd ed.). McGraw-Hill College.

Fiet, J. O. (2001). The Theoretical Side of Teaching Entrepreneurship. *Journal of Business Venturing, 16*(1), 1–24. doi:10.1016/S0883-9026(99)00041-5

Honebein, P. C. (1996). Seven goals for the design of constructivist learning environments. *Constructivist learning environments: Case studies in instructional design*, 11-24. Retrieved from http://studentcenteredlearning.pbworks.com/f/DesignConstructivistHonebein.pdf

ISCAP. (2005). *Business Simulation: Support Book*. Instituto Superior de Contabilidade e Administração do Porto.

Kato & Suzuki. (n.d.). *An Approach for Redesigning Learning Environments with Flow Theory*. Retrieved from https://www2.gsis.kumamoto-u.ac.jp/~idportal/wp-content/uploads/icome2010_kato.pdf

Kolb, D. (1999). *Experiential Learning Theory: Previous Research and New Directions*. Retrieved from https://learningfromexperience.com/downloads/research-library/experiential-learning-theory.pdf

Koltai, T., Lozano, S., Uzonyi-Kecskés, J., & Moreno, P. (2017). Evaluation of the results of a production simulation game using a dynamic DEA approach. *Computers & Industrial Engineering, 105*, 1–11. doi:10.1016/j.cie.2016.12.048

Kristian, K., Lainema, T., Freitas, S., & Arnab, S. (2014). Flow framework for analyzing the quality of educational games. *Entertainment Computing, 5*(4), 367–377. doi:10.1016/j.entcom.2014.08.002

Larréché, J.-C. (1987). On simulations in business education and research. *Journal of Business Research, 15*(6), 559–571. doi:10.1016/0148-2963(87)90039-7

Lewis, L. H., & Williams, C. J. (1994). Experiential Learning: Past and Present. In L. Jackson & R. S. Caffarella (Eds.), *Experiential Learning: A New Approach* (pp. 5–16). Jossey-Bass.

Machado, E., Inácio, H., Fortes, J., & Sousa, J. (1999). Projecto em Simulação Empresarial: Uma Experiência em Desenvolvimento. *Revista Estudos do ISCAA, 2*(5), 113–127.

McLeod, S. A. (2019, July 17). Constructivism as a theory for teaching and learning. *Simply Psychology.* Retrieved from: https://www.simplypsychology.org/constructivism.html

Nakamura, J., & Csikszentmihalyi, M. (2014). The Concept of Flow. In M. Csikszentmihalyi (Ed.), *Flow and the Foundations of Positive Psychology* (pp. 239–263). Springer Netherlands. doi:10.1007/978-94-017-9088-8_16

Newbery, R., Lean, J., Moizer, J., & Haddoud, M. (2018). Entrepreneurial identity formation during the initial entrepreneurial experience: The influence of simulation feedback and existing identity. *Journal of Business Research, 85*, 51–59. doi:10.1016/j.jbusres.2017.12.013

Oliver, K. M. (2000). Methods for developing constructivism learning on the web. *Educational Technology, 40*(6), 5–18.

Papenhausen, C. (2010). Managerial optimism and search. *Journal of Business Research, 63*(7), 716–720. doi:10.1016/j.jbusres.2009.05.007

Pinheiro, M., Sarrico, C., & Santiago, R. (2011). Competências de autodesenvolvimento e metodologias PBL num curso de contabilidade: Perspectivas de alunos, docentes, diplomados e empregadores. *Revista Lusófona de Educação, 17*(17), 147–166.

Prichard, J. S., Stratford, R. J., & Bizo, L. A. (2006). Team-Skills Training Enhances Collaborative Learning. *Learning and Instruction, 16*(3), 256–265. doi:10.1016/j.learninstruc.2006.03.005

Qualters, D. M. (2010). Bringing the Outside in: Assessing Experiential Education. *New Directions for Teaching and Learning*, (124), 55-62. Retrieved from https://onlinelibrary.wiley.com/doi/abs/10.1002/tl.421#

Robben, H. S. J., Webley, P., Elffers, H., & Hessing, D. J. (1990). Decision frames, opportunity and tax evasion: An experimental approach. *Journal of Economic Behavior & Organization, 14*(3), 353–361.

Robinson, S. (2002). General concepts of quality for discrete-event simulation. *European Journal of Operational Research, 138*(1), 103–117. doi:10.1016/S0377-2217(01)00127-8

Rocha, D. R. do R. (2016). *A Importância da Metodologia PBL nos Diplomados em Contabilidade: Estudo de Caso* [Dissertação de Mestrado]. Instituto Politécnico de Bragança.

Schwartz, M. (2012). *Experiential Learning Report*. Ryerson University. Retrieved from: https://www.ryerson.ca/content/dam/lt/resources/handouts/ExperientialLearningReport.pdf

Sheehan, D., & Katz, L. (2012). The Practical and Theoretical Implications of Flow Theory and Intrinsic Motivation in Designing and Implementing Exergaming in the School Environment. *The Journal of the Canadian Game Studies Association*, 6(9), 16.

Silva, M. de L., Martins, D., & Jesus, M. J. (2018). *O Projeto em Simulação Empresarial como um Novo Paradigma de Investigação/Experimentação no Ensino Superior. XVII AECA International Meeting*, Lisbon, Portugal.

Silva, P., & Bertuzi, R. (2015). The Contribution of Business Simulation to Improve Management Competencies. *EDULEARN 2015 - 7th International Conference on Education and New Learning Technologies*.

Silva, P., & Bertuzi, R. (2017). Students' Perception about the use of Action-Based Methodologies. *EDULEARN 2017 - 9th International Conference on Education and New Learning Technologies*.

Silva, P., & Bertuzi, R. (2019). How Business Simulation Methodologies Can Impact on the Improvement of Students' Skills. *ICERI2019 - 12th annual International Conference of Education, Research and Innovation*.

Silva, P., & Mesquita, A. (2018). The Creative Internprize International Project: Preparing Students to be Entrepreneurs. *ICERI2018 - International Conference on Education, Research and Innovation*.

Silva, P., Santos, J. F., & Vieira, I. (2014). Teaching Accounting and Management through Business Simulation: A Case Study. In E. Ariwa (Ed.), *Green Technology Applications for Enterprise and Academic Innovation* (pp. 33–47). Information Science Reference. doi:10.4018/978-1-4666-5166-1.ch003

Starkey, K., & Tempest, S. (2009). The Winter of Our Discontent: The Design Challenge for Business Schools. *Academy of Management Learning & Education*, 8, 576–586.

Teixeira, A. B., Aleixo, M. da C., & Silva, S. (2012). *Simulação Empresarial e as Novas Metodologias de Ensino: Estudo de Caso*. XV Encuentro AECA.

Teng & Huang. (2012). More Than Flow: Revisiting the Theory of Four Channels of Flow. *International Journal of Computer Games Technology*. Advance online publication. doi:10.1155/2012/724917

Warren, C. (2019). *"Soft Skills" are the Essential Skills*. Institute for Health and Human Potencial. Retrieved from https://www.ihhp.com/blog/2019/08/29/soft-skills-are-the-essential-skills/

Warren, K. (1995). The Student-Directed Classroom: A Model for Teaching Experiential Education Theory. In K. Warren (Ed.), *The Theory of Experiential Education* (pp. 249–258). Kendall/Hunt Publishing Company.

Wurdinger, S. D. (2005). *Using Experiential Learning in the Classroom*. ScarecrowEducation.

ADDITIONAL READING

Csikszentmihalyi, M. (2002). *Flow: The Classic Work on How to Achieve Happiness* (Rev. ed.). Rider.

Kiili, K., Lainema, T., Freitas, S., & Arnab, S. (2014). Flow framework for analyzing the quality of educational games. *Entertainment Computing*, *5*(4), 367–377. doi:10.1016/j.entcom.2014.08.002

Pizzini, M. (2006). The relation between cost-system design, managers' evaluations of the relevance and usefulness of cost data, and financial performance: An empirical study of US hospitals. *Accounting, Organizations and Society*, *31*(2), 179–210. doi:10.1016/j.aos.2004.11.001

Wardaszko, M. (2016). Building Simulation Game-Based Teaching Program for Secondary School Students. *Simulation & Gaming*, *47*(3), 287–303. doi:10.1177/1046878116635467

KEY TERMS AND DEFINITIONS

Business Simulation: Tool for organizational learning and development allowing participants to truly engage in a risk-free environment.

Constructivism: Learning theory focusing on how humans make meaning from their experiences. It is based on the belief that learning occurs as learners are actively involved in a process of meaning and knowledge construction.

Experiential Learning: Is a process through which students develop knowledge, skills, and values from direct experiences.

Flow (Theory): Psychological state that people will experience when engaged in an activity that is adequately challenging and often results in immersion and concentration focus on a task.

Game-Based Learning: Learning approach that use games for learning and educational purposes.

Gamification: Application of game-design elements and game principles in non-game contexts.

Simulation: Imitation of the operation of a process or a system.

Chapter 3
Digital Transformation and Work 4.0:
Preparation of Youngsters for the Job Market

Anabela Mesquita
 https://orcid.org/0000-0001-8564-4582
Polytechnic of Porto, Portugal & Algoritmi RC, Portugal

Adriana Oliveira
 https://orcid.org/0000-0003-0081-2335
CEOS.PP ISCAP, Polytechnic of Porto, Portugal

Luciana Oliveira
 https://orcid.org/0000-0003-2419-4332
CEOS.PP ISCAP, Polytechnic of Porto, Portugal

Arminda Sequeira
 https://orcid.org/0000-0003-1457-6070
CEOS.PP ISCAP, Polytechnic of Porto, Portugal

Paulino Silva
 https://orcid.org/0000-0003-1443-4961
CEOS.PP ISCAP, Polytechnic of Porto, Portugal

ABSTRACT

Changes brought by the 4th Industrial Revolution and digitalization impact directly in the way we live, shape the organizations, and change the way we work. These changes imply some challenges in the preparation of youngsters to work in such an environment due to their characteristics. All over Europe, and in order to anticipate the scope and depth of the impacts that current and emerging technologies are imposing, some projects and initiatives are being carried out. The aim of this chapter is to subsidize a reflection about this complex environment by discussing the possible changes brought by the technologies and present some of these initiatives aiming to prepare students to thrive in this world of work.

DOI: 10.4018/978-1-7998-3756-5.ch003

INTRODUCTION

Literature highlights, in a very clear way, the impact that the 4th industrial revolution is having on people's and organizations' lives. In the last decades of the 20th Century, people and institutions saw their lives transformed, due to the emergence of a digitally-immersed society, which confirms an early prediction made by Alvin Toffler at the beginning of the 80s.

Today, the Fourth Industrial Revolution and the digital transformation are an undeniable reality, with a huge impact on the way we live, socialize and work (Braña, 2019). Of course, these changes will not be the same all over the world and in all industries, but the trend is set globally. There will be depth and acceleration of change in the labour market (Guerra & de Gómez, 2019), and many of the tasks performed today by workers will not be essential in the future. Moreover, in some of the tasks, the changes will be evident sooner and faster (Guerra & de Gómez, 2019).

The most significant features of the changes concern its transforming role in general and the place of people in the production, economy, and life, having both positive and negative impacts. On the positive side, economies will potentially grow and businesses might rise profitability as the access to the global market is increasingly easier; on the negative side, many people might become unemployed if they don't update their skills and abilities. This will require additional effort from governments, on one hand, to ensure decent living conditions to those who lose their jobs and to provide conditions to those who want to keep up with the transformations and, on the other hand, from companies and educational institutions to reduce the imbalance between supply and demand on labour sources (Chala & Poplavska, 2017).

With the emergence of so many technologies and trends, such as the Internet of Things (IoT), automation, robotics, virtual reality (VR), artificial intelligence (AI), 3D printing, it is necessary to understand which tasks may be carried out by the available applications/software/robots and those that can (still) only be performed by humans. In this context, organizations and humans need to prepare to thrive in a new environment, where the motto is set by digital transformation. In other words, they need to develop (new) competencies, namely those related to communication, teamwork, problem-solving, and higher-order critical and digital skills, just to name a few. This context was advanced by Alvim Toffler when he stated that in the 21st century, the illiterate are not those who cannot read or write but those who cannot learn, unlearn and relearn (Toffler, 1980).

To contribute to the mitigation of this problem, some initiatives and projects are being carried out by different consortia in Europe. As such, the purpose of this paper is to contribute with a reflection about the Work 4.0 (which can be described as having a high degree of integration and cooperation, using a wide range of digital technologies and demanding flexible work arrangements), the preparation of youngsters for the labour market, and to present some projects that might help youngsters to be better prepared to face the challenges presented by the above-mentioned context. These projects provide answers to the needs of young people and organizations, such as: answers to the IT sector's upskilling/reskilling needs; development of an integrated curriculum for the digital age; cooperation between organizations and higher education institutions. For that purpose, the authors, first present a literature review concerning the digital transformation by addressing the technologies which enable the core changes, and its impacts at the social, organizational and individual levels. Then, a set of projects and initiatives that are being already carried out to address these problems are presented. The body of strategies to address the current challenges underlying these projects consists of a corpus with relevance for researchers, professional organizations, human resources professionals and educators/educational providers.

BACKGROUND: ARRIVING AT THE FOURTH INDUSTRIAL REVOLUTION: CONCEPTS AND IMPACTS

The 1st industrial Revolution (1760-1840) or Industry 1.0, was marked by the arrival of the steam engine, the weaving loom and the mechanization in general, innovations that changed radically the labour market with the increase of industry employees and the corresponding decrease of agricultural workers. Besides, the transport revolution at the end of the 19th century served as a trigger for other innovations and developments, enabling easier trade relations and connections which constituted a structural change rousing roughly the same kind of fears that are heard today, namely the complete replacement of man by machines (Chala & Poplavska, 2017). The 2nd Industrial Revolution (1870), brought the assembly line and the invention of electrical energy which led to the emergence of mass production which in turn, created unprecedented abundance and overcrowded markets. The 3rd Industrial Revolution takes place at the end of the sixties of the 20th century, brought automation, computers and electronics, generally speaking, and we could say that the emergence of computer robotics and internet laid the foundations for the 4th Industrial Revolution (Schwab, 2017), bringing the need for a complete turnaround of the mindset and view of the world at large. The most striking aspect of this evolution is the rapid acceleration of the sequence of events, which occurred in increasingly shorter intervals of time.

The concept of the 4.0 Industry was presented in the Hanover Industrial Fair in the context of Germany's Innovative Development Strategy, in 2011. The purpose of the German government was to highlight Germany's innovative leadership position in the world. The concept was based on the principles of ergonomics: the functional interaction between man and machine, namely with equipment directly over the Internet; the clearness and transparency of information and the capacity of systems to create a virtual copy of the physical world; the technical remote assistance of people through technology, the execution of numerous tasks by remote technology; and the ability of systems to make decisions independently and autonomously (Chala & Poplavska, 2017).

The 4th Industrial Revolution, which is frequently used as synonym for Industry 4.0, is defined, by the Technical Terminology Handbook as a being ''the current and developing environment in which disruptive technologies and trends such as the Internet of Things (loT), robotics, virtual reality (VR) and artificial intelligence (AI) are changing the way we live and work'' (Rouse, 2017). The main features of this new revolution are the exponential speed, depth, technological fusion and the interaction between physical, digital and biological domains (Schwab, 2017). Innovations, such as cyber-physical systems supported by artificial intelligence (AI), robotics, autonomous vehicles, 3D printing, new materials, and the internet as well as industries of computing, virtual reality, biotechnology, space exploration and climate control (Michaud, 2019) are so deeply world-shattering that affects every aspect of social, organizational and individual life and represent a complete shift of the way we see the world, live and work, impacting everything and everyone.

The 4th Revolution is not a synonym for a set of new technological innovations but a transition that takes us to merge with systems influenced by the digital revolution (Schwab, 2017). Digital technologies have been forcing society, altogether, and the individual, in particular, to absorb new daily behaviors, to answer to the changes that have been taking place. The depth and scope of the changes will not be the same everywhere, but the impacts will be felt everywhere.

Generally speaking, the impact of digital transformation can and will be seen in every job and occupation but in some of them, the changes will be evident sooner and faster and no occupation will be immune to the changes. Being aware of this challenging scenario, promoted by the digital transformation, it is necessary to understand how these changes will and are already affecting society, organizations, and individuals. These domains are discussed in the following subsections.

4th Industrial Revolution Impacts on Society

The challenges posed by the 4th Industrial Revolution are frequently called game-changers. Initially, game-changers were conceptualized as macro-events or trends that are perceived to shift completely rules, fields, players, how society is organized and even today's understandings about values, institutions and social relationships (Haxeltine, Pel, Dumitru, Kemp, Avelino, Jørgensen, & Bauler, 2017). Virtual reality, nanotechnologies, biotechnologies, cognitive sciences, the space sector, and many others came to radically change society. The fear of mass automation and its destructive impacts on employment is a speech that often appears at the beginning of a new period of innovation (Michaud, 2019).

Innovations and events have a direct impact in the way we perceive social structure as "relationships through which society is organized and defined, may fundamentally change in response to game-changing events and trends" (Avelino, Wittmayer, Haxeltine, Kemp, O'Riordan, Weaver, & Rotmans, 2014, p. 6). These changes impact directly on the way people interact in society and change social structures as key technological concepts and solutions to accomplish a combination of the economies of scale and mass customization, characterized by handling a high level of complexity with a total network integration of products and production processes are attained. (Dombrowski & Wagner, 2014). These technology-driven changes also create new fields of activity and new functions as the interaction between humans and machines progressively develop and expand.

The 4th Industrial Revolution particularities have led to the necessity of implementing a group of measures in the most distinct contexts, such as the political context signaled in the necessity to make modifications in the legislation of what concerns the protection of data or labour issues; the social context, with employment/unemployment issues having a central role; organizational context, with the necessity of adapting the means/tools or the development of employees; education/development context, with the necessity of (re)creating new models/educational contents which can enhance new skills, namely for young people. Other challenges that are raised by the increasingly digital society are related to the so-called digital ethics (Leonhard, 2016), as technology infiltrates every part of human life and human activity. Questions such as the right to privacy vs security issues or data protection vs availability and accessibility to data, come into question and the discussion about ethical limits and digital society.

As Leonhard (2016) highlights, in the past, each radical shift in human society has been driven fundamentally by one key enabling shift factor—from wood, stone, bronze, and iron, to steam, electricity, factory automation, and the internet. At present, however, a combined set of science and technology produces mega shifts with multiple impacts that are and will redesign commerce, culture, society, human biology, and ethics.

4th Industrial Revolution Impacts on Organizations

Technology and digitalization are a global phenomenon of vital importance for the future of companies as well as individuals. Thus, the level, quality, and conditions of technological use is as important, or even more important, than possessing access to technological knowledge (Guerrieri, Evangelista, & Meliciani, 2014). Furthermore, according to the literature, the main changes occurring in the organization of work and people are visible in the following areas: organization of work; the relationship between private and working life; the format of work, communication and collaboration; performance and talent management; organizational hierarchies.

The shift concerning the organization of work refers to the way people work and how companies organize themselves. While more traditional companies try to adapt to the technologies introducing telework and mobile work, the digital native companies present a more agile organization of work, such as projects, as well as collaboration and crowdsourcing. This flexibility is visible when we observe the work territoriality dematerialization once employees can work anywhere; the working hours as the flexible schedules allow to work any time; the relationship between employers and employees and even in the approach to the function profile as this kind of flexibility allows companies to find in the market the right person for a specific task. These changes demand the emergence of digital platforms that incorporate mechanisms to validate the identity of the service provider and the reliability of the participants. When the shift refers to the relationship between private and working life, the working hours are no longer relevant as what matters is the results achieved. And if on one hand, it seems to contribute to a better balance between private and professional life, as tasks are performed according to the convenience of the professional, on the other hand, it means that people are always connected and accessible, eliminating barriers between the work and family life, which might constitute a problem if the professional is not able to set boundaries.

Digital transformation also affects the format of work, communication, and collaboration. Teamwork gains importance to the extent that knowledge as a resource can only be developed and advanced within a group of people and knowledge becomes a key property of the organization (Irma Becerra-Fernandez, 2001). New ways of teamwork and collaboration emerged, enhanced by technologies and virtual teams, composed of multidisciplinary professionals and working from different geographies, which are already a reality with impacts at a global level that will grow in the next years. Organizational structures will increasingly be replaced by project-based work and self-organized teams as traditional hierarchies are too rigid and too slow to provide an answer to speed, interdependency and innovation challenges of society and markets.

Traditional organizational models were built on the assumption that efficiency would be achieved through the optimization of predictable, linear, deterministic systems (McChrystal, Collins, Silverman, & Fussell, 2015). Nevertheless, the world has changed and the level of adaptation and innovation required is no longer compatible with the complex, rather than complicated, contexts we live in with a high degree of volatility. The key to surviving appears to rely on being more prepared, adaptable and resilient so that people can respond effectively to unexpected events.

In terms of work coordination, the traditional structure relies on command and centralized decision making. Today's environment being complex, dynamic and demanding, doesn't comply with time-consuming decision processes and further dissemination through the structure towards the operational level. As such, organizations are and will have to evolve to much more flexible structures. The model of team-of-teams is designed to allow the team to respond rapidly to its highly-connected, fast-paced and unpredictable environment (McChrystal et al., 2015). To respond with malleability to complex environments, the team must be trained to be resilient, learn to expect ever-changing demands and be connected in flexible ways, both vertically and horizontally, allowing fast responses to new opportunities or challenges. This configures a cultural shift and not simply a digital, technological competency question.

To build teams that think and act as one unit, it is indispensable to develop a shared consciousness and to train every team member to develop the ability to understand the big picture in every situation and to frame it correctly which is not compatible to stratification, physical, psychological and geographical barriers, hierarchical agreements and secrecy. Another element that is crucial to the team to function is the lateral connectivity, based on personal relationships between individual team members. Finally, for the team to work, leaders must share power, that is to say, go beyond simple delegation and effectively nurture decision-making as the team shows signs of being in the process of developing the most needed shared consciousness (McChrystal et al., 2015). As such, organizational transformation powered by digital transformation is leading to the increase of the influence of workers in organizational hierarchies as technologies allow workers to participate more in decision making, involving them in real-time in the different subjects and decisions. The increased responsibility in one's work is facilitated by improved access to information and growing transparency of information, making it easier to find contacts, people specialized in specific topics/tasks, and disseminate information among several interlocutors, inside and outside the organization, which seems to flatten the hierarchical levels.

Building increasingly autonomous teams require the concomitant development of multiple skills and the indispensable abilities to overcome the challenges of this very complex context. The increase in the use of technologies at work leads to a growing need for digital competencies, performance and talent management. The indispensable competencies related to the use of the computer will be necessary for all occupations. Besides, as routine tasks will be automatized, the focus is and will continue to be, on cognitive competencies and those related to problem-solving and creativity to handle successfully with more complex tasks, meaning those tasks that are not automatized. Moreover, as the environment becomes more complex and dynamic, the need to develop adaptability and resilience forces people, that want to stay relevant in the labor market, to invest in lifelong learning as the knowledge life cycle is increasingly shorter.

4th Industrial Revolution Impacts on Individuals

On top of the changes caused by the 4th Industrial Revolution in the organizational structure, business models, communication and collaboration, impacts are also felt on the relationship/balance between work and private life and the work and employment concept.

According to a study carried out by Oxford University (David, 2015; Frey & Osborne, 2017), 47% of the job occupations in the United States are at risk of being replaced by technologies while automatization and work become more digital, virtual and remote. Moreover, according to the report of the WEF 2018 (WEF, 2018) "the wave of technological advancement is set to reduce the number of workers required for certain tasks" (p. v). It is also stated that there will be an increase in the "demand for new roles" and a "decrease demand for others".

Factors such as technological advancement and adoption of mobile internet, artificial intelligence, big data analytics, and cloud computing; trends in robotization; changing geographies on the way production and distribution of value in the value chain; changing employment types; a net positive outlook for jobs and the decrease of some others; emerging in-demand roles; growing skills instability and reskilling need, are transforming the labor market. Furthermore, the WEF 2018 Report (WEF, 2018) also points out the strategies for addressing the skills gap in the organizations calling the attention for the companies needs and expectations which go through hiring wholly new permanent staff already possessing skills relevant to new technologies and to seek for additional opportunities to automate completely some the work tasks and retrain existing employees.

The digital transformation, namely cloud computing and cloud data storage, provide the development of a technological network which represents a radical professional and cultural change but the possibility of access to an infinite amount of data reveals the inability of the human being to retain, to deal and dominate all the information available. Although mobile internet and cloud computing allow offering more efficient services and the opportunity to increase productivity, enabling the quick dissemination of the service models, based on the internet, the retrieval, storage, and analysis of large amounts of structured and non-structured data, raises the questions of what kind of professional as well as personal profile is needed in the future and calls the attention to opportunities and challenges on the need to re-skill or up-skill the labor force with hard and soft skills.

The economic imperatives and efficiency demands help push companies to adopt new forms of work and doing business as crowdsourcing, collaborative consumption and peer-to-peer interaction constitute technology-based processes or even robotic that expand production processes at a more convenient, precise and cheaper price, which allows companies to have access to global markets, even for SME, but also enhances the need to hire talents to cope with continuous innovations (Porter & Heppelmann, 2015) The impact of the 4th Industrial Revolution that we are witnessing and is foreseeable shortly in the transportation sector, especially with the most probable robotization of this segment, will bring ground-breaking changes.

For all these reasons, we can infer that the 4th Industrial Revolution represents a challenge that demands the constant need to re-skill or up-skill professionals with hard skills as well as soft skills, with special impact over the ICT market professionals. It also requires profound social changes to cope with the digitalization of personal and professional life (Gray & Rumpe, 2015; Rintala & Suolanen, 2005). As agreed by Susskind and Susskind (2015), traditionally, practical expertise has been held in people's heads, textbooks, and filing cabinets, but nowadays, it is being stored and represented in digital form, in multiple storage units, systems, and tools. Similarly, 3D and 4D printing allow increasing productivity to levels never seen before as 3D printing enables the adjustment of production to real-time demand, creating and improving the supply chain and global nets. The Internet of Things is and will generate large amounts of information, patterns and knowledge as never seen before and will change everything—including ourselves. This may seem like a bold statement, but no so much when considering the impact the Internet already had on education, communication, business, science, government, and humanity. The Internet is one of the most important and powerful creations in all of human history (Evans, 2011). Artificial intelligence and machine learning allow the automatization of tasks within a cognitive dimension, expanding human intelligence.

Nevertheless, no matter how complex the systems, the impact of technology on the professions can be categorized under two categories – automation, that is to say, technology-based work that improves traditional ways of operating in an organization or an industry - and innovation meaning disruptive technologies that radically change working practices (Susskind & Susskind, 2015). In automation, technologies are used to suppress some inefficient activities. The focus is on streamlining manual or administrative work. However, the old ways of operating are not ignored or discarded. Automation can be transformative, i.e., people can use technology to transform the way a task is done. In innovation, technologies enable ways of making practical expertise available that just was not possible without the system in question. Innovative systems provide services at a lower cost, or higher quality or in a more convenient way than in the past (Susskind & Susskind, 2015). In one case and the other, new skills are required and training is part of the process.

To foresee the needs of the labor market, to anticipate new ways to develop training and to envision ways to train the next generation of workers, taking into consideration the challenges of the 4th Industrial Revolution and other upcoming *revolutions,* is a big part of both social and organizational concerns.

Talented and well qualified human resources are a critical part of organizational survival and to identify a vision to attract the most talented individuals, to motivate and to retain them is essential once only through the best human resources it is possible to move the organization forward and to stand up among the competition (Topcu, 2020) but for that purpose to be achieved each organization should identify the set of competencies they will be looking for.

With this in mind, we can state that if there are tasks that require human intervention, there are also others that no longer need that intervention. Despite the breakthroughs in artificial intelligence, the cognitive-intellectual operations, such as critical thinking, knowledge management, and teamwork still require human intervention. So, it is important to notice that in some cases, individuals will be replaced by technology, in other cases, they will be required to undertake continuous, advanced, cross-functional high-tech training to respond to the digitalization of tasks. Taking into consideration the kind of scenario we are working in, soft skills seem to gain significance once collaborative cross-functional and multicultural cooperation will be increasingly needed (Gupta, 2018). Ovans (2015), based on the work of Goleman (2004), who developed a framework that introduces five components of emotional intelligence which allow individuals to recognize, connect with and learn from their own and other people's mental states. The five components are self-awareness; self-regulation; motivation - defined as a passion for work that goes beyond money and status; empathy for others and social skills, such as proficiency in managing relationships and building networks (Ovans, 2015). The author defends that understanding of what exactly constitutes emotional intelligence is very important because it represents the opportunity to assess in what domains an individual is strong and in what domains some additional *work needs to be done*.

In this scenario, time is also important because as technology grows in applicability and complexity, more time is required to learn how to handle it and to keep up with new features and new releases (Shrivastava, 1998). Therefore, it is required that professionals continue to improve their personal and technological competencies throughout life, as the current digital transformation implies a constant update of knowledge and skills (Martyakova & Gorchakova, 2019; Shrivastava, 1998). Lifelong learning, either as a competency and as an end in itself, becomes central in dealing with the challenges of the digital transformation. However, given the present and expected conditions for the future, the issue about 'training' for the 'new digital economy' or investment in skills and qualifications cannot be thought of in isolation (Degryse, 2016); (De Franceschi, 2015). The issue needs to be thought through in a more articulate way with society, meaning that youth employment requires coordination and coherent strategies based on research and dialogue with workers' and employers' organizations and youth groups (ILO). In this context, some projects and initiatives are already being implemented to overcome the challenges of digital transformation and will be presented in the next subsection.

CURRENT PROJECTS AIMED AT FACING THE CHALLENGES ENACTED BY THE DIGITAL TRANSFORMATION

In the previous sections, we reflected on Work 4.0, and preparing young people for the labor market. In this section are presented the projects that can help young people to be better prepared to face the challenges brought by the mentioned environments.

As explained in the previous section, society has suffered several changes, impacting at different domains, being at the individual or the organizational level. The transformations based on Industry 4.0, influenced by digitalization, imply reduced human or manual intervention in tasks (Kumar & Nayyar,

2020). This is a paradigm shift and organizations need to become digitalized to respond to the market technological challenges because some tasks still need human intervention, but other tasks will be replaced by technology, or they will require humans to undertake cross-functional high-tech training (Chhabra, 2018; Gupta, 2018; Martyakova & Gorchakova, 2019). In this digital context, companies have to adapt their production lines, demanding that professionals continue to improve their personal and technological competencies. Additionally, educational institutions have to adapt their curriculum/subjects to offer intensive training and high-quality critical skills, including the training of digital skills (Atiku, 2018; Martyakova & Gorchakova, 2019). In this context, some projects and initiatives are already being implemented to overcome the challenges enacted by the digital transformation (e.g. Mesquita, Oliveira, Sequeira, Oliveira & Silva, 2020). Many of these projects are designed globally and applied locally. These projects provide companies and higher education institutions with new platforms or models of work or training, tutorial actions, simulation environments and they offer youngsters the possibility to develop digital competencies, analytical and critical thinking, the capacity of being innovative, critical learning, ability to solve complex problems and reasoning. So, the projects are: (1) Project Direction Employment; (2) Project UPPScience; (3) Project Creative InternPrize; (4) Project ELSE; (5) Project YBS – Your Business Success. Although each project has its specificities, they have one element in common – their ultimate goal is to prepare youth to be competitive and employable in an ever-changing environment.

Project Direction Employment

Direction Employment (DE) is a European project, funded by the program EEA and Norway Grants for Youth Employment. The project's main objective is to prepare disadvantaged young people for the structural labor market changes and digital transition by crafting and applying, in different EU regional contexts, an experimental educational and social-professional intervention model. This project is targeted to disadvantaged NEET (not in education, employment or training) youth, aged 20-29 years, at the European level, comprising the inclusion of specific groups at the local contexts of the participating countries, such as women, LGBT, immigrants, and ROMA.

In Portugal, the DE project is focusing on NEET youth. According to OCDE data, Portugal is in 10th place among countries with a higher number of NEET youth, with a percentage of 4.49% (2017). However, when looking at the numbers from previous years, the decrease is evident, since in 2013 the percentage of not employed or educated teenagers was at 8.53%, nearly double the current rate (OECD, 2019).

The situation changes, though, when we look at national statistics, and this is mostly because of one reason: while most countries consider the NEET youth to be teenagers between the ages of 15 and 25, in Portugal of the age gap goes up to 35 years old. This was simply due to the high levels of unemployed people of this age range. Therefore, Portuguese national statistics point out to 11.2% (2017) of NEET youth, which is still a big drop when compared to the data of the previous year (13.2%). Most of these are between the ages of 20-24 (14.7%) followed by a rate of 13% for both remaining age groups of 25-29 and 30-34. The rate of NEET youth between the ages of 15-19 is the lowest, counting only 4.2% (2017 data) (Vieira, Ferreira, & Pappámikail, 2018), though these are not expected to have an active work life just be active in education. Even though Portugal seems to be on a good path to decreasing the number of unemployed youths, there are still a few problems. The factors contributing to the above rate are: too long vast training courses; inadequacy between training and companies' needs; lack of demand, by young people, in areas with higher employability, like the industrial sector; and maladjusted perspectives.

Provided the current context, the core of the project consists of improving soft skills, including knowing how to work in groups, how to communicate, how to manage work and time. All these skills are necessary for all occupations at one point or another as evidenced by the literature cited in the first part of this chapter. Another area where it is necessary to develop skills relates to the IT sector (Perez-Uribe, Ovalle-Mora, Ocampo-Guzman, & Ramirez-Salazar, 2020; Ulusoy, 2020) once, it has also become evident, IT skills are needed in all sorts of jobs, from desk work to the industries, even to agriculture because almost everything is at least partially automated (Atiku & Boateng, 2020). Of course, companies teach their employees all they need to know about technologies they will need to use in the workplace, but it is also an advantage for both parties when one already has the knowledge to work with certain applications.

The DE project provides answers to the IT sector's upskilling/reskilling needs. The consortium of the project is made up of partners from different sectors - ONGs, higher education institutions, companies - from Portugal (ISCAP P.Porto e IEFP); Bulgaria (Workshop for Civic Initiatives Foundation); Bulgaria (Code Success Foundation); Lithuania (Lithuanian Gay League); Italy (Lai-momo); Ireland (DMC-Matrix). The consortium has a proven track record of working for the social and labor market through the inclusion of young people from marginalized minorities, being particularly, focused in fulfilling a set of specific objectives: (1) Development of an experimental model of training, which matches innovative pedagogical methodology with social support structures towards NEET youth and *mentoring* programs; (2) Development of a curriculum of training, with corresponding content and evaluation instruments, specifically conceived to train NEET youth; (3) Development of a benchmark of inter-regional *mobile learning* for training and integration of potential lecturer; (4) Development of devices of social impact measures and the evaluation integrated in the training benchmark; (5) Active engagement from the community, NGOs and national and regional system, as well as the corporate structures, for the enhancement of synergies and the increase of youngsters' employability.

Attending to the project's specifications, the benchmark and methodology are shaped in synchrony with the digital labor market and aligned with global tendencies, namely in what concerns integral and democratic pedagogy, as well as the head booster of digital transition, for example, the evolution of preferences, and behaviors of the corporate sector, globalization and new labor market opportunities, the rising pressure regarding the acquisition and development of knowledge and relevant expertise, among others.

The project's methodology is organized into seven main iterative stages (Oliveira, Mesquita & Oliveira, 2019), which combine research, intervention, evaluation and informing/reporting/refinement, as illustrated in Figure 1.

The first stage of the methodology consists of an ex-ante analysis of the ICT market and NEET youth employment needs, together with existing governmental and non-governmental employment and training policies and programs. This analysis is conducted not only on current needs but also on future expectations and predictions for the ICT labor market and youth training. The research wants to establish a provisional set of domain areas, at the European level, to be included in the training curriculum. These areas include computer literacy, mathematics and logic, programming and web development. After that, the curriculum is tested with a group of 15 NEET young students and trainers using the short test-class sessions approach. Feedback and follow-ups are collected and reflected in the curriculum, which is, therefore, redesigned and adapted to local contexts.

All through each of the three series of selection, training, and placement the NEET youth will be accompanied by psychologists, vocational trainers, potential employers, and ICT professionals. This is aimed at nurturing both the personal and professional development of NEET youth, as well as building the necessary social settings for their market entry. Together with the vocational training and mentoring,

Figure 1. Overview of the 4.0 de methodology (Oliveira, Mesquita & Oliveira, 2019)

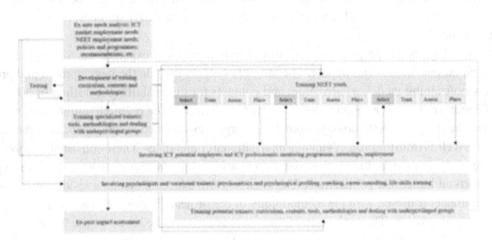

in-family work with parents and siblings, personal development support, training visits, cultural development and meetings with ICT industries are included as continuous support initiatives.

In parallel, analysis of the group and individual experiences will be conducted, and feedback to the education methodologies and trainers will be provided every month. Reports of learning metrics, such as activity, learning flow, laziness, etc., will be provided, and indexes for personal development will be introduced. The initial estimation of the trained NEET young students is 420, with at least 70% of the in-class training attended, and at least 90% of the course hours taken. The foreseen success rate of trainees is 65%.

As the final step of the preparation of training, the consortium ensures the certification of the training by appropriate EU or internationally recognized standards (i.e. ECVET, a certificate for vocational training (CP or FP), etc.).

Together with the development and implementation of training for NETT youth, a mobile smart classroom toolkit for the training of potential trainers will also be prepared. The toolkit's purpose is to train new trainers and to transfer the 4.0 DE methodology into new regions of the participating countries. At least 2 new regions per country will be approached, and short-term training will be organized in parallel with the NEET youth main training. At least one train of new trainers per take-in (three overall) will be organized using the following structure: 3 months of MOOC combined with 3 days of on-site training in preselected regions. The main criteria for the selection of a new region will be to have at least 20 trainees enrolled in the course. The course content will be based on the following ToT (training of trainers) curriculum modules: (a) how to use the curriculum; (b) how to prepare digital content; (c) mobile smart classroom toolkit utilization; and (g) working with socially vulnerable groups. The ToT also envisions the creation of synergies among trainers to improve the curriculum, contents and pedagogical strategies for NEET youth training.

An ex-post and impact analysis and assessment will be conducted at the end of each of the training cycles, and six months after the NEET youth placement in the labor market. This is to ensure proper analysis and improvement of the methodology, the convenient personal and professional follow-up of trainees in the labor market and the measurement of employment rates and social impact. To do so, the World Bank Social Safeguards methodology and the Aspen Institute Social Impact methodology will be used together with other in-house developed social impact and assessment tools, which will be informed, among others, by peer reviews and empathic deep interviews with NEET trainees, trainers, employers, and other stakeholders.

The methodology of the project envisions three main domains of expected outcomes: tangible outputs, research outputs, and social impact. The tangible outputs include the development and provision of an education/training model, a curriculum and contexts for the upskilling/reskilling of NEET youth in the ICT labor market and a toolkit/course for training trainers. The research outputs are expected to emerge from the project's methodology, from the synergies established with trainers, stakeholders, and researchers as well as from the project's annual international conferences. These consist of methodologies, current state analysis, models, forecasts, revisions, recommendations, assessments and results expressed in tools, reports and scientific publications. The most relevant expected outcome resides on the potential of the social impact achieved with the methodology of the project. This is why the methodology is key and the subject of revision. The evaluation of the social impact will be based on the following key indicators: (1) 52% of the trainees have received placements; (b) 75% of the trainees have reported changes in behavior/self-assessment; and (c) 55% of the employers have reported changes in their perception of the employability of disadvantaged NEET youth, which leads to increased sustainability.

Project ELSE

ELSE, which stands for Eco/Logical Learning and Simulation Environments in Higher Education - http://www.elseproject.eu/else/ -, is an international project that has a contribution from eleven partners of eight different countries. Mainly, the partnership is made up of a partner from the business sector, with expertise in serious games and ten higher education institutions, willing to change the way teaching and learning process is provided. It is recognized that for many higher education teachers, technology is not used fully to its capacities. Some teachers try to avoid technological tools during their classes, which can be very dangerous in a society that is flooded with technology. Students are aware of the last technological developments and for being engaged, they expect more dynamic classes, not a teacher addressing a passive audience with a monochord discourse. This is particularly common in the higher education sector of several European countries, in where the teacher is of difficult access. To change this paradigm and to prove that technology can help effectively the learning process, the ELSE project was created. Nevertheless, technology alone does not solve the existing problems. The challenges can only be surpassed by the active contribution of teachers and students. The ELSE project enabled the research of novel uses of digital technologies to provide innovative content through innovative methods to enhance the learning experience of students. The countries represented in this project are Italy, with three partners – two higher education institutions and one company, Romania, with two higher education institutions, the UK, Northern Macedonia, Poland, Spain, Cyprus, and Portugal, with one higher education institution each.

The main aim of the project is to create and disseminate a strategy to achieve the European Commission's goal of redesigning Higher Education, enabling an easier application of Bologna principles across Europe. The objective is achieved through the development of an integrated curriculum, in which the delivery of academic content is coincident with, and enhanced by the acquisition of transversal skills and abilities appropriate for the digital age. The project has three main additional objectives: 1) to know about the current activity and best practices in the learning process of participating institutions and countries; 2) to develop innovative pedagogies and offer suggestions for the best ICT applications for competence teaching in higher education, including project-based learning; 3) to design digital learning environments that support blended learning and increases the engagement and involvement of students, such as the flipped classroom methodology.

The practical tools expected to be produced by the partnership are a video tagging tool, called e-voli, a serious game web platform, called e-core, and an assessment tool called e-dashboard. All these tools are being tested by partners and also by participants of the Intensive Study Programs organized by the partnership. All these tools will be integrated into the LMS Moodle, enabling teachers from all participant institutions to use them with their students as they usually do.

The use of these tools and the creation of this technological environment can stimulate higher education teachers, as well as teachers from other levels of education, to be more motivated and engaged in an innovative learning environment based on learner-centered pedagogies (holistic, constructivist, connectivism approaches) and activate students' learning process through problem-solving, learning-by-doing, gamification, or digital information research.

Project Creative Internprize

Creative Internprize - http://creative.internprize.eu/ - was the name given to a project, whose main objective was to provide creative entrepreneurs with the necessary skills for the creation and effective management of a business. These skills include the so-called hard or technical skills and transversal or soft skills. For a world that is changing every day, soft skills have a fundamental role in the career of any professional (e.g. (Mesquita, Oliveira, & Sequeira, 2019). In practice, partners from different European countries met together to create a concept that could generate opportunities for entrepreneurs in the form of training through a web platform. Higher education institutions, companies and non-profit organizations from Portugal, Turkey, Malta, Spain, Italy, Norway, Northern Ireland, and Greece took part in the partnership.

During the project, a set of manuals was developed with the contribution of all partners and a web platform was created to manage and monitor projects that were developed by volunteer participants. For example, in Portugal, students from communication and design areas had the opportunity to develop some work for two non-profit organizations. These beneficiary nonprofit organizations were MAERA association and SPACE Network. Both organizations promote networking among its members to create synergies. MAERA – Management, Accounting, and Education Research Association is an international association that intends to connect the academic world with the business world, for example, allowing students to do practical research that can benefit enterprises in practice. SPACE network, founded in France in 1989, is an international network that brings together primarily professional higher education institutions, including universities and VET schools. In the case of the MAERA association, one of the participants developed communication materials, such as an institutional video, a flyer and some banners to be included in the social media of the organization. The other participant restructured MAERA website, updating contents and adding new ones that were in line with the mission of the association. In the case of the SPACE Network, the participants developed some communication materials to promote the organization internationally. In both cases, participants had the opportunity to apply their knowledge, mainly acquired during their graduations and could contact and interact with professionals from academic and business areas.

These experiences are important, not only for students putting in practice what they learned, but also serves as an opportunity for future work opportunities. And that was what happened with one of the participants of MAERA association experience, that was hired by a company, member of the association. During the above-mentioned experiences, the participants used the web platform that managed their activities of the project they were involved in and also had the opportunity to access the materials in a training format that was created by the partnership and that are available for free (http://creative. internprize.eu/Pages/Training).

Project UPPScience

UPPScience, which stands for Using Profiling and Publishing for the upping of Scientific Approaches - http://viscontiproject.eu/uppscience/Welcome_UPPScience -,is an international project whose main objective is to help develop competencies of youngsters related to analytical and critical thinking, the capacity of being innovative, critical learning, ability to solve complex problems and reasoning. The project also helps teachers, trainers and managers of VET to overcome their difficulties in doing research and publishing, which are activities normally exclusive for academics.

The partnership encompasses 22 organizations partners from different countries, such as Romania, Turkey, Poland, Italy, Spain, Malta, Norway, Portugal, and Palestinian Authority, including 3 Universities, 7 VET schools, 6 High Schools, 3 Civil Society Organizations, 2 NGOs working in the field of education and 1 private company. One of the main tools developed by this project was a web-based virtual workspace, that participants can use to improve the previously referred competences (http://cop. viscontiproject.eu/web/). The process of using the platform is simple, - the participant elaborates his/her paper which can be a research paper or a project. Then, two experienced reviewers will assess/review the paper and give the respective feedback. In the following step, participants can also become reviewers of other papers and projects. This process is possible thanks to the community of practice that was initially developed in a previous international project (VISConti – Viability Innovation Scientific Creativity).

Additionally, some training materials were created and provided to improve the capacity of writing, and how to use the platform. During the project lifetime, four training activities were organized comprising involving more than thirty participants from partners. More than 150 research projects and publications were produced and reviewed. Every partner organization had an "Ambassador of Change" which promoted the benefits of the project and its adoption in his / her organization and country. Aggregating both the platform and the community of practice enables teachers, for example, to use these tools to teach research methodologies or other related courses. One of the most important merits of the platform is to provide the development of analytical and critical competencies for youngsters in a risk-free environment. In this way, we can say that the project prepares youngsters for the job market.

Project YBS – Your Business Success

According to several studies from the European Commission, SMEs perform a very important role in the countries' economies. Not only because they represent a high percentage of the total enterprises, but also because they are the source of most jobs (Act, 2008). In this line, young entrepreneurs and business owners/managers of micro and small enterprises must have fundamental competencies and skills for the job and frequently they don't. To overcome this problem, an international project was created with the collaboration of organizations from six different countries, one higher education from Portugal, one company from the UK and others from Greece, one foundation from Romania, a nonprofit organization from Bulgaria and another one from the Netherlands.

The YBS – Your Business Success (https://www.ybsproject.com/pt/) is the name given to the project, which translates, in a certain way, the will of the consortium to provide success for every entrepreneur or a business owner. In this line, some important tools are being developed. The YBS VET course and the VET enterprise planning tool, which is web-based, are the most important tools for helping aspiring entrepreneurs and owners or managers from existing firms, especially in developing the entrepreneurial spirit and fundamental skills and competences for business planning and decision-making. The YBS VET course, together with the VET enterprise planning tool was translated and will be tested through pilot training in all countries of the partnership. The idea is to have feedback from real users of the tools and the comments received will help to improve them to a final version.

The main targets of this project are primarily aspiring entrepreneurs and established business owners or managers, especially from small and medium enterprises. Secondly, the project defines as target groups the teachers and trainers that are going to deliver the VET training to the primary group. Thirdly, another target group encompasses the other VET actors and stakeholders, such as governmental agencies, VET education centers, business support agencies and all entities that want to improve the effectiveness of entrepreneurs and level of enterprise survival rates.

During the development of the main tools of the project, partners considered today's need of providing essential skills for creating and managing a business. For that, it is important to provide technical skills for entrepreneurs, such as financial management or marketing, but it is also important to deliver training that can develop transversal skills such as negotiation, cooperation, teamwork, just to mention a few.

FUTURE RESEARCH DIRECTIONS

This chapter present a set of project and initiatives to provide companies and higher education institutions new platforms or models of work and training, tutorial actions, simulation environment and it gives the youngsters the possibility to develop digital competencies, analytical and critical thinking, the capacity of being innovative, critical learning, ability to solve complex problems and reasoning.

Future research is expected to collect an increased body of the medium and long term impacts projects/initiatives in the covered targets, in the companies and in higher education institutions. A subsequent research direction will rely on identifying and collecting remaining gaps between the preparation of youngsters and the demands of the labor market, as to improve/correct/devise new social/educational/organizational interventions at the European level. Future research is expected to understand the impact of these projects and initiatives in a different work context, for example concerning remote work and remote learning. It will be pertinent to check if these projects have contributed to employability issues, if organizations have become more competitive and if young people have acquired skills to respond to the digital needs presented by organizations.

Furthermore, we also point out as another research direction the analysis of how these changes are happening and what are the challenges that professionals are facing together with the identification of how they are reacting to the digital transformation and how they are envisioning their future work life and workplace.

CONCLUSION

The purpose of this paper was to contribute with a reflection about the Work 4.0, the preparation of youngsters for the labor market, and to present some projects that might help youngsters to be better prepared to face the challenges brought by digital environments.

The chapter show that there isn't a revolution with no implications for the lives of organizations and people and that the 4th Industrial Revolution or Industry 4.0 is a reality in modern societies transforming the way organizations and young people live their private and work lives. The analysis of this context shows that task automation requires human resources with an increasing range of both hard and soft skills. In this context, five projects and initiatives are already being implemented to overcome the challenges enacted by the digital transformation: (1) Project Direction Employment; (2) Project UPPScience; (3) Project Creative InternPrize; (4) Project ELSE; (5) Project YBS – Your Business Success. These projects provide answers to the needs of young people and organizations, such as: answers to the IT sector's upskilling/reskilling needs; improving soft skills, including knowing how to work in groups, how to communicate, how to improving soft skills, including; development of an integrated curriculum for the digital age; to provide creative entrepreneurs so-called hard or technical skills and transversal or soft skills; development of tools capable of helping the aspiring entrepreneurs and owners or managers from existing firms, especially in developing the entrepreneurial spirit and fundamental skills and competences for business planning and decision-making. These projects and initiatives highlight studies referred to in the literature review that showed, for example, that educational institutions have to adapt their curriculum/subjects to offer intensive training of digital skills (Atiku, 2018; Martyakova & Gorchakova, 2019), the digitalization, imply reduced human or manual intervention in tasks (Kumar & Nayyar, 2020), the organizations need to become digitalized to respond to the market technological challenges and they will require humans to undertake cross-functional high-tech training (Chhabra, 2018; Gupta, 2018; Martyakova & Gorchakova, 2019). As a conclusion we may say, that these projects provide companies and higher education institutions with new platforms or models of work or training, tutorial actions, simulation environments and they offer youngsters the possibility to develop digital competencies, analytical and critical thinking, the capacity of being innovative, critical learning, ability to solve complex problems and reasoning.

Therefore, it can be concluded that it is necessary that organizations continuously restructure themselves and, together with society at large, define which hard, soft and digital skills are needed and which digital and human resources profiles are key (Ulusoy, 2020). The chapter also allows us to conclude that schools, educators, and governments need to be aware of how jobs are rapidly changing and to able to address the current and future demands of companies, concerning the roles that these jobs will have in industry/companies (Schwarzmüller et al., 2018). This means that there is a clear need to adjust and adapt current training curricula to the alterations that have been introduced (and still are) by technology in the market, and there is also the need to foresee and prepare for future changes and impacts on the jobs that current students will occupy.

In this context, this chapter presented a set of projects and initiatives that are already being implemented in Europe, aiming to contribute to overcoming the challenges enacted by the digital transformation.

REFERENCES

Act, S. B. (2008). Think small first: A 'Small Business Act'f or Europe. Communication from the commission to the council, the European Parliament, the European Economic and Social Committee and the Committee of the Regions. *Commission of the European Communities Brussels*, *25*, 2008.

Atiku, S. O. (2018). Reshaping human capital formation through digitalization. In *Radical Reorganization of Existing Work Structures through Digitalization* (pp. 52–73). IGI Global. doi:10.4018/978-1-5225-3191-3.ch004

Atiku, S. O., & Boateng, F. (2020). Rethinking Education System for the Fourth Industrial Revolution. In *Human Capital Formation for the Fourth Industrial Revolution* (pp. 1–17). IGI Global. doi:10.4018/978-1-5225-9810-7.ch001

Chala, N., & Poplavska, O. (2017). *The 4th Industrial Revolution and Innovative Labor: Trends.* Challenges, Forecasts.

De Franceschi, A. (2015). EU Digital Single Market Strategy in Light of the Consumer Rights Directive, The. *J. Eur. Consumer & Mkt. L.*, *4*, 144.

Degryse, C. (2016). *Digitalisation of the economy and its impact on labour markets.* ETUI Research Paper-Working Paper.

Evans, D. (2011). The internet of things: How the next evolution of the internet is changing everything. *CISCO White Paper, 1*(2011), 1-11.

Gray, J., & Rumpe, B. (2015). *Models for digitalization.* Springer. doi:10.100710270-015-0494-9

Guerrieri, P., Evangelista, R., & Meliciani, V. (2014). *The economic impact of digital technologies in Europe.* Academic Press.

Irma Becerra-Fernandez, R. S. (2001). Organizational knowledge management: A contingency perspective. *Journal of Management Information Systems*, *18*(1), 23–55. doi:10.1080/07421222.2001.11045676

Martyakova, E., & Gorchakova, E. (2019). *Quality Education and Digitalization of the Economy.* Paper presented at the International Conference on the Industry 4.0 model for Advanced Manufacturing. 10.1007/978-3-030-18180-2_17

McChrystal, G. S., Collins, T., Silverman, D., & Fussell, C. (2015). *Team of teams: New rules of engagement for a complex world.* Penguin.

Mesquita, A., Oliveira, L., & Sequeira, A. (2019). *The Future of the Digital Workforce: Current and Future Challenges for Executive and Administrative Assistants.* Academic Press.

OECD. (2019). *Youth not in employment, education or training.* NEET.

Ovans, A. (2015). How emotional intelligence became a key leadership skill. *Harvard Business Review*, 28.

Perez-Uribe, R. I., Ovalle-Mora, O. O., Ocampo-Guzman, D., & Ramirez-Salazar, M. D. P. (2020). Innovation Trends in Human Management for Competitiveness in SMEs. In *Handbook of Research on Increasing the Competitiveness of SMEs* (pp. 1–25). IGI Global. doi:10.4018/978-1-5225-9425-3.ch001

Porter, M. E., & Heppelmann, J. E. (2015). How smart, connected products are transforming companies. *Harvard Business Review*, *93*(10), 96–114.

Rintala, N., & Suolanen, S. (2005). The implications of digitalization for job descriptions, competencies and the quality of working life. *Nordicom Review*, *26*(2), 53–67. doi:10.1515/nor-2017-0258 PMID:17290637

Schwab, K. (2017). *The fourth industrial revolution*. Currency.

Shrivastava, P. (1998). Management Education for the Digital Economy. *Academy of Management Proceedings*.

Susskind, R. E., & Susskind, D. (2015). *The future of the professions: How technology will transform the work of human experts*. Oxford University Press.

Topcu, M. K. (2020). Competency Framework for the Fourth Industrial Revolution. In *Human Capital Formation for the Fourth Industrial Revolution* (pp. 18–43). IGI Global. doi:10.4018/978-1-5225-9810-7.ch002

Ulusoy, B. (2020). Understanding Digital Congruence in Industry 4.0. In Business Management and Communication Perspectives in Industry 4.0 (pp. 17-31). IGI Global.

Vieira, M. M., Ferreira, T., & Pappámikail, L. (2018). *Fazer o futuro no presente?* Jovens em condição NEEF e o programa Garantia Jovem.

KEY TERMS AND DEFINITIONS

Artificial Intelligence: Machines that are programmed to work and think like humans.

Automation: Technology that allows tasks to be performed, often without human intervention.

Competencies: A combination of skills, aptitudes, knowledge that contribute to making the individual stand out for it's the difference and highlight the difference of the company.

Digital Transformation: Process of integrating digital technology in different contexts of companies and the life of individuals. Creates new ways of working, communicating and living.

Fourth Industrial Revolution: Represents new resources for people and organizations. Used as a synonym for digital transformation, the fourth industrial revolution introduces new technology and leads to new ways of working.

Internet: It is the set of computer networks that can exchange data and messages using a common protocol.

Work 4.0: Brings together high technological level technologies and methods. Represents new ways of working.

Chapter 4
Variable Fonts From Pioneer Perspectives

Liudmila Bredikhina
Geneva University, Switzerland

ABSTRACT

The impact of fonts on user experience and brand perception has been widely discussed by a variety of specialists. In 2016 a new technology called variable fonts came out with a promise of lighter font files, responsiveness, variability, and adaptability on the web across devices. This chapter reminds users of parameters that should be taken into account when choosing a font and discuss ways in which brands can implement variable fonts to increase their performance. Unique perspective on variable fonts from specialist in different domains related to variable fonts and their implementation will be proposed in this chapter as it aims to focus on providing unique insider knowledge on currently developing projects that implement this new technology as well as on ideas and possibilities that might interest future e-learning and e-business brands.

INTRODUCTION

Type designers and developers are key individuals in regard to font design and font implementations. The choice of font can have an effect on users' opinions about the brand (Mackiewicz & Moeller, 2004), generating emotions and stimulating customer demand. Responsive design is important for businesses and e-learning platforms as it enables flexibility across platforms and interfaces. Unfortunately, while web design is often flexible and responsive, regular fonts are static and do not enable smooth variations across devices. In 2016, Apple, Google, and Microsoft announced a new software that allows users to store several variable font designs in one file, making a single font behave like multiple fonts. Variable fonts are a new technology that enables glyphs' outlines to morph in between variable style shapes and offers flexibility to responsive design. Variable fonts can create better type hierarchy on websites compared to regular fonts, visual consistency, and better readability across screen interfaces, which are important aspects in web usability (Bhatia et al., 2011) and user experience. Compared to regular fonts, variable

DOI: 10.4018/978-1-7998-3756-5.ch004

fonts exist in one lighter file that encapsulates the entire font family, speeds up webpage download time, has a smaller disc footprint, requires fewer server requests, and improves performance, readability and delivery. Screen adaptability makes text more accessible and memorable; then, users' attention to the website grows, generating a positive response to the brand (Nakilcioğlu, 2013). With this new technology, clients can differentiate their businesses from others by fine-tuning fonts and creating custom styles of fonts for specific purposes and devices (Hudson, 2018). Moreover, variable fonts benefit designers and brands as they enable them to choose the exact weight and width of a font for their interfaces and displays. Variable fonts, as a responsive typography, have the potential to fine-tune digital design based on screen orientation, reading distance, or the size of the screen (Hudson, 2018), morphing the text with the responsive web layout.

Variable fonts have emerged in the recent years. However, academics have yet to study their implications. The paper attempts to contribute to the lack of literary work in the field of variable fonts and provide the field with the first academic publication on the matter. In order to demonstrate the importance of taking into account variable fonts in business and e-learning, this paper consists of two parts that aim to use different perspectives to research how variable fonts can generate a better user experience than with regular fonts. This paper will begin with a background and literature review on regular fonts, as academic research on variable fonts is almost non-existent. Researchers can transpose and adapt the hypothesis proposed by academics in regard to readability and user experience surrounding regular fonts onto the variable fonts issue. In the second section, this paper will propose an interview summary conducted among currently developing variable fonts studios, developers, and type specialists in order to acquire professional opinions on the subject of variable fonts and user experience. It is crucial to take into consideration insider knowledge from individuals who create and develop variable fonts as they take into account design-related issues that impact user experience. In summary, this paperer will summarize various aspects of variable fonts that should be taken into account to improve user experience.

BACKGROUND

In the age of globalization, cultures affect brands linguistic elements, consumer behavior, and users' responses to brands' attitudes (Schmitt et al., 1994; Zhang & Schmitt, 2001). Brand and corporate-identity elements, such as brand names, trademarks, brand personalities, logotypes, fonts, colors, and shapes, contribute to distinct consumer perception of a brand and better business performance (Grinsven & Das, 2014; Henderson et al., 2004a; Hutton, 1997; Kristensen & Grønhaug, 2007; Puškarević et al., 2014; Zaichkowsky, 2010). Brand personality (Azoulay & Kapferer, 2003) and brand names can generate favorable impressions of the product and influence consumers' behaviors (Argo et al., 2010). In marketing strategies, the most persuasive design element for accomplishing communication goals are fonts (Henderson et al., 2004b). Fonts are involved in brand perception (Childers & Jass, 2002) as "typography deals with the form, spacing and layout of words and sentences in the text written or displayed communication messages" (Mccarthy & Mothersbaugh, 2002, p. 664).

Typographic website information consists of several aspects that affect brands' success (Salehi et al., 2012) and brands' perception (Nakilcioğlu, 2013). Studies have shown that web page design (Wang et al., 2011), color (Chadwick-Dias et al., 2007; K.-C. Huang et al., 2008; Tavassoli, 2001), images, and text can have an impact on users' desires to engage with digital content (Diouf & Lemoine, 2019). Reading can provoke feelings of excitement, joy, serenity, or even distress (Bayer et al., 2010; Lemoine, 2012).

Furthermore, fonts communicate a brand's personality (Childers & Jass, 2002; Grohmann et al., 2012) and influence users' responses to visual identity and advertisement (Amar et al., 2017). Handwritten style can humanize a product (Schroll et al., 2018) and promote haptic engagement (Izadi & Patrick, n.d.). Fonts encourage consumers to pursuit their interactions with brands, improve readability (Hussain et al., 2011; Slattery & Rayner, 2010), and improve overall perception of the brand by conveying meaning (Childers & Jass, 2002), which leads to purchasing behavior (Novemsky et al., 2007).

Additionally, fonts impact users' capacity to read (Ali et al., 2013) and comprehend written content (Childers & Jass, 2002; McCarthy & Mothersbaugh, 2002). The number of words per paragraph, line, and the size of characters impact legibility (Bigelow, 2019; McCarthy & Mothersbaugh, 2002; Patching & Jordan, 2005). Legibility is the ease "of obtaining enough information to understand the words of pictures being presented" (Nilsson, 2006, p. 1445). Font legibility constitutes several elements: size (x-height, ascenders, descenders)(Beymer et al., 2008; Pušnik et al., 2016), height, weight (volume of the letter), style (serif, non-serif, italic), and width (Childers & Jass, 2002; Keage et al., 2014; Mccarthy & Mothersbaugh, 2002). Serif or non-serif fonts can impact readability at different sizes and on different devices (Arditi & Cho, 2005). Letter and word spacing contributes to semantic associations of the brand and webpage information retrieve (Ling & van Schaik, 2006); for example, increased spacing can give a feeling of purity or can hinder text legibility (Mccarthy & Mothersbaugh, 2002). User's reading ability, such as the nature of eye movement, reading skills, and reading difficulties (dyslexia), can be affected by typographic choice (Mccarthy & Mothersbaugh, 2002).

In addition, color and text attract attention, improve brand recognition, and impact the user's favorable attitudes toward the visual material (Madden et al., 2000; Moore et al., 2013; Nilsson, 2006). Typefaces, with their overall characteristics, have a strong impact on brands perceptions and message readability. Additionally, they can have a persuasive effect, making typography the central element and an integral part of the text (Amar et al., 2017; McCarthy & Mothersbaugh, 2002). The font choice can affect perceived credibility of the product, website, or application and influence users' engagements with the brand (Y. Huang, Li, et al., 2018). For example, a font that is easy to read results in positive reviews from users (Y. Huang, Wu, et al., 2018). Visual complexity and fluidity of webpages affect the user's approach and behavior toward a website (Deng & Poole, 2010). Design for usability has been the major focus of web design for several years. Moreover, user experience on webpages has direct consequences on brand's perception and consumer behavior (Deng & Poole, 2010).

The above-mentioned literature arrives to the conclusion that fonts impact users' perceptions of brands, user experience, and readability. However, these articles focus on the finished product, failing to take into account the design process of typefaces by type designers and the implementation process of typefaces by developers. Thus, the authors chose to take a unique approach compared with the literature that they reviewed. This approach focuses on filling the gap between academic perspectives and behind the scenes of the type design industry by providing an innovative and unique approach to thinking and considering fonts. In the next section, variable font design specialists and developers will present their opinions and discuss some of their current projects that involve variable fonts.

MAIN FOCUS OF THE CHAPTER

The goal of this paper is to provide readers with variable font design specialists and developers opinions on the subject of variable fonts and how this technology can improve user experience on the web.

Researchers in the above reviewed literature have written and said many things about regular fonts; however, this paper focuses on reasons why brands should opt for variable fonts in order to improve user experience on digital platforms. The goal of this paper is to answer the question of why companies should use variable fonts in order to generate better user experience, which results in a positive impression of a brand's business or facilitates e-learning.

The paper's goal is to propose a discussion panel with the pioneers in the variable fonts field; they all have their unique approach to variable fonts and have worked on different projects: from those who design the variable fonts to those who implement them in e-learning digital environments. Instead of providing yet another empirical approach to users perceptions of fonts (which should be usually done internally in the design studio), this paper wishes to provide its readers with with an understanding of the possibilities to imagine the different possibilities of variable font applications and introduce to them professionals that are specialized in the field of this technology. As variable fonts have existed only since mid-2016, there is a need to educate people about the possibilities that they offer.

For this paper, the authors conducted interviews among thirteen participants who the authors chose based on their approach and knowledge of the field. Participants were sampled among design strategist, a UX leader, a technologist, an expert in web, type designers, type consultants, AR/VR specialists, front-end developers, and teachers. They were chosen based on their novelty of work with variable fonts, their knowledge on the subject of variable fonts and their involvement with development process of the variable font technology. Small design studios or independent designers who only developed few variable fonts were disregarded from this research. The participants were limited to thirteen, as they covered the various segments of variable fonts designs and implementations. The authors interviewed each of them in person or via Skype on a semi-structured basis. The answers were analyzed and presented in the following questions as solutions and recommendations in regard to variable fonts and user experience on the web.

The questions included:

1. Are variable fonts an interesting tool for e-business and can they have a beneficial effect on their visual identity and help productivity?
2. What areas are variable fonts most useful in?
3. Can variable fonts enable a more consistent experience across devices?
4. How can variable fonts impact user experience?
5. Do variable fonts enable better readability across devices and thus a better user experience?
6. Do variable fonts enable more opportunities for branding?

SOLUTIONS AND RECOMMENDATIONS

This section provides a series of thirteen interviews from the sampled participants. The authors wish to provide readers with better understanding of the solutions that offer variable fonts for better user experience on the web. Variable fonts specialist, designers and developers provide solutions and recommendations based on the asked sections described in the previous section. The section will be organized as follows: Jason Pamental (design strategist, UX leader); ABCDinamo (type design agency offering retail and bespoke typefaces, design software, research, and consultation); Laurence Penney (consultant in dynamic font technology); Nick Sherman (type designer, web designer, typographer, and consultant); Black[Foundry] (an international team of twelve talents, including type designers, font developers, art directors, software engineers, programmers, and project managers); Mandy Michael (speaker and variable font developer); Christopher Koeberlin (designs fonts producer); Future Fonts (experimental variable font company); Underware (collective of type designers who design type, educate about type, publish about type, and give conferences); Andrew Johnson (variable font designer and font designer for augmented reality); David Jonathan Ross (variable font designers); Raphaël Verona (type designer, graphic designer, type design teacher); Ilya Ruderman (graphic and type designer).

Jason Pamental

Jason Pamental is a design strategist, UX leader, technologist, expert in web typography, and Invited Expert on the W3C Web Fonts Working Group. He works with teams and brand owners on how to set type better on digital platforms. He has spoken with organizations like Adobe, Audible, Condé Nast, GoDaddy, and IBM in addition to giving presentations and workshops all over the world. As variable fonts came out, he became interested in the new typographic possibilities that were now available for the web. He has launched production websites that have implemented variable fonts. In Pamental's opinions, variable fonts are a perfect extension of responsive design; from readability and utility of type, web design with variable fonts becomes one fluid system. With variable fonts, text can respond to ambient conditions and user's preferences. Additionally, variable fonts can apply to virtual reality and augmented reality environments (using a grey and optical size axis can be an interesting solution for better readability and user experience).

Type setting on a website is most commonly designers' suggestion to how they think the text is best set for readability. However, not all users have the same readability needs. Using a variable font that can tailor the reading experience to each user's needs allows brands to communicate their information and make it readable to any needs and capacities. It is a dramatic step forward in user experience by enabling them to have a personalized experience with the website, application, or any digital design that the brand has created. User experience has been an important topic of discussion over the past years, and now accessibility is becoming an important part of digital design. Pamental is working on an accessibility panel, which is a plug-in that can be moved from one project to another. He is also working on an educational website on Google fonts that caters to educating people about this new technology.

Usually, Jason Pamental asks clients and designers to find a typeface that they like. After this, he asks them to decide on the weights they want to use. Before they can even start to experiment, they have to limit themselves. With variable fonts, the typeface can be as light and as bold as the designer wants it to be, having one less concept and parameter to decide on. Variable fonts offer a range of possibilities, enabling the designer to focus on hierarchy that is no longer tied to the previous choices of weights, allowing them to find the most appropriate value for the specific design. Performance is really the reason why people want to use variable fonts. By purchasing a variable font, the brand can be almost sure that they will not have to purchase another weight or width as all the possibilities already exist in the one file. Another important factor is for companies with multiple desktops: with only one file to distribute to thousands of users, there is less risk of not having all previous files replaced with the new version compared to regular fonts.

With variable fonts, typography can be more adaptive to the environment the user is in and can be fluid on the web and digital applications. It is even possible to adjust the typeface based on the market. For example, in India, there is a much higher percentage of very low-cost android phones with low pixel density screen than in the USA or Europe, but those android phones can support variable fonts.

Designers and developers can program variable font to adapt to the changes of screen resolution and anticipate screen quality, bettering population's user experience. Variable fonts are key to being sensible, delivering better user experience and making content more accessible across the globe, based on the device's size and quality. Any company that is interested in e-learning has a target audience that uses a variety of devices. Pamental gave an example of such company. The product was targeted to a disadvantaged student population that is underserved at schools. Statistically, students who are in those schools come from homes that are more likely to have only one mobile device compared to students who live in middle-class families. The e-learning product had to be served and work on any screen size and resolution. Variable fonts are useful as they can tailor the learning experience based on the size of the screen and make it accessible to that specific population.

ABSDinamo

ABCDinamo is a Swiss type design agency offering retail and bespoke typefaces, design software, research, and consultation. They have offices in Basel and Berlin, as well as satellite members in several other locations as they do not limit themselves to Latin fonts. With variable fonts, typefaces can become and do so much more compared to before: they can allow designs and brands to express their vision and tell stories with fonts in an innovative manner. Previously, fonts were either serif or non-serif. However, with the new technology that offers variable fonts, ABCDinamo has designed a typeface that morphs in a range of styles, from serif to non-serif. Not only does this offer a wider range of motion, design, and style in one file between different font stylistics, but the animation is also clean throughout all of the instances. Combining two font styles that are so different and achieving a smooth range of motion is a challenging task, but when achieved, it provides users with a font that can be used in a greater variety of situations compared to regular fonts.

As most of everyday reading is done on phones, variable fonts offer a better readability than regular fonts across devices. It is possible to adjust variable font's weight and width in CSS code, resulting in the appropriate amount of words per line (i.e., the most comfortable number of words per line for readability). Usually, when users read words from a phone screen, the typeface can benefit from subtle adjustments, such as contrast and weight. With variable fonts, users can adjust text to the environment and to personal user's needs. Variable fonts not only offer more creativity, but they also offer different perspectives from type designers and developers.

Laurence Penney

Laurence Penney is a consultant in dynamic font technology based in Bristol, United Kingdom. Since 2016, he has been operating as a consultant in variable fonts, presenting the technology at conferences and universities. In 2016, he created the first website where anybody could play with variable fonts. In 2019, together with Irene Vlachou, he launched FauxFoundry, a web font service using variable font technology that provides automatic fallback fonts when the main font lacks characters. Penney thinks that with variable fonts, it is possible to invent new ways of using fonts, such as parametric font. A parametric font is a font in which the designer can directly control the width steams and separately control the movement of the horizontal axes while also separately controlling the width of counters and the x-height. A parametric font separately controls different axes, while adjusting them together.

With variable fonts, serif fonts become usable again. The main reason why designers and branding agencies prefer sans-serif fonts is because they are predictable at different sizes on different devices. However, serif-fonts are almost never readable in small size on a small screen. This results in the majority of companies using sans-serif fonts, with their visual identities becoming similar over time. By implementing an optical size axis in a variable serif font, the optical size is adjustable in CSS based on the screen and the device, making serif fonts readable at any size. Not only does this technology make serif fonts readable and the user experience better, but it also allows for brands to choose from a variety of fonts that are not limited to sans-serif fonts, creating unique brand identities and differentiating themselves from other brands.

One of the main focuses on variable fonts is on the weight-saving and fever server requests by cashing only one single file. Developers often use a font tool called "Suit," which allows them to subset variable fonts and their design spaces. The font file becomes smaller and lighter by choosing only the needed axis in a variable font. Penney gives an illustrative example: it is possible to choose the width axes based on the bold style of the typeface, making bold the new regular. Then the server decides which subset can be most sufficiently supplied to the user. This technology is particularly important in the case of a parametric font that has a large variety of axis and scripts. By creating subsets, it makes the fonts variable on a smaller design space, a smaller number of glyphs, and a lighter font file size.

Variable fonts enable brand consistency across devices and mediums. Their variability is useful for the development of the brand's identity. Reduction in font data does not result in a reduction of the typographic quality: designers can use as many font styles as they wish without creating heavier and slower websites, allowing for more room for the brand's identity expression without any compromises. Variable fonts also allow for fully responsive designs, highlighting the potential of some formatting changes. Penney gives an example: with variable fonts, it is possible to animate transitions between regular and bold styles. When text is repositioned or undergoes a stylist change, the designer can highlight the change to the user in a smoother manner for the perception. Instead of having a font change sharply, for example, by making it underlined or bluntly going from regular to bold, with variable fonts, the transition can be animated and make the user experience more pleasant.

Nick Sherman

Nick Sherman is a type designer, web designer, typographer, and consultant. He runs HEX Projects and is also a founder and designer of Fonts in Use and v-fonts.com. On v-fonts.com, he documents all of variable fonts releases. He began this project because previous websites that attempted to achieve the same project quality targeted an audience that was already familiar with variable fonts that were difficult to use or find. His goal was to create a simple, user-friendly website that would document all of the variable fonts that are available. On Fonts in Use, he documents interesting applications of fonts. Nick Sherman believes that variable fonts are useful anywhere that normal fonts are used. Specifically, they are useful in any area where the design is not fixed but more a set of parameters of how to lay out information based on context and concept. Examples include rule-based print design or responsive design.

For the Typographics conference, Nick Sherman had to print name badges. By using a variable font, it was easier to condense the letters and make the full name and surname fit on badges. Although this is an example of a printed material, it showcases how one can use variable fonts in any layout process in which there is some amount of dynamic composition involved. Since the responsive design on the web was introduced, web design became a practice of preparing logic for making compositions. The process is about making rules and parameters that adapt across different variables rather than static composition. With variable fonts, the design becomes fully responsive.

Display style variable fonts help people understand the technology and get interested in variable fonts. One can also use variable fonts for subtle animations to draw attention to a part of a text instead of using italics or bold to emphasize the change. Augmented reality is another fruitful environment where variable fonts can be interesting by adjusting letters based on the angle of view. That means that letters can change based on the users position in relation to the text, and the changes can happen in a smooth manner without the user noticing the animation. Furthermore, variable fonts make sense in the case of East Asian typefaces that have a lot of glyphs, and in any additional style usage on the web that can make a significant weight difference. Specifically, variable fonts are a valuable tool for branding. As the typefaces become easily adaptable with the technology, the brand's logo can change and vary based on size and application. From a business perspective, variable fonts can result in savings: in the case of a brand that needs a design space to be translated into different languages, it would necessitate a design that can undergo drastic variations in words length. A variable font can easily adapt to different design environment and be consistent across languages.

Black[Foundry]

Black[Foundry] was born out of the meeting of a serial French entrepreneur and type designer, Grégori Vincens, with a London-raised type designer and font engineer, Jérémie Hornus. Today, Black[Foundry] is an international team of twelve talents, including type designers, font developers, art directors, software engineers, programmers, and project managers, all working from central Paris. Once the variable font technology emerged in 2016, they quickly released one of their original fonts as a variable font. Before the variable font technology existed, the company was already interpolating extremes, making the shift to variable fonts simple for them as the families they were drawing before had already a variable like axis. However, they believe that there should not be a variety of axes to choose from in a variable font to make it interesting. This has the potential to become complicated by giving many possibilities to designers, resulting in confusion.

For custom project with clients, Black[Foundry] developed variable fonts that expressed feeling or ideas outside of the classic font variations. For example, for one client, they created a script font that simulated handwriting and, depending on the chosen axis, it expressed a different mood and style. Based on the target audience and its preferred aesthetics, the company could vary and adjust the visual of their font. Adjusting fonts based on the message, the brand wants to express to different audiences allows for personalized experiences for users. Variable fonts are most interesting on the web as they allow for adjustments and unity across platforms and screens. With fully responsive design, users can adjust text content delicately and precisely. As it has been mentioned also by other professionals, variable fonts can adapt based on the screen's luminosity, width of the column, and anything that can be responsive and necessitates adaptability. For example, text can be justified differently according to the screen size. Black[Foundry] believes that for Chinese Japanese Korean fonts, variable fonts are an interesting technology. As those files have more glyphs than Latin fonts, having a website that uses a Chinese font in several weights would result in more server requests as the font file can be heavier. However, with variable fonts, it is possible to draw Chinese, Arabic, and Japanese, typefaces in a new way: by programming variations inside the font and the glyphs.

Mandy Michael

Mandy Michael is a speaker and developer working as the Frond End Development Manager as Seven West Media in Western Australia. When Google, Apple and Microsoft announced variable fonts in 2016, she began creating demos and experimenting in ways in which they can be used. As a front developer, her job consists of creating interfaces that cannot be controlled and need to be responsive and adaptable to different parameters. Before this new technology, fonts were static and limiting in their inability to be as responsive as the rest of the web page design. Variable fonts made control and manipulation of fonts possible. Michael's goal is to see how far she can push these aspects in the front end of development. She believes that variable fonts offer a greater control over typography on the web by making it possible to fine-tune font characteristics to maximize legibility, readability, and accessibility of web text. Not only do variable fonts offer better website performance, but, if designed well and correctly, they also make it possible to make more usable, accessible, and meaningful content and a better overall user experience.

Mandy Michael also created a project called Variablefonts.dev that showcases many possibilities and opportunities that variable fonts offer. Her goal in this project was to provide developers with the necessary resources and tools needed to incorporate variable fonts into their projects. For the moment, she mostly focused on creative applications of variable fonts, but she is currently working on more practical implementations, such as responsiveness, dark modes, and performance.

Michael always designs websites with one specific perfect usage in mind; however, such design often does not respond to specific user needs, such as colorblindness and dyslexia. Variable fonts can make design suitable for everyone by modifying how the variable font is rendered based on the user experience during user's interaction with the website. Michael can adjust variable fonts for better readability: the text can respond to different environments (indoor and outdoor), making the variable font respond to ambient light. Another example is dark mode. Usually, only the background color is changed, and the typeface stays the same. By using variable fonts and creating adjustments based on the color theme of the website, the font's rendering will improve readability and overall user experience.

It is also possible to imagine users creating their own style sheets based on accessibility (color blindness, dyslexia, etc.). For example, people with dyslexia prefer reading text that has letters spaced further apart. With variable fonts, it is possible to imagine a user interface in which the user adjusts the spacing between the letters in the text for optimal readability. This is important for government websites or other websites that provide critical services for the masses because they need to provide the optimal user experience, which has to be adjusted based on the needs of different populations. Michael mentioned a creative way that variable fonts can be implemented: it would be possible to take a user's voice and change how the text is represented in the user's interface. By combining chatbot and voice recognition, it would be possible to create fonts that change and reproduce the mood of a user's voice. In the future, interfaces will not be about clicks but about technology using voice recognition, like Alexa. Michael can use variable fonts for storytelling, for practical usability requirements, or to have new, creative approaches in how text and content are reproduced on the web. Developers made web and variable fonts to be together as they offer flexibility that was not achievable before their existence.

Christoph Koerberlin

Christoph Koeberlin designs fonts produces fonts for print, Web, and apps, repairs and TrueType-hints them, and works as a consultant for typographic projects. He believes that variable fonts can solve problems. For example, variable fonts can not only reduce file size and server requests, but they can also do the following: make fonts more readable by adjusting axis and parameters; and make variations based on the surrounding light. One of the strengths of variable fonts is that they can make the layout better for user experience and accessibility without the user noticing the changes that happen. The majority of designers work on variable fonts by creating the extreme point of the design space that they then adjust in order to create a smooth interpellation.

Koeberlin defines the middle master as a center and makes all the other axes go into different directions from this center. He starts from this one style and then draws additional masters (weight, ascenders, descenders, x-height, optical compensation), that he combines to the central point. His new font, Pangea, will soon be released. Koeberlin designed Pangea in such logic and has a regular master as basis, light and bold for weight axis, regular spacing for the spacing axis, and only virtual master for the affected glyphs for extenders and apertures axes.

Koeberlin mentioned one his customers who had a large variety of fonts on their website: sans-serif, serif, text, and title. As they were not using a variable font, it became a problem to upload all of the stylistic variations on the website because the files were heavy. If the client would have used a variable font, they would not have had to compromise on their design and typographic abundance as the variable font file would have been lighter compared to all the other files combined. More generally, there are clients and designers who care about pragmatic solutions that adapt to certain environments, and there are those who are more interested in the experimental approach that translates an ambiance of the brand. Both have a place in the market and offer different solutions to clients.

Future Fonts

Future Fonts is made of Lizy Gershenzon, Travis Kochel, and James Edmondson, who help shape and grow the type design community. Their concept is a fresh voice in the type design industry. They provide a new marketplace to shop experimental typefaces as well as providing early access to useful and affordable fonts. They mention file savings and variable fonts potentially becoming a new default type file in the future as some of the aspects of variable font technology. They are more interested when the design of a variable font changes very dramatically, depending on the axis's movements. For example, "Chee" font has a yeast axis (from concave to puffed out) and a gravity axis (shifts the distribution of weight). It is an illustrative display variable font that allows for more personality and expression. Compared to the super families that enable minute choices and variations, display fonts from Future Fonts create unique designs and styles, thinking outside of the width and weight axis. Another example is "Whoa," which has four axes (zoom, shout, spinbox, and wedge) that are all very different, and yet they stay in the same style system. Future Font's variable fonts' goal is to show personality and the brand's identity by being expressive and innovative in the visual sphere.

Underware

Underware is a collective of type designers who design type, educate about type, publish about type, and give conferences. They are interested in thinking about variable fonts beyond animated design spaces that has a width and a weight axis. What happens when a font becomes fully variable and an "A" can also be a "B"? They believe that, for the moment, people talk only about a small part of what variable fonts can really do and be. The introduction of variable font format is more than what people can think about and imagine at the present day, and new technology can bring new possibilities and change society. According to Underware, there are three aspects of variable fonts: 1) replacement for current font technology (taking existing ideas and putting them in the new format); 2) variable fonts offer new possibilities, but it is not easy to imagine as it is necessary to develop new ideas (for example, HOI and Grammato) and develop a technique to execute themit; 3) is the an unknown category, it is which represents all the ideas that designers cannot imagine at the moment.

The majority of the companies are interested in the third category: taking an existing idea and rebranding it in the new variable format. Underware uses it on a large scale, and it is also an aspect that Google is interested in as they want to serve less data on their website. For the moment, it's the first aspect of technical replacement that is most common to see. The unknown category is underestimated at the moment. For example, the typewriter had a critical influence on society. What are the consequences of the introduction of variable fonts? What happens when letters become variable – when "A" becomes "B"? Although it is on a philosophical level, it contradicts everything that a letter can become the opposite of what it really is.

Next, HOI stands for higher order of interpellation. It resolves the problem of interpellation of point moving not in a straight line but in a curve (nonlinear interpellation). In this case, x needs special technology and editing tools. HOI moves multiple axes at the same time with the same values. This means that it is possible to produce smooth handwritten texts. Underware uses this technology to teach kids how to read and write, which can only be done with this variable font. Grammato is another example of a creative approach toward variable fonts. Grammato is a handwritten font that x uses in education apps to learn how to write, to introduce written word in social media, and to be implemented in operating systems. Users can also write Chinese characters stroke by stroke in a smooth animation. In the case of Chinese fonts, using Grammato to learn how to write the characters in the correct stroke order can provide new ways of learning to read and write. On a philosophical level, Grammato provides a new perspective on the human activity of "writing." Until Grammato, there was writing by hand (personal expression) and writing with fonts (use of a keyboard, effective communication). Grammato combines both of these attributes: users can transcribe thought and expression at the same time.

Andrew Johnson

Andrew Johnson is a designer who resides in the Boston area. He spent time learning at Filament Group, the MIT Mobile Experience Lab, Font Bureau, and Tank design. He views variable fonts as a responsive design system that defines curves and relationships between variables. It is of interest when users input parameters such as distance and reading goals. At most times, there is an ideal relationship between the reader and the font. However, it changes as the user moves in space, changing the relationship between the user and the text. In such a situation, fonts should adapt to the new environment and provide users with better accessibility and readability.

The introduction of augmented and virtual reality opens new possibilities for experiments with context-based typography. By taking into account the user's reading distance and their environment (for example, light) and taking advantage of variable font interpellation, it is possible to communicate in new ways. Andrew Johnson is interested in distance-based interpolations and how written text can change hierarchy of information based on users' movements towards or from the text. This can be useful for airport sections and gates, where type could shift to highlight numbers, airplanes, and walking time as people move closer. In addition, restaurant signs could adapt their written text on the menu based on users' distance. Furthermore, interfaces in games could adjust their typography hierarchy based on danger level. Any area where the physical distance and space has an impact on readability can be used to influence the behavior of type and interface. By taking into account info-tracking (light and distance) and face tracking user interfaces, written text can evolve and create an overall better user experience.

David Jonathan Ross

David Jonathan Ross is a type designed who is interested in finding solutions for typefaces that go beyond generic fonts. He believes that variable fonts allow for new ways to express typography while also being an upgrade from the existing format. Instead of just type designers having full control of the typeface, users can also adjust and choose the parameters that they are interested in and that they find most suitable for their projects. Variable fonts allow for text content to respond to different environments, and they give designers the possibility of playing with styles and being expressive in their design. Not every typeface needs animation like variations and smooth variability. Ross has typefaces in which, by moving the axis, the glyph changes. Variable font technology is a lever that allows users to access different glyph information in different spaces. This new technology asks questions about all the letter states in between defined "regular" forms. For example, users might ask, "What is between a roman and an italic?" In one font, he splits the slanted and the cursive of the letters, questioning the point at which a typeface becomes italic. This is typically a question that can only be asked with variable fonts technology as it allows type designers to go inside and in between shapes.

Variable fonts offer the possibility of storing recommendations inside the file for correct usage of the typeface based on a specific environment. For example, in the future, fonts could adapt and choose the right optical size and other parameters automatically. Variable fonts are most interesting to implement in highly sensitive typographic environments that could benefit from the adjustability of variable typefaces. He gave an example of a font he designed for computer programming, called IMPUT. In computer programming people, look at text environments in different contexts, screen sizes, resolutions, and distances. Additionally, they look at these elements of typeface all day long. This very a sensitive typographic environment that would benefit from a typeface that can be adjusted to the user's settings and preferences. Users choose the parameters they prefer and download their customized version of the typeface. In sensitive type environments, where the number of characters the user sees in a line makes a difference, giving people fine-tune control is a very affective option.

Raphaël Verona

Raphaël Verona is a type designer, graphic designer, teacher, and the founder of Altiplano Typefaces. Raphaël Verona develops the font catalog according to the evolutionary and narrative potential of alphabetic characters. He sees letters not only as a vector of meaning but also as images. The company offers typographic solutions to shape any kind of genres and media (print, Web, mobile apps, and electronic publications). Ergonomics is an important aspect of variable fonts as they make micro adjustments possible. He believes that width and weight adjustment that variable fonts offer can influence readability and user experience.

Furthermore, Raphaël Verona is interested in how text animation can become a supplementary tool for branding and visual identity creation. For example, by animating variable fonts, the designer and brand can point out a change that is happening on the web page. Without adding extra visual graphic elements that can disturb users' navigations across the web (such as underline stylistics), by animating variable font designers can facilitate users' navigations and teach them how to use the website. In a way, variable fonts allow for the brand to teach and show the user how to navigate while animating the web page's status (e.g., what changed, what stayed the same, and where to click or scroll).

Ilya Ruderman

Ilya Ruderman is a Russian graphic designer and co-founder of TypeToday. The adaptability of variable fonts across platforms is of great importance, according to Ilya Ruderman. However, he does not think that the file size is lighter. Additionally, he believes that it is worse when programmers have just one file than when they have multiple files. His programmers make each individual file smaller by cutting out glyphs. It was interesting to hear his perspective as he appears to be the only person who did not agree with the general opinion of variable fonts' file size. In the custom segment, used variable fonts across different technologies to find the final decision and the proper design for brands. Animations of variable fonts help in production and visualization of ideas, as variable fonts allow for more flexibility and variability in brands' identity creation. Variability is an interesting tool for illustrating ideas and understanding of usage based on implementations and sizes. Variable fonts are most interesting on the web, interactive devices, virtual reality, augmented reality, mobile and different apps that use camera recognition or that have any interactions between the user and the device.

The interviews with variable font specialists, designers and developers proved that variable fonts are a new technology that enables glyphs' outlines to morph in between variable style shapes and offers flexibility to responsive design. According to the interviewed specialists, variable fonts are an interesting tool for e-business as variable fonts are more suitable for websites than regular fonts. Variable fonts can create better type hierarchy on websites compared to regular fonts, visual consistency, better readability across screen interfaces, and overall improve user experience compared to regular fonts, by consequence, offering a more consistent user experience across devices. Moreover, compared to regular fonts, variable fonts exist in one lighter file that encapsulates the entire font family and speeds up webpage download time.

CONCLUSION

Professionals in the field of variable fonts have innovative and creative solutions that can be of interest to those who are involved with e-business and e-learning. In the literature review, the authors discussed reasons why and where fonts are important. Fonts impact users' perceptions of brands, user experience, and readability. The interviews confirmed the literature review section. Font developers and designers proposed their opinions in regard to variable font and user experience. There were some examples of e-learning applications as well as future ideas on variable font implementations in virtual and augmented reality environments and in voice recognition devices. In summary, variable fonts, their aesthetics, and technological solutions enable visual solutions for brands. For those developing or looking to develop an e-business and improve user experience, it is necessary to take into account thoughts and discussions of professionals of variable fonts instead of articles written by academics who do not have professional experience in the field. Variable fonts can impact user experience and future studies should consider the opportunities this technology offers for better readability, accessibility and comprehension of written words across devices.

REFERENCES

Ali, A. Z. M., Wahid, R., Samsudin, K., & Idris, M. Z. (2013). Reading on the computer screen: Does font type has effects on web text readability? *International Education Studies, 6*(3), 26. doi:10.5539/ies.v6n3p26

Amar, J., Droulers, O., & Legoherel, P. (2017). Typography in destination advertising: An exploratory study and research perspectives. *Tourism Management, 63*, 77–86. doi:10.1016/j.tourman.2017.06.002

Arditi, A., & Cho, J. (2005). Serifs and font legibility. *Vision Research, 45*(23), 2926–2933. doi:10.1016/j.visres.2005.06.013 PubMed

Argo, J. J., Popa, M., & Smith, M. C. (2010). The sound of brands. *Journal of Marketing, 74*(4), 97–109. doi:10.1509/jmkg.74.4.097

Azoulay, A., & Kapferer, J.-N. (2003). Do brand personality scales really measure brand personality? *Journal of Brand Management, 11*(2), 143–155. Advance online publication. doi:10.1057/palgrave.bm.2540162

Bayer, M., Sommer, W., & Schacht, A. (2010). Reading emotional words within sentences: The impact of arousal and valence on event-related potentials. *International Journal of Psychophysiology: Official Journal of the International Organization of Psychophysiology, 78*(3), 299–307. doi:10.1016/j.ijpsycho.2010.09.004 PubMed

Beymer, D., Russell, D., & Orton, P. (2008, September 1). An eye tracking study of how font size and type influence online reading. People and Computers XXII Culture, Creativity. *Interaction*. Advance online publication. doi:10.14236/ewic/HCI2008.23

Bhatia, S. K., Samal, A., Rajan, N., & Kiviniemi, M. T. (2011). Effect of font size, italics, and colour count on web usability. *International Journal of Computational Vision and Robotics, 2*(2), 156. Advance online publication. doi:10.1504/IJCVR.2011.042271 PubMed

Bigelow, C. (2019). Typeface features and legibility research. *Vision Research, 165*, 162–172. doi:10.1016/j.visres.2019.05.003 PubMed

Chadwick-Dias, A., Bergel, M., & Tullis, T. S. (2007). Senior surfers 2.0: A re-examination of the older web user and the dynamic web. In C. Stephanidis (Ed.), *Universal acess in human computer interaction. Coping with diversity* (pp. 868–876). Springer., doi:10.1007/978-3-540-73279-2_97.

Childers, T. L., & Jass, J. (2002). All dressed up with something to say: Effects of typeface semantic associations on brand perceptions and consumer memory. *Journal of Consumer Psychology, 12*(2), 93–106. doi:10.1207/S15327663JCP1202_03

Deng, L., & Poole, M. (2010). Affect in web interfaces: A study of the impacts of web page visual complexity and order. *Management Information Systems Quarterly, 34*(4), 711–730. doi:10.2307/25750702

Diouf, D. O., & Lemoine, J. F. (2019). *Les effets d'interaction entre les composantes atmosphériques d'un site web et les réactions des internautes: Une étude qualitative portant sur la couleur et la typographie.* Academic Press.

Grinsven, B., & Das, E. (2014). Logo design in marketing communications: Brand logo complexity moderates exposure effects on brand recognition and brand attitude. *Journal of Marketing Communications*, *22*, 1–15. doi:10.1080/13527266.2013.866593

Grohmann, B., Giese, J., & Parkman, I. (2012). Using type font characteristics to communicate brand personality of new brands. *Journal of Brand Management*, *20*. Advance online publication. doi:10.1057/bm.2012.23

Henderson, P., Giese, J., & Cote, J. (2004a). Impression management using typeface design. *Journal of Marketing*, *68*, 60–72. doi:10.1509/jmkg.68.4.60.42736

Huang, K. C., Lin, C. C., & Chiang, S. Y. (2008). Color preference and familiarity in performance on brand logo recall. *Perceptual and Motor Skills*, *107*(2), 587–596. doi:10.2466/pms.107.2.587-596 PubMed

Huang, Y., Li, C., Wu, J., & Lin, Z. (2018). Online customer reviews and consumer evaluation: The role of review font. *Information & Management*, *55*(4), 430–440. doi:10.1016/j.im.2017.10.003

Huang, Y., Wu, J., & Shi, W. (2018). The impact of font choice on web pages: Relationship with willingness to pay and tourism motivation. *Tourism Management*, *66*, 191–199. doi:10.1016/j.tourman.2017.12.010

Hudson, J. (2018, April 4). Introducing OpenType variable fonts. Medium. Retrieved from; https://medium.com/variable-fonts/https-medium-com-tiro-introducing-opentype-variable-fonts-12ba6cd2369

Hussain, W., Sohaib, O., Ahmed, A., & Khan, M. Q. (2011). *Web readability factors affecting users of all ages*. Academic Press.

Hutton, J. G. (1997). The influence of brand and corporate-identity programmes on consumer behaviour: A conceptual framework. *Journal of Brand Management*, *5*(2), 120–135. doi:10.1057/bm.1997.38

Izadi, A., & Patrick, V. M. (n.d.). The power of the pen: Handwritten fonts promote haptic engagement. *Psychology and Marketing*. Advance online publication. doi:10.1002/mar.21318

Keage, H. A. D., Coussens, S., Kohler, M., Thiessen, M., & Churches, O. F. (2014). Investigating letter recognition in the brain by varying typeface: An event-related potential study. *Brain and Cognition*, *88*, 83–89. doi:10.1016/j.bandc.2014.05.001 PubMed

Kristensen, T., & Grønhaug, K. (2007). Can design improve the performance of marketing management? *Journal of Marketing Management*, *23*(9-10), 815–827. doi:10.1362/026725707X250331

Lemoine, J. F. (2012). Pour une présentation du concept d'atmosphère des sites web et de ses effets sur le comportement des internautes. *Marche et Organisations*, *15*(1), 169–180.

Ling, J., & van Schaik, P. (2006). The influence of font type and line length on visual search and information retrieval in web pages. *International Journal of Human-Computer Studies*, *64*(5), 395–404. doi:10.1016/j.ijhcs.2005.08.015

Mackiewicz, J., & Moeller, R. (2004). Why people perceive typefaces to have different personalities. International Professional Communication Conference, 2004. IPCC 2004. Proceedings, 304–313. doi:10.1109/IPCC.2004.1375315

Madden, T. J., Hewett, K., & Roth, M. S. (2000). Managing images in different cultures: A cross-national study of color meanings and preferences. *Journal of International Marketing, 8*(4), 90–107. doi:10.1509/jimk.8.4.90.19795

McCarthy, M. S., & Mothersbaugh, D. L. (2002). Effects of typographic factors in advertising-based persuasion: A general model and initial empirical tests. doi:10.1002/mar.10030

McCarthy, M. S., & Mothersbaugh, D. L. (2002). Les effets de la typographie sur la persuasion publicitaire: Un modèle général et des tests empiriques préliminaires [Effects of typographic factors in advertising-based persuasion: A general model and initial empirical tests]. *Recherche et Applications en Marketing, 17*(4), 67–89. doi:10.1177/076737010201700404

Moore, R., Stammerjohan, C., & Coulter, R. (2013). Banner advertiser web site congruity and color effects on attention and attitudes. *Journal of Advertising, 34*(2), 71–84. doi:10.1080/00913367.2005.10639189

Nakilcioğlu, İ. H. (2013). The effects of font type choosing on visual perception and visual communication. Online Journal of Art and Design, 1(3). Retrieved from https://arastirmax.com/en/publication/online-journal-art-and-design/1/3/effects-font-type-choosing-visual-perception-and-visual-communication/arid/e1e93307-3481-44b6-a2dc-f35eed6f139f

Nilsson, T. (2006). Legibility of colored print. doi:10.1201/9780849375477.ch293

Novemsky, N., Dhar, R., Schwarz, N., & Simonson, I. (2007). Preference fluency in choice. *JMR, Journal of Marketing Research, 44*(3), 347–356. doi:10.1509/jmkr.44.3.347

Patching, G. R., & Jordan, T. R. (2005). Assessing the role of different spatial frequencies in word perception by good and poor readers. *Memory & Cognition, 33*(6), 961–971. doi:10.3758/BF03193205 PubMed

Puškarević, I., Nedeljković, U., & Pintier, I. (2014, November 13). Visual analysis of typeface management in brand identity. Academic Press.

Pušnik, N., Podlesek, A., & Možina, K. (2016). Typeface comparison – Does the x-height of lower-case letters increased to the size of upper-case letters speed up recognition? *International Journal of Industrial Ergonomics, 54*, 164–169. doi:10.1016/j.ergon.2016.06.002

Salehi, F., Abdollahbeigi, B., Langroudi, A. C., & Salehi, F. (2012). The impact of website information convenience on e-commerce success of companies. *Procedia: Social and Behavioral Sciences, 57*, 381–387. doi:10.1016/j.sbspro.2012.09.1201

Schmitt, B. H., Pan, Y., & Tavassoli, N. T. (1994). Language and consumer memory: The impact of linguistic differences between Chinese and English. *The Journal of Consumer Research, 21*(3), 419–431. doi:10.1086/209408

Schroll, R., Schnurr, B., & Grewal, D. (2018). Humanizing products with handwritten typefaces. *The Journal of Consumer Research, 45*(3), 648–672. doi:10.1093/jcr/ucy014

Slattery, T., & Rayner, K. (2010). The influence of text legibility on eye movements during reading. *Applied Cognitive Psychology, 24*(8), 1129–1148. doi:10.1002/acp.1623

Tavassoli, N. (2001). Color memory and evaluations for alphabetical and logographic brand names. *Journal of Experimental Psychology. Applied, 7*(2), 104–111. doi:10.1037/1076-898X.7.2.104 PubMed

Wang, Y., Minor, M., & Wei, J. (2011). Aesthetics and the online shopping environment: Understanding consumer responses. *Journal of Retailing, 87*(1), 46–58. doi:10.1016/j.jretai.2010.09.002

Zaichkowsky, J. L. (2010). Strategies for distinctive brands. *Journal of Brand Management, 17*(8), 548–560. doi:10.1057/bm.2010.12

Zhang, S., & Schmitt, B. H. (2001). Creating local brands in multilingual international markets. *JMR, Journal of Marketing Research, 38*(3), 313–325. doi:10.1509/jmkr.38.3.313.18869

ADDITIONAL READING

Bartram, D. (1982). The perception of semantic quality in type: Differences between designers and non-designers. *Information Design Journal, 3*(1), 38–50. doi:10.1075/idj.3.1.04bar

Brumberger, E. (n.d.). The rhetoric of typography: The awareness and impact of typeface appropriateness. Technical Communication. Retrieved June 2, 2020 from https://www.academia.edu/38391596/The_Rhetoric_of_Typography_The_Awareness_and_Impact_of_Typeface_Appropriateness

Buttle, H., & Westoby, N. (2006). Brand logo and name association: It's all in the name. *Applied Cognitive Psychology, 20*(9), 1181–1194. doi:10.1002/acp.1257

Doyle, J. R., & Bottomley, P. A. (2006). Dressed for the occasion: Font-product congruity in the perception of logotype. *Journal of Consumer Psychology, 16*(2), 112–123. doi:10.1207/s15327663jcp1602_2

Heller, S., & Meggs, P. B. (2001). *Texts on type: Critical writings on typography (Reprint).* Allworth Press.

Kinross, R. (2003). *Unjustified texts: Perspectives on typography (New title).* Hyphen Press.

Kinross, R. (2004). Modern typography: An essay in critical history (2nd Revised ed.). Hyphen Press.

Luffarelli, J., Mukesh, M., & Mahmood, A. (2019). Let the logo do the talking: The influence of logo descriptiveness on brand equity. *JMR, Journal of Marketing Research, 56*(5), 862–878. Advance online publication. doi:10.1177/0022243719845000

Mccarthy, M., & Mothersbaugh, D. (2002). Effects of typographic factors in advertising-based persuasion: A general model and initial empirical tests. *Psychology and Marketing, 19*(7-8), 663–691. doi:10.1002/mar.10030

van Leeuwen, T., & Djonov, E. (2015). Notes towards a semiotics of kinetic typography. *Social Semiotics, 25*(2), 244–253. doi:10.1080/10350330.2015.1010324

KEY TERMS AND DEFINITIONS

Accessibility: Capacity for users to easily access and comprehend any kind of content.

Readability: The quality of being legible, decipherable, easy, or enjoyable to read.

Responsive Design: Flexible layout on the web. Web pages that detect the user's screen size and adapt accordingly for better user experience.

User Experience: User experience (UX) is the user's emotions, behaviors, and attitudes towards the product.

User Interface: User interface (UI) is a panel for human-computer interactions in a digital device.

Variable Font: A variable font is a digital font that comes in one, lighter file and allows users to choose any of the axis' parameters.

Web Design: A process of creating websites on the web.

Chapter 5
An Overview of Web 2.0 and Its Technologies and Their Impact in the Modern Era

Reinaldo Padilha França
State University of Campinas (UNICAMP), Brazil

Ana Carolina Borges Monteiro
State University of Campinas (UNICAMP), Brazil

Rangel Arthur
Faculty of Technology (FT), State University of Campinas (UNICAMP), Brazil

Yuzo Iano
State University of Campinas (UNICAMP), Brazil

ABSTRACT

Web 2.0 is the evolution of the web. Seen as a new and second movement of access to information through the world wide web, Web 2.0 brings interactivity and collaboration as the main keys to its functioning. It is now possible and simpler and faster to send information at any time, by any user connected to the internet. The ease of uploading information, images, and videos on the Web 2.0 is due to the expansion of resources and codes, allowing anyone to be able to act naturally and take their own content to the internet. As the data and information shared daily is almost infinite, the search engines act even more intuitively and bring only results tailored to each user. Therefore, this chapter aims to provide an updated review and overview of Web 2.0, addressing its evolution and fundamental concepts, showing its relationship, as well as approaching its success with a concise bibliographic background, categorizing and synthesizing the potential of technology.

DOI: 10.4018/978-1-7998-3756-5.ch005

INTRODUCTION

Web 2.0 is a term used to refer to the second generation of communities and services offered on the Internet, having as its concept the Web and through applications based on social networks and information technology. The term does not refer to updating the technical specifications, but to a change in the way it is perceived by users and developers, that is, the environment of interaction and participation that today encompasses many languages (Bradley, 2007, Deitel & Deitel, 2007, McLoughlin & Alam, 2019).

Web 2.0 is the move to the internet as a platform, and an understanding of the rules to succeed in this new platform, such a concept has a fundamental rule in harnessing collective intelligence. It is conceptualized in the essentially online context. Thus, activities that were previously done offline, with the aid of traditional programs sold in specialized stores, are now done online, using free tools open to all users. With it has increased the speed and ease of use of various applications, accounting for a significant increase in existing content on the Internet (Kroski, 2008, Shuen, 2018).

The idea of Web 2.0 is to make the online environment more dynamic and make users collaborate for content organization. With the advent of Web 2.0, many sites are no longer rigid and static structures, but platforms where people can contribute their knowledge for the benefit of other users and visitors. That's because Web 2.0 brought with it collaborative content creation software, social networking, blogging, and information technology (Berger & Trexler, 2010, Sankar & Bouchard, 2009, McLoughlin & Alam, 2019).

As a result, users are no longer just viewers and can interact, produce their own content, and communicate with others. Thus, Web 2.0 enhances and facilitates knowledge acquisition, having an impact on education (Vickery & Wunsch-Vincent, 2007, Bizer et al, 2007, Ellis & Kent, 2019).

One of the principles of this evolution of the Internet is that content must be opened under creative commons licenses, the copyright of which allows a user to repost, alter, or collaborate. This is because Web 2.0 aims to generate communities, either through a social network or comments on news sites and blogs. With this, the information technology that allows such interaction between users also brought significant changes in the way Marketing is done (Lee & McLoughlin, 2011, Rigby, 2008, Ellis & Kent, 2019). One downside is that these days people don't store information so easily and search the internet for all the information already processed, which doesn't stimulate critical thinking.

One of the biggest news that changes on the internet have brought to marketing is that companies had to learn to interact with their audience. This is because communication is no longer a one-way street and now the consumer not only receives the message but also gives their opinion about it. Besides, information technology has also brought with it a new way of advertising: through online advertisements and search engine placement (Solomon & Schrum, 2007, Theimer, 2009, Kompen et al, 2019).

With this, the evolution of the internet introduced us to Performance Marketing, that is, when a company hires this type of service but only pays for the corresponding result. Finally, technological advances have also made it possible to develop cross-media strategies: when an action goes beyond the online environment and continues offline. That is, Digital Marketing as we know it today was only possible thanks to the evolution of Web 2.0 (Solomon & Schrum, 2007, Theimer, 2009, Kompen et al, 2019).

Today, for a page to fit into this "second chapter" of internet history, it must provide a content experience for the user. This content should be dynamic and open to their participation at a minimum. It must escape text blocks and provide options for reaching what the user wants. Obviously, graphics and dynamism often meet, and this union is very well-liked (literally) by users. In addition to purely graphical innovations, Web 2.0 pages have also brought some such features, such as large buttons and gradient effects. However, if the Internet user does not know what to do in a beautifully graphically developed environment, forget it does not return to the page (Lee & McLoughlin, 2011, Rigby, 2008, Teo et al, 2019).

In short, Web 2.0 pages have taken advantage of graphics, enhanced many of them, and today they do so in many cases, but this does not imply a direct relationship between them. Another great resource provided by this shift in awareness was web applications (Rich Internet Applications). These are programs with traditional software functions, but the necessary processing and data are downloaded from a server. This eliminates the need for installation and in some cases offers more security. That is, the internet is used as a platform, and the application becomes the service of many pages (Vickery & Wunsch-Vincent, 2007, Bizer et al, 2007, Teo et al, 2019).

The goal of Web 2.0 was to provide users with more creativity, information sharing, and most of all, a collaboration between them, enabling them to take part in this revolution. Based on these concepts, social networking services, pages full of videos, wikis, blogs and other services with a common trait have exploded: effective user participation in both directions of information traffic: dynamic content is provided, dynamic content is provided. same kind of information just as easily. The most interesting of all is that it is not a technological revolution or a sudden upgrade. It's simply a change in the way that a user promotes dynamic content over the internet (Berger & Trexler, 2010, Sankar & Bouchard, 2009, Teo et al, 2019).

Therefore, this chapter aims to provide an updated discussion on Web 2.0 and its technologies, showing and approaching its success, with a concise bibliographic background, categorizing and synthesizing the technological potential.

METHODOLOGY

This study was based on the research of scientific articles and books that address the theme of the present chapter and research, exploring mainly a historical review and applicability of techniques related to **Web 2.0 and its technologies**. These papers were analyzed based on the publication date of fewer than **5** years, with emphasis on publications and indexing in renowned databases, such as IEEE and Scholar Google

WEB 1.0

Web 1.0 is the first version of the internet presented to the public, it was the possibility of, for the first time, accessing content spread around the world with a few clicks, enchanting users, it was revolutionary for starting a process that evolves today, regarding democratization access to information (Cormode & Krishnamurthy, 2008, Aghaei et al, 2012, Teo et al, 2019).

It is the internet as it emerged with sites with static content with little interactivity from internet users and several link directories, where these had predominantly a passive performance in a process where few people produce and many consume, something very similar to the broadcasting model of the media industry such as TVs, radios, newspapers, and magazines. Its great virtue was the democratization of access to information (García Aretio, 2014, Shivalingaiah & Naik, 2008, Teo et al, 2019).

Evolving from its roots of military and university use, the internet began to walk and take shape in the face of people's needs, is considered the era of e-mail, simplistic search engines, and a time when every site had a section of recommended links. Web 1.0 had pages that barely interacted with Internet users. The contents were mostly institutional (Patel, 2013, Hsu & Park, 2011, Harris & Rea, 2019).

The sites were static, the navigation, however, offered very few possibilities for interaction between the visitor of a page and its content, it was not possible to leave comments and much less carry out edits, as is done today on Wikipedia, and the production of content and materials it was extremely centralized. This means that the creation of content was mainly in charge of portals of giant journalistic companies, and the search for information was carried out in directories such as Yahoo, which dominated the pre-Google period (Nath et al, 2014, Breeding, 2006, Hiremath & Kenchakkanavar, 2016, Harris & Rea, 2019).

The technologies and methods of Web 1.0 are still used for displaying content such as laws and manuals, which, similar to the era of Web 1.0, these sites in the vast majority made a very technical use of the network, the predominant sites of companies and institutions (Nath et al, 2014, Breeding, 2006, Hiremath & Kenchakkanavar, 2016, Harris & Rea, 2019).

Even though it is very different from what is currently known, the internet was a revolution for all those who depended on libraries, post offices and telephones for a lifetime to exchange information, learn or consult something, being considered the main services of that time were Hotmail, DMOZ, Yahoo! and Google (Nath et al, 2014, Breeding, 2006, Hiremath & Kenchakkanavar, 2016, McLoughlin & Alam, 2019).

It was an information distribution model similar to existing media channels, such as radio and television. This means that Web 1.0 was an environment in which many consumed, but only a handful created, a situation that was reversed over the years, until the arrival of Web 2.0 (García Aretio, 2014, Shivalingaiah & Naik, 2008, McLoughlin & Alam, 2019).

While Web 1.0 stood out for the democratization of access to information, its successor started this process in the production of content, causing users to stop being mostly passive to reach the leading role of the world wide web (Cormode & Krishnamurthy, 2008, Aghaei et al, 2012).

WEB 2.0

The term Web 2.0 is used to describe the second generation of the World Wide Web, this term was created by the American company O'Reilly Media in 2004 to designate the concept of the Web as a platform, reinforcing the concept of internet users' collaboration with websites and virtual services and exchange of information, with the idea that the online environment becomes more dynamic and that users collaborate for the organization of content, where sites no longer have a static characteristic, users have the possibility to participate in the content, insert, update, comment and rate them, personalization of the content is possible, allowing each user to filter the information important to their needs, creating their own page. From a business point of view, it refers to a phase in the evolution of the internet that profoundly impacted the way companies do Marketing, making it a fundamental concept for establishing assertive communication with the public (Berger & Trexler, 2010, Sankar & Bouchard, 2009, McLoughlin & Alam, 2019).

Web 2.0 is the second phase of the evolution of the internet that brought interaction between people to the online environment, changing the way users used it, it is also used to classify sites that follow trends of 'cleaner' and 'lighter' design ', using technologies such as Ajax (Asynchronous JavaScript and XML), being a set of development techniques aimed at the web that allows applications to work asynchronously, processing any request to the server in the background; CSS (Cascading Style Sheets), is used to style elements written in a markup language like HTML, it is he who separates the content from the visual representation of the website; and XML (Extensible Markup Language), is a markup language recommended for creating documents with hierarchically organized data, such as texts, databases or vector drawings (Kopecký et al, 2008, Reynolds, 2008, Feiler, 2007, Méndez Rodríguez et al, 2007, McLoughlin & Alam, 2019).

Before this evolution, what was seen before, was that people would enter a certain website, read the text and leave, the maximum interaction was to send an e-mail and wait for the response, which with Web 2.0 the interaction between the website and user is much greater, there is communication between the two sides and user/user communication. Even taking into account the collaboration of users on the site is possible, there is an exchange of information. In the same sense that content production is now decentralized, emerging the concept of collective intelligence (Kroski, 2008, Shuen, 2018).

That's because Web 2.0 brought with its collaborative software for creating content, social networks, blogs, and information technology. Since this profusion of sites based on the social tools that make up this "new" virtual landscape has grown exponentially, allowing levels and patterns of interaction, sharing, and exchange of opinion until recently only possible offline. Thus, users stopped being just spectators and started to be able to interact, produce their own content, and communicate with other people (Bradley, 2007, Deitel & Deitel, 2007, Kompen et al, 2019, Ellis & Kent, 2019).

Thus, Web 2.0 has essentially to do with the creation of environments conducive to the creation and maintenance of social networks (public or private, open or closed), which this spirit goes beyond the limits of a given website, and each time if more it is observed the establishment of links between several sites to provide additional functionality to the members of the respective virtual communities (Berger & Trexler, 2010, Sankar & Bouchard, 2009, Kompen et al, 2019, Ellis & Kent, 2019).

Since then, the term has been widely used to designate changes in the internet that impact the online environment and the strategies of companies today, along with the chance for the user to create material and interact with others, based on the principles of this evolution of the internet. is that the content must be opened under licenses of the type "creative commons", that is, whose copyright allows reposting, changes, or collaborations of a user (Kroski, 2008, Shuen, 2018).

It is due to this objective of openness and transparency that the Web 2.0 is also characterized, in the great majority, by the free character of the sites and tools and by the creation and availability of APIs (Application Programming Interface) that allow the communication with other sites, resulting in the creation of multiple plugins, developed especially by the user community, which allow extension of basic functionalities of a given website or application, in the same way, that it also adds content, since version 2.0 of the Web, aims to generate virtual communities, either through a social network or comments on news sites and blogs (Solomon & Schrum, 2007, Theimer, 2009, Farrell, 2009, Bae et al, 2014).

Within this context fits the Wikipedia encyclopedia, whose information is made available and edited by the Internet users themselves, this definition also includes the offer of several online services, gathering links to news, podcasts, and videos sent by the users and rated by them, featuring the best articles, videos, and original content that the web is talking about right now, combining social bookmarks, blog, and feed; YouTube, one of the largest video sharing platform; eBay was a pioneer in electronic commerce, is one of the largest sites in the world for selling and buying goods; and Google Earth, is a three-dimensional map application maintained that allows the user to walk virtually anywhere on the planet, due to the images captured by satellite (Berger & Trexler, 2010, Sankar & Bouchard, 2009, Vickery & Wunsch-Vincent, 2007, Bizer et al, 2007, Harris & Rea, 2019, Teo et al, 2019).

The main characteristics of Web 2.0 are simplicity, where everything must be intuitive and evident; sharing, since each day new collaboration tools appear based on the simple-fast-web trinomial; publication, assuming that in the world of Web 2.0, information is received, transformed and published in an infinite cycle of information generation; fast availability, since the information is updated in a much more agile way and reach users more quickly; editing and user participation, wherein Web 2.0, the user becomes an active, participative being, who acts on what he sees and consumes on the internet; opinion, linked to the democratic possibility and without barriers for users to exercise their freedom of opinion; and virtual communities, provided that through the flood of digital communities and applications that make us more speakers, it is possible to exchange information quickly (Kroski, 2008, Shuen, 2018).

As the digital universe presented greater interactivity, the reinforcement of this characteristic would be a natural movement and, one of the biggest news that the changes in the internet brought to Marketing is that companies had to learn to interact with their audience, because communication it is no longer a one-way street, where the consumer not only receives the message, but also starts to express his opinion on it. Still considering that information technology has also brought a new way of advertising, through online ads and positioning on search engines (Lee & McLoughlin, 2011, Rigby, 2008, Kopecký et al, 2008, Reynolds, 2008, Feiler, 2007, Méndez Rodríguez et al, 2007, Harris & Rea, 2019, Teo et al, 2019).

Since the evolution of the internet has presented the possibility for a company to hire this type of service and pay for the corresponding result. In this scenario, technological advances have also enabled the development of cross-media strategies, that is, when an action extrapolates the online environment and continues in an offline environment, in this way it is possible to highlight the emergence of Digital Marketing, arising through the evolution of the internet (Kroski, 2008, Shuen, 2018, Lee & McLoughlin, 2011, Rigby, 2008, Kopecký et al, 2008, Reynolds, 2008, Feiler, 2007, Méndez Rodríguez et al, 2007, Harris & Rea, 2019, Teo et al, 2019).

Web 2.0 Elements and Features

The elements and functionalities generally present in Web 2.0 sites are blogs, being sites in the form of a diary in which the texts are presented in reverse chronological order; social bookmarking, accessible from any computer with access to the Internet and which allows the user to comment and share them with others; wikis, the sites whose content is added and maintained by those who visit it; possibility of aggregating content, making available content published on other sites on one site to facilitate access or enrich it with the opinion of other users (e.g. Digg); the tags, possibility to associate one (or more) term (s) or keyword (s) to a content item (e.g. text, photo, bookmark), meaning "tag", "identification" (Kroski, 2008, Shuen, 2018, Lee & McLoughlin, 2011, Rigby, 2008, Kopecký et al, 2008, Reynolds, 2008, Feiler, 2007, Méndez Rodríguez et al, 2007, Harris & Rea, 2019, Ellis & Kent, 2019).

Before Web 2.0, there was a lot of complexity, mass audience, protection of information by a single distribution source, need to subscribe for access to information, slow availability of information, professional editing, corporate discourse, unilateral communication of information and the same product; and after Web 2.0 there is simplicity, virtual niches, information sharing, the act of publishing information for free, quick availability of information, user editing, user opinion, user participation and thus the virtual community (Nath et al, 2014, Breeding, 2006, Hiremath & Kenchakkanavar, 2016, Yamakami, 2007, O'Reilly, 2012, Harris & Rea, 2019, Ellis & Kent, 2019).

Tags

Tags are, par excellence, one of the greatest features of Web 2.0, being able to be personalized by users, facilitating the process of association and identification of the searched site, the tags are personal classifications, that is, the same site can have different tags for two or more people, as each classifies objects according to their own understanding of the world. On the current internet, it is possible to "tag" a page and not just access it through its URL, allowing searches to be made by the content of the sites and not just by keywords, which allows greater efficiency (Bradley, 2007, Deitel & Deitel, 2007, Xu et al, 2006, Adrian et al, 2007, Harris & Rea, 2019, Ellis & Kent, 2019).

Tagging has made a Web 2.0 version for the lists of preferred sites, offering users a way to link keywords to words or images they find interesting on the internet, helping to categorize them and make it easier for other users to obtain them. The online use of tagging is also classified as "folksonomy", since it creates a classified distribution, or taxonomy, of content on the web, reinforcing its usefulness (Kroski, 2008, Shuen, 2018, Lee & McLoughlin, 2011, Rigby, 2008, Kopecký et al, 2008, Reynolds, 2008, Feiler, 2007, Méndez Rodríguez et al, 2007, McLoughlin & Alam, 2019, Teo et al, 2019).

RSS (Really Simple Syndication)

RSS feeds (Really Simple Syndication) are a way to alert members and visitors to a website of changes in their content, they are produced automatically by many of the available tools and can then be read through feed readers online, on the desktop or associated with an application - email client. The abbreviation of RSS is used to refer to the following standards, such as Rich Site Summary (RSS 0.91), RDF Site Summary (RSS 0.9 and 1.0), Really Simple Syndication (RSS 2.0), this technology works under the XML language, used for share web content. Allowing a news site administrator to create an XML file with the latest headlines published, to share them more quickly with their readers, which can be read using any tool that is capable of understanding the XML format of RSS; where the RSS file includes information such as title, page (the exact address where something is new), description of the change, date, author, among other characteristics, of all the latest updates to the site to which it is attached (Barsky, 2006, Huffman, 2017, Neumann & Weikum, 2008, Ankolekar et al, 2007, Kompen et al, 2019, Teo et al, 2019).

With RSS, it became practical to distribute information through the internet, making a powerful combination of "pull" technologies, with which the web user requests the information he wants; and "push" technologies, where information is automatically sent to a user. Still considering a visit to a particular website that works with RSS, he can request that updates be sent to him (a process is known as "subscribing to a feed") (Bradley, 2007, Deitel & Deitel, 2007, Xu et al, 2006, Adrian et al, 2007, Barsky, 2006, Huffman, 2017, Neumann & Weikum, 2008, Ankolekar et al, 2007, Kompen et al, 2019, Teo et al, 2019).

AdSense

AdSense are a Google advertising plan inc. which helps website creators, including blogs, make money from their work, is a Google tool for digital content producers to earn money by displaying ads along with their content, which has become the most important source of revenue for Web 2.0 companies, along with search results, Google offers ads relevant to the content of a website, generating revenue for the website each time the ad is clicked (Farrell, 2009, Bae et al, 2014, Yamakami, 2007, O'Reilly, 2012, Kompen et al, 2019, Teo et al, 2019).

Ajax

Ajax is a broad package of technologies used to create interactive applications for the web, historically Microsoft was one of the first companies to explore the technology, but the adoption of the technique by Google, for services such as online maps, most recent and enthusiastic, is that it made Ajax one of the most used tools among the creators of websites and services on the web. Ajax is not a single technology, or even a programming language, it is a series of development techniques aimed at the web. The system is generally composed of HTML/XHTML for the main language and CSS for the presentation, the Document Object Model (DOM) for dynamic data display and interaction, XML for data exchange and XSLT for manipulation, still with the possibility of JSON insertion for being more similar to JavaScript. The XMLHttpRequest object for asynchronous communication, and finally, the JavaScript programming language to bring all these technologies together (Bradley, 2007, Deitel & Deitel, 2007, Xu et al, 2006, Adrian et al, 2007, Barsky, 2006, Huffman, 2017, Neumann & Weikum, 2008, Ankolekar et al, 2007, Mahemoff, 2006, McLoughlin & Alam, 2019, Teo et al, 2019).

These are some examples of how AJAX is currently used in Voting and Evaluation systems, where a user conducts an evaluation of a product he bought on the internet, or fills out an online form, both of which use this technology to carry out the evaluation, causing the site to update the calculations without having to reload the page. Some sites have chat channels (Chat Channels) on their home page to communicate with their customers and provide technical support services, make the user continue to browse the site while exchanging messages without them disappearing. Twitter Trending notifications, where the social network uses whenever new tweets are made on a certain trending topic, causing new figures to be automatically updated without affecting the main page. Simply put, AJAX makes the multitasking process simpler, mainly seen in situations where two operations work simultaneously, one running and the other idle (Bradley, 2007, Deitel & Deitel, 2007, Xu et al, 2006, Adrian et al, 2007, Barsky, 2006, Huffman, 2017, Neumann & Weikum, 2008, Ankolekar et al, 2007, Mahemoff, 2006, Mesbah & Van Deursen, 2009, McLoughlin & Alam, 2019, Teo et al, 2019).

Blogs and Mash-ups

Blogs are a low-cost means of publishing on the web available to millions of users, being among the first Web 2.0 tools to be used widely. Mash-ups are services created by combining two different applications for the internet, such as mixing an online mapping site with a property listings service to present a unified feature of finding homes that are for sale (Bradley, 2007, Deitel & Deitel, 2007, Xu et al, 2006, Adrian et al, 2007, Barsky, 2006, Huffman, 2017, Neumann & Weikum, 2008, Ankolekar et al, 2007, Mahemoff, 2006, Mesbah & Van Deursen, 2009, McLoughlin & Alam, 2019, Teo et al, 2019).

Wikis (Virtual Communities)

Like Wikis, which are community pages on the internet that can be changed by all users who have access rights, and these community pages have generated phenomena like Wikipedia, which is an online encyclopedia written by readers, as well as also used in companies, wikis are becoming an easy way to exchange ideas for a group of workers involved in a project (Berger & Trexler, 2010, Sankar & Bouchard, 2009, Vickery & Wunsch-Vincent, 2007, Bizer et al, 2007, McLoughlin & Alam, 2019, Teo et al, 2019).

Streaming Technology

Streaming technology is a form of instantaneous transmission of audio and video data over networks, in addition to the fact that this technology is not recent, having existed since the 1990s, however, but it has not become popular due to the low speed of connections with web, as the data took longer to load and be stored than to be displayed. Videos crashed a lot and were often shown in poor quality, which did not allow instant loading. Where through this service, it is possible to watch movies or listen to music without the need to download, which makes access to online content faster (Solomon & Schrum, 2007, Theimer, 2009, Farrell, 2009, Bae et al, 2014, Harris & Rea, 2019, Ellis & Kent, 2019).

With the arrival of broadband, technology gained more space, its popularization of streaming brought an incalculable number of possibilities, and allowed the possibility of following a live event online, even though through a twitcam or a show is broadcast directly over the internet. On-demand streaming services have enabled the user to be in control of what they are going to watch, when and where, as well as enabling the control of the display, related to the pause, forward or rewind of a video or music; still making it access data at the same time it receives it, without the need for the user to wait for a download or take up space on your hard drive with content storage (Kopecký et al, 2008, Reynolds, 2008, Feiler, 2007, Méndez Rodríguez et al, 2007, Farrell, 2009, Bae et al, 2014, Yamakami, 2007, O'Reilly, 2012, Harris & Rea, 2019, Ellis & Kent, 2019).

Cloud Computing

With Web 2.0, the advent of cloud computing has brought that not only user data, but the operating system works on online servers, making content accessible on any web access platform, making the "cloud" become a space for processing or storing data shared and interconnected through the internet, making the cloud the best backup. Cloud computing is an integral trend of Web 2.0, enabling the use of online servers and thus making the use of storage devices unnecessary and allowing the sharing of content with a web-access platform. Its advantages are related that in most cases the user does not have to worry about the operating system and the hardware he is using, and corporate work and file sharing become easier, since all the information is in the same "place", that is, in the "computational cloud" (Barsky, 2006, Huffman, 2017, Neumann & Weikum, 2008, Ankolekar et al, 2007, Guha & Al-Dabass, 2010, Sultan, 2013, Harris & Rea, 2019, Ellis & Kent, 2019).

Virtual Disk

The virtual disk is a remote storage area, that is, a space to store any type of file (texts, images, sounds, photos, programs) and there are several advantages to using this service, being possible to download files as if they were using a local disk, such as the hard disk (HD) installed on the computer, the user has access to this HD when he is on any machine connected to the network, has his digital documents always available, being able to create subfolders, making it unnecessary to deal with other types storage media, and with a greater organization when storing files as well as redundancy is desired (Barsky, 2006,

Huffman, 2017, Neumann & Weikum, 2008, Ankolekar et al, 2007, Guha & Al-Dabass, 2010, Sultan, 2013, Harris & Rea, 2019, Ellis & Kent, 2019).

Some examples of Web 2.0 applications are text editors and spreadsheets online, along with the advantages for the user of not having to save your documents, resumes or other types of files on CD's, on your computer or even in e-mails, being possible to leave the documents online, and access from any computer, modify them and save them again for a new use, and when sharing these documents, it is still possible to make important information available to certain groups, allowing other users to edit their content in the same place, avoiding rework and saving time (Lee & McLoughlin, 2011, Rigby, 2008, Kopecký et al, 2008, Reynolds, 2008, Feiler, 2007, Méndez Rodríguez et al, 2007, Harris & Rea, 2019, Ellis & Kent, 2019).

Web 2.0 is a concept that provides for interaction in the internet environment, where it has done with most companies already has some type of activity or studies the implementation of collaborative solutions aimed at the public (García Aretio, 2014, Shivalingaiah & Naik, 2008, McLoughlin & Alam, 2019, Teo et al, 2019).

People have learned that sharing information on corporate social networks is more efficient than sending documents by email to large groups of people, making these initiatives grow the concept of Enterprise 2.0, describing the process for enabling organizational success in an environment of rapid changes. Although technologies like Web 2.0 are critical aspects to make this happen, this process is much more of an organizational transformation than the technology itself (García Aretio, 2014, Shivalingaiah & Naik, 2008, Patel, 2013, Hsu & Park, 2011, McLoughlin & Alam, 2019, Teo et al, 2019).

In the search for innovation and adoption of new technologies to overcome some of these challenges, companies bet on complementary strategies using Web 2.0 solutions, focusing on collaborative environments, knowledge management, project management, rich interfaces, wikis, internal and external blogs, RSS, social bookmarking, social networks, among other features. Regarding what companies have seen in how costs have changed, the need to give people what they want, and for free, since Web 2.0 is made up of platforms for people to express themselves and not just a one-way street, as it happened on that 1.0 platform. What before the explosion of the amount of online content, the web went through a rupture phase, transition from Web 1.0 to 2.0, creating an internet of easy and free platforms (García Aretio, 2014, Aghaei et al, 2012, McLoughlin & Alam, 2019, Teo et al, 2019).

The Web 2.0 is, practically, a system of resources that can be worked on the web itself, with several users interconnected simultaneously and anywhere in the world, like the current browsers that become the work platforms of their users, however, for this to happen occurs, it is necessary that, on the work computer, there is a browser or browser, which before there was no such need, the same use of any other application (Cormode & Krishnamurthy, 2008, Shivalingaiah & Naik, 2008, Patel, 2013, Hsu & Park, 2011, McLoughlin & Alam, 2019, Teo et al, 2019).

Web 2.0 is an Internet that allows its users to access personal files only by accessing the network, which can be done from anywhere in the world, with no need to back up personal files, which is considered that some of the services available to perform these tasks, such as the text editor, spreadsheet, presentation program, collaboration, among others, gave rise to the mobile desktop or mobile PC, as they allow all content to be kept on the computer online, and can be handled at any time and from any machine, including applications and the same operating system (Cormode & Krishnamurthy, 2008, Shivalingaiah & Naik, 2008, Patel, 2013, Hsu & Park, 2011, McLoughlin & Alam, 2019, Teo et al, 2019).

Currently, the Web allows countless possibilities to multiply exponential knowledge, since everything is available on the network, creating and making the idea that everything is a raw material, everything can be worked and reworked by everyone, according to interests and needs, which can be seen from this condition, together with interactivity, pointing to the possibilities of using virtual environments for education.

LINK BETWEEN WEB 2.0 AND USER EXPERIENCE (UX)

User Experience (UX) is related to the use of the service itself, mainly in its interactions with the end customer. It is the discipline responsible for designing charming user experiences to build customer loyalty and win, i.e., it aims to study human behavior and the service offered to find ways to improve customer satisfaction and loyalty (Väänänen-Vainio-Mattila et al., 2010; Lialina, 2018).

UX refers to the method of analyzing and understanding how users interact with services, products, and the elements of a web page. Even more, correlated is the potential concerning ease, dynamism, and intuitiveness than this aspect and version of the internet offers in the practical lives of users. Provided that through the characteristics of Web 2.0, it is possible to optimize and realize, more efficiently and satisfactorily, how the user experience will be (Gómez et al., 2015; Orehovački et al., 2011).

Through a differentiated Service Design covering the entire service ecosystem; of Utility concerning how useful the service is to the customer; and taking into account the ease of use concerning how easy and fast it is to use the service and resolve whatever is necessary using it and not an alternative; still reflecting on the Pleasure meaning how pleasurable, i.e., interesting, fun, among other aspects it is to use the service and not the alternatives (Mistry et al., 2019; Nogueira et al., 2019).

This makes it possible to study these interactions at a deeper level of detail, applied both to the creation of new services and to their maintenance and management in the short, medium and long term, reaching the level of micro-interactions that will contribute, for example, in the construction ease and enchantment. Covering all aspects of a person's experience with a system, including industrial design, graphics, interface, and physical interaction, since that is when people feel satisfied or enchanted by something, being encouraged to continue consuming or trying something for the first time (Vilarinho et al., 2017; Hayek et al., 2019).

With UX efficiently applied along with the characteristics and potential of Web 2.0, or even future versions such as Web 3.0, whether it is a service, website, product, electronic device or object of personal satisfaction, the importance of UX is to make the user feel good at all times in the user experience. In other words, UX is proportional to the usability of a Web 2.0 product or service, developing the user's natural desire to buy more than the same brand, make renewals or upgrades of scalable products or services (Lopes et al., 2020; van de Sand et al., 2020).

The visual identity is what makes the user understand and consume the proposal of a 2.0 website, since it is possible to analyze and apply UX in internet pages, or in the experience of buying services or products. Satisfying the user with the navigation of a website, usability experience, or the process of buying a product, is to make him a defender of a brand, making indications and highlighting the benefits of this item over the internet. UX is suitable for any project on Web 2.0, including a blog with opinions about entertainment, news site, a career page, or even a virtual store, inclining the user to make recommendations for a company (Lopes et al., 2020; van de Sand et al., 2020; Vilarinho et al., 2017; Hayek et al., 2019).

DISCUSSION

In the early days of the Internet, the search was for both the technical and financial exploitation of all the opportunities offered by the global network, and as it matured, the Internet moved from failed technical and economic models to a web of more significant value for the user, which was so large, taking advantage of technological resources currently available, that it allowed the creation of applications extremely similar to those that run on personal computers, without the need for any additional installation.

Web 2.0 is based on simple concepts, such as simplicity, since everything must be intuitive and evident, access and use must be a pleasure and not the torture of infinite clicks, since, in it, the environments adapt to the place where they are read and "consumed", as long as Web 2.0 feeds on all available content.

Concerning content, with Web 2.0, it has become the democratic and barrier-free possibility for users to exercise their opinion, directly on the content, associated with a certain stretch of anything, an indelible, classifying and sometimes personal mark, each content can have infinite Tags and be consumed from them, showing the world the digital personas of the user. Still taking into account that Web 2.0, information is received, transformed, and published, creating an infinite cycle of information generation.

The web is a platform in constant evolution, since the sites of the 1980s, accessed only by governments, practically in 'plain text' mode, going through the excesses of the 1996s, to the clean environment of the Google era, the web has been evolving each novelty, with the creation of HTML to display documents, impacting people's lives, however still in its beginning, the lack of standard browsers and the still slow connections to the web continued to be a limited technological platform.

Today, web applications are very close to what we have installed on personal PCs, with Ajax, the re-invention of Java script associated with XML, Ruby on Rails, xmlHttpRequest, among other dozens of novelties, make it increasingly difficult to differentiate what is web than what is not.

These features allow any user to work with the same material, and with several users simultaneously, anywhere in the world, needing only a browser, without the need to load pen drives, CDs or even DVDs, allowing access to personal files having simply a point of access to the Internet, practically making the user free not only of the operating system but even of the concept of "personal computer". Since Web 2.0 ended the need for large versions of software being released annually, considering that programs run everywhere, but only exist in one place: the server.

Another element that made Web 2.0 viable was broadband, with its increasingly faster connections, enabling the availability of various and diverse services, or applications, free of charge on the Internet such as text editors, spreadsheets, presentations, photo editors, among others, developed with increasingly powerful programming technologies, such as AJAX, which allow the user to browse as if it were the preferred application on the desktop.

Web 2.0 is by nature entrepreneurial, since it was born under the focus of collaboration and multi-platform content, considering that everyone reads more, everyone creates more, everyone collaborates more, since with collaborative environments, there is the speed in the briefing cycle and greater emphasis on remote work, with the ease of working at a distance, it is possible to reach more distant clients, and even abroad, which was something very complicated before; in this context, it is worth highlighting the digital communities, wherein them, through the creation of individual profiles, the user has available various platforms for exchanging information.

Still considering the digital platforms that are everywhere reference that capitalism has transformed everything, related to streaming services, credit cards, social media, online chat rooms, reflecting the performance of American technology giants monopolizing attention in life everyday life; attracting attention to technology. When narrating the rise of platforms, it is closely related to the technological premise of the development of Web 2.0 and later Web 3.0, systematically examining all facets of digital platforms. Analyzing the immense impact of platforms on contemporary media, such as streaming music, video, and games, which fills neglected parts of society and contemporary life, with the rise of social games that mimic people's real lives, in the same way, that chat tools, and video streaming sites, as well as the development of online platforms as part of a broader transformation which is responsible as mediators of cultural life (Steinberg, 2019).

TRENDS

Web 3.0 brings together the characteristics of the internet of yesterday and today, in addition to adding elements of artificial intelligence, through continuous collaboration between man and machine, the future promises a more free, secure digital experience without centralizing power (Sein-Echaluce et al, 2019, Garg & Garg, 2019).

Also called the Semantic Web that brings together the virtues of its predecessors and adds an innovative and fundamental element, artificial intelligence, where machines nowadays become allies of users both in the production of content and in the optimization of the online experience (Ahmed, 2019, SHARAFI FARZAD et al, 2019).

The web 3.0 is also known as the smart web, with the main characteristics related to the ability of machines to undertake certain activities that today are performed manually, even considering that from the crossing of data and the development of machine learning, the Semantic Web has the ability not to only to generate and store information, but also to interpret it, thus creating a much more personalized and interactive user experience (Boudlaie et al, 2019, Tavakoli & Wijesinghe, 2019).

With Web 3.0, it is possible to solve one of the biggest concerns of today's Internet users, related to data security, since the unregulated exploitation of user information by companies such as social networks represents an excessive centralization of digital power in the hands of a few. And to combat this, the tendency is that users, with the use of technologies such as encryption, have full control over their own data, meaning that, instead of waiting for companies to personalize their experiences, Internet users will, together with artificial intelligence, shaping navigation itself (Ahmed, 2019, SHARAFI FARZAD et al, 2019, Boudlaie et al, 2019, Tavakoli & Wijesinghe, 2019). The emergence of Web 3.0 does not represent the extinction of Web 1.0 or 2.0, but another step in a long development process.

Web 4.0 will allow even greater exploration of wireless communication, creating a kind of gigantic intelligent and dynamic operating system, based on a complex artificial intelligence system. Which will be able to support the interactions of individuals, using available data, instant or historical, to propose or support decision making. Web 4.0 will further intensify communication and data storage through wireless communication, allowing for greater integration with tools such as Big Data, which means a very wide set of data so that all information in the media to be found, analyzed quickly. Web 4.0 will further emphasize the technological aspect, serving to obtain data and analyze precious insights to improve strategic directions (Choudhury, 2014; Nath & Iswary, 2015; Demartini & Benussi, 2017; Almeida, 2017).

Through Web 3.0 and in the future, Web 4.0 will result in greater optimization of all productive activity, and in processes without human intervention in the control of machines. What through this technological interaction through integration with the Internet of Things (IoT), which means the use of a large number of utensils, household appliances, smart devices, and the like connected to the internet that does tasks without any human action. Like a refrigerator sending information to a smartphone when it is necessary to buy some food, as in the case of smart homes with integration linked to the Web, various equipment and objects in the house can perform tasks that make life easier for the owner. The IoT is able to connect all machines over the internet identifying all the quality of the processes, carried out in the industry, from production analysis to the need for parts in maintenance (Ke, 2010; Murugesan et al., 2011; Robert et al., 2016; Patel et al., 2017; Okano, 2017; Ferrer et al., 2017; Hatzivasilis et al., 2018).

CONCLUSION

As was said throughout this chapter, simplicity is the backbone of Web 2.0, along with the existence of several virtual platforms, strong collaborative appeal, constant professionalization, considering that the web is the platform itself, and what counts is the content, this being text, video, audio, profiles, campaign and advertising, among others, with the user's ability and right to express an opinion.

In the beginning, information technology had fundamental elements such as hardware and software. With the creation of Web 2.0, we have a new concept, Webware, defined by Wikipedia itself as the second generation of Internet services and applications, which allows greater interaction with the user and similarity to desktop applications, to more comprehensively meet peopleware (users who use computing directly or indirectly) through Collective Intelligence.

Therefore, this new Internet reflects a significant change in the habits of users, to the point that many experts consider Web 2.0 a revolution. However, for others, Web 2.0 is still a mere evolution, because it does not structurally change the world network, but only interacts several resources and tools already existing on the web, adding value to the standard Internet user in a very intelligent way.

REFERENCES

Adrian, B., Sauermann, L., & Roth-Berghofer, T. (2007). Contag: A semantic tag recommendation system. *Proceedings of I-Semantics*, *7*, 297–304.

Aghaei, S., Nematbakhsh, M. A., & Farsani, H. K. (2012). Evolution of the world wide web: From WEB 1.0 TO WEB 4.0. *International Journal of Web & Semantic Technology*, *3*(1), 1–10. doi:10.5121/ijwest.2012.3101

Ahmed, F. (2019). *Possible uses of web 3.0 in websites of Libraries of Academic Institutions of Pakistan*. Academic Press.

Almeida, F. L. (2017). Concept and dimensions of web 4.0. *International Journal of Computers and Technology*, *16*(7), 7040–7046. doi:10.24297/ijct.v16i7.6446

Ankolekar, A., Krötzsch, M., Tran, T., & Vrandecic, D. (2007, May). The two cultures: Mashing up Web 2.0 and the Semantic Web. In *Proceedings of the 16th international conference on World Wide Web* (pp. 825-834). 10.1145/1242572.1242684

Bae, S., Cho, H., Lim, I., & Ryu, S. (2014, November). SAFEWAPI: web API misuse detector for web applications. In *Proceedings of the 22nd ACM SIGSOFT International Symposium on Foundations of Software Engineering* (pp. 507-517). 10.1145/2635868.2635916

Barsky, E. (2006). Introducing Web 2.0: RSS trends for health librarians. *Journal of the Canadian Health Libraries Association/Journal de l'Association des bibliothèques de la santé du Canada, 27*(1), 7-8.

Berger, P., & Trexler, S. (2010). *Choosing Web 2.0 tools for learning and teaching in a digital world.* Libraries Unlimited, Inc.

Bizer, C., Cyganiak, R., & Gauß, T. (2007). The RDF Book Mashup: From Web APIs to a Web of Data. *SFSW*, 248.

Boudlaie, H., & Nargesian, A., & Keshavarz Nik, B. (2019). Digital footprint in Web 3.0: Social Media Usage in Recruitment. *AD-Minister*, (34), 139–156.

Bradley, P. (2007). *How to use Web 2.0 in your library.* Facet Publishing.

Breeding, M. (2006). Web 2.0? Let's get to Web 1.0 first. *Computers in Libraries, 26*(5), 30–33.

Choudhury, N. (2014). World wide web and its journey from web 1.0 to web 4.0. *International Journal of Computer Science and Information Technologies, 5*(6), 8096–8100.

Coleman, D., & Levine, S. (2008). *Collaboration 2.0: technology and best practices for successful collaboration in a Web 2.0 world.* Happy About.

Cormode, G., & Krishnamurthy, B. (2008). Key differences between Web 1.0 and Web 2.0. *First Monday, 13*(6). Advance online publication. doi:10.5210/fm.v13i6.2125

Deitel, P., & Deitel, H. (2007). *Internet & world wide web: how to program.* Prentice-Hall Press.

Demartini, C., & Benussi, L. (2017). Do Web 4.0 and industry 4.0 imply education X. 0? *IT Professional, 19*(3), 4–7. doi:10.1109/MITP.2017.47

Ellis, K., & Kent, M. (2019). Community accessibility: Tweeters take responsibility for an accessible Web 2.0. *Fast Capitalism, 7*(1).

Farrell, S. (2009). API Keys to the Kingdom. *IEEE Internet Computing, 13*(5), 91–93. doi:10.1109/MIC.2009.100

Feiler, J. (2007). *How to do everything with Web 2.0 Mashups.* McGraw-Hill, Inc.

Ferrer, B. R., Mohammed, W. M., Chen, E., & Lastra, J. L. M. (2017, October). Connecting web-based IoT devices to a cloud-based manufacturing platform. In *IECON 2017-43rd Annual Conference of the IEEE Industrial Electronics Society* (pp. 8628-8633). IEEE. 10.1109/IECON.2017.8217516

García Aretio, L. (2014). *Web 2.0 vs web 1.0.* Academic Press.

Garg, N., & Garg, N. (2019). Next Generation Internet (Web 3.0: Block Chained Internet). *Cybernomics, 1*(6), 19–23.

Gómez, A., Ruiz, Á. A. M., & Orcos, L. (2015). UX of social network Edmodo in undergraduate engineering students. *IJIMAI*, *3*(4), 31–36. doi:10.9781/ijimai.2015.346

Guha, R., & Al-Dabass, D. (2010, December). Impact of web 2.0 and cloud computing platform on software engineering. In *2010 International Symposium on Electronic System Design* (pp. 213-218). IEEE. 10.1109/ISED.2010.48

Harris, A. L., & Rea, A. (2019). Web 2.0 and virtual world technologies: A growing impact on IS education. *Journal of Information Systems Education*, *20*(2), 3.

Hatzivasilis, G., Askoxylakis, I., Alexandris, G., Anicic, D., Bröring, A., Kulkarni, V., . . . Spanoudakis, G. (2018, September). The Interoperability of Things: Interoperable solutions as an enabler for IoT and Web 3.0. In *2018 IEEE 23rd International Workshop on Computer-Aided Modeling and Design of Communication Links and Networks (CAMAD)* (pp. 1-7). IEEE.

Hayek, M., Farhat, P., Yamout, Y., Ghorra, C., & Haraty, R. A. (2019, September). Web 2.0 Testing Tools: A Compendium. In *2019 International Conference on Innovation and Intelligence for Informatics, Computing, and Technologies (3ICT)* (pp. 1-6). IEEE.

Hiremath, B. K., & Kenchakkanavar, A. Y. (2016). An alteration of the web 1.0, web 2.0 and web 3.0: a comparative study. *Imperial Journal of Interdisciplinary Research, 2*(4), 705-710.

Hsu, C. L., & Park, H. W. (2011). Sociology of hyperlink networks of Web 1.0, Web 2.0, and Twitter: A case study of South Korea. *Social Science Computer Review*, *29*(3), 354–368. doi:10.1177/0894439310382517

Huffman, K. (2017). Web 2.0: Beyond the concept practical ways to implement RSS, podcasts, and Wikis. *Education Libraries*, *29*(1), 12–19. doi:10.26443/el.v29i1.220

Ke, H. (2010). The Key Technologies of IoT with Development & Applications. *Radio Frequency Ubiquitous Journal*, *1*(1), 33.

Kompen, R. T., Edirisingha, P., Canaleta, X., Alsina, M., & Monguet, J. M. (2019). Personal learning Environments based on Web 2.0 services in higher education. *Telematics and Informatics*, *38*, 194–206. doi:10.1016/j.tele.2018.10.003

Kopecký, J., Gomadam, K., & Vitvar, T. (2008, December). hrests: An HTML microformat for describing restful web services. In *2008 IEEE/WIC/ACM International Conference on Web Intelligence and Intelligent Agent Technology* (Vol. 1, pp. 619-625). IEEE. 10.1109/WIIAT.2008.379

Kroski, E. (2008). *Web 2.0 for librarians and information professionals*. Neal-Schuman Publishers, Inc.

Lee, M. J., & McLoughlin, C. (2011). *Web 2.0-based e-learning: Applying social informatics for tertiary teaching*. Information Science Reference. doi:10.4018/978-1-60566-294-7

Lialina, O. (2018). Rich user experience, UX and the desktopization of war. *Interface Critique*, (1), 176-193.

Lopes, B. D. C. M., & da Silva, E. P. (2020). A divulgação de acervos arquivísticos na web: potencialidades da perspectiva de User Experience aplicada ao Sistema de Informações do Arquivo Nacional. *Ciência da Informação em Revista, 7*, 70-90.

Mahemoff, M. (2006). *AJAX design patterns: creating Web 2.0 sites with programming and usability patterns*. O'Reilly Media, Inc.

McLoughlin, C. E., & Alam, S. L. (2019). A case study of instructor scaffolding using Web 2.0 tools to teach social informatics. *Journal of Information Systems Education, 25*(2), 4.

Méndez Rodríguez, E. M., Bravo, A., & López, L. M. (2007). *Microformatos: web 2.0 para el Dublin Core*. Academic Press.

Mesbah, A., & Van Deursen, A. (2009, May). Invariant-based automatic testing of AJAX user interfaces. In *2009 IEEE 31st International Conference on Software Engineering* (pp. 210-220). IEEE. 10.1109/ICSE.2009.5070522

Mistry, A., Rajan, P., & Arokia, R. (2019). Evaluation of web applications based on UX parameters. *International Journal of Electrical & Computer Engineering*, 9.

Murugesan, S., Rossi, G., Wilbanks, L., & Djavanshir, R. (2011). The future of web apps. *IT Professional, 13*(5), 12–14. doi:10.1109/MITP.2011.89

Nath, K., Dhar, S., & Basishtha, S. (2014, February). Web 1.0 to Web 3.0-Evolution of the Web and its various challenges. In *2014 International Conference on Reliability Optimization and Information Technology (ICROIT)* (pp. 86-89). IEEE. 10.1109/ICROIT.2014.6798297

Nath, K., & Iswary, R. (2015). What comes after Web 3.0? Web 4.0 and the Future. In *Proceedings of the International Conference and Communication System (I3CS'15), Shillong, India* (pp. 337-341). Academic Press.

Neumann, T., & Weikum, G. (2008). RDF-3X: A RISC-style engine for RDF. *Proceedings of the VLDB Endowment International Conference on Very Large Data Bases, 1*(1), 647–659. doi:10.14778/1453856.1453927

Nogueira, T. D. C., & Ferreira, D. J. (2019). Systematic Review of Visually-Impaired and Blind User Experience of Web Trends. *Revista de Sistemas e Computação-RSC, 8*(2).

O'Reilly, T. (2012). *What is web 2.0. Design patterns and business models for the next generation of software*. Academic Press.

Okano, M. T. (2017, September). IoT and industry 4.0: the industrial new revolution. In *International Conference on Management and Information System* (pp. 75-82). Academic Press.

Orehovački, T., Granić, A., & Kermek, D. (2011, June). Exploring the quality in use of Web 2.0 applications: the case of mind mapping services. In *International Conference on Web Engineering* (pp. 266-277). Springer.

Patel, K. (2013). Incremental journey for World Wide Web: Introduced with Web 1.0 to recent Web 5.0–a survey paper. *International Journal of Advanced Research in Computer Science and Software Engineering, 3*(10).

Patel, P., Ali, M. I., & Sheth, A. (2017). On using the intelligent edge for IoT analytics. *IEEE Intelligent Systems, 32*(5), 64–69. doi:10.1109/MIS.2017.3711653

Reynolds, F. (2008). Web 2.0–in your hand. *IEEE Pervasive Computing*, 8(1), 86–88. doi:10.1109/MPRV.2009.22

Rigby, B. (2008). *Mobilizing Generation 2.0: A practical guide to using Web 2.0: technologies to recruit, organize and engage youth*. John Wiley & Sons.

Robert, J., Kubler, S., & Le Traon, Y. (2016, August). Micro-billing framework for IoT: Research & Technological foundations. In *2016 IEEE 4th International Conference on Future Internet of Things and Cloud (FiCloud)* (pp. 301-308). IEEE.

Sankar, K., & Bouchard, S. A. (2009). *Enterprise web 2.0 fundamentals*. Cisco Press.

Sein-Echaluce, M. L., Fidalgo-Blanco, Á., & Esteban-Escaño, J. (2019). Technological ecosystems and ontologies for an educational model based on Web 3.0. *Universal Access in the Information Society*, 18(3), 645–658. doi:10.100710209-019-00684-9

Sharafi Farzad, F., Kolli, S., Soltani, T., & Ghanbary, S. (2019). Digital Brands and Web 3.0 Enterprises: Social Network Analysis and Thematic Analysis of User activities and Behavioral Patterns in Online Retailers. *AD-Minister*, (34), 119–138.

Shivalingaiah, D., & Naik, U. (2008). *Comparative Study of web 1.0, web 2.0 and web 3.0*. Academic Press.

Shuen, A. (2018). *Web 2.0: A Strategy Guide: Business thinking and strategies behind successful Web 2.0 implementations*. O'Reilly Media.

Solomon, G., & Schrum, L. (2007). *Web 2.0: New tools, new schools. ISTE*. Interntl Soc Tech Educ.

Steinberg, M. (2019). *The Platform Economy: How Japan Transformed the Consumer Internet*. U of Minnesota Press.

Sultan, N. (2013). Knowledge management in the age of cloud computing and Web 2.0: Experiencing the power of disruptive innovations. *International Journal of Information Management*, 33(1), 160–165. doi:10.1016/j.ijinfomgt.2012.08.006

Tavakoli, R., & Wijesinghe, S. N. (2019). The evolution of the web and netnography in tourism: A systematic review. *Tourism Management Perspectives*, 29, 48–55. doi:10.1016/j.tmp.2018.10.008

Teo, T., Sang, G., Mei, B., & Hoi, C. K. W. (2019). Investigating pre-service teachers' acceptance of Web 2.0 technologies in their future teaching: A Chinese perspective. *Interactive Learning Environments*, 27(4), 530–546. doi:10.1080/10494820.2018.1489290

Theimer, K. (2009). *Web 2.0 tools and strategies for archives and local history collections*. Neal-Schuman Publishers, Inc.

Väänänen-Vainio-Mattila, K., Wäljas, M., Ojala, J., & Segerståhl, K. (2010, April). Identifying drivers and hindrances of social user experience in web services. In *Proceedings of the SIGCHI Conference on Human Factors in Computing Systems* (pp. 2499-2502). 10.1145/1753326.1753704

van de Sand, F., Frison, A. K., Zotz, P., Riener, A., & Holl, K. (2020). The Intersection of User Experience (UX), Customer Experience (CX), and Brand Experience (BX). In *User Experience Is Brand Experience* (pp. 71–93). Springer. doi:10.1007/978-3-030-29868-5_5

Vickery, G., & Wunsch-Vincent, S. (2007). *Participative web and user-created content: Web 2.0 wikis and social networking. Organization for Economic Cooperation and Development.* OECD.

Vilarinho, T., Floch, J., Oliveira, M., Dinant, I., Pappas, I. O., & Mora, S. (2017, November). Developing a social innovation methodology in the web 2.0 era. In *International Conference on Internet Science* (pp. 168-183). Springer.

Xu, Z., Fu, Y., Mao, J., & Su, D. (2006, May). Towards the semantic web: Collaborative tag suggestions. In Collaborative web tagging workshop at WWW2006, Edinburgh, UK.

Yamakami, T. (2007, April). MobileWeb 2.0: Lessons from Web 2.0 and past mobile Internet development. In *2007 International Conference on Multimedia and Ubiquitous Engineering (MUE'07)* (pp. 886-890). IEEE. 10.1109/MUE.2007.155

ADDITIONAL READING

Aljawarneh, S. A. (2019). Reviewing and exploring innovative ubiquitous learning tools in higher education. *Journal of Computing in Higher Education*, 1–17.

Almeida, F. L. (2017). Concept and dimensions of web 4.0. *International Journal of Computers and Technology*, *16*(7), 7040–7046. doi:10.24297/ijct.v16i7.6446

Boulaid, F., & Moubtassime, M. (2018). *Using Web 3.0 Apps to stimulate university learners' participation: SMBUF as a case study (No. 182).* EasyChair. doi:10.29007/6pg7

Cabada, R. Z., Estrada, M. L. B., Hernández, F. G., Bustillos, R. O., & Reyes-García, C. A. (2018). An affective and Web 3.0-based learning environment for a programming language. *Telematics and Informatics*, *35*(3), 611–628. doi:10.1016/j.tele.2017.03.005

Esmaeili, L., & Hashemi, G. S. A. (2019). A systematic review on social commerce. *Journal of Strategic Marketing*, *27*(4), 317–355. doi:10.1080/0965254X.2017.1408672

Fornasari, A. (2017). Social Privacy. Informare, comunicare, educare ai tempi del web 3.0. *Mondo Digitale*, *6*(71), 1–13.

Jensen, J. (2019). A systematic literature review of the use of semantic web technologies in formal education. *British Journal of Educational Technology*, *50*(2), 505–517. doi:10.1111/bjet.12570

Khiste, G. P., & Surwade, Y. P. (2018). Publication Productivity of "Web 3.0" By Using Science Direct During 2008-2017. *International Journal for Science and Advance Research in Technology*, *4*(3), 1632–1634.

Lies, J. (2019). Marketing 4.0 als „Old School "des PR-Managements. In Digitalisierung und Kommunikation (pp. 231-252). Springer VS, Wiesbaden.

Ohei, K. N., & Brink, R. (2019). Web 3.0 and Web 2.0 technologies in higher educational institute: Methodological concept towards a framework development for adoption. *International Journal for Infonomics*, *12*(1), 1841–1853. doi:10.20533/iji.1742.4712.2019.0188

Orenga-Roglá, S., & Chalmeta, R. (2019). Methodology for the implementation of knowledge management systems 2.0. *Business & Information Systems Engineering, 61*(2), 195–213. doi:10.100712599-017-0513-1

Parveen, S., & Biswas, R. (2018). Framework for selection of Semantic Web Languages and Tools: A Prerequisite for Web 3.0. International Information Institute (Tokyo). Information, 21(7), 2007-2021.

Salamzadeh, Y., Williams, I., & Labafi, S. (2019). Guest Editorial: Media Entrepreneurship and Web 3.0, the way passed, the way forward. *AD-Minister*, (34), 7–13.

Sein-Echaluce, M. L., Fidalgo-Blanco, Á., & Esteban-Escaño, J. (2019). Technological ecosystems and ontologies for an educational model based on Web 3.0. *Universal Access in the Information Society, 18*(3), 645–658. doi:10.100710209-019-00684-9

KEY TERMS AND DEFINITIONS

AJAX: Is a technique of Web development that allows the creation of more interactive applications, one of the main objectives is to make the responses of Web pages faster by exchanging small amounts of information with the Web server. It has the philosophy of loading and rendering a page, using script resources running on the client-side, searching, and loading data in the background without the need to reload the page.

API: They are a type of "bridge" that connect applications, which can be used for the most varied types of business, by companies of different market niches or sizes, ie, they are a way of integrating systems, enabling benefits such as the security of data, ease of exchange between information with different programming languages and monetization of accesses. They are invisible to the average user, who sees only the interface of software and applications.

CSS: It is the language that will make this information beautiful, it is the layer in programming that shapes the elements of HTML, it is a language of stylization, formatting, determining the style of a text, a page with a certain background color or a block wrapped around a border and present it as a new shape in the browser.

HTML: It is the language that will display the information, in addition to displaying the information, it gives meaning, since this is important because some search engine systems will read your page, they need to understand what is each element in it and the that each of these elements means.

Information: It is a set of data that aims to reduce uncertainty or deepen the knowledge on a subject of interest based on what already exists. It constitutes a message about a particular phenomenon or event. Information makes it possible to solve problems and make decisions, taking into account that its rational use is the basis of knowledge.

Internet: The internet is a worldwide network that aims to interconnect computers to provide the user with access to various information, and is thus called the world wide web. It has revolutionized world communication by allowing, the conversation between users thousands of kilometers away.

JavaScript: It is the language that will make this information receive some behaviors, for example when creating a submenu or controlling something that appears and disappears on the screen, it is the layer in the programming that adds dynamic behaviors, it is this technology that acts when the user is in contact with the interface of a page that can at any time perform an action that results in behavior on the page, that is, as a dynamic behavior obtained when filling out a form, the user misses the email and is notified by the site.

Web: Is the term used to refer to a set of connected computers that can exchange data and messages. This is possible through a common protocol, which allows several users—private individuals, cultural bodies, libraries, or military institutes—to join in the same access.

Web 1.0: It was the first version of the Internet (called ARPANET) that emerged shortly after the Cold War, in the 1960s, with the initial purpose that served the US military objectives, providing information sharing, featuring online content delivery, in short, one of its milestones was e-mail, in 1969, the existence of the Internet Protocol (IP) and HyperText Transfer Protocol Secure (HTTP), providing data traffic by means such as radio, optical fiber and satellite (currently); sending encrypted information and commercial transactions via the Internet. The internet pages were simple, with mostly one-sided information and almost no interaction. The aim was only to discover information, the user being a mere spectator.

Web 2.0: It was the Web that gained new tools that made it more dynamic, starting phase 2.0, being marked by the 2000s with the sharing of information, where users invaded it with the production of video, text and photo content, considering the era of blogs, YouTube channels, and photo sharing networks, which has increased virtual interaction between people. It is a more intuitive and interactive Web platform, with the emergence and culmination of social networks, and video sharing sites, making it not only an entertainment platform, but also a business platform, as several companies have already started to operate virtually.

XML: It is a markup language that defines a set of rules for encoding documents, it is a set of codes that can be applied when reading data or texts made by computers or people, providing a platform to define markup elements and generate a custom language. Working to define how certain content will be viewed on the screen or how the data will be distributed, and this internal coding is done through the use of markers or tags.

Chapter 6
Cross–Cultural Study of Trust Types in Sharing Economy Organizations:
Evidence From Inside Airbnb

Jialei Li
Dongbei University of Finance and Economics, China

Tao Meng
Dongbei University of Finance and Economics, China

Chunying Li
Dongbei University of Finance and Economics, China

ABSTRACT

The sharing economy has developed very quickly. However, organizations like Airbnb and Uber have encountered crisis of trust. Academia still does not know what is the type of trust in sharing economy organizations. Therefore, the authors designed two studies, used data from Airbnb, to test 2 hypotheses: (1) the level of inter-organizational trust in sharing economy organizations is relatively positive to the level of participation, and (2) the price of the product or service being shared is relatively negative to the level of participation. The results find out that consumers are more willing to choose non-shared renting methods in China, yet the opposite in America. Under both conditions, price is an important moderator. This shows that the role of trust in China is mainly inter-organizational trust, but interpersonal in America. The theoretical contribution is to reveal the type of trust in the sharing economy organizations, collaborative relations and studies of Airbnb.

DOI: 10.4018/978-1-7998-3756-5.ch006

INTRODUCTION

In recent years, one of the major innovations of Web 2.0 technologies called the Sharing Economy has dramatically influenced the user experience in Web 2.0 technologies. In specific, Airbnb is a typical business platform based on sharing economy, it does not own many houses but enables its users to share their houses on the platform. This is different from traditional businesses and changed the user experience during this process. Users are not only consuming the products but also producing goods and services like a "producer". For example, one person can rent a house in Airbnb while traveling and lease his or her own house through this platform as well. *It is clear that sharing economy presents an important role to understand the change of user experience in Web 2.0 technologies. So research on Airbnb in this chapter will give new insights to the change of the user experience in sharing economy.*

Technically speaking, The sharing economy is a process of collaborative consumption online, so it is no doubt that there is a great risk of uncertainty in this process. In reality, several typical representatives of the sharing economy have encountered a crisis of trust during development. For example, violent incidents have repeatedly appeared in Airbnb, and two of Didichuxing's female passengers were killed years ago. Trust is an important factor in overcoming this kind of risk, but academia still does not know what is the type of trust in sharing economy organizations, neither knows little about the cultural influence under these circumstances. Although trust has always been the focus of sharing economy research (Huurne, Ronteltap, and Corten et al., 2017), relevant research is still insufficient in quantity and quality.

In this chapter, we view business platforms in sharing economy like Airbnb as growing organizations (Perren and Kozinets, 2018), and we will use "sharing economy organizations" for short in the following context. Therefore, the objective of this chapter is to find out the trust types in sharing economy organizations from a cross-cultural perspective. And the research question comes from the observation of Airbnb: Airbnb is a typical representative of the sharing economy, it should carry the main logic of sharing economy, that is, the participants would share, interact and trust each other, but the reality in China is just the opposite. This means users from different cultures in Airbnb perform differently and earn different user experiences. Why is that this counterintuitive phenomenon happened?

BACKGROUND

Research on Sharing Economy

Recently, Uber, Airbnb, and other sharing economy organizations have quickly become hot research topics in the management fields, forming a variety of concepts and theories, such as: collaborative consumption (Botsman and Rogers, 2010; Benoit et al. 2017), business sharing systems (Lamberton and Rose, 2012), access-based consumption (Bardhi and Eckhardt, 2012), gig economy (Friedman, 2014), peer-to-peer economy (Schor and Fitzmaurice, 2015), mixed economy (Scaraboto, 2015), platform economy (Kenney and Zysman, 2016), lateral exchange market (Perren and Kozinets, 2018), etc. At present, the concept of the sharing economy can accurately express this new type of resource allocation way. It has become a "big umbrella", covering the above-mentioned various theoretical explanations and phenomenon descriptions, and has formed a conceptual consensus in the theoretical world.

However, existing research on the sharing economy cannot directly reach our objective. Studies on the sharing economy are various from different perspectives. Economic researchers focus on the property rights and economic mechanisms (Bardhi and Eckhardt, 2012; Belk, 2014; Kostakis and Bauwens, 2014; Martin, 2016); Management and marketing scholars focus on the business model and operational management, value creation, consumer behavior, etc. (Lan, Ma, and Zhu et al., 2017; Camilleri and Neuhofer, 2017); Sociologists focus on participants' motivations and behaviors (Celata, Lamberton and Rose, 2012; Möhlmann, 2015; Perren and Kozinets, 2018); Legal researchers focus on government regulation and legal regulation (Zervas, Proserpio and Byers, 2017; Guttentag, 2015). However, there is no clear research on the role of trust in the sharing economy.

Moreover, in the management field, A lot of research focuses on consumers' behavior in the sharing economy. The main research involves value co-creation, knowledge sharing, human resources, and operation management. Value co-creation refers to the cooperation between producers and consumers to create value. It is a new marketing concept based on service-dominant logic after goods-dominant logic (Grönroos, 2011). The main idea of this concept is that value is not created independently by the enterprise, but is created jointly by the enterprise and the customer (Prahalad and Ramaswamy, 2004). The research by Johnson and Neuhofer (2017) combined service-dominant logic with the value creation in the sharing economy. Besides, Lan, Ma and Zhu et al. (2017) proposed that value co-creation on the study of Mobike is an important behavior for users to participate in the sharing economy.

The Dimensions of Trust

Trust itself is a multidimensional concept (Fulmer and Gelfand, 2012), which is not only a relationship between specific individuals but also at the interpersonal, organizational, and institutional levels (Welter, 2012). Trust was initially a key issue for sociologists and psychologists. As people become more aware of the shortcomings of market mechanisms and hierarchical mechanisms, the role of trust in economic transactions is becoming more and more important. Many economists and management scientists have studied trust. Trust is no longer a purely social issue. It has been deeply embedded in economic transactions and has become an economic issue of great research value. The literature on existing research trusts is mainly concentrated among individuals, but there is not much research on trust in organizations.

The differences in disciplines and orientations lead to a variety of scholars' understanding of trust, and the classification of trust is also different. For example, psychologists Rotter (1967) argues that trust is a generalized expectation of the individual's reliability of others' words, promises, and oral written statements, and points out that such expectations will have an impact on public behavioral decisions; The sociologist Deutsch (1973) believes that trust is a belief in the cooperative behavior of others. Messick and Kramer (2001) believe that the feedback behavior of individuals based on whether others' behaviors affect moral standards is trust.

Trust can be divided into three different levels: personal, inter-personal, and social. Psychologists often study from the personal dimension, they understand trust as the performance of individual personality traits. In the inter-personal level, trust is understood as the product of inter-personal relationship, which is the inter-personal attitude determined by rational calculations and emotional concepts in inter-personal relationships. On the social level, trust is a social phenomenon closely related to social structure, economic transactions, culture, and institutions. This transcends the personal level of trust as a trait that encourages individuals, and transcends the bilateral considerations of inter-personal dimensions, placing trust in the broad context of groups, organizations, and societies. Trust is seen as ethical and institutional behavior, designing individual recognition and commitment to the rules, and oriented to economic ethics. In the above three levels, a variety of trust classifications are formed.

In a word, trust can be divided into three dimensions, inter-personal trust, inter-organizational trust, and institutional trust (see table 1). Sharing economy organization's trust is one of the inter-organizational trust. The study of trust begins with inter-personal dimension, which was proposed by Luhuman (1979), based on the familiarity and relationship of inter-personal relationships. Blois (1999) believes that trust between organizations is based on inter-personal trust. Inter-organizational trust is the abbreviation of "the trust relationship between a group of individuals". That is to say, inter-organizational trust creates collective trust generated by individual members of the organization, not between organizations and organizations. Based on the trust between organizations, institutional trust is built. Zucker (1986) believes that institutional trust is based on legal, government, industry associations, and other formal organizations, using legal punishment mechanisms or prevention mechanisms to reduce the complexity of social interaction.

Table 1. The dimensions of trust

Dimensions	Meaning	Scholar
Inter-personal Trust	Based on the familiarity and the relationship between people.	Luhuman
Institutional Trust	Based on legal, government, industry associations and other formal systems and formal organizations, the legal punishment mechanism or prevention mechanism to reduce the complexity of social interaction.	Zucker
Inter-organizational Trust	the abbreviation of "the trust relationship between a group of individuals", not between organizations and organizations.	Blois

Source: (Luhuman, 1979), (Zucker, 1986), (Blois, 1999)

MAIN FOCUS OF THE CHAPTER

Trust in Sharing Economy Organizations

The trust in sharing economy is kind of inter-organizational trust. Sharing economy activities is the process of collaborative consumption on the Internet, and organizational trust is the collective accumulated by personal trust, so sharing economy organizations' trust has the characteristics of network inter-personal trust. Corritore, Kracher and Wiedenbeck (2003) define network trust as an expectation that individuals' weaknesses are not exploited in a risky network environment; some studies directly draw on the definition of offline inter-personal trust, namely individuals generalized expectations of the words, commitments, and reliability of written or oral statements established in the process of inter-personal interaction (Feng, Lazar and Preece, 2004). In network interaction, the trust of both parties can promote individual commitment (Colquitt, Scott and LePine, 2007; DeLaat, 2005), and strengthen cooperation and information exchange in the network (Pettit, 2008).

In network trust, third-party security is a simple and effective trust mechanism. In social networks, knowing others through familiar third parties can enhance the trust between unfamiliar netizens, that is, generate trust transfer (Wong and Boh, 2010). Studies have shown that using a familiar third party as an intermediate bridge can significantly reduce the risk of trust in network interactions (Beldad, DeJong and Steehouder, 2010; Benedicktus, 2011). In sharing economy organizations, the corporate platform acts as a third-party to take on this intermediate bridge role, matching and regulating both sides of the transaction while reducing the trust risk of the transaction (Celata, Hendrickson and Sanna, 2017; Miralles, Dentoni and Pascucci, 2017).

When sharing economy platform has a high degree of inter-organizational trust, user A trusts the organization B, but does not trust the sharing service provider C. Therefore, inter-personal trust between A-C is very low, but trust between A-B and B-C is relatively high, A is willing to use B to consume, and C is willing to share products or services through B, A-C does not need to spend time and energy to establish an inter-personal trust relationship, so the transaction cost of users participate in sharing economy activities will be relatively low (Williamson, 1998), which in turn promotes users' engagement, thereby proposing hypothesis 1:

Hypotheses 1: The level of inter-organizational trust in sharing economy organizations is relatively positive to the level of participation.

The Drives of Sharing Economy Organizations

Research on the pre-influence factors of the sharing economy is very rich, and the main research focuses on factors such as self-interest, utility, trust, cost, familiarity, interaction, and environment. The results of Möhlmann's (2015) study revealed the pre-influence factors that influence individuals' participation in the sharing economy, namely self-interested needs, utility, trust, cost savings, and familiarity. Tussyadiah (2015) revealed the role of social interaction in user participation in P2P online lending. Environmental motivation is another important influencing factor. The sharing economy from the perspective of resources means that idle resources are the basis for the sharing economy. The founder of Zipcar, Robin Chase (2015) emphasized that the foundation of sharing economy organizations was reusing idle resources. The new consumption concept "use rather than own" is gradually emerging, on-demand consumption is widely accepted, and receive continuous attention (Frenken, 2017; Alanne and Cao, 2017; Kopnina, 2017). Besides, there are other pre-influence factors such as social, cultural, and institutional aspects. Researches on the pre-influence factors of sharing economy provides support for research on sharing economy's behavior.

Among all kinds of influencing factors, cost savings is the foundation of everything. The basic of sharing economy is: the reuse of idle resources for profit. So the cost has a significant impact on users' participation in sharing economy activities. Reflected in real life is the price of the product or service, which raises the hypothesis 2:

Hypotheses 2: The price of the product or service being shared is relatively negative to the level of participation.

Research Design

To test the above hypotheses, this chapter designed two studies. Study 1 examined the relations among Room Type, Room Price, and Review Per Month. According to the data collected from the website of Inside Airbnb. By using the R Project for Statistical Computing (R software), to compute the corresponding relationship. There are 3 types of room, they are: tr1, entire home/apartment; tr2, private room; tr3, shared room. Different type of room indicates a different level of inter-organizational trust. Tr1 is the highest because under that occasion the users trust the sharing economy platforms more than the room providers. The level of trust for tr2 is in the middle, tr3 is the lowest.

The main data for study 1 came from Inside Airbnb (http://insideairbnb.com/). Inside Airbnb is an independent initiative and the data made available through its website are "not associated with or endorsed by Airbnb or any of Airbnb's competitors". The data utilities public information compiled from the Airbnb website from more than 30 cities. Data compiled for Beijing refers to November 2018. Two files called listings.csv and reviews.csv.gz were downloaded. These contained room type (entire home/apartment; private room; shared room), reviews per month, and room price information on each file. After deleted abnormal data, this chapter finally got 1430 groups of available data. Then to further support this study, this chapter collected data from New York City, a total of 34514 groups of available data.

Study 2 examined the moderating effect of the room price. This chapter designed an experimental study, 55 subjects were asked to make 3 decisions. The room picture and price are all from Airbnb's official website (see appendix). Firstly the authors chose three options: higher price & entire room, medium price & private room, lower price & shared room; Secondly, remained the room type unchanged, to choose from two options: higher level of trust & higher price, lower level of trust & lower price; Lastly, only changed the order of the second one: higher level of trust & lower price, lower level of trust & higher price. The main data for study 2 came from one experimental study that happened in one university in Dalian, China, 55 people are included. 7 of them are male, and all of them aged from 18 to 25 because people in this age period are most supposed to use and consume online.

Results

1. Result of Study 1.

Study 1 tested Hypotheses 1, as shown in Table 2 is the regression result based on the data from Beijing.

$$RPM(Beijing)=1462.023-0.458p-251.847rt2-338.329rt3$$

Table 2. Regression result table (Beijing)

	Estimate	**Std. Error**	**t value**	**Pr(>|t|)**	
(Intercept)	1462.023	76.099	19.212	< 2e-16	***
P	-0.458	0.106	-4.324	0.000	***
factor(RT)2	-251.847	78.812	-3.196	0.001	**
factor(RT)3	-338.329	151.420	-2.234	0.026	*

It indicates that:

a. The P-value of the F test is extremely small, indicating that the equation is significant by the F test.
b. The P-value of four factors' T-test is 0, 0, 0.001 and 0.026, indicating that under the significance level of 0.05, all four coefficients are significant.
c. Rt is a categorical variable, tr1 represents an entire home/apartment, tr2 represents a private room, and tr3 represents a shared room. -251.847 indicates that the private room on average is 252 times less than the entire home/apartment; -338.329 indicates that the shared room on average is 338 times

less than the entire home/apartment, obliviously, the entire home/apartment is the most popular one.

Thus supporting Hypothesis 1. The authors then want to check whether this is a universal result, so they selected data from New York City as a comparative, the regression result as shown in table 3.

RPM(New York)=1382.448-0.078p+126.673rt2+195.358rt3

Table 3. Regression result table (New York)

	Estimate	Std. Error	t value	Pr(>|t|)	
(Intercept)	1382.448	16.146	85.623	< 2e-16	***
P	-0.078	0.045	-1.735	0.083	.
factor(RT)RT2	126.673	19.408	6.527	0.000	***
factor(RT)RT3	195.358	60.331	3.238	0.001	**

It indicates that:

a. The P-value of the F test is extremely small, indicating that the equation is significant by the F test.
b. The P-value of four factors' T-test is 0, 0.083, 0 and 0.001, indicating that under the significance level of 0.1, all four coefficients are significant.
c. Rt is a categorical variable, tr1 represents an entire home/apartment, tr2 represents a private room, and tr3 represents a shared room. 126.673 indicates that the private room on average is 127 times more than the entire home/apartment; 195.358 indicates that the shared room on average is 195 times more than the entire home/apartment, obliviously, the shared room is the most popular one.

Compared two cities' Airbnb, we can see that the result is just the opposite, the entire home/apartment is the most popular room type in China but least popular in America. Therefore hypothesis 1 only supported in China.

Although price significantly influences the participation, Chinese consumers are more easily to be influenced(see the coefficient of P). So one question comes to our mind, whether the price factor strong enough to change Chinese participants' choice of room type? Thus this chapter design study 2 to test this.

2. Result of Study 2.

In study 2, this chapter tests Hypotheses 2. Firstly, only 5% of participants (3 out of 55) chose the shard room, even if the price is relatively low. This percentage was significantly lower than the entire room (27%) and private room (67%). And when the authors controlled the room type, even if the level of trust may change (according to the stress of interactive, Tussyadiah's study in 2015), only 11% (6 out of 55) and 7% (4 out of 55) participants would choose higher price room.

The results of study 2 show that the price significantly influences the participants' choice, but not strong enough to change users' choice of room type in China totally, thus supporting Hypothesis 2.

SOLUTIONS AND RECOMMENDATIONS

The research makes a few theoretical and managerial implications.

Firstly, this work adds to the small but growing body of research which considers the sharing economy organizations. Currently, the research about sharing economy from the organizational field has just emerged. Enterprise organization research scholars Mair and Reischauer (2017) firstly put forward the concept of sharing economy organizations. Miralles, Dentoni, and Pascucci (2017) also believe that there is not enough research on sharing economy in the field of organizations. Still, several works have been done within two years, and these researchers are mainly focused on the sharing economy organizations' patterns. Mair and Reischauer (2017) defined sharing economy organizations as a market network, a market where people use various forms of compensation to trade and access to resources, and the digital platform is operated as an organization. Miralles, Dentoni, and Pascucci (2017) studied from an organizational perspective in the context of food and agriculture and proposed six characteristics of sharing economy organizations. At the same time, according to Perren and Kozinets (2018), sharing economy organizations can also see as a lantern exchange market. However, there is still no direct study of sharing economy organizations' trust. Based on our literature review and empirical research, trust in sharing economy organizations is different from trust in other social and economic situations. This chapter is among the first to suggest and provide evidence that trust in sharing economy organizations is mainly inter-organizational trust.

Secondly, the present work extends previous research of trust in collaborative relations. Nielsen (2004) pointed out the lack of research of trust about collaboration, particularly at the inter-organizational level. Sharing economy also called collaborative consumption, is one type of collaborative relations, which is hybrid economics of collaborative networks (Scaraboto, 2015), the research on trust in this area is still scarce and thus more research is needed to understand how trust is established in this context (Ter Huurne, Ronteltap, & Buskens, 2015). However, for the main part of the research on trust in sharing economy is focusing on the driven forces of participants, in other words, to see trust as a whole to pull consumers to participant in sharing economy activities (Möhlmann's, 2015; Tussyadiah, 2015), few of them see inside of trust and clarify the type of trust. It is no doubt that this is important to understand and governance better of trust inside the sharing economy. Here, the authors have examined what is the main type of trust in a sharing economy platform like Airbnb, which gives further evidence to this research area.

Thirdly, it contributes to the ongoing conversation regarding Airbnb. Since Airbnb and online accommodation sharing went popular, many research appeared. These studies mainly focus on two sides: (1) to use online peer-to-peer accommodation platform as an example, then analyze the feature of sharing economy (Celata, Hendrickson, & Sanna, 2017); (2) to do research based on the case of Airbnb, such as the impact on hotel industry (Zervas, Proserpio & Byers, 2017), how to build trust inside Airbnb (Karlsson, Kemperman & Dolnicar, 2017; Ert, Fleischer & Magen, 2016). However, no enough consideration of the cultural difference in this area. According to our research, trust in Airbnb appeared a significant cultural difference, so when manage platforms like Airbnb globally, understand the local culture is vital.

Finally, facing sharing economy organizations, different participants need to know different things: (1) as for the manager of sharing economy enterprises, try to build a more trustworthy platform is much more important than other processes, and this is also the key to attract more participants; (2) as for the consumer of sharing economy businesses, to choose the platform with a most completely trust system, this could give you security for your transaction and cost you least transaction cost, much more importantly, to keep you safe; (3) as for the service and product provider, this could help you match the proper consumer easier. And last, price is a significant impact factor in sharing economy, use it wisely, and find the balance point between price and trust level.

FUTURE RESEARCH DIRECTIONS

This chapter has several indications for future research directions:

Firstly, the type of trust in sharing economy organizations is one type of inter-organizational trust, not an organization to organization trust, but one person to a group of people (the organization). That is to say, under the condition of sharing economy, it is not mainly because user A trusts user C, then A would choose C's product or service, the deep reason is that A and C are all trusting the platform B (a group of people, which means an organization), then A and C could make a deal.

Secondly, the transaction cost is one significant impact on users' participants. Users tend to choose products or services with higher inter-organizational trust, one important reason is that this could save transaction costs. For only the organization itself puts more forward to build a complete trust system, to make sure the service producer and consumer both reach a certain quality to that system, then users do not have to build inter-personal trust every time. And this whole process will also accelerate the forming of interpersonal trust.

Thirdly, inter-organizational trust appears a high cultural difference. Chinese Airbnb participants are more willing to trust the platform itself, however, American Airbnb participants are more willing to build interpersonal trust. The logic behind is that digital platforms build a great power in China during the development, big digital platforms in sharing economy like Airbnb, Didichuxing, Xiaozhuduanzu, Mobike, and so on formed the network between resource sharers and users, let them embedded in this exchange system.

Lastly, there are several limitations to discuss. On the one hand, only data from Beijing and New York are measured, in the future could design a broader cross-cultural study to test. On the other hand, only two methods were used, in the future could combine more different methods like QCA and case study to make future research. One more thing, this research only tested inter-organizational level trust, in the future tests for inter-personal and institutional level trust, could be designed.

CONCLUSION

In conclusion, the main purpose of this chapter is to explore the types of trust in sharing economy organizations. The authors designed two studies, Study 1 collected and analyzed data from inside Airbnb.com, selected the city of Beijing and New York to do competitive research; Study 2 is experimental research. These two studies concluded that Chinese consumers involved in Airbnb are more willing to choose the non-shared room, yet in America is the opposite, and price is an important moderator for both groups of people. Although the price factor is more significant in the Chinese situation, it is not strong enough to change their choice of room type.

This explained that the role of trust in China is mainly inter-organizational trust, rather than initial inter-personal trust. The reason is that the perfect organizational mechanism improves trust so that participants do not need to through frequent interactions to form inter-personal trust and achieve coordinated consumption. This reduces transaction costs, is a more efficient way, which is different from America. And the economic factor is an important driving force for sharing economy.

Theoretically, this is because the platform plays an important role in the Chinese sharing economy, which is more efficient by reducing transaction costs. And the economic factor is an important driving force for users to participate in sharing economy, but not strong enough to change participants' choice of trust type. The theoretical contribution is to reveal the role of trust in the collaborative relationship in the sharing economy organizations.

ACKNOWLEDGMENT

This research was supported by the National Natural Science Foundation of China [grant number 71840006]; and the National Social Science Fund of China [grant number 11&ZD153].

REFERENCES

Alanne, K., & Cao, S. (2017). Zero-energy hydrogen economy (ZEH2E) for buildings and communities including personal mobility. *Renewable & Sustainable Energy Reviews*, *71*, 697–711. doi:10.1016/j.rser.2016.12.098

Bardhi, F., & Eckhardt, G. M. (2012). Access-based consumption: The case of car sharing. *The Journal of Consumer Research*, *39*(4), 881–898. doi:10.1086/666376

Beldad, A., De Jong, M., & Steehouder, M. (2010). How shall I trust the faceless and the intangible? A literature review on the antecedents of online trust. *Computers in Human Behavior*, *26*(5), 857–869. doi:10.1016/j.chb.2010.03.013

Belk, R. (2014). You are what you can access: Sharing and collaborative consumption online. *Journal of Business Research*, *67*(8), 1595–1600. doi:10.1016/j.jbusres.2013.10.001

Benedicktus, R. L. (2011). The effects of 3rd party consensus information on service expectations and online trust. *Journal of Business Research*, *64*(8), 846–853. doi:10.1016/j.jbusres.2010.09.014

Benoit, S., Baker, T. L., Bolton, R. N., Gruber, T., & Kandampully, J. (2017). A triadic framework for collaborative consumption (CC): Motives, activities and resources & capabilities of actors. *Journal of Business Research*, *79*, 219–227. doi:10.1016/j.jbusres.2017.05.004

Blois, K. J. (1999). Trust in business to business relationships: An evaluation of its status. *Journal of Management Studies*, *36*(2), 197–215. doi:10.1111/1467-6486.00133

Botsman, R., & Rogers, R. (2010). *What's mine is yours: The rise of collaborative consumption*. HarperCollins.

Camilleri, J., & Neuhofer, B. (2017). Value co-creation and co-destruction in the Airbnb sharing economy. *International Journal of Contemporary Hospitality Management*, *29*(9), 2322–2340. doi:10.1108/IJCHM-09-2016-0492

Celata, F., Hendrickson, C. Y., & Sanna, V. S. (2017). The sharing economy as community marketplace? Trust, reciprocity and belonging in peer-to-peer accommodation platforms. *Cambridge Journal of Regions, Economy and Society, 10*(2), 349–363. doi:10.1093/cjres/rsw044

Chase, R. (2015). *Peers Inc: how people and platforms are inventing the collaborative economy and reinventing capitalism.* PublicAffairs.

Corritore, K., & Beverly, W. (2003). On-line trust: Concepts, evolving themes, a model. *International Journal of Human-Computer Studies, 58*(6), 737–758. doi:10.1016/S1071-5819(03)00041-7

De Laat, P. B. (2005). *Trusting Virtual Trust.* Kluwer Academic Publishers. doi:10.100710676-006-0002-6

Ert, E., Fleischer, A., & Magen, N. (2016). Trust and reputation in the sharing economy: The role of personal photos in airbnb. *Tourism Management, 55,* 62–73. doi:10.1016/j.tourman.2016.01.013

Feng, J. J., Lazar, J., & Preece, J. (2004). Empathy and online inter-personal trust: A fragile relationship. *Behaviour & Information Technology, 23*(2), 97–106. doi:10.1080/01449290310001659240

Frenken, K. (2017). Political economies and environmental futures for the sharing economy. *Philosophical Transactions - Royal Society. Mathematical, Physical, and Engineering Sciences, 375*(2095), 20160367. doi:10.1098/rsta.2016.0367 PMID:28461431

Friedman, G. (2014). Workers without employers: Shadow corporations and the rise of the gig economy. *Review of Keynesian Economics, 2*(2), 171–188. doi:10.4337/roke.2014.02.03

Fulmer, C. A., & Gelfand, M. J. (2012). At what level (and in whom) we trust: Trust across multiple organizational levels. *Journal of Management, 38*(4), 1167–1230. doi:10.1177/0149206312439327

Grönroos, C., & Ravald, A. (2011). Service as business logic: Implications for value creation and marketing. *Journal of Service Management, 22*(1), 5–22. doi:10.1108/09564231111106893

Guttentag, D. (2015). Airbnb: Disruptive innovation and the rise of an informal tourism accommodation sector. *Current Issues in Tourism, 18*(12), 1192–1217. doi:10.1080/13683500.2013.827159

Huurne, M., Ronteltap, A., Corten, R., & Buskens, V. (2017). Antecedents of trust in the sharing economy: A systematic review. *Journal of Consumer Behaviour, 16*(3), 485–498. doi:10.1002/cb.1667

Johnson, A. G., & Neuhofer, B. (2017). Airbnb–an exploration of value co-creation experiences in Jamaica. *International Journal of Contemporary Hospitality Management, 29*(9), 2361–2376. doi:10.1108/IJCHM-08-2016-0482

Karlsson, L., Kemperman, A., & Dolnicar, S. (2017). May I sleep in your bed? Getting permission to book. *Annals of Tourism Research, 62*(Complete), 1-12.

Kenney, M., & Zysman, J. (2016). The rise of the platform economy. *Issues in Science and Technology, 32*(3), 61.

Kopnina, H. (2017). Sustainability: New strategic thinking for business. *Environment, Development and Sustainability, 19*(1), 27–43. doi:10.100710668-015-9723-1

Kostakis, V., & Bauwens, M. (2014). *Network Society and Future Scenarios for a Collaborative Economy.* Springer. doi:10.1057/9781137406897

Lan, J., Ma, Y., Zhu, D., Mangalagiu, D., & Thornton, T. F. (2017). Enabling value co-creation in the sharing economy: The case of mobike. *Sustainability*, *9*(9), 1504. doi:10.3390u9091504

Luhmann, N. (1979). *Trust and power*. Wiley.

Mair, J., & Reischauer, G. (2017). Capturing the dynamics of the sharing economy: Institutional research on the plural forms and practices of sharing economy organizations. *Technological Forecasting and Social Change*, *125*, 11–20. doi:10.1016/j.techfore.2017.05.023

Martin, & Chris, J. (2016). The sharing economy: a pathway to sustainability or a nightmarish form of neoliberal capitalism? *Ecological Economics, 121*, 149-159.

Messick, D. M., & Kramer, R. M. (2001). *Trust as a form of shallow morality*. Russel Sage Foundation.

Miralles, I., Dentoni, D., & Pascucci, S. (2017). Understanding the organization of sharing economy in agri-food systems: Evidence from alternative food networks in Valencia. *Agriculture and Human Values*, *34*(4), 833–854. doi:10.100710460-017-9778-8

Möhlmann, M. (2015). Collaborative consumption: Determinants of satisfaction and the likelihood of using a sharing economy option again. *Journal of Consumer Behaviour*, *14*(3), 193–207. doi:10.1002/cb.1512

Nielsen, B. B. (2004). The role of trust in collaborative relationships: A multi-dimensional approach. *M@ n@ gement, 7*(3), 239-256.

Perren, R., & Kozinets, R. V. (2018). Lateral Exchange Markets: How Social Platforms Operate in a Networked Economy. *Journal of Marketing*, *82*(1), 20–36. doi:10.1509/jm.14.0250

Pettit, P. (2008). *Trust, reliance, and the internet*. Cambridge University Press.

Prahalad, C. K., & Ramaswamy, V. (2004). Co-creation experiences: The next practice in value creation. *Journal of Interactive Marketing*, *18*(3), 5–14. doi:10.1002/dir.20015

Rotter, J. B. (1967). A new scale for the measurement of interpersonal trust. *Journal of Personality*, *35*(4), 651–665. doi:10.1111/j.1467-6494.1967.tb01454.x PMID:4865583

Scaraboto, D. (2015). Selling, Sharing, and Everything In Between: The Hybrid Economies of Collaborative Networks. *The Journal of Consumer Research*, *42*(1), 152–176. doi:10.1093/jcr/ucv004

Schor, J. B., & Fitzmaurice, C. J. (2015). Collaborating and connecting: the emergence of the sharing economy. In Handbook of Research on Sustainable Consumption (pp. 410-425). Cheltenham, UK: Edward Elgar Publishing. doi:10.4337/9781783471270.00039

Ter Huurne, M., Ronteltap, A., Corten, R., & Buskens, V. W. (2017). Antecedents of trust in the sharing economy: A systematic review. *Journal of Consumer Behaviour*, *16*(3), 1–14. doi:10.1002/cb.1667

Tussyadiah, I. P. (2015). An exploratory study on drivers and deterrents of collaborative consumption in travel. In Information and communication technologies in tourism 2015 (pp. 817-830). Cham, Switzerland: Springer. doi:10.1007/978-3-319-14343-9_59

Welter, F. (2012). All you need is trust? A critical review of the trust and entrepreneurship literature. *International Small Business Journal, 30*(3), 193–212. doi:10.1177/0266242612439588

Williamson, O. E. (1998). The economic institutions of capitalism. Firms, markets, relational contracting. *Social Science Electronic Publishing, 32*(4), 61–75.

Wong, S. S., & Boh, W. F. (2010). Leveraging the ties of others to build a reputation for trustworthiness among peers. *Academy of Management Journal, 53*(1), 129–148. doi:10.5465/amj.2010.48037265

Zervas, G., Proserpio, D., & Byers, J. W. (2017). The rise of the sharing economy: Estimating the impact of Airbnb on the hotel industry. *JMR, Journal of Marketing Research, 54*(5), 687–705. doi:10.1509/jmr.15.0204

Zucker, L. G. (1986). Production of trust: Institutional sources of economic structure, 1840–1920. *Research in Organizational Behavior, 8*(2), 53–111.

KEY TERMS AND DEFINITIONS

Airbnb: Is an abbreviation of AirBed and Breakfast ("Air-b-n-b"). It is a service website that connects tourists and homeowners who have rooms for rent. It can provide users with various accommodation information.

Collaborative Consumption: Consumers use online and offline communities, salons, training, and other tools to connect to achieve an economic model of cooperation or mutually beneficial consumption, including lend, use, or exchange of goods and services.

Cross-Cultural Study: Refers to a method and activity that reveals the similarities and differences between people 's social behaviors and psychological characteristics and their development laws under different social conditions through the comparison of different cultures, to provide a basis for understanding the universality of social psychological phenomena.

Didichuxing: Is the world's premier ride-sharing platform. It provides comprehensive travel services such as taxis, special cars, luxury cars, buses, minibusses, shared bicycles, etc. for more than 450 million users.

Sharing Economy: An economic phenomena, with the help of a digital network platform, based on the transfer of using right and ownership between individuals or organizations, to maximize the usage of products and services.

Sharing Economy Organizations: The emerging enterprises based on the logic of sharing economy.

Transaction Cost: It refers to all the costs incurred to facilitate transactions. It is difficult to clearly define and enumerate because different transactions often involve different types of transaction costs.

Uber: The world's first ridesharing app, was founded by a Silicon Valley technology company.

Value Co-Creation: Refers to the cooperation between producers and consumers to create value. Value is not created independently by the enterprise but is created jointly by the enterprise and the customer.

Value Creation: Refers to a series of business activities and cost structure of an enterprise that produces and supplies products or services that meet the needs of target customers.

APPENDIX

Material for the experimental study:

    Please check these options and choose the one you most want to consume. You will have 30 seconds to read and choose.

1.   Option one.

Figure 1. Selections for option one
(Data Source: Airbnb's Official Website)

A：
整套房子/公寓：无需
与房东或房客共享空间，
独享整个房源。
价格：288元/每晚

B：
独立房间：有独立房间，
与房东或房客分享合用
空间。
价格：179元/每晚

C：
合住房间：有独立床位，
与房东或房客共享这个
房间。
价格：90元/每晚

2.   Option two.

Figure 2. Selections for option two
(Data Source: Airbnb's official website)

A：
房东描述：很好的房东，一起聊
天打牌，还做了早饭。

价格：498元/每晚

B：
房东描述：很好的房东，各忙各
的，互相不打扰。

价格：179元/每晚

3.   Option three.

Figure 3. Selections for option three
(Data Source: Airbnb's Official Website)

A:
房东描述：很好的房东，一起聊天打牌，还做了早饭。

价格：179元/每晚

B:
房东描述：很好的房东，各忙各的，互相不打扰。

价格：498元/每晚

Chapter 7
Development of a Regional Digital Strategy:
Case of the wine.alsace Domain Name

Coralie Haller
EM Strasbourg Business School, University of Strasbourg, France

Benjamin Louis
Région Grand Est, France

ABSTRACT

Wine regions constantly question their visibility on the internet to fully be able to embrace the 3.0 digitalization. Recent controversy of the geographic domain name ".vin" and ".wine" has raised awareness of the need to be proactive in Internet naming. The objective of the chapter is to understand how wine regions could develop a digital territory strategy to increase their competitive advantage by using specific geographic domain name. The chapter provides an overview of origin, role, and functioning of stakeholders involved in the internet naming industry. The specific case of Alsace wine region has been investigated with a specific focus on the digital wine territory strategy based on the development of the "wine.alsace."

INTRODUCTION

The global wine sector is changing with the emergence of mass marketing and changes in consumption practices linked to the development of the Internet. Relationship to wine consumption has become more informed, intelligent, community-based and connected. Information and communication technologies (ICT) open up tremendous opportunities for wine companies in the promotion and marketing of their products and services and in the development of their distribution channels. According to the World Internet Stats, there is an estimated 4,5 billion Internet users worldwide. The Internet has gone from a few networked computers to a network accessed by billion people, from Western phenomenon to a global one, and from research roots to an engine of commerce accounting for trillions of dollars in commerce

DOI: 10.4018/978-1-7998-3756-5.ch007

(World Internet Stats, 2020). The trend is towards disintermediation, i.e. shortening of wine distribution channels, which leads to an increase in online sales via virtual stores (ProWine, 2019). The total volume of wine sold through electronic commerce in Western Europe increased by 66% between 2010 and 2017. More than 360 million liters of wine were sold online in 2017, which represents around 4% of the total volumes of wine outside trade in Western Europe (RaboResearch, 2019). In France, online wine sales experienced an average annual growth of more than 30% between 2008 and 2015, to stabilize at 6.9% in 2020 (France Agrimer, 2020). And even if it seems to have entered a phase of maturity, the market value is estimated at 500 million euros.

In this perspective, wine regions have to question their visibility on the Internet to fully be able to embrace the 3.0 digitalization. In this context, there are approximately 362 million domain names registered worldwide .Com, managed by the American multinational Verisign, is the first extension with around 145 million domains registered (Verisign Domain Name Industry, 2019) However, a study shows that one in two companies in France have no visibility on the web compared with other European companies (McKinsey, 2014). The question is to understand how wine regions could develop a digital territory strategy to increase their competitive advantage by using specific geographic domain name. More specifically, the objective of the chapter is to know how to make « wines.alsace » a competitive advantage for the Alsace wine industry.

BACKGROUND

The Internet Naming Industry

1.   ICANN, Internet Corporation for Assigned Names and Numbers

The Internet Corporation for Assigned Names and Numbers (ICANN), founded in 1998 as a not-for-profit, multi-stakeholder organization is dedicated to manage and coordinate the Domain Name System (DNS): domain names and IP addresses. Originally, the management of DNS was privatized by the American administration to develop competition and contribute to the Internet extension. IANA (Internet Assigned Numbers Authority), ISOC (Internet Society Association) and the National Science Foundation of the United States signed contracts with the company Network Solutions to sell domain names. After much debate and multiple proposals, a different solution, based on a multi-stakeholder model, emanating from Jon Postel of the IANA has been published for public consultation. This will lead to the creation in California of ICANN as a non-profit utility company. ICANN has progressively taken over responsibility for the IANA functions (previously responsibility for the University of Southern California) (ICANN, 2020a).

ICANN foundational principles are to organize the Internet's unique identifiers around the world and to promote competition in the domain name marketplace while ensuring Internet security and stability. In other words, its role is to ensure that every address is unique, that all users of the Internet can find all valid addresses and that each domain name maps to the correct IP address. Without that coordination, it would not be possible to have a global Internet. However, ICANN has no control over content posted on the Internet, nor it cannot stop spam. ICANN is also responsible for accrediting the domain name registrars. It is a public-benefit corporation with participants from all over the world dedicated to keeping the Internet secure, stable and interoperable. ICANN is therefore the global forum to which namespace operators refer. Almost all of these operators (registrars, registries) are under contract with ICANN. ICANN is made up of several groups, each representing a different interest on the Internet and participating together in the final decisions made by ICANN. There are three "support organizations" representing: organizations that manage IP addresses; organizations that manage domain names and those responsible for national top-level domains. Additionally, there are four "advisory committees" that provide advice and recommendations to ICANN. They represent: governments, NGOs ; DNS root operators, operators concerned with Internet security and the standard Internet users. Finally, there is the technical liaison group, which works with the organizations responsible for designing the basic protocols for Internet technologies. The ICANN Board of Directors is made up of 21 members including a CEO (15 of whom are voting) from "support organizations" or appointed by an independent committee. Final decisions are made by this Board of Directors (ICANN, 2020a).

2.   The registries

The registries or NIC (Network Information Center) of a first-level Internet extension like .com .fr or .alsace is the entity (company, association or community) responsible for managing the database of domain names under its extension, the provision and updating of the Whois[1] and for defining registration policies of domain names under its extension. The registry guarantees the proper functioning of the extension. Registries have different origin and functioning (NIC, 2020).

Fist, the **two-letter-country-code TLD** (ccTLDs: .fr .de .it .es...) identifies a country or a territory. There are 250 ccTLDs, like the ccTLD for France, .fr or the .eu for European Union. Most of them have been created by scientists in the 80s and opened for trade in the 90's with more or less success and very different strategies (registration restrictions, prices, etc.). There are managed by associations (Afnic.fr), cooperatives (denic.de), scientific entities (nic.it) or companies (nominet.uk). Some ccTLDs have been hijacked like the well-known audio-visual .tv which is the TLD of the Tuvalu Islands. Also, the .io used in the world of start-ups and connected objects is the TLD of the British Isles of the Indian Ocean. Second, the Legacy LTD or **gTLD (generic Top-Level Domains)** are commercial extensions known as .com .net .mobi .pro .info .org .asia, etc. There are currently 18 legacy top-level domains names, which identify the nature of an organization operating a specific website. For example, a website with a dot-com address usually indicates a commercial organization. These gTLD are generally managed by companies without restrictions which arouse desires. Thus, in 2019, an investment fund (from the former CEO of ICANN) undertook to buy the .org, managed by the PIR (Public Interest Registry) association created by the Internet Society (ISOC). Until now. Since .org was used by NGOs and associations, the price has always been kept low and money generated by .org has funded research and development of Internet standards. The question is to know if users will now be ready to pay for an extension managed by investment funds. In 2012, ICANN has decided to expand the number of Internet extensions. Under this initiative, more extensions have been created (approximately 2000), which are called **New Domain extension (New gTLDs)**. According to ICANN GDD (Global Domain Division), there are 1235 New gTLDs on line and more to come, which represent more than 30 million domain. Four types of gTLDs can be identified: (1) The **brand extensions TLD corp** are brands that have created their own domain name (.total .google .airbus .bnpparibas .bmw ...). They cannot be sold as there are dedicated to the unique use of the registry which is the company that has registered its name or that its brand. Companies can decide to create a dedicated domain extension for marketing purpose, brand protection or innovation. (2) The **generic TLDs** are open extensions with or without a specific meaning. For example, possible generic TLDs can be .bio .guru .xyz .science .club .immo .top .shop .web .global .ooo, etc. There are different profiles of entities identified as registries for the generic TLD which mostly adopted low prices strategies based on volume. Large companies like Google has deposited more than 100 applications for generic TLD as for the Donuts company, backed up by investment funds, manages around 200 generic TLD. When several candidates are applying for the same generic TLD, ICANN conduct auctions. This resulted in millions of dollars battles: Google won the .app for $ 25 million (BBC News, 2015), Verisign won.web for $ 135 million (ICANN, 2020b). (3) the **Geographic TLDs** are dedicated to specific location, region, territory or city. There are 80 Geographic TLDs in the world (.berlin .london .nyc, etc.). including only four in France: .alsace .bzh .corsica .paris. There are mostly managed by the public local authorities, companies which have signed agreements or contracts with public authorities, associations from local authorities. These extensions are generally sold at higher price than the generic TLDs as they provide higher levels of anti-abuse and usage requirements. (4) the **Community extensions** (.gay .kiwi .tatar .bzh, etc.) are created and managed by a community. There number is limited.

3.   Registrars Domain extension resellers

The registries cannot sell directly the domain extension to the domain name holder. A distribution network is organized with an extended network of **certified registrar offices** around the world in charge for domain name registrations and renewal operations on behalf domain names registrants. They are under contract with ICANN and must provide technical quality insurances and comply with the anti-fraud guidelines. The American company listed on the Nasdaq, GoDaddy valued more than $ 12 billion (Nasdaq, 2020) is the largest certified registrar office which accounted for 19 million customers and 78 million domains (GoDaddy France, 2020). In France, there are few renowned companies like OVH, Gandi, Nameshield, Online (Free group), LWS or NordNet. Before the arrival of the new extensions (from 2014 for the first), the relationship between registrants, registrar and registries was quite easy as there were only a few new domain extensions created. Registrar had sufficient resources to manage the integration of the few new extensions and develop a strong relationship with the registrants to organize the commercial and marketing deployment. However, the massive arrival of 1,200 new domain extensions in 2014 has required the registrar to assume a considerable volume of new contracts with a need for new services developments. This has led them to provide diversified services that goes beyond conventional services like email addresses, hosting addresses, selling SSL certificates for web sites security, cloud services, cyber security, etc. Many of them had to create a website offer, either by having developed one entirely, or by using a white label builder. In this context, new website builders' platforms have emerged like Wix, Jimdo or Flazio (not ICANN accredited) and progressively take on market shares from traditional registrars. These operators provide templates for websites creation at low price integrating a domain name (ofter limited to .com .eu .fr) which fits to the needs for the majority of SMEs.

Local providers (web agencies or IP companies) are another type of resellers which are not ICANN accredited. They rely on an accredited registrar to deposit and manage domain extensions for their clients. The ccTLDs can contract directly with local providers. For example, Afnic, the .fr registry, can contract with a communication agency that would only have a few .fr domains in its portfolio. Thus, Afnic manages a considerable network of resellers and thus perfectly links the French territory. Verisign, for its .com .net and .name TLDs, can only work with accredited registrars (like new gtlds).

MAIN FOCUS OF THE CHAPTER

Territorial Wine Brand

Wine is a hedonic (Bruwer & Alant, 2009), information-intensive and complex product (Johnson & Bruwer, 2007) with intrinsic and extrinsic attributes (Bruwer & Buller, 2012). Wine attributes can have a hierarchical order of importance to the consumer: country, region, domain, producer, distributor and retailer (in descending order) (Lockshin et al, 2001). More precisely, in France price, brand and region of origin are the three most important attributes (Perrouty et al.; 2006). Region of origin appears to be one of the most important wine attributes that has a positive effect on the consumer and be considered as an important purchasing cue (Lockshin, 2000). Wine is innately related to its region of origin (Patterson et al., 2018) which makes it a more authentic product (Moulard et al., 2015) as it is associated with the grape variety and style of a specific region (Farmularo et al. 2010). Region of origin can even be considered as a territorial brand where the product cannot be created or made anywhere else, which is specifically the case for wine regions (Thode & Maskulka, 1998). The specifies of a territorial wine brand is that it has a brand manager, a common story, co-opetition among the proprietary brands, and local engagement (Charters & Spielmann, 2014). For the purpose of this study, we consider Alsace region as a territorial wine brand.

The Geographic TLD .alsace

1.   Reasons for the launch of the gTLD .alsace

The new gTLD .alsace was created to respond to several digital issues encountered by the region. First, the development of **Alsace as an attractive territory** needs to be clearly anchored in a strong regional identity and in the perception of that identity by regional stakeholders and external partners. In this perspective, the gTLD.alsace appears as a strong symbol and one of the most relevant tools to convey the Region's image, culture and identity and to reinforce the Region's economic attractiveness. The Region Alsace is one of the four French local authorities (beside Regions Brittany, Corsica, and of the city of Paris) to develop its own domain name. The gTLD .alsace positions the region at the same level as the country-code TLDs like like .fr or .eu. or generic Top-Level Domains like .com.

Moreover, the gTLD .alsace can also contribute to the **development of relationships with citizens**. As services to citizens are increasingly digitalized, local authorities' websites become complex hubs difficult to implement due to the volume of information processed. The objective is to have dedicated .alsace domain name for each local authority and to provide to citizens information about responsibilities of each one of them, projects conducted and decisions made? Example of areas initially planned to simplify these relationships are: Jeunesse.alsace, Ter.alsace, Lycees.alsace, Treshautdebit.alsace, Culture. alsace, Sport.alsace, Environnement.alsace, Innovation.alsace, Transfrontalier.alsace, Elus.alsace, President.alsace, etc. This makes it easier to access information or the service with a dedicated domain name.

The ambition is also to make the Alsace region recognized as a **unique digital territory**. Thus, the gTLD .alsace can be a regional digital policy lever to encourage local companies to develop their internet visibility. In fact, there is a gap between online usages and online presence of companies. With this dedicated regional digital identity, the future .alsace domain name holders on the Internet can enhance their global visibility and be able to assert themselves clearly as Alsatian, which is not possible with existing generic extensions. The Alsace region encourage always more companies to adopt the gTLD .alsace. In this perspective, the Alsace regional Council, together with the Consular Chambers of Alsace, have created a free digital pack for new venture creators. During the creation process with the entrepreneur will be given a free pack including a domain name in .alsace, an email addresses, a hosting space, and offers formatted with free local partners (web agencies, banks for e-commerce ....).

Another reasons of the Alsace Region's decision to create the gTLD .alsace is to give a **digital identity to the regional brand of Alsace** – la marque Alsace. This regional brand appears as a strong symbol and one of the most relevant tools to convey the region's image, culture and identity and to reinforce the region's economic attractiveness. Logic has led the region to deploy the digital counterpart of this brand. Finally, the gTLD .alsace can also be considered as a **commercial object** for the Alsace Regional Council achieving substantial turnover allowing it to operate in self-financing after a certain number of domains in stock. It then become a possible lever for funding new projects.

2.   Launch of the gTLD .alsace

In 2011, Philippe Richert president of the Alsace Regional Council has decided to apply for the gTLD. alsace to the ICANN. Information about technical infrastructure, financial strength, protection of rights holders (brands, etc.), organization and commercial strategy and a business plan were required for the application. It has been managed by Benjamin Louis, consultant at SdV Plurimedia and the Afnic for technical questions and submitted to the ICANN for instruction in 2012. The official launch of the gTLD .alsace was made in 2015 when the Alsace Regional Council's website has become « www.region.alsace » (former «www.region-alsace.eu »). Now, the official owner of the gTLD .alsace is the Region Grand Est as the Alsace Region has been merged with Lorraine and Champagne-Ardennes regions in 2016.

From January 19th to March 20th 2015, a two-month "sunrise" launch phase imposed by ICANN in the Trademark Clearinghouse (TMCH) was organized to allow trademarks to buy .alsace domain names. The Alsace regional Council expanded this phase to include local entities (companies, association and authorities) wishing to benefit from gTLD .alsace with a guarantee. The TMCH is a global central database in which each domain name extension holder registers its brand by attesting to its ownership (eg. INPI for French brands). They have to pay for a year membership. The TMCH also serves as an alert system as soon as a third party wishes to register an identical domain name. It is then possible for the brand to carry out a procedure called URS (Uniform Rapid Suspension) to quickly suspend the concerned domain name. In the launch period applicants were classified in categories with different priority levels, from the highest to the lowest priority: brands registered in the TMCH, brands registered with the INPI, companies, administrations, associations and finally other applicants. At the end of the two months, duplicates were treated according priorities and domains allocated. For example, there were two applicants for the abc.alsace domain, the one who justified his request with a TMCH document won out over the one who justified it with a Kbis or an INPI deposit and the unjustified requests were classified as "landrush" (lowest priority).

General availability of gTLD .alsace was given on the April 7th 2015. The .alsace domain names were allocated according to the rule of the « first to come, the first served» as .fr or .com. Anyone who deposit a domain name .alsace still available become the legal owner. However, the Alsace regional Council checked every registration and could delete a domain registered by a registrant who could not prove any relationship with the Alsace region. The Region have sold approximately 2200 domain names, most of them registered in Alsace. The rest, for brand protection, is registered in other French regions (approx. 160 domains) and in foreign country (approx. 90 domains USA, GB, CH, LU...).

3.   Creation of the gTLD.alsace digital space

Registration policies have been designed to give to the registry control over its domain name extensions with the objective to develop a dedicated digital territory representative of the Alsace region. In this perspective, the registry has the possibility to intervene on a domain name after its registration. Prior to registration interventions are not performed as it would require resellers to have dedicated resources leading to extra costs. The registry therefore checks each domain name extension after registration. To date, there has not been any interventions. However, if a sensitive or suspicious domain name were to be registered by a holder having no address in Alsace, the registry would investigate and intervene if necessary. Registration policies allow a foreign brand to protect its name (huawei.alsace google.alsace rolex.alsace.. ...) but if a foreign holder were to register a domain name like vin-xxx.alsace or dentiste. alsace then the registry would intervene. Finally, registration policies warn against abuse and use of the domains. A .alsace website with content that violates Alsace region image may be penalized. In fact, a robot scans the global lists of websites or domain names with fraudulent practices (spam, fishing, malware, botnet, etc.). It is required by the ICANN and allows the registry to warn domain name holders of possible hacking. The objective is to have a safe digital space faithful to what Alsace is and vector of notoriety for its terroir, its culture, its heritage (ICANN, 2012).

To avoid certain deviations, the registry has defined several lists of domains to be treated differently. Names of **small local cities and communities of cities** were blocked. Thus, only a city can register its name as it is essential that a city can benefit from its name. The registry wanted to avoid cyber-squatting or conflicts among cities. A number of domain name were blocked because of their **symbolic status that characterize the Alsace region**. Sensitive domains like vin.alsace, hotel.alsace, sauerkraut.alsace were protected and sold to companies or public/para-public entities that have respectable projects or services for the image of Alsace region, or which are aligned with community concerns. In order to avoid the privatization of certain **commercially interesting generic domains** (credit.alsace, rentcar.alsace pizza. alsace, etc) by speculators who would have sold them on the secondary market at excessive prices, the registry decided to classify those generic domain names characterizing an economic activity, in a range of premium domains. There are sold at a higher price than other domains name which will discourage potential speculators. A local player will invest in this premium domain if he thinks he can be an asset for his activity. It will only be a little extra cost compared to the amount to invest to develop a website. The other effect is to avoid giving the .alsace a reputation for squat extension that is not representative of its territory. So far, no .alsace domain name has been sold on the secondary market and the registry was able to progressively remove premiums. Prohibited domains cannot be registered. There are domain name that characterize an outlaw activity or referring to inappropriate behaviors.

The Generic TLD .wine and .vin Controversy

During the new-extension session in 2012, two applications for gTLD .wine and gTLD .vin have been respectively submitted to the ICANN by June Station, LLC and by Holly Shadow, LLC filed registered in the state of Delaware, USA. Those companies are part of the Donuts Inc. galaxy, a company supported by investment funds which applied for 300 extensions in 2012. It manages nearly 200 extensions such as: .events .movie .pub .pizza .school .ninja .sale .shoes .photos .taxi, etc. The gTLDs .wine and .vin applications did not include any specific measures to protect names, appellations, grape varieties or terroirs. The accessible information on the application show answers to ICANN questions which do not include any reflection on the subject of the TLD. The answers are the same as for any unspecific domain name extension like .ninja or .solar (ICANN, 2014).

The French government through the voice of its digital secretary of state, Axelle Lemaire, together with elected officials from the United States Congress, the European Union and representatives of world wine regions protested against these applications. Donuts' first reaction was to deny importance of appellations ad geographic indications as they are not recognized by the State of Delaware. An official objection has been made to ICANN to compel Donuts to protect appellations and geographic indications. Donuts decided to negotiate an agreement which has not been made public, as Donuts wanted to avoid future compliance issues with the ICANN. The agreement seems to present some controversies. A list of domain names has been created for Donuts to block. The names blocked refer to the appellation or geographic indication stricto sensus. For example, the Alsatian Grand Cru Kirchberg in Barr is included in the list and the domain name is: alsacegrandcrukirchbergdebarr.vin and alsacegrandcrukirchbergdebarr.wine. These domain names are too long and might no interest any potential holders. Though, the name likely to interest could be kirchberg.vin or kirchbergdebarr.vin or grandcrukirchberg.vin are not protected and therefore open to drift. Moreover, the list of domain names has only be blocked for 24 months to 3 years. After this phase, the domain names were left free for registration and many of them have been registered by speculators (Murphy, 2015).

For instance, available information (as RGPD blocks most of the Whois data) about the cheval-blanc. wine domain indicates a creation date on the 20th of October 2019, the holder is in Panama and the registrar's name is "Namecheap" which is not located in France (Namecheap, 2020).The same situation is accounted by the chevalblanc.wine domain which has been created the 11th of September 2018 by an holder in Australia and a the registrar's name is "Dreamscape Networks International Pte Ltd" which is not located in France (Namecheap, 2020).Comparatively, chateau-cheval-blanc.com has a French holder and a French registrar: Domainoo. In any case, it can raise mistrust of customers related to possible counterfeit products sold through those websites.

Applications for gTLDs .wine and .vin have obviously not been build for or with the world of wine and is purely profit oriented. The potential of those domain extensions is global and attractive, making Donuts' investment potentially very profitable. Appellations, geographic indications, wineries, chateaux, wine growers, wine merchants will have to deposit their domain name which is essential to protect them. Donuts Is not interested by the use of these specific domain name extension, as holders will undoubtedly renew their names for fear of cybersquatting.

SOLUTIONS AND RECOMMENDATIONS

A Digital Wine Territory Strategy for the Alsace Wines

1.   The context of the Alsace Wine region

The wine industry is one of the major industries in the Alsace region as it represents 15600 hectares of vineyards produced in AOP in 119 wine villages. 92% of the wine produced in Alsace is white and there are 1,15 million hectoliters produced annually in AOP (150 millions of bottles); 25% of total wine sell is done on the export market (CIVA, 2019). This regional industry is part of the French wine industry, which is important both economically and commercially. Worth around 11,7 billion euros in 2018, compared to 5.5 billion euros in 2003, wine generates the second largest export revenue in the French economy, just behind aeronautics (FEVS, 2019, Vin et société, 2019). With an estimated production of 41,9 million hectoliters of wine in 2019, France remains one of the three largest wine-producing countries, along with Italy and Spain (OIV, a, 2019). 30% of the wine produced in France is exported, for 56% to European countries (Vin et Société, 2019). Although France is 'only' the second largest wine-drinking nation in the world, after the United States, consuming 26,8 million hectoliters (OIV, b, 2019), wine remains a national drink. In this matter, France has endorsed a special protection for its « wine and viticultural terroirs» by incorporating them into France's cultural, gastronomic and landscape heritage (OIV, 2019). Vines occupy 3% of total land area in France, which makes it the world's second largest vineyard area after Spain, with 750 000 hectares of vines grown in the country in 2019 (Vin et Société, 2019).

The wine sector goes through a global transformation that places wineries against certain number of challenges (Hannin and al, 2010). They have to consider not only the emergence of mass marketing and changes in consumption practices but also the important competitive density and the strict legislation, which differs from one country to another, when producing and selling their wines. Other constraints, more local can be added, such as difficulties of settling down and transmission, land pressure or soils constraints (irrigation in particular). It appears to be necessary for the wineries of the Alsace wine industry to be aware of their environment to be able to understand and anticipate strategic issues they are facing or will be facing in the coming future. Besides, these wineries evolve within a local sector, which is characterized by an inter-organizational complex and fragmented context including various regional entities called professional wine organizations (OPV). Wine councils (AOP: appellation of certified origin and IGP: protected geographic indication), appellations labor unions, federations of independent wine growers and cooperative cellars, and public administrations are brought to exchange economic and declarative information, knowledge, know-how and innovations, but also to communicate information to their members

In this context, a regional organism, the Alsace Wine Council (CIVA) is commissioned to lead various axes of development of the sector. The CIVA represents both professionals of wine production and of wine trading. The general objective of the CIVA, defined by statutory missions, is to gather and share means to increase weight of the Alsace wine sector, to value specificities and characters of every « terroir » in Alsace through the implementation of interregional projects and global promotion of the Alsace wine through an umbrella Brand "Vins d'Alsace".

2. Development of a digital terroir strategy: From the wines.alsace and vins.alsace to all winemakers website in .alsace

In order to achieve its mission, the CIVA planned to develop a digital terroir strategy based on the domain names wines.alsace and vins.alsace. "Alsace" is the exact name of the appellation and the extension, which give a competitive advantage to the region compared to other wine region of the world. The objective of the CIVA is to migrate the existing vinsalsace.com domain name to vins.alsace (for French market) and wines.alsace (for international market) in order to take the most advantage of this gTLD .alsace in terms of promotion and communication of the Alsace Wine brand. It will increase visibility and generate traffic to the wines.alsace in comparison to existing social media and generic internet extension. The CIVA should also encourage local wine producers to adopt the gTLD.alsace for their individual company. This strategy aims to establish a relationship of trust with the consumer but also to bring a tool to fight against counterfeiting. In fact, if the customer is on a.alsace website, it will ensure the origin of the products and that it is not a counterfeit website, which might not be the case on a .com or another website. It's the beginning of what can be the digital terroir. Communicating globally in this way makes consumers aware that they have to be careful what they buy, where they buy it. This use of .alsace has a lot of similarity with the approaches of brand extensions, .brand, which, for some have created their TLD in order to switch to a well-defined namespace for its customers: emails as websites ending with the .brand means that the customer is in good contact with the company and not on a counterfeit website. Haller (2018) indicated that still 7% of the independent wine makers in Alsace do not have a website, which is quite high regarding the importance of wine sold via the Internet. However, it is necessary for the wineries develop online sale, before a disruptive actor take on the market. Hotels have missed the opportunity and ended up with a booking.com which takes more than 20% per room as for the taxi industry with Uber. The world of wine is still preserved but it is better to anticipate and initiate this digitalization of distribution. It might be difficult for a single winemaker to develop E-commerce as it requires financial and human resources. The CIVA could create a global e-commerce platform on its vin.alsace and organize online distribution by centralizing stock to facilitate shipping and export procedures. The winemaker deposits stocks and is notified of directly about online sales. The CIVA could automate the stock-winemaker relationship in order to have a restock before the liquidation of the stock. The CIVA pays the winemakers on a monthly base and takes a commission for communication and operating costs of the platform.

FUTURE RESEARCH DIRECTIONS

.Alsace Domain Portfolio Strategy

The CIVA and other stakeholders of the Alsace wines should develop a global strategy to protect the brands and the different appellations. They should first lock the important domain name on the gTLD .alsace and in different languages: vin.alsace wine.alsace wein.alsace, etc. It is recommended to define a list of extensions to protect based on sematic fields related to Alsace wine grapes, Alsace appellations, Alsace geographic indication, Alsace lieux-dits, Alsace grands crus, Alsace vendanges tardives, Alsace Grains nobles, Alsace crémant and Alsace wine tourism. An in-depth study of search trends in Google should also be conducted in order to define a list of domains to deposit. Negotiations should then start with the registry to block high value domain names, like the Alsace grands crus generating many variants (with, without dash, etc).

These specific domain names should also be protected in a number of extensions. It is important to start protecting the .fr and the .eu extension and then have a market-driven approach according to the main exporting markets of the Alsace wines and block domain name like Belgique .be, Allemagne .de Italie .it, Pays-Bas .nl, Suisse .ch et .swiss and GB .uk & .co.uk for the closest countries, but also more distant export markets like China .cn or Japan .jp. It is of course necessary to protect domains in .com as it is one of the most sensitive extension the Alsace Wines should pay attention to and lock the most domains. There might also be a need to secure extensions such as .asia .net .org (for certain corporate domains only). Typology of new extensions should also be studied and then decisions should be made base on the most relevant ones. gTLDs .wine and .vin controversial extensions need also to be protected. CIVA and other stakeholder of the Alsace wines will not be able to deposit all domain name extension. However, it is important to properly the manage domain extension portfolio, make it evolve and use the monitoring tools offered to control listed domain extensions.

CONCLUSION

The controversy of the gTLD .vin and gTLD .wine has raised awareness of the need to be proactive in Internet naming. ICANN and its stakeholders have been working for several years on the organization of a new round of new extensions which could take place in 2022 or 2023. This second round will certainly encourage many applications to be presented mostly by companies which want to create their brand extensions like the .bnpparibas .total .audi or .mma. This next round can be at the same time a threat and an opportunity for wine territories. They should worry about the protection of geographic indications as some speculators might be interested to force through even if it means entering into a long phase of conciliation. Thus, a company far removed from the world of wine has already deposited gTLDs .vin and .wine which will not prevent this same company to deposit the gTLDs .champagne or .nappa. The wine territories could then react and ask for redemption. However, the recent decision by the ICANN of gTLD .amazon to the American company of the same name despite years of battle waged by the country of the Amazonian alliance may cast doubt. It is therefore necessary for the wine regions to take the subject seriously and, beyond warding off a threat, take it as an opportunity.

Wine regions and appellations should consider applying for domain name extension at the second round and simultaneously develop a global strategy. The Champagne wine council (CIVC) has already started to work on a .champagne. countering possible counterfeit website. In fact, having a .champagne, not marketed and allocated according to strict criteria, would allow to implement a strategy similar to that of .alsace, which is to create a space of trust for online users experience. In fact, studies showed that customer consider region of origin as one the most important wine attributes that positively influence purchasing behaviours (Lockshin, 2000). Websites with a domain extension. alsace provide only wine specifically made in Alsace and thus guaranty the origin of the product to online users. By massively investing in a digital terroir through the .alsace, Alsace region will enhance both territorial brand identity and online users experience. Today Alsace is the only appellation to have an extension in the root of the Internet. Alsace must open the way, be innovative and show the way to other regions. It is necessary to take advantage of this advance to install trust with the consumer and embrace digitalization.

REFERENCES

France Agrimer. (2020). *Etudes Vin et Cidre: commercialisation du vin par internet en France, données de cadrage du circuit*. Direction Marchés, études et prospective.

BBC News. (2015). *Google buys. app web domain for $25m*. Retrieved from: https://www.bbc.com/news/technology-31659666

Bruwer, J., & Alant, K. (2009). The hedonic nature of wine tourism consumption: An experiential view. *International Journal of Wine Business Research, 21*(3), 235–257. doi:10.1108/17511060910985962

Bruwer, J., & Buller, C. (2012). Country-of-origin (COO) brand preferences and associated knowledge levels of Japanese wine consumers. *Journal of Product and Brand Management, 21*(5), 307–316. doi:10.1108/10610421211253605

Charters, S., & Spielmann, N. (2014). Characteristics of strong territorial brands: The case of champagne. *Journal of Business Research, 67*(7), 1461–1467. doi:10.1016/j.jbusres.2013.07.020

Conseil Interprofessionnel des Vins d'Alsace (CIVA). (2019). *Rapport de production 2016-2017*. Author.

Exporters of French wines and spirits. (2019). Retrieved from: https://www.fevs.com/en/the-sector/key-figures/

Famularo, B., Bruwer, J., & Li, E. (2010). Region of origin as choice factor: Wine knowledge and wine tourism involvement influence. *International Journal of Wine Business Research, 22*(4), 362–385. doi:10.1108/17511061011092410

GoDaddy France. (2020). *Découvrez pourquoi nous sommes le plus grand registraire de noms de domaine*. Retrieved from: ehttps://www.godaddy.com/fr-fr/domaines

Haller C. (2018). *La digitalisation du monde du vin: le cas des entreprises vitivinicoles*. Conférence "Auf" de la Confrérie Saint Etienne, Kientzheim.

Haller, C., Hess, I., & Méreaux, J.-P. (2019). Valorisation du vignoble alsacien à travers l'oenotourisme: création d'un écosystème d'innovation régional basé sur l'expérience oenotouristique. In Unione Giuristi della Vite e del Vino UGIVI (pp. 119-131). G.Giappichelli Editore.

Hannin, H. ; Couderc, J.-P. ; D'Hauteville, F. & Montaigne, E. (2010). *La vigne et le vin: mutations économiques en France et dans le monde*. Collection les Études de la Documentation française, La Documentation française.

Hochschule Geisenheim University. (2019). *ProWein Business Report*. Retrieved from: https://www.prowein.com/en/For_Visitors/Business_Reports/Business_Report_2019

International Organisation of Vine and Wine (OIV). (2019a). *Wine Production: first estimation*. Retrieved from: http://www.oiv.int/public/medias/7033/en-oiv-point-de-conjoncture.pdf

International Organisation of Vine and Wine (OIV). (2019b). *Statistical report on world vitiviniculture*. Retrieved from: http://www.oiv.int/public/medias/6782/oiv-2019-statistical-report-on-world-vitiviniculture.pdf

Internet Assigned Numbers Authority (IANA). (2020). *Accredited registrar list update at 2020-03-19*. Retrieved from: https://www.iana.org/assignments/registrar-ids/registrar-ids.xhtml

Internet Corporation for Assigned Names and Numbers (ICANN). (2012). *alsace application: ICANN new gTLDs program Status*. Retrieved from: https://gtldresult.icann.org/applicationstatus/application-details/313

Internet Corporation for Assigned Names and Numbers (ICANN). (2014) *Approved resolution – meeting of the new gTLD Program Committee*. Retrieved from: https://www.icann.org/resources/board-material/resolutions-new-gtld-2014-03-22-en

Internet Corporation for Assigned Names and Numbers (ICANN). (2020a). *Resources*. Retrieved from: https://www.icann.org/resources/pages/what-2012-02-25-en

Internet Corporation for Assigned Names and Numbers (ICANN). (2020b). Retrieved from: https://web.archive.org/web/20170217011554/https://gtldresult.icann.org/application-result/applicationstatus/auctionresults

Johnson, R., & Bruwer, J. (2007). Regional brand image and perceived wine quality: The consumer perspective. *International Journal of Wine Business Research, 19*(4), 276–297. doi:10.1108/17511060710837427

Lockshin, L., Rasmussen, M., & Cleary, F. (2000). The nature and roles of a wine brand. *Australia and New Zealand Wine Industry Journal, 15*(4), 50–58.

Lockshin, L., & Spawton, T. (2001). Using involvement and brand equity to develop a wine tourism strategy. *International Journal of Wine Marketing, 13*(1), 72–81. doi:10.1108/eb043371

McKinsey & Company. (2014). *Accélérer la mutation numérique des entreprises: un gisement de croissance et de compétitivité pour la France*. Retrieved from: https://www.mckinsey.com/fr/~/media/McKinsey/Locations/Europe%20and%20Middle%20East/France/Our%20Insights/Accelerer%20la%20mutation%20numerique%20des%20entreprises/Rapport_Accelerer_la_mutation_numerique_des_entreprises.ashx

Moulard, J., Babin, B. J., & Griffin, M. (2015). How aspects of a wine's place affect consumers' authenticity perceptions and purchase intentions. *International Journal of Wine Business Research, 27*(1), 61–78. doi:10.1108/IJWBR-01-2014-0002

Murphy, K. (2015). *Donuts makes private deal with wine-makers*. Retrieved from: http://domainincite.com/?s=.vin+.wine

Namecheap. (2020). *Cheval-blanc.wine Wois*. Retrieved from: https://www.namecheap.com/domains/whois/result?domain=cheval-blanc.wine

Nasdaq. (2020) *Market activitiy: GoDaddy Inc Class a Common Stock*. Retrieved from: https://www.nasdaq.com/market-activity/stocks/gddy

Network Information Center (NIC). (2020). Retrieved from https://nic.com

Patterson, T., Buechsenstein, J., & Comiskey, P. J. (2018). *Wine and Place: a terroir reader*. University of California Press.

Perrouty, J. P., d'Hauteville, F., & Lockshin, L. (2006). The influence of wine attributes on region of origin equity: An analysis of the moderating effect of consumer's perceived expertise. *Agribusiness: An International Journal, 22*(3), 323–341. doi:10.1002/agr.20089

RaboSearch. (2019). *Wine Quarterly, Q1-2019: Online wine is growing in Europe*. https://en.wikipedia.org/wiki/InterNIC

Thode, S. F., & Maskulka, J. M. (1998). Place-based marketing strategies, brand equity and vineyard valuation. *Journal of Product and Brand Management*, 7(5), 379–399. doi:10.1108/10610429810237673

Verisign Domain Name Industry. (2019). *Report Q4-2019*. Retrieved from March 2020 https://www.verisign.com/en_US/domain-names/dnib/index.xhtml

Vin et société. (2019). *Key figures of the French wine industry*. Retrieved from: https://www.vinetsociete.fr/chiffres-cles

Viot, C., & Passebois-Ducros, J. (2010). Wine brands or branded wines? The specificity of the French market in terms of the brand. *International Journal of Wine Business Research*, 22(4), 406–422. doi:10.1108/17511061011092438

World Internet Stats. (2020). *Internet Users Distribution in the World – 2020 Q1*. Retrieved from https://www.internetworldstats.com/stats.htm

KEY TERMS AND DEFINITIONS

Certified Registrar Offices: Are in charge for domain name registrations and renewal operations on behalf domain names registrants.

CIVA: Alsace Wine Council.

CIVC: Champagne Wine Council.

Community Extensions: Are created and managed by a community, examples are .gay, .kiwi, .tatar, .bzh, etc.

Domain Name System (DNS): Domain names and IP addresses.

Generic Top-Level Domains (gTLDs): Are commercial extensions, examples are .com, .net, .mobi, .pro, .info, .org, .asia, etc.

Geographic TLDs: Are dedicated to specific location, region, territory or city, examples are .berlin .london, .nyc, etc. including only four in France: .alsace, .bzh, .corsica, .paris.

IGP: Protected geographic indication.

Internet Assigned Numbers Authority (IANA): The global coordination of the DNS Root, IP addressing, and other Internet protocol resources is performed as the Internet Assigned Numbers Authority (IANA) functions.

Internet Corporation for Assigned Names and Numbers ICAAN: The global coordination of the DNS Root, IP addressing, and other Internet protocol resources is performed as the Internet Assigned Numbers Authority (IANA) functions.

Internet Society Association (ISOC): US association created 1992 for promoting the internet and network development.

Local Providers: (Web agencies or IP companies) are another type of resellers which are not ICANN accredited.

New Domain Extension or New Generic Top Level Domain (New gTLDs): Internet extension created after 2012,

NIC (Network Information Center) or Registry: Entity that manage a Top Level Domain.

OPV: Professional wine organizations.

Two-letter-country-code domains (ccTLDs): domain extension which identifies a country or a territory, examples are ccTLDs: .fr, .de, .it, .es.

Whois: Is a query and response protocol that is widely used for querying databases that store the registered users or assignees of an Internet resource, such as a domain name, an IP address block.

ENDNOTE

[1]   Whois is a directory system which asks who is responsible for a domain name or an IP address.

Chapter 8
Did AI Kill My Job?
Impacts of the Fourth Industrial Revolution in Administrative Job Positions in Portugal

Anabela Mesquita
https://orcid.org/0000-0001-8564-4582
Polytechnic of Porto, Portugal & Algoritmi RC, Portugal

Luciana Oliveira
https://orcid.org/0000-0003-2419-4332
CEOS.PP ISCAP, Polytechnic of Porto, Portugal

Arminda Sa Sequeira
https://orcid.org/0000-0003-1457-6070
CEOS.PP ISCAP, Polytechnic of Porto, Portugal

ABSTRACT

People and organizations have been witnessing tremendous changes taking place in the job market. Technologies (ex. AI, machine learning, IoT) are pushing individuals away from their comfort zone and forcing them to adapt, to develop new skills and to reinvent their job positions. Reports on the changes in the workplace and on the workforce have been raising concerns about the potential of AI to replace humans in job positions. The current challenges, brought by the 4th IR, have been providing countless opportunities for business growth, optimization and internationalization; however, tremendous concerns are currently raised regarding the sustainability of the human resources which are currently on the market and of those who are being trained to enter it. In this chapter, the authors focus on administrative job positions, which have been pointed out as one of the most prone to be taken over by AI and identify the already available technologies that can perform the job description tasks, as a current diagnose of the profession.

DOI: 10.4018/978-1-7998-3756-5.ch008

INTRODUCTION

For a great diversity of job positions, the answer to the challenges imposed by the new AI-powered workplace has relied on the devise of strategies, either to boost work performance through intensive training aimed at building skills for a higher technology absorption or to completely restructure the job position in order to reconfigure it to the contingencies of the increasingly technological immersed workplace (WEF, 2018). Life-long learning and entrepreneurship emerge as core soft skills for professionals nowadays, namely those whose core tasks are on the verge of being replaced by Artificial Intelligence (AI). Research has actually been pointing out that a great number of new job positions that have never existed, will arise in upcoming years with profile demands that are not possible to foresee at the moment. In other words, it would be necessary to, right now, train future professionals for job positions that don't even exist (WEF, 2018).

Naturally, the impact of such technologies in the workplace/workforce is progressing at a different pace around the globe, and the profoundness of these impacts is also expected to vary according to national/regional contexts, legislation, culture, industry, etc. Nevertheless, we are before a scenario where the human intervention capital is being depreciated by the added value that AI can offer organizations in performing work, efficiently, at a lower cost, greater volume and faster pace.

A climate of instability and uncertainty for the current and future workforce (Workforce 4.0) is installed, thus it is crucial to gather evidence on the impacts of AI in distinct job positions, analyse the extension of those impacts, analyse where human capital is still most valued, and develop educational and entrepreneurial strategies to aid professionals in striving during the current era.

The administrative job occupations have been, for decades, an underprivileged subject of research mainly because they are not considered as a specific domain of specialized knowledge, and, in fact, it consists of a highly technical profession, clerical for the majority, and with a level of specialization that occurs at the multi-domain of personal and technological skills, trained to assist most of the existing specialized professions.

In this chapter, we focus on administrative job positions, which, in its core essence of 'assisting others', has been pointed out as one of the most prone to be taken over by AI and automation, and to deprecate soon, if not already (WEF, 2018). Built on international human resources data, we begin by identifying which are the most frequent tasks conducted by these professionals at two levels: Administrative Assistants (AA), at the basic level, and Executive Assistants (EA), at the top level, and bring forward which of these tasks are prone to be deprecated, replaced or automated by current and emerging technologies. On a second stage, a diagnose of the profession within the Portuguese context is presented, based on a five-dimension framework of tasks, which also includes the hard and soft skills most valued by the professionals.

The local and international contexts are analysed, and recommendations are built upon the preliminary results of this exploratory study, concerning the (re)framing of the profession. The research results are of practical, methodological and managerial significance for researchers, professional organizations, human resources professionals and educators/educational providers.

BACKGROUND: DIGITAL TRANSFORMATION IN THE WORKFORCE

The 4th Industrial Revolution (4th IR) and the digitalisation are transforming the way we live, socialise and work. Besides the changes being visible in the business models, in communication and collaboration, in the relationship between our working and private life, in the structure and organisational hierarchies, technologies are also impacting the employment itself. According to a study carried out by the Oxford University (David, 2015; Frey & Osborne, 2017), 47% of the job occupations in the United States are at risk of being replaced by technologies or automatization and work becomes more digital, virtual and remote. Moreover, according to the report of the WEF 2018 (WEF, 2018), "the wave of technological advancement is set to reduce the number of workers required for certain tasks" (p. v). It is also stated that there will be an increase in the "demand for new roles" and a "decrease demand for others". Of course, these changes will not be the same all over the world and in all industries, but the trend is set globally (Arntz, Gregory, & Zierahn, 2016).

This scenario is enabled by some factors such as: 1) technological advancement and adoption (mobile internet, artificial intelligence, big data analytics and cloud computing); 2) trends in robotization; 3) changing geography or the way we produce and distribute value in the value chain); 4) changing employment types (shift on the frontier between humans and machines when it comes to emerge/grow in existing work tasks); 5) a net positive outlook for jobs (a new set of jobs will be expected to increase automation which will lead to some workforce reduction); 6) a decrease of some others; 7) emerging in-demand roles (some roles are expected to be more demanded by the market); 8) growing skills instability (by 2022 it is also expected that the skills needed to perform tasks might have changed). There will be roles that leverage distinctively human skills such as customer service workers; sales and marketing professionals; training and development; people and culture; organisational development specialists; innovation managers. Moreover, new specialist roles related to understanding and leveraging the latest emerging technologies will keep emerging: AI and machine learning specialists; big data specialists; process automation experts; information security analysts; user experience and human-machine interaction designers; robotics engineers and blockchain specialists); 9) reskilling is and will be imperative (in this scenario, the majority of the employees will be expected to re- and/or upskill) (WEF, 2018).

One of the professions where this impact will be significant in the next years is the one related with administrative tasks (administrative assistants, executive assistants, executive secretaries, etc.) (Wike & Stokes, 2018). Hence, human capital management in the 4th IR involves effective development and deployment of human resources, artificial intelligence, and robotics to achieve organisational goals and objectives (Elif, 2020; Manisha, 2018). It is expected that the principles underlying human capital management—planning, staffing, development, compensation, and investment in the digital workforce—will become more intense and complex (Kaur, Awasthi, & Grzybowska, 2020; Ninan, Roy, & Thomas, 2019; Vivence & Geoff, 2020).

Being aware of the challenging scenario, promoted by the digital transformation, it is necessary to understand what are the tasks that may be carried out by the applications/software/robots available and those that can (still) only be performed by humans. In parallel, as there are several technological possibilities in the market, how can the existing assistants make the most out of the technologies and thus making their job easier and use the spare time in tasks requiring more cognition? Of course, this will imply the development of (new) competencies, namely those related to communication, teamwork, problem-solving, critical and digital skills, just to name a few. And it is necessary to understand if the educational institutions that are preparing those professionals are ready to shift and/or upgrade the content and the pedagogical approaches needed to prepare such (new) professionals (Teng, Ma, Pahlevansharif, & Turner, 2019).

According to the literature, the main changes occurring in the organisation of work and people are visible in the following areas (Schwarzmüller, Brosi, Duman, & Welpe, 2018; Vuorikari, Punie, Gomez, & Van Den Brande, 2016):

- Organization of work – these changes concern the way people work and how the companies organise themselves. While more traditional companies try to adapt to the technologies introducing telework, mobile work, the digital native companies present a more agile organisation of work, such as projects, as well as collaborative spaces and crowdsourcing. This flexibility is visible in the place of work (the employee can work anywhere), the working hours (any time), the relationship between employers and employee and even in the approach (this kind of flexibility allows companies to find in the market the right person they need for a specific task). This led to the emergence of digital platforms that incorporate mechanisms to validate the identity of the service provider and the reliability of the participants. E.g TaskRabbits (www.taskrabbit.com), Airbnb (www.airbnb.com), UberEats (www.ubereats.com), Etsy (www.etsy.com).
- Relationship between private and working life – due to the changes in the organization of work, the activities are dissociated from a physical space, a building and a schedule. The working hours are no longer important as what matters are the results achieved. And if on the one hand, it seems to contribute to balance private and professional life, as tasks are performed according to the convenience of the professional, on the other hand, it means that people are always connected and accessible, eliminating barriers between the work and family life, which might constitute a problem if the professional is not able to set boundaries.
- Format of work, communication, and collaboration – Digital transformation also affects the way people work, communicate and collaborate. Teamwork gains importance to the extent that knowledge as a resource can only be developed and advanced within a group pf people (Schwarzmüller et al., 2018). New ways of teamwork and collaboration will emerge, enhanced by the technologies (virtual teams). The organisational structures will be replaced by project work and self-organised teams as traditional hierarchies are too rigid and slow to constitute an answer to the challenges
- Performance and talent management – the increase in the use of technologies at work leads to an increase in the need for digital competencies. The basic competencies related to the use of computer will be necessary for all occupations. Besides, routine tasks will be automatized, increasing the demand for cognitive competencies and those related to problem solving and creativity in order to handle successfully those tasks that are not automatized. Moreover, the markets will be more dynamic, demanding people to continuously adapt to new situations and forcing them to be more agile. This will lead to permanently invest in lifelong learning as the lifetime of knowledge is shorter. A certain level of resilience is also crucial.
- Organisational hierarchies – the digital transformation is leading to an increase in the influence of workers. Technologies allow workers to participate more in decision making, involving them in real-time in the different subjects and decisions. The increased responsibility in one's work is facilitated by increased access to information and increased transparency of information, making it easier to find contacts, people for specific topics/tasks, and direct contact with several interlocutors (inside and outside the organization), which seems to flatten the hierarchical levels.

Digital Transformation Technologies

In the above-mentioned context, it is relevant to consider which technologies are enabling this digital transformation, being aware that these might change every day.

Entering the era of the fourth industrial revolution, it is now the time of disruptive technologies to gain global competitiveness, prosperity and sustainability (Brynjolfsson, McAfee, & Spence, 2014; Curley & Salmelin, 2017; Schwab, 2017; Wassim, 2019). One of the technologies concerns the mobile internet and the cloud as they allow to offer more efficient services and the opportunity to increase productivity. Moreover, the cloud allows the quick dissemination of the service models, based on the internet. Big Data allows the retrieval, storage and analysis of large amounts of structured and non-structured data. This analysis is and will constitute the basis of intelligent services, requiring complex knowledge. The Internet of Things is and will generate large amounts of information, patterns and knowledge as never seen before. Crowdsourcing, collaborative consumption and peer-to-peer interaction constitute technology-based processes that allow companies to have access to talents, promote mass production and enable the emergence of small/family companies. Robotics allow that production tasks that are being developed by robots with high dexterity and intelligence to be more convenient, precise, and cheaper. Additionally, the transportation sector is witnessing changes due to the introduction of autonomous vehicles. Artificial intelligence and machine learning facilitate the automatization of tasks within a cognitive dimension, augmenting human intelligence. Finally, 3D and 4D printing allow to increase the productivity to levels never seen before as 3D printing permits an adjusted production to real-time demand, creating and improving the supply chain and global nets (Boneva, 2018; INTUI, 2010; WEF, 2018).

As expressed in the previous section, technology lies at the core of most of the changes that we may witness in professions. As for Susskind and Susskind (2015, p. 109), "traditionally, practical expertise has been held in people's heads, textbooks and filing cabinets". Nowadays, it is being stored and represented in digital form, in a variety of machines, systems and tools. Nevertheless, no matter how complex the systems, the impact of technology on the professions can be categorized under two categories - automation (sustaining technologies - those that support and enhance traditional ways of operating in an organisation or an industry) and innovation (disruptive technologies - those that fundamentally challenge and change working practices).

In automation, technologies are used to suppress some inefficient activities, in the general ability of organizations to provide more effective and efficient services (Calp, 2020). The focus is on streamlining manual or administrative work. However, old ways of operating are not ignored or discarded. Therefore, the workforce 4.0 is anticipated to comprehend the processes, connect along with the networks, digitalization, and data collection and utilization (Ras, Wild, Stahl, & Baudet, 2017). Actually, this automation can be transformative, i.e., people can use technology to transform the way a task is done (e.g. the use of Skype in a meeting - in this situation, the interaction is still real-time and face-to-face but at distance). In innovation, technologies enable ways of making practical expertise available that simply was not possible without the system in question. Innovative systems provide services at a lower cost, or at a higher quality or in a more convenient way than in the past (Anchal, 2018; Braña, 2019).

The Career Levels of Administrative job Positions

In the career of the Executive/Administrative Assistants' professionals it is possible to identify two levels: the basic level - Administrative Assistants (AA) - whose main focus is to perform operational tasks, and the top-level - Executive Assistant or Executive Secretary (EA) - whose tasks are more related with communication, problem-solving, negotiation, and support to the top-level executives of a company (Mesquita, Oliveira, & Sequeira, 2019).

At the basic level, the professional has instrumental knowledge or knowledge competence (Lyotard, 1984) consisting mainly of clerical, computer and electronics in the user perspective.

At the top-level – Executive Assistant or Executive Secretary – further knowledge, skills and abilities (O*NET, 2018a) are required, focusing especially in customer and personal service, information and data literacy; communication and collaboration, digital content creation, safety, problem-solving (Vuorikari et al., 2016) as well as mastering foreign languages and understanding and negotiating with partners from foreign cultures individuals, administration and management knowledge. The daily operations require additional skills such as service orientation – actively looking for ways to help people; coordination – adjusting actions in relation to others' actions; social perceptiveness – being aware of others' reactions and understanding the reasoning behind the behaviour; monitoring/assessing performances (self-assessment and other individuals and organizations to make corrections and/or improvements) (O*NET, 2018a).

The core tasks of these job positions, Administrative Assistants and Executive Assistants tend to focus essentially on aid/support tasks that are provided to executives of all specialized areas: management, economy, accounting, finance, marketing, human resources, etc. They consist, most of the times, in extensions of a specific job occupation in a company, providing support to the implementation wide set of diversified tasks. These job positions are, therefore, typically not domain-specific in order to be flexible enough to accommodate to the needs and demands of the broad range of jobs that they support. By not being domain-specific, AAs and AEs are not, however, unspecialised jobs. Specialisation occurs at the technical level, and on the multi-domain of personal and technological skills. However, it is precisely on the job of 'assisting others' that these jobs collide directly with the role of the current and future technological developments that have been made available to industry.

The professional intervention of AAs and EAs is centred mainly in five different domains: general management and organization tasks; liaison and business communication tasks; data generation and data management; representation tasks and operation logistics (Sequeira & Santana, 2016). Many of these tasks will suffer the impact of AI and automation either because the tasks itself became automated or because each person takes care of the task as it becomes intuitive and/or simpler, without the need of an assistant.

Typically, organising tasks consists of: database storage and maintenance; schedule management and contact selection; work trip arrangements; set up meetings (either face-to-face or remote) taking care of physical conditions of the place; data collection to minute's elaboration; data collection to support decisions; office supply management; applying rules of organisational and institutional protocol; integrated systems networks supervision; work teams coordination and concrete projects; administrative procedures implementation;

The business liaison and communication tasks consist especially of: establishing contacts with business partners, both through digital or conventional means; elaborate different messages fit to each receiver; keep up and master technological tools; develop interpersonal internal and external contacts and acts as intermediary in solving conflicts; master foreign languages and establish contacts with partners from different countries/markets.

Data generation and data management consist mainly of: preservation and grant access, through established rules, to the archives that constitutes the organisational historical memory; relevant data collection about the world, markets and competition; take decisions on delegated matters; extract relevant information from available internal data making suggestions and course of actions, aiming organisational efficiency.

The representation tasks consist especially in "acting in the name of" a person or even an organisation: hosting foreign, multicultural visitors and implementing and supervising of business meetings and contacts taking into consideration multicultural peculiarities; support and supervise the integration and socialisation in the organisational culture of foreign employees; support and provide relevant information about other cultures to employees going abroad; establish connection among geographically disperse organisational units through distant communication technologies.

In the next section, the research goals and methodology are presented, followed by the results.

Methodology

The main goals of this work consist of:

1. Identifying the core main tasks conducted by both levels of the administrative job occupations within the international context;
2. Build a framework for the diagnose of the current state of the job occupation;
3. Identify current and emerging technologies with the potential to replace the job occupation tasks that are conducted more frequently, and which can deprecate sooner;
4. Evaluate the current state of the job position within the Portuguese context regarding the risks posed by the 4th IR and digitalization, concerning the most frequently conducted tasks;
5. Reveal the most relevant hard and soft skills valued by Portuguese professionals, at the present time, for the job occupation.

In order to achieve these goals, an exploratory methodology was adopted, and divided into two main stages, each one with two steps:

Stage 1: Through desk research, the main tasks of administrative occupations were compiled, with the aim of identifying which ones are at risk of being replaced or automated by technology, absorbed by other professions or remaining as relevant tasks performed by humans during the 4th IR. For this purpose, in the first stage of the study, we began by identifying and systematizing the tasks performed by administrative professionals that are considered core. To this end, the description of career assignments under the codes of Executive Secretaries and Administrative and Executive Assistants (code 43-6011.00) and Administrative Secretaries and Assistants, except legal, medical and executive (code 43-6014.00), of the human resources portals O*Net (www.onetonline.org) (O*Net, 2018a; b), Effortless HR and Career Planner (job-descriptions.careerplanner.com), as sources of information. From the total set of tasks analysed, tasks with relevance equal or superior to 50% were considered, according to the classification that the international professionals themselves report to the human resources portals.

The second step of this stage consisted of an exploratory study in which the selected set of tasks were analysed and, considering the process(es) in which they are framed and the objective(s) they serve, a set of technologies, technological solutions, technology-based processes and applications designed for the same purpose were compiled. The research of technologies was carried out in search engines and the technologies were crossed with the identified tasks, and then a diagnosis was made for each task/process, regarding its greater or lesser propensity to be removed from the administrative career assignments.

Stage 2: The second stage of the methodology is also divided into two main steps: 1) the first consisting of the development of a framework for the assessment of the current state of the profession, based on internationally referred core tasks; and 2) the second built upon the implementation of a survey among Portuguese professionals, in order to assess (1) which of the previously identified tasks are performed more frequently, (2) if these professionals have felt any major changes in the profession recently and (3) which are the core hard and soft skills that they value the most, in order to capture the current state of work and skills necessary to perform this job. The survey was made available in social media (Facebook and LinkedIn), where it was promoted in professional groups by the researchers. The Portuguese professionals were also contacted through the Portuguese Association of Administrative and Executive Assistants (ASP), who disseminated the survey among their mailing list of associates. A total of 30 valid responses was considered for the purpose of this analysis.

As said above, a framework was developed and is was composed of five main areas of work (categories): (1) Generation and management of information tasks, (2) Organization tasks; (3) Business liaison and communication tasks; (4) Representation tasks and; (5) Operational logistics tasks. To this set of skills, 7 new skills were added, concerning 'Representation tasks', which consist of top-level attributions (EA) retrieved from Portuguese literature (Sequeira & Santana, 2016). These tasks were added because they were considered less prone deprecation and because they add comprehensiveness to the job description. This framework also included a set of 29 hard skills and 31 soft skills, considered the most relevant for the profession in the Portuguese context. The hard skills were deducted from the main content areas taught at higher education courses aimed at preparing these professionals in Portugal. The soft skills were collected from articles published by HR professionals in Portugal, retrieved from the most recent newspaper articles mentioning the subject.

The framework is presented in the Table 1, together with the internal codes assigned to each of the tasks, according to which, codes starting with: 'AA' refer to Administrative Assistants' tasks (internationally recognized as basic level tasks), 'EA' refer to Executive Assistants tasks (internationally recognized as basic top tasks), 'Both' refer to tasks performed by both job descriptions, and 'EAN" refer to the new set of tasks that were added for the Portuguese context, according to Sequeira and Santana (2016).

The results of both stages of research are presented in the next section, with reference to the international and Portuguese context. For a matter of simplicity and economy, further details about the research methods and instruments are provided in context.

RESULTS

The results presented in this section are divided into two major sections: the first presenting the results obtained within the international context, concerning the job occupation under analysis; and the second concerning the results obtained with the exploratory analysis of the Portuguese context, for the same job occupation.

Table 1. Framework for the assessment of the current state of administrative job positions

Generation and management of information	AA08	Discuss account status or activity with customers or superiors
	Both05	Record information from meetings or other formal procedures
	AA16	Search documents, databases or reference materials for necessary information
	EA01	Prepare technical or search reports
	EA02	Keep medical records
	EA05	Compile data or documentation
	EA06	Archiving documents or records
	EA08	Read materials to determine the necessary actions to implement
	EA10	Transcribing oral or written information
	AA23	Create and manage databases
	AA24	Managing electronic document management systems
	EA14	Conduct surveys, compile data and prepare documents for consideration and presentation of boards of directors
	AA03	Enter information in databases or other software/applications
	AA05	Recording personnel/collaborator information
	AA19	Develop computer applications or web applications
	AA25	Photocopying printed materials
Organization tasks	AA06	Report maintenance or equipment problems to the appropriate personnel
	AA07	Select the resources required to perform tasks
	AA10	Schedule appointments
	AA12	Distribute materials to employees or customers
	AA13	Issue documentation or identification to customers or employees
	Both07	Planning trips, accommodation or entertainment activities for others
	Both08	Schedule operational activities
	Both10	Distribute incoming mail
	Both12	Manage clerical and administrative activities
	Both13	Supervising the administrative staff
	EA04	Select and classify incoming mail
	EA09	Meet with co-workers to coordinate work activities
	AA26	Schedule, confirm and prepare face-to-face meetings
	AA27	Schedule, confirm and prepare virtual meetings
	AA30	Manage projects
	EA11	Managing the agenda of superiors
	Both09	Order office supplies or equipment

continues on following page

Table 1. Continued

Business liaison and communication tasks	Both01	Make sales or other financial transactions
	Bot0h2	Answering phones to route calls or provide information
	AA02	Collect deposits, payments or fees
	Both04	Prepare documentation for contracts, transactions or ensure regulatory compliance
	AA14	Forward mail to the appropriate destination
	AA15	Review documents, records and other documents (e.g. language, grammar, compliance with company policies, etc.) to ensure quality
	AA18	Send information, materials or documentation
	AA20	Ensure the maintenance of knowledge about work activities
	AA21	Prepare information or reference materials
	EA03	Preparing business correspondence
	EA07	Explain regulations, policies or procedures
	AA22	Answer the phone
	AA28	Coordinate internal and external communication flows
	AA29	Prepare and distribute presentations (e.g. PowerPoint)
	AA31	Send newsletters, promotional materials or other internal and external information
	EA15	Read and analyze memos, proposals and reports received to determine their importance and plan their distribution
	Both06	Coordinate operational activities
	Both14	Train employees
	EA13	Provide administrative support to other departments
Representation tasks	EAN16	Welcoming foreign visitors according to their cultural specificities on behalf of the organization
	EAN17	Representing managers in their absence at meetings and other organizational events
	EAN18	Represent the organization at trade fairs or sector events
	EAN19	Supervision and monitoring of compliance with the Organizational Protocol
	EAN20	Establishment of contacts on behalf of the organisation
	EAN21	Promote congruence and alignment between business units in dispersed geographies
	EAN22	Manage on behalf of the organisation multinational and multifunctional teams
	Both03	Receive customers, clients, superiors or visitors.
	AA09	Refer customers to the appropriate personnel/site.
Operational Logistics tasks	AA01	Operate computers or computer equipment.
	AA04	Operate office equipment.
	AA32	Learn to operate digital office technologies.

Administrative job Occupations Within the International Context

The results gathered through the analysis of the tasks conducted by the AA and AE professionals taking into consideration the description of the jobs and the evaluation of the already existing technologies with the potential to replace the identified job position's tasks are presented in Table 2 and 3. In the first column, we present the main tasks being performed by those professionals, in the second column the technologies found that might replace or complement those tasks.

Table 2. Top tasks performed by the Administrative Assistant (AA) and the diagnose

Task	Diagnose
Use computers for various applications, such as database management or word processing.	Partially deprecated. Database management will be performed by machines, using technologies such as AI. Tasks related to word processing will partially be replaced by dashboards for the generation of performance reports, for instance. Some word processing operations might still be conducted by these professionals for addressing specific purposes.
Answer telephones and give information to callers, take messages, or transfer calls to appropriate individuals.	Replaced by automatic call distribution (ACD) with applications as: Capterra (https://www.capterra.com/call-center-software) and applications for Customer Relationship Management (CMR) and Enterprise Resource Planning (ERP): most important suppliers of the CRM systems include Salesforce.com, Microsoft, SAP and Oracle, com Salesforce.com representing 18,4% of the market, Microsoft representing 6,2%, SAP representing 12,1% and Oracle representing 9,1% of the market in 2015 (Columbus, 2014).
Create, maintain, and enter information into databases.	Soon to be deprecated, as digital information is growingly available.
Set up and manage paper or electronic filing systems, recording information, updating paperwork, or maintaining documents, such as attendance records, correspondence, or other material.	Replaced by ERP. Setting up and managing systems is necessary. Digitising documents or paperwork is soon to be deprecated, as information in digital format is growingly available
Operate office equipment, such as fax machines, copiers, or phone systems and arrange for repairs when equipment malfunctions.	All information will be digital. Repairs will require specialised staff.
Greet visitors or callers and handle their inquiries or direct them to the appropriate persons according to their needs.	Replaced by automatic call distribution (ACD). As for personal contact, may be maintained or will be absorbed by other jobs.
Maintain scheduling and event calendars.	Soon to be deprecated. Replaced by PDAs.
Complete forms in accordance with company procedures.	Procedures will be enforced by SAP or other similar systems. Completing forms will be a task for every domain specialist in the organisation.
Schedule and confirm appointments for clients, customers, or supervisors.	Replaced by PDAs or absorbed.
Make copies of correspondence or other printed material.	Soon to be deprecated. Replaced by ERP and SAP systems.
Locate and attach appropriate files to incoming correspondence requiring replies.	Soon to be deprecated. Replaced by ERP and SAP systems.
Operate electronic mail systems and coordinate the flow of information, internally or with other organisations.	Soon to be deprecated. To be replaced by SAP.

continues on following page

Table 1. Continued

Task	Diagnose
Compose, type, and distribute meeting notes, routine correspondence, or reports, such as presentations or expense, statistical, or monthly reports.	Composing presentations may still be required. Automation mainly on the layout, with AI systems, such as https://www.beautiful.ai/ Several services worldwide are offering customer service though. All types of distribution tasks will be deprecated. Statistics reports will be automatically generated from digital Data-warehouse, through dashboards (models) created in applications such as Power BI (Microsoft).
Open, read, route, and distribute incoming mail or other materials and answer routine letters.	Soon to be deprecated. Replaced by ERP and SAP systems.
Provide services to customers, such as order placement or account information.	Soon to be deprecated. Replaced by ERP and SAP systems.
Review work done by others to check for correct spelling and grammar, ensure that company format policies are followed, and recommend revisions.	Technologies will conduct these operations first-hand, with no need for another person to revise. Policies will be enforced to be verification systems.
Conduct searches to find needed information, using such sources as the Internet.	Critical information gathering and organising will remain relevant, but not the ability to find information as an end in itself.
Manage projects or contribute to committee or teamwork.	As it consists of critical thinking and knowledge management tasks, the task will remain, but not specifically in this job description. It may be moved to higher levels of the hierarchy.
Mail newsletters, promotional material, or other information.	Soon to be deprecated. Replaced by CRM operations.
Order and dispense supplies.	Soon to be deprecated. Replaced by CRM and ERP and SAP operations.
Learn to operate new office technologies as they are developed and implemented.	This task will remain, but not exclusively for this job occupation. It will include not only office technologies, but productivity, team management, and information management. The need for a technological update will remain as a requirement for most jobs around the globe.

As it is possible to observe in Table 1, the great majority of tasks performed by Administrative Assistants (18 out of 21), operating at the operational level, will be deprecated soon, as they can be automated by technology, leading to the extinction of the job position. We also believe that the remaining tasks (3 out of 21), those that cannot be fully automated by technology, might be absorbed by other job positions in companies, since technology can provide greater autonomy in performing them, dismissing the role of 'the assistant'.

In Table 3 we present the analysis and results concerning the Executive Assistant/Secretary job position.

From the analysis of Table 2, concerning the job position of Executive Assistants/Secretaries, it is possible to verify that there are some tasks that are expected to deprecated soon (7 out of 15) and be automated (3 out of 15), namely the ones related to routine procedures. There are, however, other tasks (grey cells), namely the ones that require critical thinking, knowledge management and teamwork that are estimated to remain in the job description and in the tasks performed. We consider these to be higher-order tasks that will still require human intervention, despite the advances in artificial intelligence. These, however, will depend on the peculiarities of the organizational context (e.g.: business area) and on its level of digitalization.

Table 3. Top tasks performed by the Executive Assistant/Secretary (EA) and the diagnose

Task	Diagnose
Manage and maintain executives' schedules.	Soon to be deprecated. Replaced by PDA.
Make travel arrangements for executives.	Soon to be deprecated. Replaced by PDA.
Prepare invoices, reports, memos, letters, financial statements, and other documents, using word processing, spreadsheet, database, or presentation software.	Most of the documents needed will be automatically generated by information systems based on ERP and big data supported dashboards. Documents requiring critical thinking, creativity and knowledge management may still be required and, according to the time and complexity they require, may still be conducted by EAs.
Coordinate and direct office services, such as records, departmental finances, budget preparation, personnel issues, and housekeeping, to aid executives.	If coordination tasks are part of a routine process, they will be automated through ERP systems, just like any other routine tasks. Technology is propelling executives to include technological systems as the primary aid.
Answer phone calls and direct calls to appropriate parties or take messages.	Soon to be deprecated. Replaced by automatic call distribution (ACD).
Prepare responses to correspondence containing routine inquiries.	Soon to be deprecated. Routine process will be automated through ERP systems.
Open, sort, and distribute incoming correspondence, including faxes and email.	Soon to be deprecated. Routine process will be automated through ERP systems.
Greet visitors and determine whether they should be given access to specific individuals.	Personal contact may be maintained as a core task of EA or will be absorbed by other job positions, depending on how human resource costs are held at the organisation. Personal contact (as in Public Relations), will be, however, one of the core competencies of EA in terms of representing executives in meetings and other teamwork activities.
Prepare agendas and make arrangements, such as coordinating catering for luncheons, for committees, board, and other meetings.	Coordination tasks that cannot be performed by PDA will remain as competencies of EA.
Conduct research, compile data and prepare papers for consideration and presentation by executives, committees, and boards of directors.	Knowledge management and tasks requiring critical thinking such as research will remain as core competencies of EA.
Perform general office duties, such as ordering supplies, maintaining records management database systems, and performing basic bookkeeping work.	Soon to be deprecated. Routine process will be automated through ERP systems.
File and retrieve corporate documents, records, and reports.	Routine process will be automated through ERP systems. Digital information will be widely available and access to it will be managed by systems who will provide distinct access levels inside and outside the company.
Read and analyse incoming memos, submissions, and reports to determine their significance and plan their distribution.	Routine process will be automated through ERP systems. However, knowledge management and tasks requiring critical thinking, such as determining significance, will remain as a competence of the job position
Provide clerical support to other departments.	Knowledge management, critical thinking and teamwork will remain as competencies of the job position. If support is merely clerical, the task may be deprecated.
Attend meetings to record minutes.	Soon to be deprecated. Replaced by systems and transcription software: - Dragon: https://www.nuance.com/dragon.html - Software to manage meetings: https://www.meetingbooster.com/ https://www.capterra.com/meeting-software/

Administrative Job Occupation Within the Portuguese Context

The results presented in this subsection are based on the survey conducted among Portuguese AA and EA professionals and are organized according to the proposed framework (c.f. Table 1).

Generation and Management of Information Tasks

In this domain of tasks it is possible to observe (cf. Figure 1) that the most frequently conducted tasks consist of (1) 'Compile data or documentation', (2) 'Search documents, databases or reference materials for necessary information', (3) 'Archiving documents or records', (4) 'Photocopying printed materials' and (5) 'Conducting surveys, compile data and prepare documents for consideration and presentation of boards of directors'.

The least performed tasks consist of (1) 'Developing computer or web applications', (2) 'Keeping medical records', (3) 'Discuss account or activity with customers and superiors', (4) 'Record personnel/collaborator information and (5) 'Transcribing oral or written communication'.

In this category it is possible to observe that the most frequent tasks are performed, typically by EA (top-level), and that some of the operations require critical thinking or higher-order skills. However, some of these tasks, though not all, can be considered as routine tasks related to the management of documents and information/data and on its coherent forms of organization/archiving, together with tasks of collecting information for superiors to use and assess. These types of tasks could be framed into a broader category of being able to select, organize, archive and report on critical information, which is later reselected, organized and presented by their superiors.

Figure 1. Tasks conducted by Portuguese professional in the domain of Generation and management of information

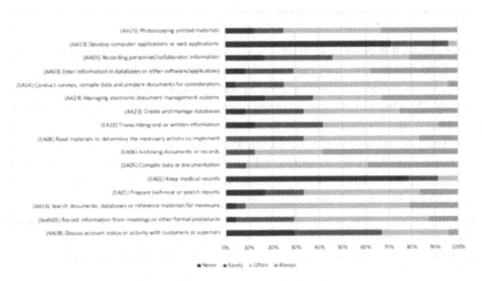

Organization Tasks

In this domain of tasks it is possible to observe (cf. Figure 2) that the most frequently conducted tasks consist of (1) 'Scheduling appointments', (2) 'Managing clerical and administrative activities', (3) 'Schedule, confirm and prepare face-to-face meetings', (4) 'Issue documents of identification to customers or employees' and (5) 'Select and classify incoming mail'.

The tendency, among the main most frequent core tasks conducted by professionals in this domain, consists of tasks of the basic level of the profession (AA), revealing attributions that do not require higher-level soft skills, on the contrary, they consist of routine operations.

Figure 2. Tasks conducted by Portuguese professional in the domain of Organization tasks

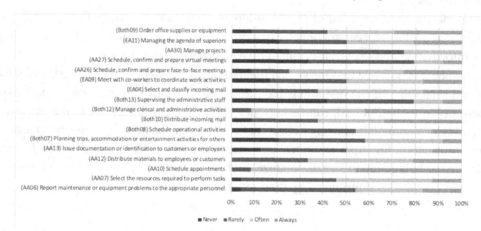

Business Liaison and Communication Tasks

In this domain of tasks, it is possible to observe (cf. Figure 3) that the most frequently conducted tasks consist of (1) 'Send information, materials and documentation', (2) 'Answer the phone', (3) 'Answer phones to route calls or provide information', (4) 'Provide administrative support to other departments', and, concurrently, (5) 'Preparing business correspondence', 'Ensuring the maintenance of knowledge about work activities' and 'Forwarding mail to the appropriate destination'. The least conducted tasks consist of (1) 'Training employees, (2) 'Collect deposits, payments or fees', (3) 'Make sales or other financial transactions', (4) 'Coordinate operational activities', and (5), concurrently, 'Prepare and distribute presentations' and 'Prepare documents for contracts, transactions or ensure regulatory compliance.

Most of the top conducted tasks are, again, at the basic level (AA) and in the domain of connecting and rerouting information among organizational members/departments. Some of these operations were previously identified as being in high risk of deprecation, namely by ACD and ERP systems, as is the case of tasks such as 'Answer phones to route calls or provide information', for example.

Figure 3. Tasks conducted by Portuguese professional in the domain of Business liaison and communication

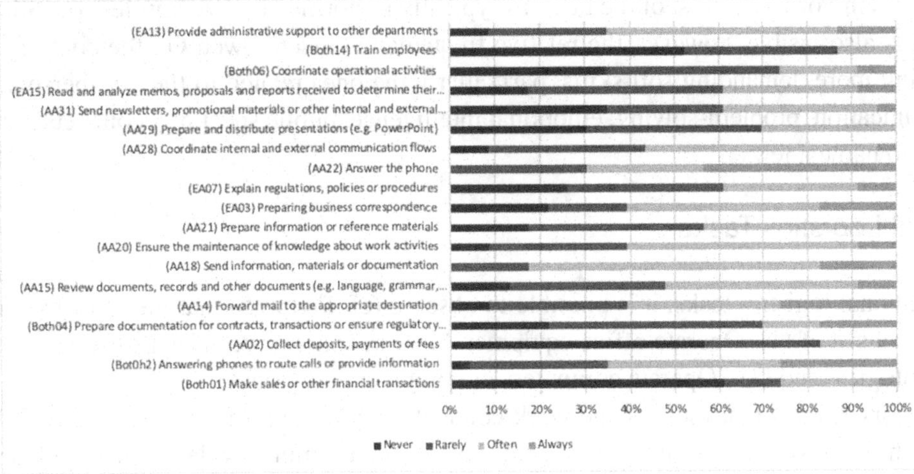

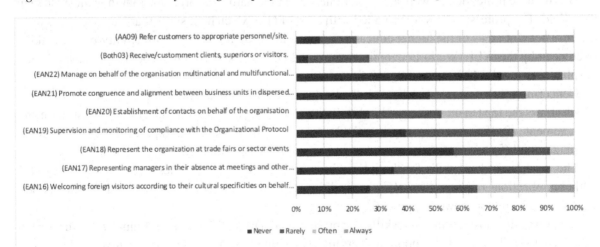

Representation Tasks

In this domain of tasks, it is possible to observe (cf. Figure 4) that the most frequently conducted tasks consist of (1) 'Referring customers to appropriate personnel/site', (2) 'Receive customers/clients/supervisors of visitors', (3) ' Establishment of contacts on behalf of the organization' and, (4) 'Welcoming visitors'. All of the remaining tasks are not part of the core work conducted by these professionals, namely: (1) 'Manage on behalf of the organization multinational and functional teams', (2) 'Represent the organization at trade fairs or sector events', (3) 'Represent managers in their absence at meetings and other organizational events', (4) ' Promote congruence and alignment between business units and dispersed geographies' and, (5) 'Supervising and monitoring the compliance of organizational protocol'.

Figure 4. Tasks conducted by Portuguese professional in the domain of Representation tasks

In comparison to the remaining areas or work, this area is the least expressive in the administrative job occupations in Portugal. Most of the tasks as typically performed by EA (top-level), and among the top five that is also visible, however, the relative frequency is much lower. On the contrary, these are tasks requiring more demanding soft skills, particularly the ones related to the intrapersonal relationship: communication, problem-solving, emotional intelligence, public speaking, conflict resolution and networking, to name a few.

Operational Logistics Tasks

As for Operational logistics tasks, it is possible to observe (cf. Figure 5) that the most frequently conducted ones consist of (1) 'Operate office equipment' and in concurrence (2) 'Learn to operate digital office technologies' and (3) ' Operate computers or computer equipment'.

This category reveals that most of the work conducted by these professionals are, in fact, clerical work in which the most basic digital applications still play a prominent role, as this work area is very expressive. This also reveals that technology is at the centre of the profession as it would be expectable nowadays and in the context of the 4th IR.

Figure 5. Tasks conducted by Portuguese professionals in the domain of Operational logistics

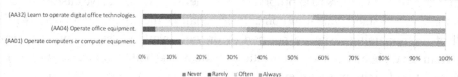

Most Relevant Hard and Soft Skills in the Portuguese Context

The Portuguese professionals were also questioned about the hard and soft skills that they most value in their field. The professionals were provided with a list of (1) sixteen hard skills that were retrieved from the core content areas of the higher education courses in Portugal, and (2) with twenty-two soft skills referenced by the WEF (World Economic Forum) and Portuguese literature as being the most relevant to subsist during the 4th Industrial Revolution.

Concerning the most relevant hard skills, Portuguese professionals have highlighted (cf. Figure 6, which shows the top ten most relevant hard skills) the following core hard skills: (1) 'Administration and management', (2) 'Document management', (3) 'Administrative practices and procedures', (4) 'Foreign languages' and (5) 'Computer equipment (e.g. computer, printer, scanner)'.

The top left out hard skills for the job position include (1) "Mathematics", (2) 'Stenography', (3) 'Other applications (e.g. image and/or video editing software)', (4) 'Transcription', and (5) 'Social networks', which are not shown in Figure 6.

Regarding the most relevant soft skills, the professional have highlighted (cf. Figure 7, for the top ten soft skills) the following: (1) 'Continuous learning', (2) 'Communication', (3) 'Ability to make decisions', these being the absolute top 3, together with (4) ' Reading comprehension/expression' and (5) 'Attitude'.

Figure 6. Rank of most relevant hard skills for AA&EA (scores)

Figure 7. Rank of most relevant soft skills for AA&EA (scores)

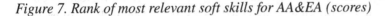
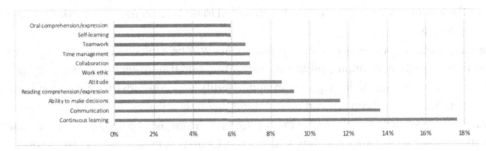

From this analysis, it is possible to capture that professionals most value training regarding hard skills in management and administration, the management of documents, the management of high volumes of digital information, and the mastery of foreign languages.

Concerning the key soft skills, the ones ranked first consist mainly of lifelong learning (LLL), communication skills, either in internal or external organizational context (reinforced by mastering foreign languages), together with the ability to make decisions and the attitude at work, some of which align with Seda and Yeşim (2020).

This analysis reinforces the main conception put forward regarding the work of these professionals: it consists of a highly technical profession, clerical for the majority, and with a level of specialization that occurs at the multi-domain of personal and technological skills.

SOLUTIONS AND RECOMMENDATIONS

Overall, in the Portuguese context, the professionals report conducting more frequently the most basic level of tasks considering the reference tasks collected for the jobs under the codes of Executive Secretaries and Executive Administrative Assistants (code 43-6011.00) and Secretaries and Administrative Assistants, Except Legal, Medical and Executive (code 43-6014.00) (O*NET, 2018a, 2018b).

In the international context, the number of tasks conducted at the basic level (AA – 21 tasks) is higher than at the top level (EA – 15 tasks). This became evident in the results from the first stage of the investigation. In the Portuguese context, the basic level tasks are also more expressive in terms of frequency of execution. These are precisely the tasks at higher risk of being deprecated already or in a near-future or replaced/automated by technology during the 4th IR, thus it is clear that the job occupation is at a very high risk of being partially or totally deprecated. As referred by Mustafa Kemal (2020) The work tasks are getting less routine and ask for continuous knowledge and skills development.

However, within the Portuguese context, at present time, professionals still report conducting these same tasks very frequently and as core of their professional attributions, thus it is possible to conclude that, in the Portuguese context, the effects of the digital transformation of professions pushed by the 4th Industrial Revolution are not visible yet and, therefore, do not have a high impact on how the work of these professionals is performed.

In fact, according to the results of the implemented survey, when the professionals were asked if they felt any major changes in the profession in the last five years, 95% of the respondents said that they had not felt major changes. Those who felt changes in the workplace refer to how the technological developments can better assist them in conducting the aforementioned tasks (mainly clerical tasks), contrary to the notion of these same technologies having the potential to replace them in the workplace, particularly when used by superiors.

It is also important to notice that, either professionals will be replaced by technology, or they will be required to undertake continuous, advanced, cross-functional high-tech training to respond to the digitalisation of tasks. As technology grows in applicability and complexity, more time is required to learn how to handle it and to keep up with new features and new releases. Time, as a determinant factor of every learning curve, will be key, either in striping tasks from these jobs or in continuously adding tasks to them, in which technology handling will be core. Considering the business field, top-level white collars, such as CEOs, senior managers, middle managers, etc. are not always available and it is not even considered in their job description to devote large amounts of time to technological or computer training. They are expected to absorb additional tasks and functions as technology offers more convenience and autonomy for operations such as: booking a meeting, managing their own schedules, make travel arrangements with the aid of a PDA, for instance. Some of the tasks performed by AS and ES will be totally performed by digital systems, such as answering and transferring calls, typing data, manage documents, etc. Operations related to handling complex technology that require hard training together with higher cognitive skills will rapidly become the core for AA/EA.

The use of technologies in the occupation of AA may imply that the current entry-level of this career might disappear, as almost all tasks can be performed or automated by technology. However, in a best-case scenario, the existing professionals will find their professional tasks facilitated as they can use the technologies as a facilitator or a complement. Nevertheless, in the worst scenario, these professionals might need to evolve to the next stage of EA. This implies performing new/other tasks and work in a more autonomous and independent way, as well as the development of new competencies such as creativity, negotiation, communication, leadership, problem-solving, creative thinking, just to name a few. However, this is only possible if the professional continuous to improve its personal and technological competencies throughout life (Miller, 2019), as digital transformation implies a constant update of knowledge and skills (Martyakova & Gorchakova, 2019).

Additionally, the AA might also specialise in one domain and become the right arm or even occupy a position in the middle of the hierarchy (e.g. human resources, marketing, financial department), as a specialisation strategy that guarantees the relevance of the tasks performed, supported by field-specific knowledge. Finally, according to the literature, these professionals might opt for a complete restructure of their careers and become virtual/remote assistants, creating their own company and providing their services at distance to a set of persons/companies in the most diverse areas.

From this exploratory analysis it is, therefore, possible to conclude that, in the Portuguese case, for the provided sample, the work carried by AA and EA has not yet suffered major changes as a consequence of the 4th Industrial Revolution that has been reported to be happening so far worldwide. There may be cultural reasons linked to the top managers of the organizations that were not subject to investigation at the stage of research, together with other cultural and technological issues that may be in the origin of the delay of the effects felt so far. These issues are to be included in future research, together with a wider and more representative sample of the local context so far.

FUTURE RESEARCH DIRECTIONS

This work has provided a ground basis for the diagnose of the administrative job occupations, covering both the international and Portuguese context, for the time being. Current results highlight the need for permanent monitoring of the evolution of the context and impacts of the changes brought by the 4th IR as, currently, its full impacts are not yet felt.

Future research in this domain is expected to pursue one or more of the following streams:

1. Improve the acquired knowledge in the Portuguese context by extending the research to a wider and more representative sample, as this is a limitation of the presented results. In this domain, the research could be stratified into different business sectors, so as to provide segmented access to professionals and cross-sector analysis of the profession.
2. Build a body of transnational results focused on the national/local current state of the profession to contribute, increasing the body of knowledge with a wider scale diagnose and recommendations that may emerge as local solutions, but with potential global impacts.
3. Develop a longitudinal analysis and documentation of the evolution of the impacts of the technological advancements in this career and on the adopted strategies to cope with change, reconfigure the work, upskill professionals or repurpose them, etc.

CONCLUSION

Provided the results presented in this work it is possible to conclude that in the Portuguese context the 4th Industrial Revolution and the full automation of tasks have not yet had a high impact on one of the most susceptible job positions to disappear in this context. This reveals that the effects of the high technological immersed workplace are impacting business and jobs at distinct paces around the globe, and that the tendency for prone-to-automation jobs has not yet reached the Portuguese context at its fullest, at least concerning the administrative jog occupations.

Although this work does not aim to establish a current state for the broader level of the impacts of the 4th IR and of digitalization within the Portuguese context, it is possible to conclude that one of the most endangered professions has not yet suffered, fully, the consequences of automation that have been put forward by several researchers and organizations as the era of the end of several professions.

The analysis of this context, before the worldwide work labour context, allows, at least for the Portuguese context, to bring forward essential knowledge about the core tasks that are still being conducted by humans, and which are the actual hard and soft skills necessary to operate in the profession.

Even in a threatened context for the survival of the profession, this work may aid educators and educational providers to better frame their course curricula in core areas of hard skills and to analyse which of the soft skills currently valued are under the risk of being deprecated, giving room to other higher-order soft sills that will be core in the near future, and therefore, should be included in the training of professionals

REFERENCES

Anchal, C. (2018). *Dynamic Workplace Revolution: Recent Digitalization Trends in Organizations. In Radical Reorganization of Existing Work Structures Through Digitalization*. IGI Global.

Arntz, M., Gregory, T., & Zierahn, U. (2016). *The risk of automation for jobs in OECD countries*. Academic Press.

Boneva, M. (2018). Challenges Related to the Digital Transformation of Business Companies. In Innovation Management, Entrepreneurship and Sustainability (IMES 2018) (pp. 101-114). Vysoká škola ekonomická v Praze.

Braña, F.-J. (2019). A fourth industrial revolution? Digital transformation, labor and work organization: A view from Spain. *Economia e Politica Industriale, 46*(3), 415–430. doi:10.100740812-019-00122-0

Brynjolfsson, E., McAfee, A., & Spence, M. (2014). New world order: Labor, capital, and ideas in the power law economy. *Foreign Affairs, 93*(4), 44–53.

Calp, M. H. (2020). *The Role of Artificial Intelligence Within the Scope of Digital Transformation in Enterprises. In Advanced MIS and Digital Transformation for Increased Creativity and Innovation in Business*. IGI Global.

Columbus, L. (2014). Gartner CRM market share update: 41% Of CRM systems are SaaS-based, Salesforce dominating market growth. *Julkaistu, 6*.

Curley, M., & Salmelin, B. (2017). *Open innovation 2.0: the new mode of digital innovation for prosperity and sustainability*. Springer.

David, H. (2015). Why are there still so many jobs? The history and future of workplace automation. *The Journal of Economic Perspectives, 29*(3), 3–30. doi:10.1257/jep.29.3.3

Elif, B. (2020). *Digitalization of Human Resources: e-HR. In Tools and Techniques for Implementing International E-Trading Tactics for Competitive Advantage*. IGI Global.

Frey, C. B., & Osborne, M. A. (2017). The future of employment: How susceptible are jobs to computerisation? *Technological Forecasting and Social Change, 114*, 254–280. doi:10.1016/j.techfore.2016.08.019

INTUI. (2010). *Twenty Trends that Will Shape the Next Decade*. Retrieved from https://http-download.intuit.com/http.intuit/CMO/intuit/futureofsmallbusiness/intuit_2020_report.pdf

Kaur, R., Awasthi, A., & Grzybowska, K. (2020). *Evaluation of Key Skills Supporting Industry 4.0—A Review of Literature and Practice. In Sustainable Logistics and Production in Industry 4.0*. Springer.

Lyotard, J.-F. (1984). *The postmodern condition: A report on knowledge* (Vol. 10). U of Minnesota Press.

Manisha, M. (2018). *Digitalization's Impact on Work Culture. In Radical Reorganization of Existing Work Structures Through Digitalization*. IGI Global.

Martyakova, E., & Gorchakova, E. (2019). *Quality Education and Digitalization of the Economy*. doi:10.1007/978-3-030-18180-2_17

Mesquita, A., Oliveira, L., & Sequeira, A. (2019). The Future of the Digital Workforce: Current and Future Challenges for Executive and Administrative Assistants. Academic Press.

Miller, C. (2019). *Leading Digital Transformation in Higher Education: A Toolkit for Technology Leaders. In Technology Leadership for Innovation in Higher Education*. IGI Global. doi:10.4018/978-1-5225-7769-0.ch001

Mustafa Kemal, T. (2020). *Competency Framework for the Fourth Industrial Revolution. In Human Capital Formation for the Fourth Industrial Revolution*. IGI Global.

Ninan, N., Roy, J. C., & Thomas, M. R. (2019). Training the workforce for industry 4.0. *International Journal of Research in Social Sciences*, 9(4), 782–790.

O*NET, N. C. f. O. N. D. (2018a). *Executive Secretaries and Executive Administrative Assistants. 43-6011.00*. Retrieved from https://www.onetonline.org/link/details/43-6011.00

O*NET, N. C. f. O. N. D. (2018b). *Secretaries and Administrative Assistants, Except Legal, Medical, and Executive. 43-6014.00*. Retrieved from https://www.onetonline.org/link/details/43-6014.00

Ras, E., Wild, F., Stahl, C., & Baudet, A. (2017). Bridging the skills gap of workers in Industry 4.0 by human performance augmentation tools: Challenges and roadmap. *Proceedings of the 10th International Conference on PErvasive Technologies Related to Assistive Environments*. 10.1145/3056540.3076192

Schwab, K. (2017). *The fourth industrial revolution*. Currency.

Schwarzmüller, T., Brosi, P., Duman, D., & Welpe, I. M. (2018). How Does the Digital Transformation Affect Organizations? Key Themes of Change in Work Design and Leadership. *Management Revue*, 29(2), 114-138.

Seda, M., & Yeşim, G. (2020). *The Nature of Digital Leadership in Managing Employees Through Organizational Culture. In Business Management and Communication Perspectives in Industry 4.0*. IGI Global.

Sequeira, A., & Santana, C. (2016). *O Trabalho Especializado do Secretariado/Assessoria: a comunicação assertiva como competência diferenciadora*. Retrieved from https://issuu.com/anavieira34/docs/anais_cisa2016

Susskind, R. E., & Susskind, D. (2015). *The future of the professions: How technology will transform the work of human experts*. Oxford University Press.

Teng, W., Ma, C., Pahlevansharif, S., & Turner, J. J. (2019). Graduate readiness for the employment market of the 4th industrial revolution. *Education + Training*, 61(5), 590–604. doi:10.1108/ET-07-2018-0154

Vivence, K., & Geoff, A. G. (2020). *Human Capital Management in the Fourth Industrial Revolution. In Human Capital Formation for the Fourth Industrial Revolution.* IGI Global.

Vuorikari, R., Punie, Y., Gomez, S. C., & Van Den Brande, G. (2016). *DigComp 2.0: The digital competence framework for citizens. Update phase 1: The conceptual reference model.* Retrieved from.

Wassim, A. (2019). *Entrepreneurship and Innovation in the Digitalization Era: Exploring Uncharted Territories. In Business Transformations in the Era of Digitalization.* IGI Global.

WEF. (2018). *The Future of Jobs Report 2018.* Retrieved from Geneva: http://www3.weforum.org/docs/WEF_Future_of_Jobs_2018.pdf

Wike, R., & Stokes, B. (2018). *Pew Research Center: In Advanced and Emerging Economies Alike, Worries About Job Automation.* Retrieved from https://www.pewglobal.org/2018/09/13/in-advanced-and-emerging-economies-alike-worries-about-job-automation/?fbclid=IwAR02CjIGbpQ1PNYepFm L6gQaK87w4lAm66EcNMsFDwnXb_dTLJBHRMR6uLY

KEY TERMS AND DEFINITIONS

Administrative Assistants: The basic level of the career of administrative job positions, in which the professional is expected to perform operational tasks, and to possess instrumental knowledge or knowledge competence mainly in clerical, computer and electronics domain.

Artificial Intelligence: Refers to the simulation of human intelligence in machines that are programmed to think like humans and mimic their actions.

Automation: Refers to the set of sustainable technologies that are used to support traditional ways of operating in an organization or an industry by technological means.

Digital Transformation: The processes by which the technology-immersed workplace affects the formats of work, communication, and collaboration. Used as a synonym for the Fourth Industrial Revolution.

Executive Assistants: The top level of the career of administrative job positions, in which the professional is expected to perform tasks related with communication, problem-solving, negotiation, and support to the top-level executives of a company/organization.

Fourth Industrial Revolution: Industrial revolution is driven by systems involving entirely new capabilities for people and machines. Represents new ways to embed technology in society and induces new ways of working and thinking for human and corporate matters. Used as a synonym for Digital Transformation.

Innovation: Refers to the set of disruptive technologies that are used to fundamentally challenge and change the work practices and the requirements of the workforce.

Skill: Understood as the proficiency developed through training or experience and is the sum of skills, knowledge and abilities. Define a specific learned activity, whereas 'ability' is the capacity of performing a task regardless of the proficiency and can be innated (not learned). Skill is used as a synonym for Competence.

Workforce 4.0: Refers to the high technological profile, requirements, and challenges of the next level workforce. Used as a synonym of Industry 4.0.

Chapter 9
Analysis of User–Experience Evaluation of French Winery Websites

Coralie Haller

EM Strasbourg Business School, University of Strasbourg, France

Daria Plotkina

EM Strasbourg Business School, University of Strasbourg, France

ABSTRACT

Wine consumption becomes more informed, smart, and connected. A website is a vitrine for wineries providing better visibility and higher attractiveness toward visitors, buyers, and business partners. Due to the increasing competition on the wine market, it is important to assess the digital development of wineries. Yet, there is no common instrument to evaluate website development of wineries. This research aims to create an evaluation grid adapted for European wineries website based on the extended Model of Internet Commerce Adoption (eMICA) and the model of Davidson. The grid comprises 108 attributes organized under eleven dimensions. A quantitative methodology based on a questionnaire was developed to evaluate user-experience of wineries websites of 255 consumers. This approach allowed to validate a grid that might be used to analyze and benchmark the digital advancement within the specific context of the French wine industry.

INTRODUCTION

Information processing and analysis capabilities offered by Information Communication Technologies (ICTs) open up tremendous opportunities for organizations in all areas. More specifically, the information-intensive nature of the wine industry suggests the important role for the Internet and Web-based technology in the promotion and marketing of wineries products, services, and channels. The total volume of wine sold through e-commerce in western Europe increased by 66% between 2010 and 2017. Over 360m liters of wine were sold online in 2017 which accounts for around 4% of the total

DOI: 10.4018/978-1-7998-3756-5.ch009

off-trade wine volumes in western Europe (RaboResearch, 2019). There is a clear trend in shortening wine procurement channels which will lead to an increase of online sales via wineries' own online stores (Hochschule Geisenheim University, 2019). The market share of e-commerce is higher in terms of value than in volume as online wine buyers are ready to pay more for the uniqueness of a product they cannot find elsewhere (RaboResearch, 2019).

With changes in consumption practices linked in particular with Information and Communication Technologies (ICT), consumers are increasingly using the Internet as a source of information in the search for products and services (Basu, 2018; Cristobal-Fransi et al., 2015). More precisely, online wine buyers are active participants and co-creators of information, offerings and value (Sigala & Haller, 2018). They are empowered and can be considered as real "decision makers" who fix the rules of the game, sometimes referred to as "ATAWAD- Any Time, Any Where, Any Device." They are looking for advice, human contact and proximity (Bressolles, 2016). The research shows that more and more wineries have websites and are using social media to create effective customer interaction (Szolnoki et al, 2016; Thach et al. 2016; Haller et al., 2020).

However, beyond simple transactions and interactions, customers are looking for an overall compelling experience. Indeed, wine is by nature a hedonic (Bruwer & Alant, 2009), information-intensive and complex product (Johnson & Bruwer, 2007). Hence, customer experience is crucial for the wine industry. The customer experience can be defined as the sensory, cognitive, emotional, social, and behavioral dimensions of all activities that connect the customer and the organisation over time across touchpoints and channels. It encompasses all activities involving the customer. (Bolton, 2016). Digital or user-experience (UX) has become a concept at stake in the field of human-computer interaction (HCI) and interface design. With the technological evolution, UX is not only focused on instrumental needs, useful information or ease of use. Digital interfaces must now engage in non-instrumental needs and experiences in a more complex sense and must entertain, impress and engage (Bargas-Avila & Hornbæk, 2011, Hassenzahl & Tractinsky, 2006). It is important to go beyond the instrumental and understand the influence of Information and Communication Technology (ICT) on affect and emotional aspects. These dimensions are of prior importance in creating customer experience and influencing brand attitude and behavior (Hassenzahl & Tractinsky, 2006). In the wine industry, UX is crucial given the hedonic nature of the product and experience that should be developed through any point of contact with the consumer. Behavior of the modern and connected consumer is explained much better by the website interactivity than by the product concerned (Bressolles & Durrieu, 2011). Digital customer experience triggers wine purchases and positive word-of-mouth, which can lead to brand loyalty (Massa & Bédé, 2018). Modern wine customers expect a rich digital experience (Muñoz et al., 2019).

Wineries are facing a growing difficulty of trying to stand out in an increasingly crowded market and they struggle to find the right approach to capitalize on the online opportunity. Even if the wine industry has been reluctant to fully embrace Web-based technology mainly due to tradition, and inability to measure direct results (Shepp, 2013), wineries are now required to continuously integrate ICTs in their work processes. One of the most important digital experiences is the winery website: it predicts trust in the winery and perceived quality of the wine (Brewer et al., 2008). Thousands of wineries around the world are beginning to use their websites and social media tools to sell wine online (Szolnoki et al., 2016). Websites can be a possible solution for capturing the market in the wine industry. They would then be considered as real alternative distribution channels providing information on the company and its offers. The use of a website allows wider dissemination of information to potential consumers, saving the business time. Moreover, the winery website is probably the first contact with potential customers. In the online environment, the website is the medium through which many potential customers are introduced to the company. As such, the website is the first reference that these customers have to form an impression of the company (Jurado et al, 2019). This makes it strategic for the wineries to develop and maintain an attractive, high-quality, up-to-date and easy-to-use website to be able to generate more revenues.

Thus, Web presence is a requirement of the wine market. A Website is a vitrine for wineries providing better visibility and higher attractiveness toward visitors, buyers, and business partners (Haller et al. 2019). At the same time studies have shown that the design of most wineries websites is still not effective (Taylor et al., 2010). Indeed, academic and managerial studies highlight the need to evaluate and improve the UX of wineries websites (Velikova et al., 2011). Former studies have developed an evaluation grid to evaluate effectiveness of wineries websites from a company's perspective (Davidson, 2009; Haller, 2018; Haller et al, 2019). However, website digital experiences were studied mainly in the context of Australian and American wineries (e.g., Davidson, 2009), using specifically created assessment frameworks. However, these frameworks are not adjusted to the european context. Law, space, and society underpin the differences among the wine industries of the old and the new world (Baker, 2004). For instance, organizational structures differ drastically between Europe dominated by small family vineyards and the new world where wine production is concentrated in a small number of top companies (Simpson, 2009). These differences bring to uneven digitalization of wine industries. Thus, the purpose of this chapter is to provide an evaluation grid for European wineries websites from a customer perspective. As there are no studies to date that have designed an evaluation grid of wineries websites in the European context, this grid will help overcome the existing gaps from constant technological change.

BACKGROUND

From the Model of Internet Commerce Adoption (eMICA) to the Website design framework (Davidson, 2009).

Numerous conceptual frameworks of how-to evaluation websites have been developed in marketing, tourism and ICT literature and applied since the creation of the World Wide Web (Web). They suggest a comprehensive list of website features in an attempt to help organizations in designing effective websites that will draw consumers to them. One of the most frequently used one to analyze websites is the extended **Model of Internet Commerce Adoption (eMICA)** developed by Burgess and Cooper (2000). This model has built on previous stages of development frameworks proposed by Cockburn and Wilson (1996), McKay et al. (2000) which focused on website functionalities. These researches have in common the highlighting of the importance of websites in the relationship that companies establish with their potential consumers. Specifically, they reveal a continuous development of websites through different stages of evolution, ranging from the sharing of basic information solely for informational purposes to the sharing of richer information based on interactivity with the consumer. The website is classified into the stage that best fits according to the presence of the functions on the list of criteria. Higher stages generally indicate higher levels of functionality (Lin et al., 2009).

In the eMICA, there are three stages of website development representing the level of interactivity of the website with online visitors. It is a road map which indicated where a company stands in its development of Internet commerce applications. The first stage is called "promotion" in which the website makes basic or rich information available to visitors without an interactivity. It mainly serves to promote company's offerings (Lin et al., 2009). The second stage is called "provision" as company website provides more dynamic information system with web front end. It is declined in three sub-levels of interactivity (low, intermediary and high). For example, in the lower interactivity level, the website only provides product catalogue. In the intermediary phase, customers can also find user support like FAQ. A website with high interactivity level provides an online chat that allow customers to ask questions directly to the company. The last stage is the "processing" stage that integrates highly innovative features. The company shows functional maturity of its website by creating an integrated function around multiple tasks: online sales, orders, delivery and payment. This implies being able to identify users, maintain individual profile and service, match offering and ensuring a high level of security. At the initial stage a firm has the lowest degree of innovation and functionality, and as the firm moves through the provision and processing stages the level of innovation and functionality increases (Burgess & Cooper, 1999). Table 1 summarizes the different stages and level of the eMICA model.

Table 1. The extended model of internet commerce adoption (eMICA)

eMICA stage and levels	Examples of functionality
Stage 1 PROMOTION	
Layer 1- basic information	Company name, physical address and contact details, area of business
Layer 2- rich information	Annual report, email contact, information on company activities
Stage 2 PROVISION	
Layer 1- low interactivity	Basic product catalogue, hyperlinks to further information, online enquiry form
Layer 2 - medium interactivity	Higher-level product catalogues, customer support (e.g., FAQs, sitemaps), industry-specific value-added features
Layer 3 - high interactivity	Chat room, discussion forum, multimedia, newsletters or updates by email
Stage 3 PROCESSING	
	Secure online transactions, order status and tracking, interaction with corporate servers

Davidson (2009) has developed a website design framework based on the Zeithaml et al. (2002, p.363) definition of electronic service quality (e-SQ) which represents "the extent to which a website facilitates efficient and effective shopping, purchases and delivery of products and services". In an extensive study conducted by the author a method of identifying and measuring e-SQ gaps was developed and tested on Australian wineries (Davidson, 2006). As a result of this study an Australian winery B2C website design framework was developed based on 10 dimensions.

By using all criteria listed in existing website evaluation frameworks of Davidson (2009) together with the criteria present in the three stages development of the eMICA, a website evaluation grid specific to European wineries was derived. There are different reasons why we decided to integrate both Davidson and eMICA. First, both approaches propose a different yet complementary integrative analytical framework based on different existing models and analytical frameworks (Cockburn and Wilson, 1996; Burgess and Cooper, 1999, 2000; McKay et al., 2000; Elliot, 2002; Gartner, 2002). On the other hand, the eMICA has been extensively tested within the tourism industry, especially to evaluate website of hotels (Ting et al., 2013) and travel agencies (Lin et al., 2009). The Davidson framework has been applied successively in 2006 and 2009 to analyze the effectiveness of the wine industry's websites (Davidson, 2006, 2009). Finally, we consider that this integrative analytical framework reports on a majority of criteria

Table 2. Website design framework (Davidson, 2009)

Company information	Company details Company person Winery Region	Off-line orders	Fill in, calculate, and print-out order form Email orders Phone orders
Product Information	Wine description Price – bottle and case Technical notes Tasting chart Bestseller list Reviews-winemaker, Professional, consumer	Content, organisation & timeliness	Title bar- name and description Contact on every page Last updated date Less than 10 second download time Security and privacy policy
On-site tasting and sales / external distributors	Cellar door hours Cellar door map Distributor details – restaurants, retail, wholesale	Value-added features	Press releases Special offers New products Best buys Wine making information Storage information Ageing information Complementary foods Show awards Photographs Local tourism promoted Contact by email or form readily available Frequently Asked Questions Wine club Electronic newsletter Contests/give-aways
On-line orders	On-line ordering Order retained – within site and between sessions Price and freight calculated Export freight prices Order confirmation Payment options Secured transmission Form validation Previous orders and customer details remembered Similar products suggested	Navigation	Site map Search facilities Relevant external links Standard link colours
Customer Service	Gift service Single bottles Mixed cases Order status on-line Wish list Deliver methods Bonuses and discounts	Aesthetics	Colourful web pages Contrasting colours Text size – easy to read, not fixed size Uncluttered pages Short pages Same menu/structure Clarity - short paragraphs, headings, lists Multiple linked pages

for evaluating the effectiveness of wine company websites, thus appearing to be the most exhaustive in the conduct of our research project.

The review of the research literature above highlights different tool or instruments use by wineries to attract and interact with the online wine consumers. Nevertheless, it seems clear that these frameworks or models present a number of limits. Davidson (2009) stresses that the evaluation grid must be adapted to regional contexts, considering the cultural specificities of the wine industry. Thus, following Davidson recommendation we created an evaluation grid considering specificities of the European context, and more specifically to France. Thus, with regard to the eMICA model we have added a supplementary stage (i.e., 2.4 which relates to the aesthetics and website navigation). With regard to the Davidson's (2009) framework we have identified the importance of recommendations (i.e., consumers, journalists, professional experts, and bloggers), which we singled out to a separate category.

MAIN FOCUS OF THE CHAPTER

1. The French Wine industry

The wine sector in France represents the second export sector of the trade balance just behind aeronautics with, in 2018, a trade surplus of 11.7 billion euros (FEVS, 2018). In addition, it has nearly 750,000 hectares of vines in production, i.e. 10% of the world surface (Vin et Société, 2019). With wine production of 49.1 million hectoliters in 2018, France is the second largest wine producer in the world after Italy and produces around 17% of the world's wine. France is also the second largest consumer of wine in the world, behind the United States and ahead of Italy, with more than 3.7 billion bottles of wine consumed (OIV,b, 2019). However, the sector is changing and losing competitiveness internationally (Pahpy, 2017). This is reflected by the emergence of mass marketing, changes in consumption practices but also in high competitive density as well as strict legislation, which differs from country to country, in terms of production and the marketing of wines. Other, more local, constraints can be added, such as difficulties in setting up and transmitting organizations, land pressure or constraints linked to appellations of origin, especially in terms of constrained production yields. Wine companies therefore have to meet a certain number of challenges (Hanin et al., 2010) in order to remain competitive and rely on different levers for promoting the marketing of their wines.

2. Data Collection

By following the Davidson (2006) procedure, we confirm the relevance of the evaluation grid for European wine-growing websites by recruiting a panel of French consumers and asking them the importance of every attribute in their user experience on the winery website. 300 respondents rated each of the 108 attributes on the scale from 1 ("Not at all important") to 7 ("Very important"). The respondents were recruited on a crowdfunding platform, as latest studies suggest that Clickworker yields valid data (Lutz, 2015). Respondents are between 18 and 79 years old, with an average of 32,4 years old. The gender distribution is very even with 49,8% of men and 50,2% of women. The recruited consumers are French and have a pronounced interest in wine (confirmed wine consumers). The questionnaire contained two attention check questions which were used to filter out the low-quality responses, as suggested by Peer et al. (2014). The attention check questions asked to fill in a certain response despite the question before it (e.g., "To what extent background music is important to you. Despite your opinion, please answer 2"). Thus, only 255 responses were analyzed. We present the results, including the mean and the standard deviation of in Table 3 below.

3. Main Results

The results made it possible to identify the less important attributes: (1) background music, (2) online auctions, (3) copyright notice, and (4) print and fill orders. Despite the empirical evidence on the positive effect of "background music" (Ding & Lin, 2012), customers indicated that this functionality is obsolete (mean = 2,21, standard deviation = 1,52). The background music was so much undervalued that it actually was identified as an attribute that is important not to have in order to not destroy the customer value. The second less important attribute is "online auctions", it the mean for its input into the customer experience is below the average (mean = 3,15, standard deviation = 1,61). Online auctions particularly concern only wines of Bordeaux or Burgundy and are organized by experts and major auction houses. This practice remains unknown to the general public and reserved for experts or wine professionals. As survey participants are not wine experts, this could be interpreted as a misunderstanding of what online auctions are. Moreover, since this criterion is specific to certain wine regions and therefore cannot be generalized, we choose to delete it. Then "copyright notice" criterion has been considered as the third less important criterion (mean = 3,63, standard deviation = 1,87). According to the French law, information present on a website (e.g. texts, images, videos) are subjected to copyright, (Directive (EU) 2018/1972 of European Parliament and of the Council, 2018). It seems that there is a lack of awareness of the obligations to include or not the legal notices on a website, which could explain why this criterion is not important for most of customers. In this context, we decided to keep "copyright notice" criterion in the grid. Finally, the fourth less important attribute is "print and fill orders" criterion (mean = 4,02, standard deviation = 1,88). Indeed, in the midst of the digital age, customers look for ease of use when they order products online. E-commerce is supposed to free companies and customers from paperwork and allow to focus on more value adding activities (Porter, 2001; Leroux et al., 2001).

The results also made it possible to identify the most important attributes: (1) secure transaction of data and (2) information on wines (including prices, description, appellation and medals). The most important attributes to consumers are related to the clarity and presentation of information, the structure of websites, information related to the description of the product and the winery. Consumers appreciate the possibility to easily contact the wineries using both electronically as well as being able to come directly to the winery. The information on the winery website should be detailed, but precise and short. Most consumers are interested in information on the possibility of purchasing: prices, delivery and special offers. Certain attributes did not receive a minimum score (i.e., no one evaluated the attribute as "1" = not important at all), which demonstrate their importance, for example: information on the cellar, transactions on the website, consistency and visibility of the text and prices.

SOLUTIONS AND RECOMMENDATIONS

The attributes have been classified into 11 categories (see table 3): (1) information on the winery, (2) information on the product, (3) information on the cellar and visits, (4) information on distribution, (5) information on orders, online and offline, (6) website content and structure, (7) advanced website options, (8) legal information on the website, (9) value-added services, (10) aesthetics, (11) reviews and recommendations. After calculating the average importance for every category, we find that the most important category for consumers is product information (mean = 6,17, standard deviation=1,09), followed by cellar (mean = 5,58, standard deviation=1,31), and winery information (mean = 5, standard deviation=1). The least important category, as expected, is legal information (e.g., legal drinking age, cookies files) (mean = 4, standard deviation=2).

Consumers have offered additional attributes that represent value to them but were not initially listed. Thus, they highlighted the importance of the **history of the owners.** Further personal information on the owners and the possibility of making a personal contact and an appointment for a visit to the cellar and the winery seem to be crucial. Indeed, a **section by the winemaker** can add authenticity and personality to the winery. Likewise, **recruitment information** is important. **A live chat** on the website and **the organization of events** such as a wine festival can create a bond and a feeling of closeness with the winemaker.

Consumers say in unison (80% of respondents leaving an open comment) that the importance of websites is becoming increasingly prevalent and has a significant impact on perceptions of winemakers, customer relationships, and purchasing decisions. In addition, respondents highlighted the importance of the website being easy, clear, and secure. The design must be refined to allow comfort in navigation. The content must be accessible and visual, with photos and videos that contribute to the creation of the image of the vineyard. If the visual and aesthetics of the website are on the level, it stimulates people to come back to the website, taste the wine and visit the winery. The function of the website is to facilitate contact with the winemaker and to inspire you to taste the wine. They lead to a good image product, confidence, and curiosity. Information is the most important thing, because transparency and detailed description help make decisions. The new elements offered by the websites, such as customer recommendations, are very much appreciated. Some consumers are drawn to features that make amusing and entertaining experience, others pay more attention to creating an impression of prestige (e.g., a castle). At the same time, a large part of consumers is afraid that the websites will become very complicated.

Table 3. Suggested and validated grid of winery website evaluation

		Avge	Standard Deviation	Stage			Avge	Standard Deviation	Stage
1	**Information on winery**	**5,58**	**1,312**		7	**Website advanced options**	**5**	**1**	
	Village name	5,16	1,519	1.2		Direct transaction	5,6	1,342	3
	Organization type	4,92	1,453	1.2		Indirect transaction via another website	4,24	1,791	3
	Cellar history	4,86	1,555	1.2		Secured transaction (SSL)	6,2	1,295	3
	Contact mode	5,07	1,497	1.1		Form validation	6,05	1,225	3
	Postal code	4,44	1,812	1.1		Previous orders and customer details remembered	4,7	1,657	3
	Postal address	4,67	1,762	1.1		Similar products suggested	4,26	1,502	3
	Email	4,86	1,822	1.1	8	**Legal information**	**4**	**2**	
	"Contact us" form	5,04	1,637	2.1		Winery name in the address line	4,53	1,606	1.2
	Online booking to visit the cellar	5,03	1,537	1.2		Information on the update	4,14	1,792	1.2
	Telephone number	5,54	1,52	1.1		Copyright declaration	3,63	1,87	1.2
	Owner or general manager	4,45	1,553	1.1		Confidentiality policies	4,09	1,984	1.2
	Winery region	5,68	1,302	1.1		Age verification	4,33	1,891	1.2
2	**Information on products**	**6,17**	**1,091**			Moderated consumption	4,34	1,851	1.2

continues on following page

Table 3. Continued

		Avge	Standard Deviation	Stage			Avge	Standard Deviation	Stage
	Wine description	6,05	1,113	2.1		Cookies use	3,8	1,921	1.2
	Appellation	5,94	1,169	2.1	9	**Added value services**	**5**	**2**	
	Grands Crus	5,62	1,347	2.1		Online auctions	3,15	1,618	3
	Prises	6,13	1,204	2.2		Client service	5,33	1,435	2.3
	Medals	5,26	1,347	2.2		Gift card	5,08	1,612	2.3
	Bottle price	6,02	1,236	2.1		Single bottles	5,86	1,34	2.2
	Price per pack	5,64	1,412	2.1		Mixed cases	5,85	1,33	2.2
	Technical notes	4,84	1,39	2.2		Order status on-line	5,84	1,317	2.3
	Taste description	5,35	1,29	2.2		Wish list	4,28	1,691	2.3
	Taste characteristics	5,29	1,258	2.2		Deliver modes	5,79	1,259	2.2
	Best sellers list	4,33	1,6	2.2		Bonuses and discounts	5,79	1,255	2.2
	Information on wine production	5,42	1,308	2.2		Additional products and services	4,64	1,521	2.2
	Information on wine conservation	5,53	1,254	2.2		Press releases	3,65	1,547	2.3
	Information on ageing	5,46	1,31	2.2		Special offers	5,08	1,51	2.3
3	**Information on cellar and visits**	**5**	**1**			New products announced	5,15	1,413	2.2
	Information on visits and tastings	5,26	1,424	1.2		Wine and food pairing	5,16	1,436	2.2
	Information on the cellar	5,39	1,229	1.2		Personalized labels	4,26	1,867	2.3
	Opening hours	5,94	1,292	1.2		Contest with prizes	4,39	1,64	2.3
	Capacity	4,93	1,647	1.2		Loyal Customers Club	4,34	1,727	2.3
	Accessibility to disabled visitors	5,54	1,557	1.2		Participation in fairs and other events	4,58	1,614	2.2
	Access map	5,07	1,593	1.2		Promotion of local tourism	4,59	1,603	2.2
4	**Distribution**	**4**	**2**			Questions and answers	4,84	1,606	2.2
	Information on distribution	4,71	1,465	2.2		Newsletter by email	3,71	1,856	2.2
	Restaurant	4,43	1,513	2.2		Presence on social networks	4,29	1,908	2.3
	Shops	4,72	1,488	2.2		Good referencing: it is easy to find the site	5,56	1,492	2.3
	Retailers	3,99	1,649	2.2		Sitemap	4,76	1,894	2.2
5	**Orders**	**5**	**2**			Search function	5,33	1,584	2.3
	Online orders	5,72	1,292	2.3	10	**Aesthetic**	**5**	**1**	
	E-commerce	5,56	1,422	2.3		Relevant external links	4,16	1,717	2.4
	Orders to pick up	5,14	1,377	2.2		Standard link colours	4,1	1,645	2.4
	Calculation of prices and distribution	5,96	1,15	2.3		Adapted design (for laptop or tablet)	5,72	1,421	2.4
	Exportation price	4,74	1,85	2.3		Charging time <3 sec	5,61	1,476	2.4
	Confirmation of the order	5,96	1,27	2.3		Content structured in a uniform manner	5,37	1,366	2.4
	Payment options	6,01	1,23	2.3		Aesthetic	5,58	1,268	2.4
	Offline orders	4,12	1,824	2.2		Use of colours	5,22	1,403	2.4

continues on following page

Table 3. Continued

		Avge	Standard Deviation	Stage			Avge	Standard Deviation	Stage
	Order files to print and fill in	4,02	1,882	2.2		Good contrast between background and text	5,64	1,259	2.4
	Prices calculated automatically	5,71	1,419	2.3		Adapted and easy-to-read text size	5,73	1,169	2.4
	Orders by email	4,72	1,759	2.2		Short pages	5,07	1,285	2.4
	Orders by telephone	4,67	1,724	2.2		Short paragraphs	5,12	1,311	2.4
6	**Website content and structure**	**4**	**2**			Numbered lists	4,11	1,623	2.4
	Content, organization, and recency	4,46	1,298	2.3		Background music	2,12	1,528	2.4
	Photographs	5,19	1,51	2.3	11	**Reviews and recommendations**	**5**	**1**	
	Videos	3,98	1,757	2.3		Professional reviews	4,8	1,284	2.3
	Virtual tour of the winery	3,9	1,71	2.3		Customer reviews	5,22	1,431	2.3
	Multiple languages	4,83	1,783	2.3		Journalists reviews	3,79	1,695	2.3
						Bloggers reviews	3,8	1,703	2.3

FUTURE RESEARCH DIRECTIONS

Future research can use the evaluation grid as a benchmark both among old world wine producing countries, like France and with new world wine producing countries. More specifically, it can be applied in order to analyze and compare the maturity of wine company websites between different wine regions of the world with the objective to understand international digital evolution of the wine industry as a whole. Wine professionals and wine destinations will be given elements enabling them to improve the efficiency of their websites and to be able to respond as effectively as possible to the needs and expectations of potential internet consumers. In any case, it is important to update the grid considering the changing demands of consumers and professionals in the wine sector.

CONCLUSION

This chapter has validated a grid to assess the digital maturity of a French winery website. The grid presented in table 3 is made up of 108 criteria which describe the website according to 11 dimensions based on the extended Model of Internet Commerce Adoption (eMICA) developed by Burgess and Cooper (2000) and Davidson (2009)'s website design framework. The evaluation grid provides some guidelines on how to evaluate the website of wineries, concluding in evaluation and potential enhancements. It is based on an extensive review of the literature, and could prove beneficial to wineries managers as they deal with how to engage with wine consumers in a digital world. This grid will help them to respond as effectively as possible to the needs and expectations of potential internet users. Thus, the grid can be used to audit the maturity of a winery or of a whole winemaking sector in a particular localization.

REFERENCES

Bargas-Avila, J. A., & Hornbæk, K. (2011). Old wine in new bottles or novel challenges? A critical analysis of empirical studies of User Experience. *Proceedings of the International Conference on Human Factors in Computing Systems.*

Barker, J. P. H. (2004). *Different worlds: law and the changing geographies of wine in France and New Zealand* (Doctoral dissertation). ResearchSpace@ Auckland.

Basu, S. (2018). Information search in the internet markets: Experience versus search goods. *Electronic Commerce Research and Applications, 30*, 25–37. doi:10.1016/j.elerap.2018.05.004

Bressolles, G. (2016). *Vente de vin sur Internet: l'avenir passe par le commerce connecté. Journal du Net. Chroniques.*

Bressolles, G., & Durrieu, F. (2011). Impact des dimensions de la qualité de service électronique sur la satisfaction et les intentions de fidélité: Différences entre acheteurs et visiteur. *La Revue des Sciences de Gestion, 6*(6), 37–45. doi:10.3917/rsg.252.0037

Bruwer, J., & Alant, K. (2009). The hedonic nature of wine tourism consumption: An experiential view. *International Journal of Wine Business Research, 21*(3), 235–257. doi:10.1108/17511060910985962

Bruwer, J., Nowak, L. I., & Newton, S. (2008). Using winery web sites to launch relationships with Millennials. *International Journal of Wine Business Research, 21*(1), 51–67.

Burgess, L., & Cooper, J. (1999). A model for classification of business adoption of internet commerce. *Proceedings of the 12th International Bled Electronic Commerce Conference,* 7-9.

Burgess, L., & Cooper, J. (2000). Extending the viability of MICA (Model of Internet Commerce Adoption) as a metric for explaining the process of business adoption of internet commerce. *Proceedings of the International Conference on Telecommunications and Electronic Commerce.*

Cockburn, C., & Wilson, T. D. (1996). Business use of the World Wide Web. *International Journal of Information Management, 16*(2), 83–102. doi:10.1016/0268-4012(95)00071-2

Cristobal-Fransi, E., Martin-Fuentes, E. Daries, N. (2015). Behavioral analysis of subjects interacting with information technology: Categorizing the behavior of e-consumers. *International Journal of Services Technology and Management, 21*(1/2/3), 163-182.

Davidson, R. (2006). *Electronic Service Quality Gaps in Australian Wineries* (PhD Thesis). Flinders University, Australia.

Davidson, R. (2009). A longitudinal study of Australian winery Websites. *Asia Pacific Management Review, 14*(4), 379–392.

Ding, C. G., & Lin, C. H. (2012). How does background music tempo work for online shopping? *Electronic Commerce Research and Applications, 11*(3), 299–307. doi:10.1016/j.elerap.2011.10.002

Elliots, S. (2002). *Electronic Commerce B2C Strategies and Model.* John Wiley and Sons.

Fédération des Exportateurs de Vins et spiritueux de France (FEVS). (2020). *Key Figures*. Retrieved from: https://www.fevs.com/en/the-sector/key-figures/

Fernández-Uclés, D., Bernal-Jurado, E., Mozas-Moral, A., & Medina-Viruel, M. J. (2019). The importance of websites for organic agri-food producers. *Economic Research-Ekonomska Istraživanja*, 1-14.

Gartner. (2002). *Gartner Web Site Evaluation Application*. Available www.gartnerg2.com

Haller, C. (2018). La digitalisation du monde du vin: le cas des entreprises vitivinicoles. *Conférence "Auf" de la Confrérie Saint Etienne*.

Haller, C., & Plotkina, D. & VoThan, T. (2019, June). *Proposition d'une grille d'évaluation de la maturité digitale d'un site Web d'entreprise vitivinicole dans le contexte européen*. Paper presented at the Conférence de l'Association Système d'information (AIM), France.

Haller, C., Thach, L., & Olsen, J. (2020). Understanding eWineTourism Practices of European and North America Wineries. *Journal of Gastronomy and Tourism*, *4*(3), 141–156. doi:10.3727/216929720X15846938923987

Hassenzahl, M., & Tractinsky, N. (2006). User experience – a research agenda. *Behaviour & Information Technology*, *25*(2), 91–97. doi:10.1080/01449290500330331

Hochschule Geisenheim University. (2019). *ProWein Business Report*. Retrieved from https://www.prowein.com/en/For_Visitors/Business_Reports/Business_Report_2019

Johnson, R., & Bruwer, J. (2007). Regional brand image and perceived wine quality: The consumer perspective. *International Journal of Wine Business Research*, *19*(4), 276–297. doi:10.1108/17511060710837427

Lanktree, C., & Briere, J. (1991, January). *Early data on the trauma symptom checklist for children (TSC-C)*. Paper presented at the meeting of the American Professional Society on the Abuse of Children, San Diego, CA.

Leroux, N., Wortman, M. S. Jr, & Mathias, E. D. (2001). Dominant factors impacting the development of business-to-business (B2B) e-commerce in agriculture. *The International Food and Agribusiness Management Review*, *4*(2), 205–218. doi:10.1016/S1096-7508(01)00075-1

Lin, D., Zongqing, Z., & Xialon, G. (2009). A study of the website performance of travel agencies based on the eMICA model. *Journal of Service Science and Management*, *3*(03), 181–185. doi:10.4236/jssm.2009.23021

Lutz, J. (2015). The validity of crowdsourcing data in studying anger and aggressive behavior. *Social Psychology*, *47*(1), 38–51. doi:10.1027/1864-9335/a000256

Massa, C., & Bédé, S. (2018). A consumer value approach to a holistic understanding of the winery experience. *Qualitative Market Research*, *21*(4), 530–548. doi:10.1108/QMR-01-2017-0031

McKay, J., Prananto, A., & Marshal, P. (2000). E-Business maturity: The SOG-e Model. *Proceedings of ACIS 2000*, 6-8.

Muñoz, R., Fernández, M., & Salinero, Y. (2019). Assessing consumer behavior in the wine industry and its consequences for wineries: A case study of a Spanish company. *Frontiers in Psychology*, *10*(2491), 1–7. PMID:31780997

Pahpy, L. (2017). *Comment rétablir la compétitivité de la viticulture française. Les propositions de l'IREF*. Etudes et Monographies, Institut de Recherches Economiques et Fiscales.

Peer, E., Vosgerau, J., & Acquisti, A. (2014). Reputation as a sufficient condition for data quality on Amazon Mechanical Turk. *Behavior Research Methods*, *46*(4), 1023–1031. doi:10.375813428-013-0434-y PMID:24356996

Porter, M. (2001). Strategy and the Internet. *Harvard Business Review*, *79*(2), 63–78. PMID:11246925

RaboSearch. (2019). *Wine Quarterly, Q1-2019: Online wine is growing in Europe*. Author.

Sheep, J. (2013). *Social Media Marketing for the Wine Industry*. Presentation at a Wine Intensive Executive MBA, Sonoma State University. Retrieved from: https://fr.slideshare.net/earthsite/social-media-for-the-wine-industry-by-joey-shepp

Sigala, M., & Haller, C. (2018). The Impact of Social Media on the Behavior of Wine Tourists: A Typology of Power Sources. In M. Sigala & R. Robinson (Eds.), *Management and Marketing of Wine Tourism Business* (pp. 139–154). Palgrave Macmillan.

Simpson, J. (2009). *Old World versus New World: the origins of organizational diversity in the international wine industry, 1850-1914*. Retrieved from: https://e-archivo.uc3m.es/bitstream/handle/10016/3742/wp-09-01.pdf?sequence=5

Szolnoki, G., Thach, L., & Kolb, D. (2016). Successful Social Media and Ecommerce Strategies in the Wine Industry. Palgrave Macmillan. doi:10.1057/9781137602985

Taylor, D. C., Parboteeah, D. V., & Snipes, M. (2010). Winery websites: Effectiveness explored. *Journal of Business Administration Online*, *9*(2), 1–11.

Taylor, D.C., Parboteeah, D.V., & Snipes, M. (2010). Winery websites: effectiveness explored. *Journal of Business Administration*, *9*(2), 1-11.

Thach, L., Lease, T., & Barton, M. (2016). Exploring the Impact of Social Media Practices on Wine Sales in US Wineries. *Journal of Direct, Data and Digital Marketing Practice*, *17*(4), 272–283. doi:10.1057/dddmp.2016.5

Ting, P.-H., Wang, S.-T., Bau, D.-Y., & Chiang, M.-L. (2013). Website evaluation of the top 100 hotels using advanced content analysis and eMICA model. *Cornell Hospitality Quarterly*, *54*(3), 284–293. doi:10.1177/1938965512471892

VandenBos, G., Knapp, S., & Doe, J. (2001). *Role of reference elements in the selection of resources by psychology undergraduates*. Retrieved from http://jbr.org/articles.html

Velikova, N., Wilcox, J. B., & Dood, T. H. (2011). Designing effective winery Websites: Marketing-oriented versus wine-oriented Website. *The 6th International Conference of the Academy of Wine Business Research*.

Zeithaml, V. A., Parasuraman, A., & Malhotra, A. (2002). Service quality delivery through Web sites: A critical review of extant knowledge. *Academy of Marketing Science Journal, 30*(4), 362–375. doi:10.1177/009207002236911

KEY TERMS AND DEFINITIONS

Aesthetics of a Website: A set of visual tools and attributes contributing to the beauty and artistic look of the website.

Customer Experience: The customer experience is the sensory, cognitive, emotional, social, and behavioral dimensions of all activities that connect the customer and the organisation over time across touchpoints and channels. It encompasses all activities involving the customer (Bolton, 2016).

eMICA: Extended Model of Internet Commerce Adoption (Davidson, 2009).

Evaluation Grid: A framework allowing to evaluate and benchmark a website.

Reviews and Recommendations: Opinions of non-winemakers on wines and wineries.

Website Attribute: Presence of a certain characteristic of the website.

Wine Industry: The market sector of wine makers and wine distributors.

Chapter 10
The Changes Brought by Digital Technology to Cognitive Learning

Anca Simona Ursu
University of Bucharest, Romania

Ion Ovidiu Panisoara
University of Bucharest, Romania

Ruxandra Claudia Chirca
University of Bucharest, Romania

ABSTRACT

The use of technological devices has become natural, which is why technology seems to become a natural learning environment. Many studies show that technologically-rich learning environments improve learning outcomes. It has been shown that technological integration helps to create more authentic learning environments, in which students are more motivated to participate. Digital world has greater opportunities for communication, collaboration, and problem-solving and have more opportunities to expand and even amplify thinking, thus changing the role of students by building knowledge rather than reproducing information. Given the possible disadvantages of using digital devices permanently, it is important to find a good balance between constructively using digital technology and keeping it to avoid distraction and concentration. However, some research shows that electronic learning does not differ in effectiveness or efficiency from traditional learning. This chapter presents an in-depth and reasoned analysis of cognitive learning of university students using Web 2.0 tools.

DOI: 10.4018/978-1-7998-3756-5.ch010

INTRODUCTION

Today's students have unlimited access to cell phones, digital cameras and the internet. They listen to music, watch and create their own videos, use blogs, play games in three-dimensional worlds, in short, live permanently in a world of technology. They feel the need for continuous access to new media to surf the internet, communicate with friends. „You see them everywhere. The teenage girl with ipod, sitting across from you on the subway, frenetically typing messages into her cell phone" (Palfrey & Gasser, 2011). According to a US study of teenage content creators and consumers (Lenhard & Madden, 2005), 57% of online teens create content on the Internet. In 2011, research on 3,000 students, from 1179 higher education institutions in the US, the EDUCAUSE Center for Applied Research found that social networks (for example, Facebook) were used much more in 2011 than in 2006, registering an increase from 65.3% to 90%. (Dahlstrom, de Boor, Grunwald & Vockley, 2011). Jones and Fox (2009) argue that students regularly use Web 2.0 applications, 75% of US adult users and 93% of adolescents. If we have such a large number of Web 2.0 users in higher education, the problem of using them in education is raised.

The use of mobile devices has become very natural, which is why mobile technology seems to become the natural learning environment (Farley, Murphy & Johnson, 2015). Applications such as blogs, wikis, social media tools and video sharing tools are most commonly used on university campuses for teaching purposes. Web 2.0 phenomenon offers students an unprecedented way to access, socialize, edit, categorize, promote and create in common. These innovations in technology and Web 2.0 sites are also changing learning, providing new support for it. Students quickly absorb information, through pictures and videos, as well as text, from multiple sources simultaneously. In Mayer's opinion (2014), introducing content through two or more forms of presentation supports the individual in assimilating more pieces of information in a shorter period of time.

Web 2.0 tools are of major importance to 21st century students, who must develop a variety of skills to meet the demands of the labor market, to place them in the service of the community (World Economic Forum, 2015). Nowadays, the outdated curriculum of higher education institutions is considered to be the cause of the lack of skills for graduates (Williams, 2015). As Mark Prensky (in Blair, K., Murphy, R. M., Almjeld, J., 2001) argues „Our students have changed radically. Today's students are no longer the people our educational system was designed to teach". Digital natives are a generation with obvious skills regarding the use of technology, who wants to be connected anytime and anywhere (Puybaraud, 2012). They are part of a social environment, driven by continuous change and transformation (Gulsecen et al., 2015). With this in mind, a refresh of the higher education program is needed, so that the graduates' competences are in line with the demands on the labour market. The need for educational reform is also mentioned by some researchers „Termed 'digital natives' or the 'Net generation', these young people are said to have been immersed in technology all their lives, imbuing them with sophisticated technical skills and learning preferences for which traditional education is unprepared. Grand claims are being made about the nature of this generational change and about the urgent necessity for educational reform in response" (Bennett, Maton & Kervin, 2008).

Technologies are used to provide simulations and real-world experiences for developing cognitive thinking and extending learning or to provide access to a wealth of improved information and communications through the Internet and other related information technologies; they are also used as productivity tools that use various programs, to manage information, to solve problems and to create sophisticated products. Applications such as databases, spreadsheets, semantic networks, multimedia / hypermedia constructs, can function as computer-based cognitive tools that function as intellectual partners for students, to expand and even amplify their thinking, thus changing the role of student by building knowledge rather than reproducing information.

To address the aforementioned issues, this study aims to analyse how Web 2.0 applications could influence the cognitive learning of university students and aims to raise awareness among teachers and students about the pedagogical benefits of Web 2.0 to supplement classroom learning through integrating them into the design and learning process and to better understand the factors that influence students' decisions to adopt these tools. This chapter presents some possible strategies for teachers to incorporate some of these Web 2.0 technologies into the student learning experience. Understanding these issues is an important first step for teachers in creating and developing an effective learning environment.

We wanted to answer the following question: Does the use of Web 2.0 applications make changes in the cognitive learning of university students?

In the following sections we aim to present an overview of the studies and opinions on this topic, as well as our own perspective on how they influence the design of enriched learning environments through Web 2.0.

BACKGROUND

Learning is a change in human disposition or capacity, which persists over a period of time and is not simply attributable to growth processes (Gagne, 1977). This is the most well-known definition of the learning given by Gagne, to which reference was made most often by scholars in the field of learning and psychology. Learning theory from a cognitive perspective is a general approach that regards learning as an active mental process of acquiring, remembering and using knowledge. Learning results in a change in knowledge, which results in a change in behaviour.

The Greek philosopher, Aristotle, developed one of the earliest theories of learning since ancient times. According to him, "the fixing, fertilizing and updating of knowledge is favoured by 3 factors: contiguity, similarity and opposition. For example, two events that are repeatedly presented to a subject successively, are likely to be memorized together, so that either of them can become the evocative / trigger signal of the other" (Pirâu, 2008, p.99). The American psychologist, Thorndike, defined learning as "the acquisition of new reactions or responses (R) to new situations (S), respectively, the elaboration and establishment of connections that education establishes between situations or events-stimulus and reactions" (Thorndike, 1983) .

Leontiev defined learning as "the process of acquiring the intellectual experience of behavior", thus understanding the assimilation of information and more than that, the formation of thought, the affective sphere, the will, thus the formation of the personality system "(Silva, 2014). Learning can also be regarded as "a process which takes place under the influence of multiple factors, the result being a set of products, embodied in knowledge, skills, abilities, beliefs, feelings, opinions, interests, attitudes, habits or ways of thinking and acting, based on which the continuous reconstruction of human behaviour takes place" (Stoica, 2001, p. 96).

What is Cognitive Learning?

Cognitive learning refers to the way students process the information and strategies used by teachers so that they understand what is being passed on to them. The working structure of human cognition is different for each student. The working structure of human cognition must be taken into account when designing messages using technology to allow learning to progress according to each student's own cognitive process. Learning is achieved by establishing connections between verbal representations and images. The new scheme involves a process of selecting and organizing relevant information and integrating it with prior knowledge; it can only be produced through cognitive involvement (Mayer, 2014).

Bloom has established that in cognitive learning the fields involve the knowledge and development of intellectual abilities. This includes recalling or recognizing facts, patterns, procedures, concepts that help develop intellectual skills. Learning processes in the cognitive field include a hierarchy of skills that involve processing information, building understanding, applying knowledge, solving problems, and conducting research. There are six levels of cognitive complexity: knowledge, understanding, application, analysis, synthesis, evaluation. Bloom's taxonomy focused on describing achievement levels, rather than process skills, and did not substantially address how the student moves from one level to another (Bloom, 1956). Later on, a former student of Bloom, L. Anderson, together with D. Krathwohl revised Bloom's taxonomy and replaced the highest level of cognitive complexity with "creation", regarded as the ability of generating new ideas and reorganising content in an innovative manner (Winge & Embry, 2013).

School learning is, for the most and significant part, a cognitive learning, since the final aim is to establish a student's cognitive system and operational structures specific to the objects studied in school. The brain and its cognitive functions shape our learning and, as we evolve, we learn to be smarter, to reach new learning thresholds, by acquiring new skills, information and ideas. Thus, it is not the brain that changes and evolves, but the people who learn how to use it. The more information you discover about how the brain works and the characteristics of the brain, the easier it will be for people to learn.

The benefits of cognitive learning:

- Cognitive learning encourages students to adopt a practical approach to learning. This allows them to explore the material and develop a deeper understanding.
- The cognitive learning approach teaches students the skills they need to learn effectively. This helps students develop transferable problem-solving and study skills that they can apply to any subject.
- The development of cognitive skills allows students to build on previous knowledge and ideas. This teaches students to make connections and apply new concepts to what they already know.
- With a deeper understanding of the topics and stronger learning skills, students can approach schoolwork with enthusiasm and confidence.
- Giving students the chance to be actively involved in learning is fun and interesting.

When carrying out an activity with pleasure, students have the opportunity to experience success easily. This helps students to love learning outside the classroom.

What is web 2.0 Tools?

The term "Web 2.0" includes web applications that facilitate the distribution of information, interaction with other users, collaboration, user-friendly design. Web 2.0 technologies "allow users to communicate, create content and share it with each other through communities, social networks and virtual worlds more easily than before" (Jussila et all., 2014, p. 607). A Web 2.0 site allows its users to interact with other users or change the content of the Web site, as opposed to non-interactive Web sites, where users are limited to passive viewing of the information provided to them. They created the idea that people who access and consume web content should not passively absorb what is available, but be active contributors. These are Web-based technology tools that focus on social, collaborative, user-oriented content and applications that facilitate a more social connection to the Internet.

There are a number of web-based services and applications that demonstrate the fundamentals of the "Web 2.0" concept and are already being used to some extent in education. These are not technologies themselves, but services (or user processes) built using the basics of open technologies and standards that underpin the Internet and the Web. Because Web 2.0 applications are capable of delivering learning experiences that are otherwise impossible, research efforts should focus on how learners use these applications for learning and how these applications provide equal access to all learners. The use of Web 2.0 applications involves a collective contribution to the creation of information, which is also called crowd wisdom.

Constructivist pedagogy focuses on students who build knowledge rather than those who acquire knowledge (Pallof and Pratt, 2004). From a social constructivist (and constructionist) perspective, this construction occurs primarily through social interactions (Vygotsky, 1978). The path to acquiring knowledge becomes an interactive and collaborative activity, in which learning is the result of the individuals' exchange of opinions on a common topic. (Bearison & Dorval, 2002, in Klopfer et al., 2009). Web 2.0 collaboration technologies promote social interaction. These allow students to read and receive feedback from a larger audience than is allowed in traditional constructivist education. Using collaborative technologies, students can communicate with classmates as well as others around the world. The comments made by this diverse and participative audience often generate discussions that improve learning.

Recent studies have underlined the significant need to adapt traditional teaching methods to new technologies, to the needs and expectations of students (Dumitrescu, 2015; Wilson, 2015). In other words, new teaching and learning methods using new technologies, especially Web 2.0, should be student-centered methods that encourage autonomy, interactivity, collaboration, creativity and critical thinking. Anastasiades & Kotsidis (2013) suggests that the use of Web 2.0 in education can develop critical thinking skills, meta-cognitive skills, and problem solving skills.

Technology can help the process of teaching and learning through its interactive, dynamic content and can provide real opportunities for individualized training. It enriches the skills, involves the students in the learning process, relates the school experiences with the practical aspects, connects the school with the surrounding world, brings major changes in the school. (Davis & Tearle, 1999; Lemke & Coughlin, 1998). The use of technology helps the school to become more efficient, generating various tools to help teachers in the educational activity (Kirschner & Woperies, 2003).

Web 2.0 applications can enhance student motivation (Karkoulia, 2016). Dumitrescu (2015) found that integrating Web 2.0 into classroom learning helps teachers to expand and diversify teaching and learning approaches and thus increases student motivation and engagement.

What is E-Learning?

Electronic learning refers to the intentional use of information technology and other types of communication technologies in teaching and learning. Electronic learning is a combination of content and training methods through computers and the Internet to facilitate the building of knowledge and skills (Rovai, 2004). They help in acquiring and understanding knowledge through interactive technology, both offline and online (Wilkinson et al., 2004).

The learning system based on formalized teaching, but with the help of electronic resources is also known as E-learning. While traditional teaching takes place in or outside the classroom, the use of computers and the Internet is the main component of e-learning. At first, this system was criticized for lacking the human element, but over time, many researchers highlighted its major benefits. The term e-learning encompasses much more than e-learning, since the letter "e" in e-learning means the word "electronic", e-learning would incorporate all educational activities carried out by individuals or groups working online or offline (Naidu, 2006).

Electronic learning can be used either to replace traditional teaching completely, or only partially to support traditional methods with access to complementary electronic information and communication possibilities (Penny, 2011).

Thus, when Web 2.0 tools are properly integrated into the education process, they are supposed to stimulate social skills, to encourage collaboration between students in higher education institutions and to foster cognitive learning.

MAIN FOCUS OF THE CHAPTER

Arguments for and Against the use of Technology in Education

Web 2.0 student experiences are clearly different from the experiences provided by the previous web versions, that is why teachers should use Web 2.0 tools to improve their students' learning experiences. In fact, some teachers state that they are a necessity for educating the Net Generation, which, they argue, differs from previous generations. „Digital natives (also known as "Generation Y" and "Millennials"), a generation born during of after introduction of digital technologies, 1980s and after, have mixed preferences for media use in personal and professional lives" (Verčič & Verčič, 2013). In addition, the researchers stated that, having grown up in an age of media saturation and convenient access to digital technologies, the Net Generation has distinctive ways of thinking, communicating and learning (Oblinger and Oblinger, 2005). They are used to the permanent interaction provided by the online environment and they prefer working in teams, rather than individually (Howe & Strauss, 2007). „The digitally enhanced person who will emerge from these developments, homo sapiens digital, differs from today's human in two key aspects: he or she accepts digital enhancement as an integral fact of human existence, and he or she is digitally wise. Digital wisdom is exhibited both in a considered use of digital enhancements to complement innate abilities and in the use of enhancements to facilitate wiser decision making in an unimaginably complex future" (Prensky, 2009).

Computers can function as cognitive technologies for amplifying and reorganizing the way students think. Web 2.0 technologies support the development of students' ability and develop critical thinking, problem solving and communication skills (Insteford & Munthe, 2017). Computer tools, unlike most tools, can function as intellectual partners who share the cognitive task of performing tasks (Solomon, 1993). Cognitive technologies are tools that can be provided by any environment and help students overcome the limitations of their mind, such as memory, thinking or problem solving (Pea, 1985). This generation „is not homogenous in its use and appreciation of new technologies and (…). There are significant variations amongst students that lie within the Net generation age band" (Jones, Ramanau, Cross & Healing, 2010).

Some research shows that e-learning does not make a significant difference in effectiveness or efficiency over traditional learning (Clark and Jones, 2001; Marttunen and Laurinen, 2001). Some research even shows that e-learning is not as good as traditional learning. Summer & Hosterler (2002) also supported that result by showing that traditional groups performed significantly better than the e-learning group. The functioning of the student learning process and how the student perceives a new form of learning should be sufficiently considered. Technological characteristics should not be added randomly to e-learning. Misuse of technology can mislead the student and distract the learner, which will negatively affect the learning outcome. However, there are some studies that show different results. Online instruction is found to have a significantly more positive effect than traditional learning (Buchanan, 2000). Some of them show that the technologically rich learning environments ensure a better development of life skills. These skills include organizational skills, problem solving, inquiry and collaboration. The learning environment is improved by providing more cooperative learning and reduced competition (Stratham and Torell, 1996). Many studies report that if the learning environment is technologically rich, self-esteem and enthusiasm for learning can increase (Fouts, 2000).

If the teaching and learning methods were controlled by teachers in the traditional environment (Strawbridge, 2010), now the focus has changed from teacher to student. This major change is possible with Web 2.0 tools (Karunasena, Deng & Zhang, 2012). Passive learning is less effective because the student learns only what the teacher transmits to them. Through active learning, the student looks for and discovers alone what he needs. Students should not only listen, but also read, write, discuss, or be involved in problem solving (Chickering & Gamson, 1987). If passive learning involves memorization by students, active learning requires higher-level tasks, such as analysis, synthesis and evaluation.

Web tools offer openness and flexibility in the learning process. If traditional learning is rigid and closed within the specific framework of classroom teaching, web technologies are open access means, and E-learning allows learning anywhere, anytime, regardless of geographical locations. Web technologies could be used effectively in distance education, as pointed out by Den Exter et. Al. (2012). This also involves flexibility in terms of time. There is no need for the student to connect simultaneously with the teacher or other colleagues.

Using Web 2.0 tools gives us the ability to collaborate with new knowledge and create connections between people. It allows us to use and creatively reuse the material in new ways (Hicks and Graber 2010). In many researches, collaboration is one of the important features. Online learning has many advantages: promoting creative, intuitive, associative and analogical thinking, increased access, social interactions (Safran, Helic and Gütl, 2007). And Karunasena, Deng and Zhang (2012) argue that web 2.0 tools are collaborative and participatory in nature. Electronic learning can make courses livelier, more enjoyable and can support collaboration, critical thinking, reflection and a variety of technological skills (Buchem and Hamelmann, 2011).

Electronic learning allows the education to be adapted to the individual needs of the students more than the traditional teaching. Each participant can set their own study pace. Electronic learning offers availability and accessibility on course materials. When education becomes more and more expensive, web tools provide inexpensive and effective solutions for communication and information exchange (Koshi, 2013). The education delivery is done to a large number of recipients at the same time or different.

Impact on Cognitive Learning

The use of the Internet is associated with the development of certain cognitive skills. Johnson highlighted a significant difference between those who frequently use the Internet and visual reasoning, compared to those who do not use it frequently and visual reasoning. The results suggest that selective use of the internet leads to increased cognitive ability to manipulate visual images. Internet users will notice visual stimuli more easily and this can be used in life (Johnson, 2008).

Technology *enhances cognitive skills*, such as information processing and perception. Cecilia and colleagues (2015) analysed the influence of games on cognitive performance. The results showed that technological exposure in childhood can promote better cognitive flexibility and increased learning; autonomy in using technological tools and / or applications is a good way to improve learning skills during development. Mobile games are also very useful tools for learning and can have a positive impact on the cognitive learning process (Schmitz, 2014). Mobile learning games are considered to have the potential to influence both cognitive and socio-affective learning in a positive way, especially among young adults (Mitchell, 2007; Schmitz, 2014). Each video game is a unique world, that the player builds step-by-step (Egenfeldt-Nielsen, 2006, in Egenfeldt-Nielsen et al., 2006). The various positive traits of video games include: the generation of strong emotional reactions (such as joy or the feeling of power), the immediate reward, the existence of a narrative, the competition with other players, the opportunity to collaborate with them, and the influence that players can have upon the virtual world (Squire, 2003). Green and Bavelier (2012) observed that online gambling causes faster processing of information. This is due to the speed with which the players have to make a decision. Online games are very demanding and this allows users to use their knowledge constructively, developing cognitive retention skills (Hagman, 1980). Along the same lines, Schlickum et al. (2009) found that medical students increased their cognitive performance due to computer games and Drew and Waters (1986) found that they caused increases in perceptual motor skills in adults. These studies show that online games have a positive impact on cognitive abilities and learning.

Sparrow, Liu, and Wegner (2011) found that the use of search engines (eg Google) affected *memory* structures in individuals. People forgot the information available externally and kept only those that were not. Rahwan (2014) found that memory is not influenced by the use of search engines, but using them helps solve cognitive problems, facilitating the spread of correct information. Furthermore, Nicholas et al. (2011) compared the memory of the Google generation with previous generations. The working memory of the Google generation was significantly lower than in previous generations. This is explained by the fact that the use of search engines, which are more readily available, makes memory very little used, and this limits the development of the memory instead of developing it.

Pitler et al. (2007) argue that students can *better understand the material presented* if they use the technology when taking notes. They can use various word processing software to observe changes, to highlight and better retain certain portions, to summarize and edit a text. Pitler also describes how conceptual maps help in understanding the material. There are certain programs (for example, Inspiration) through which teachers can create conceptual maps and use them in different types of lessons. With the help of a visual environment, students make varied and multiple connections between previous concepts, ideas, words, knowledge, meaning they understand the topic of the conceptual map better and make connections between information.

Another common concern regarding the use of the Internet is that it can lead to *superficial thinking*. One hypothesis underlying this concern is that instantaneous access to seemingly unlimited information removes the need to engage in more cognitively efficient processes. A study has been done in this regard. In this study, when graduate students had access to the answers provided by others in highly connected networks, they were more likely to correctly answer a question that requires analytical logic, but they were less likely to use analytical logic in subsequent situations that required this cognitive strategy. These findings indicate that individuals who are part of a highly connected network (such as the Internet) are less likely to adopt the kind of cognitive strategy needed to reach a solution when the solution is immediately available (Rashwan et al., 2014).

Some educational research shows that the use of mobile devices and social networks when learning new materials *reduces understanding and affects academic performance* (Froese et al., 2012). The mere presence in the room of one's own smartphone can induce "brain drain", by occupying the cognitive resources with limited capacity, for the purpose of attentional control. Because the same finite group of attentional resources accepts both attentional control and other cognitive processes, the resources recruited to inhibit the automatic attention of a phone are unavailable for other tasks as well, and the performance of these tasks will suffer. The use of attentional resources for a cognitive process or task leaves fewer resources available for other tasks; in other words, the use of cognitive resources reduces the available cognitive capacity (Ward, Duke, Gneezy & Bos, 2017). Specific cognitive ability measures used are associated with general abilities that support fundamental processes such as learning, logical thinking, abstract thinking, problem solving, and creativity (Cattell, 1987; Kane et al., 2004).

There is a lot of research into improving the teaching process using online video distribution tools (eg YouTube). One of them argues that YouTube can be an effective online tool for language learning, being easy to use and having many videos that not only help to learn a language, but also provide cultural contexts in which the language can be applied (Balcikanli, 2009).

Regarding social media tools, „the majority of the digital-native preservice teachers reported that the scope of their use of Web 2.0 technologies was limited to mainly social-networking Web sites, and they lacked the experiences and expertise in using Web 2.0 technologies with great potential for classroom application" (Lei, 2009). In another study, which included 606 Facebook users, Mazman and Usluel (2010) found that a variety of non-educational purposes could mediate the relationship between the initial adoption of Facebook and the use of Facebook for educational purposes. Such a mediated relationship could support Facebook's integration into teaching and learning. On the other hand, Kirschner and Karpinski (2010) found that users who do not use Facebook may have better results in academia than Facebook users. The mixed results regarding the effect of Facebook on learning could be determined by several external factors. Thomas (2010) argued that the reason we cannot deduce the effect of social networking tools for learning is our inability to detach "learning processes" from conventional learning spaces and to reactivate them to Facebook's virtual environments.

Although it has been found that the use of smart devices can have a major impact on cognitive tasks, the results on the long-term impact of online tools are insufficient. However, most researchers agree with some secure benefits of Web 2.0 applications for learning (Wilmer et al., 2017).

The Advantages of Web 2.0 Applications for Learning

a.   Creation of knowledge

This emerging technology, characterized by increased functionality, interoperability and connectivity, contributes to the creation of knowledge through open communication and collaboration. Using it changes the role of the users, who become active participants in the construction of knowledge. Students not only receive knowledge, but they also create, edit and distribute learning materials. Web 2.0 tools give learners the opportunity to engage in higher-order thinking skills, which involves not only understanding and applying knowledge but also participating in high-level skills, such as critically evaluating information, synthesizing information objects with different formats and working independently and collectively with contributors, from peer to peer. These promise students new opportunities to be independent in their study and research and encourage greater ability to express themselves. They have common goals and form the basis of a learning community.

b.   Collaboration

Web 2.0 promotes learning in an extremely interactive and complex environment. Learners from these environments need to interact with other learners and the interactive system to discover and gain new information. People who learn in these interactive environments generally exercise a high degree of control in decision-making processes. Web 2.0 allows users to participate in collective and collaborative learning activities through applications such as blogs, wikis, social networking sites, online games, online video distribution and engaging in virtual environments etc. (Daniela et al. 2018). In turn, collaboration with other users promotes group and debate learning, highlighting the contributions and opinions of all participants. For training purposes, Web 2.0 students can interact with others synchronously or asynchronously, solve collaborative problems at their own pace, provide instant feedback between them, clarify misunderstandings, and build knowledge.

Collaboration with Web tools. 2.0 facilitates the exchange of ideas and resources, the development of active listening, the debate of ideas in a constructive way, the responsibility for their own tasks within the groups, the possibility of presenting their own opinions. Some students can help others who did not understand, by providing explanations and support. Thus, both those who receive the information and those who provide it are in advantage, as they reorganize and restructure information mentally, thus developing a better cognitive understanding.

c.   Interaction

Interaction refers to the exchange of ideas between students through the use of social networks, such as Facebook, Twitter, etc., which allow students to engage with friends, colleagues and teachers by making educational contributions in an online learning environment, and namely, an online discussion forum. Web 2.0 applications allow any member of the group to interact with all the other members, individually or at once. When a new student joins a learning community, not only does he benefit from it, but existing students also benefit indirectly, as they can interact with new members.

d.   Social support

According to Wenger (1998), learning occurs when it is socially situated, when students are involved in learning groups and communities. Web 2.0 applications can support this type of learning because they allow learners to participate in communities, communicate with each other and edit their own content. Applications for online distribution of video and social media on the network can offer such social support.

e.   Accessibility

The relatively simple and intuitive use of Web 2.0 tools gives students the chance to contribute and experiment in online learning communities. The "Web 2.0" world has become possible only through an open mind where developers and companies offer open and transparent access to their applications and content. The tools and often massive amounts of user-generated content that they create and organize are characterized by being available for free on the Internet.

This feature allows participants to use and produce content at any time and from anywhere in the world. With this feature, interactions are easier and cheaper.

f.   Involvement

Involvement is a proof of the active participation of students in the learning process (Ivala & Gachago, 2012). Finally, Web 2.0 tools function "to a great extent, as Ullrich also suggests, as a pedagogical tool", characterized by social learning and active participation (Ullrich et all. 2008, p. 709). In a general sense, motivation determines student involvement and thus student involvement increases learning. There are many factors that motivate students to learn, and motivation is a key component of learning. The more motivated a person is, the more involved they are in what they learn. Therefore, the longer the information is processed or repeated in working memory, the greater the likelihood of becoming long-term memory.

In addition, Web 2.0 tools offer other benefits:

- flexibility in choosing technology;
- control of access to resources through user authentication;
- distribution of online learning resources (texts, images, sounds, videos, animations) through Web 2.0 tools.
- low level of complexity required for use (minimum internet usage skills)
- can empower the student to become self-guided and self-organized
- promotes initiative, creativity and critical thinking. (Grosseck, 2009)

Disadvantages

a)   Low control

Learning environments can actually inhibit learning if they fail to respond and manage increased cognitive demands. To be effective, these learning environments must balance an interactive, stimulating environment with manageable levels of mental effort for the learner. In the online learning process, it is more difficult to respond to students' needs because teachers have limited control over students' perceptions and learning processes.

However, the availability of technology applications does not guarantee that users will really learn from the interaction with the applications. Only users who have the intention and ability to use the applications can benefit from Web 2.0 applications (Hughes, 2009). Factors such as extrinsic motivation, attitude, and anxiety about technology use all play a role in technology use (Venkatesh et al., 2003). Using a wiki as an example, constantly changing the content or critical views of other contributors can make some wiki users feel restless and unwilling to participate in the process of building knowledge in collaboration. Therefore, this reluctance to share and collaborate prevents users from contributing to and learning from it (White, Gurzick, & Lutters, 2009).

Finally, other factors, such as learning strategies, communication, interaction, flexibility, involvement and means of assessment are also related to learning effectiveness through the use of online learning environments (Simonson et al, 2006; Richardson and Newby, 2006).

Also, other challenges related to information overload, intellectual property and copyright, as well as the development of personal archives and personal learning environment are discussed.

b)   High requirements

These applications can add richness to the content, opportunities for collaboration and new opportunities for communication in courses. However, the same characteristics could impose an excessive level of cognitive requirements for some students. From a cognitive point of view, Web 2.0 users need to acquire the skills necessary to navigate and interrogate this new knowledge space.

c)   Time

The use of Web 2.0 tools does not mean that traditional pedagogical strategies are simply integrated into providing courses on the Internet, but complex pedagogical approaches such as Web 2.0 may take a long time to develop, but have the potential to provide students with hands-on experiences of more engaging learning.

There are disadvantages to prolonged exposure to digital devices. Research is still being done on the impact of excessive exposure on technology. Some researchers have hypothesized that children's attention is changing, others are concerned that their brain is developing differently, and some even claim that exposure to technology has accelerated evolution so that children are a new species of people. Virtual environments have a very strong impact on people and especially on children. They can be very interactive and appealing to children and separating them from their online lives can be difficult - which can lead to problems in offline life. Block states that "Internet addiction leads to behavioral disorders and psychological dysfunctions in everyday life" (Block, 2008, p. 306-307). Control strategies are needed to prevent these problems.

The recent phenomenon of media multitasking has raised serious concerns about the negative impact of digital media on attention. Research has shown that divided attention can hinder information retention, learning, and metacognition (Bergen, Grimes, & Potter, 2005, pp. 311-336). E. and K. Petersen (2000) point out that the online world of the child should not replace his real world and, online friends, while important, should not replace school friends. Homework Help should not replace the library, a real book, or personal parenting support. In short, internet education, even if it is of extraordinary importance, should not be a substitute for our personal and interpersonal world.

Some unexpected side effects also begin to appear after several hours of watching the screen. Studies show that backlit screens suppress melatonin levels in our brain by up to 22% (Rensselaer Polytechnic Institute Lighting Research Center, 2012). There is empirical evidence that addiction behaviors, including video games / computer games and Internet use, are a growing problem (Mitchell, Becker-Blease, & Finkelhor, 2005, pp. 498-509). Dependence phenomena and side effects have become significant social problems. Dependence on mobile phones has direct symptoms of psychological anxiety, avoiding communication, weakening social adaptations and withdrawal symptoms, similar to those of drug or alcohol dependence (Kim, 2013, p. 2). This often leads to ophthalmological problems.

Movement is an essential component of a child's life. The more active and experienced the child is in various physical activities, the faster his or her neural system will develop; the neural development of the brain allows the child to effectively take advantage of the possibilities in his environment. Through movement, a child even learns to show initiative, independence and responsibility (Walter & Hen, 2012, pp. 20-30). Sherborne (2001) argues that there is a strong connection between movement and emotion. Each movement appears in combination with other movements and functions closely with them and with cognitive and emotional-social functioning, such as self-confidence, self-control, empathy, independence and leadership (Nabal-Heller, Raviv, Lidor & Levianne, 1999).

SOLUTIONS AND RECOMMENDATIONS

Thus, by introducing Web 2.0 tools into the educational process, it is important to keep in mind that students are not a homogeneous group of digitally developed students. The digital divide must be identified between those with access and skills and those who do not. Other challenges that need to be considered when using Web 2.0 tools are student characteristics, such as the level of knowledge in the field and learning experience using Web 2.0, as well as the context of the learning tasks. These factors can significantly influence the interactions and success of students in learning.

Higher education institutions should use Web 2.0 tools because they promote cognitive learning and develop the skills required by the current labour market, while they are also more interactive and attractive to students. In order to avoid obstacles for some students in this process, conditions should be created, and instructions given for using Web 2.0 tools as early as possible. For teachers, institutions should be encouraged to provide opportunities for professional development and supportive environments to experiment with technologies in their content areas (Nelson, Voithofer & Cheng, 2019). There are researchers who claim that teacher training programs on the use of Web 2.0 digital tools will help them to integrate them more effectively in the teaching process (Mata, Panisoara, Fat, Panisoara & Lazar, 2019).

In order to influence the belief of university teachers regarding the value of technology, it is important, in addition to providing knowledge, to also consider changing their pedagogical beliefs from traditional to constructivist. Then there is a good chance that technology will be integrated into their teaching (Taimalu & Luik, 2019). Although Web 2.0 technologies are successful, stimulating participation, the teacher must continue to play an active role as a discussion mediator. Active participation and collaboration can have negative educational effects when teachers do not maintain the role of mediators of the discussion. Technologies require teachers to be thoughtful practitioners. They should recognize the difference between collaboration as the adoption and exchange of information, as well as collaboration as a productive exchange and the construction of ideas that lead to learning gains (Angeli 2008).

As far as over-exposure is concerned, the existence of rules for using the Internet has a positive impact on young people. Establishing good habits from an early age - and keeping communication lines open as children grow - builds a solid foundation when teens become more independent web users. It is important that these rules are for the whole family, as children are expected to have time limits on their online games, and parents should also agree that they should turn off their phones while on family trips, for example. Ideally there should be a program in this regard. For example, without technology

1-2 hours before sleep and without phones in the room where you sleep because there are some studies that support the harmful effects on sleep, without screens during the meal, topics, reading.

Technology can be a very valuable friend if it is used for educational or entertainment purposes but it can also be a dangerous enemy by distracting from daily life, without having to play anymore, face-to-face discussions with friends, walks in outdoors, moments spent with family members.

In order not to become the slaves of technology we must balance the virtual life with the real one and take everything that has good to offer the technology and avoid what is not useful or which can negatively affect our life.

FUTURE RESEARCH DIRECTIONS

Considering the above, we have learnt that Web.20 are already widely used by university students and yet rigorous systematic research in this area is limited. Future research should address questions such as: To what extent are Web 2.0 tools integrated among students to promote their cognitive learning? Which tools do I or should I use more often? Are teachers ready to keep up with new media evolution and use these technologies in classrooms? Which one would be the most appropriate for the development of cognitive learning? What are the differences in terms of cognitive learning between students who use Web 2.0 and those who do not?

CONCLUSION

Technology has had a huge impact on people's lives. This impact has affected every aspect of society. It also had a major impact on education. It has made our world more and more complex, which has changed the requirements for people entering the workforce. This change made it necessary to create learning environments to support the development of higher-level thinking skills. Technological integration has also shown that it helps to create more authentic learning environments, where students are more motivated to participate, have greater opportunities for communication and collaboration, and have more opportunities to use higher thinking skills to solve problems related to real-world situations. These tools provide new inputs to the field of education and a new way of thinking.

Given the potential disadvantages of the ongoing existence of smartphones and other digital devices, Web 2.0 tools might need to pay more attention to pedagogical issues. It is important to find a good balance between using digital technology in a constructive way, which is driven by a learning purpose and helps students better focus on their tasks, and using it only for entertainment purposes or as a distraction tool. As long as these issues are overcome, the use of Web 2.0 tools in the educational process will prove to have multiple benefits for both students and teachers.

REFERENCES

Anastasiades, P. S., & Kotsidis, K. (2013). The challenges of web 2.0 for education in Greece. *International Journal of Web-Based Learning and Teaching Technologies*, 8(4), 19–33. doi:10.4018/ijwltt.2013100102

Angeli, C. (2008). Distributed Cognition: A framework for understanding the role of computers in classroom teaching and learning. *Journal of Research on Technology in Education, 40*(3), 271–279. doi:10.1080/15391523.2008.10782508

Balcikanli, C. (2009). Long live, YouTube: L2 stories about YouTube in language learning. *E-Proceeding of the International Online Language Conference (IOLC),* 91–96.

Bearison, D. J., & Dorval, B. (2002). *Advances in discourse processes. Collaborative cognition: Children negotiating ways of knowing.* Ablex Publishing.

Bennett, S., Maton, K., & Kervin, L. (2008). The 'digital natives' debate: A critical review of the evidence. *BJET, 39*(5), 775–786. doi:10.1111/j.1467-8535.2007.00793.x

Bergen, L., Grimes, T., & Potter, D. (2005). How attention partitions itself during simultaneous message presentations. *Human Communication Research, 31*(3), 311–336. doi:10.1111/j.1468-2958.2005.tb00874.x

Blair, K., Murphy, R. M., & Almjeld, J. (2001). Cross Currents: Cultures, Communities, Technologies. New York: Cengage Learning.

Block, J. J. (2008). Issues for DSM-V: Internet addiction. *The American Journal of Psychiatry, 165*(3), 306–307. doi:10.1176/appi.ajp.2007.07101556 PMID:18316427

Bloom, B. S., Engelhart, M. D., Furst, E. J., Hill, W. H., & Krathwohl, D. R. (1956). *Taxonomy of educational objectives: The classification of educational goals. Handbook 1: Cognitive domain.* David McKay.

Buchanan, T. (2000). The Efficacy of a World Wide Web. *Computing Research, 23*(2), 203–216.

Buchem, I., & Hamelmann, H. (2011). Developing 21st century skills: Web 2.0 in higher education: A Case Study. *E-learning papers,* (24). Available at: http://elearningpapers.eu/sites/default/files/media25535

Cattell, R. B. (1987). *Intelligence: Its Structure, Growth and Action.* Elsevier.

Cecilia, R., Di Giacomo, D., Vittorini, P., & De la Prieta, F. (Eds.). (2015). Influence of gaming activities on cognitive performances. Methodologies & Intelligent Systems for Technology Enhanced Learning, 374. Springer. doi:10.1007/978-3-319-19632-9_9

Chickering, A. W., & Gamson, Z. F. (1987). Seven principles for good practice. *AAHE Bulletin, 39,* 3–7.

Clark, R. A., & Jones, D. (2001). A Comparison of Traditional and Online Formats in a Public Speaking Course. *Communication Education, 50*(2), 109–124. doi:10.1080/03634520109379238

Dahlstrom, E., de Boor, T., Grunwald, P., & Vockley, M. (2011). *The ECAR study of undergraduate students and information technology.* EDUCAUSE Center for Applied Research. Available from http://www.educause.edu/Resources/ECARNationalStudy ofUndergradua/238012

Daniela, L., Visvizi, A., Gutierrez-Braojos, C., & Lytras, M. (2018). Sustainable higher education and technology-enhanced Learning (TEL). *Sustainability, 10*(11), 3883. doi:10.3390u10113883

Davis, N. E., & Tearle, P. (Eds.). (1999). *A core curriculum for telematics in teacher training.* Teleteaching 98 Conference, Vienna. https://files.eric.ed.gov/fulltext/ED432260.pdf

Den Exter, K., Rowe, S., Boyd, W., & Lloyd, D. (2012). Using Web 2.0 technologies for collaborative learning in dis-tance education—Case studies from an Australian University. *Future Internet*, *4*(4), 216–237. doi:10.3390/fi4010216

Drew, B., & Waters, J. (1986). Video games: Utilization of a novel strategy to improve perceptual motor skills and cognitive functioning in the non-institutionalized elderly. *Cognitive Rehabilitation*, *4*(2), 26–31.

Dumitrescu, V. M. (2015). *One step ahead: From Web 1.0 to web 2.0 technologies in higher education.* Paper presented at the 4th International Scientific Conference: eLearning and Software for Education: eLSE. Bucharest. Romania: CAROLI, National Defence University Publishing House.

Egenfeldt-Nielsen, S. (2006). Understanding the educational potential of commercial computer games through activity and narratives. In *Understanding Video Games*. http://game-research.com/index.php/articles/understanding-the-educational-potential-of-commercial-computer-games-through-activity-and-narratives/

Farley, H., Murphy, A., Johnson, C., Carter, B., Lane, M., Midgley, W., Hafeez-Baig, A., Dekeyser, S., & Koronios, A. (2015). How do students use their mobile devices to support learning? A Case study from an Australian Regional University. *Journal of Interactive Media in Education*, *2015*(1), 14. doi:10.5334/jime.ar

Fouts, J. T. (2000). *Research on computers and education: Past, present, and future. A report to the Bill and Melinda Gates Foundation*. Seattle Pacific University.

Froese, A. D., Carpenter, C., Inman, D. A., Schooley, J., Barnes, R., Brecht, P. W., & Chacon, J. D. (2012). Effects of Classroom Cell Phone Use on Expected and Actual Learning. *College Student Journal*, *46*(2), 323–332.

Gagne, R. M. (1977). *The Conditions of Learning*. Holt, Rinehart and Winston.

Green, C. S., & Bavelier, D. (2012). Learning, Attentional Control, and Action Video Games. *Current Biology*, *22*(6), R197–R206. doi:10.1016/j.cub.2012.02.012 PMID:22440805

Grosseck, G. (2009). To use or not to use web 2.0. in higher education? *Procedia: Social and Behavioral Sciences*, *1*(1), 478–482. doi:10.1016/j.sbspro.2009.01.087

Gulsecen, S., Ozdemir, S., Gezer, M., & Akadal, E. (2015). The Good Reader of Digital World, Digital Natives: Are They Good Writer Also? *Procedia: Social and Behavioral Sciences*, *191*, 2396–2401. doi:10.1016/j.sbspro.2015.04.444

Hagman, J. D. (1980). *Effects of Presentation and Test Trial Training on Acquisition and Retention of Movement End Location*. DTIC Document. doi:10.21236/ADA100867

Hicks, A., & Graber, A. (2010). Shifting paradigms: Teaching, learning and Web 2.0. *RSR. Reference Services Review*, *38*(4), 621–633. doi:10.1108/00907321011090764

Howe, N., & Strauss, W. (2007). *Millennials & K-12 Schools: Educational Strategies for a New Generation*. LifeCourse Associates.

Hughes, G. (2009). Social software: New opportunities for challenging social inequalities in learning? *Learning, Media and Technology, 34*(4), 291–305. doi:10.1080/17439880903338580

Insteford, E. J., & Munthe, E. (2017). Educating digitally competent teachers: A study of integration of professional digital competence in teacher education. *Teaching and Teacher Education, 67,* 37–45. doi:10.1016/j.tate.2017.05.016

Ivala, E., & Gachago, D. (2012). Social media for enhancing student engagement: The use of Facebook and blogs at a University of Technology. *South African Journal of Higher Education, 26*(1), 152–166.

Johnson, G. M. (2008). Cognitive processing differences between frequent and infrequent Internet users. *Computers in Human Behavior, 24*(5), 2094–2106. doi:10.1016/j.chb.2007.10.001

Jones, S., & Fox, S. (2009). *Generations online in 2009.* Pew Internet and American Life Project. Available at: https://pewinternet.org/PPF/r/251/presentation_display.asp

Jussila, J. J., Kärkkäinen, H., & Aramo-Immonen, H. (2014). Social media utilization in business-to-business relationships of technology industry frms. *Computers in Human Behavior, 30,* 606–613. doi:10.1016/j.chb.2013.07.047

Kane, M. J., Hambrick, D. Z., Tuholski, S. W., Wilhelm, O., Payne, T. W., & Engle, R. W. (2004). The Generality of Working Memory Capacity: A Latent-Variable Approach to Verbal and Visuospatial Memory Span and Reasoning. *Journal of Experimental Psychology. General, 133*(2), 189–217. doi:10.1037/0096-3445.133.2.189 PMID:15149250

Karkoulia, K. C. (2016). Teachers' attitudes towards the integration of Web 2.0 tools in EFL teaching. *Research Papers in Language Teaching and Learning, 1*(7), 46–73.

Karunasena, A., Deng, H., & Zhang, X. (2012). *A Web 2.0 based e-learning success model in higher education.* Available at: http://www.ier-institute.org/2070-1918/lnit23/v23/177.pdf

Kim, H. B. (2013). The study on the relationship between smartphone addiction and cyber-crime. *Korean Association of Addiction Crime Review, 3*(2), 1–21.

Kirschner, P., & Woperies, I. G. J. H. (2003). Mind tools for teacher communities: A European perspective. *Technology, Pedagogy and Education, 12*(1), 127–149. doi:10.1080/14759390300200148

Kirschner, P. A., & Karpinski, A. C. (2010). Facebook® and academic performance. *Computers in Human Behavior, 26*(6), 1237–1245. doi:10.1016/j.chb.2010.03.024

Klopfer, E., Osterweil, S., Groff, J., & Haas, J. (2009). *Using the technology of today, in the classroom today. The Instructional Power of digital games, social networking, simulations and How Teachers Can Leverage Them.* Massachusetts Institute of Technology, The Education Arcade.

Koshi, L. (2013). Web based education. *University News, 51*(29), 14–16.

Lei, J. (2009). Digital Natives As Preservice Teachers What Technology Preparation Is Needed? *Journal of Computing in Teacher Education, 25*(3), 87–97.

Lemke, C., & Coughlin, E. C. (1998). *Technology in American Schools. Seven dimensions for gauging progress.* Milken Exchange Commission on Educational Technology. Available at. https://files.eric.ed.gov/fulltext/ED460677.pdf

Lenhard, A., & Madden, M. (2005). *Pew Internet & American Life Project. Reports. Family, friends & community. Teen content creators and consumers.* Retrieved December 10th, 2006 from http://www.pewinternet.org/pdfs/PIP_Teens_Content_Creation.pdf

Marttunen, M., & Laurinen, L. (2001). Learning of Argumentation Skills in Networked and Face-to-face environments. *Journal of Instructional Science, 29*(2), 127–153. doi:10.1023/A:1003931514884

Mata, L., Panisoara, G., Fat, S., Panisoara, I. O., & Lazar, I. (2019). Exploring the Adoptions by Students of Web 2.0 Tools for E-Learning in Higher Education: Web 2.0 Tools for E-Learning in Higher Education. Advanced Web Applications and Progressing E-Learning 2.0 Technologies in Higher Education, 128-149.

Mayer, R. E. (2014). Cognitive theory of multimedia learning. In The Cambridge Handbook of multimedia learning. Cambridge University Press. doi:10.1017/CBO9781139547369.005

Mazman, S. G., & Usluel, Y. K. (2010). Modeling educational usage of Facebook. *Computers & Education, 55*(2), 444–453. doi:10.1016/j.compedu.2010.02.008

Mitchell, A. (2007). Get real! – Reviewing the design of a mobile learning game. In N. Pachler (Ed.), *Mobile learning – Towards a research agenda* (pp. 75–104). The WLE Centre.

Mitchell, K. J., Becker-Blease, K. A., & Finkelhor, D. (2005). Inventory of problematic internet experiences encountered in clinical practice. *Professional Psychology, Research and Practice, 36*(5), 498–509. doi:10.1037/0735-7028.36.5.498

Nabal-Heller, N., Raviv, S., Lidor, R., & Levianne, Z. (1999). *Guided movement activity aimed at motor development.* Reches.

Naidu, S. (2006). *E-Learning: A Guidebook of Principles, Procedures and Practices* (2nd Revised Edition). CEMCA.

Nelson, M. J., Voithofer, R., & Cheng, S.-L. (2019). Mediating factors that influence the technology integration practices of teacher educators. *Computers & Education, 128*, 330–344. doi:10.1016/j.compedu.2018.09.023

Nicholas, D., Rowlands, I., Clark, D., & Williams, P. (2011). Google Generation II: Web behaviour experiments with the BBC. *Aslib Proceedings, 63*(1), 28–45. doi:10.1108/00012531111103768

Oblinger, D., & Oblinger, J. L. (2005). *Educating the Net Generation.* Boulder, CO: Educause. Retrieved March 19, 208, from https://www.educause.edu/educatingthenetgen/

Palfrey, J. G., & Gasser, U. (2011). Born Digital: Understanding the First Generation of Digital Natives. New York: ReadHowYouWant.com.

Palloff, R. M., & Pratt, K. (2004). *Collaborating Online: Learning Together in Community* (1st ed.). Jossey-Bass.

Pea, R. D. (1985). Beyond amplification: Using the computer to reorganize mental functioning. *Educational Psychologist, 20*(4), 167–182. doi:10.120715326985ep2004_2

Penny, K. I. (2011). Factors that Influence Student E-learning Participation in a UK Higher Education Institution. *Interdisciplinary Journal of E-Learning and Learning Objects, 7,* 81–95. doi:10.28945/1377

Petersen, E., & Petersen, K. (2000). E-Parenting: Using the Internet and Computers to be a Better Parent. Macmillan Published Co

Pirâu, M. (2008). Introducere în pedagogie. Editura Risoprint.

Pitler, H., Hubbell, E., Kuhn, M., & Malenoski, K. (2007). *Using technology with classroom instruction that works*. ASCD.

Prensky, M. (2009). H. Sapiens Digital: From Digital Immigrants and Digital Natives to Digital Wisdom. *Innovate: Journal of Online Education, 5*(3). Retrieved March 4, 2020 from https://www.learntechlib.org/p/104264/

Puybaraud, M. (2012). *Digital Natives: A Tech-Savvy Generation Enters the Workplace*. WorkDesign Magazine. http://workdesign.com/2012/02/digital-natives-a-tech-savvy-generation-enters-the-workplace/

Rahwan, I., Krasnoshtan, D., Shariff, A., & Bonnefon, J.-F. (2014). Analytical reasoning task reveals limits of social learning in networks. *Journal of the Royal Society, Interface/the Royal Society, 11*(93).

Rensselaer Polytechnic Institute Lighting Research Centre. (2012). *Can't sleep? Turn off your iPad*. The Times.

Rovai, A. P. (2004). A constructivist approach to online college learning. *The Internet and Higher Education, 7*(2), 79–93. doi:10.1016/j.iheduc.2003.10.002

Safran, C., Helic, D., & Gütl, C. (2007*). E-Learning practices and Web 2.0. In Proceedings of the International Conference of 'Interactive computer aided learning' ICL2007: E-Portofolio and Quality in e-Learning*. Available at: https://halshs.archives-ouvertes.fr/hal-00197260/

Salomon, G. (1993). On the nature of pedagogic computer tools. The case of the wiring partner. In S. P. LaJoie & S. J. Derry (Eds.), *Computers as cognitive tools* (pp. 179–196). Lawrence Erlbaum Associates.

Schlickum, M. K., Hedman, L., Enochsson, L., Kjellin, A., & Felländer-Tsai, L. (2009). Systematic video game training in surgical novices improves performance in virtual reality endoscopic surgical simulators: A prospective randomized study. *World Journal of Surgery, 33*(11), 2360–2367. doi:10.100700268-009-0151-y PMID:19649553

Schmitz, B. (2014). *Mobile games for learning: A pattern-based approach* (PhD thesis, Open University, SIKS Dissertation Series No. 2014-45, Datawyse). Retrieved from http:// dspace.ou.nl/bitstream/1820/5833/6/Thesis%20BSZ_print.pdf

Sherborne, V. (2001). *Developmental movement for children*. Worth Publishing Ltd.

Silva, A.L. (2014). *A. N. Leontiev And The Critical To "Learning To Learn"*. School Physical Education Teaching.

Sparrow, B., Liu, J., & Wegner, D. M. (2011). Google effects on memory: Cognitive consequences of having information at our fingertips. *Science, 333*(6043), 776–778. doi:10.1126cience.1207745 PMID:21764755

Squire, K. (2003). *Video Games in Education. International Journal of Intelligent Games & Simulations.* https://pdfs.semanticscholar.org/72fa/723394b80532947b19ecf9aa3039d12af5e3.pdf?_ga=2.260854669.1850271032.1583530991-573723792.1583530991

Stoica, M. (2001). *Pedagogie și Psihologie pentru Examenele de definitivare și Grade didactice: profesori, institutori / învățători, studenți și elevi ai școlilor normale.* Editura Gheorghe Alexandru.

Stratham, D. S., & Torell, C. R. (1996). *Computers in the classroom: The impact of technology on student learning.* Army Research Institute.

Strawbridge, F. (2010). *Is there a case for Web 2.0 in higher education? Do the benefits outweigh the risks?* Available at: http://online.education.ed.ac.uk/gallery/strawbridge_web_2.pdf

Summer, M., & Hosterler, D. (2002). A Comparative Study of Computer Conferencing and Face-to-face Communications in Systems Designs. *Journal of Interactive Learning Research, 13*(3), 277–291.

Taimalu, M., & Luik, P. (2019). The impact of beliefs and knowledge on the integration of technology among teacher educators: A path analysis. *Teaching and Teacher Education, 79*, 101–110. doi:10.1016/j.tate.2018.12.012

Thomas, H. (2010). Learning spaces, learning environments and the dis'placement' of learning. *British Journal of Educational Technology, 41*(3), 502–511. doi:10.1111/j.1467-8535.2009.00974.x

Thorndike, E. L. (1983). *Învățarea umană.* EDP.

Ullrich, C., Borau, K., Luo, H., Tan, X., Shen, L., & Shen, R. (2008). Why Web 2.0 is Good for Learning and for Research: Principles and Prototypes. In *Proceedings of the 17th International World Wide Web Conference* (pp. 705-714). ACM. 10.1145/1367497.1367593

Venkatesh, V., Morris, M. G., Davis, G. B., & Davis, F. D. (2003). User acceptance of information technology: Toward a unified view. *Management Information Systems Quarterly, 27*(3), 425–478. doi:10.2307/30036540

Verčič, A. T., & Verčič, D. (2013). Digital natives and social media. *Public Relations Review, 39*(5), 600–602. doi:10.1016/j.pubrev.2013.08.008

Vygotsky, L. (1978). *Mind in society: The development of higher psychological processes.* Harvard University Press.

Walter, O., & Hen, M. (2012). Sherborne Developmental Movement (SDM) teaching model for pre service teachers. *Support for Learning, 27*(1), 20–30.

Ward, A. F., Duke, K., Gneezy, A., & Bos, M. W. (2017). Brain Drain: The Mere Presence of One's Own Smartphone Reduces Available Cognitive Capacity. *Journal of the Association for Consumer Research, 2*(2), 140–154. doi:10.1086/691462

Wenger, E. (1998). *Communities of practice: Learning, meaning and identity*. Cambridge University Press. doi:10.1017/CBO9780511803932

White, K. F., Gurzick, D., & Lutters, W. G. (2009). Wiki anxiety: Impediments to implementing wikis for IT support groups. *Proceedings of the 2009 Symposium on Computer Human Interaction for the Management of Information Technology*, 64. 10.1145/1641587.1641597

Wilkinson, A., Forbes, A., Bloomfield, J., & Gee, C. F. (2004). An exploration of four webbased open and flexible learning modules in post-registration nurse education. *International Journal of Nursing Studies*, *41*(4), 411–424. doi:10.1016/j.ijnurstu.2003.11.001 PMID:15050852

Williams, A. M. (2015). *Soft Skills perceived by students and employers as relevant employability skills* (Doctoral dissertation). Walden University.

Wilmer, H. H., Shermann, L. E., & Chein, J. M. (2017). Smartphones and Cognition: A Review of Research Exploring the Links between Mobile Technology Habits and Cognitive Functioning. *Frontiers in Psychology*, *8*, 605. doi:10.3389/fpsyg.2017.00605 PMID:28487665

Wilson, A. (2015). *YouTube in the Classroom* (Unpublished Master thesis). The University of Toronto, Toronto, Canada.

Winge, T. M., & Embry, M. C. (2013). Fashion Design Podcast Initiative: Emerging Technologies and Fashion Design Teaching Strategies. In Increasing Student Engagement and Retention Using Mobile Applications: Smartphones, Skype and Texting Technologies. Cutting-Edge Technologies in Higher Education. Volume 6D. Emerald Group Publishing Limited. doi:10.1108/S2044-9968(2013)000006D008

World Economic Forum. (2015). *New Vision for Education: Unlocking the Potential of Technology*. Author.

ADDITIONAL READING

Bingimlas, K. A. (2017, July). Learning and Teaching with Web 2.0 Applications in Saudi K-12 Schools. *The Turkish Online Journal of Educational Technology*, *16*(3), 100–115.

Duffy, P. (2008). Engaging the YouTube Google-eyed generation: Strategies for using Web 2.0 in teaching and learning. *Electronic Journal of E-learning*, *6*(2), 119–130.

Elzarka, S. (2012). Technology use in higher education instruction. The Claremont Graduate University. CGU Theses & Dissertations. Paper 39. doi:10.5642/cguetd/39

Faboya, O. T., & Adamu, B. J. (2017). Integrating Web 2.0 Tools into Teaching and Learning Process through Mobile Device Technology in Nigerian Schools: Current Status and Future Directions. *International Journal of Education and Research*, *5*(5), 113–124.

Grosseck, G. (2009). To use or not to use web 2.0 in higher education? *Procedia: Social and Behavioral Sciences*, *1*(1), 478–482. doi:10.1016/j.sbspro.2009.01.087

Huang, W.-H. D., Hood, D. W., & Yoo, S. J. (2013). Gender divide and acceptance of collaborative Web 2.0 applications for learning in higher education. *The Internet and Higher Education, 16,* 57–65. doi:10.1016/j.iheduc.2012.02.001

Malecela, I. O., & Syed Hassan, S. S. (2019). Investigating web 2.0 tools use and students cognitive engagement in selected Tanzanian higher institutions: preparing towards 21st learning. International Journal of Advanced Engineering Research and Science (IJAERS), 6 (1). pp. 173-183. ISSN 2349-6495 E-ISSN 2456-1908

Malhiwsky, D. R. (2010). *Student achievement using web 2.0 technologies: a mixed methods study.* Public Access Theses and Dissertations from the College of Education and Human Sciences. 58. https://digitalcommons.unl.edu/cehsdiss/58

Newland, B., & Byles, L. (2014). Changing academic teaching with Web 2.0 technologies. *Innovations in Education and Teaching International, 51*(3), 315–325. doi:10.1080/14703297.2013.796727

Paily, M. U. (2013). *Creating Constructivist Learning Environment: Role of "Web 2.0" Technology.* International Forum of Teaching and Studies Vol. 9, 1.

KEY TERMS AND DEFINITIONS

Cognitive Learning: is a type of active, constructive, and long-lasting learning that engages students in the learning processes, teaching them to use their brains more effectively and to make connections when learning new things.

Digital Technologies: Represent information used or disseminated through a computer, mainly aimed at developing intelligent processes.

Net Generation: Refers to students who were born after 1980 and were digitally literate.

Technological Device: Means any computer, mobile phone, smartphone, which helps in carrying out school tasks.

Technological Integration: Is defined as the use of technological tools in the educational environment to improve and support the teaching-learning-evaluation process.

University Students: Are persons who take the courses of a university or a higher education institute.

Web 2.0 Tools: Are web applications that facilitate the interactive exchange of information, user-centred designs and collaboration on the Internet.

Chapter 11
Customer Experience:
The New Competitive Advantage for Companies That Want Their Customer at the Center of Their Business

Ilenia Vidili

The Smarter Crew, Italy

ABSTRACT

The impact of increasing advancement in digital technologies is driving massive changes in contemporary business enterprises affecting every dimension of society, especially the way individuals buy, research, and interact with one another and with leading brands. This chapter explores case studies of specific leading brands to illustrate this principle with the purpose of better understanding how end-to-end customer experiences (CXs) can be maintained and improved. It begins with a detailed example of the cost of not adapting to the evolving changes in consumer behaviour, specifically the expectations of new generations of "digital natives" with a focus on the user experience (UX). This is followed by an analysis of six customer experience (CX) principles that deliver value, relevance, and superior CXs. Finally, this chapter highlights the importance of embracing a holistic customer-centric culture and offers valuable considerations for businesses seeking to make customer experience their new competitive advantage.

INTRODUCTION

The advent of the internet and the consequent digital revolution has provided every industry with a vast proliferation of businesses selling similar products and services. Over the years research shows the "paradox of choice", whereby more options for consumers lead to poorer outcomes (Scheibehenne et al., 2010). Across contemporary industries, the main differentiator is no longer products, but experiences that complement products (Abramovich, 2018). For centuries businesses ruled by logical, rational decision makers, with no room for emotions, (Norman, 2004, p.10) even as customers were driven by impulse, by emotions and by subconscious compulsions (Zaltman, 2003, p.8). This chapter argues for

DOI: 10.4018/978-1-7998-3756-5.ch011

the importance of embracing a customer experience strategy within organizations, which requires an understanding of the customer's needs and wants where circumstances change with time. This chapter analyzes how and why Waveix (fictitious name) a technology camera-related empire with historic basis on photography missed the turn and filed for bankruptcy in 2012. Many companies stubbornly follow the same strategy for decades without realizing that the land under their feet changes quickly. This is exactly what happened to the photography company.

This chapter introduces some issues and concepts that lie at the heart of the shift in business dynamics, especially that of the changes in consumer behavior. As such an understanding of multi-generational behavior is very important for the success of customer experience planning. Therefore, the author will briefly examine two important generations, Millennials and Generation Z, and how these generations have been transforming the way businesses operate. The main aim is to deliver a strong understanding of the customer experience with a focus on the user experience in this time of increasingly complex and changing consumer behavior. After years of research, the author of this chapter wants to describe how customer experience consultants helped We Love Dogs (fictitious name), a dog accessories brand to regain trust and relevance by integrating six important principles for a superior customer experience strategy. The customer experience strategy was a plan of 12 months that included constant hard work from both teams and continuous improvement over time.

BACKGROUND

Three industrial revolutions and the rise of new technologies and novel ways of perceiving the world have together caused a deep change in modern economic and social structures (Schwab, 2016, p.11). In the contemporary milieu, autonomous vehicles, digital personal assistants, robots in restaurants and clinics, wearable technologies, smart homes, 3D printing, and voice activated devices are fundamentally changing not only the lives of individuals but also the way businesses operate. In fact, Jagdish Seth (1972) predicted that the theory of buyer behavior grows rapidly and broadens alongside these changes. Unfortunately, many companies today are not agile enough to reconfigure, re-engineer or adapt to consumer expectations and market demand or as fast as their competitors (Goodwin, 2018, p.2). For centuries big companies benefited by the advantage of their size, however the internet and the changes in business dynamics means that historical heritage is becoming more of a liability for brands as it makes the change and adaptation harder. Today, the main challenge for businesses is to deal with the repercussions of the ever evolving digital era: specifically, the loss of customer relationships, increased competition and the speed in which companies may lose their competitive advantage in this commoditized world (Ernst & Young, pp.1-8).

MAIN FOCUS OF THE CHAPTER

When the Land Turns Upside Down for Waveix

Over the past few decades technology brought many changes and led to great opportunities such as greater flexibility, reactivity and product individualization, however it has also brought significant challenges in the 2010s, such as rapid technological change, increased legal requirements and changing customer preferences. As a result of this, companies can achieve success in terms of reduced costs, experiencing optimized resource utilization, increased employee productivity, increased customer loyalty and satisfaction and optimized supply chains (Rachinger et al., 2019, pp.1143-1160)

Digital disruption describes a process whereby a smaller company with fewer resources is able to successfully challenge established incumbent businesses (Christensen et al., 2015). In this phenomenon new business models replace traditional ones in ever shorter time intervals. Many established companies are struggling as they underestimate the dynamics, react not quick enough and persist with their existing business models (Matzler et al., 2018).

In the past decades businesses and individuals have seen three stages of the digital evolution. In the first stage the world-wide-web was not spread yet and information was only available on tangible paper. Companies set up in this phase, also called incumbents, have a very good basis of their products, service and organization but lack in the understanding of how digital can help both technically and the customer side of the company. In the second stage, the birth of the internet and mobile technologies started to influence (Belleghem, 2017, p.1981) customers, with pervasive access to information and multiple channels to choose from. Companies that were set up in this phase still have early technologies as their foundations that quickly became obsolete, facing the innovation dilemma. In the last stage, automation and artificial intelligence are largely part of companies. Those companies that are set up in this phase are the youngest generation of companies, also called disruptors, created in response to the latest technological developments (Belleghem, 2017, p.1981). The key feature of these companies is that they are fully digitized and have drastically disrupted established companies and industries by putting digital technology at the center of their businesses. With a focus on convenient services, appetible content that caters to millennials and personalized customer experiences, these companies are growing incredibly fast (Morgan, 2019). Slow technological adoption by market incumbents coupled with the fast paced changes in consumer behavior, leave a massive opportunity for disrupters to shape agile business models, as a result that the existing ones become obsolete (Souto, 2015; Matzler et al., 2016). Companies can be successful over time if they can adapt to their environment. To increase the success of the designed business model on the market, the company must analyze various alternatives and have a good understanding of customer requirements so as to deliver what customers need as cost-effectively as possible and on time (Teece, 2018)

Waveix was a film and photography company born in the first phase that enjoyed a sheltered and highly lucrative market position in the industry. Its products, machinery and expertise were not easy to imitate, however the digital cameras do not use film technology, therefore easily replicable by competitors. The power of the digital camera was immense and opened a new phase in the evolution of photography, providing customers a more compact, convenient and versatile piece of technology (Price et al 2018) In 2007 a smartphones brand offered the ability to take increasingly clear and high-quality images and by 2008 third-party picture sharing tools enabled users to share them digitally on various social media platforms (Ratner, 2019)

Waveix was aware of the threat of digital imaging and spent considerable time and resources trying to catch up with the storm but unfortunately more agile disruptors were quicker to understand the industry and adapt. Users no longer had to take a photo and wait for days or months before seeing their photos. Moreover, users could take as many photos as they'd like with the only restrictions being their battery life and/or storage capacity (Ratner, 2019). The traditional camera and the technologies that complemented it were largely swept (Jackson, 2011).

The circumstances of Waveix's fall were similar to those of many other companies that were victims of the digital disruption. The digital change and consumer behavior shift hit the ground so fast that the photography brand had to quickly choose whether framing itself as a chemical film company vs. an imaging company vs. a moment-sharing company. The real disruption occurred with the advent of smartphones and when market behavior shifted from printing pictures to posting them on social media (Anthony, 2016)

It is important to underline though that a strategy that worked well in the past may not work as well in the future because of the constant changes that shape consumer behavior (Blythe, 2013)

According to Bennett (1995) *"the dynamic interaction of affect and cognition, behavior and environmental events by which human beings conduct the exchange aspects of their lives"* can be summarized into consumer behavior. While Waveix invented the digital cameras, it also opted not to invest in it, completely ignoring changes in the needs and wants of its customers as technology advanced. Understanding and adapting to consumer behavior is one of the crucial aspects to the success of a superior CX and UX, which reveals consumer satisfaction or dissatisfaction. The first clear signals of this erosion came visible after a decline in market share, then a more serious undermining in customer satisfaction and eventually the inevitable bankruptcy of Waveix. The digitalization of products created new patterns of consumer behavior which made it possible for older patterns to gradually become obsolete over time. The problem was not so much caused by the shift in technology but rather in the one by the lack of understanding the changes in consumer behavior coupled with the resistance of Waivex to adapt to these changes (Belleghem, 2017, p.1779). With a blind optimism the photography company wasn't able to manage the digital wave of disruption. Although the photography brand invented digital cameras, coming first and being a pioneer was not kind to the company born in this phase.

Consumer Behavior and the Customer Experience

In a world where the smartphone did not exist consumers used to rely on shop assistants for suggestions on products they barely knew existed. The advent of the smartphone, connected devices interrelated in the system of Internet of Things (IoT) and virtual communities have completely revolutionized consumer behavior, societies and organizations with widespread access to information, better social networking, enhanced communication (Kucuk & Krishnamurthy, 2007) and advanced new models of customer power. Today customers are no longer passive receivers of marketing messages - instead, they are using social media channels to spread their positive and negative opinions and emotions (Sinclaire & Vogus, 2011). As new technologies evolved over the past decade to modern-day-multi-tools new patterns of consumer behavior became the new normal (Deloitte, 2019). This means that if decades ago consumers used to go through a linear marketing funnel, today intent-rich moments are creating unique customer journeys (Thygesen, 2018). Therefore brands cannot be managed in a traditional way because traditional marketing no longer influences customer behavior. Brands should manage what drives the brand perception which is the customer experience. Customer and user experience are the reason why a brand is perceived positively or negatively because customers and users gauge the perception of brands upon the experiences they provide (Klaus, 2020)

Bolton (2016) states that *"The customer experience is the sensory, cognitive, emotional, social and behavioral dimensions of all activities that connect the customer and the organization over time across touchpoints and channels. It encompasses all activities involving the customer."*

Over the years many factors comprising the customer experience have changed, these are: the time, place, technology and social dimension. Customer experience includes pre-purchase, purchase and post-purchase activities across different channels, technologies and locations (i.e. the real store, website or mobile application) and also in relation to the people inside and outside the organization, such as other customers, employees, friends or virtual community members (Koetz, 2019). The user experience is the process of increasing customer satisfaction by improving the usability and ease of use - be it a product or website and the interaction with the customer. i.e. how easy it is for the user to complete the desired task (Pappas et al., 2018, p.1683)

Customer journeys include many interactions that happen before, during, and after the sale of a product or service. Customer journeys can be long and can be stretched by the consumer across multiple channels and touchpoints (Maechler et al., 2016). However, these customer journeys are quickly becoming obsolete given the dynamic advancement in digital technologies, changes in customer behavior, and the competitive landscape. This is happening in both business-to-consumer and business-to-business models. Consumers compare their prior perception of the business and have their opinion of the business only when they interact with the touchpoints (Stein & Ramaseshan, 2016). Perceptions and opinions of customers are mainly influenced by the interaction with the touchpoints, which can be positive or negative (Meyer & Schwager, 2007). Customer perception is considered a strong predictor of buying behavior and it increases customers' willingness to buy and increases loyal behavior (Makri, 2019)

Customer experience's main focus is engaging with humans and that means understanding their behavior, their needs, their wants and their emotions. Large enterprises manage customer experience by employing advanced technologies based on virtual, non-human interactions with customers. On the contrary, small businesses with fewer financial and human resources for managing customer experience have the ability to offer human-oriented experiences. Customer experiences are led by two main factors of customer engagement: the first factor is based on establishing long-lasting customer relationships, while the second factor is based on the brand's ability to deliver customized service, flexibility, convenience and accessibility (Gilboa et al., 2019, p.152). Companies and customers interact among the customer journey with a variety of online and offline channels. This interaction between the two has been identified as customer engagement which in marketing practice can be associated with omni-channel experience (Koetz, 2019, p.11)

Relationships morph into long-term collaborations to satisfy customer needs. In this ever-evolving competitive landscape, both technology and customer expectations change fast and retaining existing customers is difficult due to the proliferation of competitive offers and relatively low switching costs. Businesses' success is led by interacting with existing and potential customers and delivering superior customer experiences (Ciuchita et al., 2019, p.130). Successful customer and user experiences lead to customer satisfaction which consequently establishes a brand trust relationship with the customer (Yasin, 2019, p.5). They occur when the gap between customers' expectations and their subsequent experiences has been closed (Meyer, & Schwager, 2007). Oliver et al., (1997) revealed that positive emotions lead to higher levels of customer satisfaction and increase repurchase intentions which is equal to loyalty. Consumer trust is central to online and offline loyalty as trusting a brand leads customers toward increasing their loyalty to that brand (Yasin, 2019, p.5)

The very essence of a company is that it delivers on its promises, however consumer trust in brands has declined around the world in recent decades, especially among the new generations of consumers. In a study conducted by Edelman (2019) among 16,000 respondents only 34 percent said that they trust brands. Only 21 percent of respondents know from personal experience that the brands they use keep the best interests of society in mind and 56 percent said that too many brands are using societal issues as a marketing tool. As a result, trust has become a major concern among companies and it is one of the key factors to consider when improving customer experience (Rajavi et al., 2019, p.651) and user experience.

Today consumers trust information from online sources, including anonymous internet users, more than information from the company itself. This means that electronic word of mouth is perceived to have more credibility and have more influence over purchasing decisions than traditional marketing, assuming the same level of exposure to the message (Nowak & McGloin, 2014). The way consumers research products and services into their daily life is completely changed. Online information of any kind (i.e. blogs, emails, online communities, and social media) is integrated into their purchasing decision and gives consumers the chance to interact, read information, share opinions and influence beliefs and behaviors.

Fishbein & Ajzen (1975) study shows that humans are rational rather than impulsive and their consumption would also be made by a rational decision-making process, however consumers are often non-rational. People often purchase a product or service not because they need it but because they want it (Kang, 2020). Theories of motivation are useful for businesses as they provide insights into the motives of customers. Maslow's hierarchy of needs studies how humans stipulate a natural progression from physiological needs to higher, self-actualization wants (Maslow,1954). In the case of the photography brand, if taking traditional photos for its customers was a belongingness need as described in level three of Maslow's hierarchy, the technological and behavioral shift to digital cameras and smartphone cameras subsequently moved customers' needs to the higher level of Maslow's hierarchy. This level is called *Esteem* and it symbolizes the desire for status, importance and respect from others, which is exactly what sharing digital photos on social media channels may be able to do. In his paper Abraham Maslow revealed that human needs formed a hierarchy from the most basic to the most complex need. He suggested that the most basic needs must be fulfilled before higher level needs can be met satisfactorily (Maslow,1943)

Figure 1. Maslow's hierarchy of needs, represented as a pyramid with the more basic needs at the bottom
Source: Figure adapted by the author from (Maslow, 1943)

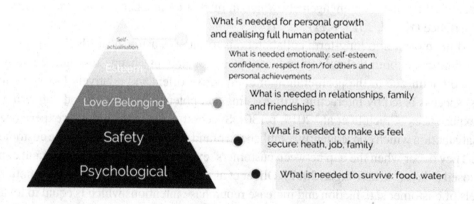

Human desire for self-expression and socialization often push consumers' decisions as customers are emotionally attached to a product (Kang, 2020)

Lerner et al (2015) research reveals that emotions play a vital role in decision-making. Business value is created when a customer is led by emotional activation and perceptions. In order to create this, businesses should understand the cognitive processes and emotions that drive customers toward and away from the brand. By driving customers' emotions, brands can observe how changes to their customer and user experience move customers up or down in the sales funnel (Forrester, 2019). Emotions are essential factors for the customer experience, evaluations and actions of consumers and can be triggered when considering buying, or using a product or services. However, customer emotions don't just drive purchase but they are also very communicative (Kranzbühler et al., 2019). Consumer trust and emotions have an important influence on loyalty and satisfaction which are strong predictors of word-of-mouth (Zenger, 2019). As technology evolves, the number of touchpoints a brand has with their customers increases. This has led to a more immediate communication with consumers but especially to a two-way communication. In this hyper competitive landscape brands need to make sure that every touch point delivers the best customer and user experience possible. This also includes the most important UX factor; a company's website. Decades ago, brands were the only ones to communicate about their products and services to their customers through their means of advertising. Today customers have the voice and power to let brands know how they feel about a certain product or service in a public and effective way.

Perceived credibility of online customer reviews determines customer purchasing behavior. Companies across all industries are steadily building and improving their competitive strategies leveraging the availability and the power of social media platforms. Social media has become one of the most direct and interactive online environments where businesses, their customers and potential customers are able to have a two-way communication providing both business and consumers with many opportunities (Yasin et al., 2020, p.1). The proliferation of channels, especially social media, comes at a very costly price. Negative emotions have a stronger effect on sharing than on purchase behavior, which is potentially alarming for companies (Kranzbühler et al., 2019). Unpleasant online reviews prevent customers to purchase goods or use services in order to avoid the potential risks that's explained and shown in the unpleasant reviewer's experience. Therefore, the likelihood of purchase decreases (Guo & Wu, 2020). When customers are satisfied and feel positive emotions about a product or service this strengthens the customer engagement with the brand and customer engagement creates customer advocacy. Customer advocacy is the tendency of customers to share favorable recommendations of experiences acting as a customer advocate. This behavior comes from a positive engagement and relationship with a brand (Arguello et al., 2020, P.182) and builds trust (Monferrer et al., 2020, p.463). Trust is the foundational element that lies on any emotional connection and relationship between customer-brand (Zenger, 2019)

The Human-Technology Interaction (UX)

Now more than ever, the promise of electronic commerce and online shopping will depend to a great extent upon the interface of how people interact with the computer (Lohse & Spiller, 1998, p.81)

Nowadays the customer experience often comprises the human-machine interaction as a specific emotional experience, (Hassenzahl et al., 2010) also as previously mentioned in this chapter as the user experience.

Desktop and mobile websites with better user experience entice the customer to return to the website and to make e-commerce consumers to remain loyal and to purchase from it. Usability, user-friendliness of the interface, and the rationality of the content displayed on the website all have a positive impact on the user experience during the purchasing process (Cai et al., 2018).

The relation between emotional experience and user experience in human-technology interaction (Mahlke & Thuring, 2007) is affected by the quality of information and system (Zhou et al., 2010). The user experience is believed to cover all aspects of a human-technology experience including design, graphics, interfaces, information quality, system quality, security and privacy. It includes all the emotions, beliefs, preferences, perceptions, physical and psychological behaviors and achievements that occurred before, during and after using something (Bevan, 2009). The user experience has a wide range of theories and research that have been developed across different dimensions. In this chapter the author aims to analyze the information quality, efficiency (mentioned later in this chapter as frictionless), attractiveness and overall customer satisfaction. Website information quality is the perception of a customer toward the quality of information about the product or service provided on the website, which is also the ability to provide its users the information they are looking for (Park & Kim, 2003)

E-commerce site interruptions are equal to lack of efficiency on the sites which often exert a negative effect on user behavior. Interruptions are a break in task activity which distracts the user from continuing the original task and often to a task switch (Zhang et al., 2020)

User experience is associated with User Interface (UI) which has a tangible aspect in e-commerce (Van Riel., 2001) and it is part of the user experience. UX focusses on anything that affects users journeys and solves problems, while UI focusses on the visual appearance, so the attractiveness and design of a website (Muslim et al., 2019) which are the first things that are seen by a user when interacting with an e-commerce site. A good user interface has a positive effect on a customer's intention. If users can use the interface well, they perceive a good user experience and therefore an overall good customer experience, which is the result of higher sales. The quality of an e-commerce website is the key success factor in a user's evaluation of that website which increases customer satisfaction and trust. Customers are satisfied when their needs and wants are fulfilled and satisfied. Customers who are not fully satisfied with an e-commerce brand lack trust which leads them to switch to another competitor (Perrault & McCarthy, 2002)

As with Maslow's hierarchy of needs previously mentioned in this chapter it is essential for a user experience to meet the lowest need on the pyramid before progressing to meet further needs. Figure 2 represents that for a user experience to meet any need it must work and must meet the basic need of the user (*functionality*), however it must also function in a reliable manner and present a consistent experience (*reliability*). This increases the user's perception of the user experience but the design should also be simple and free from any interruptions for a user to have a greater perception (*usability*). Furthermore, a user experience should help the user to do more and achieve more which helps the user to fulfil their needs more effectively (*proficiency*). Lastly, the final step of the pyramid, the user experience should fulfill all other needs with products and systems that are beautiful in terms of interaction, design and function (*creativity*).

The Rise of Customer Expectations and the new Generations of Consumers

As the cultural anthropologist Margaret Mead stated *"Because all the peoples of the world are part of one electronically based, intercommunicating network, young people everywhere share a kind of experience that none of the elders ever had. . . . This break between generations is wholly new: it is planetary and universal."* new generations behave in a completely different way than older generations used to do (Cuzzort & King, 1995)

Figure 2. Maslow's hierarchy of needs represented and adapted to the user experience starting with the more basic user's needs at the bottom
Source: Figure adapted by the author from (Interaction Design Foundation, 2017)

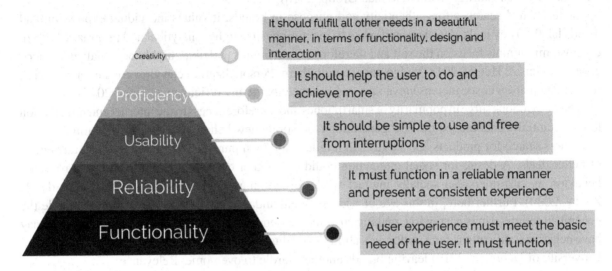

Generations are shaped by the context in which they emerged. The internet economy has enhanced that the age of an individual is an important factor in consumer expectations and has shaped different categories of consumers (Priporas et al., 2017, p.374)

Baby boomers, born between 1940 and 1959, lived in the post–World War II context, grew up as the computer revolution was taking hold and are best represented by consumption as an expression of ideology. Gen Xers, born between 1960 and 1979 consumed status (Francis & Hoefel, 2018). Millennials, born between 1980 and 1994 grew up during the internet explosion (Dimock, 2019) and consumed experiences over things. Generation Z, born between 1995 and 2010 is growing up during the rise of artificial intelligence. The main encouragement to consumption for this generation is the search for the truth in a personal and communal form (Francis & Hoefel, 2018)

This paper analyses the last two generations of consumers applied with the success of customer and user experience, also mentioned in this paper as the new generations. New generations have higher expectations, in fact research shows that only 32 percent of customers say that brands exceed expectations (Miller Heiman Group, 2018). Customer expectations are indicators of customer perception and satisfaction and are customers' beliefs before they can make a purchase about a product or service (Priporas et al., 2017, p.374). However, Klaus (2020) argues that consumers compare their expectations with their experiences or the experience of others.

Over the past two decades the number of consumers shopping online has increased significantly due to the difference in how people exchange information, research and communicate which is mainly through their internet powered devices. New technologies, the rapid evolution of how people communicate and interact shaped these new generations which buy quite differently than older generations do. This requires brands to understand their decision making, priorities and consumption behaviors, (Woo, 2018) as well as adapting to the shifts. What these new generations of consumers want, of course, varies from person to person and especially by culture. However, a number of common wishes can be identified; the first being they want *"experiences"* rather than *"things"* as this would also allow them to interact with the brand and with other consumers. Younger generations are self-educated when it comes to knowing exactly what and where they want things from, meaning that brands have to match their selling process with the customer journey (Miller Heiman Group, 2018)

Generation Z searches for authenticity and purpose in brands, it values individual expression and avoids labels. They make decisions and relate to institutions in a highly analytical and pragmatic way. In contrast, millennials focus on the self and therefore expect brands to deliver highly personalized experiences (Francis & Hoefel, 2018) and to engage with them. Personalization can alter consumer behavior, reduce acquisition costs, increase revenues and enhance marketing efficiency (Ariker, 2015)

The tremendous surge in popularity of smartphones and therefore access to the internet and information has substantially encouraged the new generations to adopt a new behavior called showrooming, where customers search for products and services in retailers and then purchase them online to get advantage of better deals. A desire for social interaction could be another cause that explains the showrooming behavior, as customers can socially interact while researching and purchasing online (Schneider & Zielke, 2020). Furthermore, in this age of widespread abundance of content of any kind available the general attention span is narrowing, making customer patience and time for brands very little. This may have negative implications for a customer's ability to evaluate the information they consume, (Technical University of Denmark, 2019) leaving brands another hurdle to overcome: Relevance

As previously mentioned in this chapter, numerous studies have shown that new generations are less trusting of brands and advertising, and highly likely to turn to friends, family and anonymous social media users for buying recommendations (TrustRadius, 2018). This means that competitiveness for brands gets even harder as trust is low and today it is very easy for customers to switch from one brand to another. The new purchasing behaviors influence the relationship these new generations have with brands. The convergence of the mobile, social and big data megatrends have shaped more empowered consumers, where the balance of power shifted away from the companies and towards the consumers, allowing unprecedented price and choice control. This trend is facing a highly informed, hyper connected, very loyal and extremely global consumer (Venkatachalam, 2014)

Companies should be attuned to four main important things about these two generations: 1) be accessible and responsive at any time showing relevance and value to their customers (Jenkins, 2019), 2) replace mass production for personalization in favor of consumption as an expression of individual identity, 3) as a matter of ethical principles, businesses must have a clear purpose and deliver on their promise to regain trust (Francis & Hoefel, 2018) and 4) providing an omni-channel and frictionless experience (Venkatachalam, 2014)

We Love Dogs Customer Experience

An emphasis on creating a positive customer experience has become a top priority for businesses of different industries across the world. Customer experience has also become one of the top research priorities for the Marketing Science Institute for 2018-2020 (Marketing Science Institute, 2018). As customers' expectations have risen and technologies have evolved in the last decade, customer experience has become a complex strategy to manage that involves the integration of different dimensions and people and constant adaptation to new consumer behavior, business practices as new technologies emerge in the experience economy. Pine & Gilmore (1999) coined the term "experience economy" to refer to the shift in economic value from the focus on products and services to eventually experiences. This paper examines the case study and best practices of customer experience strategy management of We Love Dogs, an e-commerce brand selling dog accessories worldwide. Considering the different elements that a company can map as its touchpoints and adjust them to the evolving consumer behavior and technologies, companies don't have complete control over all touchpoints as some of these can be generated externally by the customer (i.e. online customer reviews), partners (i.e. deliveries) and social (i.e. online communities) (Lemon & Verhoef, 2016). With the help of The Smarter Crew customer experience consultants, We Love Dogs mapped and adjusted a multitude of touchpoints ranging from internal to external and from physical to non physical of the company. It developed a dynamic process of continuously improving engaging touchpoints across the different steps of the customer journey and managed them in a consolidated way to provide a positive omni-channel experience. We Love Dogs was founded by a strong love for a rescued puppy. The company sells home made dog collars, leashes and name tags worldwide providing high quality products. We Love Dogs directly targets the new generations of consumers, millennials and generation Z, women and men between 18 to 39 years old and indirectly targets men and women older than 39 and younger than 18 years of age. The former cohort exerts because these two generations account for 62% of all pet owners in North America, bringing pets in their household earlier than previous generations and delay marriage and babies (Lee, 2019). Furthermore, according to data from market research firm Edge by Ascential shows that sales exceeded $225 billion in 2018 in North America alone, with that number expected to rise to $281 billion by 2023 (Taylor, 2019). By focusing on this cohort We Love Dogs aligns its passion and values with the new generations of consumers for whom a digital lifestyle and technology attitude are expected.

Methodology

Help was needed as We Love Dogs was experiencing poor sales performance and high churn rate, therefore they wanted to improve their end-to-end customer and user experience to increase customer acquisition and conversion, reduce customer churn and improve advocacy.

We Love Dogs conducted a deep research into their customer journey and customer reviews and feedback to determine the customer pain points and unmet needs. One significant core that stood out from the business logic was the need to build trust as the pillar of their CX strategy. With this critical core in mind We Love Dogs used a combination of six principles across four dimensions as the central engine for building their new competitive advantage. The six pillars are not exclusive to one specific dimension but have simultaneously contributed to one or even all dimensions.

Dimension 1: develop a brand purpose based on the customer experience
Dimension 2: create virtual communities
Dimension 3: gain trust and to bond with customers
Dimension 4: create a customer-centric culture in the company

The customer experience plan was split into four stages. The first stage was to reinvigorate the business purpose, the second stage was to focus on identifying what was broken, the third stage was based on adjusting what was creating customer churn and lastly the fourth stage was based on regaining trust and adopting a customer-first strategy across the organization.

Customer experiences based on the below principles are carefully curated and architected; their success lies on the execution of small details as well as on the careful planning and management.

Figure 3. Representation of We Love Dogs customer experience strategy schema

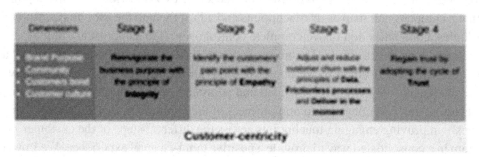

1. Stage one: Reinvigorating

This stage is one of the most important stages of this strategy because it creates an advantage over competitors. Reinvigorating the core of the business creates a company that is purposeful, authentic and deliberate in the experiences it creates. At the heart of the successful delivery of the six principles is an all consuming sense of purpose. In this stage the company embraced the principle of integrity.

a. Principle of Integrity

This is the principle by which a brand finds its mission and its reason for being alive. The modern customer and especially the younger generations of consumers are not just making decisions based on the product selection or price but they prefer to be influenced and associated with brands that have a purpose and that contribute positively to society (Barton et al., 2018). Millennials and Generation Z, are drawn to companies that display values beyond simply the state of convenience. They want to buy from brands that communicate their core beliefs openly and credibly and that are built around a strong and compelling purpose. Customers today have thousands of interactions with companies and through these interactions are looking for a perceived moral code – the core purpose that must align with the values of the consumer (Hernandez et al., 2018)

Purpose is the unique, authentic and defining characteristic that sets the customer and user experiences apart from all others. While it sounds like a big threat for brands. We Love Dogs saw the opportunity to be more authentic and build a deeper relationship with its customers. A foster care program was launched in different cities and resulted in a highly successful program. It built affinity between the customers and the brand, helped dogs in need and helped families find their pet. Customers recognized the meaning of such an initiative and attributed a strong value to the company.

Driven by these values We Love Dogs were very focused on creating an emotional link with their customers. Through the power of social media platforms they committed to creating virtual dog lovers communities which were dedicated to matching dogs from shelters with caring owners. Once a week, an alert of a dog in need was sent out through the social media groups to each member of the communities, where it could be viewed by thousands of like-minded people in hopes that a new home could be found for the pet. When a home couldn't be found, a foster home temporarily adopted the dog in need until an adopter was available. Social media community groups were more effective than traditional advertising methods. Virtual communities exposed the adoptable dogs to thousands of potential new homes, pet lovers or their close friends. Through interactions in the social community a strong bond was formed even between complete strangers which created a strong emotional support within the community. Emotional support is referred to as encouragement, empathy or understanding that is shown between members of a community. Studies show that members that develop emotional support tend to develop emotional reactions which ties them to a community (Handarkho, 2020, p.53). We Love Dogs' brand purpose changed from selling dog accessories to creating meaningful connections dog-dog lover and customer-company. The new generation of consumers don't invest their time, money and attention in companies that just sell products but they rather buy from companies that stand for a purpose which matches with their values. By instilling a sense of brand belonging through a clear and relevant purpose, We Love Dogs was able to create loyalty and affinity, increase market share and gain competitive advantage.

2. Stage two: Identifying

The company had various problems with the service and products that they were providing, customer complaints were increasing, and online reviews were deteriorating. By identifying the customer pain points the company could understand that customers were looking for dog accessories on multiple devices and wanted end-to-end experiences that were relevant and without disjointed issues. We Love Dogs identified what was needed for the e-commerce site to provide a unique and delightful customer and user experience for each of the individuals. The customer experience strategy started by an audit of the customer and user journey to understand the customers' purchasing flow which taught the touchpoints that worked well and those that did not, looking at the internal, external, physical and digital factors. The audit made the customer journey issues visible, showing that problems emerged at the system quality, conversion and the advocacy. In this stage the company embraced the principle of empathy.

a. Principle of Empathy

Empathy allows businesses to walk in their customers' shoes. In customer experience design, this means understanding customers' needs and desires and taking care of them before they reach a potential "pain point" in their customer journey. The rapid rise of artificial intelligence followed by automation of processes means that empathy and the ability to understand consumers on a deeper level became a crucial factor of the nature of customer experience (KPMG Nunwood, 2018). The customer experience strategy for the pet brand included reviewing thousands of customer comments over the web as well as building an empathy map which helped to understand customers' emotions. This is tied within four buckets: what they think and feel; see; say and do; and hear (Rembach, 2017). The empathy map helped the pet brand to develop the emotional capacity to understand their customers' experience. This was crucial to establishing a deep rapport and involved reflecting back to the customer, understanding their circumstances and doing an extra step as a result. We Love Dogs restructured the company and used new technologies with the aim of getting closer to the customer, focusing on understanding their customers' expectations and connecting across channels to deliver them. It also realigned their model in developing positive connections with customers and fostering long-term relationships. To achieve this, it designed a loyalty program that offers products rewards which motivates people to spend more. The company made personalized product recommendations based on previous shopping behavior and on personal information, such as dog type, size, color etc. shared by the user, in order to make the loyalty program more appealing and tailored to the customer's needs and wants. Customers earned points when referring friends, when purchasing for the first time, when sharing their purchases on social media. The accumulation of points awarded customers with available pet accessories of their choice. This system rewarded the most loyal customers and created a bond with the customer.

3.   Stage three: Adjusting

This stage was about fixing what wasn't working and what was stopping customers to buy products from We Love Dogs. Three important principles were successfully applied to do this stage. We Love Dogs successfully integrated its website, mobile and social media presence to provide an enhanced shopping experience focused on digital engagement. This was done across all stages of the customer and user journey: pre-purchase, during-purchase and post-purchase touchpoints. The company connected technology and the following three principles across all stages of the CX strategy plan to constantly follow their consumers trends, meeting and exceeding expectations and minimizing customer effort.

a.   Principle of Data

Customer research has shown that messages, ads and products that match consumers characteristics are viewed more favorably and made ads more persuasive. Research in human-computer interaction suggests an increase in sales when information quality was adjusted to a users cognitive style based on mainstream data (De Bellis et al 2019). Since today's customers expectations are increasing, companies should develop big-data analytical capabilities for understanding and potentially personalizing the customer and user journey (Kooge & Walk, 2016; Wedel & Kannan, 2016). Customers' emotions and trust are critical for a successful personalized online user experience and better assess on customers' purchase intentions. However, if the customer is not happy about the offered personalized service, trusting a brand alone is not enough (Pappas et al., 2018). We Love Dogs constantly interacted with their customers to capture their preferences and emotions which could have been mixed based on the user experience, therefore the company invested in mechanisms that captured emotions with mouse clicking mapping. This helped to determine the reason between high, medium and low intention to buy and adjust accordingly. A forecast carried out by Statista Research Department (2019) suggests that by 2020 there will be 6.58 connected devices per person. Data from customers' connected devices has enabled We Love Dogs to create a seamless and omnichannel experience. Using the power of data coupled with innovative technologies such as Natural Language Processing (NLP) the company could dig deeper than ever before, analyzing new data sets and gaining a comprehensive view of the user journey. Collecting and analyzing customer data allowed the pet brand to implement data segmentation activities in order to communicate more relevant messages to each segment identified. However, segmenting clusters of customers is an obsolete practice that worked well in the past, since the modern customers today expect high levels of personalization, We Love Dogs made good use of all the collected data to deliver a highly personalized experience. The pet brand capitalized on this principle, increasing brand presence in their customers' everyday lives to better understand their behaviors and preferences in order to deliver personalized experiences and build brand trust. We Love Dogs embedded new technologies that helped with the use of customer name, individualized attention, knowledge of preferences and past interactions. It adopted high-tech algorithms that made it possible to recommend appropriate products based on a customer's previous purchases and browsing history. The company now demonstrates that it understands the customers' specific circumstances and can adapt their user experience accordingly. All this delivered a high level of user experiences that felt personal, predicted behaviors and created a stronger relationship with the customer. Collecting and analyzing data also showed the pet company what wasn't working in their user journey, for example both websites (desktop and mobile).

b.   Principle of Frictionless processes

As technology developments have expanded expectations, (Larivière et al., 2017) by improving how customers and users interact with the product through new design and features may enhance the user experience (Barrett, 2015) and therefore customer experience altogether. User Experience is the process of increasing customer satisfaction by improving the usability and ease of use - be it a product or website and the interaction with the customer. i.e. how easy it is for the user to complete the desired task. Shopping online induces various emotions to customers: i.e. happiness, anxiety, sadness, anger. These emotions are determined by user behavior when using interfaces and websites, therefore customer behavior is likely to differ based on these emotions. Happiness will most likely increase intention to shop online, while anger or anxiety may lead to the opposite (Pappas et al., 2018, p.1683)

When a company provides a new version of a product or website, it creates change in how the e-service looks and what customers can do with it. Customers must then use the new version in order to complete the task for which they have been using the e-service (Ciuchita et al., 2019, p.131) - i.e. shopping online.

We Love Dogs' websites presented a lack of efficiency, with multiple frictions and interruptions during the buying process, which decreased sales and customer satisfaction. As customers have less time and are constantly looking for instant gratification, it was necessary to remove obstacles and impediments to enable them to achieve their objectives quickly and easily which has shown to increase customers loyalty. Optimizing customers' time during their purchasing processes and showing them that the company valued their time was a source of added value for We Love Dogs. The elements that contributed to the overall success of the user experience were: 1) the re-design of the desktop website and the mobile website to increase their attractiveness, 2) increased efficiency with effortless purchasing steps: these were reduced from 12 unclear steps to 5 easy and intuitive steps. 3) improved speed of both websites' versions, 4) personalization of products and content. A whole new branding and attractiveness work was done for both the company's website and mobile site to increase user attraction and user performance using colors that were more appealing to pet accessories consumers and a design that was clean and focused on the e-commerce user experience design. Consumers associate different colors with different meanings, which create different effects on the user experience evaluation (Xu et al 2019). The navigation of the sites was simplified, better organized and more responsive. The product detail pages were less cluttered but informative with visible "add to cart button" and beautiful images and videos of the products. To reinforce the above, according to Adobe 38% of online shoppers will leave a website if they find the design to be unattractive, 61 percent of users are unlikely to return to a website they had trouble accessing, and 40 percent end up visiting a competitor's website instead (Aufreiter et al., 2014)

c.   Principle of Delivering in the moment

By combining a strong focus on a real-time presence the pet brand could achieve two things which enhanced the brand: 1) it delighted customers right then, and 2) showed responsiveness. We Love Dogs created a real-time functionality that met the needs of its tech savvy consumers, offering them the function that if an information or product of their interest became available, when they accumulated points in the loyalty program and when products where available to purchase they would be notified in real-time. Support tickets issued in case of lack of functionality were actioned immediately. The company restructured their content plan to convey clearer and more concise information quality that was relevant to their customer's needs at the right moment in order to connect them to exactly what they were looking for. Both desktop and mobile user experiences were re-designed in an easy and intuitive manner that allowed customers to a) create a personalized profile of their pet based on the dog's characteristics, b) obtain information about products, c) access the loyalty program, d) receive offers and of course e) shop. We Love Dogs created an omnichannel strategy that met customers right where they were, with the right communication or offer that was appropriate for the customer situation in real-time, regardless of the channel or device that was used.

The modern consumer and user journey is composed of hundreds of real-time, intent-driven micro-moments that occur when individuals research from their device – increasingly a smartphone – to act on a need to learn something, do, discover, watch, or buy something. They are intent-rich moments when purchasing decisions are taken (Ramaswamy, 2015). Today's consumers are bombarded by content, ads, offers, emails, texts, tweets, push notifications which is causing distraction. Also, as Postman (1985) believes, the attention span of humans is decreasing as a result of using modern technology and proliferation of information. This means that brands have a few seconds to capture the attention of their target audience. Social media offered customers the opportunity to socialize with other dog owners in virtual communities that were created by the company, write and read reviews about products, post pictures and watch videos to learn more about dog grooming. We Love Dogs increased its presence in the social environment to create a social shopping experience. This was well accepted by its targeted tech-savvy customers who are often connected on social media and are eager to make shopping a social event. This strategy aligned very well with the original customer experience plan since the social concept had a proactive and reactive approach with the customers.

In the first stage We Love Dogs understood that customers' needs and expectations were volatile, therefore keeping abreast of this required continually meeting customer needs by providing a brand presence into the life of their customer in real-time, staying connected with them and evolving alongside them all the time.

4. Stage four: Regaining

Across the previous stages the pet brand aimed to identify customers' pain points, fixing what wasn't working and finally re-building those relationships where trust faded away but also creating new relationships based on the principle of trust.

a. Principle of Trust

The last but not least principle for a superior customer experience is what wraps up the five principles above. Trust is the customer's confidence that his/her needs will be satisfied by a business (Genesan & Hess, 2004) and it provides the foundation for future customer and business relationships (Geyskens et al., 1998). As previously cited in this chapter, the new generations of consumers are quickly losing trust for institutions, brands and politicians (Daneshkhu, 2018)

Trust in business relationships involves the belief in a company and the perception of that company to be credible. It is aligned with the customers' expectations that the company will deliver on its promise according to what is expected by the customer (Rosa Pulga et al, 2019). According to a global consumer study carried out by Eldelman (2019) 81 percent of customers say that trusting a brand is a deciding factor in their purchase decisions and they'll also advocate on the brand's behalf.

We Love Dogs made sure to improve every step along the customer journey where trust fell flat. By implementing the five principles the pet brand was able to regain trust, which now lies at the heart of their customers emphasis, and it is the foundation to which the organization consistently delivers on its promises. When brands build consumer trust as a result of delivering on their promises, this eases customers' decision making process and it reduces cost of information gathering and processing information (Rajavi et al., 2019, p.651). We Love Dogs followed the virtuous cycle, that was engineered into five phases by their consultants (figure 4): 1) customer satisfaction (positive emotion) 2) customer engagement 3) customer relationship 4) customer loyalty 5) customer advocacy

The cycle of trust reinforced itself through a loop. By successfully going through these five important phases the brand established a two-way relationship with their customers, encouraging them to be involved as active shapers of the experiences that improved their lives. The brand adopted the cycle of trust where customer satisfaction creates engagement, customer engagement creates relationship, relationship creates loyalty and therefore customer advocacy. Customers wouldn't act as advocates to friends and family if they don't feel they can trust the brand. This mechanism successfully worked over the customer retention and customer acquisition processes.

Figure 4. Representation of the cycle of trust adopted by We love Dogs.
Source: Ilenia Vidili

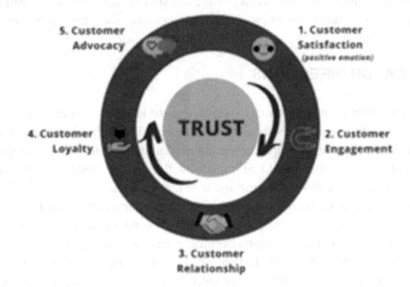

SOLUTIONS AND RECOMMENDATIONS

Prahalad and Ramaswamy (2004) estimated that the internet era would shift from company-centric to a more customer-centric perspective where value is created and co-created in an age of constant connectivity and brand-consumer real-time interaction. The concept of customer-centricity and the value creation it generates is the result of an in-depth appreciation of the customer rather than the old product-centric view which tends to create a war within the company and among its competitors (Christensen, 2016)

To build a customer-centric culture companies should: 1) operationalize customer empathy, so the ability to identify a customer's emotional need, understanding the reason behind it and responding effectively and appropriately. 2) every employee must understand the company's customers. While decades ago customer insights were only taken into consideration by the marketing department, today every department should understand customer wants and needs (Lee Yohn, 2018) and 3) focus on building relationships with customers that are designed to maximize their experience and all those people who are directly or indirectly in contact with the company.

A customer-centric strategy is based on putting customers first and at the core of a business. Each of the six principles that We Love Dogs implemented were based on creating customer value and really putting customers first, beyond what was the initial simple customer focus. This was expanded past the existing customers and extended across potential buyers, customers of customers, readers of the company's content, social connections, virtual community members and especially employees of the company. A positive customer experience is created by the whole company, meaning that companies are required to integrate their activities in the department of information technology, services, logistics, marketing, human resources as well as external partners (Lemon & Verhoef, 2016). A customer-centric culture across the pet company generated longer lasting business value. Organizations should be focusing on customer centricity as a strategy that aligns a company's products and services with the needs of its most valuable customers to maximize the long term financial value of those customers (Fader, 2012). Furthermore, to instill a customer-centric vision businesses should take a deliberate shift from product-focus to a customer-focus mindset that emphasizes customer emotions in this experience economy.

FUTURE RESEARCH DIRECTIONS

This chapter lays the importance of customer experience as the key factor for creating value to customers. To compete successfully businesses should set customer value as the overall customer experience strategy. Members of an organization: employees, managers and stakeholders must become value creators and customer experience strategies should be implemented to delight customers. A customer-centric culture provides focus and direction while making sure that customer value is provided across every interaction with the customer. Customer value is defined as the perception of what a product or service is worth to a customer which can increase customer trust and brand reputation (Andersson et al., 2020)

Given the limited research to date on customer-centricity and the growing importance of this phenomenon the author is particularly interested in further researching the implementation of customer-centric models within organizations and the shift from product-focus towards customer-focus as the driver for shaping and re-shaping a company's competitive advantage.

CONCLUSION

To create a superior customer experience and to promote engagement with customers, companies should thoroughly connect with them on a deeper level, aligning with their values and identities and create strong emotional ties. In the current hyper competitive landscape designing valuable customer and user experiences is led by new technologies but the outcome of the most important principles of *Integrity* and *Trust* are the basis of long-lasting relationships and consequently of exceptional customer experiences. We Love Dogs strategy perfectly matches its target characteristics and business specificities. The pet industry is driven by emotional rather than rational decisions and this explains the reason behind creating virtual communities that share their experiences with their dogs and genuinely have passion for helping homeless dogs. This paper explains the successful implementation of We Love Dogs customer experience strategy, however it is important to highlight that the strategy was tailored to match the company's unique characteristics, values and consumers. This means that each company needs to follow its own way when developing a customer experience strategy based on its business model, specific market characteristics and customer profiles. Despite this it is relevant and useful to take into consideration the six principles listed in this paper that are the result of a customer experience plan based on customer centricity. In this age of mistrust managing a customer experience strategy requires businesses to pay careful attention at every stage of the customer lifecycle and examine the whole customer journey with humble eyes. Companies that adopt technologies, customer experience and culture need to have the capacity to rapidly change and adjust to new consumers desires and market moves. In conclusion, managing customer experience is a difficult idea which combines external factors such as consumer psychology, technology advancement, economic behavior, and internal factors such as employees, culture and efficient processes. Success comes from being able to join each of these factors as one concept that guarantees integrity as a whole.

REFERENCES

Abramovich, G. (2018). *People Buy Experiences, Not Products.* https://www.cmo.com/features/articles/2018/3/27/adobe-ceo-people-buy-experiences-not-products-summit18.html#gs.fv9o0o

Adobe (2015). *The state of content: expectations on the rise.* https://blogs.adobe.com/creative/files/2015/12/Adobe-State-of-Content-Report.pdf

Allen, J., Frederick, F. R., Barney, H., & Markey, R. (2005). How to achieve true customer-led growth. Closing the delivery gap. Academic Press.

Andersson, S., Awuah, G., Aagerup, U., & Wictor, I. (2020). How do mature born globals create customer value to achieve international growth? *International Marketing Review, 37*(2), 185–211. doi:10.1108/IMR-11-2018-0340

Anthony, S. (2016). *Harvard Business Review: Kodak's Downfall Wasn't About Technology.* https://hbr.org/2016/07/kodaks-downfall-wasnt-about-technology#comment-section

Arguello, M., Monferrer Tirado, D., & Estrada Guillén, M (2019). Service quality in a post-crisis context: Emotional effects and behaviours. *International Journal of Bank Marketing, 38*(1), 175–198. doi:10.1108/IJBM-02-2019-0045

Ariker, M., Heller, J., Diaz, A., & Perry, J. (2015). How marketers can personalize at scaler. *Harvard Business Review*.

Aufreiter, N., Boudet, J., & Weng, V. (2014). *Why marketers should keep sending you e-mails.* https://www.mckinsey.com/business-functions/marketing-and-sales/our-insights/why-marketers-should-keep-sending-you-emails

Barrett, M., Davidson, E., Prabhu, J., & Vargo, S. L. (2015). Service innovation in the digital age: Key contributions and future directions. *Management Information Systems Quarterly, 39*(1), 135–154. doi:10.25300/MISQ/2015/39:1.03

Barton, R., Ishikawa, M., Quiring, K., & Theofilou, B. (2018). *From Me to We: The Rise of the Purpose-Led Brand.* https://www.accenture.com/_acnmedia/thought-leadership-assets/pdf/accenture-competitiveagility-gcpr-pov.pdf

Belleghem, S. V. (2019). *Customers the day after tomorrow.* Lannoo, Uitgeverij.

Bennett, P. D. (1995). *Dictionary of Marketing Terms.* American Marketing Association.

Bevan, N. (2009). What is the difference between the purpose of usability and user experience evaluation methods. *Proceedings of the workshop UXEM 9,* 1-4.

Blythe, J. (2013). *Consumer Behaviour.* SAGE Publications.

Bolton, R. N. (2016). *Service Excellence: Creating Customer Experiences that Build Relationships.* Business Expert Press.

Cai, L., He, X., Dai, Y., & Zhu, K. (2018). Research on B2B2C E-commerce Website Design Based on User Experience. *Journal of Physics: Conference Series, 1087*(6), 5. doi:10.1088/1742-6596/1087/6/062043

Christensen, C. M., Dillon, K., Hall, T., & Duncan, D. S. (2016). *Competing Against Luck: The Story of Innovation and Customer Choice.* Harper Collins.

Christensen, C. M., Raynor, E. M., & McDonald, R. (2015). *What is Disruptive Innovation?* https://hbr.org/2015/12/what-is-disruptive-innovation

Ciuchita, R., Mahr, D., & Odekerken-Schröder, G. (2019). Deal with it: How coping with e-service innovation affects the customer experience. *Journal of Business Research, 103,* 130–141. doi:10.1016/j.jbusres.2019.05.036

Cuzzort, R. P., & King, E. W. (1995). *Twentieth-century social thought.* Harcourt Brace College Publishers.

Daneshkhu, S. (2018). *How millennials' taste for 'authenticity' is disrupting powerful food brands.* https://www.ft.com/content/09271178-6f29-11e8-92d3-6c13e5c92914

De Bellis, E., Hildebrand, C., Ito, K., Herrmann, A., & Schmitt, B. (2019). Personalizing the Customization Experience: A Matching Theory of Mass Customization Interfaces and Cultural Information Processing. *JMR, Journal of Marketing Research, 56*(6), 1050–1065. doi:10.1177/0022243719867698

Deloitte (2019). Smartphone: the center of life A study on Nordic mobile consumer behaviour. Deloitte Global Mobile Consumer Survey 2019: The Nordic cut.

Dimock, M. (2019). *Defining generations: Where Millennials end and Generation Z begins.* https://www.pewresearch.org/fact-tank/2019/01/17/where-millennials-end-and-generation-z-begins/

Edelman, R. (2019). *2019 Edelman Trust Barometer Special Report: In Brands We Trust?* https://www.edelman.com/sites/g/files/aatuss191/files/2019-06/2019_edelman_trust_barometer_special_report_in_brands_we_trust.pdf

Ernst & Young LLP (n.d.). *The Digitalisation of Everything. How organisations much adapt to changing consumer behaviour.* https://www.ey.com/Publication/vwLUAssets/The_digitisation_of_everything_-_How_organisations_must_adapt_to_changing_consumer_behaviour/%24file/EY_Digitisation_of_everything.pdf

Fader, P. (2012). *Customer Centricity: Focus on the Right Customers for Strategic Advantage.* Wharton Digital Press.

Forrester (2019). *How Customers Think, Feel, And Act: The Paradigm Of Business Outcomes.* https://cloud.kapostcontent.net/pub/d2a85d5e-c053-4bfc-ae8d-f1a9c0b2af31/whitepaper-how-customers-think-feel-and-act-the-paradigm-of-business-outcomes?kui=MtTZamfFfmzvSS4fnSaD4Q

Francis, T., & Hoefel, F. (2018). *True Gen: Generation Z and its implications for companies.* https://www.mckinsey.com/industries/consumer-packaged-goods/our-insights/true-gen-generation-z-and-its-implications-for-companies#

Genesan, S., & Hess, R. (2004). Dimensions and levels of Trust: Implications for commitment to a relationship. *Marketing Letters*, 8(4), 439–448. doi:10.1023/A:1007955514781

Geyskens, I., Jan-Benedict, E.M. Steenkamp, & Nirmalya, K. (1998). Generalisations about trust in marketing channel relationships using Meta-Analysis. *International Journal of Research in Marketing*, 15(3), 223-248.

Gilboa, S., Seger-Guttmann, T., & Mimran, O. (2019). The unique role of relationship marketing in small businesses' customer experience. *Journal of Retailing and Consumer Services*, 51, 152–164. doi:10.1016/j.jretconser.2019.06.004

Goodwin, T. (2018). Digital Darwinism: Survival of the Fittest in the Age of Business Disruption. Academic Press.

Guo, J., Wang, X., & Wu, Y. (2020). Positive emotion bias: Role of emotional content from online customer reviews in purchase decisions. *Journal of Retailing and Consumer Services*, 52, 2–4. doi:10.1016/j.jretconser.2019.101891

Handarkho, Y. (2020). Impact of social experience on customer purchase decision in the social commerce context. *Journal of Systems and Information Technology*, 22(4).

Hassenzahl, M., Diefenbach, S., & Goritz, A. (2010). Needs, affect and interactive products-facets of user experience. *Interacting with Computers*, 22(5), 353–362. doi:10.1016/j.intcom.2010.04.002

Hernandez, J.J., Conway, D., & Knight, T. (2018). *Tomorrow's experience, today. Harnessing a customer first approach in a changing world.* Academic Press.

Interaction Design Foundation (2017). *Needs Before Wants in User Experiences – Maslow and the Hierarchy of Needs.* https://www.interaction-design.org/literature/article/needs-before-wants-in-user-experiences-maslow-and-the-hierarchy-of-needs#:~:text=Abraham%20Maslow%20developed%20a%20deep,be%20motivated%20to%20do%20so

Jackson, T. (2011). *Kodak fell victim to disruptive technology.* https://www.ft.com/content/f49cb408-ecd8-11e0-be97-00144feab49a

Jagdish, S. (1972). The future of buyer behaviour. *Proceedings of the Third Annual Conference of the Association for Consumer Research,* 562-575.

Jenkins, R. (2019). *5 Need-To-Know Characteristics of the New Millennial Buyer.* https://www.inc.com/ryan-jenkins/selling-to-millennial-buyers-5-things-you-need-to-know.html

Kang, J., Hong, S., & Hubbard, G. (2020). The role of storytelling in advertising: Consumer emotion, narrative engagement level, and word-of-mouth intention. *Journal of Consumer Behaviour, 19*(1), 47–56. doi:10.1002/cb.1793

Klaus, P. (2020). Customer experience, not brands will be on the iron throne. *International Journal of Market Research, 62*(1), 6–8. doi:10.1177/1470785319858570

Koetz, C. (2019). Managing the customer experience: A beauty retailer deploys all tactics. *The Journal of Business Strategy, 40*(1), 10–17. doi:10.1108/JBS-09-2017-0139

KPMG (2018). *Growing Pains: 2018 Global CEO Outlook.* https://assets.kpmg/content/dam/kpmg/jm/pdf/2018-ceo-outlook-report-final-low.pdf

Kranzbühler, A., Zerres, A., Kleijnen, M., & Verlegh, P. (2019). Beyond valence: a meta-analysis of discrete emotions in firm-customer encounters. *Journal of the Academy of Marketing Science,* 1-21.

Kucuk, S. U., & Krishnamurthy, S. (2007). An Analysis of Consumer Power on the Internet. *Technovation, 27*(1-2), 47–56. doi:10.1016/j.technovation.2006.05.002

Larivière, B., Bowenb, D., Andreassenc, T. W., Kunzd, W., Siriannie, N. J., Voss, C., & De Keyserh, A. (2017). Service Encounter 2.0: An investigation into the roles of technology, employees and customers. *Journal of Business Research, 79,* 238–246. doi:10.1016/j.jbusres.2017.03.008

Lee, B. (2019). *As Millennials Choose Pets Over Babies, Pet Tech Is Silicon Valley's Unlikely Industry.* https://www.forbes.com/sites/forbestechcouncil/2019/10/22/as-millennials-choose-pets-over-babies-pet-tech-is-silicon-valleys-unlikely-industry/#66f5df7d48b6

Lee Yohn, D. (2018). *In Harvard Business Review: 6 Ways to Build a Customer-Centric Culture.* https://hbr.org/2018/10/6-ways-to-build-a-customer-centric-culture

Lemon, K. N., & Verhoef, P. C. (2016). Understanding customer experience through the customer journey. *Journal of Marketing, 80*(6), 69–96. doi:10.1509/jm.15.0420

Lerner, J., Valdesolo, P., & Kassam, K. (2015). Emotion and Decision Making. *Annual Review of Psychology, 66*(1), 799–823. doi:10.1146/annurev-psych-010213-115043 PMID:25251484

Lohse, G. L., & Spiller, P. (1998). Electronic Shopping. *Communications of the ACM, 41*(7), 81–87. doi:10.1145/278476.278491

Maechler, N., Neher, K., & Park, R. (2016). *From touchpoints to journeys: Seeing the world as customers do*. https://www.mckinsey.com/business-functions/marketing-and-sales/our-insights/from-touchpoints-to-journeys-seeing-the-world-as-customers-do#

Mahlke, S., & Thuring, M. (2007) Studying antecedents of emotional experiences in interactive contexts. *Proceedings of the SIGCHI Conference on Human Factors in Computing Systems (CHI '07)*, 915-918. 10.1145/1240624.1240762

Makri, K., Papadas, K. K., & Schlegelmilch, B. B. (2019). Global-local consumer identities as drivers of global digital brand usage. *International Marketing Review, 36*(5), 708. doi:10.1108/IMR-03-2018-0104

Marketing Science Institute (2018). *Research Priorities 2018-2020*. Marketing Science Institute.

Maslow, A. H. (1943). A theory of human motivation. *Psychological Review, 50*(4), 370–396. doi:10.1037/h0054346

Matzler, K., Bailom, F., Von den Eichen, S. F., & Anschober, M. (2016). Digital Disruption. Wie Sie Ihr Unternehmen auf das digitale Zeitalter vorbereiten, Vahlen, München.

Matzler, K., Friedrich von den Eichen, S., Anschober, M., & Kohler, T. (2018). The crusade of digital disruption. *The Journal of Business Strategy, 39*(6), 13–20. doi:10.1108/JBS-12-2017-0187

McClinton, D. (2019). *Global attention span is narrowing and trends don't last as long, study reveals*. https://www.theguardian.com/society/2019/apr/16/got-a-minute-global-attention-span-is-narrowing-study-reveals

Meyer, C., & Schwager, A. (2007). *Understanding Customer Experience*. https://hbr.org/2007/02/understanding-customer-experience

Miller Heiman Group (2018). *The Growing Buyer-Seller Gap: Results of the 2018 Buyer Preferences Study*. https://www.csoinsights.com/wp-content/uploads/sites/5/2018/06/Growing-Buyer-Seller-Gap-White-paper_FINAL.pdf

Monferrer, D., Moliner, M., & Estrada, M. (2019). Increasing customer loyalty through customer engagement in the retail banking industry. *Spanish Journal of Marketing, 23*(3), 461-484.

Morgan, B. (2019). *The Customer of the Future*. HarperCollins Leadership. Edition.

Muslim, E., Moch, B., Wilgert, Y., Utami, F., & Indriyani, D. (2019). User interface redesign of e-commerce platform mobile application (Kudo) through user experience evaluation to increase user attraction. *IOP Conference Series. Materials Science and Engineering, 508*(1), 6. doi:10.1088/1757-899X/508/1/012113

Norman, D. A. (2004). Emotional Design. New York: Academic Press.

Nowak, K. L., & McGloin, R. (2014). The Influence of Peer Reviews on Source Credibility and Purchase Intention in Societies. *Societies (Basel, Switzerland)*, 690.

Nunwood, K. P. M. G. (2018). *Developing empathy in customer experience design: Why this challenge is more important than you think.* https://www.nunwood.com/excellence-centre/blog/2016/developing-empathy-in-customer-experience-design-why-this-challenge-is-more-important-than-you-think/

Oliver, R. L., Rust, R. T., & Varki, S. (1997). Customer delight: Foundations, findings, and managerial insight. *Journal of Retailing, 73*(3), 311–336. doi:10.1016/S0022-4359(97)90021-X

Pappas, I. (2018). User experience in personalized online shopping: A fuzzy-set analysis. *European Journal of Marketing, 52*(7/8), 1679–1703. doi:10.1108/EJM-10-2017-0707

Park, C. H., & Kim, Y. G. (2003). Identifying key factors affecting consumer purchase behavior in an online shopping context. *International Journal of Retail & Distribution Management, 31*(1), 16–29. doi:10.1108/09590550310457818

Perrault, W. D., & McCarthy, E. J. (2002). *Principios de Marketing.* LTC.

Pine, J. B. II, & Gilmore, J. H. (1999). *The Experience Economy: Work is theatre and every business a stage.* Harvard Business School Press.

Postman, N. (1985). *Amusing ourselves to death.* Penguin Group USA.

Prahalad, C. K., & Ramaswamy, V. (2004). *The future of competition: Co-creating unique value with customers.* Boston Harvard Business School Press.

Pride, W. M., Ferrell, O. C., Lukas, A. B., Schembri, S., Niininen, O., & Casidy, R. (2018). *Marketing Principles.* Cengage Learning Australia.

Priporas, C., Stylos, N., & Fotiadis, A. (2017). Generation Z consumers' expectations of interactions in smart retailing: A future agenda. *Computers in Human Behavior, 77,* 374–381. doi:10.1016/j.chb.2017.01.058

Provost, F., & Fawcett, T. (2013). *Data science for business.* Academic Press.

Rachinger, M., Rauter, R., Müller, C., Vorraber, W., & Schirgi, E (2019). Digitalization and its influence on business model innovation. *Journal of Manufacturing Technology Management, 30*(8), 1143–1160. doi:10.1108/JMTM-01-2018-0020

Rajavi, K., Kushwaha, T., & Steenkamp, J. M. (2019). In Brands We Trust? A Multicategory, Multi-country Investigation of Sensitivity of Consumers' Trust in Brands to Marketing-Mix Activities. *The Journal of Consumer Research, 46*(4).

Ramaswamy, S. (2015). *How Micro-Moments Are Changing the Rules.* https://www.thinkwithgoogle.com/marketing-resources/micro-moments/how-micromoments-are-changing-rules/

Ratner, N. (2019). *The Rise of the Smartphone Ecosystem and Kodak's Fall.* https://digital.hbs.edu/platform-digit/submission/the-rise-of-the-smartphone-ecosystem-and-kodaks-fall/

Rembach, J. (2017). *What is a Customer Empathy Map.* https://customerthink.com/what-is-a-customer-empathy-map/

Rosa Pulga, A., Basso, K., Viacava, K., Pacheco, N., Ladeira, W., & Dalla Corte, V. (2019). The link between social interactions and trust recovery in customer–business relationships. *Journal of Consumer Behaviour, 18*(6), 496–504. doi:10.1002/cb.1788

Scheibehenne, B., Greifeneder, R., & Todd, P.M. (2010). Can There Ever Be Too Many Options? A Meta-Analytic Review of Choice Overload. *Journal of Consumer Research, 37*(3), 409-425.

Schneider, P., & Zielke, S. (2020). Searching offline and buying online – An analysis of showrooming forms and segments. *Journal of Retailing and Consumer Services, 52*, 52. doi:10.1016/j.jretconser.2019.101919

Schwab, K. (2016). *The Fourth Industrial Revolution: what it means, how to respond.* https://www.weforum.org/agenda/2016/01/the-fourth-industrial-revolution-what-it-means-and-how-to-respond/

Sinclaire, J., & Vogus, C. E. (2011). Adoption of social networking sites: An exploratory adaptive structuration perspective for global organizations. *Information Technology Management, 12*(4), 293–314. doi:10.100710799-011-0086-5

Souto, J. E. (2015). Business model innovation and business concept innovation as the context of incremental innovation and radical innovation. *Tourism Management, 51*(December), 142–155. doi:10.1016/j.tourman.2015.05.017

Statista Research Department (2019). *Number of network connected devices per person around the world from 2003 to 2020.* https://www.statista.com/statistics/678739/forecast-on-connected-devices-per-person/

Stein, A., & Ramaseshan, B. (2016). Towards the identification of customer experience touch point elements. *Journal of Retailing and Consumer Services, 30*, 8–19. doi:10.1016/j.jretconser.2015.12.001

Taylor, K. (2019). *The $225 billion pet care industry is exploding, as millennials delay marriage and babies while turning to pets to 'fill that void.* https://www.businessinsider.com/pet-care-industry-grows-as-millennials-elevate-pets-2019-5?IR=T

Technical University of Denmark (2019). *Abundance of information narrows our collective attention span.* https://www.eurekalert.org/pub_releases/2019-04/tuod-aoi041119.php

Teece, D. J. (2018). Business models and dynamic capabilities. *Long Range Planning, 51*(1), 40–49. doi:10.1016/j.lrp.2017.06.007

Thygesen, A. (2018). *Beyond the traditional marketing funnel – a new formula for growth.* https://www.thinkwithgoogle.com/intl/en-145/perspectives/global-articles/beyond-traditional-marketing-funnel-new-formula-growth/

TrustRadius (2018). *The 2018 B2B Buying Disconnect An in-depth study on buyer preferences, vendor impact, and the persistent trust gap in B2B technology.* http://go.trustradius.com/rs/827-FOI-687/images/TrustRadius_2018_B2B_Buying_Disconnect.pdf

Van Riel, A. C., Liljander, V., & Jurriens, P (2001). Exploring customer evaluation of e-services: A portal site. *International Journal of Service Industry Management, 12*(4), 359–377. doi:10.1108/09564230110405280

Venkatachalam, S. (2014). *Five things that make you an empowered consumer.* https://www.weforum.org/agenda/2014/11/five-things-that-make-you-an-empowered-consumer/

Verhoef, P., Kooge, E., &Walk N., (2016). *Creating Value with Big Data Analytics: Making Smarter Marketing Decisions.* Academic Press.

Wedel, M., & Kannan, P. K. (2016). Marketing Analytics for Data-Rich Environments. *Journal of Marketing, 80*(6), 97–121. doi:10.1509/jm.15.0413

Woo, A. (2018). *Understanding The Research On Millennial Shopping Behaviors.* https://www.forbes.com/sites/forbesagencycouncil/2018/06/04/understanding-the-research-on-millennial-shopping-behaviors/#82758d75f7ab

Xu, C., & Zhang, Q. (2019). The dominant factor of social tags for users' decision behavior on e-commerce websites: Color or text. *Journal of the Association for Information Science and Technology, 70*(9), 943.

Yasin, M., Liébana-Cabanillas, F., Porcu, L., & Kayed, R. (2020). The role of customer online brand experience in customers' intention to forward online company-generated content: The case of the Islamic online banking sector in Palestine. *Journal of Retailing and Consumer Services, 52*, 52. doi:10.1016/j.jretconser.2019.101902

Young, & Rubicam (2017). *The decline of trust.* Academic Press.

Zaltman, G. (2003). How Customers Think: Essential Insights into the Mind of the Market. Academic Press.

Zenger, J., & Folkman, J. (2019). *The 3 Elements of Trust.* https://hbr.org/2019/02/the-3-elements-of-trust

Zhang, Y., Liu, L., & Ho, S. (2020). How do interruptions affect user contributions on social commerce? *Information Systems Journal, 30*(3), 535–565. doi:10.1111/isj.12266

Zhou, T., Li, H., & Liu, Y. (2010). The system effect of flow experience on mobile SNS users' loyalty. *Industrial Management & Data Systems, 110*(6), 930–946. doi:10.1108/02635571011055126

ADDITIONAL READING

Belleghem, S. V. (2015). *When Digital Becomes Human.* Kogan Page. doi:10.1057/dddmp.2015.36

Dixon, M. (2013). The Effortless Experience. Penguin Books Ltd. Harari, Y. N. Homo Deus: A brief history of tomorrow. Random House.

Heath, C., & Heath, D. (2017). *The Power of Moments.* Transworld.

Leonhard, G. (2019). *Technology vs. Humanity: The coming clash between man and machine.* The Futures Agency.

Pennington, A. (2016). *The customer experience book: How to design, measure and improve customer experience in your business.* Pearson.

Solis, B. (2015). *X: The Experience when business meets design.* Wiley.

Watkinson, M. (2012). *The Ten Principles Behind Great Customer Experiences.* Financial Times

KEY TERMS AND DEFINITIONS

Consumer Behavior: Consumer behavior is how customers decide to purchase, research and interact with a brand and its products. It also involves how needs and wants of consumers arise and how consumers make decisions to fulfill these needs and wants.

Customer Experience: Customer experience is the impression that a brand leaves to a customer based on what they think of the brand across every touchpoint or interaction with that brand.

Customer Relationship: Customer relationship is the development of an ongoing relationship between a company and its customers. This is measured by the level of customer satisfaction.

Customer-Centricity: Customer-centricity is the approach of an organization to put its customers at the center of the business strategy. This approach is tied to delivering a positive customer experience.

Digital Disruption: Digital disruption occurs when digital technologies adopted by smaller companies in a market are able to revolutionize the business model of bigger and more established organizations. Often this leads to a change in consumer behavior and expectations in a market.

Touchpoint: A touchpoint is a way or channel that a customer can interact with a brand. Whether it is through face-to-face or through a digital form, be it a website, a mobile app, or any other form of communication.

User Experience: User experience is the perception of a customer when using a particular product, system or service.

Chapter 12
Online Inter@ctivity via Web 3.0

Ali Sallemi Hrichi

New World Marketing Association, Tunisia

ABSTRACT

The end of the 20th century was marked by the advent of the internet along with the transformation of the consumer behavior into an information behavior. As a matter of fact, our daily life becomes centered on a multitude of informational exhibitions through which brands have invested this cutting-edge information technology, tending for delivering the perfect service by adopting the multichannel communication strategies. The advent of interactive marketing has brought new features to the web, allowing online companies to configure websites and manage smarter, more social, and more personalized interactions and communications. Accordingly, this chapter aims to make a synthetic study of the concept of online interactivity and to present a review of the literature, and to better explain the concept and to how to achieve the role of Web 3.0.

INTRODUCTION

The field of marketing is changing in exponential manner. For several decades, the primary role of marketing was to orchestrate the mix of product, price, promotion and place (Shankar & Malthouse, 2018). Currently, the customer expectations are changing fast, to the extent that retailers wouldn't be able keep up get left behind. A consumer, enjoying online shopping at an e-store automatically, expects the same level of service from every virtual point of sale. Therefore, the expectation loop is born. So, it becomes incumbent upon retailers, for getting ahead with the curve, to innovate (Popov, 2019). As a process, interactivity refers to the responsiveness and communication between consumers and manufacturers, and between consumers and advertisers (Park & Yoo, 2020).

Kotler & al (2017) believe that the deep changes in the market and hyper competition are changing the managerial approaches of companies, shifting from the product portfolio management to client portfolio management. So that, companies are moving towards a customer-oriented management, and are interested in the digital relationship with the client. At the same time, the relational characteristics of the website and the web 3.0 platform are shaking up the traditional models of marketing and more precisely the notion of customer loyalty. According to Genimon & Kennedy (2020), the web 3.0 and artificial

DOI: 10.4018/978-1-7998-3756-5.ch012

intelligence, applications and networking technologies, popped up as new challenges and opportunities for today's businesses. Thus, some companies have built their own strategies to consumer-centered ones. And moved from a product-orientated to a customer-orientated approach. Indeed, the relational marketing is going beyond the transaction boundaries to creating long-term and profitable relationships with the customer. The relational marketing focuses on specific notions such as relational proximity, interaction, personalization, and the dyadic relationship. The success of relational marketing becomes heavily relying on the rapid diffusion and development of information and communication technologies

Therefore, in this chapter, we will provide an overview of this literature to tackle the phenomenon of online interactivity through a synthesis.

BACKGROUND

Interactive marketing is a one-to-one marketing practice that focuses on the individual customer and the prospects' actions. The interactive marketing covers the marketing initiatives that are triggered by the customers' behaviors and preferences; therefore, it represents a substitute for the traditional campaign-based marketing efforts.

The Notion of Interactivity in Marketing

Direct marketing is the distribution of products information and promotion by aiming integrative communication with the consumers (Jobber & Lancaster, 2009). Working on media and its interactive characteristics will emerge accordingly, and borrowing massively from the theories developed in the sociology of media and the theories of communication (Park & Yoo, 2020). As a process, interactivity refers to responsiveness and the communication between consumers and manufacturers and between consumers and advertisers. As a feature, interactivity focuses on technological features and website characteristics that allow user control and mutual communication (McMillan & Hwang, 2002).

Mechant (2012) had identified three perspectives of interactivity in the literature. These perspectives can be summarized in "structure", "process" and "users". The first perspective, "structure", considers marketing interactivity as a characteristic of media technologies, "a measure of the potential capacity of a media that will allow the user to influence the content and /or the mediated communication" (Jensen & Toscan, 1999). The second perspective, "process," identifies interactivity as a communication process. Here, the focus is on the study of interactivity as a form of information exchange between different parts. The third perspective, "users", presents interactivity as "an information-driven process that takes place within the individual" (Newhagen, 2004). This view investigates the effect of interactive communication channels and emphasizes user experience.

Interactive Marketing: An Aspect of Direct and Relational Marketing

With the growing competition in all channels of interaction, especially the Internet, brands have focused on engaging in personal conversations with their customers, targeting to gain customer loyalty to avoid seeing their portfolio gradually shift to competition (Hrichi & Ben Rached, 2018). Indeed, the increasing use of client-oriented computer applications and new information and communication technologies (NICT) offered new relational possibilities and a better knowledge of customers (Vanheems, 2012). It becomes important for the managers in companies to cope with an increasing amount of information that should be processed, and to face more complex coordination problems in organizations due to the multiplication of time units and places, especially in industrialized countries. Facing with these problems, companies have sought for new information and communication technologies that would make it possible for them to understand, process, store and communicate information.

Interactivity as an Aspect of Direct Marketing

The term "Direct Marketing" has changed over the years. Originally, Kotler & Dubois (2003) explain that it is a distribution circuit without intermediary between the manufacturer and the consumer. Direct marketing is therefore, a marketing communication tool that fosters two-way direct engagement with customers (Zephaniah& al, 2020). Subsequently, direct marketing designates any form of mail order or catalog sales. Mail order companies, that are highly interested in the identity and characteristics of each of its customers, are considered as pioneers and experts in direct marketing. Today, the term of direct marketing is strongly linked to the notion of interactivity.

According to the Direct Marketing Association; "An interactive marketing uses one or more media to obtain a response and/or transaction". Two key elements can be extracted from this definition: the measurability of the response and the multi-media character. Since 1998, the Journal of Direct Marketing has become the Journal of Interactive Marketing, and assimilated interactivity with direct marketing. We cannot talk about the concept of interactive marketing without referring to the "one-to-one".

Interactivity as an Aspect of Relational Marketing

During the relational marketing era, the technological revolution allowed firms to gather, store, and analyze information about customers in an unprecedented step (Edwards & al, 2020). The buying and selling relationship becomes interactive when an item produced during the buyer-seller interaction is integrated into the consumer's buying decision process (David & Stenger, 2000). Indeed, the interactive nature of the buying relationship leads to a structuring of buyer preferences and a learning process. For example, telephone interaction, web site navigation, face-to-face dialogue or email exchange help the consumer defining a method for selecting attributes, structuring its set of references, and defining its preferences or improving one's knowledge of a product.

Relational marketing considers all the dimensions and aspects of life of the individual at any time and under any circumstances. It tries to decode the complexity and the relativity of behaviors in order to build marketing strategies that are efficiently piloted (Yazid & Zghal, 2015).

DIMENSIONS OF MARKETING INTERACTIVITY

Three dimensions appear frequently in the marketing interactivity literature; Two-way communication, control over participation in communication, and time (Jensen, 1998).

Bidirectional Communication

In one part of the literature, bidirectional communication is characterized as being mutual discourse (Burgoon & al, 2000). By making their websites user-friendly, marketers can facilitate this kind of interpersonal interactivity and can generate positive Word of Mouth (BAO) for their businesses (Hoffman & Novak, 2000). Bidirectional communication via the web also facilitates other types of business relationships such as customer service and supply chain management (Berthon & al, 2000).

Controlling Participation in Communication

The web often provides users with more content and navigation tools than traditional media (McMillan & Hwang, 2005). Indeed, much of the literature focuses on the way people control their computers. Reeves and Nass (2000) noted that some control studies about participation in communication focused on how the individual and others perceive the computer design. Human-centered studies, on the one hand, examine the way the individuals interpret the personality of the computer (Moon & Nass, 1996), the level of agentivity (ability to act on the other side) perceived by the individual (Huhtamo, 1999), and the goals individuals bring to the system (Xie, 2000). On the other hand, computer-focused studies examine the problems of interfaces and input devices (Nielsen, 2000), navigation tools (Heeter, 2000), choice features (Mahood & al, 2000).

Time

Time is a key element in the online interaction; the perception of interaction through human-based or computer-assisted messages is influenced by the speed of delivering messages and the speed of the response of the individual (Nielsen, 2000). Time of interaction indicates the amount of time until a page is first expected to be usable and the quick response of the user's input. It can be the suitable unit of measurement to determine the expected users' interaction with a page. However it is important to understand how much time is taken to interact, and to define the right metric to monitor an application.

ONLINE INTERACTIVITY

Online interactivity is often associated with new technologies that provide the user with new experiences in different forms of communication and information allowing the user to exchange and to share its ideas and orientations, and to enhance the cooperation between the actors to set and progress social relationships, and to achieve the objectives by modifying or adapting content to one's preferences and behaviors (Yazid & Zghal, 2015). Therefore, interactivity is a crucial factor in the formation of reactions and the creation of web browsing behaviors. As a matter of fact, the interactivity of the site allows the consumer to interact with a personalized environment and to choose among different hyperlinks that generate a feeling of pleasure and freedom.

In their empirical study, Cyr and al (2007) validated the relationship of perceived interactivity with efficiency, pleasure and trust towards the website. Along the same lines as Lee (2005), they explain that the specific elements and dimensions of perceived interactivity, including user control and connection, certainly lead to trust in the website. According to Cho (2004) perceiving interactivity positively influences attitudes towards websites, attitudes toward brands, and buying intentions. The results of the empirical study of Teo and al (2003) confirmed the positive impact of the high degree of interactivity on the satisfaction and usability of websites by providing options that help in making the proper search and the effective reception of information for the website user. It gives fun and motivation, and offers the possibility of controlling the interaction.

Online Interactivity at the Time of web 3.0

The Internet of things has emerged as allowed the appearance of a multitude of things of everyday life connected to the Internet. Now, it becomes possible to talk about the coexistence of several webs. In the context of the following developments, we will focus more specifically on the "web 3.0" that is called semantic web.

After 1.0, There is 2.0, and After 3.0, What Will There be?

The web 1.0 had been the first generation of websites, which content (text, image, video, and sound) were produced and hosted by the company the owner of the site. These sites were the information systems of the early history of the Internet. They were static; the content of the pages had been rarely updated. With the emergence of new scripting languages coupled with a database, some sites have become dynamic. That is, the content is managed by a Content Management System. It allows multiple individuals to work and edit information on a single document. These technologies allow the separation of management from the form and content.

Web 2.0, i.e., "participatory web" or "collaborative web", combines various complex social systems such as blogs, wikis or social networks. It refers to a certain vision of the Internet as a space of socialization. The interaction establishes action and ensures continuous production of the content. In this context, the public is considered a producer, aggregator, sharer or linker.

Web 3.0 is the third phase of web development; it is a relatively new concept. It is commonly called a semantic web because it allows understanding and interpreting the contents of the internet for easy access and for more efficient exploitation.

The web 3.0 is not limited to human machine interaction, it provides the best access to the huge pools of digitized information available throughout modeling the path of the human brain and allowing the exchange of databases through interoperable applications. It gives machines the ability to easily understand the meaning of data through the network of links between them. These contents are accessible intelligently. The command of the web 3.0 gives a competitive advantage to the company that uses it in terms of comparison to its competitors. Indeed, the web 3.0 that makes the semantics of data, i.e., the meaning attributed to data and the pivot of the web, is increasingly appearing as the most prominent and basic element of the web that is used and highlighted in more active and visible spheres.

The challenge for the semantic web is not to build data consultation platforms, but to make reference information accessible in formats making them subject for review and dissemination in other dimensions of the web. In these conditions, semantic web technologies make it possible to establish links between corpora that had been isolated from each other, also to allow unexpected discoveries. Thus, the digital economy is based on the exchange of data, mass of data or "Big Data". This data exchange is beneficial for both the individual, who makes them available, and for the user experience. The new service and data consumer are useful for users; the producing system would realize its competitive position is strengthened throughout increasing the dependence of the market on its services.

The Main Axes of the web 3.0

The changes to web 3.0 are represented in three distinct axes; semantic web, mobile web and web applications. We will examine these three tools in detail.

The Semantic web

The semantic web, more technically called "the data web", allows machines to understand semantics i.e., the meaning of information on the web. It extends the network of hyperlinks between conventional web pages by a network of structured data links allowing automated agents to access the different data sources contained on the web more intelligently and, in this way, to perform tasks (research, learning, etc.) more accurately.

One of the main purposes of the semantic web is allowing users to use the full potential of the web: so, they will be able to find, share and to combine information easily. Today, everyone is able to use forums and social networks, chatting, browsing or buying different products. Nevertheless, it would be better for the machine to do all this on behalf of man. Actually, the machines need the man to perform these tasks. The main reason is that current web pages are designed to be readable by humans, not by machines. The main goal of the semantic web is enabling these very machines to perform all these tasks, such as searching for or associating information and acting on the web.

The Mobile web

The French Mobile Multimedia Association (AFMM) defines "mobile marketing" as "the fact of using the mobile phone to reach the consumer and to react in a targeted way, at the right moment, wherever he is". The mobile Internet market is exploding. Unlimited DATA packages are starting to have reasonable prices, and phones are making it easier to browse on the Internet. In the second quarter of 2014, the global sales of iPhone show an annual increase of 13% (source: Apple), which has inspired many sites to develop specific versions, such as Facebook, Google or LinkedIn. Many describe the mobile web as a full-fledged revolution of the web 3.0.

Krum (2010) distinguishes 4 distinctive advantages of "mobile marketing". First of all, it can be personalized and extremely targeted. Beyond presenting an advertising message to a homogeneous audience, mobile marketing is a direct marketing channel capable of providing personalized advertising directly to customer, who is targeted and chosen in a particular situation or location. Secondly, its portability is attractive; mobile phones are constant companions for many consumers, especially young consumers. Third, such messages are persistent and can reach a form of permanence in the smart phone's memory more than the paper and electronic media that cannot do this job. Finally, mobile devices show intelligence by allowing interaction between the recipient and the sender. So, it can contribute to build a relationship with the company, the product and the brand image and it may enrich a campaign.

Web Applications

Currently, one of the important trends of the web is to develop and adapt applications that are known so far, in our local offices. For some time now, a lot of web applications have flourished on the web: word processing, spreadsheets, photo editing, video editing, etc. Most of these sites have used and still use conventional web technologies: html, css, ajax, etc. However, to obtain a very dynamic site, these languages are hindering development and are presenting many problems: compatibility problems between browsers, very difficult development and debugging before the heterogeneity of languages, the lower quality of graphical interfaces in comparison to those usually seen on local applications. It becomes evident that the information technology and communication techniques are evolving to overcome the defects of previous versions. All major players have jumped into the market for web applications and "Cloud Computing": Google, Microsoft, Adobe, etc. They have many advantages: requiring no installation, being adaptable with any computer, not hackable, updating is not problematic, etc. For all these reasons, web applications are increasingly prominent on the web.

The Rise of Interactive Products

People like to experience things before buying, and desire to touch, feel, see and hear. This is what the interactive product visualization is all about. In a world dominated by digital interfaces, interactive product visualization gives consumers the opportunity to experience, see, and understand products before buying them (Wagner, 2019).

Interactive 3D Product Experiences

"Interactive 3D product experiences provide consumers with the freedom to explore products online as though they were in a store, while getting direct access to enriched content and customization capabilities," said Aurélien Vaysset, CEO of Emersya. These experiences empower online consumers to fully interact with products to discover every detail, animate the moving parts, visualize interior parts, switch among color and material options on the fly, customize components and to get informed about the special features (Wagner, 2019).

"By providing intuitive interactive product visualization, you are essentially giving the consumer full control of the process and access to the product in a new way," said Travis Keith, account director for Column Five.

Successful interactive product visualization is ultimately the one that gives a true-to-life experience of a product, and is a key part of this experience with an intuitive user interface.

Avatars as Artificial Intelligence Solutions

From now on, there's little to no doubt that the future of e-commerce lies with artificial intelligence. From personalized 3D avatars and virtual fashion advisors for increased interactivity, to AI-gathered never-seen-before data for boosting sales. AI is at the helm of an e-commerce revolution. Virtual fashion assistants still have a long way to go, however what was considered as fiction just a few years ago has now turned into reality. With the insights gathered by AI, e-commerce merchants will be able to improve

Figure 1. 3D Product Visualization
Source: www.deepskystudios.com

product visualization, choose winning color combinations, and put bestsellers at the forefront of their offerings (Popov, 2018).

FUTURE RESEARCH DIRECTIONS

In the nearest future, we will witness much more use of virtual reality and augmented reality as it relates to product visualization and user experience design. IKEA has recently released an application where you can use augmented reality to see how products would look like at your house before buying them. Interactive product visualizations are increasingly coming to the mobile space, and the technologies, which allow the exploration of these visualizations via mobile devices, will also be the key to the field's success (Wagner, 2019). The contributions of online interactivity can be extensible to other potential areas of research, since it turns out that online interactivity may still have various effects on the behavior of cyber-consumers. Therefore, this phenomenon can be applied in various fields and sectors of activity, and plays fundamental roles and may be exploited especially by marketers by applying more extensive research on the empirical level to explore the way that leads to the new web 4.0 generation and to illustrate its impact on the online users' experience.

CONCLUSION

A commercial or non-commercial website competes with thousands of sites on the network. In this case, marketers and site designers face a difficult question: how to make sites more attractive and to optimize its performance in order to cope with new trends before the challenging modern consumer behavior? Accordingly, to answer to this question, this chapter sought to describe the marketing interactivity and the notion of web 3.0. It was necessary to examine the notion of online interactivity that has often focused on the effectiveness and contribution of its application in web 3.0.

REFERENCES

Berthon, P., Holbrook, M. B., & Hulbert, J. M. (2000). Beyond market orientation: A conceptualization of market evolution. *Journal of Interactive Marketing*, *14*(3), 50–66. doi:10.1002/1520-6653(200022)14:3<50::AID-DIR4>3.0.CO;2-L

Burgoon, J. K., Bonito, J. A., Bengtsson, B., Ramirez, A. Jr, Dunbar, N. E., & Miczo, N. (1999). Testing the interactivity model: Communication processes, partner assessments, and the quality of collaborative work. *Journal of Management Information Systems*, *16*(3), 33–56. doi:10.1080/07421222.1999.11518255

Cho, P. (2004). *Interactivity in Cinema-Based Media Art: a Phenomenology-Influenced Discussion*. Academic Press.

Cyr, D., Head, M., & Ivanov, A. (2007). Perceived Interactivity Leading to E-Loyalty: An Empirical Investigation of Web-Poll Design. *SIGHCI 2007 Proceedings, 16*.

Edwards, C. J., Bendickson, J. S., Baker, B. L., & Solomon, S. J. (2020). Entrepreneurship within the history of marketing. *Journal of Business Research*, *108*, 259–267. doi:10.1016/j.jbusres.2019.10.040

Heeter, C. (2000). Interactivity in the context of designed experiences. *Journal of Interactive Advertising*, *1*(1), 3–14. doi:10.1080/15252019.2000.10722040

Hoffman, D. L., & Novak, T. P. (2000). How to acquire customers on the web. *Harvard Business Review*, *78*(3), 179–188. PMID:11183979

Hrichi, A. S., & Rached, K. B. (2017). La fidélité envers la marque de «Deal» à travers une atmosphère inter@ctive: Une étude qualitative exploratoire «Le cas d'achat groupé en ligne». *La Revue Gestion et Organisation*, *9*(2), 131–142. doi:10.1016/j.rgo.2017.04.001

Jensen, J. F. (1998). Interactivity. *Nordicom Review, Nordic research on media and comunication review*, *19*(2), 191.

Jensen, J. F. (1999). *Interactive Television: TV of the Future or the Future of TV?* Aalborg Universitetsforlag.

Jobber, D., & Lancaster, G. (2009). Selling and sales management. 8. painos. Harlow: Pearson Education.

Joseph, G. V., & Thomas, K. A. (2020). Volatility of Digital Technology Enabled Learning through Social Media: Educators" Apprehensions. *Test Engineering and Management*, *82*, 5832–5839.

Kaplan, A. M., & Haenlein, M. (2010). Users of the world, unite! The challenges and opportunities of Social Media. *Business Horizons*, *53*(1), 59–68. doi:10.1016/j.bushor.2009.09.003

Kotler, P. (2003). Marketing *Management*. Academic Press.

Kotler, P., Kartajaya, H., & Setiawan, I. (2016). *Marketing 4.0: Moving from traditional to digital*. John Wiley & Sons.

Krum, C. (2010). *Mobile marketing: Finding your customers no matter where they are*. Pearson Education.

Mahood, C., Kalyanaraman, S., & Sundar, S. S. (2000, August). *The effects of erotica and dehumanizing pornography in an online interactive environment*. In Annual conference of the Association for Education in Journalism and Mass Communication, Phoenix, AZ.

McMillan, S. J., & Hwang, J. S. (2002). Measures of perceived interactivity: An exploration of the role of direction of communication, user control, and time in shaping perceptions of interactivity. *Journal of Advertising*, *31*(3), 29–42. doi:10.1080/00913367.2002.10673674

McMillan, S. J., & Hwang, J. S. (2002). Measures of perceived interactivity: An exploration of the role of direction of communication, user control, and time in shaping perceptions of interactivity. *Journal of Advertising*, *31*(3), 29–42. doi:10.1080/00913367.2002.10673674

Mechant, P. (2012). An illustrated framework for the analysis of Web2. 0 interactivity. *Contemporary Social Science*, *7*(3), 263–281. doi:10.1080/21582041.2012.716524

Moon, Y., & Nass, C. (1996). How "real" are computer personalities? Psychological responses to personality types in human-computer interaction. *Communication Research*, *23*(6), 651–674. doi:10.1177/009365096023006002

Nielsen, J. (2000). *Designing Web Usability. New Riders Publishing*.

Park, M., & Yoo, J. (2020). Effects of perceived interactivity of augmented reality on consumer responses: A mental imagery perspective. *Journal of Retailing and Consumer Services*, *52*, 101912. doi:10.1016/j.jretconser.2019.101912

Popov. (2018). https://www.ecommercetimes.com/story/85620.html

Reeves, B., & Nass, C. (2000). Perceptual user interfaces: Perceptual bandwidth. *Communications of the ACM*, *43*(3), 65–70. doi:10.1145/330534.330542

Shankar, V., & Malthouse, E. C. (2009). *A peek into the future of interactive marketing*. Academic Press.

Teo, H. H., Oh, L. B., Liu, C., & Wei, K. K. (2003). An empirical study of the effects of interactivity on web user attitude. *International Journal of Human-Computer Studies*, *58*(3), 281–305. doi:10.1016/S1071-5819(03)00008-9

Vivian Wagner. (2019). https://www.ecommercetimes.com/story/86012.html

Xie, H. (2000). Shifts of interactive intentions and information-seeking strategies in interactive information retrieval. *Journal of the American Society for Information Science*, *51*(9), 841–857. doi:10.1002/(SICI)1097-4571(2000)51:9<841::AID-ASI70>3.0.CO;2-0

Yazid, S., & Zghal, M. (2015). *L'Interactivité en Ligne: un Etat de l'Art*. Le 6ème Colloque de l'URAM (Printemps du Marketing), Hammamet.

Zephaniah, C. O., Ogba, I. E., & Izogo, E. E. (2020). Examining the effect of customers' perception of bank marketing communication on customer loyalty. *Scientific African*, e00383.

Chapter 13
Incorporating Classroom Blogs in Teaching

Dennis Relojo-Howell
Psychreg, UK

ABSTRACT

There are 1,518,207,412 websites in the world as of January 2019. These websites can be a personal, commercial, government, or non-profit organisation website. Websites are typically dedicated to a particular topic or purpose, ranging from entertainment and social networking to providing news and education. Blogs are another form of website and they have been in use for years, but it is more recently that teachers are including them as a learning tool in the classroom – as it provides many positive aspects to their students. When speaking about blogging in the classroom, we are running away from the academic writing and practising informal writing, which in many occasions takes off pressure and gives a voice to our students in a 'safe environment'. This does not mean that it may be also used to publish assignments and essays, which do contribute to share and educate in particular topics and to practice writing.

WHAT IS A BLOG?

It is estimated that as of September 2020, there are about 2 billion websites (Hosting Tribunal, n.d.). These websites can be a personal, commercial, government or non-profit organisation website. Websites are typically dedicated to a particular topic or purpose – ranging from entertainment and social networking to providing news and education (Baker, 2019).

Many people would have heard of blogs, but do not fully understand what it is, or how creating or reading blogs can improve their lives.

A blog is an online diary or journal located on a website. The content of a blog typically includes texts, pictures, videos, animated GIFs, and even scans from old physical offline diaries or journals and other hard copy documents. Since a blog can exists merely for personal use, sharing information with an exclusive group or to engage the public, a blog owner (blogger) can set their blog for private or public access (Jamie, n.d).

DOI: 10.4018/978-1-7998-3756-5.ch013

Blogs are another form of website and they have been in use for years, but it is only recently that teachers are incorporating them as a learning tool in the classroom, because it provides many positive outcomes for students (CRISS, n.d.).

When speaking about blogging in the classroom, essentially we are running away from the more traditional formal academic writing and instead we are practising a more informal way of writing. By doing this, in many occasions, it allows us to take off pressure and gives a voice to students in a 'safe environment'. This does not mean that this style of writing may be also used to publish assignments and essays. In spite of that, the informal writing that can be found within blogs does contribute to sharing and educating in particular topics and to practise writing.

HISTORY OF BLOGS

The early years of blogging came about from 1994 to 1999. The very first blog (Links.net) can be traced to the year 1994, created by Justin Hall, a US freelance journalist. During this time he was a student at Swarthmore University and the content he created was not referred to as a blog. It was just listed as a personal homepage (Rioja, 2019).

The next milestone taken towards the invention of blogs occurred in 1997. The word 'weblog' was invented on 17th December 1997 by Jorn Barger who also invented his own blog labelled *Robot Wisdom*. The name was believed to have been derived from the act of logging the web during browsing hence 'web' and 'log' (Rioja, 2019).

The *Charlotte Observer* posted a blogpost on their news website during the same year. The journalist behind this was Jonathan Dube who covered the tragic Hurricane Bonnie (Rioja, 2019).

Just as the cumbersome, code-heavy blogs of the late 90s began to give way to more accessible solutions, in 1999 the word 'weblog' was dropped in favour of a simpler term: 'blog' by Peter Merholz. This year also saw the advent of three new blogging platforms: Xanga, LiveJournal, and Blogger. Xanga, a site that focused more on the social side of blogging (similar to MySpace), boasted 300,000 users at its peak but faded out of the blogging scene entirely (Themeisle, 2019).

As blogging became more popular, tools appeared to help people curate their blog reading list or market their own blogs. 2002 was a particularly big year for the blogosphere. People also started to monetise their blogs with sites like BlogAds, a precursor to Google AdSense (Themeisle, 2019). The first-ever blog search engine, Technorati, launched that November.

With the rise of blogging came a whole new style of blog: video blogs, or vlogs. The first vlog entry was created in 2000 by Adam Kontras. It's a short video that doesn't seem like much, but it was the beginning of a new form of content, and even more, a new industry (Themeisle, 2019).

The design aspect of blogs has evolved and grown more important, with each new iteration of the concept. Early platforms like LiveJournal and Blogger offered limited but simple customisation. This allowed people with no coding experience to create unique sites. Popular LiveJournal layouts also introduced some elements of design that are still common in WordPress themes (Themeisle, 2019).

The history of blogging is far from over. According to different estimates, there are millions of blogs live today. Plus, blogs are especially important to marketing: 85% of B2C companies and 91% of B2B companies use blogs or other forms of content marketing (Themeisle, 2019).

USE OF BLOGS

The application of blogging is varied and limitless. Blogs can be used for anything that involves digital communication and its most common use can be found within the education sector. However, blogs can also be used in project management. Many companies also have their own company blogs to update people about their products and services (Clayborne, 2018).

Blogs impact three primary groups of people. When these people get confused about the purpose of their blog, we end up with blogs that have trouble meeting their goals – whatever that is – but understanding the purpose means better content and real, measurable results (Clayborne, 2018).

- **For people who just want to share ideas.** It is an outlet for emotions, opinions and ideas, some of which they may not feel comfortable expressing otherwise. It can be a way to advocate or connect with like-minded people. It becomes a hobby.
- **For searchers.** They are a source of information and entertainment. People turn to blogs to help them find solutions and make decisions on products and services.
- **For business and entrepreneurs.** They are effective for personal/business branding.

Bloggers can create better blogs when they understand why searchers read blogs to more effectively connect with an audience. When they treat blogging like a hobby or don't build blogs around topics that people are really searching for they create ineffectual articles. But the great news is that there are clear ways to create a more effective business blog that meets goals (Clayborne, 2018).

Through blogging you can also establish yourself as an expert. Anybody can start a blog on any subject they like. So you don't get a lot of respect just for saying, 'I have a website about that.'

But over time, as you write more posts and share more of your expertise, your website will change from 'just another blog' into a powerful demonstration of your knowledge in a field. When somebody visits your site and sees the insights you've shared on a subject, along with the community of people who respect and seek that insight, it will be clear that you're genuinely an expert in the field. Being an expert is an excellent thing; you may get consideration for careers, awards, or consulting opportunities (Scheidies, n.d.). This holds especially true within the field of education.

Educators are using blogs in many ways including as online portfolios, for student personal reflective journals, as a record of field notes, as discipline specific spaces for knowledge sharing, as a space for student dialogue and for class administration. To keep up with cutting edge research as it happens (Centre for Excellence in Enquiry-Based Learning, n.d.)

HOW TO USE BLOGS IN THE CLASSSROOM

Pappas (2013) outlines a variety of ways that blogs can be used in the classroom:

1. Teachers can use blogs to publish assignments, resources, and keep students and even parents up to date on class events, due dates, and content being covered.
2. Teachers can also use blogs to help students gain mastery of content and improve their writing skills.
3. Students can use blogs to publish their writing and educate others on a particular topic.

4. Students can also create blogs for the chess club or the dance club, the football team or the upcoming event.

Blogging Platforms

The popularity of blogging (which originally derives from 'personal web log') continues, whether for profit, or just to have a voice on the web, since over a decade ago when it first captured the internet as the 'next big thing. Some blogs are standalone sites, but others are a more personal section that fits into a larger, corporate website (DeMuro, 2020).

In order to blog, a blogging platform is required, which takes care of formatting the content in the form of text and images, and provides a framework for getting it onto a website. The blogging platform also makes it easier for a search engine to categorize the blog entries, and to be able to take advantage of marketing and advertising opportunities (DeMuro, 2020).

There are a number of blogging platforms available: WordPress, Edublog, and Kidblog. These are secure sites and are free.

Let's look at these platforms in more details:

1. **WordPress.** This is an elegant platform for education professionals looking to create a website for their class, and there is also a specialised platform for educators known as 'WordPress Classrooms'. Whether you need a group blog for you high school history project, or to keep your 3rd grade students' parents up to date about the next school trip, you will find the solution at WordPress (Moore, 2013).
2. **Edublog.** Since 2005, Edublog has grown into the largest educational blogging network in the world. They believe that blogging transforms the educational experience of students and have seen first-hand how blogging increases ownership of learning, engages students, and becomes a source of pride in the classroom. Edublog is a project of the prominent WordPress company Incsub, the same team behind CampusPress and WPMU DEV (Edublogs, n.d.).
3. **Kidblog.** This platform provides K-12 teachers with tools to safely publish student writing. Teachers can monitor all activity within a community of authors. Posts can even be public, but nothing goes live until a teacher approves it (Kidblog, n.d.).

Applications of Educational Blogging

Blogging with your students in the classroom can be a fun and positive way to connect and share with parents on a regular basis. There are also many educational benefits that your students can gain from blogging (Victoria, 2016). Blogging can be more than just a hobby: it has its applications within the classroom (Morris, 2018).

1. **Owning your content.** Blogging is a safe option to house all your work and the n use other platforms in ancillary ways.
2. **Online hub.** A blog can be a place where all the bits and pieces you create and explore in the online and offline world can be housed. This could include videos, podcasts, graphic designs, articles, links, etc.

3. **Traditional literacy.** Through integrating blogging into literacy curriculum, not only can students' literacy skills improve, but engagement levels can also be increased.
4. **New literacies.** These new literacies include things like digital citizenship, curation, critical evaluation, visual literacies, and so on. And then there are essential skills like problem solving, critical thinking and the opportunity to explore different topics. But there is also the aspect of problem solving and coming up with different solutions (a skill a blogger always needs).

Educational blogs or edublogs are good for keeping everyone in your class on the same page It is just the platform for student writing and digital creation. How good it is for learning depends on the types of meaningful experiences that teachers create for the students and the level of collaboration that takes place. If teachers can provide authentic experiences, allow students to interact in rigorous ways, and get students thinking about digital citizenship, then the potential for learning is there (Trautman, 2016).

Use of Blogs in the Classroom

Although people often think of social media as a space for non-academic interactions, blogs can be helpful tools for instructors interested in enhancing their students' communication skills and increasing their students' investment in learning (Oliver & Coble, 2016).

Blogs can be spaces for informal or formal writing by students, and the capacity of blogs to support multiple forms of media (images, videos, links, and so on) can help students bring creativity to their communication. Most blogs includes tools for commenting and discussion, enabling students to engage their ideas in conversation with others, either within their local learning communities or on the open Web (Oliver & Coble, 2016).

Student writing is often seen by just one person on the planet (their instructor), which can make writing assignments feel like "busy work." The dynamic interaction between writer and audience that blogs facilitate can help students see real value in their academic writing and take that writing more seriously. Moreover, the public, persistent nature of blogs can help students practice more integrative learning, finding connections among their personal, professional, and academic experiences (Oliver & Coble, 2016). Also, one of the best benefits that come as a result of blogging is that it allows people to express and hone their creativity. This can turn a boring paper into a fun creative process (Thomson, 2018).

When writing for blogs, students can experiment and interact digitally in a relaxed and low-risk environment. Blogs can be an excellent balance between the rigor and structure of a formal written assignment and the freedom to experiment with ideas and arguments (Oliver & Coble, 2016).

Reading and writing texts online are basic skills that students need to be literate citizens in the 21st century. Teaching with blogs provides the opportunity to engage students in both of these literacy activities, and the strategy has the additional benefit of enabling students to publish their writing easily and to share their writing with an authentic audience (ReadWriteThink, n.d).

When students write entries and comment on the entries of their peers, blogs become an integral part of a lively literacy community. Students can post on such topics as journal/diary entries, reflections on their writing process, details on their research projects, commentary on recent events or readings, and drafts for other writing they are doing. Once a student posts an entry, others in the class can respond, provide supportive feedback, and offer additional suggestions or perspectives. By writing and commenting on blogs, students write for real readers (not just for their teachers). As a result, students focus on clear communication and get immediate feedback on whether they communicate effectively (ReadWriteThink, n.d).

Blogging for Student Engagement

As you know, students of most ages and levels enjoy being online in just about any form. So, with the help of blogging, you can motivate students in your classroom to take an active part in their learning With this technology tool, students can work online completing writing projects, journalling, collaborating with other students, and even keeping track of and turning in assignments (Botts, n.d.).

You could create one blog for the entire class, or you could have students create their own blog, using online platforms. You will likely want to decide which platform works best for you and your class, depending on student age and level. Spend some time familiarising yourself with the different formats (Botts, n.d.).

As you can imagine, with all the uses for blogs, you can transform your classroom into an educational playground (Botts, n.d.).

Other Forms of Blogging

In the blogging world, there are different kinds of blogs and bloggers who blog to reach specific goals. If you decided to start a blog, but you're not sure what your blog is going to tackle, then identifying the type of blogger you want to become can help. There are personal blogs, business blogs, professional blogs, niche blogs, and reverse blogs (Skrba, 2019).

Microblogging

Social media in the form of microblogging can also be useful tool in education. Social media in education encompasses the practice or act of using social media platform as a way of enhancing the education of students. Many educational institutions are now adopting the use of social media into their teaching platforms to improve the educational system which makes it easier for a student to learn and communicate well. It also provides educational institutions easy and fast way to dispense information and also to receive feedback from students. More and more educators now connect with themselves on social media e.g., Facebook, Instagram, Skype, Twitter, WhatsApp, and many more.

Research has shown that over 80% of teachers, principals, school librarians, and students are engaged in social networking on social media and with the help of education specialist, it has been acknowledged that social media is of great benefit to both teachers and students. The most common social media platforms are: Facebook, Instagram, Snapchat, and Twitter.

Benefits of Social Media in Education

Social media empowers everyone including parents, teachers, and students (Wade, n.d.). It is an effective way to share information and build a community. According to one study (Anderson & Jiang, 2018), 95% of students use at least one social network, with Instagram and YouTube being the most popular online platforms among teens. Fully 95% of teens have access to a smartphone, and 45% say they are online 'almost constantly'. Some of them use it only for entertainment but it can also promote positive and useful activities. For instance, students use it to find information, promote a positive story, share something useful and collaborate with projects.

Starting from secondary school up until university graduation, social media has the role to empower parents, students, and teachers to use new ways of sharing information and build a community. Statistics show that 96% of the students who have internet access are using at least one social network (Best Master in Education, n.d.). What is even more extraordinary is that even though some of the students use social network for entertainment and other purposes, there are many of them that actually use it to promote many positive and useful activities – from finding a summer internship, promoting a success story about how to win the student-loan competition or collaborate in international projects, everything is made possible (Wade, n.d.)

Social Media Implementation in Schools

These days, teachers, coaches and principals are facing an ever-present challenge: No matter how many rules they create or punishments they mete out, school administrators cannot seem to get students to put down their smartphones. Whether children are watching the latest viral videos on YouTube or attempting to create the latest viral videos on Vine, there is always something more interesting on their phones than what is happening in the classroom. In at least one instance, though, it might be better to adhere to the adage that suggests: 'If you can't beat them, join them.' When it comes to promoting your school events and garnering student interest in them, meeting kids where they frequent are – on their phones – is a great way to catch their attention, especially if you can master one of the fastest-growing social media platforms, students will be even more likely to receive the message. Snapchat, for instance, is a free app that allows its users to share pictures and videos with their followers. Each 'snap' is only available for up to 10 seconds before it disappears and cannot be seen again unless the viewer takes a screenshot. With more than 150 million users worldwide, Snapchat has recently overtaken Twitter as the most popular social media platform (Doshan, 2016).

School have different policies when it comes to adopting social media. It is a basic concern that it uses personal data to share information and organise tasks. But is also a reason form lack of attention students pay to their class and teachers. The increase in adoption of social media is high as ever and students devote a considerable portion of their time to social media; they connect on it during and after school. It is acceptable for teachers, but they cannot stand children using it during class. It is a matter of practicality because teachers can use an online tool to communicate with their students. There is no use for a case study on the use of social media in educational institutions. You need to walk down the hallway and see children of all ages are lost in their smartphones. They are busy browsing their feeds, sharing contents on Instagram and send each other Snapchat messages. This has become an important part of their lives.

How Can Teachers Make Their Place in This Realm?

Various learning management systems have been utilising the concept of online learning for years. These systems have been in place for more than a decade. This is nothing new but it never enjoyed mainstream adoption, and we intend to change it. Teachers need to use changed technology to improve the learning process for their students. It helps the students to react positively.

It is crucial that teachers adapt to the way students are doing things. It is an important part of the whole educational process. It makes sense when a teacher is strict about homework but does little to nothing to ensure the students follow suit.

This helps the teacher get an insight into what their students are doing. It is also lets students open up and share their opinion on important matters.

Some of the Educational Blogs

Here are some educational blogs that you might consider reading or sharing to your class.

1. **Teacher Toolkit.** Originally founded in 2008 from a simple Twitter account, Ross Morrison McGill moved towards a team approach in 2017 when demand for his teaching and learning ideas outweighed his capacity to continue solo. Alongside the 10 million readers to this site, you can meet small team and their key aim is to support teachers worldwide (Teacher Toolkit, n.d.).
2. **Michael Smith's Principals Page.** This blog is about school administration. The resource is a collection of forms, letters, and surveys that have been catalogued so they are available as needed for principals and superintendents.
3. **Teach Junkie.** A blog dedicated to educators who want a one-stop shop for all the best education blogs and resources on the Web. They arrange posts by categories, so teachers looking for ideas in a certain subject can find content quickly and easily (TeachThought, 2020).
4. **Curriculum Corner.** The goal of this blog to be the first place to stop when lesson planning for your elementary classroom. Through conversations about classrooms and curriculum, the website grew to recognise the need for a free website for busy teachers.
5. **The Organized Classroom Blog.** The Organized Classroom is a blog primarily for teachers who need help making their classroom functional and efficient. The website offers free resources, tips, and ideas from local teachers (TeachThought, 2020).
6. **Polka Dotted Teacher.** A fun and whimsical education site for teachers who need to add some colour and creativity into their classroom. Her site is in the style of Dr Jessica Seuss (TeachThought, 2020).
7. **Teacherhead.** The blog is managed by Tom Sherrington. He is an experienced former headteacher and teacher and, having worked in schools for 30 years starting my training in 1986. Tom is I now exploring the world of education consultancy.
8. **The Learning Spy.** The Learning Spy was created by David Didau back in 2011 when he became frustrated with the state of education and needed a place to share the constraints and irritations of the ordinary teacher. Since then, The Learning Spy has grown into a hugely popular education blog, leading to David consulting on the Ofsted Inspection Handbook in 2014 (Pirilla, 2019).
9. **Learning with 'e's.** Steve Wheeler is the brains behind this blog, bringing together his years of experience and passion for learning technology. Learning with 'e's covers the changes technology is bringing to the education system and into the classroom, from the importance of teachers blogging to making virtual reality part of a lesson (Pirilla, 2019).
10. **Resourceaholic.** This blog was created by Jo Morgan back in April 2014 as a place to share her teaching ideas and help students discover their love for maths. Jo made the move from the city to the classroom back in 2009 and never looked back, turning her mathematical experience in statistics into fun lessons for her class (Pirilla, 2019).

Guidelines for Improving Blog User's Experience

Similar to many internet-based tools, blogs should take into account user experience in order to ensure optimum benefits from using it.

Dean (n.d.) out line fundamental principles for improving blog user's experience:

1. **Increase font size.** Font size is one of those little details that make a huge difference in how people consume your content. In fact, some people won't even read a blogpost if the typography is too small or hard to read.
2. **Increase page margins.** This is especially important for posts with 1,000 words or more. Small margins make your eyes work harder to read (they have to travel a larger distance when going back and forth).
3. **Add functional design elements.** When it comes to livening up a dense blogpost, nothing beats pretty (yet functional) design elements. This does not only include the usual suspects of images and embedded YouTube videos.
4. **Cut down on options.** This is a CRO (conversion rate optimisation) / UX (user experience) one-two punch. No one likes to see busy pages with a thousand and one banners and links.
5. **Space things out.** This is a general rule of thumb for any page with lots of text: add as much space as you possibly can. When people read your content they want to be able to sit back, relax, and read away.

FUTURE TRENDS AND CONCLUSION

The academic benefits of blogging toward education and teaching are numerous. However, there are some things to keep in mind in order to effectively execute their use, at whatever level. First, student blog entries must relate back to the course objectives. If they do not, then there is little purpose for the blog itself. Second, students need to feel they are providing accurate, easy-to-understand information. Teachers need to allow for a draft process so the student's final product is a blog they are comfortable with and is academically appropriate. Lastly, making sure there is adequate technical support for the blogs is key. Teachers should decide ahead of time what type of platform to use. If not, blogs may be difficult to upload, or lack accessibility. When done meeting some basic requirements, student blogs have endless potential (Zinger & Sinclair, 2013).

Indeed, it is remarkable that many teachers today are implementing digital technology in the classroom such as blogging and it is undeniably opening doors to new ways of learning. Teachers who are looking to adopt digital technology should not dismiss the power of blogs to revolutionise learning inside the classroom.

Whether it is used for a class website or as stand-alone student projects, blogging in the classroom can easily connect students, parents, and teachers. Encouraging students to blog helps them see the connection between what they learn from the class and the different aspects of their lives, and ultimately realise that reflective writing – through blogging – is a worthwhile skill in any field. Also, teachers who incorporate weblog development in teaching initiatives should be aware of privacy and voyeurism considerations as students reveal personal information; however, weblog construction can be useful in conveying new dimensions of identity construction and plagiarism issues in social constructivist frameworks (Oravec, 2003).

Blogging, just like any other medium of instruction, is an imperfect platform. Its advantages and disadvantages have been laid out in this chapter. The teacher, therefore, must consider this dynamic nature of blogs in order to fully optimise its benefits within the classroom.

REFERENCES

Baker, G. (2019, October 16). What is blog psychology? *Free Malaysia Today.* Retrieved from https://www.freemalaysiatoday.com/category/leisure/2019/10/16/what-is-blog-psychology/

Botts, V. (n.d.). *Blogging in the classroom.* Retrieved from https://study.com/academy/lesson/blogging-in-the-classroom.html

Centre for Excellence in Enquiry-Based Learning. (n.d.). Retrieved from http://www.ceebl.manchester.ac.uk/events/archive/aligningcollaborativelearning/Blog.pdf

Clayborne, L. (2018, January 18). What are the uses of blogs? *Quora.* Retrieved from https://www.quora.com/What-are-the-uses-of-blogs

CRISS. (n.d.). *Benefits of using blogs in the classroom.* Retrieved from https://www.crissh2020.eu/benefits-using-blogs-classroom

Dean, B. (n.d.). 5 guidelines for improving your blog's user experience. *Usability Geek.* Retrieved from https://usabilitygeek.com/5-guidelines-blog-user-experience

DeMuro, J. (2020, January). *Best blogging platforms of 2020.* Retrieved from https://www.techradar.com/uk/news/best-blogging-platform

HostingTribunal. (n.d.). How many websites are there? How many are active in 2020? Retrieved from https://hostingtribunal.com/blog/how-many-websites/

Jamie. (n.d.). *What is a blog? – A guide to understanding the concept of blogging.* Retrieved from https://makeawebsitehub.com/what-is-a-blog

Moore, C. (2013, February 20). *Create an A+ site with WordPress.com Classrooms.* Retrieved from https://en.blog.wordpress.com/2013/02/20/classrooms

Morris, K. (2018, March). *Why teachers and students should blog: 18 benefits of educational blogging.* Retrieved from http://www.kathleenamorris.com/2018/03/14/benefits-blogging

Oliver, K. H., & Coble, R. R. (2016). *Teaching with blogs.* Vanderbilt University Center for Teaching. Retrieved from https://cft.vanderbilt.edu/teaching-with-blogs/

Oravec, J. A. (2003). Weblogs as an emerging genre in higher education. *Journal of Computing in Higher Education, 14*(2), 21–44. doi:10.1007/BF02940937

Pappas, C. (2013, September 26). *How to use blogs in the classroom.* Retrieved from https://elearningindustry.com/how-to-use-blogs-in-the-classroom

Pirilla, C. (2019, August 21). Education blogs UK top 10. *Vuelio*. Retrieved from https://www.vuelio. com/uk/social-media-index/top-10-uk-education-blogs/

ReadWriteThink. (n.d.). *Teaching with blogs*. Retrieved from http://www.readwritethink.org/professional-development/strategy-guides/teaching-with-blogs-30108.html

Relojo, D. (2017). Blog psychology: Insights, benefits, and research agenda on blogs as a dynamic medium to promote the discipline of psychology and allied fields. *Psychreg Journal of Psychology*, *1*(2), 70–75. doi:10.5281/zenodo.1289165

Rioja, A. (2019, July 27). *The evolution and history of blogging*. Retrieved from https://alejandrorioja. com/blog/history-of-blogging/

Samuel-Azran, T., & Ravid, G. (2016). Can blogging increase extroverts' satisfaction in the classroom? Lessons from multiple case studies. *Interactive Learning Environments*, *24*(6), 1097–1108. doi:10.108 0/10494820.2014.961483

ScheidiesN. (n.d.). *The 20 biggest benefits of blogging*. Retrieved from https://www.incomediary.com/ biggest-blogging-benefits

Skrba, A. (2019, July 15). *8 types of blogs and bloggers. What type is yours?* Retrieved from https:// firstsiteguide.com/blogging-types-revealed/

Teacher Toolkit. (n.d.). *About us*. Retrieved from https://www.teachertoolkit.co.uk/about

TeachThought. (2020, January 15). *52 Education blogs you should follow*. Retrieved from https://www. teachthought.com/pedagogy/52-education-blogs-you-should-follow

Themeisle. (2019, June 3). *The history of blogging: From 1997 until now (with pictures)*. Retrieved from https://themeisle.com/blog/history-of-blogging

Thomson, M. (2018, April 23). *Why your students should blog: 6 powerful benefits*. Retrieved from https://www.emergingedtech.com/2018/04/why-your-students-should-blog-6-powerful-benefits

TrautmanS. (2016, October). *Edublogs*. Retrieved from https://www.commonsense.org/education/ website/edublogs

Victoria. (2016, August 24). *7 benefits of blogging in the classroom*. Retrieved from https://www.teach-starter.com/gb/blog/7-benefits-blogging-classroom-gb

Wallagher, M. (2015, September 8). *How blogging is being used in the classroom today: Research results*. Retrieved from https://www.emergingedtech.com/2015/09/the-state-of-blogging-in-the-classroom

Zinger, L., & Sinclair, A. (2013). Using blogs to enhance student engagement and learning in the health sciences. *Contemporary Issues in Education Research*, *6*(3), 349–352. doi:10.19030/cier.v6i3.7907

Chapter 14
Motivational Factors of the Usage of Web 2.0 Tools for E-Learning in Business

Cosmin Malureanu
Ascendia SA, Romania

Adriana Malureanu
University of Bucharest, Romania

Gabriel Lazar
Ascendia SA, Romania

ABSTRACT

The reasons for introducing Web 2.0 tools into the business area are multiple, from efficiency to better time management. The provision of online services by companies develops the computer skills of team members, and the materials provided through Web tools 2.0 can be accessed by a larger number of end users and their quality can be permanently evaluated. This chapter proposes to investigate the motivational factors of the usage of Web tools 2.0 by companies' team members. In particular, the research is focused on e-learning based on Web 2.0 tools for training sessions organized by companies in Romania. The in-depth analysis revealed that this generally positive perception of using the e-learning course is founded on a series of objective aspects, identified in a multiple linear regression model, ranging from the perception of the benefit of professional development to the subjective character given by user experience (UX).

INTRODUCTION

Originally thought primarily for personal use, Web 2.0 technologies are at this time, to a very large extent, a part of everyday professional activity. Web 2.0 technologies and tools have created the framework in which the writing, transmission, and consultation of information is done quickly and with minimal technical means. Today, with smartphones practical in the provision of any active person, regardless of

DOI: 10.4018/978-1-7998-3756-5.ch014

the field in which they work, when the internet is present anywhere, and at relatively low prices, social networks and content distribution platforms are increasingly being used, we can say that Web 2.0 technologies are a habit in our daily lives.

It was therefore normal for this technology to be used more and more in the economic sector. Online marketing, for example, is currently used by virtually all companies, from the largest to the smallest. Since 2016, revenues from online advertising have exceeded those from television advertising in the US (PricewaterhouseCoopers, 2017). In a report by Mordor Intelligence (2020), the online advertising market and its expected evolution is described as: *The Online Advertising Market was valued at USD 304.0 billion in 2019 and is expected to reach USD 982.82 billion by 2025, at a CAGR of 21.6% over the forecast period 2020 - 2025.*

Web 2.0 tools have also become working tools within companies. They allowed collaborative work, rapid communication, and transmission of information between employees, sometimes faster and more efficiently than through classic email. We must bear in mind that Web 2.0 tools are online software applications that allow, among other things, easy content generation, online content consultation, feedback and two-way communication, storage, and data creation on online activity. Therefore, looking at these activities, we can say that we are dealing practically with what we have become accustomed to calling e-learning.

E-learning activities are another particularly important component of the business related to Web 2.0 tools. The e-learning market emerged from the demand of the educational institutions combined with the need for new learning approaches in training for the human resources of companies. Online training has the benefit of being continuous, effective at an optimal price, and the content is easy to customize to meet the specific requirements of different clients. Due to constant IT industry progress, the online training method is becoming more and more attractive to many companies and provides sustained market dynamics and expanding opportunities for market players for both experienced and innovative companies. Learning is a continuous and dynamic process, and last-minute changes in the technology area point to profound changes, driven by the use of smartphones, cloud technologies, expanded internet connectivity, or augmented reality / virtual reality technologies. The success in this market is thus determined by the ability of suppliers to adapt to the new and to adopt innovation as it becomes available.

Apart from technology, the market is also evolving due to changes in people's perceptions and actions, so new products must also address innovation from a psycho-social and pedagogical point of view. Switching to microlearning, increasing the gamification role and integrating with social media are just a few of the directions that innovation must take into account, all related to the web 2.0 instruments. Service providers that introduce technology tools that can facilitate user engagement, motivate learners, and contribute to collaborations will be successful by increasing market share and attracting new consumers to the market.

The objective of this chapter is to present some motivational factors of the usage of Web 2.0 tools for e-learning in business, based on an experience of more than 13 years in the e-learning industry and as it emerged from a study conducted by questioning participants in an e-learning course.

BACKGROUND

The Use

The first steps in using information and communications technologies (ICTs) as a tool in education were made for reasons related to sustainability and comfort (Calvo & Villarreal, 2018). The need to reduce paper consumption has led to an increasing use of online bibliographic resources. The next step was not directly related to education either. The development of social and communication tools and platforms has enabled the possibility of collaborative and implicit work of individual and group learning activities, online and offline. Continuous progress in ICT has led on the one hand to a very wide accessibility of the different types of hardware devices and the possibility of cheap Internet connection, and on the other hand to the emergence of a huge range of applications, platforms and online activities, many of which have already entered into the daily routine of the majority of the world's population (Tvenge & Martinsen, 2018). This diversification has inevitably led to the development of different approaches in the field of eLearning and a wide field of study for researchers. One of the concepts they propose is, for example, Personal Learning Environments (PLEs) based on Web 2.0 services (Torres Kompen, Edirisingha, Canaleta, Alsina, & Monguet, 2019).

In a recently published study, Choudhury and Pattnaik (2020) presented the topical themes of eLearning as it emerged from questioning beneficiaries, from learners and instructors to content developers, IT technology providers and education institutions. They identified as the main advantage of eLearning its special flexibility in several ways: rhythm, workplace, used tools. The biggest disadvantage identified was the lack of feedback, but it should be stressed that this disadvantage is largely eliminated by the use of web 2.0 tools that allow much wider communication between all participants in the learning act. The authors' final conclusion is that (Choudhury & Pattnaik, 2020, p. 9):

E-learning undoubtedly is a source of competitive advantage, however, as discussed in the paper stakeholders need to observe the changing dynamics of the learning environment and should be ready to adapt to the factors that enable adoption and diffusion of e-learning tools.

As is normal, the use of web 2.0 tools in education first began in universities. Numerous studies have sought to analyse how this new type of education influences the quality of learning, how online education is viewed and accepted by students, but also by teachers.

Some studies have highlighted how the new learning environment can increase students' motivation. They are increasingly turning from passive participants in the learning process, from information receptors, into protagonists of the educational process (Torres Kompen et al., 2019). Communication opportunities, usually encouraged by educators, allow students to communicate a lot and constructively with each other or with teachers. In this way they have access to much more diverse information and ideas, being able to identify completely new aspects and correlations for the studied topics. Also, the enhancement of the communication allows the use of the peer-review system, found as a main way to enhance the teaching-learning process (Mora, Signes-Pont, Fuster-Guilló, & Pertegal-Felices, 2020).

Many studies have focused on the aspect related to the motivation of the use of digital tools in education and eLearning, on the aspects that ensure the satisfaction of the user, whether we are talking about the teacher or the student, and on the acceptance of the use of these tools. To analyse these aspects many different instruments and theories were developed a number of different theories and models on acceptance of IT technologies like the Theory of Reasoned Action (TRA), Technology Acceptance Model (TAM), Theory of Planned Behaviour (TPB), Decomposed Theory of Planned Behaviour (DTPB), Uses and Gratifications Theory (UGT), The unified theory of acceptance and use of technology (UTAUT), Innovation Diffusion Theory (IDT), Expectation-Confirmation Theory (ECT) (Abdous, 2019; Dunn & Kennedy, 2019; Harandi, 2015; Ifinedo, 2017; Liao, Chen, & Shih, 2019).

But the effects of social media on education are proving to be not only positive, but also negative (Zannettou, Sirivianos, Blackburn, & Kourtellis, 2019). A study published in 2020 identified and analysed several such negative aspects (Neelakandan, Annamalai, Rayen, & Arunajsmine, 2020), three of which are considered the main ones. Firstly, excessive use of social networks in the learning process leads to a decrease in academic performance due to the ease with which answers are found. Students thus lose the concentration and the need to synthesize information, resulting in superficial and short-term learning. Another negative aspect is the one related to the management of time. In particular, social networks such as Facebook, YouTube and Tweeter present a lot of adjacent information that disrupts the normal learning process (Lloro & Hunold, 2020). The information is diluted and takes an impermissible long time, the student jumps from one subject to another away from the original theme. Finally, one aspect that should not be neglected is given by the personal aspects of interaction on social networks that become and remain public. There are many situations where activity and social media posts have influenced a university or an employer in their relationship with a potential student or employee (Neelakandan et al., 2020).

The Problem

Consumer behaviour in the field of information has changed radically in recent years. The switch from traditional printed sources to digital ones is not just a change in the support on which the information is delivered, but also in the user's behaviour, and learning makes no exception. According to recent studies on the subject of the eLearning systems used mainly for corporate training, the market is facing significant technological and pedagogical changes. The analysis of the market trends identified four main necessary changes presented in Figure 1. So, this is a broad market transformation opportunity that targets both the way the content of the digital courses is presented to users, but also the way the digital platforms hosting those courses need to function.

In the study *Elearning market trends and forecasts 2017-2021*, Docebo (2016), an important eLearning player worldwide, identified the industry trends:

Broadly, the entire eLearning landscape around the globe is changing rapidly and new trends continue to emerge. Some of these trends are related to the eLearning industry itself, while others have been generated by the transformation of the human resources management across enterprise. Additionally, a number of significant consumers trends that directly or indirectly impact the eLearning landscape have arisen.

In a study published on October 19, 2018, Aura Interactiva company identified 10 necessary things which must characterize a modern professional training system (Figure 2) (Aura Interactiva, 2018). A good solution should be designed to answer to (almost) all these requests but should be concentrated on four main directions/trends, identified in Fig. 1.

The first one is the necessity to shift from a **fixed learning system** to an **adaptive learning path**. The client defines his expectations, in terms of skills and abilities and the system guides him to complete only the relevant courses. The second important change is from **passive learning** to **active learning**. The courses must become more and more interactive, requesting the active intervention of the learner and his active participation in the training process. The third aspect that must be considered by any company delivering enterprise-class software solutions is that the client wants usually **multi-platform** and **personalized solutions**. More and more activities are transferred from desktop computers and laptops

Figure 1. Top 4 changes in the corporate training domain based on eLearning systems identified from the market analysis

to smartphones and tablets and the training activity is not an exception. The information must be ready to be delivered at any moment of the day and on any device, the activity started on a device must be available to be continued on another. Another aspect that must be considered by any company delivering enterprise-class software solutions is that the client wants usually personalized solutions. Starting from a basic product, this customization can require a lot of resources, both in terms of programming effort as well as hardware, basically for each customer being made a different product. Also, any update must be made separately for each customer, making it a very expensive and inefficient process.

According to a study by Hossain and Shirazi (2015), one important Software as a Service (SaaS) players managed to achieve a double profit margin compared to the average of the industry by adopting a multi-tenant architecture for its products.

The fourth strategy change, one of the most important from all, is generated by the **microlearning** approach. With web 2.0 and social media becoming common working tools the concept of microlearning has become a standard, not just in private life, but also in the professional activity. With definitions from very simple *"the delivery of bite-sized content nuggets"* (Work-Learning Research Inc., 2017), to very elaborate ones, the concept is of great currentness. The enormous amount of information, the extreme accessibility, the easy-to-filter variants according to the topics of interest have led to a change in the way the user interacts with the information. Information needs to be sent quickly, as condensed as possible, so the user can quickly decide whether it is of interest. Whether you want to learn to use a function in Excel or how to change a bulb in a car headlight, a quick search on the Internet generates hundreds of results, but there are only a few of the relevant ones that you have to choose rapidly. One of the advantages of microlearning that has made it so popular is the perfect combination of small volumes of information and the flexibility of the used technology (Jomah, Masoud, Kishore, & Aurelia, 2016). For any beneficiary, the key to making microlearning efficient is having a wide portfolio of such courses, targeting various soft or hard skills, thus being able to provide the learners with a learning path that will utterly provide for each learner the needed skills mixture.

Figure 2. Corporate training: 10 Things Modern L&D Professionals Should Be Doing. Source: https://www.shiftelearning.com

It is now the right moment for the eLearning strategy to refine, using the advantages of microlearning strategies, as some innovative companies have done over the past few years (Emerson & Berge, 2018).

The State-of-Art

The eLearning systems market is very wide and diverse. From the open source solutions to very expensive products, the market shows many ways to solve the issues related to eLearning.

To be sure that all customers benefit from the advantages of distance learning, the chosen eLearning solution must be complete. An eLearning system is composed of two inseparable components: a) the learning and evaluation platform which is the Learning Management System (LMS), and b) the digital courses, which must be interactive and to present conclusive information in an attractive way. To be precise, the eContent (or the digital modules) for training are of two kinds: off-the-shelf (ready-made, one size fits all approach – ex: international compliance, security, management, etc.) or best-spoke (tailor-made, made to the needs and specificities of the beneficiary – ex: beneficiary's products, procedures).

The learning platform must incorporate the latest technologies and to eliminate the weaknesses identified in the current platforms, assuring the four main necessary changes presented in Figure 1 (adaptative learning path, active learning, multi-device functionality, microlearning implementation) and presenting also at least a multi-tenant architecture, a responsive behaviour and compliant with the TinCan standard (the official successor of industry's veteran standard SCORM 2004). Shareable Content Object Reference Model (SCORM) is a specification of the Advanced Distributed Learning (ADL) and has been the de facto eLearning standard for packaging eLearning content (Batt). Tin Can API or standard is also known as The Experience API (or xAPI) and is an eLearning software specification that allows learning content and learning systems to speak to each other in a manner that records and tracks all types of learning experiences (Brandon, 2012).

Table 1. Comparison between the proposed solution and the existing market

Feature	Docebo	Adobe Captivate Prime	Litmos LMS	iSpring Learn	Talent LMS	Gnosis Connect	360 Learning LMS	The Academy LMS
Adaptive learning path	No	No	No	No	No	No	No	No
Personal AI assistant	No	No	No	No	No	No	No	No
Responsive (multi-device)	Yes	Yes	Yes	Yes	No	No	No	No
Multi-tenant architecture	NI	No	No	Yes	Yes	No	No	No
Gamification features	Yes	Yes	Yes	Yes	Yes	Yes	Yes	Yes
Micro learning implementation	NI	NI	NI	NI	NI	NI	NI	NI
Off-the-shelf content	Yes	No	Yes	No	Yes	No	No	No
On demand content	No	No	No	No	No	No	No	No
One type of user account	No	Yes	No	No	No	No	No	No

* NI – No information

In addition, the platform's functionalities need to be modulated and manageable from an administration panel and to have only one type of user account with specific rights, based on custom user profiles.

Because of the big diversity of the commercial solutions, the presentation of the existing market is constructed starting from the identification of the main products made by Christopher Pappas (Pappas, 2014) and updated in 2019. Starting from these recognized world-leading products, a comparison is presented in Table 1. The identification of the different characteristics was made analysing the product presentation page. The main characteristics were established based on the analysis presented above.

A very quick analysis of data from Table 1 shows that all major market players have not considered several aspects considered important for a modern eLearning platform: an adaptive learning path, a personal AI assistant and on-demand content.

The Market

Apart from technology, the market is also evolving due to changes in people's perceptions and actions, so new products must also address innovation from a psycho-social and pedagogical point of view. Switching to microlearning, increasing the gamification role, and integrating with social media are just a few of the directions that innovation must take into account. Service providers that introduce technology tools that can facilitate user engagement, motivate learners, and contribute to collaborations will be successful by increasing market share and attracting new consumers to the market.

According to Androulla Vassiliou - European Commissioner for Education, Culture, Multilingualism and Youth (European Commission, 2014), the online and open education world is changing how education is resourced, delivered and taken up. Over the next 10 years, eLearning is projected to grow fifteen-fold, accounting for 30% of all educational provision.

According to the "*E-learning Market - Global Outlook and Forecast 2018-2023*" report (Arizton, 2019), the global eLearning market size is expected to reach USD 65.41 billion by 2023. Another research report by Global Market Insights (Wadhwani & Gankar, 2019) estimated the eLearning market size at USD 200 billion by 2024, and according to Stratistics MRC cited by the European Commission (2018), the global eLearning market is expected to reach USD 275.10 billion by 2022. The study published in 2017 by a major player on this market, Docebo (2016), estimates the size of the eLearning market to more than USD 40 billion in 2023. There are no public backed studies about the dimension of this market at an international level.

More important than the dimension is the dynamics of the market, estimated by all studies to 5 - 7.5% by year in the next period.

At the European level, according to cited reports (Arizton, 2019; DOCEBO, 2016), the Western European market was estimated at USD 8 billion in 2018, with a growth rate around 13%, and the Eastern European market USD 1 billion, with a growth rate around 17%.

According to the latest market study released by Technavio and cited by Business Wire (2018), the size of the global corporate eLearning market is predicted to reach an approximate amount of USD 31 billion in revenue by the end of 2020. Also, the corporate eLearning market is expected to grow at a Compound Annual Growth Rate (CAGR) of 11.41% during the 2016 to 2020 period, according to Technavio's analysts (Business Wire, 2018).

According to Research and Markets Report, the global content authoring tools market is expected to grow at a CAGR of 7.72% over the 2016-2020 period (Arizton, 2019). The Learning Authoring Tools market continues to be dominated by desktop tools, with Articulate and iSpring claiming a total aggregate user base around 90.000 organizations (European Commission, 2018).

Apart from this evident substantial demand, the market shows a clear willingness to pay for innovation. The market is characterized by an important tendency to change the used eLearning systems, looking for innovation in content delivery. While most companies that need learning management already have LMS products, there is a significant churn trend, as they can now easily switch to another supplier. As a matter of fact, according to Docebo study, long-term contracts for LMS products are now quite rare and switching vendors are relatively painless for buyers.

THE STUDY CASE

As a provider of e-learning services, but also as a manufacturer of working tools, such as Coffee LMS and e-learning authoring tool LIVRESQ, Ascendia SA has been and is always interested in assessing the motivational factors of the usage of Web 2.0 tools for e-learning in business. In this chapter are presented the results from the evaluation of a questionnaire regarding the attitude of students regarding one e-learning course, built using LIVRESQ instruments and hosted by the Coffee LMS platform.

The questionnaire had 14 questions and was applied to the students from a pharma company in Romania, employed in pharmacies spread throughout the country. The students spend 459h:13m:50s on LMS platform with an average of 1h:3m:56s. From the initial number total of 617 students, 483 (78%) have accessed the course, and 431 (70%) finished it. The questionnaire was applied to all 483 students who have completed at least part of the course and 438 valid responses were received. That means more than 90% of the students responded, assuring the statistical validity of the analysis. The questionnaire was applied online, at the end of the course, and contained 14 statements. The students have expressed their agreement on those claims on a five-point Likert scale, from 1 (total disagreement) to 5 (total agreement).

The corresponding assertion were:

Q1. The course is useful for my daily work
Q2. I consider such courses beneficial for my professional development
Q3. I will recommend the course to my colleagues
Q4. It is easy to access and complete the online course
Q5. The duration of the course is appropriate to the information transmitted
Q6. The graphic presentation is dynamic and impactful
Q7. The course helped me understand the feature – action – benefit recommendation
Q8. It would help me find other information that would help me make the best recommendations
Q9. The electronic format for the course is convenient and useful
Q10. We learned a lot of information in a short time
Q11. I easily understood the information
Q12. Feature-action-benefit method is effective to memorize and recommend products
Q13. I managed to keep my attention throughout the course
Q14. I want to have access to similar online courses to help me learn products easier.

The first analysis was made regarding the proportion of each type of response as an indication of the global attitude of the students towards the e-learning module. The results of each of the 14 questions are presented in Figure 3. More than 75% of the respondents of each item were in a total agreement with the assertion and very little information can be obtained from this analysis.

Advanced statistical analysis was performed to obtain relevant information on the motivational factors of the usage of Web 2.0 tools for e-learning in business. As the analysis method, an Enter type multiple linear regression analysis was chosen. Each variable has the same initial weight due to the fact that the literature study did not reveal situations in which the studied predictors were described. In this analysis, the first item was chosen as a dependent variable because it describes the motivation for the usage of this online instrument (*The course is useful for my daily work*). In conclusion, the linear regression was started with a dependent variable (Q1) and 13 predictors (Q2 – Q14). The characteristic data of the chosen regression model are presented in Table 2.

Figure 3. The proportion of each type of response from 1 (total disagreement) to 5 (total agreement) regarding the 14 items

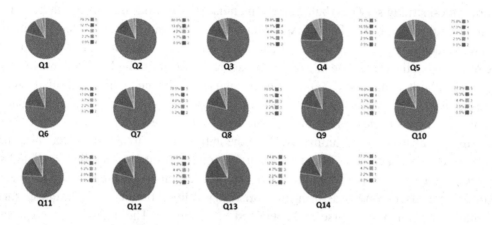

Table 2. The multiple linear regression model summary

Model Summary[a]							
Model	R	R Square	Adjusted R Square	Std. Error of the Estimate	Change Statistics		
					R Square Change	F Change	df1
1	.880[b]	.775	.769	.308	.775	131.011	11

Model Summary[a]			
Model	Change Statistics		Durbin-Watson
	df2	Sig. F Change	
1	419[b]	.000	2.040

a. Dependent Variable: Q1

b. Predictors: (Constant), Q13, Q3, Q6, Q4, Q10, Q12, Q7, Q2, Q11, Q9, Q8

Analyzing the results from Table 2, it can be seen that two predictors (Q5 and Q14) were excluded from the final model because the analysis indicated that their significance to the modes was very low. The chosen multiple linear regression model explains 77.5% of the total variation of the dependent variable. The Durbin-Watson coefficient, which is an indicator of the quality of the model has a value of 2.040, very close to the ideal value, 2.00. The model is also validated by the value of the Sig. F Change coefficient of .000. The values of the regression coefficients and their statistical significance are presented in Table 3. The results indicate that only for five external variables, the calculated factors are significant from the mathematical point of view. The discussion is made solely for these five factors.

The most significant predictor is Q2, with the biggest standardized coefficient, .469. Q2 item was *"I consider such courses beneficial for my professional development"* and is an indication of the generally positive perception of using the e-learning course. The Q3 predictor (I *will recommend the course to my colleagues*) had a standardized coefficient of .294 and was the second as weight in the model. He strengthens the positive perception of the students, who are very much in agreement that they will recommend the course to other colleagues. The Q8 predictor is very important from the analysis point of view (*It would help me find other information that would help me make the best recommendations*). The presence of this predictor in the final model is an indication of the motivation of students to extend their study with the help of Web 2.0 instruments. The next positive coefficient is corresponding to the 13th predictor (*I managed to keep my attention throughout the course*). It is an indicator of the interest and motivation for the usage of this online instrument, without moments of loss of attention and concentration, as would have happened if the students had not been motivated to follow the course. The only significative regression coefficient corresponds to the Q6 item (*The graphic presentation is dynamic and impactful*). These results indicate that the students they want a more dynamic and impactful graphic representation from e-learning courses, as they are used to from other Web 2.0 tools that they usually use.

Table 3. Calculated coefficients of the multiple linear regression

	Coefficients						
Model		**Unstandardized Coefficients**		**Standardized Coefficients**	**t**	**Sig.**	**Correlations**
		B	**Std. Error**	**Beta**			**Zero-order**
1	(Constant)	-.287	.138		-2.082	**.038**	
	Q2	.557	.064	**.469**	8.718	**.000**	.846
	Q3	.317	.050	**.294**	6.288	**.000**	.810
	Q4	.035	.044	.037	.801	.424	.690
	Q6	-.107	.045	**-.102**	-2.390	**.017**	.671
	Q7	.028	.064	.027	.440	.660	.758
	Q8	.155	.078	**.141**	1.998	**.046**	.787
	Q9	-.098	.056	-.105	-1.747	.081	.669
	Q10	.019	.059	.019	.329	.742	.720
	Q11	-.042	.055	-.043	-.758	.449	.717
	Q12	.063	.049	.058	1.286	.199	.721
	Q13	.128	.040	**.138**	3.152	**.002**	.694

To confirm the unidimensionality of the regression model found for the significant items of the model, the Cronbach's Alpha coefficient indicating the fidelity of the scale was calculated. The obtained values are presented in Table 4, where we see that both the value of the coefficient calculated for the direct calculated items, and that calculated for standardized items are very close to the maximum value, 1. This indicates that the chosen items express the same dimension, converge to the same dimension.

Table 4. Calculated Cronbach's Alpha coefficient

Reliability Statistics		
Cronbach's Alpha	**Cronbach's Alpha Based on Standardized Items**	**N of Items**
.947	.949	6

In order to further verify the necessity of each of the items kept in the final model, the item-total statistics was calculated, the results being presented in Table 5. It is noticed that if we remove any of the items, except for Q13, the new value of the Cronbach's Alpha coefficient decreases, which means that this reduces the accuracy of the model. Only in the case of removing item Q13, the new value of the Cronbach's Alpha coefficient is identical to that calculated for the entire model. From Table 5 can also be observed that all Corrected Item-Total Correlation coefficients have values over .765, well above the minimum .20 indicated in the literature as the limit to which each item can be used in the model.

As a next step of the statistical analysis, the correlations between the selected items were calculated, and the results are presented in Table 6. It should be emphasized that all values are statistically significant, for all correlations the Sig (2-tailed) coefficient being equal to .000, under the conditions where for a significant correlation, the considered threshold was .010.

The strongest correlation was found between items Q1 and Q2, with a Pearson correlation coefficient of .846. This is not surprising because always is a strong link between a positive perception of daily work and professional development. The weakest correlation was found between items Q3 *I will recommend the course to my colleagues a*nd Q13 *I managed to keep my attention throughout the course*, but the values of Pearson Correlation coefficient remains high, having a value of .666.

Table 5. Item-Total Statistics

	Scale Mean if Item Deleted	Scale Variance if Item Deleted	Corrected Item-Total Correlation	Squared Multiple Correlation	Cronbach's Alpha if Item Deleted
Q1	23.64	7.305	.846	.771	.936
Q2	23.60	7.687	.892	.815	.932
Q3	23.63	7.512	.852	.755	.935
Q6	23.65	7.569	.803	.691	.941
Q8	23.62	7.444	.897	.814	.930
Q13	23.69	7.298	.765	.596	.947

The unidimensionality of the model found was actually confirmed by the exploratory factor analysis that indicated a value of Kaiser-Meyer-Olkin Measure of Sampling Adequacy of .917, very close to the maximum value of 1.0, as can be seen in Table 7.

The Kaiser-Meyer-Olkin and Bartlett's Test expresses the convergence of model variables. As shown in Table 8, a single item, Q1, explains 79.904% of the model, so the identified items shape a single dimension.

The non-parametric Mann-Whitney test was chosen to compare the average of each variable of the model according to the respondent's gender. The obtained results are presented in Table 9 and Table 10.

According to the analysis, the respondent's gender is statistically significant only in the case of Items Q2 *I consider such courses beneficial for my professional development*, Q3 *I will recommend the course to my colleagues* and Q8 *It would help me find other information that would help me make the best recommendations*. The values of the mean rank calculated in Table 9 show that for all three items, the perception of the women was strongest, indicating a more positive motivation of using the e-learning course.

Table 6. Calculated correlations between model variables

		Q1	Q2	Q3	Q6	Q8	Q13
Q1	Pearson Correlation	1	**.846****	.810**	.671**	.787**	.694**
	Sig. (2-tailed)		.000	.000	.000	.000	.000
	Sum of Squares and Cross-products	176.144	125.390	132.524	112.868	126.353	132.346
	Covariance	.410	.292	.308	.262	.294	.308
	N	431	431	431	431	431	431
Q2	Pearson Correlation	**.846****	1	.818**	.764**	.838**	.707**
	Sig. (2-tailed)	.000		.000	.000	.000	.000
	Sum of Squares and Cross-products	125.390	124.798	112.550	108.158	113.246	113.517
	Covariance	.292	.290	.262	.252	.263	.264
	N	431	431	431	431	431	431
Q3	Pearson Correlation	.810**	.818**	1	.719**	.816**	**.666****
	Sig. (2-tailed)	.000	.000		.000	.000	.000
	Sum of Squares and Cross-products	132.524	112.550	151.847	112.260	121.640	117.970
	Covariance	.308	.262	.353	.261	.283	.274
	N	431	431	431	431	431	431
Q6	Pearson Correlation	.671**	.764**	.719**	1	.809**	.676**
	Sig. (2-tailed)	.000	.000	.000		.000	.000
	Sum of Squares and Cross-products	112.868	108.158	112.260	160.589	124.095	123.021
	Covariance	.262	.252	.261	.373	.289	.286
	N	431	431	431	431	431	431
Q8	Pearson Correlation	.787**	.838**	.816**	.809**	1	.742**
	Sig. (2-tailed)	.000	.000	.000	.000		.000
	Sum of Squares and Cross-products	126.353	113.246	121.640	124.095	146.413	128.944
	Covariance	.294	.263	.283	.289	.340	.300
	N	431	431	431	431	431	431
Q13	Pearson Correlation	.694**	.707**	.666**	.676**	.742**	1
	Sig. (2-tailed)	.000	.000	.000	.000	.000	
	Sum of Squares and Cross-products	132.346	113.517	117.970	123.021	128.944	206.524
	Covariance	.308	.264	.274	.286	.300	.480
	N	431	431	431	431	431	431

**. Correlation is significant at the 0.01 level (2-tailed).

Table 7. Calculated KMO and Bartlett's Test

Kaiser-Meyer-Olkin Measure of Sampling Adequacy.		.917
Bartlett's Test of Sphericity	Approx. Chi-Square	2562.160
	df	15
	Sig.	.000

Table 8. Total variance explained

Component	Initial Eigenvalues			Extraction Sums of Squared Loadings		
	Total	% of Variance	Cumulative %	Total	% of Variance	Cumulative %
1	4.794	79.904	79.904	4.794	79.904	79.904
2	.384	6.406	86.310			
3	.341	5.692	92.002			
4	.195	3.242	95.244			
5	.151	2.516	97.760			
6	.134	2.240	100.000			

Table 9. Calculate ranks of the Mann-Whitney Test

	Gender	N	Mean Rank	Sum of Ranks
Q1	Female	389	218.08	84833.50
	Male	42	196.73	8262.50
	Total	431		
Q2	Female	389	218.98	85181.50
	Male	42	188.44	7914.50
	Total	431		
Q3	Female	389	219.07	85220.00
	Male	42	187.52	7876.00
	Total	431		
Q6	Female	389	217.68	84679.00
	Male	42	200.40	8417.00
	Total	431		
Q8	Female	389	219.10	85228.50
	Male	42	187.32	7867.50
	Total	431		
Q13	Female	389	217.72	84693.50
	Male	42	200.06	8402.50
	Total	431		

Table 10. Mann-Whitney Test Statistics

			Q1	Q2	Q3
Mann-Whitney U			7359.500	7011.500	6973.000
Wilcoxon W			8262.500	7914.500	7876.000
Z			-1.544	-2.255	-2.252
Asymp. Sig. (2-tailed)			.123	**.024**	**.024**
Monte Carlo Sig. (2-tailed)	Sig.		.132[b]	.027[b]	.025[b]
	99% Confidence Interval	Lower Bound	.123	.023	.021
		Upper Bound	.140	.031	.028
Monte Carlo Sig. (1-tailed)	Sig.		.068[b]	.018[b]	.020[b]
	99% Confidence Interval	Lower Bound	.062	.015	.016
		Upper Bound	.075	.022	.023
			Q6	Q8	Q13
Mann-Whitney U			7514.000	6964.500	7499.500
Wilcoxon W			8417.000	7867.500	8402.500
Z			-1.193	-2.259	-1.185
Asymp. Sig. (2-tailed)			.233	**.024**	.236
Monte Carlo Sig. (2-tailed)	Sig.		.243[b]	.020[b]	.234[b]
	99% Confidence Interval	Lower Bound	.232	.017	.223
		Upper Bound	.254	.024	.245
Monte Carlo Sig. (1-tailed)	Sig.		.119[b]	.017[b]	.126[b]
	99% Confidence Interval	Lower Bound	.110	.014	.117
		Upper Bound	.127	.020	.134

FUTURE RESEARCH DIRECTIONS

Today, the use of e-learning courses and platforms is a necessary step to have trained employees. The research of the parameters that influence in a positive way the perception of students on this type of activity must continue because advances in technology and the increasing use of Web 2.0 tools are rapidly changing people's perceptions and habits. Only by taking this into account can be provided the necessary framework for an efficient and quality online preparation.

CONCLUSION

Corporate culture is increasingly adopting "investing in people" by training them. More and more companies are turning to specialized services for the integration of an LMS-type platform. Online courses are a good way to improve the knowledge and performance of learners, employees of a company, and by increasing the personal level improves the performance of the entire team. However, employee training does not have only the formal component. Through the interaction and communication within social groups and networks such as Facebook, LinkedIn, Slack or other workgroups, individuals are exposed to learning, access information, share knowledge. Analysis of the attitude and motivational factors of the usage of Web 2.0 tools for e-learning must be a continuing concern for both e-learning providers and employers, who must choose the most effective working tools. This chapter presents such an analysis. The general conclusion of the analysis was that the students have a dominant positive attitude towards the use of the e-learning course. The in-depth analysis revealed that this generally positive perception of using the e-learning course is founded on a series of objective aspects, identified in a multiple linear regression model.

A very important result of the analysis, useful in designing future activities, is that the students want to work with materials with a more dynamic and impactful graphic, as they are used to from other Web 2.0 tools that they usually use.

AUTHOR CONTRIBUTION STATEMENT

All authors contributed equally to the work.

REFERENCES

Abdous, M. (2019). Influence of satisfaction and preparedness on online students' feelings of anxiety. *The Internet and Higher Education*, *41*, 34–44. doi:10.1016/j.iheduc.2019.01.001

Arizton. (2019). *E-learning Market - Global Outlook and Forecast 2019-2024*. Retrieved from https://www.researchandmarkets.com/reports/4825750/e-learning-market-global-outlook-and-forecast?utm_code=b7dx72&utm_medium=CI

Aura Interactiva. (2018). *10 Things Modern L&D Professionals Should Be Doing*. Retrieved from https://www.shiftelearning.com/blog/10-ways-to-make-ld-cool-again

Batt, B. (n.d.). *How to Explain AICC, SCORM 1.2, and SCORM 2004 to Anyone*. Retrieved from https://www.elearningfreak.com/how-to-explain-aicc-scorm-12-and-scorm-2004-to-anyone/

Brandon, B. (2012). Making History: mLearnCon 2012 Rocks Attendees. *Learning Solutions Magazine*. Retrieved from https://web.archive.org/web/20120806005118/http://www.learningsolutionsmag.com/articles/958/

Business Wire. (2018). *Global Corporate e-Learning Market to Post 11% CAGR During 2018-2022*. Retrieved from https://www.businesswire.com/news/home/20180630005028/en/Global-Corporate-e-Learning-Market-Post-11-CAGR

Calvo, N., & Villarreal, Ó. (2018). Analysis of the growth of the e-learning industry through sustainable business model archetypes: A case study. *Journal of Cleaner Production*, *191*, 26–39. doi:10.1016/j.jclepro.2018.04.211

Choudhury, S., & Pattnaik, S. (2020). Emerging themes in e-learning: A review from the stakeholders' perspective. *Computers & Education*, *144*, 103657. doi:10.1016/j.compedu.2019.103657

DOCEBO. (2016). *Elearning market trends and forecasts 2017-2021*. Retrieved from https://www. docebo.com/resource/elearning-market-trends-and-forecast-2017-2021/

Dunn, T. J., & Kennedy, M. (2019). Technology Enhanced Learning in higher education; motivations, engagement and academic achievement. *Computers & Education, 137*, 104–113. doi:10.1016/j. compedu.2019.04.004

Emerson, L. C., & Berge, Z. L. (2018). *Microlearning: Knowledge management applications and competency-based training in the workplace*. UMBC Faculty Collection.

European Commission. (2014). *New modes of learning and teaching in higher education*. Retrieved from https://ec.europa.eu/education/library/reports/modernisation-universities_en.pdf

European Commission. (2018). *Promoting Online Training Opportunities for the Workforce in Europe*. Retrieved from https://repositorio-aberto.up.pt/bitstream/10216/121228/2/343305.pdf

Harandi, S. R. (2015). Effects of e-learning on Students' Motivation. *Procedia: Social and Behavioral Sciences, 181*, 423–430. doi:10.1016/j.sbspro.2015.04.905

Hossain, A., & Shirazi, F. (2015). *Cloud Computing: A Multi-tenant Case Study*. Paper presented at the International Conference on Human-Computer Interaction.

Ifinedo, P. (2017). Examining students' intention to continue using blogs for learning: Perspectives from technology acceptance, motivational, and social-cognitive frameworks. *Computers in Human Behavior, 72*, 189–199. doi:10.1016/j.chb.2016.12.049

Intelligence, M. (2020). *Online Advertising Market - Growth, Trends, and Forecast (2020 - 2025)*. Retrieved from https://www.researchandmarkets.com/reports/4602258/online-advertising-market-growth-trends-and

Jomah, O., Masoud, A. K., Kishore, X. P., & Aurelia, S. (2016). Micro learning: A modernized education system. *BRAIN. Broad Research in Artificial Intelligence and Neuroscience, 7*(1), 103–110.

Liao, C.-W., Chen, C.-H., & Shih, S.-J. (2019). The interactivity of video and collaboration for learning achievement, intrinsic motivation, cognitive load, and behavior patterns in a digital game-based learning environment. *Computers & Education, 133*, 43–55. doi:10.1016/j.compedu.2019.01.013

Lloro, T., & Hunold, C. (2020). The public pedagogy of neighborhood Facebook communities: Negotiating relations with urban coyotes. *Environmental Education Research, 26*(2), 189–205. doi:10.1080 /13504622.2019.1690637

Mora, H., Signes-Pont, M. T., Fuster-Guilló, A., & Pertegal-Felices, M. L. (2020). A collaborative working model for enhancing the learning process of science & engineering students. *Computers in Human Behavior, 103*, 140–150. doi:10.1016/j.chb.2019.09.008

Neelakandan, S., Annamalai, R., Rayen, S. J., & Arunajsmine, J. (2020). Social Media Networks Owing To Disruptions For Effective Learning. *Procedia Computer Science, 172*, 145–151. doi:10.1016/j. procs.2020.05.022

Pappas, C. (2014). *The 20 Best Learning Management Systems (2019 Update).* Retrieved from https://elearningindustry.com/the-20-best-learning-management-systems

PricewaterhouseCoopers. (2017). *IAB internet advertising revenue report: 2016 full year results.* Retrieved from https://www.iab.com/wp-content/uploads/2016/04/IAB_Internet_Advertising_Revenue_Report_FY_2016.pdf

Torres Kompen, R., Edirisingha, P., Canaleta, X., Alsina, M., & Monguet, J. M. (2019). Personal learning Environments based on Web 2.0 services in higher education. *Telematics and Informatics, 38,* 194–206. doi:10.1016/j.tele.2018.10.003

Tvenge, N., & Martinsen, K. (2018). Integration of digital learning in industry 4.0. *Procedia Manufacturing, 23,* 261–266. doi:10.1016/j.promfg.2018.04.027

Wadhwani, P., & Gankar, S. (2019). *Global eLearning Market Size worth over $300bn by 2025.* Retrieved from https://www.gminsights.com/pressrelease/elearning-market

Work-Learning Research Inc. (2017). *Definition of MicroLearning.* Retrieved from https://www.worklearning.com/2017/01/13/definition-of-microlearning/

Zannettou, S., Sirivianos, M., Blackburn, J., & Kourtellis, N. (2019). The web of false information: Rumors, fake news, hoaxes, clickbait, and various other shenanigans. *Journal of Data and Information Quality, 11*(3), 1–37. doi:10.1145/3309699

ADDITIONAL READING

Baporikar, N. (2019). E-Learning Strategies for Emerging Economies in the Knowledge Era. In *Advanced Web Applications and Progressing E-Learning 2.0 Technologies in Higher Education* (pp. 150–171). IGI Global. doi:10.4018/978-1-5225-7435-4.ch008

Giannakos, M. N., Mikalef, P., & Pappas, I. O. (2019). *Technology-Enhanced Organizational Learning: A Systematic Literature Review.* Paper presented at the Conference on e-Business, e-Services and e-Society. 10.1007/978-3-030-29374-1_46

Kravčík, M. (2019). Adaptive Workplace Learning Assistance. In *Proceedings of the 23rd International Workshop on Personalization and Recommendation on the Web and Beyond* (pp. 33-33). Academic Press.

Lin, C. H., Wang, W. C., Liu, C. Y., Pan, P. N., & Pan, H. R. (2019). Research into the E-learning model of agriculture technology companies: Analysis by deep learning. *Agronomy (Basel), 9*(2), 83. doi:10.3390/agronomy9020083

Lin, C. Y., Huang, C. K., & Zhang, H. (2019). Enhancing employee job satisfaction via E-learning: The mediating role of an organizational learning culture. *International Journal of Human-Computer Interaction, 35*(7), 584–595. doi:10.1080/10447318.2018.1480694

Menolli, A., Tirone, H., Reinehr, S., & Malucelli, A. (2019). Identifying organisational learning needs: An approach to the semi-automatic creation of course structures for software companies. *Behaviour & Information Technology*, 1–16. doi:10.1080/0144929X.2019.1653372

KEY TERMS AND DEFINITIONS

Corporate Trainer: Instructor responsible for designing and constructing training content for corporates, organization, SME's, etc.

E-Learning Market: The marketplace for online learning as a business opportunity.

Livresq: An eLearning Authoring Tool created by Ascendia SA. With it you can create eLearning courses and interactive lessons. Everything is done online, and you do not have to download or install anything.

LMS Platform: A Learning Management System is the "place" where eLearning is performed, having several instruments used for creating, managing and delivering courses, authenticating users, serving data and notifications, and a user interface that runs inside your browser as a website used for interaction between administrators, instructors and students.

Microlearning: Small learning units which involved learning activities for short-term.

Online Resources: Practical tools for online teaching and learning.

Platform's Functionalities: Functional requirements, additional constraints, and restrictions of virtual platforms.

Chapter 15
User Experience Measurement:
Recent Practice of E–Businesses

Oryina Kingsley Akputu
(iD) https://orcid.org/0000-0003-4520-0084
Ritman University, Nigeria

Kingsley Friday Attai
(iD) https://orcid.org/0000-0002-2199-5049
Ritman University, Nigeria

ABSTRACT

User experience (UX) measurement has become a powerful component in determining the usability success or failure of products or services that are marketed via e-business channels. Succcess in the e-business does not only depend on building stellar software interfaces but also on competitive receptiveness to customers experience or feedback. Only e-businesses that can effectively measure the UX to forecast and understand the future are able to stay afloat and not get drown in the highly competitive market. The development of various UX metrics and measurement techniques have helped to quantify user feedack but most of these rely on different contextual assumptions. As a result, choosing appropriate UX techniques that match a particular business need becomes difficult for most e-business concerns. This chapter provides an overview of recent UX measurement techniques that are relevant to the e-business settings in the Web 2.0 era. The objective is to elaborate on what tools that have been employed in literature to measure UX and possibly how these can be employed in practice.

INTRODUCTION

An e-business refers to a company that does most of its commerce of buying and selling electronically or over the internet, using sales and marketing information systems. Typical examples of such businesses as shown in fig.1, with no preferential order, include, Zara, Jumia, Konga, ebay, Walmart and many others. About 80% of a chunk of data and product information for similar line of businesses which are however, brick and mortar, in the past were unstructured and found in many forms (Alalwan

DOI: 10.4018/978-1-7998-3756-5.ch015

& Weistroffer, 2012). Information assets of those businesses such as product sale, purchase and usage of products or services were neglected as employees and customers alike had to search extensively for the information they needed.

For someone searching what information is available, where to find it, and what information is consistent, up-to-date, and correct often experienced information overload. However, the current era of web 2.0 has offered convenient techniques in the collection of customer experience data regarding usage of products or services. The e-business systems now are improved in information search accuracy and speed with reported reduction in overload issues (Gan et al., 2020; Tang, Wang, Guo, Xiao, & Chi, 2018; Wu, Huang, & Jiang, 2019). One concern of most e-business applications has remained making products and services more customer centered, hence the emergence of "user experience (UX)" concept. The UX concept is successor to "usability"- a widely accepted measure of quality of most products and services in the information system domains. Most e-business outlets have succeeded today partly on the basis that, they offer a stellar UX for their products and services; others have failed due to a terrible UX. It is no longer myth that UX can make or break any potentially great e-business; a good UX management has contributed to many success stories in the e-business market.

Therefore, the first critical consideration for any e-business concern is for their product or service to meet customer's needs and expectations. The business offering has to be highly usable, look, and feel good, the way the customers expect it to be.

Figure 1. Selected examples of e-businesses

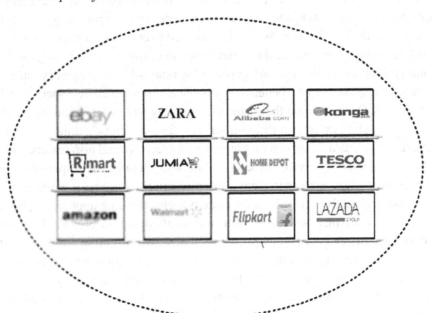

In 2018, Forbes.com, a renowned global media company published an article describing why Zara, the world's largest clothing retailer, succeeds above its competitors. Zara had introduced an Augmented Reality technology to improve customer UX in shopping in its online outlets. The Augmented Reality is a technology that offers capability of superimposing a computer-generated image on the user's view of the actual world, thus creating a composite view (Azuma et al., 2001; Carmigniani et al., 2011). By analyzing customers purchase behavior over time, Zara professionals discover patterns that could be used to interpret buying habits of each shopper. The shoppers could engage their mobile phones to view models wearing a variety of selected fashion styles by clicking on sensors displayed on AR-enabled shop windows. The AR-enabled technology was initially launched in 120 stores worldwide irresistibly pulling customers, mostly the millennial and other customer segments into the stores. With the AR application and in many other ways Zara excels more than its closest competitor H&M that remained fixed on old form of market model for success. Two more case studies for Amazon and Walmart can be found in Appendix 1.

The Zara's kind of customer centered approach to success underscores the need for measuring UX data or feedbacks in the e-business market setting. Most e-businesses have continued to exploit recent technological advances to revamp their sales and marketing information systems centering on customer's needs. Technically speaking, it is possible for an online retail outlet to have important information about its users through "tracking points" embedded in the point of sales system. These tracking points mine UX and feedbacks from variety of sources (usage metrics); these may include transaction history, page views, click-through rates for the ads as well as rate of user sign-ups to the system. Some new entrants, for instance, Jumia, a startup effort by German-based Rocket Internet have unique metrics for measuring shopper experience. The company's customer support department measure success by the number of complaints resolved and the amount of time spent in the resolutions. Nevertheless, like road sensors in a highway, the tracking points of most e-business monitor product usage data precisely and comprehensively using a recent proven marketing philosophy. According to this philosophy, building a product or service that inspires long-term loyalty and engages customers more deeply over time requires a collection of usage data and measure of the UX. In other words, there is need to collect customers feedback and conduct user research to learn why customers are doing what they're doing. Understanding the UX timely will not only pinpoint problem areas to work and improve the brands but also identify, quantify, and communicate the UX to stakeholders to get better clarity about positioning and competitive advantages that win satisfied customers. Once satisfied the customers probably will recommend the product. For these reasons, the UX of a product or service that is marketed via e-business setting is vital to commercial success of the business concern. If we can measure almost precisely and also understand what the user feels while using the product or service, we can continuously improve his experience. Following this idea, several studies related to the measurement of user experience have been written and disseminated using qualitative and quantitative analysis. In practice however, finding appropriate UX measurement techniques that match a particular business needs can be challenging for both the UX practitioners and the business concerns. This chapter addresses this challenge by presenting a rich head start overview of recent UX measurement techniques that are relevant to the e-business setting especially in the web 2.0 era. The objective is to elaborate on what tools that have been employed in literature to measure UX and possibly how they can be employed in practice. In order to achieve this objective, the following steps were taken, in what could be considered as a methodology. First, is the article inclusion step. The literature sources of interest in the databases explored are mostly those included under the classification of CNRS (Center national de la recherche scientifique)- French National Centre for Scientific Research. The CNRS is believed to be the largest fundamental research agency in Europe. Selection of literature sources using CNRS classification is to ensure both validity and quality of the research contributions. The articles published from 2009 (the last 11 years), in reputable websites, conferences, magazines, journals and book chapters available to read and written in English were used. A second consideration was a search for the articles related to the topic from four prestigious research databases namely, IEEE Xplore, ACM Springer links and Science Direct. The authors used the search string: ("user experience metric") AND ("Measurement" OR "evaluation"). Using this approach, a set of UX metrics and measurement techniques are identified and classified. What follows next is the selection of the UX techniques that the authors consider applicable to the e-business settings.

The Chapter is organized into six main sections. The first section is the introduction which provides an overview on the contextual concentration of the chapter. The e-business, user experience (UX) metrics and the value of UX measurement are some of the contextual concentrations discussed with few case studies. The second section constitutes background. Here discussions center on product or service usability with a contrast to UX. Also included in the background is discussion on the UX related disciplines as well as how the UX impacts the e-business sector. The third section is the main focus of the chapter-UX measurement. This section begins with discussion on the fundamental concept of measurement. The UX metrics, the UX data, and recent techniques that are used to assemble the UX data are also discussed. The section concludes by highlighting issues, controversies and problem surrounding the UX measurement realistic settings. The fourth section provides authors suggested solutions as well as recommendation to most UX measurement challenges. The fifth section discusses potentially viable future research directions that might be expected in related research trends. The last section is the conclusion that summarizes the chapter with remarks on the key concepts covered.

BACKGROUND

Since the invention of the first piece of computer software, at 11 am 21 June 1948, at the University of Manchester, on the Manchester Baby computer; people had begun to learn how to use the software and speak the language of the machines. A more interesting era however, began in the late 1980s when a new emphasis on users came to fruition. Till date, Human Computer Interaction (HCI) has been advancing. An important goal of the HCI community is to develop quality measures for interactive products and services. Among well-known and widely accepted quality measure in a task-oriented setting is 'usability'. The usability of a product or service could be defined as the "capability it to be used by humans easily "(ISO, 2019); or the effectiveness, efficiency and satisfaction with which specified users achieve defined goals in particular environments using the product or service (Shackel, 2009).The quantities such as effectiveness, efficiency and satisfaction are commonly referred to as UX metrics. A metric could be viewed as a way of quantifying a particular phenomenon or thing. Contextually, the UX metrics are the tools used for quantifying, measuring and improving the design of a product or service.

The beginning of 1990 and later years, recorded inclusion of new UX metrics like emotional usability (Logan, 1994), pleasure (Jordan, 2000) or hedonic qualities (Hassenzahl, 2001) –to also measure non-utilitarian qualities of products and services subsumed in the research field of UX. In the e-business settings, measuring the UX offers so much for an organization. With a suitable selection of UX metrics, it is possible to measure and possibly show whether a business is actually improving from one product line to the next.

What is UX?

Before we concentrate discussions in later parts of the chapter, it is fundamentally important to first understand what UX is and what it isn't. Don Norman, an electrical engineer and cognitive scientist at Apple was the first to coin the term "User Experience Architect". In an interview, Norman has been attributed the following explanation: "I invented the term [User Experience] because I thought human interface and usability were too narrow. I wanted to cover all aspects of the person's experience with the system including industrial design graphics, the interface, the physical interaction and the manual" (Merholz, 2007). Alternatively, the International organization for Standardization (ISO) defines the term as "a person's perceptions and responses that result from the use and (or) anticipated use of a product, system or service"(ISO, 2014). Essentially, the UX of a product or service could be seen as the level of user's satisfaction derivation in terms of interactivity and usage among other key factors. One should not however limit the meaning of UX to just making user interfaces look pretty. Now for a question of whether do the UX designers wants interfaces to look visually appealing? Of course. But what is the need of visually stunning designs if it would not be user centered or friendly? In short, the UX is all about easing usage complexity of a product or service.

Contrasting UX from Usability

Originally the UX study as a discipline began with usability; however, its umbrella has expanded to include more qualitative attributes that completes the characterization of a typical UX scenario compared to just the concept of usability. Unlike classical usability study, user experience is something purely subjective and thus cannot be evaluated by observation or expert's adjudication alone. Moreover, there are other aspects of the UX that extend its coverage beyond scope of the usability (Sonnleitner, Pawlowski, Kässer, & Peissner, 2013):

Holistic: focuses on task related (pragmatic) aspects and their accomplishment, whereas UX takes a more holistic approach, including non-task related (hedonic) aspects of product possession and use, such as beauty, challenge, stimulation or self-expression.

Subjective: has its origin from psychology and human factors. Usability evaluation with "objective" measurement methods (e.g. eye-tracking) rests primarily on observation. The "subjective" UX is explicitly interested in the way people experience and judge products they use. It may not matter how good a product is objectively, but it must also be experienced to have an impact.

Positive: usability focuses on problems, barriers, frustration or stress and how they can be overcome. The UX stresses the importance of positive outcomes of technology use or possession, e.g. positive affect or emotions such as joy, pride, and excitement or simply value. This does not imply that usability is unessential. It rather emphasizes that positive does not necessarily equate with an absence of the negative.

Although the above three additional aspects of UX might sound like a common understanding on the subject, in the existing literature, the UX is associated with a broad range of fuzzy and dynamic concepts, including affective, experiential, hedonic, and aesthetic variables. But most importantly, in the e-businesses world, winning customers positive affective feedbacks is perhaps the first momentary impression to long-lasting reputation about the product. The goal of most UX designers and marketing teams is therefore to shape positive affective responses and reactions from the customer.

Disciplines of User Experience

User Experience design has many subdisciplines that include, Visual Design, Interaction Design, Information Architecture, Content Design etc. As demonstrated in fig. 2, the fields are tightly intertwined and interdependent. Excellent UX design practice requires working with regards to and on the intersection of all these various fields to ensure an all-encompassing creative process that is inextricably intertwined and defined by five product or service quality components for usage:

Learnability: pertains to how fast and painless the learning process for new users is; does the system teaches the users through interaction or is it predominantly a trial-and-error process? Do customers need to read manuals to understand and learn the system?

Efficiency: upon getting a sufficient experience with the system, can customers perform the tasks in reasonable and satisfactory time?

Memorability: pertains to how easy it is for a returning user to remember the system and resume the activities with ease after some time of inactivity. How hard is it to re-establish the proficiency of use?

Errors: pertains to how often do users make errors while interacting with the system; how serious are the errors? Do users recognize them as errors? And how easy can the errors be resolved?

Satisfaction: how pleasant is the system to use so that users are subjectively satisfied when using it; they like it.

Figure 2. the fields of UX design

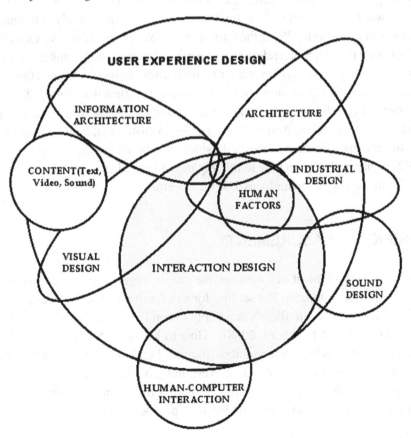

How UX Impact E-Businesses

Now that you have some ideas about what the UX is or not and its disciplinary boundary, it is important to specifically address two critical questions: why does knowledge of UX matter a lot? and how exactly does it impact Return on Investment (ROI) of the business? The first question could be answered by considering an e-business trying to attract new customers via an online sales and marketing system embedded on the company's website or app. That website is now akin to someone walking into your brick and mortal store or office. If they have a bad experience, such as not being able to find what they needed and came for, or can't reach someone to attend to them; they are going to leave and possibly not return. This could also be thought of this way: the more resources and effort you commit to making the systems fantastic upfront, the less you might have to deal with reported bugs and changes after it has been release. If your content is not optimized, chances are that a great percent of visitors will leave and never return to search again. Also, from experience, mobile users are more likely to abandon a task if your website is not optimized for their device. Not to forget that most of these mobile customers might be looking to make a purchase that day, so you do not want them to leave.

Nevertheless, on the question of how exactly UX impact on ROI; it should be noted that product or service branding and UX could be considered as two sides of the same coin. With the growing focus on UX design industry, one should expect the experience of the consumer overtaking price and product as the number one brand differentiator in no distant time. This is because a good UX investment generally enhances customer satisfaction and satisfied customers are loyal, trustful to the company's products or have good perception for the brand. Thus, most e-businesses create brand perception when customers interact with their digital assets. In a research conducted by Harvard Business Review (Dixon, Freeman, & Toman, 2010), It was reported how satisfied customers are much more likely to recommend a product to others. According to the report, 23% of the customers who expressed positive experience reportedly referred at least 10 other people. Since referrals and personal recommendations carry more weight than any other form of marketing, increase in customer volume would indirectly bring a faster ROI. However, this is not to say only a good UX design "runs" the business, rather it implies UX design is a highly influential force that, when effectively integrated with a good marketing strategy, can help the company stand out in front of its competitors. And by staying close to customers, handsome price premiums can be commanded. But the main concern of most e-businesses is no longer the question of whether the UX impact on the ROI or not; rather is on how to reliably measure the UX and make sense of the data. The next section shall buttress on the -main focus-UX measurement.

USER EXPERIENCE MEASUREMENT

To understand the UX measurement as a concept, the reader might perhaps need to understand fundamentally the purpose of measurement. But settling for a definition of measurement is akin to clinching on a definition of UX. In this regard there's inevitably (often heated) disagreement. A good definition is offered by Douglas Hubbard (Hubbard, 2008): "How to Measure Anything is a set of observations expressed as a quantity that reduces uncertainty". It could be noted that the purpose of measurement under hubbard's definition is not about to reduce everything to a single number neither is it to generate an exact amount or have 100% accuracy to perfectly predict the future. Notably, measurements in real sense don't guarantee success; rather, they only improve prospects of the success.

The fundamental purpose of measurement can be overly extended to UX measurement. For instance, you could observe users' scuffle to complete a task, making mistakes, or taking longer time duration, and expressing negative affects like frustration. This gives the UX expert some idea about the experience to relate to business stakeholders. Thus, rather than saying a UX was "bad" or "good," or "better" or "worse," we preferably express these more precisely with quantities such frustration, difficult, long completion time etc.

Therefore, by UX measurement, we mean the assemblage of skills, evaluation metrics and techniques in discovering how the user views or observes a particular service, product or system. It takes into consideration a holistic reaction and viewpoint of the end-user before, during and after working with (using) the system. Essentially, the UX measurement is about quantifying observations and attitudes about an experience to reduce our uncertainty about how difficult or successful it actually was. To achieve an effective UX measurement for a product or service, relevant metrics, and techniques must be employed.

UX Metrics

No single standard measurement instrument for the UX quantities like thermometer is for Temperature or tape for Length; rather what we have is a collection of all-embracing types of metrics. To select a suitable set of metrics for a particular case, most business concerns normally rely on a combination of what customers do (actions) and what they think (attitudes). We can group UX metrics under three broad categories: study-level metrics, task-level metrics and web-analytic metrics. It should be noted that the list given here might not be exhaustive as there are endless ways to measure the UX of product and service but the grouping here appears to be the most common and effective.

Study-Level Metrics

The first category of the UX Metrics is the study-level; this represents those metrics that cover a broader experience of the user. The Standardized User Experience Percentile Rank Questionnaire (SUPR-Q), System Usability Scale (SUS), Single Ease Question (SEQ), After-Scenario Questionnaire (ASQ), Subjective Mental Effort Questionnaire (SMEQ), NASA Task Load Index (NASA-TLX), Brand Attitude Metric, Net Promoter Score (NPS) are all study-level metrics. Each of these metrics is further discussed below.

Standardized User Experience Percentile Rank Questionnaire (SUPR-Q)

The SUPR-Q (Standardized User Experience Percentile Rank Questionnaire), is a standardized and widely acceptable questionnaire designed by Jeff Sauro (Sauro Jeff, 2015).The SUPR-Q is an 8-element questionnaire that emphasizes on usability, appearance, reliability and trustworthiness. See Fig.3 in Appendix 2 for a copy of the SUPR-Q. Question numbers 1 to 7 are to be used by the participants to rate their answers from strongly disagree to strongly agree and question 8 is used to know how likely the respondent is to recommend the website to others. The SUPR-Q can be used to quantify the overall quality of an online UX of a product or service.

System Usability Scale (SUS)

The SUS is a standard 10-item questionnaire powered metric that quantifies the perceived usability of UX for a product and service. See fig.4 in Appendix 2 for a copy of the SUS. The SUS metric has been in existence for more than 30 years and it is specially used for measuring software or hardware interfaces. The average SUS metric score is 68.

Single Ease Question (SEQ)

The SEQ is often recommended for quantifying the ease of use in correlation with other usability metrics.
It consists of just a single question at the end of a task. See fig. 5 in Appendix 2 for a copy of the SEQ. It is a 7-point rating scale used to quantify how difficult users find a task. The SEQ metric is preferably measured immediately after a user attempts a task in a usability test.

After-Scenario Questionnaire (ASQ)

The After-Scenario Questionnaire (ASQ) is a three-item metric that UX evaluators have developed for quantification of customer level of satisfaction after the completion of each interaction scenario. The three items on the ASQ must address the three key components of the customer satisfaction with the system usability viz., ease of task completion, time to complete a task, and adequacy of support information (online customer care supports, messages and products manuals or documentation). See fig.6 in Appendix 2 for a copy of the ASQ. Because the questionnaire is very short, it takes very little time for participants to complete – an important practical consideration for usability studies.

Subjective Mental Effort Questionnaire (SMEQ)

SMEQ is made up of just one scale, and it measures the mental effort that people feel was involved in a certain task (Sauro & Dumas, 2009). See fig.7 in Appendix 2 for a copy of the SMEQ. According to Jeff Sauro in Quantifying the UX, SMEQ correlates highly with SUS scores, as well as completion time, completion rates, and errors.

NASA Task Load Index (NASA-TLX)

The NASA-TLX is "a widely-used, subjective, and multidimensional assessment tool that rates perceived workload in order to assess a task, system, or team's effectiveness or other aspects of performance." It has been cited in well over 9,000 studies in the UX literature. See fig.8 in Appendix 2 for a copy of the NASA-TLX. The NASA-TLX questionnaire is divided into two parts. The first part referred to as total workload, consists of six subjective subscale divisions that are represented on a single page that serv as one part of the questionnaire: Mental Demand, Physical Demand, Temporal Demand, Performance, Effort and Frustration. This part also contains a description for each of these subscales that the subject should read before rating. The second part of TLX makes provision for an individual weighting of the six subscales by letting the subjects compare them pairwise based on perceived importance. This requires choosing which measurement is more relevant to workload. The number of times each is chosen is recorded as the weighted score.

Brand Attitude Metric

Brand attitude happens to be one of the strongest influencers of other UX metrics. It quantifies an understanding of what people think about the business (e.g. Facebook, Amazon, Walmart). In practice Brand Attitude metric help explains a lot of variations among other attitudinal metrics (like SEQ, SUPR-Q, SUS, and satisfaction) and words people associate with the brand. Thus, we have consistently seen this as a key driver of UX metrics in most industry reports. See Appendix 2, Table 3, for a copy of the Brand Attitude Metric.

Net Promoter Score (NPS)

NPS metric to say the list isn't in the same category with other questionnaires-based study-level metrics. However, since it is specially developed for e-businesses it is good to add it to our tool kits of UX metrics. Another reason for its choice hinges on its popularity and effectiveness in measuring the UX and user satisfaction in particular. Notably it is one of the questions on the SUPR-Q scale. The scale is calibrated between the range of -100 to 100 that quantifies the willingness of customers to recommend a brand to others. In other words, the NPS metric could be seen as a proxy for ranking the customer's overall satisfaction as well as loyalty for the brand.

Task-Level Metrics

The second category of UX metrics pertains to study-based task of the user; this group is known as task-level metrics. UX metrics under this category are used to quantify task-level satisfaction. In practice, the UX is seen more reliable when Task-level metrics quantification is done immediately after the customer completes a task (whether or not they achieve the set goal). The Task Time, SUM, Confidence, Disasters and some of the most common task-level metrics that could be of relevance in the e-business setting. For benchmarking a study with tasks (versus only retrospective studies), the each of these metrics provide a granular view of the user experience and usually offer more clues as to what needs to be fixed.

Task Time

The Task Time metric is a fundamental measure of efficiency that provides a sensitive way to quantify the length of time it takes an online customer in context to complete (or fail) tasks. With this metric, a business provider can measure from average task completion time (successfully completed attempts), to average task time (average time of all participants) or even the mean time of failure (average time till participants fail a task).

SUM Metric

The SUM metric quantifies the average of standardized versions of the following three important metrics namely completion rates, ease of use, and length of time integrated form a single measure that describes the UX report of a task. It's ideal especially when a business concerns desires to gather multidimensional knowledge of task-level engagement of customers under a single measure especially in a competitive benchmark.

Confidence

The confidence metric measured using a 7-point scale immediately after a user completes a task. Generally, confidence translates to competence (higher completion rates). In practice customers are generally over-confident, often men more than women. But low confidence could be an indication of problems. This measure of user's confidence should not be mistaken for the confidence interval.

Disasters

The disasters metric combines confidence ratings with task completion rate to numerically quantify disasters. A disaster rating represents scenario where the customer user fails a task but rate that they were extremely confident. By interpretation, any failure rating of 7 out of 7 on task confidence is a disaster. The only thing worse than failing in this case thus is thinking the user did it correctly but really failed.

Web-Analytic metrics

The third category of the UX metric is the web-analytic metrics. Metrics under this category are those embedded in websites and apps of certain e-business applications whose usage is in objective quantification of specific user activities or experiences with the e-business applications. Every time a user's browser or device requests data or information from an e-business website or app; the web server collects relevant details about the user (e.g. address, what was requested, when it was requested etc.). In the recent web technology, the "web cookie"– message that is sent to web browser by the web servers- triggers to identify if the user device may have accessed the site before, and a number of other facts about the connection. All these about the user are stored a text files called log files and can be evaluated or measured by an e-business concern to show certain behavior about the user such as transaction history, frequency of visit to their online store among other enquiries. The Site-Wide Metrics, Session based metrics and Click Streams are all grouped under the web-analytics metrics.

Site-Wide Metrics

These metrics are used to quantify a global window of information within website. The metrics includes several crude measures of site traffic, the number of active users in a given time period, total number of pages viewed in a given period, search engine referrers and search key words and so on.

Session Based Metrics

Session metrics are used to quantify a richer set of user behaviors than other site-wide statistics. Recent measures used by e-business outlets to collect customer browsing behavior includes average number of page views within a single session, first and last visited pages within a session etc.

Click Streams

The click streams are one of the most recent type of UX web-analytic metric. These metrics have far reaching collection of the UX compared to other forms of web-analytic metrics like session-based metrics. They not only study users by looking at what pages they visited, but in addition, they also measure the sequence in which online content was accessed. Basically, it is a measure of the paths people take in surfing to uncover common ways customers move through it. Most e-business outlet like Konga-the biggest e-commerce business of African descent exploits previous surf-paths online to recommend products based on browsing history.

The UX Data

In order to understand and measure UX in the e-business settings, it is essential to collect data from the users who are the actual buyers of the product or service. Generally, the UX data gets its source from the metrics of measurement discussed in the previous subsection. When collecting the UX data, an e-business concern should know what type of data they want or are to deal with and what they can and can't do with each type. Now a carefully selected and relevant UX data can provide detailed answers to most of these questions. For the e-business that could mean a lot of data, of course, with more coming in every second. To keep from getting overwhelmed, you should begin by learning what kind of data the company collects for UX measurement and which of these their stakeholders view as important. The UX data can be categorized under various dimensions with each with its types of data. The first categorization of data is qualitative or quantitative; another is seen as objective or subjective. In practice it possible to have both objective and subjective data as either qualitative or quantitative data. A good example for this is the questionnaires discussed in later sections, which are usually both subjective and quantitative in nature.

Quantitative vs. Qualitative Data

The quantitative data are numeric in nature and usually originates from measurements whose objective is to assess a level of achievement. One of the most common kinds of quantitative data is that collected during or from objective user performance measured against a benchmark task. Another kind of quantitative data is that collected from subjective user opinion and measured using questionnaires. To put in short, quantitative data can easily be counted, expressed, measured or evaluated numerically. They are used to quantify as precise as possible the nature or measure of the UX. The qualitative data on the other hand are only descriptive and conceptual and can be categorized based on trait and characteristic of the UX quantity being measured. The qualitative data for UX measurement describes the usability problems or issues observed or experienced during product or service usage. While the quantitative data are collected via the metric based approached whereas the qualitative data are usually collected via specialized techniques such as the critical incident identification, the think-aloud technique, as well as UX inspections methods.

Objective vs. Subjective Data

Objective data in UX measurement basically are those observed directly. This category of data arises from observations carried out by either the UX evaluator or the user of the product or service based guided by some acceptable standards of data collection. The objective data are usually associated with empirical methods. The subjective UX data represent opinions, judgments, and other feedback of the users or the evaluator of the product or service regarding the UX and satisfaction with the product and service. Analytic UX measurement technique is one good example of the source of qualitative subjective data. On the other hand, the questionnaires technique yields quantitative and subjective data.

Types of UX Data

Either the objective or subjective data can be measured using one of four general types of data: nominal, ordinal, interval, and ratio. Each of these uniquely supports specific types UX measurement techniques. Practitioners of UX study and e-business concerns in particular must understand the type of data to collect from users for UX related business decisions.

Nominal Data

Nominal (categorical) data are unordered groups or categories. Without order between the categories, it can be said only that they are different, not that one is any better than the other. For example, different types of grains, maize, millets, rice and sorghum. They are just different; no one particular grain is inherently better than the other. Likewise, in UX, nominal data might be the characteristics of different types of users. These might typically be independent variables that allow you to segment data by these different groups.

Ordinal Data

Ordinal data are ordered groups or categories. They are data that is organized in a certain way. However, the intervals between measurements are not meaningful. One can think of the ordinal data as ranked data. In UX, the most common examples of ordinal data come from user self-reported feedback data. For example, a user might rate an e-business's transaction system as excellent, good, fair, or poor. These are relative rankings: The distance between excellent and good is not necessarily the same distance between good and fair.

Interval Data

Interval data are continuous data. The differences between the values are meaningful, but there is no natural zero point. An example of interval data familiar to most of us is temperature. Defining 0° Celsius or 32° Fahrenheit based on when water freezes is completely arbitrary. In UX, the System Usability Scale (SUS) is one example of interval data. SUS, described in later section is based on self-reported data from a series of questions about the overall usability of any system. Scores range from 0 to 100, with a higher SUS score indicating better usability. The distance between each point along the scale is meaningful in the sense that it represents an incremental increase or decrease in perceived usability.

Ratio Data

Ratio data are the same as interval data but with the addition of an absolute zero. This means that the zero value is not arbitrary, as with interval data, but has some inherent meaning. With ratio data, differences between the measurements are interpreted as a ratio. Examples of ratio data are age, height, and weight. In each example, zero indicates the absence of age, height, or weight. In user experience, the most obvious example of ratio data is time. Zero seconds left to complete a task would mean no time or duration remaining. Ratio data let you say something is twice as fast or half as slow as something else. For example, you could say that one user is twice as fast as another user in completing a task.

UX Measuring Techniques

Any technique can be used to assemble data concerning specific concepts of end-user experience in a e-business scenario. But knowing the appropriate technique to use will guide both the designer and business concern in discovering the best end-user experience. However, it is difficult to measure user experience. First, because several factors influence the user experience, like feelings, culture and communicability(Maia & Furtado, 2016). Furthermore, the user experience is multidimensional(Huang, Hong, & Xu, 2020), consisting of various elements, and there is still no consensus among authors about these elements of user experience. There have been several UX measurement techniques in the literature most of which are still in the developmental stages. The UX measurement techniques can be broadly classify into three approaches based on their nature, purpose of use and the development stage of the product and service: formative, summative and specialized implicit measurement techniques. Even though the first two (formative and summative) techniques originated from educational theory, where they are used to describe and assess student learning process, they have however formed part of understanding in the UX design field.

Formative User Experience Measurement

The formative UX measurement are also refers to as qualitative formative techniques since they are diagnostic and uses qualitative data collection with the sole objective of finding users feedback to fix UX problems. This entails thoroughly checking the design to identify or diagnose the problems, improving on the implementation recommendations in the process, and then measuring again. There are some important questions the UX experts should answer while embarking on a formative measurement:

1. What are most recorded UX issues preventing users from achieving their goals?
2. What aspects of the current versions of the product or service in use work well for the users?
3. What aspect of the product or service reported seems frustrating?
4. What are the most common errors or mistakes users make?
5. Are there recorded improvements from one design iteration to another?

It should be emphasized that formative measurement must be utilized at onset in the product creation cycle. Perhaps the most appropriate time is when an obvious opportunity to improve the design presents itself. Events such as customer queries or recommendations; need to switch over to improved technologies or even a change in company's corporate policy are the best times to improve UX designs and measurement by extension. The formative measurement techniques can be grouped under empirical or analytic techniques.

Empirical UX Measuring Techniques

The empirical measurement techniques mostly depend on the data collection in the performance of real user participants and data coming directly from them. These techniques include all qualitative research techniques such as Interviews, Web or App Analytics, Expert reviews and Video tools as illustrated and "thinking aloud" studies as illustrated in Table 1. The Table 1, highlights recent qualitative research techniques, their usefulness and application tools. Moreover, the reader could refer to appendix 2 for a summary of previous studies on empirical formative (qualitative) UX techniques.

Analytic Techniques

Analytic UX measurement techniques examine inherent attributes of the design of the product or service rather than study this design in use. Except in situations here numerical ratings and similar data are required, most analytic UX techniques yield qualitative subjective data. An advantage of this over the empirical techniques is in fastness and cost effectiveness in implementation. However, their application is rigorously and correspondingly more slowly compared to the empirical results. Analytic methods include design reviews, design walkthroughs, and inspection methods, such as heuristic evaluation (HE).

Summative User Experience Measurement

The summative UX measurement techniques can also be referred to as quantitative summative techniques since they use quantitative data and are run with the objective of summing up or assessing the success of a UX design. Summative UX measurement makes an assessment of the product or service and checks if its productivity meets its objectives. There are some important questions the UX experts need to answer while embarking on a summative measurement:

1. Has the UX goals of the project been met yet?
2. What is considered as the overall UX of the product or service in question?
3. How does the UX measure for the product or service fare against competition?
4. Are there recorded improvements from one product release to the next?

In the summative measurement process, UX is assessed at the later stages of the project with the sole focus of measuring it against a set criterion. The Summative UX techniques can either be formal summative or informal summative techniques.

Formal Summative Techniques

The Formal summative (quantitative) UX techniques are empirical methods that produce statistically significant results. The term "formal" sterns from the notion that the process is statistically rigorous. These methods utilize experimental designs for controlled comparative hypothesis testing. A drawback of these techniques comes from their high cost (expenses and time consumption) due to general demand for a proper summative measurement. For this reason, even though the formal summative UX measurement is an important HCI research skill, it is rarely adopted in practice. Consequently, we exclude the formal summative studies from the scope of this chapter.

Informal Summative Technique

Informal summative (quantitative) UX techniques, unlike their formal summative counterparts, are not statistically rigorous and do not produce statistically significant results. Informal summative measurement does not usually demand experimental controls, and requires smaller numbers of user participants, with just summary descriptive statistics (such as average values). At the end of each phase or iteration of a product version, the informal summative measurement is used as an acceptance test to compare with the company's UX targets to ensure both business goals and customer user recommendations are considered in design of the product or service. Informal summative includes various quantitative techniques including, Click/Mouse, A/B Testing, and Questionnaire(survey). Table 2 highlights these quantitative techniques and their usefulness as well as example application tools.

Table 1. Empirical qualitative techniques

Qualitative Formative Techniques	Usefulness	Tools
Expert Review	It feeds the researcher with comments, responses and criticisms about a product or system's usability from a group of experts. Experts also identify issues and make suggestions that can improve the usability of the product. This qualitative method saves cost, shorten completion time date especially when there is no ample fund and time.	Concept Feedback
Web or App Analytics	Qualitative analysis regardless of whether it is web or app analysis guides the researcher in the comprehension of end-user behavior. These tools can guide researchers in learning end-user's preferences by simply observing end-user's interactions with system.	Bugsee, Appsee, Full Story, Hotjar etc
Video Tools	Used to gather a first-rate series of vital data on end-user's experience in a video format and the researcher can then extract useful information from the data and carry out appropriate analysis.	OpenHallway, Userlytics, UserTesting.com etc
Interview	This is a fact-finding technique where data is collected from individuals through face-to-face interrogation	Face-to-face and Google hangouts, Skype, and VidCruiter (remote interviews)
Rapid Iterative Testing and Evaluation (RITE)	RITE is a fast user-based UX measurement approach that is focused on fixing the problems as soon as they are identified. Problem reporting occurs while the UX specialist team still on ground, so they are already informed and immersed in the process.	

Specialized and Implicit UX Techniques

In addition to the two (i.e. formative and summative) "standard" UX measurement techniques discussed earlier, there are a number of other specialized techniques which are implicit in application. Their implicitness and specialized usage sterns from their ability to capture nonverbal expressions of the user that cannot be easily communicated to the UX specialist. Nevertheless, these nonverbal expressions are imperative and highly essential in understanding UX. Observation, Eye tracking and Electroencephalography (EEG) are some of the important implicit techniques that will described under the subsections below.

Table 2. Analytical quantitative techniques

Quantitative Summative Techniques	Usefulness	Tools
Click/Mouse	A useful tool for testing the awareness of key aspects in the system, such as the perception of navigation and what captures the end-user's attention when using the system.	FiveSecondTest, ClickTale, Usabilla, Chalkmark etc.
A/B Testing	A/B Testing is used to compare two types of system or product. Comparing product, A and B from quantitative data that has been collected helps researcher or designer find possible issues that needs fixing in the system.	AB Tasty, Omni convert, Crazy Egg, VWO, Optimizely etc.
Questionnaire/Survey	Questionnaire are well structured questions with the intention of gathering useful information from end-user of a system in a survey	Qualtrics, SurveyMonkey, SurveyGizmo, Survey Planet, Zoho Survey, Client Heartbeat, Google Forms, SoGoSurvey etc.
Early design reviews and design walkthroughs	They are demos of the design UX run to get early reactions and feedback from stakeholders. presentations evolve from an early stage with the use of scenarios and storyboards for evaluating the ecological views, to use of click-through wireframe prototypes.	Asana,Humanity,Pinterest, Autopilot, Innovate etc.
Heuristic evaluation technique	Is one of the best-known analytical inspection techniques. Inspectors are guided by an empirically derived list of about 20 "heuristics" or rules that govern good UX design.	8 C Framework, Nielsen's heuristics, Gerhardt-Powal's cognitive engineering principles, Weinschenk and Barker classification etc.

Observation

Observation is a technique wherein a researcher either observes an activity in order to learn and gather useful information about UX. The observer checks and examines the participant's emotional responses such as facial expression, voice tone and other physical gestures.

Eye Tracking

It is used to measure the motion of an eye relative to the head also referred to as the point of gaze-direction in which the eye is staring. An eye tracking device or eye tracker is a device that measures eye movements and positions. This usability technique exposes end-user's point of gaze and directional pattern on a particular interface. It gives researchers detailed feedbacks of attention-grabbing aspects of the system and the aspects with poor visibility. The UX information obtained through this technique can guide the system designer in the improvement of certain aspects of the system.

Electroencephalography (EEG)

The Electroencephalography (EEG) is an electrophysiological monitoring approach that picks up voltages produced by series of brain activities. EEG captures the activities of end-user's brain to know what they want. EEG is important in UX design because when an end-user wears the scanner on the head and performs a given task, it captures the end-user's brain activities and checks with the excitement, attention and frustration parameters. The neuro-feedback from the end-user is used to observe whether a certain task gets an end-user's attention, excitement or frustration.

Issues, Controversies and Problems

The field of UX design like every other discipline has its set of issues and UX measurement of course is a topical issue. To avoid sounding too academic, in the e-business settings there are additional issues that tend to generate some passionate discussions which will be discussed only in briefs.

Issues in UX Measurement

There several common issues associated with UX measurement. In this subsection we have pinpointed just a selected few believed to be more elaborate key concern.

Not Knowing Where to Start

A common issue for most organizations that adopt or are ready to embrace good UX measurement to improve the UX of an offering is knowing where to start. This is mostly the case since there is a tendency to jump into counting the number of UX problems identified, instead of first planning how to go about the UX measurement schedule. This issue could seem even worse when a business concern has yet to settle on what UX measurement technique to understand her customers. Choosing the most trusted and adequate technique to enhance the user experience within the organization can indeed become an overwhelming process.

Misconceptions by Specialist About What To Do

Certain business issues or customer requirements that are communicated to the UX designers might appear much vague that they lack understanding about what to do. To most managers the term UX design is just synonymous with just "making things look good" therefore, management decisions to utter changes in the UX designs could be done as easily as putting new products on the shelf in a brick and mortar store. Thus, often than not one finds out that the business value of UX design is overlooked. While the UX evaluation designer understands there's more to it than sketching wireframes, or gathering UX data and if the key stakeholders don't fully understand what all that means or the UX designer is there to do, it can be a serious issue.

No One-Size Fits-All-UX Designs

One of the biggest problems facing the adoption of UX measurement techniques by both e-business concerns and UX practitioners in the industry is the fact that no single UX measurement technique can fit all business design requirements. This issue is generally referred to as 'no one-size-fits-all set of design criteria'. Another side to the other half is knowing the tradeoff in choosing between usability methods for requirements gathering and evaluation. What many practitioners may find surprising is the fact that several tried-and-true techniques out there reportedly have limitations, pertaining to every context of usage in which they are applied. For instance, many usability methods are originally created for use in certain cultures and therefore might not be as effective when adopted to other settings.

Controversies in UX measurement

There are some hot-button controversies in the adoption of UX measurement. We discuss a selected few of some that tend to spark some passionate discussion.

Quantifying User Experience

The UX measurement is all about quantifying the user (i.e. people). Merely talking about using numbers to quantify user experience with a product and service can get managers of the business upset. To many business owners, usability should typically remain a qualitative activity and not a cold-number crunching task. Throw some probability and statistics and you really have some executive turn off. Another issue in this regard is deciding appropriate sample size or the number of user population needed to test in a UX measurement. Some suggests "a lot sample size", others say moderate and other avoid discussion on sample size completely. Nevertheless, the real answer hovers on many factors in which the mathematical foundation behind it could again upset many.

Metrics Rarely Help Businesses Understand Causes

There have been some arguments that metrics don't help businesses understand the root causes of UX problems. They assume incorrectly that the UX metrics is only to highlight the magnitude of the problem. Concentrating only on success rates or task completion time data of UX measurement, it will be understood going by this perception. But in practice metrics, can actually tell much more about the root cause of UX issues than one might think. It is possible to analyze verbatim comments of UX data to reveal the source of the problem and how many users experience it. It is also possible to identify where within the product or service design users experience encountered a problem and use the UX measurement metrics to tell where and even why some problems occur. Moreover, depending on how the UX data is encoded and the technique used, there is a wealth of UX data that can help reveal the root cause of most UX issues.

Long-Standing Debate: Formative vs. Summative Techniques

The academic debate to distinguish between formative techniques and summative techniques has been a long-standing tradition in the related literature for these concepts. Perhaps the best way to contribute on this debate is to use day to day real-world scenario. When running a UX study, the UX specialist could be likened to house wife who sets up for a party. She selects the costumes that looks appropriate for the gathering, then carefully does facial makeovers while periodically watching herself in the mirror. She steps out satisfied but would customarily request her man pass some final validation checks to know her appearance fits the party.

Now the process the house wife uses to costume up, is likened to formative measurement and her man's validation is likened to summative measurement. Now the man is likened to users or UX evaluators the house wife who checks the mirror periodically while being dressed is likened to UX specialist. In in context, an e-business concern who evaluates product or service periodically in-house or passes it to users to collect their UX and makes recommendations while it is being created. Generally speaking, what distinguishes formative summative techniques from summative techniques is the iterative nature of the measurement or testing and when it occurs. The goal is to make improvements in the design prior to release. This way the e-business concern is able to identify shortcomings, and repeats the process if need be, until, ideally, the product comes out in accordance with customers feedback first and then the business needs.

Problems in UX Measurement

There are a lot of problems associated with the UX measurement. Here we describe few of such problems

Reliability in Measurement

In simple terms, the reliability of a UX evaluation method means repeatability, and it's a problem with both empirical and analytic methods (Hartson, Andre, & Williges, 2003). It means that, if you use the same formative evaluation method with several different user participants (for empirical methods) or several different UX inspectors (for analytic methods), you won't get the same list of UX problems each time. In fact, the differences can be fairly large. We have to live with imperfect reliability.

Gathering Marketing Data Without Interruption

Most e-businesses today tends to collect all kinds of customer data to aid usability decisions and also effect new corporate strategies, or policies. However, most techniques used in collecting this data are often intrusive or questionable to the consumer (i.e. Facebook's latest data collection fiasco). What ought to be known is that data collection is certainly not going away, but will remain a precursor to personalization of relevant aspect of the product or service to customer's needs. However, the data collection process must be done without interruption or putting valuable information of the customer at risk.

UX Measurement is Mostly Undervalued

Owners of the e-business often than not will question the usefulness of the UX metrics or measurement techniques especially if only fairly small improvements are needed. some may say it's best to focus on a narrow set of improvements and not worry about metrics or costly evaluations. They may not dedicate any extra resource or budget to run UX measurement project. They are likely going to say that metrics have no place in a rapid-pace iterative design process.

UX Metrics are Too Noisy

Another problem with the UX measurement is the big criticism that UX data are mostly too "noisy." It is inherently contaminated with too many variables that might prevent getting a clear picture of what is being measured. One classic example of the "noisy" data can be seen in measuring task completion time in an automated usability study when the participant goes out for a cup of coffee.

SOLUTIONS AND RECOMMENDATIONS

For every problem, there is a solution as well as recommendation to solving it. Here we described possible ways to solving most of the UX issues and problems described earlier. We also give some recommendations for possible improvement were necessary.

Solution to Intrusive Data Collection

The issue of user intrusion during UX measurements can be solved by devising novel ways that does not interrupt with the user. For an e-business concern, instead of soliciting the consumer's data through opt-in forms or web cookies and web analytics, the UX designers can device other engaging and subtle UX data collection techniques. A good example of how to engage nonintrusive technique is to use an interactive content, such as quizzes, polls, or surveys to gather valuable data.

No Perfect UX Measurement but Reliability Exist

It is understood that no perfect UX measurement techniques exists, but there can be reliability in the measurement process if run properly. Nevertheless, the good news is that even UX measurement techniques that have low reliability can still show much effectiveness. Most often than not, the low reliability in a technique is not always a serious drawback. This is because much of each iteration in the formative measurement is about learning as much about the UX design issues as possible and at the lowest cost and then moving on. So, while it would be nice to have perfect reliability, as a practical matter if the method is reasonably effective, the process still works.

Create a Strategy to Solve UX Problems

Most of the UX measurement issues of e-businesses are birthed from lack of proper organizational strategy on ground to approach customer centered issues. Starting with a good organizational plan that is customer focused and proven can help solve many of the UX problems or issues regarding best metrics and techniques to achieve the company's goals. To achieve a strategic planning, the best way is to begin by creating the plan, the marketing team or the management should start with the big picture (a top-down approach) which could be identifying how the company measures success. Just like the professional business management study, in which the concern is to optimize efforts around things that matter. Thus, by keeping watch on these success measures, most e-business concerns are able to produce outcomes that relate to meaningful dimensions. Now associating relevant UX metrics to the business success and with the quantitative chain of accountability in place, even the ROI for the business can be achieved or calculated.

Avoid Misuse of UX Metrics

The UX metric as important as they are, each have a time and a place of application or relevance. Misapplication of the metrics has the potential of undermining a company's entire UX design program. A misapplication could be taken for a situation where the metrics are used or applied on scenarios that are not relevant or needed. In some situations, it is probably better not to apply the UX metrics. If the goal of the business is just looking for some qualitative feedback from customers at the start of a project, metrics might just not be appropriate to use.

Benchmark Product or Service

There is a general understanding that the UX metrics are relative in practice. Moreover, there is no absolute standard out there to measure a "good UX" and "bad UX." For this reason, it is essential for a business provider to benchmark the UX of their product or service. To establish a set of benchmarks, first, the business concern must determine which UX metrics would be collected over time. In our opinion it is good to collect data around three aspects of UX: effectiveness (i.e., task success), efficiency (i.e., task completion time), and satisfaction (i.e., ease-of-use ratings). Next, they have to determine their unique strategy for collecting the metrics. This may include how often the data is going to be collected and how the metrics are going to be applied and presented. Finally, the type of customer participants to include in the benchmark must be identified. The customer selection requirement may run from breaking the available population into distinct groups, to how many needed and how they are going to be recruited. Perhaps the most important thing to remember is to be consistent from one benchmark to another.

FUTURE RESEARCH DIRECTIONS

In light of this overview on UX measurement in the e-business sector, discussions have been focused presenting a first picture on used and known UX measurement approaches. But we believe there is still need for a clearer understanding of what characterizes a UX measurement techniques compared to a usability method. We therefore foresee a great future for the UX studies; potentially viable future research directions that might be expected in the following trends:

Systematic Studies of User Design Feedback

It is likely seen from the overview study in this chapter, that the usefulness or impact of the customer feedback across the UX design process is dependent on the stage of development process that it was conducted. Therefore, further works will require broadening on the current UX measurement techniques and metrics so that different stages of the development process may require different ways of collecting and analyzing user design feedback. A lot of technological advancement could be taken advantage of to achieve this fit (e.g. Artificial Intelligent (AI) discussed next).

Artificial Intelligence (AI) and Machine Learning (ML)

Perhaps every business's dream would be to have the technical capability, not just to analyze customers feedbacks but also have an individually tailored design according to a customer's precedence such as previous recommendation or buying habit or history. This might feel like a far-fetched concept, but it is already here. The emerging new technologies in related fields of AI and Machine Learning (ML) can be used to actualize the dream. With the AI and ML UX, designers can design personalize ads based on the customer's online search precedent, social media interests and online activities. Today people rarely get random ads pop up, they usually see something related to their interest and when that happens, there is a high probability they will click on them or even make a purchase. In recent times, users prefer suitability and comfort when using a system and when this experience aligns with their behavior and needs, they feel great. The AI and ML tools can assist companies create a personalized experience for their customers each time they interact with their marketing or sales systems with even improved UX.

Advancement of AR for E-Business Stores

The introduction section of this chapter narrates how deployment of the AR enhanced UX by Zara, the fashion designer brand resulted in a historic increase in their customer base as well as sale volume. Perhaps because of Zara's market turnover with the use of AR enabled UX shopping, the technology has received a widespread adoption in the e-businesses market. However, it is generally believed that the AR influences unplanned purchases and most will avoid online stores using it. For this reason, we don't think so far, the AR has disrupted existence of retail stores. But we believe the technology contributes to the growing decline in the brick and mortar stores. In the foreseeable future, even though, there will still be certain products (e.g. cars, planes etc.) or services that will still be purchased in the brick and mortar stores but shopping experience in any type of store will be improved tremendously. Imagine a moment you have just walked into the HOME DEPOT store to buy a new pair of shoes. If you have AR contacts glass on, then you will be directed to where you can view shoes. You will be able to see previous buyer reviews, shoe varieties and so on.

Micro-Interaction

In the near future, well designed micro interactive interfaces may become the trend in the field of UX design, tremendously impacting on the e-business applications. The Micro-interactive apps can perhaps bring further improvement in the end-user's experience in the online commerce but when inadequately designed, can impair UX. The most important features of micro-interaction are that it can be used to improve the usability of a system, improve UX and give feedbacks to end-users through visual cues making them feel in control of the system. The improvement of micro-interactions can really help shape and advance UX.

CONCLUSION

Generally speaking, measuring the UX of any product or service comes with a lot of challenges. These challenges range from finding what aspect of the UX to measure, what approach to use for the measurement as well as what should be the goal of the measurement. Unfortunately, there is no single best technique for measuring UX of any product or service. Rather, a few metrics are used to quantify different aspects of the UX and a handful of reliable techniques exist as well to run the measurement and pass opined business decisions. In this chapter we have discussed some of the recently used approaches for measuring UX with a particular consideration for e-businesses. We believe the e-business sector of the economy need much exploration for possible improvement in the UX study as it impacts much on the ROI of the business concerns. As the e-business sector matures and move beyond the level of questioning the value ROI of the UX projects, individual businesses will need to have strategic plans in place towards making the most use of investment promises on user centered marketing. The best plans will be those organized around the goal of linking customer research metrics to how the company defines success through proven Key Performance Indicators (KPIs). This will require using the right methods including emerging technologies that helps in the understanding of user buying patterns and brand perceptions. It should be noted however, that the UX domain is fairly young and incorporates practitioners from distinct backgrounds with differing views about the concept. Therefore, a unified understanding to match theory and practice is lacking in the e-business settings.

REFERENCES

Alalwan, J. A., & Weistroffer, H. R. (2012). Enterprise content management research: A comprehensive review. *Journal of Enterprise Information Management*, *25*(5), 441–461. doi:10.1108/17410391211265133

Azuma, R., Baillot, Y., Behringer, R., Feiner, S., Julier, S., & MacIntyre, B. (2001). Recent advances in augmented reality. *IEEE Computer Graphics and Applications*, *21*(6), 34–47. doi:10.1109/38.963459

Carmigniani, J., Furht, B., Anisetti, M., Ceravolo, P., Damiani, E., & Ivkovic, M. (2011). Augmented reality technologies, systems and applications. *Multimedia Tools and Applications*, *51*(1), 341–377. doi:10.1007/s11042-010-0660-6

Dixon, M., Freeman, K., & Toman, N. (2010). Stop Trying to Delight Your Customers. Harvard Business Review. Retrieved from https://hbr.org/2010/07/stop-trying-to-delight-your-customers

Dotson, J. P., Fan, R. R., Feit, E. M. D., Oldham, J. D., & Yeh, Y. H. (2017). Brand Attitudes and Search Engine Queries. *Journal of Interactive Marketing*, *37*, 105–116. doi:10.1016/j.intmar.2016.10.002

Gan, W., Lin, J. C.-W., Zhang, J., Fournier-Viger, P., Chao, H.-C., & Yu, P. S. (2020). Fast Utility Mining on Sequence Data. IEEE Transactions on Cybernetics, 1–14. doi:10.1109/TCYB.2020.2970176 PubMed

Hartson, H. R., Andre, T. S., & Williges, R. C. (2003). Criteria for evaluating usability evaluation methods. In *International Journal of Human-Computer Interaction* (Vol. 15, pp. 145–181). Taylor and Francis Inc., doi:10.1207/S15327590IJHC1501_13

Hassenzahl, M. (2001). The effect of perceived hedonic quality on product appealingness. *International Journal of Human-Computer Interaction*, *13*(4), 481–499. doi:10.1207/S15327590IJHC1304_07

Huang, Z., Hong, Y., & Xu, X. (2020). Design and research on evaluation model of user experience on mobile terminal products. In *Advances in Intelligent Systems and Computing* (Vol. 972, pp. 198–206). Springer Verlag., doi:10.1007/978-3-030-19135-1_20

Hubbard, D. W. (2008). How to measure anything: finding the value of "intangibles" in business. Choice Reviews Online, 45(12), 45-6882-45–6882. doi:10.5860/choice.45-6882

ISO. (2014). ISO - ISO/IEC 25063:2014 - Systems and software engineering — Systems and software product Quality Requirements and Evaluation (SQuaRE) — Common Industry Format (CIF) for usability: Context of use description. Retrieved from https://www.iso.org/standard/35789.html

ISO. (2019). Ergonomics of human-system interaction — Part 210: Human-centred design for interactive systems (2). ISO - ISO 9241-210:2019. Retrieved from https://www.iso.org/standard/77520.html

Jeff, S. (2015). SUPR-Q: A Comprehensive Measure of the Quality of the Website User ExperienceJUS. *Journal of Usability Studies*, *10*(2), 68–86. https://uxpajournal.org/supr-q-a-comprehensive-measure-of-the-quality-of-the-website-user-experience/

Jordan, P. W. (2000). Designing Pleasurable Products | An Introduction to the New Human Factors | Taylor & Francis Group. Lodon: Taylor & Francis, Imprint CRC Press. Retrieved from https://www.taylorfrancis.com/books/9780429219962

Logan, R. J. (1994). Behavioral and emotional usability: Thomson Consumer Electronics. In M. E. Wiklund (Ed.), *Usability in practice: how companies develop user-friendly products* (pp. 59–82). Academic Press Professional Inc., Retrieved from https://dl.acm.org/doi/10.5555/180981.180984

Maia, C. L. B., & Furtado, E. S. (2016). A systematic review about user experience evaluation. In *Lecture Notes in Computer Science (including subseries Lecture Notes in Artificial Intelligence and Lecture Notes in Bioinformatics)* (Vol. 9746, pp. 445–455). Springer Verlag., doi:10.1007/978-3-319-40409-7_42.

Sauro, J., & Dumas, J. S. (2009). Comparison of three one-question, post-task usability questionnaires. In Conference on Human Factors in Computing Systems - Proceedings (pp. 1599–1608). ACM Press. doi:10.1145/1518701.1518946

Shackel, B. (2009). Usability – Context, framework, definition, design and evaluation. *Interacting with Computers*, *21*(5–6), 339–346. doi:10.1016/j.intcom.2009.04.007

Sonnleitner, A., Pawlowski, M., Kässer, T., & Peissner, M. (2013). Experimentally manipulating positive user experience based on the fulfilment of user needs. In Lecture Notes in Computer Science (including subseries Lecture Notes in Artificial Intelligence and Lecture Notes in Bioinformatics) (Vol. 8120 LNCS, pp. 555–562). Springer. doi:10.1007/978-3-642-40498-6_45

Tang, Y., Wang, H., Guo, K., Xiao, Y., & Chi, T. (2018). Relevant Feedback Based Accurate and Intelligent Retrieval on Capturing User Intention for Personalized Websites. *IEEE Access : Practical Innovations, Open Solutions*, *6*, 24239–24248. doi:10.1109/ACCESS.2018.2828081

Wu, F., Huang, X., & Jiang, B. (2019). A Data-Driven Approach for Extracting Representative Information From Large Datasets With Mixed Attributes. IEEE Transactions on Engineering Management, 1–17. Advance online publication. doi:10.1109/TEM.2019.2934485

ADDITIONAL READING

Alalwan, J. A., & Weistroffer, H. R. (2012). Enterprise content management research: A comprehensive review. *Journal of Enterprise Information Management*, *25*(5), 441–461. doi:10.1108/17410391211265133

Azuma, R., Baillot, Y., Behringer, R., Feiner, S., Julier, S., & MacIntyre, B. (2001). Recent advances in augmented reality. *IEEE Computer Graphics and Applications*, *21*(6), 34–47. doi:10.1109/38.963459

Carmigniani, J., Furht, B., Anisetti, M., Ceravolo, P., Damiani, E., & Ivkovic, M. (2011). Augmented reality technologies, systems and applications. *Multimedia Tools and Applications*, *51*(1), 341–377. doi:10.1007/s11042-010-0660-6

Dixon, M., Freeman, K., & Toman, N. (2010). Stop Trying to Delight Your Customers. Havard Business Review. Retrieved from https://hbr.org/2010/07/stop-trying-to-delight-your-customers

Dotson, J. P., Fan, R. R., Feit, E. M. D., Oldham, J. D., & Yeh, Y. H. (2017). Brand Attitudes and Search Engine Queries. *Journal of Interactive Marketing, 37*, 105–116. doi:10.1016/j.intmar.2016.10.002

Gan, W., Lin, J. C.-W., Zhang, J., Fournier-Viger, P., Chao, H.-C., & Yu, P. S. (2020). Fast Utility Mining on Sequence Data. IEEE Transactions on Cybernetics, 1–14. doi:10.1109/TCYB.2020.2970176 PubMed

Hartson, H. R., Andre, T. S., & Williges, R. C. (2003). Criteria for evaluating usability evaluation methods. In *International Journal of Human-Computer Interaction* (Vol. 15, pp. 145–181). Taylor and Francis Inc., doi:10.1207/S15327590IJHC1501_13

Hassenzahl, M. (2001). The effect of perceived hedonic quality on product appealingness. *International Journal of Human-Computer Interaction, 13*(4), 481–499. doi:10.1207/S15327590IJHC1304_07

Huang, Z., Hong, Y., & Xu, X. (2020). Design and research on evaluation model of user experience on mobile terminal products. In *Advances in Intelligent Systems and Computing* (Vol. 972, pp. 198–206). Springer Verlag., doi:10.1007/978-3-030-19135-1_20

Hubbard, D. W. (2008). How to measure anything: finding the value of "intangibles" in business. Choice Reviews Online, 45(12), 45-6882-45–6882. doi:10.5860/choice.45-6882

ISO. (2014). ISO - ISO/IEC 25063:2014 - Systems and software engineering — Systems and software product Quality Requirements and Evaluation (SQuaRE) — Common Industry Format (CIF) for usability: Context of use description. Retrieved from https://www.iso.org/standard/35789.html

ISO. (2019). Ergonomics of human-system interaction — Part 210: Human-centred design for interactive systems (2). ISO - ISO 9241-210:2019. Retrieved from https://www.iso.org/standard/77520.html

Jeff, S. (2015). SUPR-Q: A Comprehensive Measure of the Quality of the Website User ExperienceJUS. *Journal of Usability Studies, 10*(2), 68–86. https://uxpajournal.org/supr-q-a-comprehensive-measure-of-the-quality-of-the-website-user-experience/

Jordan, P. W. (2000). Designing Pleasurable Products | An Introduction to the New Human Factors | Taylor & Francis Group. Lodon: Taylor & Francis, Imprint CRC Press. Retrieved from https://www.taylorfrancis.com/books/9780429219962

Logan, R. J. (1994). Behavioral and emotional usability:Thomson Consumer Electronics. In M. E. Wiklund (Ed.), Usability in practice: how companies develop user-friendly products (pp. 59–82). 525 B Street Suite 1900 San Diego, CA United States: Academic Press Professional Inc. Retrieved from https://dl.acm.org/doi/10.5555/180981.180984

Maia, C. L. B., & Furtado, E. S. (2016). A systematic review about user experience evaluation. In *Lecture Notes in Computer Science (including subseries Lecture Notes in Artificial Intelligence and Lecture Notes in Bioinformatics)* (Vol. 9746, pp. 445–455). Springer Verlag., doi:10.1007/978-3-319-40409-7_42.

Merholz, P. (2007). Peter in conversation with Don Norman about UX & innovation.

Sauro, J., & Dumas, J. S. (2009). Comparison of three one-question, post-task usability questionnaires. In *Conference on Human Factors in Computing Systems - Proceedings* (pp. 1599–1608). ACM Press., doi:10.1145/1518701.1518946.

Shackel, B. (2009). Usability – Context, framework, definition, design and evaluation. *Interacting with Computers*, *21*(5–6), 339–346. doi:10.1016/j.intcom.2009.04.007

Sonnleitner, A., Pawlowski, M., Kässer, T., & Peissner, M. (2013). Experimentally manipulating positive user experience based on the fulfilment of user needs. In Lecture Notes in Computer Science (including subseries Lecture Notes in Artificial Intelligence and Lecture Notes in Bioinformatics) (Vol. 8120 LNCS, pp. 555–562). Springer, Berlin, Heidelberg. doi:10.1007/978-3-642-40498-6_45

Tang, Y., Wang, H., Guo, K., Xiao, Y., & Chi, T. (2018). Relevant Feedback Based Accurate and Intelligent Retrieval on Capturing User Intention for Personalized Websites. *IEEE Access : Practical Innovations, Open Solutions*, *6*, 24239–24248. doi:10.1109/ACCESS.2018.2828081

Wu, F., Huang, X., & Jiang, B. (2019). A Data-Driven Approach for Extracting Representative Information From Large Datasets With Mixed Attributes. IEEE Transactions on Engineering Management, 1–17. Advance online publication. doi:10.1109/TEM.2019.2934485

KEY TERMS AND DEFINITIONS

Augmented Reality: A technology that has to do with computer induced scenario of an interactive real-world environment where object residing in it are enhanced with perceptual information across multiple sensory cues (e.g., visual, auditory, haptic, etc.).

Business Concern: A commercial enterprise and its labor force including the executives.

Customer: An individual that pays for a product or service.

Experience: Knowledge acquired when using a system or product or due to a person's participation in an activity.

Expert: An individual that is highly skilled or has great knowledge in a particular area or field.

Feedback: Remarks made by a user as a reaction or as an opinion to offer useful information on how to improve a product or service.

Machine: An electronic device that is programmable; it is capable of executing a programmed list of instructions given to it.

Machine Learning: Application of AI that makes systems to instinctively learn and get better from experience without the use of explicit instructions.

Micro Interactions: Either events, transformations, or animations that creates engaging moments when an end-user interacts with the UI of an electronic device.

Product: A thing that is manufactured or bought for sale by a business concern.

Return on Investment: A business condition when investment cost compares lower to its gains or profits.

User: Someone that uses a product or service such as sales app.

APPENDIX 1

Amazon's User Experience

Every end-user appreciates an appealing and operational website or App. Therefore, creating a user experience that meets the needs all age group can be very tasking. Younger audience would appreciate websites and apps that are appealing and senior citizens can hardly keep up with technology and their evolution. So, pleasing this vast audience would always be a challenging task for e-commerce businesses. A survey was conducted by Baymard Institute on Amazon's e-commerce user experience (UX) performance. A comprehensive performance review of 620 design elements and 59 other websites were benchmarked for a complete representation of the e-commerce UX view. The UX Performance are broken down as follows: 43.6% Product Lists & Filtering, 34.9% Product page, 7.6% Cart and Checkout, 74.7% Account and Self-Service, 21.0% Mobile E-commerce and 97.9% On-Site Search. The UX performance ratings above shows that Amazon's e-commerce website has a good "On-Site Search" and decent "Accounts & Self-Service" performances with a poor "Cart & Checkout" as well as a mediocre "Mobile E-Commerce" performances. The website is search-driven and its usability enables a user to shop in 60+ currencies and eight (8) different languages. One of the website's unique features is the ability to personalize the homepage based on end-user's search behavior in order to guide them in future shopping. The survey shows that Amazon has an Overall UX Performance of 40.1%, which is an acceptable rating meaning that the website still need improvement especially in areas like "Cart and Checkout", and "Mobile E-commerce".

Walmart's User Experience

Walmart is one of America's largest retailers. A survey was carried out by Baymard Institute on Walmart's UX performance with a comprehensive performance review of 620 design elements and 59 other websites were benchmarked for a representation of the e-commerce UX view. The UX Performance are as follows: 42.8% Product Lists & Filtering, 35% Product page, 67.4% Cart and Checkout, 31.4% Account and Self-Service, 47% Mobile E-commerce and 88.7% On-Site Search. The UX performance rating of Walmart's website shows that only "On-Site Search" has a good rating while others have low ratings. According to the survey, Walmart has an Overall UX Performance of 52.9%, which is an acceptable rating. There are a few tweaks that Walmart will have to implement to improve their UX performance. Walmart's website has a good "On-Site Search" performance, meaning that users can find whatever commodity they want with so much ease. Their filter and product listing are not impressive and Walmart has to overhaul its online grocery shopping experience. Its Product page, mobile e-commerce as well as their Account and Self-Service features need improvement. Walmart will need to apply a few usability testings measures in order fix these issues and also improve these UX performance ratings.

APPENDIX 2

A copy of the SUPR-Q

Figure 3. The SUPR-R

QUESTIONS	Strongly Disagree				Strongly Agree
1. This website is easy to use.	○	○	○	○	○
2. It is easy to navigate within the website	○	○	○	○	○
3. The information on the website is credible	○	○	○	○	○
4. The information on the website is trustworthy	○	○	○	○	○
5. I feel comfortable purchasing from this site	○	○	○	○	○
6. I found the website to be attractive	○	○	○	○	○
7. The website has a clean and simple presentation	○	○	○	○	○

8. How likely are you to recommend this website to a friend?

Not at all likely   Neutral   Extremely like

○ ○ ○ ○ ○ ○ ○ ○ ○ ○

A copy of the SUS

Figure 4. The SUS questionnaire

1. I think that I would like to use this system frequently

1. Strongly Disagree	2	3	4	5. Strongly Agree
○	○	○	○	○

2. I found the system unnecessarily complex

1. Strongly Disagree	2	3	4	5. Strongly Agree
○	○	○	○	○

3. I thought the system was easy to use

1. Strongly Disagree	2	3	4	5. Strongly Agree
○	○	○	○	○

2. I found the system unnecessarily complex

1. Strongly Disagree	2	3	4	5. Strongly Agree
○	○	○	○	○

4. I think that I would need the support of a technical person to be able to use this system

1. Strongly Disagree	2	3	4	5. Strongly Agree
○	○	○	○	○

5. I found the various functions in this system were well integrated

1. Strongly Disagree	2	3	4	5. Strongly Agree
○	○	○	○	○

6. I thought there was too much inconsistency in this system

1. Strongly Disagree	2	3	4	5. Strongly Agree
○	○	○	○	○

7. I would imagine that most people would learn to use this system very quickly

1. Strongly Disagree	2	3	4	5. Strongly Agree
○	○	○	○	○

8. I found the system very cumbersome to use

1. Strongly Disagree	2	3	4	5. Strongly Agree
○	○	○	○	○

9. I felt very confident using the system

1. Strongly Disagree	2	3	4	5. Strongly Agree
○	○	○	○	○

10. I needed to learn a lot of things before I could get going with the system

A copy of the SEQ.

Figure 5. The SEQ

Overall, this task was?

Very Difficult						Very Easy
1	2	3	4	5	6	7
○	○	○	○	○	○	○

A Copy of the ASQ

Figure 6. The ASQ

Scenario

1. Overal, I am satisfied with the ease of completing this task.

Strongly Agree   1   2   3   4   5   6   7 **Strongly Agree**

2. Overal, I am satisfied with the amount of time it took to complete this task.

Strongly Agree   1   2   3   4   5   6   7 **Strongly Agree**

3. Overal, I am satisfied with the support information when completing this task.

Strongly Agree   1   2   3   4   5   6   7 **Strongly Agree**

A copy of the SMEQ

Figure 7. The SMEQ
Source:(Sauro & Dumas, 2009)

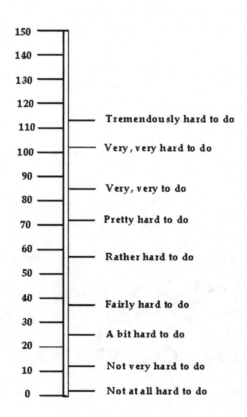

A copy of the NASA-TLX

Figure 8. The NASA-TLX questionnaire

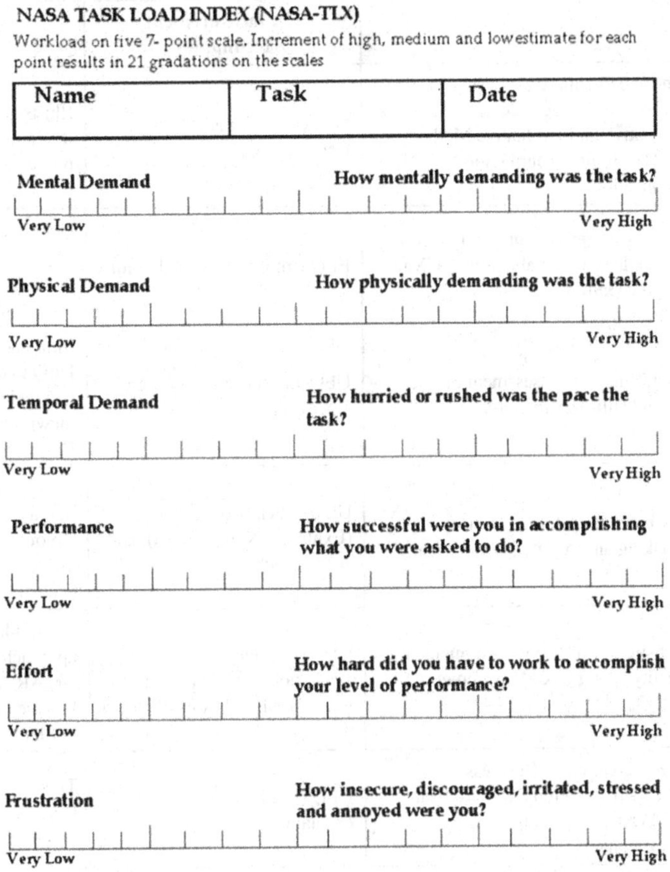

NASA TASK LOAD INDEX (NASA-TLX)

Workload on five 7- point scale. Increment of high, medium and low estimate for each point results in 21 gradations on the scales

Name	Task	Date

Mental Demand   How mentally demanding was the task?

Very Low   Very High

Physical Demand   How physically demanding was the task?

Very Low   Very High

Temporal Demand   How hurried or rushed was the pace the task?

Very Low   Very High

Performance   How successful were you in accomplishing what you were asked to do?

Very Low   Very High

Effort   How hard did you have to work to accomplish your level of performance?

Very Low   Very High

Frustration   How insecure, discouraged, irritated, stressed and annoyed were you?

Very Low   Very High

Table 3. Brand attitude metric questionnaire

Metric	Survey
Recognition (Aided Awareness)	Thinking about brand related to (category) of the following are you aware of?
Recall (Unaided Awareness)	When you think of (category), which three brands come to mind first
Familiarity	Which of the following brands would you say are familiar with?
Consideration	Would you consider purchasing this brand when you buy your next [category]
	If you were making the purchase today, which of the following[category] brands would you be most likely to purchase?

Source: (Dotson, Fan, Feit, Oldham, & Yeh, 2017)

A summary of previous studies on empirical formative techniques are highlighted in table

Table 4. Previous studies on empirical formative

Author(s)	Work	UX measurement techniques	Remark
Wardhani et al. (2019)	An Implementation of User Experience Design: Discovery, Formative and Evaluative Method for Developing Tour Guide Service Application	Interview (Explicit UX evaluation)	Illustrates use of formative usability measure during the initial design phase
Carofiglio et al. (2019)	Applying Brain-Computer Interface Technology for Evaluation of UX in Playing Games	EEG (Implicit UX evaluation)	electroencephalogram extracts data from end-users while playing a computer game and these data is used to discover emotions (UX)
Krisnawati et al. (2019)	First Time UX Assessment on Web based Online Examination	UEQ and Interview (Explicit UX evaluation)	Implemented both interview and UEQ to conclusively examine detailed specifics about user-user' viewpoints of the Web-based Online Examination website.
Souza et al. (2019)	UX Evaluation Using Mouse Tracking and Artificial Intelligence	UEQ, Click/Mouse Tracking (Explicit UX evaluation), and AI method	Compares the UX of an end-user interacting with a website using a mouse tracking UX tool, an AI method with a traditional UX evaluation tool (UEQ).
Satti et al. (2019)	Holistic UX in Mobile Augmented Reality Using UX Measurement Index	UEQ (Explicit UX evaluation) Observation and EEG (Implicit UX evaluation)	uses multiple UX evaluation approach to capture the UX in a MAR App. It can also capture holistic UX of several systems or products.
Limantara et al.(2019).	The Evaluation of Business Process Simulation Software from UX Perspective using the UX Questionnaire	UEQ (Explicit UX evaluation)	This study used UEQ to evaluate the UX of a business process simulation Software (BeeCEO)
Wicahyono et al. (2019)	Pregnancy Monitoring Mobile Application User Experience Assessment	UEQ (Explicit UX evaluation)	Discussed the user experience in implementing a mobile application for pregnancy monitoring and in the UX evaluation

Chapter 16
Sharing Economy as a New Organization Model:
Visualization Map Analysis and Future Research

Jialei Li
Dongbei University of Finance and Economics, China

Tao Meng
Dongbei University of Finance and Economics, China

Muhammad Zahid Nawaz
Dongbei University of Finance and Economics, China

ABSTRACT

Although the sharing economy's commercial practice is booming, the study on the formation mechanism is fragmented. This chapter captures a whole picture of sharing economy's research and gives suggestions for future interesting studies. Based on the method of the Prisma protocol for systematic literature review, with the help of CiteSpace software, the authors map out the structure of existing literature. Current research found out that sharing economy as a new organization model is the current developing trend, sharing economy could be a strong method in the organization's management area. The definition of sharing economy can be included as a new economic phenomenon based on the internet, including peer-to-peer-based activities of obtaining, giving, or sharing the access to goods and services to maximize the utilization. This chapter concluded the connotation of sharing economy, based on the resource view, property right view, and technique view, and several future research plans are generated.

DOI: 10.4018/978-1-7998-3756-5.ch016

INTRODUCTION

Web 2.0 technologies have a great impact on businesses, shaped the model of organizations, and changed the logic of consumption. These factors dramatically influence the user experience in Web 2.0 technologies. For example, sharing economy is a new economic pattern derived by Web 2.0 technologies, many new types of businesses like Uber and Airbnb perform differently from traditional economic organizations, they do not own much of resources but cooperate with their users to build a social-economic system. Moreover, users feel differently in the sharing economy, because they are not only consuming the goods and services from the sharing economy businesses, but also be a "producer" to produce goods and services. For example, Uber drivers can share their car and time with strangers to earn some money, Airbnb hosts can shortly rent their houses or even idle beds to get some income. *It is clear that sharing economy presents an important role to understand the change of user experience in Web 2.0 technologies. So a systematic study on the sharing economy is necessary for further research.*

The concept of sharing economy rose with the foundation of Zipcar in the year 2000 by Robin Chase, and then rapidly raised right after the global financial crises in the year 2008. Today the sharing economy concept is extensively developed in China, the United States, South Korea, the European Union, Japan, and many other regions and countries. At present, the sharing economy has been greatly developed in terms of sharing scale, sharing fields and sharing subjects. Just in a few years, Airbnb, a representative enterprise from the field of online short rent, has been able to match the size of the Hilton Hotel. Sharing domain varies from the original cars, houses, financial, etc. to skill, space, catering, logistics, education, health, infrastructure, also accelerated to the agriculture, energy, manufacturing, and many more fields such as urban construction expansion. The sharing subject is no longer limited to the individual and begins to extend to organizations, enterprises, and governments.

The sharing economy attracted more and more attention from different subjects, such as management, economics, and sociology, and has formed a research boom. Heo (2016) Found that the studies on sharing economy mainly divided into four aspects: Psychological aspect, Policy and Financial aspect, P2P sharing aspect, and Domain of Sharing aspect. However, the above research perspectives failed to reveal the connotation to the concept of sharing economy and the root causes of the formation mechanism at the organizational level. Previous researchers mainly focused on practical aspects of sharing economy. Besides, the study on sharing, collaborative consumption, peer production, and the network organization provided new theoretical perspectives to the sharing economy, but it cannot simply copy to this research system. Although some scholars have tried to put forward the concept of sharing economy, the research on the connotation of sharing economic concept has been based on a single point of view, without properly considering all the complexities of the real environment.

Visibly, the sharing economy research is in its infancy. It is not so clear about the structured definition of sharing economy. Although the commercial practice of sharing economy is rapidly booming, without the guidance of the theory, the future of sharing economy is bound to enter the bottleneck of development and there will be a lack of transformational directions and motivations. Through the deep study of the literature review, this paper will capture a whole elucidated picture of sharing economy research and will provide suggestions for the future interesting studies within the field of sharing economy.

BACKGROUND

At present, there is no unified definition of sharing economy and sharing economy research carried out under different themes, its research has a lot of diversity. Sharing economy research brought certain challenges, to define sharing economy connotation provides a certain reference significance. Based on the previous literature, through comparative analysis, scholars have mainly defined the concept of sharing economy in three perspectives: resource-based view, property right view, and technology view.

In the View of Resource

The sharing economy from the perspective of resource view refers to that idle resources or overcapacity is the root of sharing economy. The founder of Zipcar Robin Chase (2015) in his book emphasizes the collaborative sharing enterprises are the basis of excess capacity, sharing economy can make full use of knowledge assets and the idle resources of new economic form. In this context, the new consumption concept, which is used rather than occupied, is gradually emerging, and sustainable development and consumption are widely accepted, and it has received continuous attention (Frenken, 2017; Kari & Sunliang, 2017; Kopnina, 2017).

First of all, the background of sharing economy's emergence. In the context of the world financial crisis in 2008, the economies of all countries were badly hurt, and then the new economic growth points were urgently needed. Inflation leads to reduced purchasing power and increased sensitivity to prices, and consumption was considered as an important tool to stimulate economic growth. So sharing economy as consumption innovation has driven economic development and adapted to the needs of the time. At the same time, the deterioration of the living environment has enhanced the consciousness of environmental protection and the consciousness of worry.

On the other hand, sharing economy and collaborative consumption. The original sharing economy featured "collaborative consumption". Collaborative Consumption was first proposed by Felson and Spaeth (1978). It refers to the process of consuming an economic product or service together with others. Understanding collaborative consumption has three main perspectives. From the perspective of consumers, the Bozeman and Rogers (2010) point out that collaborative consumption is on the Internet, the rise of a new business model. Consumers could share the products and services with others through the way of cooperation, without having to hold the ownership of the products and services. Belk (2014) argued that the definition was too broad, limiting it to collaborative consumption only when people paid a certain amount of money to obtain the corresponding resources.

In the View of Property Right

Sharing economy performance under the perspective of property rights is the sharing of ownership and the right to use. World population is growing rapidly so as the shortage of resources environment, this phenomenon firstly put forwarded and supported by Harvard University scholar Professor Benkler, he says only by using peer production, is likely to ease or even solve the global problems. And further put forward the concept of shareable goods (Benkler, 2004) in sharing economy the construction of sustainable society become mankind's common goal (Tussyadiah, 2015).

Hamari, Sjöklint, and Ukkonen (2016) share from the Angle of technology, this paper discusses the issue of ownership in the economy, the enterprise of the type 254 share network analysis can be divided into two kinds, the first kind is to use rather than have (access over ownership), mainly for the lease, the owner of the products and services for consumers right to the use of products and services (Bardhi & Eckhardt, 2012). The first type is about the use under certain conditions to give or to assign to others, the owner of rights may not relinquish ownership, which is currently the major form of sharing economy. The other type is the transfer of ownership, which is mainly manifested in exchange, donation and second-hand goods transactions.

In the View of Technique

The core technique in sharing economy is a network technology, based on it, organizations and individuals can form a network, in this network, the boundaries of the enterprises are no longer fixed, and the traditional internal and external forms of the organizations have been changed. The interaction between the technical network and the social network is very important in this network. For economic activity is embedded into the social structure (Uzzi, 1997), the trading paradigm of sharing economy representatives is typical of strong social relations transactions, namely embedded transactions. Based on the embedded transactions, sharing economy can build trust between strangers within in a short time and could achieve mutual benefit.

It is worth mentioning that the continuous upgrading of new media and network technologies, the continuous improvement of virtual communities and the continued blurring of online and offline boundaries provided fertile soil for the sharing economy's development. The progress of information technology with the pursuit of social existence in human nature (Fitz, Nadler, Manogaran, Chong, & Reiner, 2014) has represented by social software platforms to develop a social network, the point to point, personal to personal communication and exchanges become frequent (Matzler, Veider, & Kathan, 2015). Technology network, together with the economic and social networks as important influence factors of network organization, and gradually get attention in the field of organization and management, providing a new thought and method for network organization governance.

Connotation of Sharing Economy

To sum up, the sharing economy is an economic phenomenon produced in the background of the Internet era, which is endowed with various labels in concept (Belk, 2013). There are differences in the view of the three at the same time have a certain convergence, involves redistribution via the Internet technologies, the use or sharing of product, service, spare parts, for individuals, businesses, non-profit organizations, government, to participate in the sharing and distribution in the process, to maximize the use of resources (Cohen & Kietzmann, 2014; Hamari et al., 2016). Therefore, when defining the sharing economy, this chapter should not only analyze it from a single perspective but integrate three perspectives and embody the comprehensive characteristics.

Combined with the above research, sharing economy can be defined as: with the help of a digital network platform, based on the transfer of using right and ownership between individuals or organizations, to maximize the usage of products and services. As shown in Table 1 below, the concept of sharing economy is summarized.

Table 1. The connotation of sharing economy.

Perspective	Resource	Property right	Technique
Feature	Change of consumption view Profit from the assignment of right to use Transfer ownership profits Conducive to the maximization of resources and the sustainable development of the environment.	Assignment right Assignment of title Interpersonal relationships System of trust Social identity Interaction and mutual benefit	Transparent online communities. Internet technology Economies of scale Transaction cost reduction Consumer roles change. Establish a connection

Source: Based on Relevant Studies

The realistic reflection of the sharing economy can be shown in Table 2. This paper summarized the following three categories: Goods sharing (Physical objects), Services sharing (Intangible objects) and Money sharing (Financial products).

Table 2. The realistic reflection of sharing economy.

Category	Industry	China	America
Goods sharing	Secondary goods Short accommodation rental City travel	Xianyu Tujia.com Didichuxing, ofo	Yerdle, Swaptree Airbnb Uber
Service sharing	Enterprise crowdsourcing Personal assistant Private consultant Skills exchange Private chef Private logistics	Weike Ninshuowoban Dedao Jinengjiaohuan Mishi Renren	Innocentive TaskRabbit Quora / Opentable /
Money sharing	Internet finance	Yixin	Lending Club, Prosper

Source: Based on Relevant Studies

Visualization Map Analysis

The current study is based on the prism literature analysis method as suggested by (Moher, Liberati, Tetzlaff, Altman, & Group, 2009) because it can provide a clear literature review process. The method has four steps: Identification stage, Selection stage, Determine the qualification stage and Selection stage. Then, as a supplement, this chapter adopted the "snowball" method to expand the relevant literature. After reading the literature which has been obtained through the above steps, the main topics and keywords in the field were determined. Based on the Web of Science database, retrieval keywords taken were: TS (Topics) = ("sharing economy" OR "collaborative economy" OR "collaborative consumption" OR "peer-to-peer economy" OR "hybrid economy" OR "lateral exchange markets" OR "access-based consumption" OR "commercial sharing systems" OR "Uber" OR "Airbnb" OR "Zipcar" OR "Car2go" OR "Lyft" OR "Mobike"), after screening, to get a total of 516 articles. By using the CiteSpace V.5.0.R4 SE software, visualize this core literature, and grasp the main research fields. After the clustering analysis, there are 28 knowledge clusters. This research removed the duplicate clusters, and found under mentioned clustering network map, as shown in Figure 1.

Figure 1. Cluster diagram of sharing economy research field
Source: Produced by CiteSpace Software

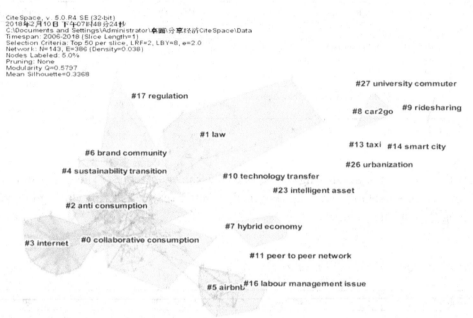

As mentioned in figure 1, #0 is the collaborative consumption, this research mainly focuses on the concept of sharing economy, and there are some core scholars such as Belk, it is also similar to the research of #7 and #11. #1 is the law, the research mainly focuses on the regulation and governance of sharing economy, and #17 is similar to that. #2 is the anti-consumption, mainly from the perspective of marketing, pay attention to consumption, the transfer rights of ownership and access, dual identity like "prosumption", tightly linked with # 0, and also appeared very influential scholars such as Bardhi. #3 is the Internet. It primarily focuses on the influence of network technology, and the research of #10, #16 and #23 are similar to that. #4 labels for the sustainability transition, focus on the environmental sustainability and business model. Ridesharing is the main research case for (#8, #9, #13, #14, #26, #27), and online renting is another one #5. The label of #6 is the brand community, focusing on the value creation process, and the main research case is Airbnb.

Apparently, the base clusters have very strong connections and the relatively isolated clusters are supplements of the base clusters. However, sharing economy organizations-related studies have not formed a cluster. Although, in reality, sharing economy organizations and organizing have played a vital role, the corresponding organization management theory does not have very good explanatory power.

Currently, the sharing economy research from the organizational field has just emerged, and the major research work has been published in the last two years. Enterprise organization research scholars Mair and Reischauer (2017) Firstly put forward the concept of sharing economy organizations. Miralles, Dentoni, and Pascucci (2017) Also believe that there is not enough research on sharing economy in the field of organizations. However, some scholars have begun to pay attention to this research area, although the overall number is small.

The main research work is as follows: forthcoming researchers are mainly on the sharing economy organizations' patterns. Mair and Reischauer (2017) Defined sharing economy organizations as a market network, a market where people use various forms of compensation to trade and access to resources, and the digital platform is operated as an organization. Miralles et al. (2017) Studied from an organizational perspective in the context of food and agriculture, and proposed six characteristics of sharing economy organizations: the collection of goods and services (building demand and supply pool), such as mass production organization, Linux is a typical example of individual intellectual resource gathering and redistributing according to supply and demand; the decentralization of power (which is conducive to the fairness of power); small participants (mainly individual participation); trust between participants; innovation and better use of resources. According to Perren and Kozinets (2018), based on case analysis, sharing economy organizations can be defined as a lantern exchange market. The basic definition of the sharing economy organization is not yet clear. So the study on sharing economy organizations' models and mechanisms is not enough and there is still a gap.

Future Research Directions

The whole system of sharing economy studies can be summed up by the IMOI (input-process-output-input) model (Ilgen, Hollenbeck, Johnson, & Jundt, 2005). Our research orientation can be reflected in this model (Figure. 2). From the perspective of organization theory, this paper focuses on the nature, mode and governance mechanism of the sharing economy organizations, which is the process part in Figure 2.

In detail, two main questions still remain to be solved: What is the nature and model of sharing economy organizations? How do different resources in sharing economy organize together? By solving these two questions, several "black boxes" will be uncovered. Such as organizational characteristics, organizational subjects, organizational structure, organizational elements, and organizational boundaries. Then on the basis of classification, various modes of sharing economy organizations could be summed up. And finally, according to the nature and model of sharing economy organizations, this chapter can discuss the governance mechanisms of it.

Figure 2. The research system of sharing economy
Source: Ilgen, Hollenbeck, Johnson, & Jundt, 2005

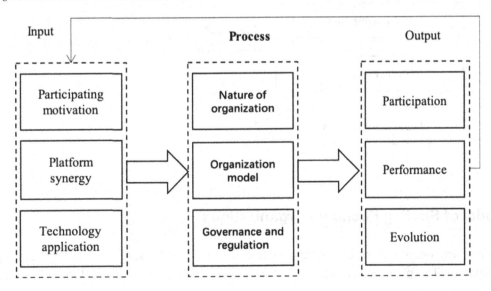

The Nature of Sharing Economy Organizations

Compared with traditional economy organizations, sharing economy organizations are complementary and alternative to the market and enterprise and are based on virtual community organizations, P2P organizations, network organizations, and platform organizations (See Figure. 3).

Firstly, in terms of organizational characteristics, the sharing economy organization is characterized by the following five characteristics, many of which are not available to ordinary enterprise organizations or non-profit organizations: dynamic, diversity, legitimacy (adaptation to the environment), complexity and spontaneity, all of which need to be further analyzed in future research.

Secondly, in terms of organizational structure, compared with traditional organizations, sharing economy organizations are a supplement and replacement for markets and enterprises and based on the logic of platform organizations, such as peer production organizations, virtual community organizations, and network organizations.

Thirdly, on the main body of this type of organization, the platform built by the sharing economy organization is an enterprise organization operated by the enterprise. And finally, on the organizational elements, the core elements of the sharing economy are refined into: a wide market (sufficient individual participants), idle resources (formation of supply and the demand side), a variety of forms of compensation (including the separation of the right to use and ownership), the technical carrier of the operation of the enterprise.

Figure 3. Nature of sharing economy organizations.
Source: Based on relevant studies

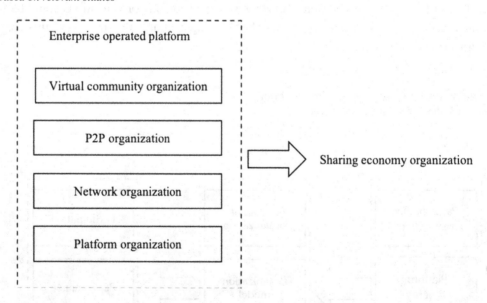

The Model of Sharing Economy Organizations

Sharing economy organizations can be divided into three types: Hierarchy type, Platform type, and Community type The platform type mainly occurs between users and users (both consumers and producers), which is more general, it is an innovative form of organization. Community type (or C-form) is a special form of platform type, which is an organizational form, composed entirely of consumers and has the same kernel as peer production. And the hierarchical model mainly occurs between enterprises and consumers (B2C). As seen in Table 3.

Table 3. Model of sharing economy organizations.

Model	Characteristic	Exchange subject	Cases
Platform	Lateral exchange market	C2C & B2C & C2B	Airbnb, Uber, Lending Club
Community	Lateral exchange market	C2C	Wiki, TaskRabbit
Hierarchy	Vertical exchange market	B2C	Car2go, ofo, Zipcar

Source: Based on relevant studies

Firstly, the platform type (C2C & B2B & C2B): in the market type as a lateral exchange market; in the exchange subject mainly occurs between users. Due to the dual identity characteristics of the users, according to the different identities, different kinds of platforms are created. The platform here is a third-party enterprise proprietary platform, which is an organizational innovation model, which is currently widely used, such as Airbnb mentioned above, second-hand item trading platform, network platform, etc. However, assets such as second-hand houses and cars are professional and require professional inter-vening intervention, which is different from the general platform-based mode in terms of performance.

Secondly, the community type (C2C): is a special form of platform type, is an organizational form composed entirely of consumers, and has the same core as peer production, mainly in the field of knowl-edge product innovation, such as Wiki and TaskRabbit.

And finally, the hierarchical type (B2C): in the market type as a vertical exchange market; in the user category mainly occurs between the enterprise and the user; mainly represented by shared bicycles as ofo bike, the corresponding platform is the enterprise's platform.

The Governance Mechanism of Sharing Economy Organizations

The rapid development of the sharing economy poses a serious challenge to the management of the organization. The participants in the sharing economy have never met, and how can they effectively solve the economic surplus through Internet communication? What is the mechanism behind this? In the following two mechanisms are discussed as examples, which are openness, trust, interaction, and reciprocity. They are closely related to the connotation of sharing economy and can give an inspiration for the governance of sharing economy organizations.

1.   Openness.

The primal instinct of human beings in cognition causes individuals to make decisions based on other people's behaviors and opinions, which is the law of social identity. Social identity is an important motivation for people to participate in the sharing economy, and it is also the internal cause of sharing economy to attract people, and the formation and spread of this identity benefit from the development of

Internet technology. On the one hand, the Internet reduces the time and spread the cost of identity formation from the technical level, expands the scope of identity coverage, and thus forms the scale effect. On the other hand, it significantly reduces the transaction costs between organizations, between enterprises, between individuals and individuals. Web 2.0 has interactive information flow, each person can receive and publish the information at the same time. With the help of network technology, the link between users is not one-way but becomes a network. The network is open, individuals and organizations are able to access anywhere and anytime. And the network has become a new type of social organization or economic organization. Under the perspective of organizational behavior, "network" is synonymous with "cooperation". Based on this, participants in the sharing economy show the characteristics of collaboration and sharing through the Internet in an open network environment (Hamari, Sjoklint & Ukkonen, 2015).

2.   Trust.

Trust is very important to strangers in sharing economy because the exchange environment is more complex in the Internet era (Beldad, De Jong & Steehouder., 2010). People cannot see each other, and don't even know whether there is a real person or not behind the computer. Trust is a multi-dimensional concept and can help customers to overcome the uncertainty risk awareness, increase customer enthusiasm to participate in the network transaction (McKnight, Choudhury & Kacmar, 2002). A good network community tends to have good Internet trust, which is reflected in good interpersonal trust and system trust (Benlian & Hess, 2011; Pizzutti & Fernandes, 2010) among them. In a perfect transparent community, everyone has the responsibility to keep the trust and behave themselves. This will cause more interaction among people inside the sharing economy, help the sharing economy organizations gain more users, and extend their business.

3.   Interaction

Bruhn et al. (2014) defined interaction between multiple customers as the process of collaborative exchange of resources using the same brand through the B2B community platform. This process is consistent with the sharing economy. It can be said that the sharing economy is a generalized exchange process. Interaction is an important factor in promoting the development of the sharing economy. Kim et al. (2015) used the theoretical framework of social exchange to explain the reason why people want to use but not own in the sharing economy is to maximize personal benefits. In the research, trust is considered as a cost and consumers' perceivable risks are the factors affecting trust. Positive interactions between customers can reduce their perceived risks, and the community-based sharing economy enterprises make interactions between customers more easily. It is also because consumers in the network society gradually gather different roles together such as producer, consumer, and sharer. This unity of roles gives new life to collaborative producers and consumers. Scaraboto's (2015) research answered the reasons and steps for the formation of the mixed economy, and the role of consumers in it. Consumers participate in collaborative consumption and collaborative production, and reduce the uncertainty of the mixed economy by increasing the reciprocity interval in the collaborative production and consumption framework, thereby increasing the frequency of interaction between participating entities.

4.   Reciprocity

The important background of the origin of the sharing economy is the global economic crisis and the deteriorating of the global natural environment. All sectors of society urgently need a new, environmentally friendly income growth point. The sharing economy is a fusion of friendly economy, ecological economy, and inclusive economy. The characteristics of idle resources and income sharing are meeting this demand. Idle resources prompt people to change their consumption habits to "no possession", and form a new, sustainable and green concept of property rights from the social level. Cohen and Kietzmann (2014) used a principal-agent theory to explain the relationship between service providers and local governments in the sharing economy business model. This theory advocates the idea of separating ownership from operating rights and fully transferring operating rights. It has been applied in the "sharing economy", that is, the separation of ownership and accessing rights, and full transfer of accessing rights. The new consumption concept derived from idle resources keeps people open, both physically and mentally. It is mainly manifested by greatly improving the availability of products, services, skills, funds, etc., and allowing individuals, enterprises, non-profit organizations, governments, and other parties jointly participate and play multiple roles including producers, consumers, lenders, etc., allowing individuals who did not have the opportunity to occupy or use a resource to share through idle resources In a cost-effective and efficient way, all parties can benefit from it (Leismann et al., 2013). This green ecological concept of property helps to create a sustainable society through the innovation of a sharing economy business model, such as electric vehicle sharing, public bicycle sharing, work sharing, and risk-sharing. Just as Martin and Chris (2016) proposed that the sharing economy is the key to a sustainable development road, however, it may also be a nightmare. No matter whether it is for the benefit or the disadvantage, it will have a great impact on the existing society, and will inevitably bring changes.

CONCLUSION

Through the literature review, this chapter mapped out the structure of existing studies, and find out that sharing economy as a new organization model is one potential developing trend in the coming future. At the same time, this chapter concluded the connotation of sharing economy, based on the resource view, property right view, and technique view. The definition of sharing economy can be included as a new economic phenomenon based on the Internet, including peer-to-peer-based activities of obtaining, giving, or sharing the access to goods and services, to maximize the utilization. Finally, this study generated several future research plans as references, mainly from the perspectives of sharing economy's nature, model and governance mechanisms.

ACKNOWLEDGMENT

This research was supported by the National Natural Science Foundation of China [grant number 71840006]; and the National Social Science Fund of China [grant number 11&ZD153].

REFERENCES

Alanne, K., & Cao, S. (2017). Zero-energy hydrogen economy (ZEH2E) for buildings and communities including personal mobility. *Renewable & Sustainable Energy Reviews*, *71*, 697–711. doi:10.1016/j.rser.2016.12.098

Bardhi, F., & Eckhardt, G. M. (2012). Access-based consumption: The case of car sharing. *The Journal of Consumer Research*, *39*(4), 881–898. doi:10.1086/666376

Beldad, A., De Jong, M., & Steehouder, M. (2010). How shall I trust the faceless and the intangible? A literature review on the antecedents of online trust. *Computers in Human Behavior*, *26*(5), 857–869. doi:10.1016/j.chb.2010.03.013

Belk, R. (2014). Sharing versus pseudo-sharing in Web 2.0. *The Anthropologist*, *18*(1), 7–23. doi:10.1080/09720073.2014.11891518

Belk, R. W. (2013). Extended self in a digital world. *The Journal of Consumer Research*, *40*(3), 477–500. doi:10.1086/671052

Benkler, Y. (2004). Sharing nicely: On shareable goods and the emergence of sharing as a modality of economic production. *The Yale Law Journal*, *114*(2), 273. doi:10.2307/4135731

Benlian, A., & Hess, T. (2011). The signaling role of IT features in influencing trust and participation in online communities. *International Journal of Electronic Commerce*, *15*(4), 7–56. doi:10.2753/JEC1086-4415150401

Botsman, R., & Rogers, R. (2011). *What's Mine Is Yours: The Rise of Collaborative Consumption*. HarperCollins.

Bruhn, M., Schnebelen, S., & Schäfer, D. (2014). Antecedents and consequences of the quality of e-customer-to-customer interactions in B2B brand communities. *Industrial Marketing Management*, *43*(1), 164–176. doi:10.1016/j.indmarman.2013.08.008

Chase, R. (2015). *Peers Inc: how people and platforms are inventing the collaborative economy and reinventing capitalism*. PublicAffairs.

Cohen, B., & Kietzmann, J. (2014). Ride on! Mobility business models for the sharing economy. *Organization & Environment*, *27*(3), 279–296. doi:10.1177/1086026614546199

Felson, M., & Spaeth, J. L. (1978). Community structure and collaborative consumption: A routine activity approach. *The American Behavioral Scientist*, *21*(4), 614–624. doi:10.1177/000276427802100411

Fitz, N. S., Nadler, R., Manogaran, P., Chong, E. W., & Reiner, P. B. (2014). Public attitudes toward cognitive enhancement. *Neuroethics*, *7*(2), 173–188. doi:10.100712152-013-9190-z

Frenken, K. (2017). Political economies and environmental futures for the sharing economy. *Philosophical Transactions - Royal Society. Mathematical, Physical, and Engineering Sciences*, *375*(2095), 20160367. doi:10.1098/rsta.2016.0367 PMID:28461431

Hamari, J., Sjöklint, M., & Ukkonen, A. (2016). The sharing economy: Why people participate in collaborative consumption. *Journal of the Association for Information Science and Technology, 67*(9), 2047–2059. doi:10.1002/asi.23552

Heo, Y. (2016). Sharing economy and prospects in tourism research. *Annals of Tourism Research, 58*, 166–170. doi:10.1016/j.annals.2016.02.002

Ilgen, D. R., Hollenbeck, J. R., Johnson, M., & Jundt, D. (2005). Teams in organizations: From input-process-output models to IMOI models. *Annual Review of Psychology, 56*(1), 517–543. doi:10.1146/annurev.psych.56.091103.070250 PMID:15709945

Kim, J., Yoon, Y., & Zo, H. (2015). Why People Participate in the Sharing Economy: A Social Exchange Perspective. *PACIS, 76.*

Kopnina, H. (2017). Sustainability: New strategic thinking for business. *Environment, Development and Sustainability, 19*(1), 27–43. doi:10.100710668-015-9723-1

Leismann, K., Schmitt, M., Rohn, H., & Baedeker, C. (2013). Collaborative consumption: Towards a resource-saving consumption culture. *Resources, 2*(3), 184–203. doi:10.3390/resources2030184

Mair, J., & Reischauer, G. (2017). Capturing the dynamics of the sharing economy: Institutional research on the plural forms and practices of sharing economy organizations. *Technological Forecasting and Social Change, 125*, 11–20. doi:10.1016/j.techfore.2017.05.023

Martin, & Chris, J. (2016). The sharing economy: a pathway to sustainability or a nightmarish form of neoliberal capitalism? *Ecological Economics, 121*, 149-159.

Matzler, K., Veider, V., & Kathan, W. (2015). Adapting to the sharing economy. *MIT Sloan Management Review, 56*(2), 71.

McKnight, D. H., Choudhury, V., & Kacmar, C. (2002). Developing and validating trust measures for e-commerce: An integrative typology. *Information Systems Research, 13*(3), 334–359. doi:10.1287/isre.13.3.334.81

Miralles, I., Dentoni, D., & Pascucci, S. (2017). Understanding the organization of sharing economy in agri-food systems: Evidence from alternative food networks in Valencia. *Agriculture and Human Values, 34*(4), 833–854. doi:10.100710460-017-9778-8

Moher, D., Liberati, A., Tetzlaff, J., & Altman, D. G. (2009). Preferred reporting items for systematic reviews and meta-analyses: The PRISMA statement. *Annals of Internal Medicine, 151*(4), 264–269. doi:10.7326/0003-4819-151-4-200908180-00135 PMID:19622511

Perren, R., & Kozinets, R. V. (2018). Lateral Exchange Markets: How Social Platforms Operate in a Networked Economy. *Journal of Marketing, 82*(1), 20–36. doi:10.1509/jm.14.0250

Pizzutti, C., & Fernandes, D. (2010). Effect of recovery efforts on consumer trust and loyalty in e-tail: A contingency model. *International Journal of Electronic Commerce, 14*(4), 127–160. doi:10.2753/JEC1086-4415140405

Sawyer, S., & Tapia, A. (2005). The sociotechnical nature of mobile computing work: Evidence from a study of policing in the United States. *International Journal of Technology and Human Interaction*, *1*(3), 1–14. doi:10.4018/jthi.2005070101

Scaraboto, D. (2015). Selling, sharing, and everything in between: The hybrid economies of collaborative networks. *The Journal of Consumer Research*, *42*(1), 152–176. doi:10.1093/jcr/ucv004

Tussyadiah, I. P. (2015). An exploratory study on drivers and deterrents of collaborative consumption in travel. In Information and communication technologies in tourism 2015 (pp. 817-830). Cham, Switzerland: Springer. doi:10.1007/978-3-319-14343-9_59

Uzzi, B. (1997). Social structure and competition in interfirm networks: The paradox of embeddedness. *Administrative Science Quarterly*, *42*(1), 35–67. doi:10.2307/2393808

KEY TERMS AND DEFINITIONS

CiteSpace Software: It is a freely available Java application for visualizing and analyzing trends and patterns in the scientific literature.

Governance Mechanisms: Refers to the structural relationship and operation mode between various elements. In his chapter indicates the vital factors for running the sharing economy.

Prism Literature Analysis Method: This method has four steps: identification stage, selection stage, determine the qualification stage, and selection stage. It can provide a clear literature review process.

Prosumer: Refers to consumers involved in production activities.

Sharing Economy: An economic phenomena, with the help of a digital network platform, based on the transfer of using right and ownership between individuals or organizations, to maximize the usage of products and services.

Sharing Economy Organizations: The emerging enterprises based on the logic of sharing economy.

Snowball Method: This method can help to expand the relevant literature. The way to expand literature is like making a snowball.

Chapter 17
Academic Motivation of University Students Towards the Usage of Web 2.0 Technologies:
Undergraduate Motivation Among Web 2.0 Tool Use

Iulia Mihaela Lazar

Bucharest University, Romania

ABSTRACT

Web 2.0 technologies refer to useful and modern tools to motivate students for actively engaging in learning activities. However, there are difficulties to Web 2.0 technologies adoption among university students. Understanding users' motivation could enhance the adoption of Web 2.0 technologies. The aim of this chapter was to use the multivariate methods to quantitative describe the student's user experience (UX) regarding the acceptance of Web 2.0 technologies in higher education. An excellent validity of the structural model for testing the intention to use Web 2.0 technologies by university students was revealed. The data indicate that the intrinsic motivation was composed by users' expectations and educational aspirations. Moreover, the findings revealed that the extrinsic motivation can influence the intention to use Web 2.0 educational tools. This study completed the current knowledge on behavioral intention to use digital tools across university students and released new opportunities for UX investigations.

INTRODUCTION

Human behavior is dynamic, constantly changing, adapting, and most often depending by social, economical, cultural, and educational contexts. Consequently, behaviour is only rarely predictable. However, for the understanding and subsequent prediction of behavior it is necessary to know as accurately as possible the internal and external factors that influence it.

DOI: 10.4018/978-1-7998-3756-5.ch017

Motivation (Panisoara & Panisoara, 2005), from the perspective of subsequent behavior is the selection, orientation and maintenance of a path justified by the purpose and objectives of each person (Ifinedo, 2017). Briefly, the motivation is appreciated to be a set of internal and external factors that influences the behavior of a person (Böheim, Knogler, Kosel, & Seidel, 2020; Sun, 2008; Wu, 2020). It would be particularly interesting to be able to find out, in the greatest possible proportion, which are the motivational factors who influence the behavioral intention to use web-based technologies (Moon & Kim, 2001) into an educational environment. The academic motivation of university students is considered to have a significant effect on the intention to use Web 2.0 technologies by researchers (Ellison & Wu, 2008). In the current socio-economic context, the digital users' orientation is evident in the direction of increasing the use of Web 2.0 technologies. Therefore, a deeply understanding of the effects of motivational factors on human behaviours is necessary to be performed (Brown, 2002).

Motivation is a fundamental psychological concept and represents a set of aspirations, personal beliefs, desires, intentions with the purpose of fulfilling an aspiration (Lazar, 2019a, 2019b). Precisely, human action is usually based on motivation. On the other hand, professional motivation and success are closely linked. According to Chon & Shin motivation brings together "*subscales ranging from poor to more strong forms of motivation on a continuum (e.g., amotivation, extrinsic motivation, intrinsic motivation), where intrinsic motivation has mostly been found to be the most robust form of motivation that can promote learning and achievement*" (Chon & Shin, 2019). From Zeynali and collaborators perspective, academic motivation represented the tendency of a student "*to find academic activities meaningful and worthwhile and to try to derive the intended academic benefits from them*" (Zeynali, Pishghadam, & Hosseini Fatemi, 2019). Motivation can also be interpreted as an external factor, as a result of which behavioral changes can occurred. In this direction remained the research carried out by Maulana, Opdenakker, & Bosker who believed that "*students are capable of performing certain tasks (self-efficacy), and tend to be more engaged academically, use more cognitive strategies*" (Maulana, Opdenakker, & Bosker, 2016).

During the present investigation, two research hypotheses were identified, such as:

H1: University students' intention to use web-based technologies was strongly and directly influenced by her/his perceived challenges of Web 2.0 tools and applications.

H2: Intrinsic motivation was the most important form of motivation that can influence intention to use the Web 2.0 tools and applications across university students.

In order to be able to answer such questions, it is necessary to model the behaviour of students in the context of adopting Web 2.0 technologies to identified predictive factors in each specific context. Web 2.0 commonly used by undergraduate students who voluntary participated at experimental study case described in this chapter were the following:

- Web 2.0 applications (e.g. Google Docs)
- Web 2.0 educational tools (e.g. Microsoft Photo Story 3)
- social networking sites (Facebook)
- online Web 2.0 services like video hosting sites (e.g. YouTube)

The study of motivation as a predictive factor on the intention to use Web 2.0 technologies started from the need to understand human behavior in different contexts of digital learning explaining the users interests, perception of utility (Sivarajah, Irani, & Weerakkody, 2015), ease of use and attitude (Ulrich & Karvonen, 2011) to these technologies.

The present investigation is an extension of a complex research carried out by the author during PhD studies (Lazar, 2019b). The purpose of this study, who promoted interdisciplinary and transdisciplinary investigations, was to examine the relationships between the intrinsic/extrinsic motivation and university student's intention to use Web 2.0 technologies.

BACKGROUND

Intrinsic and Extrinsic Academic Motivation

The conceptualization of present research is based on motivational theories applied in an educational context (Graham, 2020; Koenka, 2020; Wigfield & Koenka, 2020; Wu, 2020). Some of the motivational factors recognized by literature are responsibility, autonomy in completing the proposed tasks and satisfaction resulting from the completion of the student's assignments designated by the instructor (Dong, Huang, Hou, & Liu, 2020; Slemp, Field, & Cho, 2020; Zhang, Oo, & Lim, 2019). The motivation varies according to several specific factors of the educational environment, including expectations of evaluation and possible rewards associated with the academic success. Theory and practical applications have highlighted the coexistence of the two motivational factors, intrinsic and extrinsic. What is particularly noticeable are the different effects that extrinsic motivation (*which results from the desires to acquire finalities other than those obtained by usual work*) and intrinsic motivation (*which occurs from the personal values of the individual*) (Amabile, 1993) can have on the affective factors (Kim & Lee, 2019), that ultimately affect the quality of academic performance. Most often researchers investigate the resulting relationship between intrinsic and extraneous motivation as personality traits. The direction and meaning of the resulting factor of the two main practical motivational components affected the final orientation of the user.

The definitions of extrinsic and intrinsic academic motivation are multiple and not always converging. Reporting to Hill statements it can be observed that university students have several types of motivation: autonomous motivation, controlled motivation or amotivation (Hill, 2013). The academic motivation is essentially as internal and external stimulating factors that can influences human behavior during educational activities. From the perspective of Meens, Bakx, Klimstra, & Denissen the academic motivation predicted *academic achievement* (Meens, Bakx, Klimstra, & Denissen, 2018) and from Tuominen, Niemivirta, Lonka, & Salmela-Aro perspective, the academic motivation predicted academic well-being (*school commitment and school burnout*) (Tuominen, Niemivirta, Lonka, & Salmela-Aro, 2020). The extrinsic motivation may act in the same way as the intrinsic motivation or in the opposite direction. Depending on the blend of personality traits and educational context, intrinsic and external motivation can be combined synergistically to achieve high levels of academic performance (Amabile, 1993). Negative evaluations have a much greater effect on academic motivation than positive evaluations. The negatives are perceived to be much more rigorous and implicit are more credible (Amabile, 1983). Kee and Lee (2019) demonstrated that "*negative feedback provided students the opportunity of more accurate self-assessment, but also produced negative emotional responses and less self-efficacy*" (Kim & Lee, 2019). However, there are contradictory studies on this subject, a reality that supports the need to draw up new studies on this research directive.

The acceptance of Web 2.0 technologies in academic settings and motivating factors to its use is also explored by researchers (Santosh, 2017). The educational environment shows an extent of investigating motivational factors in relation to other dimensions such as well-being, and life satisfaction (Muro, Soler, Cebolla, & Cladellas, 2018) or perceived self-efficacy and personal outcome expectations (Ifinedo, 2017). Most university students look for new ways of personal or professional development through the opportunities offered by the Web 2.0 tools and applications. From this perspective, it is necessary to examine the influence of internal and external academic motivational factors that lead to the adoption of Web 2.0 technologies.

Several studies have shown that extrinsic motivation does not manifest for the long term (Jovanovic & Matejevic, 2014; Ramseier, 2001). In the beginning of educational activities, university students may be particularly interested in a subject, but in time they lose their interest. This remarque confirms the complexity of human behaviour. This conclusion has also been reached by the research carried out by other authors (Stone & Baker-Eveleth, 2013).

Litalien, Gillet, Gagné, Ratelle, & Morin presented intrinsic motivation correlated with self-esteem (Litalien, Gillet, Gagné, Ratelle, & Morin, 2019). Self-determination theory (SDT) modelled the changing aspects of motivation (Chang, Hou, Wang, Cui, & Zhang, 2020). SDT separates motivation into three classes: intrinsic motivation, extrinsic motivation and amotivation (R.M. Ryan & E.L. Deci, 2000). Intrinsically motivations were generated by external sources (e.g. perceived playfulness) and extrinsically motivations were generated by external sources (e.g. perceived usefulness, perceived ease of use) or by the nature of the activity they carry out (Dedeurwaerdere et al., 2016; Ifinedo, 2017).

The educational management plays an important role in determining the dimensions that influence motivation. Also, the manager support seems to be a key facet of the work environment for improvement of teaching strategies based on creativity (Amabile & Pratt, 2016; Amabile, Schatzel, Moneta, & Kramer, 2004; Cromwell, Amabile, & Harvey, 2018). People are more creative when they are motivated mainly by the curiosity, enjoyment, happiness and challenge of the work itself (Amabile & Pratt, 2016). However, all facets of motivation can influence the adoption level of digital resources among different kind of academic users (Ceipek, Hautz, Petruzzelli, De Massis, & Matzler, 2020; Mehta, Morris, Swinnerton, & Homer, 2019; J. Wang, Tigelaar, & Admiraal, 2019; Yu, Lin, & Liao, 2017).

During practical activities teachers get to know intrinsic and extrinsic motivational aspects of digital tools users. Understanding how motivation works, the mechanisms by which motivation is influenced, and how the motivational factors can be used in the practice activities are some of the research objectives of this chapter. Briefly, various external and mediator factors, like academic motivational factors (Nikou & Economides, 2017), perceived usefulness, prior experiences, affective factors, or perceived ease of use can influenced users' attitude towards Web 2.0 technologies and the behavioral intention to use these tools (Rogers-Estable, 2014). All these factors are usually correlated, but their role and importance depend on a context. This research aimed to clarify these aspects using a validated scale described in the following sub-chapter.

Active Learning

Active learning involves permanent collaboration between students enhancing their role in educational process by promoting intra-group and inter-group interaction. However, the content chosen by the teacher to be taught must be adapted to be compatible with the active learning. This adjustment is facilitated by expansion of information and communication technologies.

More specifically, in recent years, social web applications turned out to be an important tools for active learning, which becomes more attractive to students than static learning and may keep students more time involved in different activities, along with increasing their motivation. Active learning is perceived to be a multidimensional construction with psychological and behavioural components and it is integrated into blended learning activities (Molinillo, Aguilar-Illescas, Anaya-Sánchez, & Vallespín-Arán, 2018).

Blended learning (López-Pérez, Pérez-López, & Rodríguez-Ariza, 2011) is a mix of face-to-face and distance learning process, in which a written or spoken message can be transmitted together with images, animations, narrative and video to better understand the notions taught through synchronous or asynchronous activities (C. Wang, Fang, & Gu, 2020).

Distance learning (Romano, Wallace, Helmick, Carey, & Adkins, 2005; Tuckman, 2007) is increasingly used in a singular mode or along with traditional methods managing mixed learning resources. Moreover, distance learning requires more learner self-management than a blended course (Romano et al., 2005). Promoting active learning is a major achievement of distance learning and a step forward in the development of cognitive theories useful for modeling users' behaviour (Belk, Papatheocharous, Germanakos, & Samaras, 2013).

Digital tools such as Web 2.0 technologies facilitate active learning (Alsaif, Li, Soh, & Alraddady, 2019; Aydede & Matyar, 2009; Bennett, Bishop, Dalgarno, Waycott, & Kennedy, 2012; Huang, Hood, & Yoo, 2013; Kam & Katerattanakul, 2014; Rahimi, van den Berg, & Veen, 2015; Torres Kompen, Edirisingha, Canaleta, Alsina, & Monguet, 2019) due to the connections between images and verbal information. Thus, different types of digital educational resources like Web 2.0 technologies can play a significant role in virtual environments, enhance design and practice in teaching and learning (Luckin et al., 2012). From the perspective of Luis, Gutiérrez, & Marrero *"a higher dynamic, a more collaborative, and more open environment for problem-solving learning processes was reached"*, if university students used Web 2.0 technologies within an active learning environment (Luis, Gutiérrez, & Marrero, 2014). Web 2.0 technologies are widely used in higher education activities, but the correlations with psychological factors are not deeply understood. Therefore, a case study to test the effects of academic motivation on university student's usage of Web 2.0 technologies was performed.

CASE STUDY: ACADEMIC MOTIVATION FOR USING WEB 2.0 TECHNOLOGIES ACROSS STUDENTS FROM TWO PUBLIC UNIVERSITIES FROM ROMANIA

This case study was based on quantitative research that measures the intention to use Web 2.0 technologies (e.g. Web 2.0 applications (e.g. Google Docs); Web 2.0 educational tools (e.g. Microsoft Photo Story 3); social networking sites (Facebook) and online Web 2.0 services like video hosting sites (e.g. YouTube)) of students enrolled at two universities in Romania, in university years 2017-2018 and 2018-2019.

In this context, different categories of information obtained through a research tool designed and subsequently validated as content and structure were required. The questionnaire developed and tested in a doctoral thesis by the authors:" *Investigation on the relationship between the aspirational learners and acceptance of modern technology in education*" (Lazar, 2019b) was adapted to assess the adoption of Web 2.0 technologies across university students. This research tool is presented in Table 1.

Table 1. Scale to measure behavioral intention to use Web 2.0 technologies among university students'

Scale	Strongly disagree	Disagree	Neither agree nor disagree	Agree	Strongly agree
Subscale: Intrinsic motivation					
Challenge					
IC1. I like to use the Web 2.0 technologies due to the implied challenges.	1	2	3	4	5
IC2. I must complete all specified steps to use the Web 2.0 technologies.	1	2	3	4	5
IC3. I like the challenge of any new Web 2.0 technology.	1	2	3	4	5
IC4. I like the new Web 2.0 technology that require to find solutions.	1	2	3	4	5
IC5. I like the opportunities to develop my experience through the usage of the new Web 2.0 technology.	1	2	3	4	5
IC6. I like those Web 2.0 technologies that challenges me to make my own decisions.	1	2	3	4	5
Educational aspiration					
IE1: I am interested in acquiring new skills using Web 2.0 technologies, in the immediate future.	1	2	3	4	5
IE3: My main goal now is to get additional knowledge using Web 2.0 technologies.	1	2	3	4	5
IE4: I would be more motivated to use Web 2.0 technologies, if I am convinced that my acquired skills help me to obtain easier a job.	1	2	3	4	5
Subscale: Extrinsic motivation					
Help					
HP1: When I do not understand something related to Web 2.0 technologies, I want the teacher to tell me the answer immediately.	1	2	3	4	5
HP2: I like to receive help from my family members during the usage of Web 2.0 technologies.	1	2	3	4	5
HP3: I like to receive help from my teacher during the usage of Web 2.0 technologies.	1	2	3	4	5
HP4: When I make a mistake during the usage of Web 2.0 technologies, I like to ask the teacher how to correct it.	1	2	3	4	5
HP5: If I fail to solve a problem during the usage of Web 2.0 technologies, I will ask the teacher for help.	1	2	3	4	5
Subscale: I intend to use….					
R2: *users' applications*: ….Web 2.0 applications (e.g. Google Docs)	1	2	3	4	5
R3: *software tools*: …Web 2.0 educational tools (e.g. Microsoft Photo Story 3)	1	2	3	4	5
R4: *people to people:* …social networking sites (Facebook)	1	2	3	4	5
R8: *online Web 2.0 services*: …online Web 2.0 services like video hosting sites (e.g. YouTube)	1	2	3	4	5

The overall aim of the study was to investigate the relationship between intrinsic motivation, extrinsic motivation, and the intention to use Web 2.0 technologies. The study examined why Web 2.0 technologies are attractive to use its and whether their acceptance is influenced under certain conditions by the intrinsic and external motivations of university students.

Briefly, the main aim of the research is the evaluation of the significance and intensity of the degree of correlation between latent factors characterising the acceptance of Web 2.0 technologies and the intrinsic/extrinsic motivation of university students. Based on theory, hypotheses developed to test the acceptance of Web 2.0 technologies by university students and the relation between model dimensions are presented in introduction.

To test these research hypotheses, a methodology proper for examining the research hypothesis was used. A relational survey model was applied to perform the research (Celik & Yesilyurt, 2013). Data collected from 490 participants from two universities in Romania during the university years 2017-2018 and 2018-2019 were used for the purpose of primary statistical characterisation and interpretation, supplemented by other criteria (e.g. saturation, consistency, etc.), described by the Bank and Balog (Banciu & Balog, 2013; Lazar, 2019b). The exploratory analyses (EFA), confirmatory analysis (CFA) and the partial least squares structural equation modelling (PLS-SEM) were used to validate the structural research model and to test the relationships between model dimensions (Lazar, 2019a; Lazar, Panisoara, & Panisoara, 2020).

The data collected were analysed statistically using the licensed SPSS software version 20. Each research participant as voluntary was asked to express their opinion regarding the questionnaire topics using a scale from 1 to 5, where: 1-total disagreement, 2-disagreement, 3-indifferent, 4-agreement, 5-total agreement. The presentation of the mean values, the coefficient of asymmetry (Skewness) and the bolting coefficient (Kurtosis) associated with the answers on the intention to use different Web 2.0 technologies is presented in Table 2.

Table 2. Description of the mean values, the coefficient of asymmetry (Skewness) and the bolting coefficient (Kurtois) associated with the answers on the use of different Web 2.0 applications and tools

	N	Minimum	Maximum	Mean	Standard deviation	Skewness		Kurtosis	
	Statistic	Statistic	Statistic	Statistic	Statistic	Statistic	Standard Error	Statistic	Standard Error
R2: Web 2.0 applications (e.g. Google Docs)	490	1	5	3.41	1.150	-.447	.110	-.520	.220
R3: Web 2.0 educational tools (e.g. Microsoft Photo Story 3)	490	1	5	3.36	1.187	-.424	.110	-.599	.220
R4: social networking sites (Facebook)	490	1	5	*3.84*	1.059	-.899	.110	.374	.220
R8: online Web 2.0 services like video hosting sites (e.g. YouTube)	490	1	5	3.70	1.099	-.652	.110	-.182	.220

It is remarked that Web technology 2.0 indicated to be the most used (Table 2) by university students in this case study is social networking sites. Additional comments from students show some lack of enthusiasm to use other Web 2.0 educational tools, probably due to the specific digital knowledge needed to use these kinds of resources. However, an increasingly attractive feature is digital audio-video applications, which are much easier to access and have a great impact on the audience following the presentation of the results.

The values obtained for KMO and Bartlett's test (.848) confirm the appropriateness of the sample of items (Table 1) chosen to describe the factors, which are higher than the minimum value required by .50 to apply the factorial analysis (Darling-Churchill & Lippman, 2016). The analysis of the dimensionality of the subsets of the model was carried out using the analysis of the principal components and the rotation of the factors by the Promax method, method frequently used by researchers (Banciu & Balog, 2013; Labar, 2008; Lazar, 2019a, 2019b).

Eigenvalues values greater than the unit, the communalities greater than 0.3 and items with values of factor coefficients greater than 0.4 are the reference criteria that its must have taken into account in retaining the final items (Lazar, 2019a, 2019b; R. M. Ryan & E. L. Deci, 2000). Therefore, factors who respected all statistical requirements were extracted for each subscale, thus verifying their unidimensionality. For the entire scale the four principal components have been identified explaining the percentage variation of 65.63% (Table 3).

Items for the first component who explain 32.09% from total variation describes the intrinsic motivation (*perceived challenges*) (IC). These items are the following: IC1, IC2, IC3, IC4, IC5 and IC6 (Table 3).

Items for the second component who explain 14.83% from total variation describes the extrinsic motivation (*need of external help*) (HP). These items are the following: HP1, HP2, HP3, HP4 and HP5 (Table 3).

Items for the third component who explain 12.27% from total variation describes the intention to use Web 2.0 technologies (R). These items are the following: R2, R3, R4 and R8 (Table 3).

Items for the fourth component who explain 6.44% from total variation describes the intrinsic motivation (*educational aspiration*) (IE). These items are the following: IE1, IE3, IE4 (Table 3).

Values for each extracted principal component are presented in Table 3 and the results of the exploratory analysis are presented in Table 4.

Table 3. Values for each component extracted by the Principal Component Analysis and cumulative variance percentages.

Total Variance Explained							
Component	Initial Eigenvalues			Extraction Sums of Squared Loadings			Rotation Sums of Squared Loadings[a]
	Total	% of Variance	Cumulative %	Total	% of Variance	Cumulative %	Total
IC	5.455	32.089	32.089	5.455	32.089	32.089	4.642
HP	2.521	14.829	46.917	2.521	14.829	46.917	3.078
R	2.085	12.266	59.183	2.085	12.266	59.183	3.063
IE	1.096	6.444	65.628	1.096	6.444	65.628	3.688

Table 4. Component matrix after rotation. Method of Principal Component Analysis for the bidimensional scale consists of two factors: motivation and acceptance of Web 2.0 technologies. Rotation method: Promax.

	Pattern Matrix[a]			
	Component			
	1	**2**	**3**	**4**
IC3	.915			
IC4	.866			
IC1	.838			
IC2	.808			
IC5	.705			
HP3		.829		
HP2		.818		
HP1		.695		
HP4		.691		
HP5		.668		
R3			.896	
R2			.883	
R4			.737	
R8			.617	
IE4				.842
IE1				.803
IE3				.723
Extraction Method: Principal Component Analysis. Rotation Method: Promax with Kaiser Normalization.				
a. Rotation converged in 5 iterations.				

The bidimensional scale of the two factors: motivation and acceptance of Web 2.0 technologies is characterized by four factors, and some of them are related to each other. Particularly interesting data was provided by exploring the weighting of principal components (Table 3). Therefore, it can be observed that both intrinsic factors explain 38.52% of the total variation of items, more than a half of the total variance.

The standardised regression indicators and coefficients resulting from the confirmatory analysis (CFA) using the Structural Modeling Equation (SEM) through the IBM SPSS AmosTM Free Version 26 were examined for the purpose of testing the convergent and divergent validity of the mentioned scale. The SEM-tested measurement model identified from the four related constructions and 18 items from the exploratory analysis performed on the volunteer group that completed the online questionnaires.

Based on the SEM analyse, it can be estimated the quality attributed to each model (Lazar, 2019a, 2019b) as derived from the CFA results of the subsets (Table 5 and Table 6).

The results are presented in Table 5 and Table 6 show very good quality structural models, confirming the construction validation of both subscales.

Table 5. Indicators resulting from the SEM analysis for the intrinsic motivation and acceptance of Web 2.0 technologies

	CMIN/DF	GFI	TLI rho2	CFI	RMSEA	PCLOSE
Thresholds	< 3	> .9	> .9	> .9	< .08	> .05
	1.979	.968	.978	.984	.045	.730

Table 6 Indicators resulting from the SEM analysis for the extrinsic motivation and acceptance of Web 2.0 technologies

	CMIN/DF	GFI	TLI rho2	CFI	RMSEA	PCLOSE
Thresholds	< 3	> .9	> .9	> .9	< .08	> .05
	1.430	.985	.991	.994	.030	.941

Both structural models helped to identify the associations between significant statistical variables, including the direct and indirect effects between them. In addition, results are useful for highlighting the original points of our study compared to other studies from the literature.

The measurement model using Confirmatory Factor Analyses is presented in Figure 1 and the structural models of the relationships between the latent variables are presented in Figure 2 and Figure 3. The directional relationships between variables are expressed by arrows the meaning of which is consistent with the theoretical main research question: *Are significant associations between intrinsic, extrinsic motivational factors, and the adoption of Web 2.0 technologies by university students?*

Exploratory factor analysis (EFA), confirmatory factor analysis (CFA) and structural equation modelling (SEM) were used to understand the common variation of each principal dimension of measurement model (Table 3 and Table 4) and structural models (Figure 2 and Figure 3). Therefore, four latent variables were investigated (two internal motivational factors, an external motivational factor and a factor that measures the intention to use). The indicators values (Table 5 and Table 6) revealed an excellent validity of the structural model for testing the intention to use Web 2.0 technologies across the university students under the influence of motivational factors. A total effect of extrinsic motivation on intention to use Web 2.0 educational tools (e.g. Microsoft Photo Story 3) was validated ($\beta = .302; p = .000$) using SEM analyses. The intrinsic motivation was composed by challenge ($\beta = .155; t = 1960; p = .050$) and educational aspirations ($\beta = .192; t = 2.311; p = .021$). According to the results both research hypotheses were confirmed. Thus, the intrinsic and extrinsic motivational factors significantly affect the acceptance of Web 2.0 technologies by university students. These results are consistent with prior findings that underline the motivation for the student's active learning (Molinillo et al., 2018; Owens, Sadler, Barlow, & Smith-Walters, 2020). The findings highlighted a medium intensity effect of both type of motivation on the intention to use Web 2.0 technologies cross university students. The decreasing order of the internal motivational factors was the following: Web 2.0 educational tools (e.g. Microsoft Photo Story 3), Web 2.0 applications (e.g. Google Docs), social networking sites (Facebook) and the last one, online Web 2.0 services like video hosting sites (e.g. YouTube). Briefly, the resultant of motivational factors, and not each factor, orient human behavior by guiding it towards the desired goals. In conclusion, it can be said that the intention to use Web 2.0 among university students was mainly influenced by intrinsic

Figure 1. Standardized factor loadings of the CFA model composed by 4 latent factors of the bidimensional scale (N = 490)

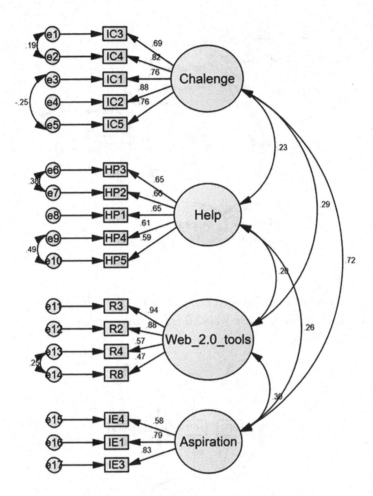

motivational factors by calculating the amount of the two dimensions and secondly by extrinsic ones, similar with results obtained by Chon & Shin (2019) in case of middle school learners.

CONCLUSION

User experience (UX) as university student's point of view and reactions related to the anticipated use of Web 2.0 technologies was explored. Four latent variables were investigated (two internal motivational factors, an external motivational factor and a factor that measures the intention to use). More date regarding the performance of Web 2.0 tools and the strategies based on digital resources are crucial for enhancing user experience (UX). The validated structural model facilitated the explanation of motivational factors who directly and indirectly influenced the intention to use Web 2.0 technologies by university students. The intrinsic motivation represented by the desire for professional and personal development has a positive, direct, and medium influence on the intention to use Web 2.0 technologies. In this case study the

Figure 2. Structural model of relations between components of the subscale including intrinsic motivational factors and behaviour intention to use Web 2.0 technologies (N = 490)

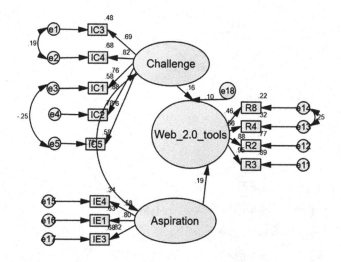

Figure 3. Structural model of relations between components of the subscale including extrinsic motivational factor and behaviour intention to use Web 2.0 technologies (N = 490)

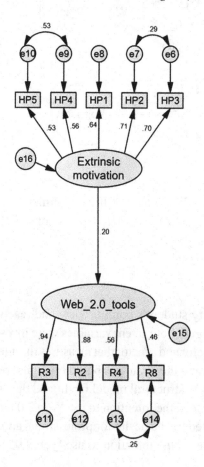

decreasing order of the internal motivational factors was the following: Web 2.0 educational tools, Web 2.0 applications, social networking sites and online Web 2.0 services. In conclusion, it can be said that the intention to use Web 2.0 technologies among university students was mainly influenced by intrinsic motivational factors (perceived challenges and aspirations) secondly by extrinsic ones (requesting external help). This preliminary investigation completed the current knowledge regarding behavioral intention to use Web 2.0 technologies across university students and releases new opportunities for researchers in user experience (UX) direction.

ACKNOWLEDGMENT

This book chapter was written with the contribution of the staff of Doctoral School in Psychology and Education Sciences from Bucharest University who provided support by encouraging debates related to the main subjects of the author doctoral study in Science Education.

REFERENCES

Alsaif, S., Li, A. S., Soh, B., & Alraddady, S. (2019). The Efficacy of Facebook in Teaching and Learning: Studied via Content Analysis of Web Log Data. *Procedia Computer Science*, *161*, 493–501. doi:10.1016/j.procs.2019.11.149

Amabile, T. M. (1983). Brilliant but cruel: Perceptions of negative evaluators. *Journal of Experimental Social Psychology*, *19*(2), 146–156. doi:10.1016/0022-1031(83)90034-3

Amabile, T. M. (1993). Motivational synergy: Toward new conceptualizations of intrinsic and extrinsic motivation in the workplace. *Human Resource Management Review*, *3*(3), 185–201. doi:10.1016/1053-4822(93)90012-S

Amabile, T. M., & Pratt, M. G. (2016). The dynamic componential model of creativity and innovation in organizations: Making progress, making meaning. *Research in Organizational Behavior*, *36*, 157–183. doi:10.1016/j.riob.2016.10.001

Amabile, T. M., Schatzel, E. A., Moneta, G. B., & Kramer, S. J. (2004). Leader behaviors and the work environment for creativity: Perceived leader support. *The Leadership Quarterly*, *15*(1), 5–32. doi:10.1016/j.leaqua.2003.12.003

Aydede, M., & Matyar, F. (2009). The Effect of Active Learning Approach in Science Teaching on Cognitive Level of Student Achievement. *Journal of Turkish Science Education, 6*.

Banciu, D., & Balog, A. (2013). *Calitatea sistemelor și serviciilor de e-learning*. Agir.

Belk, M., Papatheocharous, E., Germanakos, P., & Samaras, G. (2013). Modeling users on the World Wide Web based on cognitive factors, navigation behavior and clustering techniques. *Journal of Systems and Software*, *86*(12), 2995–3012. doi:10.1016/j.jss.2013.04.029

Bennett, S., Bishop, A., Dalgarno, B., Waycott, J., & Kennedy, G. (2012). Implementing Web 2.0 technologies in higher education: A collective case study. *Computers & Education, 59*(2), 524–534. doi:10.1016/j.compedu.2011.12.022

Böheim, R., Knogler, M., Kosel, C., & Seidel, T. (2020). Exploring student hand-raising across two school subjects using mixed methods: An investigation of an everyday classroom behavior from a motivational perspective. *Learning and Instruction, 65*, 101250. doi:10.1016/j.learninstruc.2019.101250

Brown, I. T. J. (2002). Individual and Technological Factors Affecting Perceived Ease of Use of Web-based Learning Technologies in a Developing Country. *The Electronic Journal on Information Systems in Developing Countries, 9*(1), 1–15. doi:10.1002/j.1681-4835.2002.tb00055.x

Ceipek, R., Hautz, J., Petruzzelli, A. M., De Massis, A., & Matzler, K. (2020). A motivation and ability perspective on engagement in emerging digital technologies: The case of Internet of Things solutions. *Long Range Planning, 101991*, 101991. Advance online publication. doi:10.1016/j.lrp.2020.101991

Celik, V., & Yesilyurt, E. (2013). Attitudes to technology, perceived computer self-efficacy and computer anxiety as predictors of computer supported education. *Computers & Education, 60*(1), 148–158. doi:10.1016/j.compedu.2012.06.008

Chang, Y., Hou, R.-J., Wang, K., Cui, A. P., & Zhang, C.-B. (2020). Effects of intrinsic and extrinsic motivation on social loafing in online travel communities. *Computers in Human Behavior, 109*, 106360. doi:10.1016/j.chb.2020.106360

Chon, Y. V., & Shin, T. (2019). Profile of second language learners' metacognitive awareness and academic motivation for successful listening: A latent class analysis. *Learning and Individual Differences, 70*, 62–75. doi:10.1016/j.lindif.2019.01.007

Cromwell, J. R., Amabile, T. M., & Harvey, J.-F. (2018). An Integrated Model of Dynamic Problem Solving Within Organizational Constraints. In R. Reiter-Palmon, V. L. Kennel, & J. C. Kaufman (Eds.), *Individual Creativity in the Workplace* (pp. 53–81). Academic Press. doi:10.1016/B978-0-12-813238-8.00003-6

Darling-Churchill, K. E., & Lippman, L. (2016). Early childhood social and emotional development: Advancing the field of measurement. *Journal of Applied Developmental Psychology, 45*, 1–7. doi:10.1016/j.appdev.2016.02.002

Dedeurwaerdere, T., Admiraal, J., Beringer, A., Bonaiuto, F., Cicero, L., Fernandez-Wulff, P., Hagens, J., Hiedanpää, J., Knights, P., Molinario, E., Melindi-Ghidi, P., Popa, F., Šilc, U., Soethe, N., Soininen, T., & Luis Vivero, J. (2016). Combining internal and external motivations in multi-actor governance arrangements for biodiversity and ecosystem services. *Environmental Science & Policy, 58*, 1–10. doi:10.1016/j.envsci.2015.12.003 PMID:28149197

Dong, L., Huang, L., Hou, J., & Liu, Y. (2020). Continuous content contribution in virtual community: The role of status-standing on motivational mechanisms. *Decision Support Systems, 132*, 113283. doi:10.1016/j.dss.2020.113283

Ellison, N. B., & Wu, Y. (2008). Blogging in the classroom: A preliminary exploration of student attitudes and impact on comprehension. *Journal of Educational Multimedia and Hypermedia, 17*(1), 99–122.

Graham, S. (2020). An attributional theory of motivation. *Contemporary Educational Psychology, 101861*. Advance online publication. doi:10.1016/j.cedpsych.2020.101861

Hill, A. P. (2013). Motivation and university experience in first-year university students: A self-determination theory perspective. *Journal of Hospitality, Leisure, Sport and Tourism Education, 13*, 244–254. doi:10.1016/j.jhlste.2012.07.001

Huang, W.-H. D., Hood, D. W., & Yoo, S. J. (2013). Gender divide and acceptance of collaborative Web 2.0 applications for learning in higher education. *The Internet and Higher Education, 16*, 57–65. doi:10.1016/j.iheduc.2012.02.001

Ifinedo, P. (2017). Examining students' intention to continue using blogs for learning: Perspectives from technology acceptance, motivational, and social-cognitive frameworks. *Computers in Human Behavior, 72*, 189–199. doi:10.1016/j.chb.2016.12.049

Jovanovic, D., & Matejevic, M. (2014). Relationship between Rewards and Intrinsic Motivation for Learning – Researches Review. *Procedia: Social and Behavioral Sciences, 149*, 456–460. doi:10.1016/j.sbspro.2014.08.287

Kam, H.-J., & Katerattanakul, P. (2014). Structural model of team-based learning using Web 2.0 collaborative software. *Computers & Education, 76*, 1–12. doi:10.1016/j.compedu.2014.03.003

Kim, E. J., & Lee, K. R. (2019). Effects of an examiner's positive and negative feedback on self-assessment of skill performance, emotional response, and self-efficacy in Korea: A quasi-experimental study. *BMC Medical Education, 19*(1), 142. doi:10.118612909-019-1595-x PMID:31088436

Koenka, A. C. (2020). Academic motivation theories revisited: An interactive dialog between motivation scholars on recent contributions, underexplored issues, and future directions. *Contemporary Educational Psychology, 101831*, 101831. Advance online publication. doi:10.1016/j.cedpsych.2019.101831

Labar, A. V. (2008). *SPSS pentru Științele Educației*. Editura Polirom.

Lazar, I. (2019a). *A guide for statistical analysis of data in the educational research* [Ghid pentru analiza statistica a datelor in cercetarea educationala, in Romanian]. Presa Universitara Clujeana.

Lazar, I. (2019b). Investigation on the relationship between the aspirational learners and the acceptance of modern technology in education [Investigații privind relația dintre nivelului aspirațional al cursanților și acceptarea tehnologiilor moderne în procesul de învățământ, in Romanian] (PhD in Science Education). Bucharest University.

Lazar, I., Panisoara, G., & Panisoara, I. O. (2020). Adoption of digital storytelling tool in natural sciences and technology education by pre-service teachers using the technology acceptance model. *Journal of Baltic Science Education, 19*(3), 429–453. doi:10.33225/jbse/20.19.429

Litalien, D., Gillet, N., Gagné, M., Ratelle, C. F., & Morin, A. J. S. (2019). Self-determined motivation profiles among undergraduate students: A robust test of profile similarity as a function of gender and age. *Learning and Individual Differences, 70*, 39–52. doi:10.1016/j.lindif.2019.01.005

López-Pérez, M. V., Pérez-López, M. C., & Rodríguez-Ariza, L. (2011). Blended learning in higher education: Students' perceptions and their relation to outcomes. *Computers & Education, 56*(3), 818–826. doi:10.1016/j.compedu.2010.10.023

Luckin, R., Bligh, B., Manches, A., Ainsworth, S., Crook, C., & Noss, R. (2012). *Cambridge professional development qualifications for Teaching with Digital Technologies: Decoding Learning: The Proof, Promise and Potential of Digital Education.* Nesta.

Luis, C. E. M., Gutiérrez, J. M., & Marrero, A. M. G. (2014). Using mobile devices and internet technologies in problem-based learning: Design of a suitable active and collaborative learning environment in engineering education. *2014 IEEE Frontiers in Education Conference (FIE) Proceedings.* 10.1109/FIE.2014.7044184

Maulana, R., Opdenakker, M.-C., & Bosker, R. (2016). Teachers' instructional behaviors as important predictors of academic motivation: Changes and links across the school year. *Learning and Individual Differences, 50*, 147–156. doi:10.1016/j.lindif.2016.07.019

Meens, E. E. M., Bakx, A. W. E. A., Klimstra, T. A., & Denissen, J. J. A. (2018). The association of identity and motivation with students' academic achievement in higher education. *Learning and Individual Differences, 64*, 54–70. doi:10.1016/j.lindif.2018.04.006

Mehta, A., Morris, N. P., Swinnerton, B., & Homer, M. (2019). The Influence of Values on E-learning Adoption. *Computers & Education, 141*, 103617. doi:10.1016/j.compedu.2019.103617

Molinillo, S., Aguilar-Illescas, R., Anaya-Sánchez, R., & Vallespín-Arán, M. (2018). Exploring the impacts of interactions, social presence and emotional engagement on active collaborative learning in a social web-based environment. *Computers & Education, 123*, 41–52. doi:10.1016/j.compedu.2018.04.012

Moon, J.-W., & Kim, Y.-G. (2001). Extending the TAM for a World-Wide-Web context. *Information & Management, 38*(4), 217–230. doi:10.1016/S0378-7206(00)00061-6

Muro, A., Soler, J., Cebolla, À., & Cladellas, R. (2018). A positive psychological intervention for failing students: Does it improve academic achievement and motivation? A pilot study. *Learning and Motivation, 63*, 126–132. doi:10.1016/j.lmot.2018.04.002

Nikou, S. A., & Economides, A. A. (2017). Mobile-Based Assessment: Integrating acceptance and motivational factors into a combined model of Self-Determination Theory and Technology Acceptance. *Computers in Human Behavior, 68*, 83–95. doi:10.1016/j.chb.2016.11.020

Owens, D. C., Sadler, T. D., Barlow, A. T., & Smith-Walters, C. (2020). Student Motivation from and Resistance to Active Learning Rooted in Essential Science Practices. *Research in Science Education, 50*(1), 253–277. doi:10.100711165-017-9688-1

Panisoara, G., & Panisoara, I. O. (2005). *Motivarea Eficienta. Ghid Practic.* Polirom.

Rahimi, E., van den Berg, J., & Veen, W. (2015). Facilitating student-driven constructing of learning environments using Web 2.0 personal learning environments. *Computers & Education, 81*, 235–246. doi:10.1016/j.compedu.2014.10.012

Ramseier, E. (2001). Motivation to learn as an outcome and determining factor of learning at school. *European Journal of Psychology of Education*, *16*(3), 421–439. doi:10.1007/BF03173191

Rogers-Estable, M. (2014). Web 2.0 Use in Higher Education. *European Journal of Open. Distance and E-Learning*, *17*. Advance online publication. doi:10.2478/eurodl-2014-0024

Romano, J., Wallace, T. L., Helmick, I. J., Carey, L. M., & Adkins, L. (2005). Study procrastination, achievement, and academic motivation in web-based and blended distance learning. *The Internet and Higher Education*, *8*(4), 299–305. doi:10.1016/j.iheduc.2005.09.003

Ryan, R. M., & Deci, E. L. (2000). Intrinsic and Extrinsic Motivations: Classic Definitions and New Directions. *Contemporary Educational Psychology*, *25*(1), 54–67. doi:10.1006/ceps.1999.1020 PMID:10620381

Ryan, R. M., & Deci, E. L. (2000). Self-determination theory and the facilitation of intrinsic motivation, social development, and well-being. *The American Psychologist*, *55*(1), 68–78. doi:10.1037/0003-066X.55.1.68 PMID:11392867

Santosh, S. (2017). Adoption of Web 2.0 Applications in Academic Libraries in India. *DESIDOC Journal of Library and Information Technology*, *37*(3), 192–198. doi:10.14429/djlit.37.3.10918

Sivarajah, U., Irani, Z., & Weerakkody, V. (2015). Evaluating the use and impact of Web 2.0 technologies in local government. *Government Information Quarterly*, *32*(4), 473–487. doi:10.1016/j.giq.2015.06.004

Slemp, G. R., Field, J. G., & Cho, A. S. H. (2020). A meta-analysis of autonomous and controlled forms of teacher motivation. *Journal of Vocational Behavior*, *103459*, 103459. Advance online publication. doi:10.1016/j.jvb.2020.103459

Stone, R. W., & Baker-Eveleth, L. (2013). Students' expectation, confirmation, and continuance intention to use electronic textbooks. *Computers in Human Behavior*, *29*(3), 984–990. doi:10.1016/j.chb.2012.12.007

Sun, S. (2008). An examination of disposition, motivation, and involvement in the new technology context computers in human behavior. *Computers in Human Behavior*, *24*(6), 2723–2740. doi:10.1016/j.chb.2008.03.016

Torres Kompen, R., Edirisingha, P., Canaleta, X., Alsina, M., & Monguet, J. M. (2019). Personal learning Environments based on Web 2.0 services in higher education. *Telematics and Informatics*, *38*, 194–206. doi:10.1016/j.tele.2018.10.003

Tuckman, B. W. (2007). The effect of motivational scaffolding on procrastinators' distance learning outcomes. *Computers & Education*, *49*(2), 414–422. doi:10.1016/j.compedu.2005.10.002

Tuominen, H., Niemivirta, M., Lonka, K., & Salmela-Aro, K. (2020). Motivation across a transition: Changes in achievement goal orientations and academic well-being from elementary to secondary school. *Learning and Individual Differences*, *79*, 101854. doi:10.1016/j.lindif.2020.101854

Ulrich, J., & Karvonen, M. (2011). Faculty instructional attitudes, interest, and intention: Predictors of Web 2.0 use in online courses. *The Internet and Higher Education*, *14*(4), 207–216. doi:10.1016/j.iheduc.2011.07.001

Wang, C., Fang, T., & Gu, Y. (2020). Learning performance and behavioral patterns of online collaborative learning: Impact of cognitive load and affordances of different multimedia. *Computers & Education*, *143*, 103683. doi:10.1016/j.compedu.2019.103683

Wang, J., Tigelaar, D. E. H., & Admiraal, W. (2019). Connecting rural schools to quality education: Rural teachers' use of digital educational resources. *Computers in Human Behavior*, *101*, 68–76. doi:10.1016/j.chb.2019.07.009

Wigfield, A., & Koenka, A. C. (2020). Where do we go from here in academic motivation theory and research? Some reflections and recommendations for future work. *Contemporary Educational Psychology*, *101872*. Advance online publication. doi:10.1016/j.cedpsych.2020.101872

Wu, D. (2020). Empirical study of knowledge withholding in cyberspace: Integrating protection motivation theory and theory of reasoned behavior. *Computers in Human Behavior*, *105*, 106229. doi:10.1016/j.chb.2019.106229

Yu, T.-K., Lin, M.-L., & Liao, Y.-K. (2017). Understanding factors influencing information communication technology adoption behavior: The moderators of information literacy and digital skills. *Computers in Human Behavior*, *71*, 196–208. doi:10.1016/j.chb.2017.02.005

Zeynali, S., Pishghadam, R., & Hosseini Fatemi, A. (2019). Identifying the motivational and demotivational factors influencing students' academic achievements in language education. *Learning and Motivation*, *68*, 101598. doi:10.1016/j.lmot.2019.101598

Zhang, Q., Oo, B. L., & Lim, B. T. H. (2019). Drivers, motivations, and barriers to the implementation of corporate social responsibility practices by construction enterprises: A review. *Journal of Cleaner Production*, *210*, 563–584. doi:10.1016/j.jclepro.2018.11.050

ADDITIONAL READING

Allam, H., Bliemel, M., Spiteri, L., Blustein, J., & Ali-Hassan, H. (2019). Applying a multi-dimensional hedonic concept of intrinsic motivation on social tagging tools: A theoretical model and empirical validation. *International Journal of Information Management*, *45*, 211–222. doi:10.1016/j.ijinfomgt.2018.11.005

Baby, A., & Kannammal, A. (2020). Network Path Analysis for developing an enhanced TAM model: A user-centric e-learning perspective. *Computers in Human Behavior*, *107*, 106081. doi:10.1016/j.chb.2019.07.024

Nikou, S. A., & Economides, A. A. (2017). Mobile-Based Assessment: Integrating acceptance and motivational factors into a combined model of Self-Determination Theory and Technology Acceptance. *Computers in Human Behavior*, *68*, 83–95. doi:10.1016/j.chb.2016.11.020

Sánchez, R. A., & Hueros, A. D. (2010). Motivational factors that influence the acceptance of Moodle using TAM. *Computers in Human Behavior*, *26*(6), 1632–1640. doi:10.1016/j.chb.2010.06.011

Scherer, R., Siddiq, F., & Tondeur, J. (2019). The technology acceptance model (TAM): A meta-analytic structural equation modeling approach to explaining teachers' adoption of digital technology in education. *Computers & Education, 128,* 13–35. doi:10.1016/j.compedu.2018.09.009

Wu, B., & Chen, X. (2017). Continuance intention to use MOOCs: Integrating the technology acceptance model (TAM) and task technology fit (TTF) model. *Computers in Human Behavior, 67,* 221–232. doi:10.1016/j.chb.2016.10.028

Zhang, S., Zhao, J., & Tan, W. (2008). Extending TAM for Online Learning Systems: An Intrinsic Motivation Perspective. *Tsinghua Science and Technology, 13*(3), 312–317. doi:10.1016/S1007-0214(08)70050-6

KEY TERMS AND DEFINITIONS

Digital Competences: Term used to illustrate or explain the skill to use Information and communications technology (ICT) tools.

Digital Learning Strategies: Strategies that utilizes digital tools to reach one or more learning objectives.

Digital Technologies: Information and communications technology (ICT) tools used to simulate and modelling real experiments and to facilitate the interactivity and collaboration between users.

Educational Aspiration: Educational objectives that learner establishes for himself or herself.

Perceptions of Technology: Beliefs, attitudes, and behaviour towards the user's technology.

Technical Support: Support that individuals or organisations provide help for usage of products or services.

Web 2.0 Tools for E-Learning: Tools to share data, as well as increasing the creativity and innovation as essential skills of learners for the 21st century.

Chapter 18

UX and E–Commerce:
Comparing the Best Practices in Europe, Asia, North America, South America, and Africa

Silvia Carter

To Web Or Not To Web, France

ABSTRACT

E-commerce is expected to see considerable growth in the next years anywhere all over the world. A trend that has been accelerated by the COVID-19. To succeed in this increasingly global and increasingly competitive landscape, e-commerce companies need to attract more and more traffic, the condition for getting clients. The questions "How important is UX for increasing the e-commerce sales?" and "Do geography and culture impact the UX performance?" are therefore essential. This chapter on the one hand analyzes the specific e-commerce UX elements and dimensions, and on the other hand compares strengths and weaknesses in Europe, Asia, Africa, North and South America to find UX international best practices. Keywords: Ecommerce, Online Sales, Cross-Border, International, Marketplaces, Geo-Cultural Adaptation, Ux Elements, Ux Dimensions, Worldwide, Global

INTRODUCTION

With the development of high-speed Web, mobile Internet, dematerialized payments, multichannel functions, advanced delivery and logistics solutions, e-commerce is expected to see tremendous growth in the next years in any sector worldwide. In May 2019 eMarketer estimated that global e-commerce will approach 5 trillion USD by 2021, which represents a growth rate of approximately 40% from 2019. But the health crisis triggered by the COVID-19 worldwide had an unpredicted impact on the global economy. During the lockdown, businesses had to shut down their mortar shops for several weeks and people had to replace them with online shopping. Then, after the lockdown, the social distancing measures turned physical shopping into a not-as-agreeable-as-before experience. As a result of that, the global

DOI: 10.4018/978-1-7998-3756-5.ch018

e-commerce is expected to see a much faster growth, as April 2020 statistics already reported a jump of 209% compared to the same period in 2019 (ACI Worldwide Research, May 2020).

In this new increasingly global and increasingly competitive landscape, it will be critical for e-commerce providers to focus their investments on attracting more traffic on their website and on improving the Click-Through-Rate (CTR) of it. The CTR measuring the transformation rate of the traffic into customers, it is one of the most important Key Performance Indicators (KPI) for online sales.

But before making investing decisions, some considerations must be gauged. Among all, two issues are analyzed in this chapter:

1. Among all the factors that impact the e-commerce sales performance, is the User Experience (referred to as UX in the rest of this chapter) the most important one?
2. How geography and culture impact e-commerce UX and how should they be managed to maximize the international online sales performance?

This chapter aims to help exporting companies and decision makers in their UX strategy to improve the cross-border performance of their e-commerce websites. It also offers support to further discussions about UX best practices for cross-border e-commerce based on the analysis of same global and local cases.

BACKGROUND: AN EXPLANATION OF UX - USER EXPERIENCE

The word UX, which stands for User Experience, was coined by Don Norman in the 90s while he was Vice President of the Advanced Technology Group at Apple (Donald Norman, 1988 and Merholz, Peter, 2007). As he explained, he "wanted to cover all aspects of the person's experience with the system including industrial design, graphics, the interface, the physical interaction, and the manual." Since then the term has spread widely, blending with other words and generating some confusion among non-web experts.

J. J. Garrett contributed to the UX definition by explaining through a diagram that UX is composed by many layers (Jesse James Garret, 2000):

- **Language:** English, French, Portuguese, etc.
- **Visual Design, i.e. the graphic interface:** esthetics, pictures, colors, symbolisms, etc.
- **Motion & Audio Design:** music, voice, videos, animations, etc.
- **Content Requirements:** for an e-commerce they concern the brand style and tone delivered throughout the website.
- **Information Design, i.e. how contents are presented for user's comprehension:** for an e-commerce it can concern for example the way product descriptions, USP and benefits are presented.
- **Interface Design, i.e. the elements that facilitate users' interaction with the website's:** for example, how users fill out their personal information at the checkout, or how they search for a product.
- **Interaction Design, i.e. how tasks are delivered to the users interacting with the website:** for an e-commerce it can be an alert for the expiring cart, or the confirmation screen after the payment.
- **Navigation Design, i.e. the elements to facilitate users' move through the pages of the website:** for example, how users select a product to view, or choose a size to add to their cart.

- **Information Architecture, i.e. the structure of the contents:** for an e-commerce it is for example, the category and subcategories organization in the main menu and the product pages included in each one.
- **Functional Specifications, i.e. the website's functionalities to meet user needs:** for example, the e-commerce payment and delivery options.
- **User Needs, i.e. the goals for the website:** in the case of an e-commerce they are about easily find and buy what users are searching.
- **Website Objectives:** for an e-commerce website the objectives are not only about selling as much as possible, they are also about delivering the sold items in the due form and in the due time to fully satisfy the clients and to avoid the problems related with possible returns. Therefore an e-commerce final objective should be to provide customers – the users – with a whole excellent experience, from the first visit on the website until the reception of their purchase, so that they will come back and tell their friends about how great it was shopping there.

Though most website developers use these elements, normal internet users are unable to distinguish them and to experience them separately. They can only perceive them as a unique interactive system, which value and performance are greater than the elements taken individually.

FIRST FOCUS OF THE CHAPTER: THE UX PECULIARITIES FOR E-COMMERCE AND MARKETPLACES, NATIONAL AND CROSS-BORDER

As statistics show (Statista2014-2023), the number of online shops is increasing year after year and made a global jump of 209% in April 2020 due to the COVID-19 (ACI Worldwide Research, May 2020). Consequently, e-commerce success in a such increasingly competitive environment depends on suppliers' capability to use the UX elements, textual and visual, that most effectively attract, stimulate, and convert visitors into buyers (Schlosser et al. 2006). However, managers' intuitions are mainly used for selecting the so-thought most effective UX elements, instead of using analysis on how such elements influence customer experiences and their purchase decisions.

Unlike with brick-and-mortar retail, online shoppers choose products not through physical interaction but through the UX elements presented on the websites. Although there are several researches that have formulated offline retail UX as consisting of the combination of cognitive, affective, sensory, social, and physical dimensions (Schmitt 1999; Verhoef et al. 2009; Brakus, Schmitt, and Zarantonello 2009; Lemon and Verhoef 2016), online retail UX doesn't have such extensive researches (Novak, Hoffman, and Yung 2000; Steenkamp, Jan-Benedict E.M. and Geyskens 2006).

Inspired by the offline UX dimensions, Bleier, Harmeling, and Palmatier (2019), have conceptualized e-commerce UX as consisting of four experience dimensions:

- **Cognitive and informative**: this is the information that a website provides to consumers. It is the primary dimension of the e-commerce UX because it is the websites direct contribution to helping consumers take a purchase decision, which involves thinking, conscious mental processing, and problem solving (Gentile, Spiller, and Noci 2007; Lim and Ting 2012). This dimension is generally impersonal, fact-based, outcome oriented, and objective (Schlosser, White, and Lloyd 2006).

- **Affective and entertaining**: this dimension concerns the interactions that customers can have with the online offer. The e-commerce can entertain and generate affective responses, whatever its power to facilitate purchasing. This e-commerce entertainment power is a key UX dimension because it shows the consumers' appreciation for the website beyond the purchase opportunities, helping increase the number of visitors (Hsieh et al. 2014) and reduce cart abandonment (Kukar-Kinney and Close 2010).

- **Social**: this dimension refers to the human feeling and warm contact that an e-shop can provide to its visitors. To establish this dimension, online shops provide more and more social functions on their website. Researches have shown that such social UX dimension for e-commerce can increase the feelings of closeness to a product, the pleasure during online shopping, the purchase intentions, and the loyalty (Darke et al. 2016; Wang and al. 2007; Hassanein and Head 2007; Cyr et al. 2007).

- **Sensory**: this UX dimension concerns the elements that can stimulate any sense online among sight, sound, smell, taste, or touch (Gentile, Spiller, and Noci 2007). Perception of beauty and aesthetic stimuli are part of this dimension as well as the sensations that can be produced by pictures or videos (Elder et al. 2017). As a result, the sensory dimension contributes to affect the consumers' product perceptions (Weathers, Sharma, and Wood 2007) and their purchase intentions (Schlosser 2003).

Based on Bleier, Harmeling, and Palmatier's research (2019), effective e-commerce UX, in terms of driving purchase decisions, can be created by using UX elements consistently with the above four UX dimensions, and accordingly to the type of product or service and to the reliability of the brand. In particular, they observed that:

- **Cognitive experience** is most effective for online offerings that require little physical interaction for being appreciated, and for brands that are already well-trusted. Bulleted features and comparison matrix are strong UX elements in this case, much stronger than on any other experience dimension.

- **Entertaining experience** is especially important for less reliable brands. No UX element appears to be particularly stronger in this dimension than in others.

- **Social experience** is most effective for online offerings that require a lot of interaction for being appreciated. A more conversational semantic style with adjectives, self-reflective questions, "you, your" pronouns, and lifestyle pictures featuring the product in use are the UX elements that perform best in this dimension. On the other hand, content filters, such as a "show more" button, should be avoided because they let visitors choose how much content is shown on the webpage and they might miss out on key interactive content.

- **Sensory experience** is also effective for online offerings that require a lot of interaction for being appreciated. Videos presenting the products and zooming functions highlighting key attributes are the UX elements that have the strongest effects on this dimension.

Bleier, Harmeling, and Palmatier's research (2019) offers some guidelines to managers on how they can generate online sales through, first determining the best UX dimension based on the level of online interaction their offerings require for being appreciated and the reliability of their brand; then optimizing the effectiveness of that dimension by applying the relevant UX elements to their web pages. This second step should be deployed consistently with the business' digital assets, avoiding the more-is-better approach that implies the use of UX elements just because they're already available in their digital inventory.

A last point regarding Bleier, Harmeling, and Palmatier's research (2019) worth mentioning is that their four-dimension approach can help businesses choose the best options their offerings require on third online retailers and marketplaces, which usually involve additional financial investments. Amazon sellers, for example, can choose among several packages (e.g., Basic A+, Premium A+) that offer different UX elements and configurations. However, for products which best perform in the cognitive dimension, choosing a package that provides social or sensory UX elements can be an unnecessary and counterproductive investment.

Besides Bleier, Harmeling, and Palmatier's four-dimension model, and unlike offline trade, there are three more e-commerce UX peculiarities that are worth to be highlighted (Dimoka, Hong, and Pavlou 2012; Pavlou, Liang, and Xue 2007):

1. **The lack of "touch and feel"**: this can create uncertainty for online purchase (Kim and Krishnan 2015), and its degree is directly correlated to the level of physical interaction a product requires for being appreciated (Hong and Pavlou 2014; Weathers, Sharma, and Wood 2007). The intensity of uncertainty can be influenced by the four-dimension e-commerce UX. For example, products with a high uncertainty because of a high physical interaction needed for being appreciated should be presented not only through full cognitive elements but also through effective sensory information to appeal the senses.

2. **The physical distance between the shoppers and the e-commerce**: to overcome such distance, either customers fully believe and trust the accuracy of the website or they fully rely on the honesty of the brand (Pavlou, Liang, and Xue 2007). Trust is a very important factor for online business. Many researches have shown that the sellers' reliability has a direct impact on online purchase decisions (Gefen, Karahanna, and Straub 2003), and that this reliability is closely related with the e-commerce UX and the web design (Urban, Amyx, and Lorenzon 2009). That means that low reliability can be overcome through powerful effective web design and/or through customized content to please customers' preferences and/or through specific online entertainment and/or through strong social presence (Schlosser, White, and Lloyd 2006; Urban et al. 2009).

3. **The multilayered distance in cross-border e-commerce**: this additional and very specific feature doesn't subsist in offline commerce or national e-commerce. In cross-border e-commerce, the distance between the online shoppers and the products or services they want to buy is not only geographical but also institutional - such as legal system, taxes, currency, etc. - cultural - such as language, history, education, etc. - and seasonal - as seasons happen at different times around the world. Therefore, such elaborate distance can impact the cross-border e-commerce UX by users' fear of transportation costs, their unfamiliarity with payment systems, VAT, and foreign currencies, their apprehension of non-adapted terms and conditions, their issues with using incomprehensible customer service, their getting annoyed with finding skiing products in summer, etc. Cross-border e-commerce should therefore deploy the best UX elements to reduce such distance. There are three main UX elements that can be used for this purpose:

    a. Information: by adapting the products and supplier's information to the local demand, and by simplifying the search and the comparison of local and international offers, through either the supplier's website or external ones, such as customer ratings websites, this improved information can reduce multilayered distance.

b.   Delivery cost: cross-border e-commerce can reduce such complex distance by adapting their delivery pricing strategies through yield management, or flat average standard price, or through prices per level of shipping service, or through free shipping for expensive purchases, etc.

c.   Delivery time: by offering reliable express delivery options, or effective tracking solutions, cross-border e-commerce can also reduce distance with their online customers.

In the following picture an example on how information is used in a product page UX on Macy's e-commerce:

SECOND FOCUS OF THE CHAPTER: THE IMPORTANCE OF INFORMATION AND COUNTRY-OF-ORIGIN FOR CROSS-BORDER E-COMMERCE UX

Due to people's differences in language, culture, history, and habits from one country to another, cross-border e-commerce attract various levels of consumers' attention, which is a key issue for driving purchases. Cross-border e-commerce must maximize visitors' perception of their offer, or they will leave the website without any intention to buy or to come back.

In general, the information shared on the Internet has an important effect on visitors during their online transaction decisions. Internet and adequate UX can lower the operational costs of making information accessible to and sharable by anyone anywhere in the world: the better the Information Design (ID) in the UX, the more effective the e-commerce can be in its cross-border sales. Consequently, the ID has become a key element for cross-border e-commerce UX, and even the promotional information, either direct (i.e. product descriptions) or indirect (i.e. mother-day discount), can influence the purchase decisions of international e-shoppers.

In their study about purchase behavior on cross-border e-commerce, W. Zhu, J. Mou, and M. Benyoucef (2019) found that high-quality product descriptions have very positive impact and help lower the barriers due to language, culture, history, and habits differences. In particular, a well-adapted ID can reduce foreign clients' doubts and perceived risk about the cross-border e-commerce offers, and as a result it can enhance their trust.

This study also demonstrated that cross-border e-commerce interactions with clients has a very positive effect on perceived trust. Facilitating such interactions between clients and suppliers, the formers will spend more time on the website and will get more involved with the products or services offered. This longer time and higher involvement increase consumers' trust towards the e-commerce, which will consequently improve their purchase intentions.

Emotions also play a key role on cross-border e-shoppers' product perception and purchase intention. In particular, W. Zhua, J. Moub, and M. Benyoucef (2019) explain that cross-border e-commerce consumers follow sequential steps from product awareness, discovery through description, perception, and involvement, to trust, emotion, and purchase intention if the earlier steps were positive. In non-cross-border e-commerce, product description and perception are less key for purchase intentions. Due to multilayered distance, in cross-border e-commerce that is very different as product description and perception are the sine qua non elements to create emotion and to let clients move towards the purchase intention.

Figure 1.

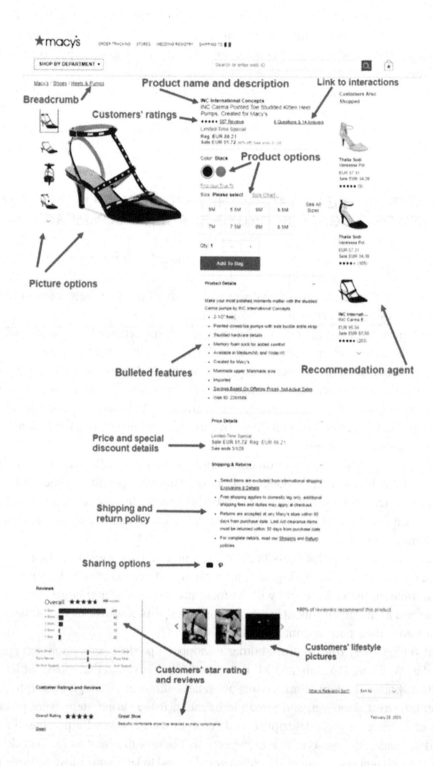

Figure 2.

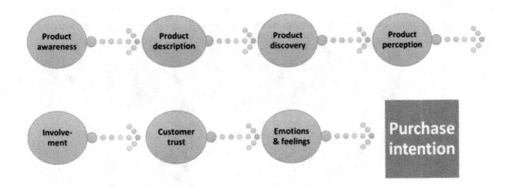

Among all the different types of promotional information, the Country-of-Origin (CO) is key in the global online trade environment and has an important role in the purchasing decisions of cross-border e-shoppers, based on its enhancing power for the brands' equity value.

The CO plays an essential role when the cross-border e-commerce ID is asymmetric. This case is particularly frequent in international marketplaces where the filling out of the information is made in a decentralized and individual way by several different sellers across the world.

Marketplaces offer three main UX levels:

1.   A central UX that is managed directly by the marketplace platform.
2.   The UX managed by the single brands within the marketplace platform.
3.   The UX for the products managed by sellers with no brand or with a little-known one.

For the cases 2 and 3, given the increasingly online competition within the marketplace platforms, success depends on sellers' ability to use information, verbal and visual (i.e., product descriptions, pictures, logo elements, etc.) on the product page to effectively convert visitors into buyers (Schlosser et al. 2006). In case 2, a well know brand will be an important visual element that will help sellers raise their conversion power.

Due to this UX decentralization, the ID, especially the products or services' information, can be inconsistent from one seller to another. In such situation, the CO can provide global e-shoppers with an additional and more objective element for evaluating the foreign brand and its online offer (Da Huo, Ken Hung, Haibo Wang, and Xu Xiaoli, 2018).

These studies provided some interesting practical implications. It is evident that cross-border e-commerce need to implement additional marketing actions to improve the description and perception of their offer. The cross-border e-commerce information must be as easy to access and to understand as possible to attract consumers' attention. The UX will therefore need to be adapted to include extra elements such as videos, pictures, music, etc. Cross-border e-commerce UX should also include specific shopping functions adapted to their target countries to make consumers get involved and spend as much time as possible on the website. That can be done for example by providing extra information about how to use the website, how to ond products, how to follow a delivery, how to get in touch with the customer service, how to easily purchase products, etc. An example of that is provided by eMag in the following

Figure 3.

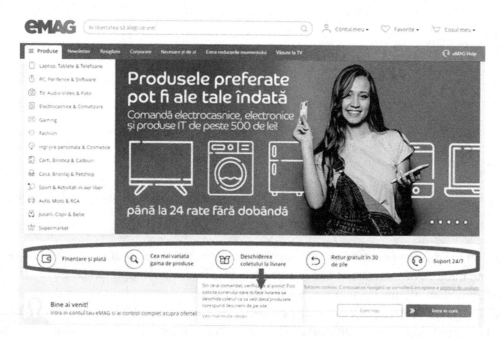

image: the Romanian e-commerce offers five explanatory buttons just underneath the main slide show to describe payments systems, product range, delivery conditions, return policy, and customer support.

THIRD FOCUS OF THE CHAPTER: THE CROSS-BORDER E-COMMERCE ORGANIZATION AND GEOGRAPHICAL STRATEGY

It is proof that cross-border e-commerce can help international businesses sell more overseas and overcome geographic distance as it can be cheaper than building a physical presence in several foreign countries. The development of cross-border e-commerce has encouraged companies to be more involved in global online business (Da Huo, Ken Hung, Haibo Wang, and Xu Xiaoli, 2018) and creating effective UX across countries has become critical. How such UX should be orchestrated internationally, however, is still unclear.

The type and the quantity of resources of a company are the key variables that can impact the level of globalization vs. localization of an e-commerce. We can find three examples:

1.   The large multichannel corporation: it operates local sales divisions in different countries, that oversee local resellers and other distributors. In this case, there can be two options: either a global e-commerce UX strategy managed through a central template and local content; or several local e-commerce UX strategies managed by the country divisions under their local budget. The former is Coca-Cola's approach in the following example for Brazil, Italy, and Russia.

Figure 4.

Figure 5.

2. The pure-player e-commerce: in this case the company doesn't have any direct or indirect "brick and mortar" sales organization and it only operates online. The global vs. local UX internationalization choice will be taken based on the company's financial capabilities, being the UX local strategy per country the most expensive one. The following example is the Lithuanian Vinted, a C-to-C marketplace that is been internationalized for operating in 12 countries.

Figure 6.

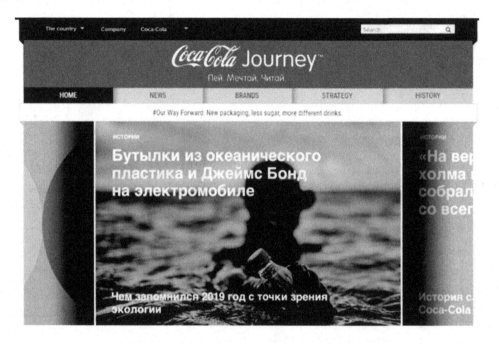

Figure 7.

3.   The small and medium enterprise (SME): unlike for the pure-player, in this case the company can have other direct or indirect "brick and mortar" sales organizations. As before, the global vs. local UX internationalization choice will be taken based on the company's financial capabilities. Nevertheless, the SME has an additional option that is almost impossible for the pure-player. The SME can also sell its products or services through cross-border marketplaces, in which case the global vs. local UX choice will depend on the chosen marketplaces' strategy. The following Kipli's mattresses is the example of selling through one's own cross-border e-commerce and international marketplaces.

Figure 8.

Figure 9.

SOLUTIONS AND RECOMMENDATIONS: HOW DOES THE WORLD SHOP? SOME E-COMMERCE UX APPROACHES AROUND THE WORLD

E-Commerce UX in the World: Amazon *Glocal* Case

In 2019, Amazon is projected to account for almost 14% of global retail e-commerce sales (Statista). Although his large global market share, its success in the United States is not to be seen anywhere else in the world as here Amazon is expected to account for over half of the local e-commerce market.

With about 200 million monthly e-shoppers worldwide and more than 3 billion products on its websites, Amazon UX's goal is to increase the number of visitors who buy something, which is also the goal of mainly any other e-commerce around the world. For that, Amazon focuses not only on its logistics performance, managing more than 175 fulfillment centers around the world, the majority of which located in North America and in Europe (Amazon), but also on the "search" performance, which is Amazon's UX key element.

On Amazon's website, searches can be performed in several ways:

1. From the top search bar, that will suggest a result as soon as a character is keyed in, like many other search engines. This search field is available on any page and it can be used throughout the whole website or by category if one has been selected among those in the search bar's left-side button.
2. From the scroll-down menu at the top left side of the website. This search menu is also available on any page, but unlike before the search can only be run by category and sub-category rather than by keyword.
3. From the left-side vertical menu. This menu is only available once an item has been previously selected. Being this type of search only by subcategory, it allows to filter the results through several criteria.
4. From the main window by browsing the items page by page. This search option can only be performed when an item has been selected, and the results can be sorted by "Featured", "Price: Low to High", "Price: High to Low", "Avg. Customer Review" and "Newest Arrivals".
5. From the half-page and bottom horizontal menus where similar or featured or sponsored products are shown. These search menus are only available when an item has been selected, and the search can be performed by scrolling left or right on the same page.

Because of the reduced space, these search options can differ in Amazon's mobile website and applications. For example: the mobile website and applications run a specific algorithm to simplify the suggestion list in the search bar; options 3 is not in the same position as in the laptop website format but compacted into a button for a scroll-down menu; the top left side scroll-down menu has been shortened in terms of number of choices; etc.

Concerning Amazon's cross-border features, it is important to underline that the geographical options, such as the language and country selectors, are clearly visible and in the same position for any Amazon website's formats, be it the computer, tablet, mobile or application format.

Apart the search element, Amazon UX is designed to suit multiple cultures and multiple generations. Some examples of Amazon UX localization are as follow:

1. Its localized brand: Amazon's logo on its USA website is "Amazon.com" while in the UK it becomes "Amazon.co.uk", in Germany "Amazon.de", etc.
2. Language localization: a language selector is accessible from any web page in any websites so that users can switch from one country to another if they need.
3. Visual, motion and audio design adaptation: for example, even if the homepage focus is always on Kindle, the UK website highlights the best titles to buy, while the USA website highlights the device.
4. Functional Specifications adaptation: users can choose among different currencies, delivery terms and costs, depending on the country website on which they are shopping.
5. Information architecture localization: product categories, subcategories and add-on services can vary from one country website to another.

Figure 10.

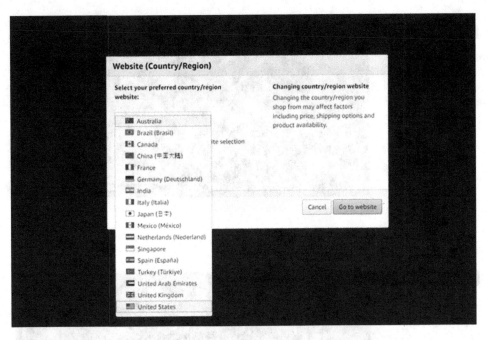

In the following pictures some examples of the different information architectures in the main left-side drop-down menu for Amazon's Brazil, Germany, India and USA websites. The Top 10 categories are different (as they are also in the rest of the list under the Top 10, which is not showed here for space reasons): the "Fußball Live" for example is a special category in the German website.

For the other UX elements, Amazon has adopted a straightforward strategy, keeping an identical information, interface, interaction, and navigation designs across countries.

Figure 11.

Figure 12.

Figure 13.

Figure 14.

Interestingly, after successfully starting in UK and Germany in 1998, then France in 2000, Italy in 2010, Spain in 2011, and many other in the following years, Amazon had to adopt a different strategy to succeed in a new key market, India. Unlike in the USA and in Europe, where the business model was based on similar UX with identical services such as Prime, Kindle, Drive, etc., Amazon had to adapt to the Indian demographics: 67% of the people live in very rural areas, only 35% have internet access, and most of them use cash for their payments.

After launching the Indian website in 2013, Amazon invested in developing local partnerships. By using special programs, such as the "Chai Cart", Amazon went as far as door-to-door to teach businessmen about e-commerce. Through such special programs, Amazon was able to tailor local offerings with specific UX, and specially the information architecture, recognizing the diversity of Indian consumers and their need to satisfy the loyal relationships they have with Indian suppliers (Blake A. Garner, 2018).

Apart India, since its inception in 1994, Amazon's UX has changed little, confirming the company's approach: 'if it ain't broke, don't fix it'.

E-Commerce UX in Europe: Fighting Against Distance

Europe represents a very large market for e-commerce counting a population of almost 750 million people, bigger than North America and third after Asia and Africa. One in four Europeans with internet access shops online at least once a week and 60% once a month (Mastercard survey, 2017). But Europe is formed by many countries that differ in terms of language, economy, politics, geography and culture. UK, Germany, France, are the largest markets for online spending followed by Italy, Spain, Benelux, and the Nordics. This ranking shows a correlation between market value and number of people. Clothing and footwear are the most popular product categories, followed by home electronics and books (Eurostat, 2019).

In such a patchworked market, what are the key UX elements for European e-commerce?

In their study about European e-commerce, Kim, Dekker, and Heij (2017) described that online purchasers can be negatively impacted if the lead time between placing their order and receiving the products is too long.

E-shops' customers still experience various consequences due to the distance between them and their online suppliers. Such a distance issue is also affected by institutional trade barriers and other country-specific elements such as income, delivery charges, borders' times, etc.

Kim, Dekker, and Heij (2017) explain that there are several ways for European e-commerce to reduce their online customers' perceived distance. These measures include, for example, shortening the delivery time by using different transporters that are more adapted to online shopping, or improving the conditions with their current logistics providers, or balancing the costs and benefits of their products by applying the yield price management.

Another important barrier for European e-commerce that is analyzed in this study is the one based on subjective factors. The study emphasizes how European e-commerce can reduce this type of barrier through effective communication and service policies, such as using the writing tone that is best adapted to their target clients, offering the purchasing functions that they use most, providing clear return policies and an easy-to-access customer service, etc. In the following pictures an example from John Lewis UK e-commerce offering many delivery options to reassure consumers about the shipping quality.

In a similar way, MediaMarkt Germany shows another example on how to reassure consumers about the shipping quality by indicating the stock availability and the lead-time for the pick-up of each product directly in the result list. The store pick-up is one of the most preferred delivery options in Germany.

Figure 15.

Figure 16.

E-Commerce UX in the U.S.: The Omnichannel Way

Omnichannel and multichannel became key game changers for the retail industry almost anywhere in the world and in particular in the United States. Often considered as the evolution from multichannel, omnichannel takes a broader perspective on integration allowing ubiquitous and real time interactions between customers, brand and stores across all channels. With less or no ubiquitous and real time factors, multichannel concerns a similar integration but on separate channels each pushing its sales neglecting the sales on other channels. Retailers use such integrations to improve their customers' experience across all channels, by erasing the boundary between physical offline and digital online shopping.

The parallel rise of new technologies like smartphones and high-speed internet enabled the access to no-stop real-time information allowing retailers to deploy new business models such as the click-and-collect, consumer-to-consumer services, online-to-offline promotions, etc.

Unlike multichannel, omnichannel, when properly implemented, offers coherent and full integration across all channels, national and international, looking completely unified to customers all over the world. Under the more and more border free global retail landscape, traditional retailers are not protected by geographical or cultural barriers anymore.

According to Y. Ye, K.H. Lau and L.K.Y. Teo (2018), it is possible to identify that the key drivers for retailers going omnichannel are:

- Mobile technology: not only in terms of devices, e.g., smartphones, tablets, etc. but also in terms of internet speed and quality. The combination of these technologies enables retailers to reach more and more consumers online and offline.

In the following pictures the example from REI omnichannel strategy from the stores to desktop UX, mobile UX and 8 apps UX. In the US, 80% of people use their mobile while shopping in off-line stores, for checking a product or a price or the availability, etc. When anyone of these 80% people cannot get the information online when he's searching in the store, then he will leave the store long with bad UX. Instead, REI makes sure that each of its shopping channels work instantaneously with one another.

- Big data: retailers can now access better and larger consumer information allowing them to improve their offers by creating enhanced and personalized shopping experience.
- Ubiquity: consumers can also get better and larger information about product brand, quality, price, and availability anywhere and at any time. Retailers can offer additional technologies, such as QR codes, dematerialized payment systems, social networks, etc. to help consumers make better purchase decisions and enhance their UX.

Figure 17.

Figure 18.

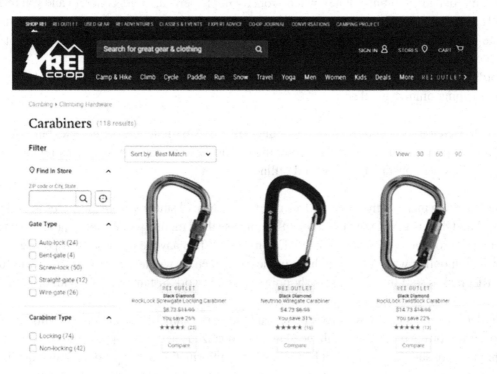

Figure 19.

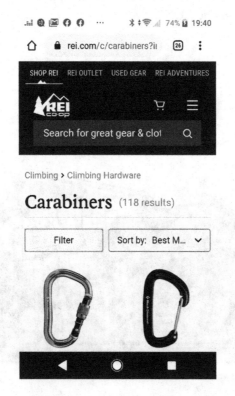

Figure 20.

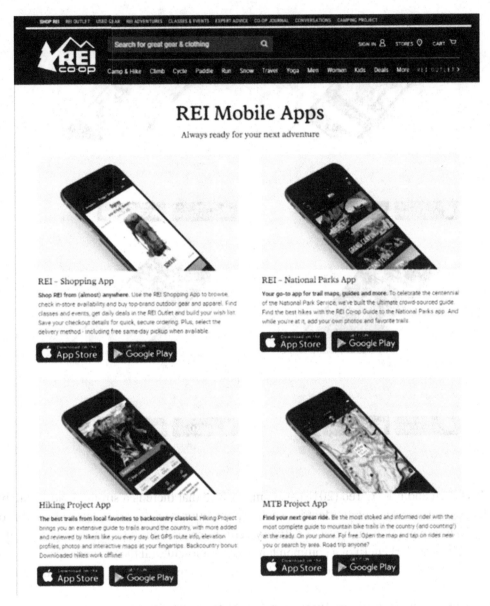

- Smart supply chains: resulting from the first two points above, retailers' supply chain is now more efficient. Able to track products in a better way, retailers can shorten their supply chains, improving both customer deliveries and stock management, including returns.

At the same time, the main barriers for retailers to go omnichannel are of two types:

- Strategy-related: issues with adapting the organization, the culture and the management strategy.
- Development-related: such as adapting the product mix, IS and technology systems, the logistics and delivery routines, the customer service and the CRM, etc.

Figure 21.

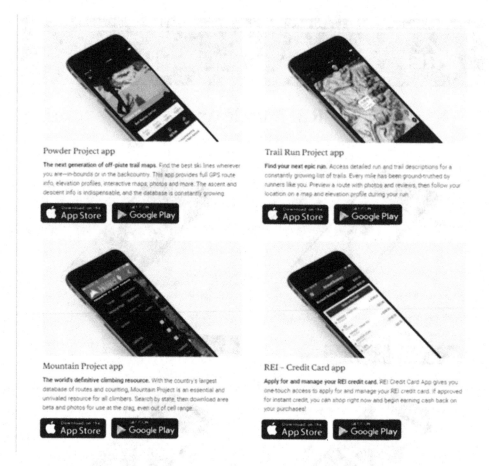

Y. Ye, K.H. Lau and L.K.Y. Teo (2018) also emphasized that there is a strong relationship between these challenges and country specifics factors, such as population density, social and cultural factors, and consumer behavior (e.g. different types of delivery, return expectations, etc.). The large size of the US market combined with the benefit of a common language, socio-cultural factors and consumer behavior, is one of the main reasons why omnichannel has been deployed much faster here than in other countries.

E-Commerce UX in Brazil: Enhancing Security and Trust

Given the global interest in e-commerce sales development, there is a continuous search to understand the key factors that help consumer buy online beyond national borders. This is true especially in emerging markets, which different characteristics can unveil new insights, useful also in mature markets.

Emerging countries are often characterized by heterogeneous markets, sociopolitical instability, strong and sometimes unfair competition with unbranded goods, lack of resources, infrastructure problems, less demanding and low-income consumers. This environment may be a barrier to new entrants in such markets, and, as a result, consumers can behave differently from those in mature markets as their online purchasing decisions are influenced in a different way (Thongpapanl et al. 2018).

Figure 22.

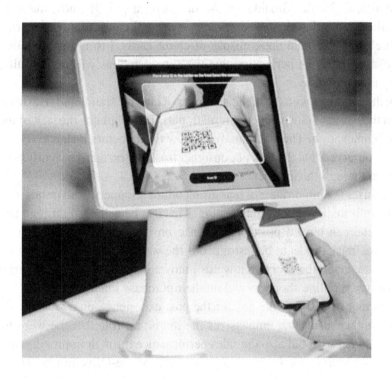

Brazil, although the eighth largest economy in the world and the largest in Latin America (Bianchi, Carneiro, and Wickramasekera 2018), is among those emerging countries. Its e-commerce is still nascent, as only 40% of the households have an internet access, a percentage that lowers to 20% and 30% in the northern regions.

E. W. Mainardes, C. M. de Almeida and M. de-Oliveira (2019) studied Brazilian e-commerce for analyzing the impact of country-specific elements on UX and sales performance. They considered e-commerce as computer operated mainly, as mobile internet operations were still less executed. The study examined:

- The impact of lack of consumer trust, website identification, and website quality on purchase intentions.
- Whether the perceived risks impact the lack of consumer trust.
- Whether consumer resistance to innovations impacts the lack of consumer trust and perceived risk.

In emerging countries such as Brazil, in addition to the characteristics mentioned in the previous pages, there is a high asymmetry of information as companies are not completely clear about their online operations. Since that is combined to a fragile consumer protection legislation, it results in low internet adoption as consumers prefer traditional physical stores (Malaquias and Hwang 2016).

In E. W. Mainardes, C. M. de Almeida and M. de-Oliveira (2019) study, the lack of online buyer trust is defined as the feeling that the website low control will cause problems during the purchasing process, such as breach of personal data, misuse of credit cards, losing parcel delivery, etc. In other words, online purchasers have the perception that the agreed actions will not be fulfilled and because of that they abandon the purchase.

Brazil is among the countries with the highest number of internet frauds and with the highest perceived corruption index in the world (Transparency International). That explains the lack of trust in consumers, and their aversion to innovation. The study analyzed how these factors influence e-commerce, directly and indirectly. It was observed that the lack of consumer trust in Brazil has a significantly negative effect on purchase intention through the internet.

This result emphasizes the importance of reassuring online shoppers from frauds, corruption, precarious logistics, scarce information, and counterfeiting. That can be achieved through the website quality, which, on the opposite, can have a positive influence on consumers' purchase intentions in Brazil. However, that positive impact risks to be restrained if the website is presented with a too high level of innovation. In that case, given the aversion towards innovation in developing countries like Brazil, the impact will be negative on online shoppers and on their purchase intentions.

The study also demonstrated that the greater the past experience on a website, the lower the lack of consumer trust, another result that emphasizes the important role that the website quality plays to increase not only consumer trust but also the sales performance through improving purchase intentions.

In conclusion, E. W. Mainardes, C. M. de Almeida and M. de-Oliveira (2019) study suggests that the UX strategy for e-commerce in Brazil should offer high website quality, through qualitative content, information and design, but avoid too high degree of innovation. These actions help create positive experience for the Brazilian consumers, who will trust the e-commerce in question, and will, therefore, be more willing to go back to.

Some pragmatic examples on how it can be achieved are: offering traditional payments at the delivery, warranties on new products, fast deliveries, products tracking from the order confirmation up to the delivery, easy-to-reach customer service, etc. These elements will help online shops eventually increase consumer's trust and reduce their perception of risk.

In the following pictures, two examples from Touratech and MercadoLivre.

E-Commerce UX in Africa: The Micro-Localization of Cross-Border

Distribution for goods and services in Africa is notoriously challenging because for consumers it is harder to find goods and to shop than anywhere else. In the past few years, however, thanks to mobile and internet technology, consumers have found a new and better way to shop.

With more than 400 million internet users, Africa has the second most digitally connected populations in the world after China. The e-commerce sector is expected to grow exponentially in the next years, with already 39% of Nigerians, 61% of Kenyans, or 69% of South Africans shopping online, most of whom through a mobile phone. Mobile UX therefore plays a major role in e-commerce usability across a wide range of countries, languages, and cultures.

Figure 23.

Figure 24.

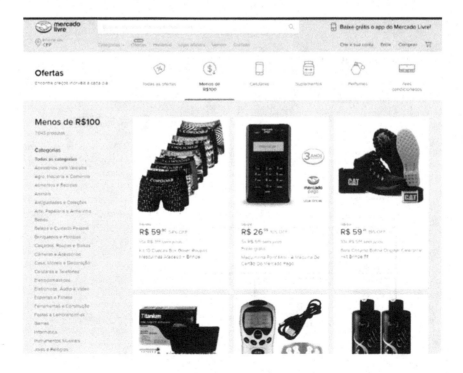

For African e-commerce, these are some of the key points to consider for effective UX:

- People often do not live in urban areas but in small villages. With internet access being provided almost everywhere in Africa, consumers are more and more enthusiastic of the large choice they can have online even when they live in isolated areas where otherwise it would be impossible for them to access the same wide range of products. Because of that, and because African consumers want the same things as any other consumer in the world, i.e. good quality, good price, good service, and quick deliveries, logistics is the biggest challenge for e-commerce in Africa. This is not only the consequence of geographical distance and poor infrastructure, it is also due to the lack of standard address system: to find a person for a delivery, local transporters need to find out where, by relying on subjective network information. For example, when someone says, "I live in the third house in the second street on the right side of the main square" that's the address. E-commerce for Africans should consider such peculiarity and adapt the UX, such as the filling out of a customer account, accordingly. Jumia is an example: this marketplace not only offers several local payment systems, including on-delivery, it also allows to enter all the destination details for the delivery. Jumia partnered with local providers in 11 African countries who can find consumers everywhere and who, by using Jumia specific tools, can easily operate their last-mile door-to-door business.

Figure 25.

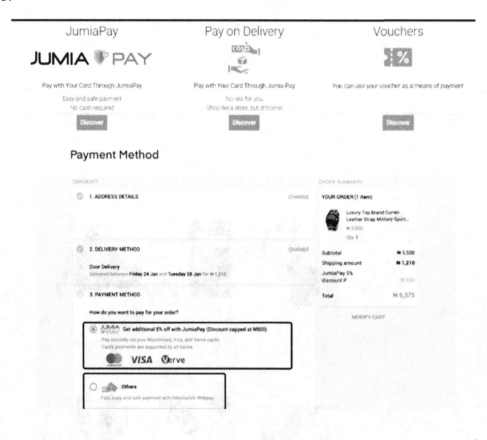

Figure 26.

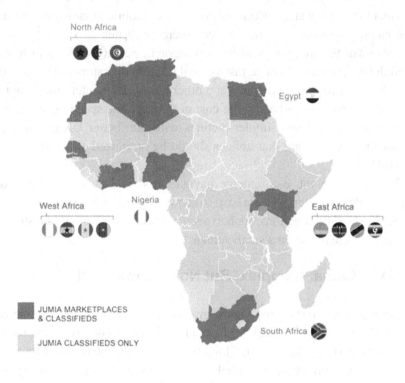

Figure 27.

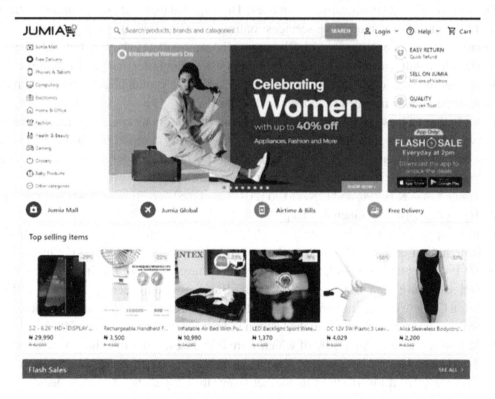

- Africa is a cashless society; its population adopted Mobile Money and e-wallets very quickly, due to the lack of material money and banking infrastructure. Mobile money services are therefore UX elements that cannot be missed on African e-commerce websites.

- 67% of Africans owns feature phones with a resolution of 320px by 480px or lower. Smartphone adoption is on the rise, but it will not go fast as local telecom operators bill by the consumed bytes. Websites with big high-resolution pictures and other heavy rich content might not be appreciated by Africans who are very concerned by the cost of data and the speed of the mobile connection. On the opposite, simple text and simpler pictures will offer better UX on smaller devices. The practical implications of that are that images should be optimized and compressed to 500 kb or even to 120-80 kb.

- Related to the previous point, e-commerce navigation should also be optimized for the small screens. Over complicated interfaces are hard to browse from a mobile phone. Instead, the product web pages and the standard functions, such as search, filter or sort, should be streamlined to make them as easy as possible to use on a small screen.

E-Commerce UX in China: Complex, But Not Complicated

The Chinese market represents one of the fastest growing retail markets in the world (Euromonitor International, 2014). Unlike in other countries where large big-boxers dominate the retail industry (e.g. Walmart, Carrefour, MediaMarkt, Zara, etc.), China is highly fragmented with a market that is mainly composed by small-and-medium retailers divided in different segments upon demographic, economic and cultural factors (PwC, 2017; Yeand Lau, 2018; Hedley, 2017). With the development of the technological giants like Alibaba and Tencent, e-commerce boomed and created many new opportunities for any retailers, especially the small-and-medium ones. This injected new technology allowed the massive deployment and adoption of innovative services: online-to-offline (O2O) using geo-localized mobile apps; dematerialized mobile payments with QR codes; click-and-collect to buy an item online and pickup it in store; etc. The small-and-medium retailers, in particular, were faster and proner to implement such technologies than the large ones, such as department stores or big capital chains, that faced more challenges due to their already installed rigid technical systems.

The result is that Chinese websites look complex, but they are not more complicated than in other parts of the world. Naturally foreigners see Chinese websites as very complex because they can only look at a Chinese website without understanding it or to using it. And anything that one doesn't understand, unsurprisingly is considered complicated. But that is not the case.

In their study Y. Ye, K.H. Lau and L.K.Y. Teo (2018) analyzed two prominent apparel retailers while they were deploying their e-commerce strategy.

The Chinese apparel industry has been going through major channel transformations. This industry in China, as in the rest of the world, is characterized by short product lifespans, high unpredictability, and recurrent impulse purchases. But, while offline stores have seen sales declining in the past years, online apparel sales have been growing steadily (Fung Business intelligence, 2017; PwC, 2017).

Retailer A, a Chinese casual and sport wear retailer, started as a wholesaler before launching its own brand, becoming a prominent business in the fashion industry by 1995. By the late 2000s, it had around 3,000 physical stores across China, 93% of which were franchises. After that, however, sales started to decline as the market got more competitive. Retailer A did not pay much attention to its product quality and design, and by 2012 it lost much of its market share. In that year the company decided to shift to direct sales by owning 100% of all the stores in the first-tier cities in China and to start selling online: more than 1bn USD was invested to build its e-commerce, as well as O2O, mobile applications, and an ERP system. Unfortunately, that created significant conflicts between direct stores, franchise stores, and the online channel. This cross-channel issues ultimately led to worsening the supply chain operations as well as to a loss in vision and leadership from the management.

Retailer B was founded in 2001 in Guangzhou under the Denmark Apparel Group, which entered the Chinese market in 1997. Within ten years, it grew its retail from first-tier cities to third-tier cities by using the franchise model, and in 2010 it decided to develop e-commerce. Unlike Retailer A, its project involved using third-party business-to-consumer (B2C) platforms such as Tabao.com and Tmall.com. Apart from online sales, Retail B also launched a mobile app also by working with another third-party media company, Tencent and its WeChat: that made Retailer B one of the first cases in fashion with e-commerce UX enhanced through social media. By collaborating with third-party service providers to build new digital channels, instead of investing like Retailer A to directly develop its own applications, the company was able to reach more consumers with lower cost and financial risk. Launched in 2011, the company become one of the top sellers in the Chinese fashion market.

Comparing Retailer A and Retailer B, it can be seen that they faced different challenges.

Retailer A faced more difficulties from marketing, supply chain, logistics, and management, having to cope with several conflicts between franchised stores, own stores and online store. Although investing heavily on the development of new channels to extend its retail network, Retail A neglected to build a unified interaction framework between customers, the brand and its retail network.

On the opposite, Retailer B outsourced the digital project to third-party e-commerce and computing providers leaving a larger portion of its resources to focus on brand awareness, products, pricing, customer experience, customer service, and supply chain. A decision that proved right because it allowed to rise its sales performance.

In summary, the study reveals that e-commerce is not an automatic panacea for retailers in China. Several challenges, such as supply chain, IT development, system integration, management's leadership, need to be overcome. If implemented correctly, even in volatile sectors like fashion, the adding of more channels can rise sales.

When considering developing a website for China, it's essential to forget the western UX. Chinese UX has evolved over the years and now meets Chinese users' needs. Understanding these Chinese UX's needs is therefore indispensable. For Chinese e-commerce, the key UX recommendations are:

- Consumers use mobile devices to buy anything from foods to luxury products. And this trend is even higher for shopping across border.
- Chinese people are used and expect a lot of content. Such expectation concerns e-commerce websites and marketplaces as well. On Tmall for example, there are thousands of brands selling millions of products and each of these products has a webpage offering various types of content: not only the product description, but also plenty of technical details, including cleaning or maintenance instructions, packaging and delivery features, customer reviews, etc.

Figure 28.

- Since 71% of Chinese consumers are using online-to-offline services such as click-and-collect ordering and online restaurant bookings, businesses must make sure that their channels are well integrated and managed. McDonald's China is an example: it does the same things all over the world but in China it adapts its online business to the big key local UX element, the QR code. This code can take Chinese users to any landing page, whether McDonald's WeChat public account, or a discount coupon, or the self-service ordering app, or in-app payment, etc.

- Chinese retailers of any size are adding as many channels and consumer contact points as possible for sales expansion, but with little focus on product development and on supply chain that pushes quality and prices lower. Although this creates a high level of pressure on online profitability, Chinese retailers are not renouncing multiple channels, and among all one is the most important, WeChat. This channel has been omnipresent for so many years that nowadays websites serve more a secondary supportive role to WeChat.

- The WeChat phenomenon had also an effect on the UX approach and on the websites' look, many of which are out-of-date and stuck in the 1990s. Since WeChat and other online channels are more successful for sales, retailers are reluctant to put efforts into their website UX, which is not considered critical, being it for China or for cross-border.

The example below shows Wingfly Textile Co., a Chinese denim manufacturer based in Shenzhen: its website is in 11 foreign languages but not in Chinese, with a very basic web design and UX elements, and without e-commerce functions as online transactions are done through other channels.

- Bright orange and other warm colors are culturally preferred. For example, the top Chinese e-commerce, such as Tabao.com, JD.com, or AliExpress, all use warm colors as the following pictures show.

Figure 29.

Figure 30.

PRODUCTS

Figure 31.

Figure 32.

CONCLUSION

In the increasingly competitive landscape of e-commerce all over the world, to achieve online sales success, businesses must understand their websites' UX elements and how to use them to match the UX expectations of their visitors in order to effectively attract, stimulate, and convert them into clients.

This chapter brought some insights to help companies manage their UX elements and improve their online sales performance, in the national as well as cross-border markets. In particular, the author has analyzed the following issues:

1. The reasons why the UX, among all the factors that impact the e-commerce sales performance, is the most important one;
2. The influence of geography and culture on e-commerce UX and how they should be managed to maximize the international online sales performance.

After explaining the general definition of UX, as coined by Don Norman in the 90s, then enhanced by J. J. Garrett through his multi-layers diagram in 2000, this chapter covered the UX peculiarities for e-commerce and marketplaces, in both national and cross-border outlook. Additional focus was also made on the one hand on the importance of information and country-of-origin for cross-border e-commerce UX, and on the other hand on the cross-border e-commerce organization and geographical strategy. Finally, the author provided use-cases on how people shop online around the world, showing the key UX differences in Europe, North and South America, Africa and China.

The conclusion of this analysis is that e-commerce companies have several UX elements that they can use to optimize and grow their online sales performance, both locally and overseas, but they must avoid over-designing. Instead, each e-commerce company must carefully select the UX elements and adapt them to its internal and external factors, meaning: the type of clients the company targets, the type of business it runs – taking into consideration its values, its business model, its sector as well as the specifics of its products or services – the human, organizational, technical and financial resources it can use, and the geo-cultural context it faces in its target markets.

FUTURE RESEARCH DIRECTIONS

Based on this chapter analysis, it is undeniably important that further discussions and research continue for bringing additional insights on cross-border e-commerce UX.

Especially comparative studies of global and local online business cases will be fundamental in order to provide companies with greater support to the best practices they can deploy around the world.

ACKNOWLEDGMENT

This research was supported by ToWebOrNotToWeb.

REFERENCES

Angelika, D., Hong, Y., & Pavlou, P. A. (2012). On Product Uncertainty in Online Markets: Theory and Evidence. *Management Information Systems Quarterly*, *36*(2), 395–426. doi:10.2307/41703461

Bianchi, C., Carneiro, J., & Wickramasekera, R. (2018). Internationalisation commitment of emerging market firms: A comparative study of Chile. *Journal of Small Business and Enterprise Development*, *25*(2), 201–221. doi:10.1108/JSBED-07-2017-0221

Bleier, A., Harmeling, C. M., & Palmatier, R. W. (2019). Creating Effective Online Customer Experiences. *Journal of Marketing*, *83*(2), 98–119. doi:10.1177/0022242918809930

Brakus, J. J., Schmitt, B. H., & Zarantonello, L. (2009, May). Brand Experience: What Is It? How Is It Measured? Does It Affect Loyalty? *Journal of Marketing*, *73*(3), 52–68. doi:10.1509/jmkg.73.3.052

Business Intelligence, F. U. N. G. (2017). *In Depth – China's Apparel Market.* https://www.fbicgroup.com/?q=reports/china-distribution-and-retail-0

Chiara, G., Spiller, N., & Noci, G. (2007). How to Sustain the Customer Experience: An Overview of Experience Components that Co-Create Value with the Customer. *European Management Journal*, *25*(5), 395–410.

Da Huo, K. H., Wang, H., & Xu, X. (2018). Country of origin and online promotion in cross-border e-business: A study of consumer behavior for quality management. *The International Trade Journal*, *32*(1), 140–149. doi:10.1080/08853908.2017.1387082

Darke, P. R., Brady, M. K., Benedicktus, R. L., & Wilson, A. E. (2016). Feeling Close from Afar: The Role of Psychological Distance in Offsetting Distrust in Unfamiliar Online Retailers. *Journal of Retailing*, *92*(3), 287–299. doi:10.1016/j.jretai.2016.02.001

Dianne, C., Hassanein, K., Head, M., & Ivanov, A. (2007). The Role of Social Presence in Establishing Loyalty in E-Service Environments. *Interacting with Computers*, *19*(1), 43–56. doi:10.1016/j.intcom.2006.07.010

Dianne, C., Head, M., Larios, H., & Pan, B. (2009). Exploring Human Images in Website Design: A Multi-Method Approach. *Management Information Systems Quarterly*, *33*(3), 539–566. doi:10.2307/20650308

Elder, R. S., Schlosser, A. E., Poor, M., & Xu, L. (2017). So Close I Can Almost Sense It: The Interplay Between Sensory Imagery and Psychological Distance. *The Journal of Consumer Research*, *44*(4), 877–894. doi:10.1093/jcr/ucx070

eMarketer. (2019). *Global Ecommerce 2019*. https://www.emarketer.com/content/global-ecommerce-2019

Euromonitor International. (2014). *China to overtake US as largest apparel market by 2017*. https://blog.euromonitor.com/video/china-to-overtake-us-as-largest-apparel-market-by-2017/

Eurostat. (2019). *Online purchases, EU-28*. https://ec.europa.eu/eurostat/statistics-explained/index.php?title=File:Online_purchases,_EU-28,_2019.png

Gan, C., & Wang, W. (2017). The influence of perceived value on purchase intention in social commerce context. *Internet Research*, *27*(4), 772–785. doi:10.1108/IntR-06-2016-0164

Garner. (2018). Amazon in the Global Market. *Journal of Marketing Management*, *9*(2), 63-73.

Gefen, D., Karahanna, E., & Straub, D. W. (2003). Trust and TAM in online shopping: An integrated model. *Management Information Systems Quarterly*, *27*(1), 51–90. doi:10.2307/30036519

Hauser, J. R., Urban, G. L., Liberali, G., & Braun, M. (2009). Website morphing. *Marketing Science*, *28*(2), 201–401. doi:10.1287/mksc.1080.0459

Hedley, M. B2B International. (2017). *Entering Chinese business-to-business markets: the challenges and opportunities*. www.b2binternational.com/publications/china-market-entry/

Hoffman, D. L., Novak, T. P., & Peralta, M. (1999). Building Consumer Trust Online. *Communications of the ACM*, *42*(4), 80–85. doi:10.1145/299157.299175

Hong, Y., & Pavlou, P. A. (2014). Product Fit Uncertainty in Online Markets: Nature, Effects, and Antecedents. *Information Systems Research*, *25*(2), 328–344. doi:10.1287/isre.2014.0520

Hsieh, J.-K., Hsieh, Y.-C., Chiu, H.-C., & Yang, Y.-R. (2014). Customer Response to Web Site Atmospherics: Task-Relevant Cues, Situational Involvement and Pad. *Journal of Interactive Marketing*, *28*(3), 225–236. doi:10.1016/j.intmar.2014.03.001

Hsieh, M., & Tsao, W. (2014). Reducing perceived online shopping risk to enhance loyalty: A website quality perspective. *Journal of Risk Research*, *17*(2), 241–261. doi:10.1080/13669877.2013.794152

Hsieh, M.-H., Pan, S.-L., & Setiono, R. (2004). Product-, Corporate-, and Country-Image Dimensions and Purchase Behavior: A Multicountry Analysis. *Journal of the Academy of Marketing Science*, *32*(3), 251–270. doi:10.1177/0092070304264262

Jesse James Garret. (2000). *The Elements of User Experience*. New Riders.

Khaled, H., & Head, M. (2007). Manipulating Perceived Social Presence Through the Web Interface and its Impact on Attitude Towards Online Shopping. *International Journal of Human-Computer Studies*, *65*(8), 689–708. doi:10.1016/j.ijhcs.2006.11.018

Kim, Dekker, & Heij. (2017). Cross-Border Electronic Commerce: Distance Effects And Express Delivery in European Union Markets. *International Journal of Electronic Commerce*, *21*(2), 184-218.

Kukar-Kinney, M., & Close, A. G. (2010). The Determinants of Consumers' Online Shopping Cart Abandonment. *Journal of the Academy of Marketing Science*, *38*(2), 240–250. doi:10.100711747-009-0141-5

Lemon, K. N., & Verhoef, P. C. (2016). Understanding Customer Experience Throughout the Customer Journey. *Journal of Marketing*, *80*(6), 69–96. doi:10.1509/jm.15.0420

Lim, W. M., & Ting, D. H. (2012). E-Shopping: An Analysis of the Uses and Gratifications Theory. *Modern Applied Science*, *6*(5). Advance online publication. doi:10.5539/mas.v6n5p48

Lin, X., Wang, X., & Hajli, N. (2019). Building ECommerce Satisfaction and Boosting Sales: The Role of Social Commerce Trust and Its Antecedents. *International Journal of Electronic Commerce*, *23*(3), 328–363. doi:10.1080/10864415.2019.1619907

Lu, Zhao, & Wang. (2010). From virtual community members to C2C e-commerce buyers: Trust in virtual communities and its effect on consumers' purchase intention, *Electronic Commerce Research and Applications*, *9*(4), 346-360.

Mainardes, E. W., Marcio de Almeida, C., & de-Oliveira, M. (2019). e-Commerce: An analysis of the factors that antecede purchase intentions in an emerging market. *Journal of International Consumer Marketing*, *31*(5), 447–468. doi:10.1080/08961530.2019.1605643

Mastercard. (n.d.). *MASTERINDEX 2017 Pan-European e-commerce and new payment trends.* https://newsroom.mastercard.com/wp-content/uploads/2017/03/Masterindex-2017.pdf

Merholz, P. (2007). *Peter in Conversation with Don Norman About UX & Innovation.* Adaptative Path.

Norman, D. (1988). *The Design of Everyday Things.* MIT Press.

Novak, T. P., Hoffman, D. L., & Yung, Y.-F. (2000). Measuring the Customer Experience in Online Environments: A Structural Modeling Approach. *Marketing Science*, *19*(1), 22–42. doi:10.1287/mksc.19.1.22.15184

Pavlou Paul, A., Liang, H., & Xue, Y. (2007). Understanding and Mitigating Uncertainty in Online Exchange Relationships: A Principal-Agent Perspective. *Management Information Systems Quarterly*, *31*(1), 105–136. doi:10.2307/25148783

PwC. Total Retail. (2017). *Ecommerce in China – the future is already here.* https://www.pwccn.com/en/retail-and-consumer/publications/total-retail-2017-china/total-retail-survey-2017-china-cut.pdf

Schlosser, A. E., White, T. B., & Lloyd, S. M. (2006). Converting Web Site Visitors into Buyers: How Web Site Investment Increases Consumer Trusting Beliefs and Online Purchase Intentions. *Journal of Marketing*, *70*(2), 133–148. doi:10.1509/jmkg.70.2.133

Schlosser Ann, E. (2003). Experiencing Products in the Virtual World: The Role of Goal and Imagery in Influencing Attitudes Versus Purchase Intentions. *The Journal of Consumer Research*, *30*(2), 184–198. doi:10.1086/376807

Schmitt, B. H. (1999). Experiential Marketing. *Journal of Marketing Management*, *15*(1-3), 53–67. doi:10.1362/026725799784870496

Statista. (n.d.). *Retail e-commerce sales worldwide from 2014 to 2023*. https://www.statista.com/statistics/379046/worldwide-retail-e-commerce-sales/

Steenkamp, J.-B. E. M., & Geyskens, I. (2006). How Country Characteristics Affect the Perceived Value of Web Sites. *Journal of Marketing*, *70*(3), 136–150. doi:10.1509/jmkg.70.3.136

Thongpapanl, N. T., Ashraf, A. R., Lapa, L., & Venkatesh, V. (2018). Differential effects of customers' regulatory fit on trust, perceived value, and m-commerce use among developing and developed countries. *Journal of International Marketing*, *26*(3), 22–44. doi:10.1509/jim.17.0129

Transparency International. (n.d.). *Corruption Perception Index*. https://www.transparency.org/en/cpi

Urban, G. L., Amyx, C., & Lorenzon, A. (2009). Online Trust: State of the Art, New Frontiers, and Research Potential. *Journal of Interactive Marketing*, *23*(2), 179–190. doi:10.1016/j.intmar.2009.03.001

Verhoef, P. C., Lemon, K. N., Parasuraman, A., Roggeveen, A., Tsiros, M., & Schlesinger, L. A. (2009). Customer Experience Creation: Determinants, Dynamics and Management Strategies. *Journal of Retailing*, *85*(1), 31–41. doi:10.1016/j.jretai.2008.11.001

Wang, C. L., He, J., & Barnes, B. R. (2017). Brand management and consumer experience in emerging markets: Directions for future research. *International Marketing Review*, *34*(4), 458–462. doi:10.1108/IMR-01-2016-0009

Weathers, D., Sharma, S., & Wood, S. L. (2007). Effects of Online Communication Practices on Consumer Perceptions of Performance Uncertainty for Search and Experience Goods. *Journal of Retailing*, *83*(4), 393–401. doi:10.1016/j.jretai.2007.03.009

Worldwide, A. C. I. (2020). *Global eCommerce Retail Sales Up 209 Percent in April*. https://www.aciworldwide.com/news-and-events/press-releases/2020/may/global-ecommerce-retail-sales-up-209-percent-in-april-aci-worldwide-research-reveals

Ye, Y., & Lau, K. H. (2018). Designing a demand chain management framework under dynamic uncertainty: An exploratory study of the Chinese fashion apparel industry. *Asia Pacific Journal of Marketing and Logistics*, *30*(2), 198–234. doi:10.1108/APJML-03-2017-0042

Ye, Y., Lau, K. H., & Leon, K. Y. T. (2018). Drivers and barriers of omnichannel retailing in China. A case study of the fashion and apparel industry. *International Journal of Retail & Distribution Management*, *46*(7), 657–689. doi:10.1108/IJRDM-04-2017-0062

Youngsoo, K., & Krishnan, R. (2015). On Product-Level Uncertainty and Online Purchase Behavior: An Empirical Analysis. *Management Science*, *61*(10), 2281–2547.

Zhu, W., Mou, J., & Benyoucef, M. (2019). Exploring purchase intention in cross-border E-commerce: A three stage model. *Journal of Retailing and Consumer Services*, *51*(C), 320–330. doi:10.1016/j.jretconser.2019.07.004

Chapter 19
Successful Implementation of Web 2.0 in Non-Profit Organisations:
A Case Study

Sara Pífano
Information Society Research Lab, Portugal

Pedro Isaias
University of New South Wales, Australia

Paula Miranda
ⓘ https://orcid.org/0000-0002-5327-1598
Setubal School of Technology, Polytechnic Institute of Setubal, Portugal

ABSTRACT

Non-profit organizations are becoming aware of the resourcefulness of Web 2.0 in terms of user engagement, communication, collaboration, and fundraising. Nonetheless, within the context of these organizations, the full potential of Web 2.0 technologies remains unrealized. This chapter explores the aspects that contribute to the successful implementation of Web 2.0 in non-profit organizations by using a case study of an international non-profit entity. The case study is based on an online questionnaire that was distributed among the members of the organization. The findings place an emphasis on the importance of the user-friendliness of the application, the participation of the users, on the availability of relevant content, and on the existence of features to create/exchange content in a multiplicity of formats.

DOI: 10.4018/978-1-7998-3756-5.ch019

INTRODUCTION

In a digital era, an organisation's lack of internet presence reflects poorly on its image, by transmitting the idea that it is not up-to-date, and results in a loss of potential users (Krueger & Haytko, 2015). As such, non-profit entities are gradually resorting to digital technologies to attain their objectives in terms of communication (Seo & Vu, 2020) .Social media can assist organisations to communicate and interact with their audience, to increase their stakeholders' involvement and to build a community based on their mission. In the particular case of non-profit organisations, social media can be used for the purpose of information collection, community creation, promotion and mobilisation (Yuan Wang & Yang, 2017).

Social technology can be used as a resource to promote an organisation's interaction with and engagement of stakeholders at the same time that it allows for communication opportunities that are fundamentally different from the traditional organisational websites (Lovejoy & Saxton, 2012). Web 2.0 can be used to enlarge the audience of non-profit entities and to appeal to new populations (Ingenhoff & Koelling, 2009). Being that interactivity is essential to support relationships online, organisations need to move beyond the conventional online donation requests and the interchange of email contacts, and present their events and activities to enable the engagement of people in online and offline environments (Waters, Burnett, Lamm, & Lucas, 2009). The management of an organisation's presence in social media requires time and effort which might prove difficult to entities with reduced dimension and resources and might result in a limited use (Young, 2017). Hence the need to examine the aspects that can assist these organisations to maximise the potential of Web 2.0 to its fullest extent. The contribution of the users plays a critical part in this aspect and it is important that organisations take into account the opinions of their users in terms of their preferences, interests and participation patterns, in order to better understand what will make their applications enhance the user experience. The identification of the core factors for the success of the Web 2.0 application enables a more positive and fruitful user experience and enhances the possibility of user participation, which is so vital for the propagation of the application.

This paper begins by examining the use of Web 2.0 in the context of non-profit organisations and reviewing existing best practices for the implementation of Web 2.0. It then proceeds to describe the methods that were used for the empirical research in the organisation, that for anonymity reasons will be designated as Entity Delta, and it concludes with the presentation and discussion of the findings of the online questionnaires.

WEB 2.0 IN NON-PROFIT ORGANISATIONS

Web 2.0's value in the business arena (Gagliardi, 2011; Isaías, Pífano, & Miranda, 2012; Li, He, & Zhang, 2020; Murugesan, 2007; Shuen, 2008; Yun Wang, Rod, Deng, & Ji, 2020; Wijaya, Spruit, Scheper, & Versendaal, 2011) is equally valid for non-profit organisations (Asencio & Sun, 2015; Dong & Rim, 2019; Kim, Jeong, & Lee, 2010; Lovejoy & Saxton, 2012; Sun & Asencio, 2019; Waters et al., 2009). The existence of several free social media platforms is particularly advantageous for entities that due to limited financial resources cannot invest in a significant technological infrastructure (Young, 2017). Social media is a free tool that can be harnesses for purposes of diffusion and well as broadcasting (McCabe & Harris, 2020). These online resources are, moreover, an important alternative to expensive offline marketing campaigns for fundraising (Nageswarakurukkal, Gonçalves, & Moshtari, 2019).

Introduced by O'Reilly (2007), Web 2.0 has been amply defined by numerous authors. Eikelmann et al. (2007) offer a definition that is both clear and concise: "The term "Web 2.0" describes online activities, sites, and applications that allow individuals to interact in online communities, directly exchange information with one another, and create their own content online."(p. 1). Hence, Web 2.0 is associated with tools such as social networks, blogs, forums, wikis and several other platforms and services that endow the users with the possibility to create their own content and exchange information in a multiplicity of formats. Within the non-profit sector Web 2.0 represents a twofold benefit: it can be used for service dissemination and relationship management (Kim et al., 2010). Additionally, the Social Web, as it is also known, has demonstrated great potential for the foment of two-way communication and as a stage for the engagement of internet users (Ingenhoff & Koelling, 2009). It goes beyond traditional websites that are mainly static, and provides organisations with the opportunity to engage in a dialogue (Young, 2017). Through social media, it is possible for non-profit entities to disseminate information to their users, which in turn can react to and share that information with their social networks' contacts (Appleby, 2016).

In a study where Waters et al. (2009) scrutinised the Facebook profile of 275 institution in the non-profit sector, it became evident that most of the organisations were using the tools that were available to them in a very limiting fashion. A significant finding of their study concerned the fact that in spite of having an extensive knowledge of the value of online social networking platforms, the organisations were incapable of fully engaging their users. Their participation was restricted to sharing external news' links, using photos and writing posts on their message boards (Waters et al., 2009). Ingenhoff and Koelling (2009), conducted a study on the employment of internet resources by 134 non-profit Swiss entities. In line with what Waters et al. (2009) established, the authors' study revealed that the majority of the non-profit organisations were employing Internet resources and Web 2.0 in a restrictive manner. Another study revealed that almost all of the non-profit organisations that the authors scrutinised had websites, but these were poorly equipped in terms of interactive features (Campbell & Lambright, 2019) .Most of the organisations are equally aware of the potential that Web 2.0 has of engaging the stakeholders and future donors, nonetheless they were unable to seize that potential. They did use the internet efficiently with concern to information requirements, however in terms of Web 2.0, the organisations were completely marginal to the employment of the social tools that were available, like chat rooms and message boards, as means to form relationships with their stakeholders. Furthermore, when it comes to media relations, their websites failed to appropriately market them (Ingenhoff & Koelling, 2009).

In another study Lovejoy and Saxton (2012) examined how the 100 largest non-profit organisations in the USA were using Twitter and they found that microblogging can be resourceful with concern to providing information, building a community and eliciting action. They postulated that non-profit entities are growingly interacting with Web 2.0 and making an investment on that engagement at a superior level, in comparison to their conventional websites. With regards to the use of Twitter itself, the authors concluded that even though a small part of the organisations were fully benefiting from the advantages of Twitter, the majority of these organisations were still "missing the bigger picture of its uses as a community building and mobilization tool... [and] not using Twitter to its full capacity as a stakeholder-engagement channel" (Lovejoy & Saxton, 2012, p. 351). In addition, a study featuring the use of Twitter in both for-profit and non-profit entities concluded that while the first privilege the dialogic loop precept, non-profit organizations tend to concentrate on the usefulness of information and in keeping their visitors (Yuan Wang & Yang, 2020).

The use of Web 2.0 technologies by non-profit entities can have a positive impact on their performance. It argued that organisations that have a more significant presence online and in social media can gather more contributions and funds to attain their mission (Shin, 2019). Despite the fact that Web 2.0 has resulted in unprecedented opportunities for non-profit organisations, it is equally a platform affected by information overflow. The amount of information and users on social media, sometimes hinder the capacity that non-profit entities have to voice their missions. Hence, "understanding what makes for successful communication in this arena is thus important." (Guo & Saxton, 2018, p. 23).

SUCCESSFUL IMPLEMENTATION OF WEB 2.0

Web 2.0 represents the access to a formerly untapped audience. Social media has billions of worldwide users, so it is crucial for non-profit organisations to successfully master its use (Appleby, 2016). While there is a panoply of individuals and institutions exploring its public relations value, it is important to understand that merely ensuring a presence in Web 2.0 websites will not per se improve awareness and educe user participation (Waters et al., 2009). There is a need for non-profit organisations to develop a strategy for the employment of social media (Young, 2017).

This research uses the work of Isaías, Miranda, and Pífano (2009), who developed a framework for the success of Web 2.0, as a guide to structure Entity Delta's Web 2.0 application. The authors postulated that the success of Web 2.0 applications can be determined by seven core factors: 1) Users' inputs – concerns the fundamental role of the user's participation; 2) Users' critical mass figures – regards the significance of achieving a critical mass of users; 3) Ease of use of component – refers to the need for user friendly applications; 4) Availability of content to justify users' access – stands for the importance of having content available on the application; 5) User content addition features – concerns the need for the inclusion of features to create content in multiple formats (text, audio, image, video); 6) User content development tools – refers to the deployment of technology that facilitates the creation of content by users, like dynamic programming languages; 7) Revenue models – regards the importance of selecting an appropriate revenue model (Isaías et al., 2009). The reason for using this framework pertains to the fact that it employs Web 2.0's core features to foment its success. In the context of this study three of the factors of this framework were disregarded. Entity Delta does not wish to build a new Web 2.0 application, but rather to incorporate an existing one. As such the user content development tools factor, which concerns the technology behind the application and is more relevant for designers, was not considered. Also, since the application will be offered for free, revenue models were also disregarded. Finally, the number of Entity Delta's active members cannot be considered enough to create critical mass, so this aspect was equally omitted. Hence, for the purpose of this study, it is relevant to examine these core four factors: users' inputs, ease of use of component, availability of content to justify users' access and user content addition features.

In terms of users' input, when using social media, non-profit organisations must provide users with the opportunity to participate and encourage them to share that participation with their contacts to create a growing network of people (Appleby, 2016). To promote the input of users, organisations must not only post content to initiate conversation, but equally to maintain and reacting to existing ones (Cole, 2014). The key role of the participation of the users has equally been supported by previous studies (Chen, Yen, & Hwang, 2012; Constantinides & Fountain, 2008; Yang, Hsu, & Tan, 2010).

The ease of use of the application is key to its success. People are more receptive to innovation is it is intuitive and easy to use and that don't present any complexity (Young, 2017). Organisations should choose interfaces that are intelligible (Moreno, Navarro, Tench, & Zerfass, 2015), since the uptake of communication tools is swifter of their have a user-friendly nature (Stewart, Procter, Williams, & Poschen, 2013).

With respect to content, the online marketing strategy that non-profit organisations employ needs to include content that appeals to the user and compels them to act (Krueger & Haytko, 2015). Web 2.0 demands a user-centred approach and as such, a crucial element for an organisation success with it is to know its intended audience, to know the users and the type of content that will interest them (Appleby, 2016). In light of the amount of competing organisations and information sources, the content that is posted should add value and concentrate on the users' interests (Cole, 2014).

It is equally valuable for this content to assume a variety of forms, such as posts, tweets, articles (Krueger & Haytko, 2015) and for it to be offered to the users on a regular basis (Appleby, 2016). Also, non-profit entities are not maximising the potential of their websites. It is important to include in their websites, links to their profiles in social media, in order to generate engagement (Young, 2017). The impact that visual communication is greater than the use of text, so it is advisable to use images infographics and other visual supports to deliver content to the users (Appleby, 2016). Moreover, the organisations should encourage the users to generate content themselves (Cole, 2014).

Besides the abovementioned core factors, prior to initiating any activity in social media, it is important for organisations to define the objectives that they aim to achieve with the use of social media. These objectives should be specific to this type of communication and to the organisation's mission. Also, another key aspect is the selection of what social media tools to use. The tools should be chosen according to the objectives of the organisation (Cole, 2014). There are several tools and platforms that can be used in the context of non-profit organisations. Facebook can be used for information dissemination, for community building and for user engagement (Krueger & Haytko, 2015). Twitter is a free platform, which is particularly advantageous for non-profit entities and represents a valuable alternative to other less financially effective promotional services. Also, since people can react to the posts by retweeting and signalling as favourite, it is possible for an organisation to assess the posts that are more appealing to their audience (Yuan Wang & Yang, 2017). Youtube is also a valuable tool for digital marketing, as it can help non-profit entities to build their public image, it includes live streaming features and it can be used as an informative channel (Krueger & Haytko, 2015). Forums, are used to promote communication between users, usually around a specific subject. They have the advantage of being organised into thread, which facilitates the division of the information into topics (Cole, 2014). With respect to blogs, although other users can often interact with post on blogs (Alkhateeb, Clauson, Khanfar, & Latif, 2008), they mainly assume the shape of online journals (Constantinides & Fountain, 2008). They are regarded as being more suitable for one-way communication, since they do not provide the users with the possibility of a high degree of feedback nor with back-and-forth sharing (Go & You, 2016). Wikis can be regarded as public or private workspaces for the collaborative creation or edition of content in documents, webpages or other formats, in an ongoing fashion (Cole, 2014).

Given the very nature of Web 2.0, the user assumes a critical role in any Web 2.0 application or technology. Users are valuable to any website, but within the context of Web 2.0 they assume an even more central part, since they create, edit and share content and with their participation enrich the application. Hence, it is fundamental, for a Web 2.0 application to thrive, that users have a positive experience. Web 2.0 applications "literally get better the more people use them, harnessing network effects not only to acquire users, but also to learn from them and build on their contributions." (O'Reilly & Battelle, 2009, p. 1). The consultation of the users before the creation of the Web 2.0 application is in line with an attempt to involve the all the stakeholders in participatory design. Unlike, the conventional user-centred design, participatory design, engages the users directly (Vandekerckhove, de Mul, Bramer, & de Bont, 2020). Participatory design is inclusive of the end user in the design process and, as such, it is more receptive to accounting to user experience (Rosenzweig, 2015). The development of an ideal Web 2.0 application needs to be guided by several principles not only usability. User experience goes beyond the notion of usability and includes a wide assortment of users' perceptions when they use a service (Saavedra, Rusu, Quiñones, & Roncagliolo, 2019). Enhancing user experience is essential in the context of Web 2.0. A positive user experience translates into user satisfaction and given the diverse parameters to assess user experience (Mistry, Rajan, & Arokia, 2019) it is paramount to understand which parameters or factors are favoured by the users of Entity Delta.

METHODOLOGY

The empirical research for this paper consisted in the administration of an online questionnaire intended to collect the opinion of Entity Delta's members about Web 2.0 applications. The main goal of the questionnaire was to assist this entity to create an application that would suit its users. The use of online questionnaire is beneficial at a variety of levels, it is associated with lower costs, increased geographical reach and more accurate data input (Denscombe, 2009). Entity Delta is an international association, non-profit, with a focus on research and conference organisation in the area of the Information Society. Entity Delta was selected by a sample of convenience. This type of sampling selects subjects that can be more easily accessed (Kelley, Clark, Brown, & Sitzia, 2003). At the time of this research Entity Delta was releasing its new Portal and it wished to incorporate a Web 2.0 application to foster the interaction among its members. The participants were selected via random sampling, from a population of 18,930, which was the total of people who had ever registered for a conference with Entity Delta, since 2001, the year of its creation. From this number an ideal random sample of 582 individuals was calculated, by applying a 4% error margin and a 95% confidence interval. Assuming a 20% completion rate, the questionnaire was distributed by email to 2910 people. Random sampling is more representative and it allows for a generalisation to a wider population (Creswell, 2008). The questionnaire had 28 questions that were designed to evaluate the relationship that the members had with Entity Delta and its various web resources; to understand their common patterns of use of Web 2.0 and to probe the respondents' viewpoints about the development of a future Web 2.0 component for Entity Delta's portal. This instrument of data collection was critical to this study in the sense that it enabled the organisation's members to voice their opinions about a technology that was being design and implemented for their use and benefit. The participation via an anonymous and safe environment allowed them to express their views openly and contribute as co-creators of the application. The questionnaire was validated prior to its final distribution by a pilot questionnaire conducted with 15 people, who enabled a more perfected version of the questionnaire, by identifying some of its limitations.

RESULTS

In total, the online questionnaire had 255 valid responses. In order to understand the familiarity of the respondents with Entity Delta, the first aspects of the profile of the respondents concern their relation with Entity Delta. While 11.1% of the respondents stated that they have been interacting with the organisation for less than 6 months and 7.1% for 6 months, most of them report a longer relation: 1-2 years, 39.1%; 3-5 years, 32%; 6-8 Years, 10.7%. This indicates the suitability of the sample with respect to their knowledge and familiarity of Entity Delta's context.

Experience With Web 2.0 Websites

Before implementing a Web 2.0 application, it was important to assess the members' own usage of these applications. The results show that an expressive majority of the participants (92%) do use Web 2.0. From the respondents that stated to use Web 2.0, 54.2% indicated that they had been using Web 2.0 for over 3 years, 40.9% said that they use it 3 times a day or more and 50.3% of them characterised their participation as being active. For the purpose of including a Web 2.0 application on Entity Delta's portal it was pertinent to assess the participants' motivations to use Web 2.0. When asked about the main reasons behind their use of Web 2.0 the respondents were asked to limit their answers to three options to identify solely the most important reasons (Table 1).

Table 1. Reasons behind Web 2.0 websites' use

Reasons for using Web 2.0 websites	Percentage
Research	72.7%
Staying updated on news	50.2%
To stay informed about new events	49.8%
Staying in contact with friends	46.3%
Business networking	31.7%
To reach people you're not normally in contact with	27.8%
Sharing your thoughts	25.4%
For entertainment (games, funny applications, etc)	13.7%
To feel connected with people	12.2%
To meet new people	9.3%
For recruitment	5.4%
Other	2.4%

Their main choices included research (72.7%), staying updated on news (50.2%), to stay informed about new events (49.8%) and staying in contact with friends (46.3%). With regards to the content of Web 2.0 websites, in general, Entity Delta's members said that they rather see informative content (96.6%), despite the fact that a substantial fraction of the sample (40.7%) stated that they like to see entertaining content. In terms of the Web 2.0 sites that the respondents use more often, Google leads the list with

87.7%, followed by Wikipedia (75.9%), YouTube (69%), Facebook (58.6%) and LinkedIn (42.9%). Twitter, where Entity Delta also has a page was selected only by 27.6% of the respondents. With concern to the tools that the sample used in Web 2.0 sites downloads (56.3%), photos (49.2%), video (45.7%), file sharing (42.2%) and profile information (41.7%) were selected as being the ones used more often. The participants were also asked to specify the reasons they used certain Web 2.0 platforms (Figure 1).

Figure 1. Reasons for using specific Web 2.0 websites

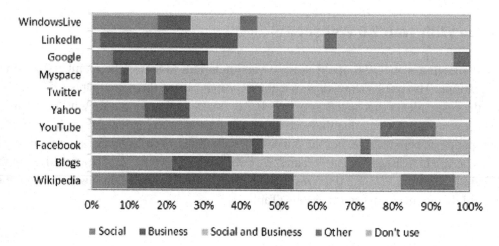

The figure highlights the predominant use of Facebook for social reasons, with 37.5% of the responses, followed by YouTube (31.7%) and Blogs (18.3%). For business reasons, Wikipedia was at the lead with 40.4% of the responses, followed by LinkedIn (30.8%) and Google (23.6%). Google was the website that had the highest score in terms of respondents who claimed to use it for both social and business reasons (60.1%). Myspace (61.1%), WindowsLive (42.8%) and Twitter (42.3%) were the websites that registered a higher percentage of non-users.

Online Engagement With Entity Delta

When the questionnaire was distributed, Entity Delta used four online communication channels: Entity Delta's website, each conferences websites (circa 20), Twitter and Facebook. The conferences' websites were the resource that the respondents stated to use more often with 59.1% vs. only 36.9% of people using Entity Delta's website. This lack of access to the Entity Delta's central website is partly the reason why a Web 2.0 application is necessary. There is a tendency to visit a particular conference website rather than using the main website, which leads to a decentralisation of the services and conduces the members to be more focused on the conference itself than on the organisation and the information about all the different conferences it organises.

In terms of Entity Delta's social media presence, the respondents were asked if they would use Entity Delta' Facebook and Twitter pages (Figure 2).

Figure 2. Facebook and Twitter actual and intended use

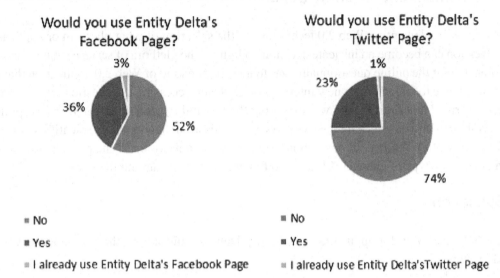

Only 2.7% of the participants stated that they already use its Facebook page, 36% said that they would use it, but most of the participants indicated that they would not use it (52.4%). With regards to Twitter, only 1.3% of the sample was already using it and the cleavage between the respondents that would use it and those who would not was even more substantial: 21.3% of the respondents said that they would use it, but 68% said they would not use it. The difference between Facebook and Twitter might be the reflection of their differing levels of popularity. In a previous question, 58.6% of the respondents had selected Facebook as one of the websites that they use more often, while only 27.6% selected Twitter. As can be seen in figure 1, although Facebook was selected by 22,6% of the participants as being for both social and business reasons, 37.5% selected it exclusively for social purposes and only 2.4% selected it exclusively for business. The same happened with Twitter, despite with more reduced percentages. With regards to Entity Delta's possible existence in other Web 2.0 services, 34.2% stated that they did not know, 31.6% said it should be present in other websites, such as LinkedIn, Google and YouTube, and 24.4% believed that it should not have an account in other websites.

The participants who were open to a potential use of Facebook and Twitter were asked to select the content that they would prefer to see on these platforms. For Facebook, their main choices included: call for papers for papers (78.6%), information on prospective conferences (73.8%), news pertaining to the information society (70.2%) and reminders related to call for papers deadlines (58.3%). With regards to Twitter, they selected: call for papers (69.4%), reminders for deadlines of the call for papers (55.1%), research projects and project proposals and partners (51%), news regarding technological innovations (46.9%) and new related to the information society (46.9%).

In terms of the format of the content, the participants' choices for both Facebook and Twitter were quite similar: Text (92% for both Facebook and Twitter), photos (64.4% for Facebook and 44%for Twitter) and video (50.6% for Facebook 34% for Twitter).

A Web 2.0 Component for Entity Delta's

The first stage of implementing Web 2.0 technology is the selection of what platform or application to use. This decision can become an intricate decision, in light of the plethora of services that are available. The key objective of the online questionnaire was to identify the kind of Web 2.0 application that Entity Delta should choose to include in its new internet portal. When accessing the questionnaire, the respondents were informed that Entity Delta was exploring the possibility of including a Web 2.0 application on their portal in order to enhance interactivity. As an organisation that organises scientific conferences, networking is essential. While communication between the organisation and the participants can be assured via email, this type of channel is limited to foment interaction among the members.

The Application

With regards to the Web 2.0 application that Entity Delta should adopt, the participants' views are portrayed in Figure 3.

Figure 3. Web 2.0 application preferences

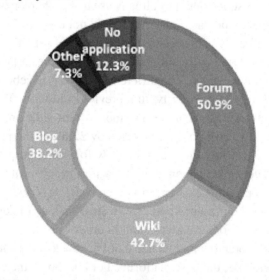

The majority of the sample selected a forum (50.9%), a wiki was chosen by 42.7% and a blog by 38.2%. The participants who did not agree with the adoption of a Web 2.0 application (12.3%) were excluded from further questions concerning the features of the application, while the remaining respondents were asked to provide more detail, namely in terms what should be its most important characteristics (Table 2).

An unequivocal majority (88.5) of the participants selected ease of use as one of the most important features. The participants equally underlined the significance of having regularly updated content (56.8%), confirming the relevance of content. Content was also central in other choices of the participants: possibility of subscribing updates (37.5%), information society related content (31.3%), variety of features to add content (30.7%) and moderation features to prevent abusive content (26.6%). Interaction among users was third on this table (52.6%), reiterating the significance of other users' contributions, which had

Table 2. Future application's most important characteristics

Most important characteristics	Percentage
Easy to use	88.5%
Content regularly updated	56.8%
Allow interaction with other users	52.6%
Possibility of subscribing updates	37.5%
Information society related content	31.3%
Variety of features to add content (photo, video, text, etc.)	30.7%
Attractive design	28.6%
Moderation features to prevent abusive content	26.6%
Uncluttered design	25.5%
Safe	24.5%
Clear Help options	23.4%
Advanced privacy settings	19.8%
Other	1.6%

already been made clear by table 1, portraying the participants' motivations for using Web 2.0 websites: staying in contact with friends (46.3%), business networking (31.7%) and to reach people you're not normally in contact with (27.8%). As such, in order to successfully implement their Web 2.0 application, it is fundamental that Entity Delta foments user participation.

An important aspect of access to the application is the need for registration, so it was relevant to understand the participants' views in this subject. The majority of the respondents expressed their preference for an access that is protected by a password (56.1%), against 38.4% that did not wish to register to access the application.

Following the list of main characteristics, it was important to establish the type of content that would be more relevant according to the participants. Entity Delta's type of organisation endows it with a more informative nature. In terms of content that the participants want to see in the new portal, the majority of the participants selected call for papers information (82.7%), forthcoming conferences (69.1%), reminders of call for papers deadlines (68.1%) and resources on how to prepare and write research papers (58.6%). All the items that were listed in this question (select all that apply multiple choice) had a high score, with the lowest score being 30.4% for information regarding tourism about the hosting countries. With concern with the tools that should be available in the portal, most of the respondents (64.2%) preferred downloads, 48.4 selected photos, file sharing was chosen by 46.8% and search features by 44.7%.

DISCUSSION

Similarly to what the existing literature portrays about non-profit organisations, Entity Delta is using Web 2.0 resources scarcely. The online questionnaire was a useful tool in the identification of Entity Delta's members. As advised in the literature, it is important to know the audience to maximise a successful engagement with Web 2.0. It offered a deeper insight into their preferences with relation to Web 2.0 platforms and it assessed their openness to engaging with Entity Delta in such platforms.

The majority of the sample was already using Web 2.0 websites frequently and for over 3 years and characterised its participation as being active. The claimed to use Web 2.0 websites mainly for research purposes, staying updated on news and new events and for staying in contact with friends. They showed a preference for informative content and as stated in the literature they used different types of content in multiple formats, such as photos, videos and profile information. It also became clear that they use some sites specifically for business, some for social reasons and others they use both in business and socially. Google, Wikipedia, YouTube, Facebook and LinkedIn were the sites that the respondents used more often.

In terms of their engagement with Entity Delta on online channels, the respondents mostly use each of the conferences' websites rather than the main website and the majority stated that they would not use Entity Delta's Twitter or Facebook account. It is important to account for the fact that Entity Delta's presence on both websites was recent and not very active. Another factor that might impact these choices is the fact that some Web 2.0 platforms are used for specific purposes.

With concern to the Web 2.0 application that Entity should integrate in its portal, most respondents selected a forum. Although a wiki or a blog were also popular choices among the participants they would be very limiting to fomenting discussion. The features of a forum, make this application the most adequate to accomplish Entity Delta's objective of promoting discussion and interactivity among the users. They allow all users to initiate and respond to discussion threads and to exchange information and ideas. The characteristics of the prospective application that the sample considered to be most important were, in order, ease of use, having regularly updated content, interaction with other users, possibility of subscribing updates, information society related content, and variety of features to add content. Their preferences of content for the application were call for papers information, forthcoming conferences, reminders of call for papers deadlines and resources on how to prepare and write research papers. In terms of tools they preferred downloads, photos, file sharing and search features.

In brief, in order for Entity Delta to successfully implement a Web 2.0 application it must choose an application that is easy to use, the content must be regularly updated, it must encourage the participation of users and there should be a variety of features to add content in multiple formats. Defining these essential factors or parameters, maximises the possibilities for a more positive and constructive user experience and increases the possibility of user participation, which is so fundamental for the proliferation of the application.

CONCLUSION

The main reasons to resort to social media are the promotion of the organisation and their services, engagement of the community, communication and collaboration (Young, 2017). Entity Delta, as many other non-profit entities, has yet to benefit from the full potential of Web 2.0.

The most significant contribution of this paper is the outline of guiding strategies for the implementation of Web 2.0 applications and the emphasis that it places on the user's role in determining their success. The respondents highlighted the importance of the ease of use of the application, the participation of the users, the availability of relevant content and the existence of features to create/exchange content in a multiplicity of formats. Their opinions were coherent with previous studies and help to establish guidelines for successfully implementing Web 2.0 application in non-profit organisations.

With concern to this paper's limitations, they relate to the size of the sample, which could have been bigger to provide a more complete depiction of what the members' preferences were, and the impossibility of testing Entity Delta's Web 2.0 application. Further research should focus on implementing the Web 2.0 application with the features and conditions that the respondents specified, to provide additional validation of the guidelines that were outlined. Also, future research ventures can resort to the use of in-depth inquiry, namely interviews to provide further insight into the reasons why people use Web 2.0 applications and how these can be used in multiple sectors of society.

REFERENCES

Alkhateeb, F. M., Clauson, K. A., Khanfar, N. M., & Latif, D. A. (2008). Legal and regulatory risk associated with Web 2.0 adoption by pharmaceutical companies. *Journal of Medical Marketing*, *8*(4), 311–318. doi:10.1057/jmm.2008.20

Appleby, M. (2016). Nonprofit Organizations and the Utilization of Social Media: Maximizing and Measuring Return of Investment. *SPNHA Review*, *12*(1), 4.

Asencio, H., & Sun, R. (2015). Introduction. In H. Asencio & R. Sun (Eds.), *Cases on Strategic Social Media Utilization in the Nonprofit Sector*. IGI Global. doi:10.4018/978-1-4666-8188-0

Campbell, D. A., & Lambright, K. T. (2019). Are You Out There? Internet Presence of Nonprofit Human Service Organizations. *Nonprofit and Voluntary Sector Quarterly*, *48*(6), 1296–1311. doi:10.1177/0899764019852673

Chen, S.-C., Yen, D. C., & Hwang, M. I. (2012). Factors influencing the continuance intention to the usage of Web 2.0: An empirical study. *Computers in Human Behavior*, *28*(3), 933–941. doi:10.1016/j.chb.2011.12.014

Cole, C. (2014). Social Media Best Practices for Nonprofit Organizations: A Guide. *Canadian Coalition for Global Health Research*. Available from: https://www.ccghr.ca/wp-content/uploads/2014/2006/CCGHR-Social-Media-Modules_Complete.pdf

Constantinides, E., & Fountain, S. J. (2008). Web 2.0: Conceptual foundations and marketing issues. *Journal of Direct, Data and Digital Marketing Practice*, *9*(3), 231–244. doi:10.1057/palgrave.dddmp.4350098

Creswell, J. W. (2008). *Research design: Qualitative, quantitative, and mixed methods approaches* (2nd ed.). Sage.

Denscombe, M. (2009). Item non-response rates: A comparison of online and paper questionnaires. *International Journal of Social Research Methodology*, *12*(4), 281–291. doi:10.1080/13645570802054706

Dong, C., & Rim, H. (2019). Exploring nonprofit-business partnerships on Twitter from a network perspective. *Public Relations Review*, *45*(1), 104–118. doi:10.1016/j.pubrev.2018.11.001

Eikelmann, S., Hajj, J., Hasbani, G., Marsch, C., Peterson, M., & Sabbagh, K. (2007). *The Urgent Need for Companies to Adapt to Web 2.0: New Models of Online Consumer Behavior Demand Changes in Corporate Strategy*. Booz Allen Hamilton.

Gagliardi, D. (2011). Next Generation Entrepreneur: How Web 2.0 Technologies Creep into SMEs. In P. Cunningham & M. Cunningham (Eds.), *eChallenges e-2011 Conference Proceedings*. Dublin, Ireland: IIMC International Information Management Corporation Ltd.

Go, E., & You, K. H. (2016). But not all social media are the same: Analyzing organizations' social media usage patterns. *Telematics and Informatics*, *33*(1), 176–186. doi:10.1016/j.tele.2015.06.016

Guo, C., & Saxton, G. D. (2018). Speaking and being heard: How nonprofit advocacy organizations gain attention on social media. *Nonprofit and Voluntary Sector Quarterly*, *47*(1), 5–26. doi:10.1177/0899764017713724

Ingenhoff, D., & Koelling, A. M. (2009). The potential of Web sites as a relationship building tool for charitable fundraising NPOs. *Public Relations Review*, *35*(1), 66–73. doi:10.1016/j.pubrev.2008.09.023

Isaías, P., Miranda, P., & Pífano, S. (2009). Critical success factors for web 2.0–A reference framework. In A. A. Ozok & P. Zaphiris (Eds.), *Online Communities and Social Computing* (pp. 354–363). Springer. doi:10.1007/978-3-642-02774-1_39

Isaías, P., Pífano, S., & Miranda, P. (2012). Social Network Sites: Modeling the New Business-Customer Relationship. In M. Safar & K. Mahdi (Eds.), *Social Networking and Community Behavior Modeling: Qualitative and Quantitative Measures* (pp. 248–265). IGI Global. doi:10.4018/978-1-61350-444-4.ch014

Kelley, K., Clark, B., Brown, V., & Sitzia, J. (2003). Good practice in the conduct and reporting of survey research. *International Journal for Quality in Health Care*, *15*(3), 261–266. doi:10.1093/intqhc/mzg031 PMID:12803354

Kim, W., Jeong, O.-R., & Lee, S.-W. (2010). On social Web sites. *Information Systems*, *35*(2), 215–236. doi:10.1016/j.is.2009.08.003

Krueger, J. C., & Haytko, D. L. (2015). Nonprofit adaptation to Web 2.0 and digital marketing strategies. *Journal of Technology Research*, *6*, 1.

Li, X., He, X., & Zhang, Y. (2020). The impact of social media on the business performance of small firms in China. *Information Technology for Development*, *26*(2), 346–368. doi:10.1080/02681102.2019.1594661

Lovejoy, K., & Saxton, G. D. (2012). Information, community, and action: How nonprofit organizations use social media*. *Journal of Computer-Mediated Communication*, *17*(3), 337–353. doi:10.1111/j.1083-6101.2012.01576.x

McCabe, A., & Harris, K. (2020). Theorizing social media and activism: Where is community development? *Community Development Journal: An International Forum*, bsz024. Advance online publication. doi:10.1093/cdj/bsz024

Mistry, A., Rajan, P., & Arokia, R. (2019). Evaluation of web applications based on UX parameters. *International Journal of Electrical & Computer Engineering, 9*.

Moreno, A., Navarro, C., Tench, R., & Zerfass, A. (2015). Does social media usage matter? An analysis of online practices and digital media perceptions of communication practitioners in Europe. *Public Relations Review*, *41*(2), 242–253. doi:10.1016/j.pubrev.2014.12.006

Murugesan, S. (2007). Understanding Web 2.0. *IT Professional, 9*(4), 34–41. doi:10.1109/MITP.2007.78

Nageswarakurukkal, K., Gonçalves, P., & Moshtari, M. (2019). Improving Fundraising Efficiency in Small and Medium Sized Non-profit Organizations Using Online Solutions. *Journal of Nonprofit & Public Sector Marketing*, 1–26. doi:10.1080/10495142.2019.1589627

O'Reilly, T. (2007). What is web 2.0, design patterns and business models for the next generation of software. *Communications & Stratégies, 65*, 17–37.

O'Reilly, T., & Battelle, J. (2009). *Web squared: Web 2.0 five years on. Special Report*. O'Reilly Media, Inc.

Rosenzweig, E. (2015). UX Thinking. In E. Rosenzweig (Ed.), *Successful User Experience: Strategies and Roadmaps* (pp. 41–67). Morgan Kaufmann. doi:10.1016/B978-0-12-800985-7.00003-X

Saavedra, M.-J., Rusu, C., Quiñones, D., & Roncagliolo, S. (2019). *A Set of Usability and User eXperience Heuristics for Social Networks*. Paper presented at the International Conference on Human-Computer Interaction. 10.1007/978-3-030-21902-4_10

Seo, H., & Vu, H. T. (2020). Transnational Nonprofits' Social Media Use: A Survey of Communications Professionals and an Analysis of Organizational Characteristics. *Nonprofit and Voluntary Sector Quarterly*, (4), 849–870. Advance online publication. doi:10.1177/0899764020908340

Shin, N. (2019). The Impact of the Web and Social Media on the Performance of Nonprofit Organizations. *Journal of International Technology and Information Management, 27*(4), 17–35.

Shuen, A. (2008). *Web 2.0: A Strategy Guide: Business thinking and strategies behind successful Web 2.0 implementations* (1st ed.). O'Reilly Media, Inc.

Stewart, J., Procter, R., Williams, R., & Poschen, M. (2013). The role of academic publishers in shaping the development of Web 2.0 services for scholarly communication. *New Media & Society, 15*(3), 413-432.

Sun, R., & Asencio, H. D. (2019). Using Social Media to Increase Nonprofit Organizational Capacity. *International Journal of Public Administration, 42*(5), 392–404. doi:10.1080/01900692.2018.1465955

Vandekerckhove, P., de Mul, M., Bramer, W. M., & de Bont, A. A. (2020). Generative Participatory Design Methodology to Develop Electronic Health Interventions: Systematic Literature Review. *Journal of Medical Internet Research, 22*(4), e13780. doi:10.2196/13780 PMID:32338617

Wang, Y., Rod, M., Deng, Q., & Ji, S. (2020). Exploiting business networks in the age of social media: The use and integration of social media analytics in B2B marketing. *Journal of Business and Industrial Marketing*. Advance online publication. doi:10.1108/JBIM-05-2019-0173

Wang, Y., & Yang, Y. (2017). How do Organizations Use Social Media to Build Dialogic Relationships? A Comparison between Nonprofit and For-profit Organizations. In B. R. Yook, Y. G. Ji & Z. F. Chen (Eds.), *Proceedings of the 20th International Public Relations Research Conference - "Looking Back, Looking Forward: 20 Years of Developing Theory & Practice"* (pp. 390-401). Academic Press.

Wang, Y., & Yang, Y. (2020). Dialogic communication on social media: How organizations use Twitter to build dialogic relationships with their publics. *Computers in Human Behavior*, *104*, 106183. doi:10.1016/j.chb.2019.106183

Waters, R. D., Burnett, E., Lamm, A., & Lucas, J. (2009). Engaging stakeholders through social networking: How nonprofit organizations are using Facebook. *Public Relations Review*, *35*(2), 102–106. doi:10.1016/j.pubrev.2009.01.006

Wijaya, S., Spruit, M., Scheper, W., & Versendaal, J. (2011). Web 2.0-based webstrategies for three different types of organizations. *Computers in Human Behavior*, *27*(4), 1399–1407. doi:10.1016/j. chb.2010.07.041

Yang, C., Hsu, Y.-C., & Tan, S. (2010). Predicting the determinants of users' intentions for using YouTube to share video: Moderating gender effects. *Cyberpsychology, Behavior, and Social Networking*, *13*(2), 141–152. doi:10.1089/cyber.2009.0105 PMID:20528269

Young, J. A. (2017). Facebook, Twitter, and blogs: The adoption and utilization of social media in nonprofit human service organizations. *Human Service Organizations, Management, Leadership & Governance*, *41*(1), 44–57. doi:10.1080/23303131.2016.1192574

ADDITIONAL READING

Blank, G., & Reisdorf, B. C. (2012). The participatory web: A user perspective on Web 2.0. *Information Communication and Society*, *15*(4), 537–554. doi:10.1080/1369118X.2012.665935

Brengarth, L. B., & Mujkic, E. (2016). WEB 2.0: How social media applications leverage nonprofit responses during a wildfire crisis. *Computers in Human Behavior*, *54*, 589–596. doi:10.1016/j.chb.2015.07.010

Edwards, H. R., & Hoefer, R. (2010). Are social work advocacy groups using Web 2.0 effectively? *Journal of Policy Practice*, *9*(3-4), 220–239. doi:10.1080/15588742.2010.489037

Greenleaf, J. (2016). Nonprofit use of social media: Insights from the field. *Global Journal of Community Psychology Practice*, *7*(3), 1–16. doi:10.7728/0703201603

Haddar, E., & Belkhir, M. (2018, May). The Practices of Nonprofit Organizations in the New Age of Social Media: A Qualitative Study of Donors' Receptiveness. In *International Conference on Digital Economy* (pp. 48-63). Springer. 10.1007/978-3-319-97749-2_4

Lee, R. L., & Blouin, M. C. (2019). Factors affecting web disclosure adoption in the nonprofit sector. *Journal of Computer Information Systems*, *59*(4), 363–372. doi:10.1080/08874417.2017.1370988

Song, F. W. (2010). Theorizing web 2.0: A cultural perspective. *Information Communication and Society*, *13*(2), 249–275. doi:10.1080/13691180902914610

Steiss, A. W. (2019). *Strategic management for public and nonprofit organizations*. Routledge. doi:10.4324/9781482275865

Vedel, I., Ramaprasad, J., & Lapointe, L. (2020). Social Media Strategies for Health Promotion by Nonprofit Organizations: Multiple Case Study Design. *Journal of Medical Internet Research*, *22*(4), e15586. doi:10.2196/15586 PMID:32250282

Williams, B. D., Valero, J. N., & Kim, K. (2018). Social media, trust, and disaster: Does trust in public and nonprofit organizations explain social media use during a disaster? *Quality & Quantity*, *52*(2), 537–550. doi:10.100711135-017-0594-4

KEY TERMS AND DEFINITIONS

Non-Profit Organisations: Entities that do not operate for profit and that are usually centred around a shared interest or cause. They are diverse in nature and can include research, scientific, educational, environmental, religious organisations.

Public Relations: Set of practices and precepts that are used to promote a positive public image by an organisation, with a focus on the relationship with its public.

Social Media: Stems from Web 2.0's principles and a new generation of participatory and editable media, where users can generate and share their own content online.

Social Media Strategy: Set of plans and principles that guide an entity's social media presence and shapes their contribution. It includes all the strategies used by a company to achieve its goals in social media websites and assert its identity.

User Engagement: It refers to the participation of the users on a specify website and all their contributions (downloads, uploads, clicks, shares) in various formats.

User-Centred Applications: It defines applications that are specifically designed to focus on the users, their needs, and how and why they use these applications.

Web 2.0: It is also known as the Read Write Web or Social Web and it is used to describe the second generation of web platforms that empower the everyday user, not just the experts, to create, publish and share content online. It includes, for example, social networks, blogs, wikis, and forums.

Compilation of References

Abdous, M. (2019). Influence of satisfaction and preparedness on online students' feelings of anxiety. *The Internet and Higher Education, 41*, 34–44. doi:10.1016/j.iheduc.2019.01.001

Abramovich, G. (2018). *People Buy Experiences, Not Products.* https://www.cmo.com/features/articles/2018/3/27/adobe-ceo-people-buy-experiences-not-products-summit18.html#gs.fv9o0o

Act, S. B. (2008). Think small first: A 'Small Business Act'f or Europe. Communication from the commission to the council, the European Parliament, the European Economic and Social Committee and the Committee of the Regions. *Commission of the European Communities Brussels, 25*, 2008.

Adler, R. W., & Milne, M. J. (1997). Improving the quality of accounting students' learning through action-oriented learning tasks. *Accounting Education, 6*(3), 191–215. doi:10.1080/096392897331442

Adobe (2015). *The state of content: expectations on the rise.* https://blogs.adobe.com/creative/files/2015/12/Adobe-State-of-Content-Report.pdf

Adrian, B., Sauermann, L., & Roth-Berghofer, T. (2007). Contag: A semantic tag recommendation system. *Proceedings of I-Semantics, 7*, 297–304.

Aghaei, S., Nematbakhsh, M. A., & Farsani, H. K. (2012). Evolution of the world wide web: From WEB 1.0 TO WEB 4.0. *International Journal of Web & Semantic Technology, 3*(1), 1–10. doi:10.5121/ijwest.2012.3101

Ahmed, F. (2019). *Possible uses of web 3.0 in websites of Libraries of Academic Institutions of Pakistan.* Academic Press.

Akputu, K., & Attai, F. (2020). User Experience Measurement: Recent Practice of E-Businesses. In J.-É. Pelet (Ed.), *User Experience in Web 2.0 Technologies and Its Impact on Universities and Businesses.* IGI Global. doi:10.4018/978-1-7998-3756-5

Alalwan, J. A., & Weistroffer, H. R. (2012). Enterprise content management research: A comprehensive review. *Journal of Enterprise Information Management, 25*(5), 441–461. doi:10.1108/17410391211265133

Alanne, K., & Cao, S. (2017). Zero-energy hydrogen economy (ZEH2E) for buildings and communities including personal mobility. *Renewable & Sustainable Energy Reviews, 71*, 697–711. doi:10.1016/j.rser.2016.12.098

Aleixo, M. da C., Teixeira, A. B., & Silva, S. (2012). *Simulação empresarial: Um caso de sucesso.* XXII Jornadas Luso-Espanholas de Gestão Científica.

Ali, A. Z. M., Wahid, R., Samsudin, K., & Idris, M. Z. (2013). Reading on the computer screen: Does font type has effects on web text readability? *International Education Studies, 6*(3), 26. doi:10.5539/ies.v6n3p26

Alkhateeb, F. M., Clauson, K. A., Khanfar, N. M., & Latif, D. A. (2008). Legal and regulatory risk associated with Web 2.0 adoption by pharmaceutical companies. *Journal of Medical Marketing, 8*(4), 311–318. doi:10.1057/jmm.2008.20

Allen, J., Frederick, F. R., Barney, H., & Markey, R. (2005). How to achieve true customer-led growth. Closing the delivery gap. Academic Press.

Almeida, F. L. (2017). Concept and dimensions of web 4.0. *International Journal of Computers and Technology, 16*(7), 7040–7046. doi:10.24297/ijct.v16i7.6446

Alsaif, S., Li, A. S., Soh, B., & Alraddady, S. (2019). The Efficacy of Facebook in Teaching and Learning: Studied via Content Analysis of Web Log Data. *Procedia Computer Science, 161*, 493–501. doi:10.1016/j.procs.2019.11.149

Alves, J., Moutinho, N., Pires, A., & Ribeiro, N. (2013). A motivação dos alunos em simulação empresarial: Análise de um ano lectivo. *XIV Congresso Internacional de Contabilidade e Auditoria.*

Amabile, T. M. (1983). Brilliant but cruel: Perceptions of negative evaluators. *Journal of Experimental Social Psychology, 19*(2), 146–156. doi:10.1016/0022-1031(83)90034-3

Amabile, T. M. (1993). Motivational synergy: Toward new conceptualizations of intrinsic and extrinsic motivation in the workplace. *Human Resource Management Review, 3*(3), 185–201. doi:10.1016/1053-4822(93)90012-S

Amabile, T. M., & Pratt, M. G. (2016). The dynamic componential model of creativity and innovation in organizations: Making progress, making meaning. *Research in Organizational Behavior, 36*, 157–183. doi:10.1016/j.riob.2016.10.001

Amabile, T. M., Schatzel, E. A., Moneta, G. B., & Kramer, S. J. (2004). Leader behaviors and the work environment for creativity: Perceived leader support. *The Leadership Quarterly, 15*(1), 5–32. doi:10.1016/j.leaqua.2003.12.003

Amar, J., Droulers, O., & Legoherel, P. (2017). Typography in destination advertising: An exploratory study and research perspectives. *Tourism Management, 63*, 77–86. doi:10.1016/j.tourman.2017.06.002

Anastasiades, P. S., & Kotsidis, K. (2013). The challenges of web 2.0 for education in Greece. *International Journal of Web-Based Learning and Teaching Technologies, 8*(4), 19–33. doi:10.4018/ijwltt.2013100102

Anchal, C. (2018). *Dynamic Workplace Revolution: Recent Digitalization Trends in Organizations. In Radical Reorganization of Existing Work Structures Through Digitalization.* IGI Global.

Andersson, S., Awuah, G., Aagerup, U., & Wictor, I. (2020). How do mature born globals create customer value to achieve international growth? *International Marketing Review, 37*(2), 185–211. doi:10.1108/IMR-11-2018-0340

Angeli, C. (2008). Distributed Cognition: A framework for understanding the role of computers in classroom teaching and learning. *Journal of Research on Technology in Education, 40*(3), 271–279. doi:10.1080/15391523.2008.10782508

Angelika, D., Hong, Y., & Pavlou, P. A. (2012). On Product Uncertainty in Online Markets: Theory and Evidence. *Management Information Systems Quarterly, 36*(2), 395–426. doi:10.2307/41703461

Ankolekar, A., Krötzsch, M., Tran, T., & Vrandecic, D. (2007, May). The two cultures: Mashing up Web 2.0 and the Semantic Web. In *Proceedings of the 16th international conference on World Wide Web* (pp. 825-834). 10.1145/1242572.1242684

Anthony, S. (2016). *Harvard Business Review: Kodak's Downfall Wasn't About Technology.* https://hbr.org/2016/07/kodaks-downfall-wasnt-about-technology#comment-section

Appleby, M. (2016). Nonprofit Organizations and the Utilization of Social Media: Maximizing and Measuring Return of Investment. *SPNHA Review, 12*(1), 4.

Arditi, A., & Cho, J. (2005). Serifs and font legibility. *Vision Research, 45*(23), 2926–2933. doi:10.1016/j.visres.2005.06.013 PubMed

Argo, J. J., Popa, M., & Smith, M. C. (2010). The sound of brands. *Journal of Marketing, 74*(4), 97–109. doi:10.1509/jmkg.74.4.097

Arguello, M., Monferrer Tirado, D., & Estrada Guillén, M (2019). Service quality in a post-crisis context: Emotional effects and behaviours. *International Journal of Bank Marketing, 38*(1), 175–198. doi:10.1108/IJBM-02-2019-0045

Ariker, M., Heller, J., Diaz, A., & Perry, J. (2015). How marketers can personalize at scaler. *Harvard Business Review.*

Arizton. (2019). *E-learning Market - Global Outlook and Forecast 2019-2024.* Retrieved from https://www.research-andmarkets.com/reports/4825750/e-learning-market-global-outlook-and-forecast?utm_code=b7dx72&utm_medium=CI

Arntz, M., Gregory, T., & Zierahn, U. (2016). *The risk of automation for jobs in OECD countries.* Academic Press.

Asencio, H., & Sun, R. (2015). Introduction. In H. Asencio & R. Sun (Eds.), *Cases on Strategic Social Media Utilization in the Nonprofit Sector.* IGI Global. doi:10.4018/978-1-4666-8188-0

Atiku, S. O. (2018). Reshaping human capital formation through digitalization. In *Radical Reorganization of Existing Work Structures through Digitalization* (pp. 52–73). IGI Global. doi:10.4018/978-1-5225-3191-3.ch004

Atiku, S. O., & Boateng, F. (2020). Rethinking Education System for the Fourth Industrial Revolution. In *Human Capital Formation for the Fourth Industrial Revolution* (pp. 1–17). IGI Global. doi:10.4018/978-1-5225-9810-7.ch001

Aufreiter, N., Boudet, J., & Weng, V. (2014). *Why marketers should keep sending you e-mails.* https://www.mckinsey.com/business-functions/marketing-and-sales/our-insights/why-marketers-should-keep-sending-you-emails

Aura Interactiva. (2018). *10 Things Modern L&D Professionals Should Be Doing.* Retrieved from https://www.shift-elearning.com/blog/10-ways-to-make-ld-cool-again

Aydede, M., & Matyar, F. (2009). The Effect of Active Learning Approach in Science Teaching on Cognitive Level of Student Achievement. *Journal of Turkish Science Education, 6.*

Azoulay, A., & Kapferer, J.-N. (2003). Do brand personality scales really measure brand personality? *Journal of Brand Management, 11*(2), 143–155. Advance online publication. doi:10.1057/palgrave.bm.2540162

Azuma, R., Baillot, Y., Behringer, R., Feiner, S., Julier, S., & MacIntyre, B. (2001). Recent advances in augmented reality. *IEEE Computer Graphics and Applications, 21*(6), 34–47. doi:10.1109/38.963459

Bae, S., Cho, H., Lim, I., & Ryu, S. (2014, November). SAFEWAPI: web API misuse detector for web applications. In *Proceedings of the 22nd ACM SIGSOFT International Symposium on Foundations of Software Engineering* (pp. 507-517). 10.1145/2635868.2635916

Baker, G. (2019, October 16). What is blog psychology? *Free Malaysia Today.* Retrieved from https://www.freemalaysiatoday.com/category/leisure/2019/10/16/what-is-blog-psychology/

Balcikanli, C. (2009). Long live, YouTube: L2 stories about YouTube in language learning. *E-Proceeding of the International Online Language Conference (IOLC),* 91–96.

Banciu, D., & Balog, A. (2013). *Calitatea sistemelor și serviciilor de e-learning.* Agir.

Bardhi, F., & Eckhardt, G. M. (2012). Access-based consumption: The case of car sharing. *The Journal of Consumer Research, 39*(4), 881–898. doi:10.1086/666376

Bargas-Avila, J. A., & Hornbæk, K. (2011). Old wine in new bottles or novel challenges? A critical analysis of empirical studies of User Experience. *Proceedings of the International Conference on Human Factors in Computing Systems.*

Barker, J. P. H. (2004). *Different worlds: law and the changing geographies of wine in France and New Zealand* (Doctoral dissertation). ResearchSpace@ Auckland.

Barrett, M., Davidson, E., Prabhu, J., & Vargo, S. L. (2015). Service innovation in the digital age: Key contributions and future directions. *Management Information Systems Quarterly, 39*(1), 135–154. doi:10.25300/MISQ/2015/39:1.03

Barsky, E. (2006). Introducing Web 2.0: RSS trends for health librarians. *Journal of the Canadian Health Libraries Association/Journal de l'Association des bibliothèques de la santé du Canada, 27*(1), 7-8.

Barton, R., Ishikawa, M., Quiring, K., & Theofilou, B. (2018). *From Me to We: The Rise of the Purpose-Led Brand.* https://www.accenture.com/_acnmedia/thought-leadership-assets/pdf/accenture-competitiveagility-gcpr-pov.pdf

Barzilai & Blau. (2014). Scaffolding game-based learning: Impact on learning achievements, perceived learning, and game experiences. *Computers & Education, 70*(1), 65–79.

Basu, S. (2018). Information search in the internet markets: Experience versus search goods. *Electronic Commerce Research and Applications, 30*, 25–37. doi:10.1016/j.elerap.2018.05.004

Batt, B. (n.d.). *How to Explain AICC, SCORM 1.2, and SCORM 2004 to Anyone.* Retrieved from https://www.elearningfreak.com/how-to-explain-aicc-scorm-12-and-scorm-2004-to-anyone/

Bayer, M., Sommer, W., & Schacht, A. (2010). Reading emotional words within sentences: The impact of arousal and valence on event-related potentials. *International Journal of Psychophysiology: Official Journal of the International Organization of Psychophysiology, 78*(3), 299–307. doi:10.1016/j.ijpsycho.2010.09.004 PubMed

BBC News. (2015). *Google buys. app web domain for $25m.* Retrieved from: https://www.bbc.com/news/technology-31659666

Bearison, D. J., & Dorval, B. (2002). *Advances in discourse processes. Collaborative cognition: Children negotiating ways of knowing.* Ablex Publishing.

Beldad, A., De Jong, M., & Steehouder, M. (2010). How shall I trust the faceless and the intangible? A literature review on the antecedents of online trust. *Computers in Human Behavior, 26*(5), 857–869. doi:10.1016/j.chb.2010.03.013

Belk, M., Papatheocharous, E., Germanakos, P., & Samaras, G. (2013). Modeling users on the World Wide Web based on cognitive factors, navigation behavior and clustering techniques. *Journal of Systems and Software, 86*(12), 2995–3012. doi:10.1016/j.jss.2013.04.029

Belk, R. (2014). Sharing versus pseudo-sharing in Web 2.0. *The Anthropologist, 18*(1), 7–23. doi:10.1080/09720073.2014.11891518

Belk, R. (2014). You are what you can access: Sharing and collaborative consumption online. *Journal of Business Research, 67*(8), 1595–1600. doi:10.1016/j.jbusres.2013.10.001

Belk, R. W. (2013). Extended self in a digital world. *The Journal of Consumer Research, 40*(3), 477–500. doi:10.1086/671052

Belleghem, S. V. (2019). *Customers the day after tomorrow.* Lannoo, Uitgeverij.

Benedicktus, R. L. (2011). The effects of 3rd party consensus information on service expectations and online trust. *Journal of Business Research, 64*(8), 846–853. doi:10.1016/j.jbusres.2010.09.014

Benkler, Y. (2004). Sharing nicely: On shareable goods and the emergence of sharing as a modality of economic production. *The Yale Law Journal, 114*(2), 273. doi:10.2307/4135731

Benlian, A., & Hess, T. (2011). The signaling role of IT features in influencing trust and participation in online communities. *International Journal of Electronic Commerce, 15*(4), 7–56. doi:10.2753/JEC1086-4415150401

Bennett, P. D. (1995). *Dictionary of Marketing Terms.* American Marketing Association.

Bennett, S., Bishop, A., Dalgarno, B., Waycott, J., & Kennedy, G. (2012). Implementing Web 2.0 technologies in higher education: A collective case study. *Computers & Education, 59*(2), 524–534. doi:10.1016/j.compedu.2011.12.022

Bennett, S., Maton, K., & Kervin, L. (2008). The 'digital natives' debate: A critical review of the evidence. *BJET, 39*(5), 775–786. doi:10.1111/j.1467-8535.2007.00793.x

Benoit, S., Baker, T. L., Bolton, R. N., Gruber, T., & Kandampully, J. (2017). A triadic framework for collaborative consumption (CC): Motives, activities and resources & capabilities of actors. *Journal of Business Research, 79,* 219–227. doi:10.1016/j.jbusres.2017.05.004

Ben-Zvi, T. (2010). The efficacy of business simulation games in creating Decision Support Systems: An experimental investigation. *Decision Support Systems, 49*(1), 61–69. doi:10.1016/j.dss.2010.01.002

Bergen, L., Grimes, T., & Potter, D. (2005). How attention partitions itself during simultaneous message presentations. *Human Communication Research, 31*(3), 311–336. doi:10.1111/j.1468-2958.2005.tb00874.x

Berger, P., & Trexler, S. (2010). *Choosing Web 2.0 tools for learning and teaching in a digital world.* Libraries Unlimited, Inc.

Berthon, P., Holbrook, M. B., & Hulbert, J. M. (2000). Beyond market orientation: A conceptualization of market evolution. *Journal of Interactive Marketing, 14*(3), 50–66. doi:10.1002/1520-6653(200022)14:3<50::AID-DIR4>3.0.CO;2-L

Bevan, N. (2009). What is the difference between the purpose of usability and user experience evaluation methods. *Proceedings of the workshop UXEM 9,* 1-4.

Beymer, D., Russell, D., & Orton, P. (2008, September 1). An eye tracking study of how font size and type influence online reading. People and Computers XXII Culture, Creativity. *Interaction.* Advance online publication. doi:10.14236/ewic/HCI2008.23

Bhatia, S. K., Samal, A., Rajan, N., & Kiviniemi, M. T. (2011). Effect of font size, italics, and colour count on web usability. *International Journal of Computational Vision and Robotics, 2*(2), 156. Advance online publication. doi:10.1504/IJCVR.2011.042271 PubMed

Bianchi, C., Carneiro, J., & Wickramasekera, R. (2018). Internationalisation commitment of emerging market firms: A comparative study of Chile. *Journal of Small Business and Enterprise Development, 25*(2), 201–221. doi:10.1108/JSBED-07-2017-0221

Bigelow, C. (2019). Typeface features and legibility research. *Vision Research, 165,* 162–172. doi:10.1016/j.visres.2019.05.003 PubMed

Bizer, C., Cyganiak, R., & Gauß, T. (2007). The RDF Book Mashup: From Web APIs to a Web of Data. *SFSW,* 248.

Blair, K., Murphy, R. M., & Almjeld, J. (2001). Cross Currents: Cultures, Communities, Technologies. New York: Cengage Learning.

Bleier, A., Harmeling, C. M., & Palmatier, R. W. (2019). Creating Effective Online Customer Experiences. *Journal of Marketing, 83*(2), 98–119. doi:10.1177/0022242918809930

Block, J. J. (2008). Issues for DSM-V: Internet addiction. *The American Journal of Psychiatry, 165*(3), 306–307. doi:10.1176/appi.ajp.2007.07101556 PMID:18316427

Blois, K. J. (1999). Trust in business to business relationships: An evaluation of its status. *Journal of Management Studies*, *36*(2), 197–215. doi:10.1111/1467-6486.00133

Bloom, B. S., Engelhart, M. D., Furst, E. J., Hill, W. H., & Krathwohl, D. R. (1956). *Taxonomy of educational objectives: The classification of educational goals. Handbook 1: Cognitive domain*. David McKay.

Blythe, J. (2013). *Consumer Behaviour*. SAGE Publications.

Böheim, R., Knogler, M., Kosel, C., & Seidel, T. (2020). Exploring student hand-raising across two school subjects using mixed methods: An investigation of an everyday classroom behavior from a motivational perspective. *Learning and Instruction*, *65*, 101250. doi:10.1016/j.learninstruc.2019.101250

Boller, S. (2014). Games vs Simulations: Choosing the Right Approach for Learning. *The Knowledge Guru*. Retrieved from http://www.theknowledgeguru.com/games-vs-simulations-choosing-right-approach/

Bolton, R. N. (2016). *Service Excellence: Creating Customer Experiences that Build Relationships*. Business Expert Press.

Boneva, M. (2018). Challenges Related to the Digital Transformation of Business Companies. In Innovation Management, Entrepreneurship and Sustainability (IMES 2018) (pp. 101-114). Vysoká škola ekonomická v Praze.

Botsman, R., & Rogers, R. (2010). *What's mine is yours: The rise of collaborative consumption*. HarperCollins.

Botsman, R., & Rogers, R. (2011). *What's Mine Is Yours: The Rise of Collaborative Consumption*. HarperCollins.

Botts, V. (n.d.). *Blogging in the classroom*. Retrieved from https://study.com/academy/lesson/blogging-in-the-classroom.html

Boudlaie, H., & Nargesian, A., & Keshavarz Nik, B. (2019). Digital footprint in Web 3.0: Social Media Usage in Recruitment. *AD-Minister*, (34), 139–156.

Bradley, P. (2007). *How to use Web 2.0 in your library*. Facet Publishing.

Brakus, J. J., Schmitt, B. H., & Zarantonello, L. (2009, May). Brand Experience: What Is It? How Is It Measured? Does It Affect Loyalty? *Journal of Marketing*, *73*(3), 52–68. doi:10.1509/jmkg.73.3.052

Braña, F.-J. (2019). A fourth industrial revolution? Digital transformation, labor and work organization: A view from Spain. *Economia e Politica Industriale*, *46*(3), 415–430. doi:10.100740812-019-00122-0

Brandon, B. (2012). Making History: mLearnCon 2012 Rocks Attendees. *Learning Solutions Magazine*. Retrieved from https://web.archive.org/web/20120806005118/http://www.learningsolutionsmag.com/articles/958/

Breeding, M. (2006). Web 2.0? Let's get to Web 1.0 first. *Computers in Libraries*, *26*(5), 30–33.

Bressolles, G. (2016). *Vente de vin sur Internet: l'avenir passe par le commerce connecté. Journal du Net. Chroniques.*

Bressolles, G., & Durrieu, F. (2011). Impact des dimensions de la qualité de service électronique sur la satisfaction et les intentions de fidélité: Différences entre acheteurs et visiteur. *La Revue des Sciences de Gestion*, *6*(6), 37–45. doi:10.3917/rsg.252.0037

Brown, I. T. J. (2002). Individual and Technological Factors Affecting Perceived Ease of Use of Web-based Learning Technologies in a Developing Country. *The Electronic Journal on Information Systems in Developing Countries*, *9*(1), 1–15. doi:10.1002/j.1681-4835.2002.tb00055.x

Bruhn, M., Schnebelen, S., & Schäfer, D. (2014). Antecedents and consequences of the quality of e-customer-to-customer interactions in B2B brand communities. *Industrial Marketing Management*, *43*(1), 164–176. doi:10.1016/j.indmarman.2013.08.008

Bruwer, J., & Alant, K. (2009). The hedonic nature of wine tourism consumption: An experiential view. *International Journal of Wine Business Research*, *21*(3), 235–257. doi:10.1108/17511060910985962

Bruwer, J., & Buller, C. (2012). Country-of-origin (COO) brand preferences and associated knowledge levels of Japanese wine consumers. *Journal of Product and Brand Management*, *21*(5), 307–316. doi:10.1108/10610421211253605

Bruwer, J., Nowak, L. I., & Newton, S. (2008). Using winery web sites to launch relationships with Millennials. *International Journal of Wine Business Research*, *21*(1), 51–67.

Brynjolfsson, E., McAfee, A., & Spence, M. (2014). New world order: Labor, capital, and ideas in the power law economy. *Foreign Affairs*, *93*(4), 44–53.

Buchanan, T. (2000). The Efficacy of a World Wide Web. *Computing Research*, *23*(2), 203–216.

Buchem, I., & Hamelmann, H. (2011). Developing 21st century skills: Web 2.0 in higher education: A Case Study. *E-learning papers*, (24). Available at: http://elearningpapers.eu/sites/default/files/media25535

Burch, G., Giambatista, R. C., Batchelor, J., Hoover, J. D., Burch, J., Heller, N., & Shaw, J. (2017, November 30). (2017). Do Experiential Learning Pedagogies Effect Student Learning? A Meta-Analysis of 40 Years of Research. *Academy of Management Journal*. Advance online publication. doi:10.5465/ambpp.2016.127

Burgess, L., & Cooper, J. (1999). A model for classification of business adoption of internet commerce. *Proceedings of the 12th International Bled Electronic Commerce Conference*, 7-9.

Burgess, L., & Cooper, J. (2000). Extending the viability of MICA (Model of Internet Commerce Adoption) as a metric for explaining the process of business adoption of internet commerce. *Proceedings of the International Conference on Telecommunications and Electronic Commerce.*

Burgoon, J. K., Bonito, J. A., Bengtsson, B., Ramirez, A. Jr, Dunbar, N. E., & Miczo, N. (1999). Testing the interactivity model: Communication processes, partner assessments, and the quality of collaborative work. *Journal of Management Information Systems*, *16*(3), 33–56. doi:10.1080/07421222.1999.11518255

Business Intelligence, F. U. N. G. (2017). *In Depth – China's Apparel Market*. https://www.fbicgroup.com/?q=reports/china-distribution-and-retail-0

Business Wire. (2018). *Global Corporate e-Learning Market to Post 11% CAGR During 2018-2022*. Retrieved from https://www.businesswire.com/news/home/20180630005028/en/Global-Corporate-e-Learning-Market-Post-11-CAGR

Cai, L., He, X., Dai, Y., & Zhu, K. (2018). Research on B2B2C E-commerce Website Design Based on User Experience. *Journal of Physics: Conference Series*, *1087*(6), 5. doi:10.1088/1742-6596/1087/6/062043

Calp, M. H. (2020). *The Role of Artificial Intelligence Within the Scope of Digital Transformation in Enterprises. In Advanced MIS and Digital Transformation for Increased Creativity and Innovation in Business*. IGI Global.

Calvo, N., & Villarreal, Ó. (2018). Analysis of the growth of the e-learning industry through sustainable business model archetypes: A case study. *Journal of Cleaner Production*, *191*, 26–39. doi:10.1016/j.jclepro.2018.04.211

Camilleri, J., & Neuhofer, B. (2017). Value co-creation and co-destruction in the Airbnb sharing economy. *International Journal of Contemporary Hospitality Management*, *29*(9), 2322–2340. doi:10.1108/IJCHM-09-2016-0492

Campbell, D. A., & Lambright, K. T. (2019). Are You Out There? Internet Presence of Nonprofit Human Service Organizations. *Nonprofit and Voluntary Sector Quarterly*, *48*(6), 1296–1311. doi:10.1177/0899764019852673

Carmigniani, J., Furht, B., Anisetti, M., Ceravolo, P., Damiani, E., & Ivkovic, M. (2011). Augmented reality technologies, systems and applications. *Multimedia Tools and Applications*, *51*(1), 341–377. doi:10.1007/s11042-010-0660-6

Cattell, R. B. (1987). *Intelligence: Its Structure, Growth and Action*. Elsevier.

Cecilia, R., Di Giacomo, D., Vittorini, P., & De la Prieta, F. (Eds.). (2015). Influence of gaming activities on cognitive performances. Methodologies & Intelligent Systems for Technology Enhanced Learning, 374. Springer. doi:10.1007/978-3-319-19632-9_9

Ceipek, R., Hautz, J., Petruzzelli, A. M., De Massis, A., & Matzler, K. (2020). A motivation and ability perspective on engagement in emerging digital technologies: The case of Internet of Things solutions. *Long Range Planning, 101991*, 101991. Advance online publication. doi:10.1016/j.lrp.2020.101991

Celata, F., Hendrickson, C. Y., & Sanna, V. S. (2017). The sharing economy as community marketplace? Trust, reciprocity and belonging in peer-to-peer accommodation platforms. *Cambridge Journal of Regions, Economy and Society, 10*(2), 349–363. doi:10.1093/cjres/rsw044

Celik, V., & Yesilyurt, E. (2013). Attitudes to technology, perceived computer self-efficacy and computer anxiety as predictors of computer supported education. *Computers & Education, 60*(1), 148–158. doi:10.1016/j.compedu.2012.06.008

Centre for Excellence in Enquiry-Based Learning. (n.d.). Retrieved from http://www.ceebl.manchester.ac.uk/events/archive/aligningcollaborativelearning/Blog.pdf

Chadwick-Dias, A., Bergel, M., & Tullis, T. S. (2007). Senior surfers 2.0: A re-examination of the older web user and the dynamic web. In C. Stephanidis (Ed.), *Universal acess in human computer interaction. Coping with diversity* (pp. 868–876). Springer., doi:10.1007/978-3-540-73279-2_97

Chala, N., & Poplavska, O. (2017). *The 4th Industrial Revolution and Innovative Labor: Trends*. Challenges, Forecasts.

Chang, Y., Hou, R.-J., Wang, K., Cui, A. P., & Zhang, C.-B. (2020). Effects of intrinsic and extrinsic motivation on social loafing in online travel communities. *Computers in Human Behavior, 109*, 106360. doi:10.1016/j.chb.2020.106360

Chapman, S., McPhee, P., & Proudman, B. (1995). What is Experiential Education? In K. Warren (Ed.), *The Theory of Experiential Education* (pp. 235–248). Kendall/Hunt Publishing Company.

Charters, S., & Spielmann, N. (2014). Characteristics of strong territorial brands: The case of champagne. *Journal of Business Research, 67*(7), 1461–1467. doi:10.1016/j.jbusres.2013.07.020

Chase, R. (2015). *Peers Inc: how people and platforms are inventing the collaborative economy and reinventing capitalism*. PublicAffairs.

Chen, J. (2007). Flow in Games (and Everything Else). *Communications of the ACM, 50*(4), 31–34. doi:10.1145/1232743.1232769

Chen, S.-C., Yen, D. C., & Hwang, M. I. (2012). Factors influencing the continuance intention to the usage of Web 2.0: An empirical study. *Computers in Human Behavior, 28*(3), 933–941. doi:10.1016/j.chb.2011.12.014

Chiara, G., Spiller, N., & Noci, G. (2007). How to Sustain the Customer Experience: An Overview of Experience Components that Co-Create Value with the Customer. *European Management Journal, 25*(5), 395–410.

Chickering, A. W., & Gamson, Z. F. (1987). Seven principles for good practice. *AAHE Bulletin, 39*, 3–7.

Childers, T. L., & Jass, J. (2002). All dressed up with something to say: Effects of typeface semantic associations on brand perceptions and consumer memory. *Journal of Consumer Psychology, 12*(2), 93–106. doi:10.1207/S15327663JCP1202_03

Cho, P. (2004). *Interactivity in Cinema-Based Media Art: a Phenomenology-Influenced Discussion*. Academic Press.

Chon, Y. V., & Shin, T. (2019). Profile of second language learners' metacognitive awareness and academic motivation for successful listening: A latent class analysis. *Learning and Individual Differences*, *70*, 62–75. doi:10.1016/j.lindif.2019.01.007

Choudhury, N. (2014). World wide web and its journey from web 1.0 to web 4.0. *International Journal of Computer Science and Information Technologies*, *5*(6), 8096–8100.

Choudhury, S., & Pattnaik, S. (2020). Emerging themes in e-learning: A review from the stakeholders' perspective. *Computers & Education*, *144*, 103657. doi:10.1016/j.compedu.2019.103657

Christensen, C. M., Raynor, E. M., & McDonald, R. (2015). *What is Disruptive Innovation?* https://hbr.org/2015/12/what-is-disruptive-innovation

Christensen, C. M., Dillon, K., Hall, T., & Duncan, D. S. (2016). *Competing Against Luck: The Story of Innovation and Customer Choice*. Harper Collins.

Ciuchita, R., Mahr, D., & Odekerken-Schröder, G. (2019). Deal with it: How coping with e-service innovation affects the customer experience. *Journal of Business Research*, *103*, 130–141. doi:10.1016/j.jbusres.2019.05.036

Clark, R. A., & Jones, D. (2001). A Comparison of Traditional and Online Formats in a Public Speaking Course. *Communication Education*, *50*(2), 109–124. doi:10.1080/03634520109379238

Clayborne, L. (2018, January 18). What are the uses of blogs? *Quora*. Retrieved from https://www.quora.com/What-are-the-uses-of-blogs

Cockburn, C., & Wilson, T. D. (1996). Business use of the World Wide Web. *International Journal of Information Management*, *16*(2), 83–102. doi:10.1016/0268-4012(95)00071-2

Cohen, B., & Kietzmann, J. (2014). Ride on! Mobility business models for the sharing economy. *Organization & Environment*, *27*(3), 279–296. doi:10.1177/1086026614546199

Cole, C. (2014). Social Media Best Practices for Nonprofit Organizations: A Guide. *Canadian Coalition for Global Health Research*. Available from: https://www.ccghr.ca/wp-content/uploads/2014/2006/CCGHR-Social-Media-Modules_Complete.pdf

Coleman, D., & Levine, S. (2008). *Collaboration 2.0: technology and best practices for successful collaboration in a Web 2.0 world*. Happy About.

Columbus, L. (2014). Gartner CRM market share update: 41% Of CRM systems are SaaS-based, Salesforce dominating market growth. *Julkaistu, 6*.

Conseil Interprofessionnel des Vins d'Alsace (CIVA). (2019). *Rapport de production 2016-2017*. Author.

Constantinides, E., & Fountain, S. J. (2008). Web 2.0: Conceptual foundations and marketing issues. *Journal of Direct, Data and Digital Marketing Practice*, *9*(3), 231–244. doi:10.1057/palgrave.dddmp.4350098

Cormode, G., & Krishnamurthy, B. (2008). Key differences between Web 1.0 and Web 2.0. *First Monday*, *13*(6). Advance online publication. doi:10.5210/fm.v13i6.2125

Corritore, K., & Beverly, W. (2003). On-line trust: Concepts, evolving themes, a model. *International Journal of Human-Computer Studies*, *58*(6), 737–758. doi:10.1016/S1071-5819(03)00041-7

Creswell, J. W. (2008). *Research design: Qualitative, quantitative, and mixed methods approaches* (2nd ed.). Sage.

CRISS. (n.d.). *Benefits of using blogs in the classroom.* Retrieved from https://www.crissh2020.eu/benefits-using-blogs-classroom

Cristobal-Fransi, E., Martin-Fuentes, E. Daries, N. (2015). Behavioral analysis of subjects interacting with information technology: Categorizing the behavior of e-consumers. *International Journal of Services Technology and Management, 21*(1/2/3), 163-182.

Cromwell, J. R., Amabile, T. M., & Harvey, J.-F. (2018). An Integrated Model of Dynamic Problem Solving Within Organizational Constraints. In R. Reiter-Palmon, V. L. Kennel, & J. C. Kaufman (Eds.), *Individual Creativity in the Workplace* (pp. 53–81). Academic Press. doi:10.1016/B978-0-12-813238-8.00003-6

Csikszentmihalyi, M. (1990). *Flow: The Psychology of Optimal Experience.* Harper & Row.

Csikszentmihalyi, M. (1993). *The Evolving Self: A Psychology for the Third Millennium.* Harper Collins.

Curley, M., & Salmelin, B. (2017). *Open innovation 2.0: the new mode of digital innovation for prosperity and sustainability.* Springer.

Cuzzort, R. P., & King, E. W. (1995). *Twentieth-century social thought.* Harcourt Brace College Publishers.

Cyr, D., Head, M., & Ivanov, A. (2007). Perceived Interactivity Leading to E-Loyalty: An Empirical Investigation of Web-Poll Design. *SIGHCI 2007 Proceedings, 16.*

Da Huo, K. H., Wang, H., & Xu, X. (2018). Country of origin and online promotion in cross-border e-business: A study of consumer behavior for quality management. *The International Trade Journal, 32*(1), 140–149. doi:10.1080/08853908.2017.1387082

Dahlstrom, E., de Boor, T., Grunwald, P., & Vockley, M. (2011). *The ECAR study of undergraduate students and information technology.* EDUCAUSE Center for Applied Research. Available from http://www.educause.edu/Resources/ECARNationalStudy ofUndergradua/238012

Daneshkhu, S. (2018). *How millennials' taste for 'authenticity' is disrupting powerful food brands.* https://www.ft.com/content/09271178-6f29-11e8-92d3-6c13e5c92914

Daniela, L., Visvizi, A., Gutierrez-Braojos, C., & Lytras, M. (2018). Sustainable higher education and technology-enhanced Learning (TEL). *Sustainability, 10*(11), 3883. doi:10.3390u10113883

Darke, P. R., Brady, M. K., Benedicktus, R. L., & Wilson, A. E. (2016). Feeling Close from Afar: The Role of Psychological Distance in Offsetting Distrust in Unfamiliar Online Retailers. *Journal of Retailing, 92*(3), 287–299. doi:10.1016/j.jretai.2016.02.001

Darling-Churchill, K. E., & Lippman, L. (2016). Early childhood social and emotional development: Advancing the field of measurement. *Journal of Applied Developmental Psychology, 45*, 1–7. doi:10.1016/j.appdev.2016.02.002

David, H. (2015). Why are there still so many jobs? The history and future of workplace automation. *The Journal of Economic Perspectives, 29*(3), 3–30. doi:10.1257/jep.29.3.3

Davidson, R. (2006). *Electronic Service Quality Gaps in Australian Wineries* (PhD Thesis). Flinders University, Australia.

Davidson, R. (2009). A longitudinal study of Australian winery Websites. *Asia Pacific Management Review, 14*(4), 379–392.

Davis, N. E., & Tearle, P. (Eds.). (1999). *A core curriculum for telematics in teacher training.* Teleteaching 98 Conference, Vienna. https://files.eric.ed.gov/fulltext/ED432260.pdf

De Bellis, E., Hildebrand, C., Ito, K., Herrmann, A., & Schmitt, B. (2019). Personalizing the Customization Experience: A Matching Theory of Mass Customization Interfaces and Cultural Information Processing. *JMR, Journal of Marketing Research*, *56*(6), 1050–1065. doi:10.1177/0022243719867698

De Franceschi, A. (2015). EU Digital Single Market Strategy in Light of the Consumer Rights Directive, The. *J. Eur. Consumer & Mkt. L.*, *4*, 144.

De Laat, P. B. (2005). *Trusting Virtual Trust*. Kluwer Academic Publishers. doi:10.100710676-006-0002-6

Dean, B. (n.d.). 5 guidelines for improving your blog's user experience. *Usability Geek.* Retrieved from https://usabilitygeek.com/5-guidelines-blog-user-experience

Debold, E. (2002). Flow with soul: An interview with Dr. Mihaly Csikszentmihalyi. *What Is Enlightenment Magazine.* Retrieved from http://www.wie.org/j21/cziksz.asp

Dedeurwaerdere, T., Admiraal, J., Beringer, A., Bonaiuto, F., Cicero, L., Fernandez-Wulff, P., Hagens, J., Hiedanpää, J., Knights, P., Molinario, E., Melindi-Ghidi, P., Popa, F., Šilc, U., Soethe, N., Soininen, T., & Luis Vivero, J. (2016). Combining internal and external motivations in multi-actor governance arrangements for biodiversity and ecosystem services. *Environmental Science & Policy*, *58*, 1–10. doi:10.1016/j.envsci.2015.12.003 PMID:28149197

Degryse, C. (2016). *Digitalisation of the economy and its impact on labour markets*. ETUI Research Paper-Working Paper.

Deitel, P., & Deitel, H. (2007). *Internet & world wide web: how to program*. Prentice-Hall Press.

Deloitte (2019). Smartphone: the center of life A study on Nordic mobile consumer behaviour. Deloitte Global Mobile Consumer Survey 2019: The Nordic cut.

Demartini, C., & Benussi, L. (2017). Do Web 4.0 and industry 4.0 imply education X. 0? *IT Professional*, *19*(3), 4–7. doi:10.1109/MITP.2017.47

DeMuro, J. (2020, January). *Best blogging platforms of 2020*. Retrieved from https://www.techradar.com/uk/news/best-blogging-platform

Den Exter, K., Rowe, S., Boyd, W., & Lloyd, D. (2012). Using Web 2.0 technologies for collaborative learning in distance education—Case studies from an Australian University. *Future Internet*, *4*(4), 216–237. doi:10.3390/fi4010216

Deng, L., & Poole, M. (2010). Affect in web interfaces: A study of the impacts of web page visual complexity and order. *Management Information Systems Quarterly*, *34*(4), 711–730. doi:10.2307/25750702

Denscombe, M. (2009). Item non-response rates: A comparison of online and paper questionnaires. *International Journal of Social Research Methodology*, *12*(4), 281–291. doi:10.1080/13645570802054706

Dewey, J. (1938). *Experience and Education*. Collier Books.

Dianne, C., Hassanein, K., Head, M., & Ivanov, A. (2007). The Role of Social Presence in Establishing Loyalty in E-Service Environments. *Interacting with Computers*, *19*(1), 43–56. doi:10.1016/j.intcom.2006.07.010

Dianne, C., Head, M., Larios, H., & Pan, B. (2009). Exploring Human Images in Website Design: A Multi-Method Approach. *Management Information Systems Quarterly*, *33*(3), 539–566. doi:10.2307/20650308

Dimock, M. (2019). *Defining generations: Where Millennials end and Generation Z begins*. https://www.pewresearch.org/fact-tank/2019/01/17/where-millennials-end-and-generation-z-begins/

Ding, C. G., & Lin, C. H. (2012). How does background music tempo work for online shopping? *Electronic Commerce Research and Applications*, *11*(3), 299–307. doi:10.1016/j.elerap.2011.10.002

Diouf, D. O., & Lemoine, J. F. (2019). *Les effets d'interaction entre les composantes atmosphériques d'un site web et les réactions des internautes: Une étude qualitative portant sur la couleur et la typographie.* Academic Press.

Dixon, M., Freeman, K., & Toman, N. (2010). Stop Trying to Delight Your Customers. Harvard Business Review. Retrieved from https://hbr.org/2010/07/stop-trying-to-delight-your-customers

DOCEBO. (2016). *Elearning market trends and forecasts 2017-2021.* Retrieved from https://www.docebo.com/resource/elearning-market-trends-and-forecast-2017-2021/

Dogramaci, A., & Nabil, R. A. (1979). Applications of simulations. In R. A. Nabil & A. Dogramaci (Eds.), *Current Issues in Computer Simulation* (pp. 101–109). Academic Press. doi:10.1016/B978-0-12-044120-4.50012-X

Dong, C., & Rim, H. (2019). Exploring nonprofit-business partnerships on Twitter from a network perspective. *Public Relations Review*, *45*(1), 104–118. doi:10.1016/j.pubrev.2018.11.001

Dong, L., Huang, L., Hou, J., & Liu, Y. (2020). Continuous content contribution in virtual community: The role of status-standing on motivational mechanisms. *Decision Support Systems*, *132*, 113283. doi:10.1016/j.dss.2020.113283

Dörschner, T., & Musshoff, O. (2015). How do incentive-based environmental policies affect environment protection initiatives of farmers? An experimental economic analysis using the example of species richness. *Ecological Economics*, *114*, 90–103. doi:10.1016/j.ecolecon.2015.03.013

dos Santos W. O., Bittencourt, I. I., Dermeval, D., Isotani, S., Marques, L. B., & Silveira, I. F. (2018). Flow Theory to Promote Learning in Educational Systems: Isit Really Relevant? *Brazilian Journal of Computers in Education (Revista Brasileira de Informática na Educação -RBIE)*, *26*(2), 29-59.

Dotson, J. P., Fan, R. R., Feit, E. M. D., Oldham, J. D., & Yeh, Y. H. (2017). Brand Attitudes and Search Engine Queries. *Journal of Interactive Marketing*, *37*, 105–116. doi:10.1016/j.intmar.2016.10.002

Drew, B., & Waters, J. (1986). Video games: Utilization of a novel strategy to improve perceptual motor skills and cognitive functioning in the non-institutionalized elderly. *Cognitive Rehabilitation*, *4*(2), 26–31.

Drouillat, B. (2019). *Comment l'UX a tué le design.* Published 4 décembre 2019 retrieved the 16th of June 2020 from https://blog.fastandfresh.fr/benoit-drouillat-pourquoi-lux-tue-le-design/

Dumitrescu, V. M. (2015). *One step ahead: From Web 1.0 to web 2.0 technologies in higher education.* Paper presented at the 4th International Scientific Conference: eLearning and Software for Education: eLSE. Bucharest. Romania: CAROLI, National Defence University Publishing House.

Dunn, T. J., & Kennedy, M. (2019). Technology Enhanced Learning in higher education; motivations, engagement and academic achievement. *Computers & Education*, *137*, 104–113. doi:10.1016/j.compedu.2019.04.004

Edelman, R. (2019). *2019 Edelman Trust Barometer Special Report: In Brands We Trust?* https://www.edelman.com/sites/g/files/aatuss191/files/2019-06/2019_edelman_trust_barometer_special_report_in_brands_we_trust.pdf

Edwards, C. J., Bendickson, J. S., Baker, B. L., & Solomon, S. J. (2020). Entrepreneurship within the history of marketing. *Journal of Business Research*, *108*, 259–267. doi:10.1016/j.jbusres.2019.10.040

Egenfeldt-Nielsen, S. (2006). Understanding the educational potential of commercial computer games through activity and narratives. In *Understanding Video Games*. http://game-research.com/index.php/articles/understanding-the-educational-potential-of-commercial-computer-games-through-activity-and-narratives/

Eikelmann, S., Hajj, J., Hasbani, G., Marsch, C., Peterson, M., & Sabbagh, K. (2007). *The Urgent Need for Companies to Adapt to Web 2.0: New Models of Online Consumer Behavior Demand Changes in Corporate Strategy*. Booz Allen Hamilton.

Elder, R. S., Schlosser, A. E., Poor, M., & Xu, L. (2017). So Close I Can Almost Sense It: The Interplay Between Sensory Imagery and Psychological Distance. *The Journal of Consumer Research, 44*(4), 877–894. doi:10.1093/jcr/ucx070

Elif, B. (2020). *Digitalization of Human Resources: e-HR. In Tools and Techniques for Implementing International E-Trading Tactics for Competitive Advantage*. IGI Global.

Elliots, S. (2002). *Electronic Commerce B2C Strategies and Model*. John Wiley and Sons.

Elliott, S. N., Kratochwill, T. R., Littlefield Cook, J., & Travers, J. (2000). *Educational psychology: Effective teaching, effective learning* (3rd ed.). McGraw-Hill College.

Ellis, K., & Kent, M. (2019). Community accessibility: Tweeters take responsibility for an accessible Web 2.0. *Fast Capitalism, 7*(1).

Ellison, N. B., & Wu, Y. (2008). Blogging in the classroom: A preliminary exploration of student attitudes and impact on comprehension. *Journal of Educational Multimedia and Hypermedia, 17*(1), 99–122.

eMarketer. (2019). *Global Ecommerce 2019.* https://www.emarketer.com/content/global-ecommerce-2019

Emerson, L. C., & Berge, Z. L. (2018). *Microlearning: Knowledge management applications and competency-based training in the workplace*. UMBC Faculty Collection.

Ernst & Young LLP (n.d.). *The Digitalisation of Everything. How organisations much adapt to changing consumer behaviour*. https://www.ey.com/Publication/vwLUAssets/The_digitisation_of_everything_-_How_organisations_must_adapt_to_changing_consumer_behaviour/%24file/EY_Digitisation_of_everything.pdf

Ert, E., Fleischer, A., & Magen, N. (2016). Trust and reputation in the sharing economy: The role of personal photos in airbnb. *Tourism Management, 55*, 62–73. doi:10.1016/j.tourman.2016.01.013

Euromonitor International. (2014). *China to overtake US as largest apparel market by 2017*. https://blog.euromonitor.com/video/china-to-overtake-us-as-largest-apparel-market-by-2017/

European Commission. (2014). *New modes of learning and teaching in higher education*. Retrieved from https://ec.europa.eu/education/library/reports/modernisation-universities_en.pdf

European Commission. (2018). *Promoting Online Training Opportunities for the Workforce in Europe*. Retrieved from https://repositorio-aberto.up.pt/bitstream/10216/121228/2/343305.pdf

Eurostat. (2019). *Online purchases, EU-28*. https://ec.europa.eu/eurostat/statistics-explained/index.php?title=File:Online_purchases,_EU-28,_2019.png

Evans, D. (2011). The internet of things: How the next evolution of the internet is changing everything. *CISCO White Paper, 1*(2011), 1-11.

Exporters of French wines and spirits. (2019). Retrieved from: https://www.fevs.com/en/the-sector/key-figures/

Fader, P. (2012). *Customer Centricity: Focus on the Right Customers for Strategic Advantage*. Wharton Digital Press.

Famularo, B., Bruwer, J., & Li, E. (2010). Region of origin as choice factor: Wine knowledge and wine tourism involvement influence. *International Journal of Wine Business Research, 22*(4), 362–385. doi:10.1108/17511061011092410

Farley, H., Murphy, A., Johnson, C., Carter, B., Lane, M., Midgley, W., Hafeez-Baig, A., Dekeyser, S., & Koronios, A. (2015). How do students use their mobile devices to support learning? A Case study from an Australian Regional University. *Journal of Interactive Media in Education*, *2015*(1), 14. doi:10.5334/jime.ar

Farrell, S. (2009). API Keys to the Kingdom. *IEEE Internet Computing*, *13*(5), 91–93. doi:10.1109/MIC.2009.100

Fédération des Exportateurs de Vins et spiritueux de France (FEVS). (2020). *Key Figures*. Retrieved from: https://www.fevs.com/en/the-sector/key-figures/

Feiler, J. (2007). *How to do everything with Web 2.0 Mashups*. McGraw-Hill, Inc.

Felson, M., & Spaeth, J. L. (1978). Community structure and collaborative consumption: A routine activity approach. *The American Behavioral Scientist*, *21*(4), 614–624. doi:10.1177/000276427802100411

Feng, J. J., Lazar, J., & Preece, J. (2004). Empathy and online inter-personal trust: A fragile relationship. *Behaviour & Information Technology*, *23*(2), 97–106. doi:10.1080/01449290310001659240

Fernández-Uclés, D., Bernal-Jurado, E., Mozas-Moral, A., & Medina-Viruel, M. J. (2019). The importance of websites for organic agri-food producers. *Economic Research-Ekonomska Istraživanja*, 1-14.

Ferrer, B. R., Mohammed, W. M., Chen, E., & Lastra, J. L. M. (2017, October). Connecting web-based IoT devices to a cloud-based manufacturing platform. In *IECON 2017-43rd Annual Conference of the IEEE Industrial Electronics Society* (pp. 8628-8633). IEEE. 10.1109/IECON.2017.8217516

Fiet, J. O. (2001). The Theoretical Side of Teaching Entrepreneurship. *Journal of Business Venturing*, *16*(1), 1–24. doi:10.1016/S0883-9026(99)00041-5

Fitz, N. S., Nadler, R., Manogaran, P., Chong, E. W., & Reiner, P. B. (2014). Public attitudes toward cognitive enhancement. *Neuroethics*, *7*(2), 173–188. doi:10.100712152-013-9190-z

Forrester (2019). *How Customers Think, Feel, And Act: The Paradigm Of Business Outcomes*. https://cloud.kapostcontent.net/pub/d2a85d5e-c053-4bfc-ae8d-f1a9c0b2af31/whitepaper-how-customers-think-feel-and-act-the-paradigm-of-business-outcomes?kui=MtTZamfFfmzvSS4fnSaD4Q

Fouts, J. T. (2000). *Research on computers and education: Past, present, and future. A report to the Bill and Melinda Gates Foundation*. Seattle Pacific University.

France Agrimer. (2020). *Etudes Vin et Cidre: commercialisation du vin par internet en France, données de cadrage du circuit*. Direction Marchés, études et prospective.

Francis, T., & Hoefel, F. (2018). *True Gen: Generation Z and its implications for companies*. https://www.mckinsey.com/industries/consumer-packaged-goods/our-insights/true-gen-generation-z-and-its-implications-for-companies#

Frenken, K. (2017). Political economies and environmental futures for the sharing economy. *Philosophical Transactions - Royal Society. Mathematical, Physical, and Engineering Sciences*, *375*(2095), 20160367. doi:10.1098/rsta.2016.0367 PMID:28461431

Frey, C. B., & Osborne, M. A. (2017). The future of employment: How susceptible are jobs to computerisation? *Technological Forecasting and Social Change*, *114*, 254–280. doi:10.1016/j.techfore.2016.08.019

Friedman, G. (2014). Workers without employers: Shadow corporations and the rise of the gig economy. *Review of Keynesian Economics*, *2*(2), 171–188. doi:10.4337/roke.2014.02.03

Froese, A. D., Carpenter, C., Inman, D. A., Schooley, J., Barnes, R., Brecht, P. W., & Chacon, J. D. (2012). Effects of Classroom Cell Phone Use on Expected and Actual Learning. *College Student Journal*, *46*(2), 323–332.

Fulmer, C. A., & Gelfand, M. J. (2012). At what level (and in whom) we trust: Trust across multiple organizational levels. *Journal of Management*, *38*(4), 1167–1230. doi:10.1177/0149206312439327

Gagliardi, D. (2011). Next Generation Entrepreneur: How Web 2.0 Technologies Creep into SMEs. In P. Cunningham & M. Cunningham (Eds.), *eChallenges e-2011 Conference Proceedings*. Dublin, Ireland: IIMC International Information Management Corporation Ltd.

Gagne, R. M. (1977). *The Conditions of Learning*. Holt, Rinehart and Winston.

Gan, W., Lin, J. C.-W., Zhang, J., Fournier-Viger, P., Chao, H.-C., & Yu, P. S. (2020). Fast Utility Mining on Sequence Data. IEEE Transactions on Cybernetics, 1–14. doi:10.1109/TCYB.2020.2970176 PubMed

Gan, C., & Wang, W. (2017). The influence of perceived value on purchase intention in social commerce context. *Internet Research*, *27*(4), 772–785. doi:10.1108/IntR-06-2016-0164

García Aretio, L. (2014). *Web 2.0 vs web 1.0*. Academic Press.

Garg, N., & Garg, N. (2019). Next Generation Internet (Web 3.0: Block Chained Internet). *Cybernomics*, *1*(6), 19–23.

Garner. (2018). Amazon in the Global Market. *Journal of Marketing Management*, *9*(2), 63-73.

Gartner. (2002). *Gartner Web Site Evaluation Application*. Available www.gartnerg2.com

Gefen, D., Karahanna, E., & Straub, D. W. (2003). Trust and TAM in online shopping: An integrated model. *Management Information Systems Quarterly*, *27*(1), 51–90. doi:10.2307/30036519

Genesan, S., & Hess, R. (2004). Dimensions and levels of Trust: Implications for commitment to a relationship. *Marketing Letters*, *8*(4), 439–448. doi:10.1023/A:1007955514781

Geyskens, I., Jan-Benedict, E.M. Steenkamp, & Nirmalya, K. (1998). Generalisations about trust in marketing channel relationships using Meta-Analysis. *International Journal of Research in Marketing*, *15*(3), 223-248.

Gilboa, S., Seger-Guttmann, T., & Mimran, O. (2019). The unique role of relationship marketing in small businesses' customer experience. *Journal of Retailing and Consumer Services*, *51*, 152–164. doi:10.1016/j.jretconser.2019.06.004

GoDaddy France. (2020). *Découvrez pourquoi nous sommes le plus grand registraire de noms de domaine*. Retrieved from: ehttps://www.godaddy.com/fr-fr/domaines

Go, E., & You, K. H. (2016). But not all social media are the same: Analyzing organizations' social media usage patterns. *Telematics and Informatics*, *33*(1), 176–186. doi:10.1016/j.tele.2015.06.016

Gómez, A., Ruiz, Á. A. M., & Orcos, L. (2015). UX of social network Edmodo in undergraduate engineering students. *IJIMAI*, *3*(4), 31–36. doi:10.9781/ijimai.2015.346

Goodwin, T. (2018). Digital Darwinism: Survival of the Fittest in the Age of Business Disruption. Academic Press.

Graham, S. (2020). An attributional theory of motivation. *Contemporary Educational Psychology*, *101861*. Advance online publication. doi:10.1016/j.cedpsych.2020.101861

Gray, J., & Rumpe, B. (2015). *Models for digitalization*. Springer. doi:10.100710270-015-0494-9

Green, C. S., & Bavelier, D. (2012). Learning, Attentional Control, and Action Video Games. *Current Biology*, *22*(6), R197–R206. doi:10.1016/j.cub.2012.02.012 PMID:22440805

Grinsven, B., & Das, E. (2014). Logo design in marketing communications: Brand logo complexity moderates exposure effects on brand recognition and brand attitude. *Journal of Marketing Communications*, *22*, 1–15. doi:10.1080/13527 266.2013.866593

Grohmann, B., Giese, J., & Parkman, I. (2012). Using type font characteristics to communicate brand personality of new brands. *Journal of Brand Management*, *20*. Advance online publication. doi:10.1057/bm.2012.23

Grönroos, C., & Ravald, A. (2011). Service as business logic: Implications for value creation and marketing. *Journal of Service Management*, *22*(1), 5–22. doi:10.1108/09564231111106893

Grosseck, G. (2009). To use or not to use web 2.0. in higher education? *Procedia: Social and Behavioral Sciences*, *1*(1), 478–482. doi:10.1016/j.sbspro.2009.01.087

Guerrieri, P., Evangelista, R., & Meliciani, V. (2014). *The economic impact of digital technologies in Europe*. Academic Press.

Guha, R., & Al-Dabass, D. (2010, December). Impact of web 2.0 and cloud computing platform on software engineering. *In 2010 International Symposium on Electronic System Design* (pp. 213-218). IEEE. 10.1109/ISED.2010.48

Gulsecen, S., Ozdemir, S., Gezer, M., & Akadal, E. (2015). The Good Reader of Digital World, Digital Natives: Are They Good Writer Also? *Procedia: Social and Behavioral Sciences*, *191*, 2396–2401. doi:10.1016/j.sbspro.2015.04.444

Guo, C., & Saxton, G. D. (2018). Speaking and being heard: How nonprofit advocacy organizations gain attention on social media. *Nonprofit and Voluntary Sector Quarterly*, *47*(1), 5–26. doi:10.1177/0899764017713724

Guo, J., Wang, X., & Wu, Y. (2020). Positive emotion bias: Role of emotional content from online customer reviews in purchase decisions. *Journal of Retailing and Consumer Services*, *52*, 2–4. doi:10.1016/j.jretconser.2019.101891

Guttentag, D. (2015). Airbnb: Disruptive innovation and the rise of an informal tourism accommodation sector. *Current Issues in Tourism*, *18*(12), 1192–1217. doi:10.1080/13683500.2013.827159

Hagman, J. D. (1980). *Effects of Presentation and Test Trial Training on Acquisition and Retention of Movement End Location*. DTIC Document. doi:10.21236/ADA100867

Haller C. (2018). *La digitalisation du monde du vin: le cas des entreprises vitivinicoles*. Conférence "Auf" de la Confrérie Saint Etienne, Kientzheim.

Haller, C. (2018). La digitalisation du monde du vin: le cas des entreprises vitivinicoles. *Conférence "Auf" de la Confrérie Saint Etienne*.

Haller, C., & Plotkina, D. & VoThan, T. (2019, June). *Proposition d'une grille d'évaluation de la maturité digitale d'un site Web d'entreprise vitivinicole dans le contexte européen*. Paper presented at the Conférence de l'Association Système d'information (AIM), France.

Haller, C., Hess, I., & Méreaux, J.-P. (2019). Valorisation du vignoble alsacien à travers l'oenotourisme: création d'un écosystème d'innovation régional basé sur l'expérience oenotouristique. In Unione Giuristi della Vite e del Vino UGIVI (pp. 119-131). G.Giappichelli Editore.

Haller, C., Thach, L., & Olsen, J. (2020). Understanding eWineTourism Practices of European and North America Wineries. *Journal of Gastronomy and Tourism*, *4*(3), 141–156. doi:10.3727/216929720X15846938923987

Hamari, J., Sjöklint, M., & Ukkonen, A. (2016). The sharing economy: Why people participate in collaborative consumption. *Journal of the Association for Information Science and Technology*, *67*(9), 2047–2059. doi:10.1002/asi.23552

Handarkho, Y. (2020). Impact of social experience on customer purchase decision in the social commerce context. *Journal of Systems and Information Technology, 22*(4).

Hannin, H. ; Couderc, J.-P. ; D'Hauteville, F. & Montaigne, E. (2010). *La vigne et le vin: mutations économiques en France et dans le monde.* Collection les Études de la Documentation française, La Documentation française.

Harandi, S. R. (2015). Effects of e-learning on Students' Motivation. *Procedia: Social and Behavioral Sciences, 181,* 423–430. doi:10.1016/j.sbspro.2015.04.905

Harris, A. L., & Rea, A. (2019). Web 2.0 and virtual world technologies: A growing impact on IS education. *Journal of Information Systems Education, 20*(2), 3.

Hartson, H. R., Andre, T. S., & Williges, R. C. (2003). Criteria for evaluating usability evaluation methods. In *International Journal of Human-Computer Interaction* (Vol. 15, pp. 145–181). Taylor and Francis Inc., doi:10.1207/S15327590IJHC1501_13

Hassenzahl, M. (2001). The effect of perceived hedonic quality on product appealingness. *International Journal of Human-Computer Interaction, 13*(4), 481–499. doi:10.1207/S15327590IJHC1304_07

Hassenzahl, M., Diefenbach, S., & Goritz, A. (2010). Needs, affect and interactive products-facets of user experience. *Interacting with Computers, 22*(5), 353–362. doi:10.1016/j.intcom.2010.04.002

Hassenzahl, M., & Tractinsky, N. (2006). User experience – a research agenda. *Behaviour & Information Technology, 25*(2), 91–97. doi:10.1080/01449290500330331

Hatzivasilis, G., Askoxylakis, I., Alexandris, G., Anicic, D., Bröring, A., Kulkarni, V., . . . Spanoudakis, G. (2018, September). The Interoperability of Things: Interoperable solutions as an enabler for IoT and Web 3.0. In *2018 IEEE 23rd International Workshop on Computer-Aided Modeling and Design of Communication Links and Networks (CAMAD)* (pp. 1-7). IEEE.

Hauser, J. R., Urban, G. L., Liberali, G., & Braun, M. (2009). Website morphing. *Marketing Science, 28*(2), 201–401. doi:10.1287/mksc.1080.0459

Hayek, M., Farhat, P., Yamout, Y., Ghorra, C., & Haraty, R. A. (2019, September). Web 2.0 Testing Tools: A Compendium. In *2019 International Conference on Innovation and Intelligence for Informatics, Computing, and Technologies (3ICT)* (pp. 1-6). IEEE.

Hedley, M. B2B International. (2017). *Entering Chinese business-to-business markets: the challenges and opportunities.* www.b2binternational.com/publications/china-market-entry/

Heeter, C. (2000). Interactivity in the context of designed experiences. *Journal of Interactive Advertising, 1*(1), 3–14. doi:10.1080/15252019.2000.10722040

Henderson, P., Giese, J., & Cote, J. (2004a). Impression management using typeface design. *Journal of Marketing, 68,* 60–72. doi:10.1509/jmkg.68.4.60.42736

Heo, Y. (2016). Sharing economy and prospects in tourism research. *Annals of Tourism Research, 58,* 166–170. doi:10.1016/j.annals.2016.02.002

Hernandez, J. J., Conway, D., & Knight, T. (2018). *Tomorrow's experience, today. Harnessing a customer first approach in a changing world.* Academic Press.

Hicks, A., & Graber, A. (2010). Shifting paradigms: Teaching, learning and Web 2.0. *RSR. Reference Services Review, 38*(4), 621–633. doi:10.1108/00907321011090764

Hill, A. P. (2013). Motivation and university experience in first-year university students: A self-determination theory perspective. *Journal of Hospitality, Leisure, Sport and Tourism Education, 13*, 244–254. doi:10.1016/j.jhlste.2012.07.001

Hiremath, B. K., & Kenchakkanavar, A. Y. (2016). An alteration of the web 1.0, web 2.0 and web 3.0: a comparative study. *Imperial Journal of Interdisciplinary Research, 2*(4), 705-710.

Hochschule Geisenheim University. (2019). *ProWein Business Report.* Retrieved from https://www.prowein.com/en/For_Visitors/Business_Reports/Business_Report_2019

Hochschule Geisenheim University. (2019). *ProWein Business Report.* Retrieved from: https://www.prowein.com/en/For_Visitors/Business_Reports/Business_Report_2019

Hoffman, D. L., & Novak, T. P. (2000). How to acquire customers on the web. *Harvard Business Review, 78*(3), 179–188. PMID:11183979

Hoffman, D. L., Novak, T. P., & Peralta, M. (1999). Building Consumer Trust Online. *Communications of the ACM, 42*(4), 80–85. doi:10.1145/299157.299175

Honebein, P. C. (1996). Seven goals for the design of constructivist learning environments. *Constructivist learning environments: Case studies in instructional design*, 11-24. Retrieved from http://studentcenteredlearning.pbworks.com/f/DesignConstructivistHonebein.pdf

Hong, Y., & Pavlou, P. A. (2014). Product Fit Uncertainty in Online Markets: Nature, Effects, and Antecedents. *Information Systems Research, 25*(2), 328–344. doi:10.1287/isre.2014.0520

Hossain, A., & Shirazi, F. (2015). *Cloud Computing: A Multi-tenant Case Study.* Paper presented at the International Conference on Human-Computer Interaction.

HostingTribunal. (n.d.). How many websites are there? How many are active in 2020? Retrieved from https://hosting-tribunal.com/blog/how-many-websites/

Howe, N., & Strauss, W. (2007). *Millennials & K-12 Schools: Educational Strategies for a New Generation.* LifeCourse Associates.

Hrichi, A. S., & Rached, K. B. (2017). La fidélité envers la marque de «Deal» à travers une atmosphère inter@ ctive: Une étude qualitative exploratoire «Le cas d'achat groupé en ligne». *La Revue Gestion et Organisation, 9*(2), 131–142. doi:10.1016/j.rgo.2017.04.001

Hsieh, J.-K., Hsieh, Y.-C., Chiu, H.-C., & Yang, Y.-R. (2014). Customer Response to Web Site Atmospherics: Task-Relevant Cues, Situational Involvement and Pad. *Journal of Interactive Marketing, 28*(3), 225–236. doi:10.1016/j.intmar.2014.03.001

Hsieh, M.-H., Pan, S.-L., & Setiono, R. (2004). Product-, Corporate-, and Country-Image Dimensions and Purchase Behavior: A Multicountry Analysis. *Journal of the Academy of Marketing Science, 32*(3), 251–270. doi:10.1177/0092070304264262

Hsieh, M., & Tsao, W. (2014). Reducing perceived online shopping risk to enhance loyalty: A website quality perspective. *Journal of Risk Research, 17*(2), 241–261. doi:10.1080/13669877.2013.794152

Hsu, C. L., & Park, H. W. (2011). Sociology of hyperlink networks of Web 1.0, Web 2.0, and Twitter: A case study of South Korea. *Social Science Computer Review, 29*(3), 354–368. doi:10.1177/0894439310382517

Huang, K. C., Lin, C. C., & Chiang, S. Y. (2008). Color preference and familiarity in performance on brand logo recall. *Perceptual and Motor Skills, 107*(2), 587–596. doi:10.2466/pms.107.2.587-596 PubMed

Huang, W.-H. D., Hood, D. W., & Yoo, S. J. (2013). Gender divide and acceptance of collaborative Web 2.0 applications for learning in higher education. *The Internet and Higher Education*, *16*, 57–65. doi:10.1016/j.iheduc.2012.02.001

Huang, Y., Li, C., Wu, J., & Lin, Z. (2018). Online customer reviews and consumer evaluation: The role of review font. *Information & Management*, *55*(4), 430–440. doi:10.1016/j.im.2017.10.003

Huang, Y., Wu, J., & Shi, W. (2018). The impact of font choice on web pages: Relationship with willingness to pay and tourism motivation. *Tourism Management*, *66*, 191–199. doi:10.1016/j.tourman.2017.12.010

Huang, Z., Hong, Y., & Xu, X. (2020). Design and research on evaluation model of user experience on mobile terminal products. In *Advances in Intelligent Systems and Computing* (Vol. 972, pp. 198–206). Springer Verlag., doi:10.1007/978-3-030-19135-1_20

Hubbard, D. W. (2008). How to measure anything: finding the value of "intangibles" in business. Choice Reviews Online, 45(12), 45-6882-45–6882. doi:10.5860/choice.45-6882

Hudson, J. (2018, April 4). Introducing OpenType variable fonts. Medium. Retrieved from; https://medium.com/variable-fonts/https-medium-com-tiro-introducing-opentype-variable-fonts-12ba6cd2369

Huffman, K. (2017). Web 2.0: Beyond the concept practical ways to implement RSS, podcasts, and Wikis. *Education Libraries*, *29*(1), 12–19. doi:10.26443/el.v29i1.220

Hughes, G. (2009). Social software: New opportunities for challenging social inequalities in learning? *Learning, Media and Technology*, *34*(4), 291–305. doi:10.1080/17439880903338580

Hussain, W., Sohaib, O., Ahmed, A., & Khan, M. Q. (2011). *Web readability factors affecting users of all ages*. Academic Press.

Hutton, J. G. (1997). The influence of brand and corporate-identity programmes on consumer behaviour: A conceptual framework. *Journal of Brand Management*, *5*(2), 120–135. doi:10.1057/bm.1997.38

Huurne, M., Ronteltap, A., Corten, R., & Buskens, V. (2017). Antecedents of trust in the sharing economy: A systematic review. *Journal of Consumer Behaviour*, *16*(3), 485–498. doi:10.1002/cb.1667

Ifinedo, P. (2017). Examining students' intention to continue using blogs for learning: Perspectives from technology acceptance, motivational, and social-cognitive frameworks. *Computers in Human Behavior*, *72*, 189–199. doi:10.1016/j.chb.2016.12.049

Ilgen, D. R., Hollenbeck, J. R., Johnson, M., & Jundt, D. (2005). Teams in organizations: From input-process-output models to IMOI models. *Annual Review of Psychology*, *56*(1), 517–543. doi:10.1146/annurev.psych.56.091103.070250 PMID:15709945

Ingenhoff, D., & Koelling, A. M. (2009). The potential of Web sites as a relationship building tool for charitable fundraising NPOs. *Public Relations Review*, *35*(1), 66–73. doi:10.1016/j.pubrev.2008.09.023

Insteford, E. J., & Munthe, E. (2017). Educating digitally competent teachers: A study of integration of professional digital competence in teacher education. *Teaching and Teacher Education*, *67*, 37–45. doi:10.1016/j.tate.2017.05.016

Intelligence, M. (2020). *Online Advertising Market - Growth, Trends, and Forecast (2020 - 2025)*. Retrieved from https://www.researchandmarkets.com/reports/4602258/online-advertising-market-growth-trends-and

Interaction Design Foundation (2017). *Needs Before Wants in User Experiences – Maslow and the Hierarchy of Needs*. https://www.interaction-design.org/literature/article/needs-before-wants-in-user-experiences-maslow-and-the-hierarchy-of-needs#:~:text=Abraham%20Maslow%20developed%20a%20deep,be%20motivated%20to%20do%20so

International Organisation of Vine and Wine (OIV). (2019a). *Wine Production: first estimation*. Retrieved from: http://www.oiv.int/public/medias/7033/en-oiv-point-de-conjoncture.pdf

International Organisation of Vine and Wine (OIV). (2019b). *Statistical report on world vitiviniculture*. Retrieved from: http://www.oiv.int/public/medias/6782/oiv-2019-statistical-report-on-world-vitiviniculture.pdf

Internet Assigned Numbers Authority (IANA). (2020). *Accredited registrar list update at 2020-03-19*. Retrieved from: https://www.iana.org/assignments/registrar-ids/registrar-ids.xhtml

Internet Corporation for Assigned Names and Numbers (ICANN). (2012). *alsace application: ICANN new gTLDs program Status*. Retrieved from: https://gtldresult.icann.org/applicationstatus/applicationdetails/313

Internet Corporation for Assigned Names and Numbers (ICANN). (2014) *Approved resolution – meeting of the new gTLD Program Committee*. Retrieved from: https://www.icann.org/resources/board-material/resolutions-new-gtld-2014-03-22-en

Internet Corporation for Assigned Names and Numbers (ICANN). (2020a). *Resources*. Retrieved from: https://www.icann.org/resources/pages/what-2012-02-25-en

Internet Corporation for Assigned Names and Numbers (ICANN). (2020b). Retrieved from: https://web.archive.org/web/20170217011554/https://gtldresult.icann.org/application-result/applicationstatus/auctionresults

INTUI. (2010). *Twenty Trends that Will Shape the Next Decade*. Retrieved from https://http-download.intuit.com/http.intuit/CMO/intuit/futureofsmallbusiness/intuit_2020_report.pdf

Irma Becerra-Fernandez, R. S. (2001). Organizational knowledge management: A contingency perspective. *Journal of Management Information Systems*, *18*(1), 23–55. doi:10.1080/07421222.2001.11045676

Isaías, P., Miranda, P., & Pífano, S. (2009). Critical success factors for web 2.0–A reference framework. In A. A. Ozok & P. Zaphiris (Eds.), *Online Communities and Social Computing* (pp. 354–363). Springer. doi:10.1007/978-3-642-02774-1_39

Isaías, P., Pífano, S., & Miranda, P. (2012). Social Network Sites: Modeling the New Business-Customer Relationship. In M. Safar & K. Mahdi (Eds.), *Social Networking and Community Behavior Modeling: Qualitative and Quantitative Measures* (pp. 248–265). IGI Global. doi:10.4018/978-1-61350-444-4.ch014

ISCAP. (2005). *Business Simulation: Support Book*. Instituto Superior de Contabilidade e Administração do Porto.

ISO. (2014). ISO - ISO/IEC 25063:2014 - Systems and software engineering — Systems and software product Quality Requirements and Evaluation (SQuaRE) — Common Industry Format (CIF) for usability: Context of use description. Retrieved from https://www.iso.org/standard/35789.html

ISO. (2019). Ergonomics of human-system interaction — Part 210: Human-centred design for interactive systems (2). ISO - ISO 9241-210:2019. Retrieved from https://www.iso.org/standard/77520.html

Ivala, E., & Gachago, D. (2012). Social media for enhancing student engagement: The use of Facebook and blogs at a University of Technology. *South African Journal of Higher Education*, *26*(1), 152–166.

Izadi, A., & Patrick, V. M. (n.d.). The power of the pen: Handwritten fonts promote haptic engagement. *Psychology and Marketing*. Advance online publication. doi:10.1002/mar.21318

Jackson, T. (2011). *Kodak fell victim to disruptive technology*. https://www.ft.com/content/f49cb408-ecd8-11e0-be97-00144feab49a

Jagdish, S. (1972). The future of buyer behaviour. *Proceedings of the Third Annual Conference of the Association for Consumer Research*, 562-575.

Jamie. (n.d.). *What is a blog? – A guide to understanding the concept of blogging*. Retrieved from https://makeawebsitehub.com/what-is-a-blog

Jeff, S. (2015). SUPR-Q: A Comprehensive Measure of the Quality of the Website User ExperienceJUS. *Journal of Usability Studies, 10*(2), 68–86. https://uxpajournal.org/supr-q-a-comprehensive-measure-of-the-quality-of-the-website-user-experience/

Jenkins, R. (2019). *5 Need-To-Know Characteristics of the New Millennial Buyer.* https://www.inc.com/ryan-jenkins/selling-to-millennial-buyers-5-things-you-need-to-know.html

Jensen, J. F. (1998). Interactivity. *Nordicom Review, Nordic research on media and comunication review, 19*(2), 191.

Jensen, J. F. (1999). *InteractiveTelevision: TV of the Future or the Future of TV?* Aalborg Universitetsforlag.

Jesse James Garret. (2000). *The Elements of User Experience.* New Riders.

Jobber, D., & Lancaster, G. (2009). Selling and sales management. 8. painos. Harlow: Pearson Education.

Johnson, A. G., & Neuhofer, B. (2017). Airbnb–an exploration of value co-creation experiences in Jamaica. *International Journal of Contemporary Hospitality Management, 29*(9), 2361–2376. doi:10.1108/IJCHM-08-2016-0482

Johnson, G. M. (2008). Cognitive processing differences between frequent and infrequent Internet users. *Computers in Human Behavior, 24*(5), 2094–2106. doi:10.1016/j.chb.2007.10.001

Johnson, R., & Bruwer, J. (2007). Regional brand image and perceived wine quality: The consumer perspective. *International Journal of Wine Business Research, 19*(4), 276–297. doi:10.1108/17511060710837427

Jomah, O., Masoud, A. K., Kishore, X. P., & Aurelia, S. (2016). Micro learning: A modernized education system. *BRAIN. Broad Research in Artificial Intelligence and Neuroscience, 7*(1), 103–110.

Jones, S., & Fox, S. (2009). *Generations online in 2009.* Pew Internet and American Life Project. Available at: https://pewinternet.org/PPF/r/251/presentation_display.asp

Jordan, P. W. (2000). Designing Pleasurable Products | An Introduction to the New Human Factors | Taylor & Francis Group. Lodon: Taylor & Francis, Imprint CRC Press. Retrieved from https://www.taylorfrancis.com/books/9780429219962

Joseph, G. V., & Thomas, K. A. (2020). Volatility of Digital Technology Enabled Learning through Social Media: Educators" Apprehensions. *Test Engineering and Management, 82*, 5832–5839.

Jovanovic, D., & Matejevic, M. (2014). Relationship between Rewards and Intrinsic Motivation for Learning – Researches Review. *Procedia: Social and Behavioral Sciences, 149*, 456–460. doi:10.1016/j.sbspro.2014.08.287

Jussila, J. J., Kärkkäinen, H., & Aramo-Immonen, H. (2014). Social media utilization in business-to-business relationships of technology industry frms. *Computers in Human Behavior, 30*, 606–613. doi:10.1016/j.chb.2013.07.047

Kam, H.-J., & Katerattanakul, P. (2014). Structural model of team-based learning using Web 2.0 collaborative software. *Computers & Education, 76*, 1–12. doi:10.1016/j.compedu.2014.03.003

Kane, M. J., Hambrick, D. Z., Tuholski, S. W., Wilhelm, O., Payne, T. W., & Engle, R. W. (2004). The Generality of Working Memory Capacity: A Latent-Variable Approach to Verbal and Visuospatial Memory Span and Reasoning. *Journal of Experimental Psychology. General, 133*(2), 189–217. doi:10.1037/0096-3445.133.2.189 PMID:15149250

Kang, J., Hong, S., & Hubbard, G. (2020). The role of storytelling in advertising: Consumer emotion, narrative engagement level, and word-of-mouth intention. *Journal of Consumer Behaviour, 19*(1), 47–56. doi:10.1002/cb.1793

Kaplan, A. M., & Haenlein, M. (2010). Users of the world, unite! The challenges and opportunities of Social Media. *Business Horizons, 53*(1), 59–68. doi:10.1016/j.bushor.2009.09.003

Karkoulia, K. C. (2016). Teachers' attitudes towards the integration of Web 2.0 tools in EFL teaching. *Research Papers in Language Teaching and Learning, 1*(7), 46–73.

Karlsson, L., Kemperman, A., & Dolnicar, S. (2017). May I sleep in your bed? Getting permission to book. *Annals of Tourism Research, 62*(Complete), 1-12.

Karunasena, A., Deng, H., & Zhang, X. (2012). *A Web 2.0 based e-learning success model in higher education.* Available at: http://www.ier-institute.org/2070-1918/lnit23/v23/177.pdf

Kato & Suzuki. (n.d.). *An Approach for Redesigning Learning Environments with Flow Theory.* Retrieved from https://www2.gsis.kumamoto-u.ac.jp/~idportal/wp-content/uploads/icome2010_kato.pdf

Kaur, R., Awasthi, A., & Grzybowska, K. (2020). *Evaluation of Key Skills Supporting Industry 4.0—A Review of Literature and Practice. In Sustainable Logistics and Production in Industry 4.0.* Springer.

Keage, H. A. D., Coussens, S., Kohler, M., Thiessen, M., & Churches, O. F. (2014). Investigating letter recognition in the brain by varying typeface: An event-related potential study. *Brain and Cognition, 88*, 83–89. doi:10.1016/j.bandc.2014.05.001 PubMed

Ke, H. (2010). The Key Technologies of IoT with Development & Applications. *Radio Frequency Ubiquitous Journal, 1*(1), 33.

Kelley, K., Clark, B., Brown, V., & Sitzia, J. (2003). Good practice in the conduct and reporting of survey research. *International Journal for Quality in Health Care, 15*(3), 261–266. doi:10.1093/intqhc/mzg031 PMID:12803354

Kenney, M., & Zysman, J. (2016). The rise of the platform economy. *Issues in Science and Technology, 32*(3), 61.

Khaled, H., & Head, M. (2007). Manipulating Perceived Social Presence Through the Web Interface and its Impact on Attitude Towards Online Shopping. *International Journal of Human-Computer Studies, 65*(8), 689–708. doi:10.1016/j.ijhcs.2006.11.018

Kim, Dekker, & Heij. (2017). Cross-Border Electronic Commerce: Distance Effects And Express Delivery in European Union Markets. *International Journal of Electronic Commerce, 21*(2), 184-218.

Kim, J., Yoon, Y., & Zo, H. (2015). Why People Participate in the Sharing Economy: A Social Exchange Perspective. *PACIS, 76*.

Kim, E. J., & Lee, K. R. (2019). Effects of an examiner's positive and negative feedback on self-assessment of skill performance, emotional response, and self-efficacy in Korea: A quasi-experimental study. *BMC Medical Education, 19*(1), 142. doi:10.118612909-019-1595-x PMID:31088436

Kim, H. B. (2013). The study on the relationship between smartphone addiction and cyber-crime. *Korean Association of Addiction Crime Review, 3*(2), 1–21.

Kim, W., Jeong, O.-R., & Lee, S.-W. (2010). On social Web sites. *Information Systems, 35*(2), 215–236. doi:10.1016/j.is.2009.08.003

Kirschner, P. A., & Karpinski, A. C. (2010). Facebook® and academic performance. *Computers in Human Behavior, 26*(6), 1237–1245. doi:10.1016/j.chb.2010.03.024

Kirschner, P., & Woperies, I. G. J. H. (2003). Mind tools for teacher communities: A European perspective. *Technology, Pedagogy and Education, 12*(1), 127–149. doi:10.1080/14759390300200148

Klaus, P. (2020). Customer experience, not brands will be on the iron throne. *International Journal of Market Research*, *62*(1), 6–8. doi:10.1177/1470785319858570

Klopfer, E., Osterweil, S., Groff, J., & Haas, J. (2009). *Using the technology of today, in the classroom today. The Instructional Power of digital games, social networking, simulations and How Teachers Can Leverage Them*. Massachusetts Institute of Technology, The Education Arcade.

Koenka, A. C. (2020). Academic motivation theories revisited: An interactive dialog between motivation scholars on recent contributions, underexplored issues, and future directions. *Contemporary Educational Psychology*, *101831*, 101831. Advance online publication. doi:10.1016/j.cedpsych.2019.101831

Koetz, C. (2019). Managing the customer experience: A beauty retailer deploys all tactics. *The Journal of Business Strategy*, *40*(1), 10–17. doi:10.1108/JBS-09-2017-0139

Kolb, D. (1999). *Experiential Learning Theory: Previous Research and New Directions*. Retrieved from https://learningfromexperience.com/downloads/research-library/experiential-learning-theory.pdf

Koltai, T., Lozano, S., Uzonyi-Kecskés, J., & Moreno, P. (2017). Evaluation of the results of a production simulation game using a dynamic DEA approach. *Computers & Industrial Engineering*, *105*, 1–11. doi:10.1016/j.cie.2016.12.048

Kompen, R. T., Edirisingha, P., Canaleta, X., Alsina, M., & Monguet, J. M. (2019). Personal learning Environments based on Web 2.0 services in higher education. *Telematics and Informatics*, *38*, 194–206. doi:10.1016/j.tele.2018.10.003

Kopecký, J., Gomadam, K., & Vitvar, T. (2008, December). hrests: An HTML microformat for describing restful web services. In *2008 IEEE/WIC/ACM International Conference on Web Intelligence and Intelligent Agent Technology* (Vol. 1, pp. 619-625). IEEE. 10.1109/WIIAT.2008.379

Kopnina, H. (2017). Sustainability: New strategic thinking for business. *Environment, Development and Sustainability*, *19*(1), 27–43. doi:10.100710668-015-9723-1

Koshi, L. (2013). Web based education. *University News*, *51*(29), 14–16.

Kostakis, V., & Bauwens, M. (2014). *Network Society and Future Scenarios for a Collaborative Economy*. Springer. doi:10.1057/9781137406897

Kotler, P. (2003). Marketing *Management*. Academic Press.

Kotler, P., Kartajaya, H., & Setiawan, I. (2016). *Marketing 4.0: Moving from traditional to digital*. John Wiley & Sons.

KPMG (2018). *Growing Pains: 2018 Global CEO Outlook*. https://assets.kpmg/content/dam/kpmg/jm/pdf/2018-ceo-outlook-report-final-low.pdf

Kranzbühler, A., Zerres, A., Kleijnen, M., & Verlegh, P. (2019). Beyond valence: a meta-analysis of discrete emotions in firm-customer encounters. *Journal of the Academy of Marketing Science*, 1-21.

Kristensen, T., & Grønhaug, K. (2007). Can design improve the performance of marketing management? *Journal of Marketing Management*, *23*(9-10), 815–827. doi:10.1362/026725707X250331

Kristian, K., Lainema, T., Freitas, S., & Arnab, S. (2014). Flow framework for analyzing the quality of educational games. *Entertainment Computing*, *5*(4), 367–377. doi:10.1016/j.entcom.2014.08.002

Kroski, E. (2008). *Web 2.0 for librarians and information professionals*. Neal-Schuman Publishers, Inc.

Krueger, J. C., & Haytko, D. L. (2015). Nonprofit adaptation to Web 2.0 and digital marketing strategies. *Journal of Technology Research*, *6*, 1.

Krum, C. (2010). *Mobile marketing: Finding your customers no matter where they are.* Pearson Education.

Kucuk, S. U., & Krishnamurthy, S. (2007). An Analysis of Consumer Power on the Internet. *Technovation, 27*(1-2), 47–56. doi:10.1016/j.technovation.2006.05.002

Kukar-Kinney, M., & Close, A. G. (2010). The Determinants of Consumers' Online Shopping Cart Abandonment. *Journal of the Academy of Marketing Science, 38*(2), 240–250. doi:10.100711747-009-0141-5

Labar, A. V. (2008). *SPSS pentru Științele Educației.* Editura Polirom.

Lan, J., Ma, Y., Zhu, D., Mangalagiu, D., & Thornton, T. F. (2017). Enabling value co-creation in the sharing economy: The case of mobike. *Sustainability, 9*(9), 1504. doi:10.3390u9091504

Lanktree, C., & Briere, J. (1991, January). *Early data on the trauma symptom checklist for children (TSC-C).* Paper presented at the meeting of the American Professional Society on the Abuse of Children, San Diego, CA.

Larivière, B., Bowenb, D., Andreassenc, T. W., Kunzd, W., Siriannie, N. J., Voss, C., & De Keyserh, A. (2017). Service Encounter 2.0: An investigation into the roles of technology, employees and customers. *Journal of Business Research, 79*, 238–246. doi:10.1016/j.jbusres.2017.03.008

Larréché, J.-C. (1987). On simulations in business education and research. *Journal of Business Research, 15*(6), 559–571. doi:10.1016/0148-2963(87)90039-7

Lazar, I. (2019b). Investigation on the relationship between the aspirational learners and the acceptance of modern technology in education [Investigații privind relația dintre nivelului aspirațional al cursanților și acceptarea tehnologiilor moderne în procesul de învățământ, in Romanian] (PhD in Science Education). Bucharest University.

Lazar, I. (2019a). *A guide for statistical analysis of data in the educational research* [Ghid pentru analiza statistica a datelor in cercetarea educationala, in Romanian]. Presa Universitara Clujeana.

Lazar, I., Panisoara, G., & Panisoara, I. O. (2020). Adoption of digital storytelling tool in natural sciences and technology education by pre-service teachers using the technology acceptance model. *Journal of Baltic Science Education, 19*(3), 429–453. doi:10.33225/jbse/20.19.429

Lee Yohn, D. (2018). *In Harvard Business Review: 6 Ways to Build a Customer-Centric Culture.* https://hbr.org/2018/10/6-ways-to-build-a-customer-centric-culture

Lee, B. (2019). *As Millennials Choose Pets Over Babies, Pet Tech Is Silicon Valley's Unlikely Industry.* https://www.forbes.com/sites/forbestechcouncil/2019/10/22/as-millennials-choose-pets-over-babies-pet-tech-is-silicon-valleys-unlikely-industry/#66f5df7d48b6

Lee, M. J., & McLoughlin, C. (2011). *Web 2.0-based e-learning: Applying social informatics for tertiary teaching.* Information Science Reference. doi:10.4018/978-1-60566-294-7

Lei, J. (2009). Digital Natives As Preservice Teachers What Technology Preparation Is Needed? *Journal of Computing in Teacher Education, 25*(3), 87–97.

Leismann, K., Schmitt, M., Rohn, H., & Baedeker, C. (2013). Collaborative consumption: Towards a resource-saving consumption culture. *Resources, 2*(3), 184–203. doi:10.3390/resources2030184

Lemke, C., & Coughlin, E. C. (1998). *Technology in American Schools. Seven dimensions for gauging progress.* Milken Exchange Commission on Educational Technology. Available at. https://files.eric.ed.gov/fulltext/ED460677.pdf

Lemoine, J. F. (2012). Pour une présentation du concept d'atmosphère des sites web et de ses effets sur le comportement des internautes. *Marche et Organisations, 15*(1), 169–180.

Lemon, K. N., & Verhoef, P. C. (2016). Understanding customer experience through the customer journey. *Journal of Marketing*, *80*(6), 69–96. doi:10.1509/jm.15.0420

Lenhard, A., & Madden, M. (2005). *Pew Internet & American Life Project. Reports. Family, friends & community. Teen content creators and consumers.* Retrieved December 10th, 2006 from http://www.pewinternet.org/pdfs/PIP_Teens_Content_Creation.pdf

Lerner, J., Valdesolo, P., & Kassam, K. (2015). Emotion and Decision Making. *Annual Review of Psychology*, *66*(1), 799–823. doi:10.1146/annurev-psych-010213-115043 PMID:25251484

Leroux, N., Wortman, M. S. Jr, & Mathias, E. D. (2001). Dominant factors impacting the development of business-to-business (B2B) e-commerce in agriculture. *The International Food and Agribusiness Management Review*, *4*(2), 205–218. doi:10.1016/S1096-7508(01)00075-1

Lewis, L. H., & Williams, C. J. (1994). Experiential Learning: Past and Present. In L. Jackson & R. S. Caffarella (Eds.), *Experiential Learning: A New Approach* (pp. 5–16). Jossey-Bass.

Lialina, O. (2018). Rich user experience, UX and the desktopization of war. *Interface Critique*, (1), 176-193.

Liao, C.-W., Chen, C.-H., & Shih, S.-J. (2019). The interactivity of video and collaboration for learning achievement, intrinsic motivation, cognitive load, and behavior patterns in a digital game-based learning environment. *Computers & Education*, *133*, 43–55. doi:10.1016/j.compedu.2019.01.013

Lim, W. M., & Ting, D. H. (2012). E-Shopping: An Analysis of the Uses and Gratifications Theory. *Modern Applied Science*, *6*(5). Advance online publication. doi:10.5539/mas.v6n5p48

Lin, D., Zongqing, Z., & Xialon, G. (2009). A study of the website performance of travel agencies based on the eMICA model. *Journal of Service Science and Management*, *3*(03), 181–185. doi:10.4236/jssm.2009.23021

Ling, J., & van Schaik, P. (2006). The influence of font type and line length on visual search and information retrieval in web pages. *International Journal of Human-Computer Studies*, *64*(5), 395–404. doi:10.1016/j.ijhcs.2005.08.015

Lin, X., Wang, X., & Hajli, N. (2019). Building ECommerce Satisfaction and Boosting Sales: The Role of Social Commerce Trust and Its Antecedents. *International Journal of Electronic Commerce*, *23*(3), 328–363. doi:10.1080/10864415.2019.1619907

Litalien, D., Gillet, N., Gagné, M., Ratelle, C. F., & Morin, A. J. S. (2019). Self-determined motivation profiles among undergraduate students: A robust test of profile similarity as a function of gender and age. *Learning and Individual Differences*, *70*, 39–52. doi:10.1016/j.lindif.2019.01.005

Li, X., He, X., & Zhang, Y. (2020). The impact of social media on the business performance of small firms in China. *Information Technology for Development*, *26*(2), 346–368. doi:10.1080/02681102.2019.1594661

Lloro, T., & Hunold, C. (2020). The public pedagogy of neighborhood Facebook communities: Negotiating relations with urban coyotes. *Environmental Education Research*, *26*(2), 189–205. doi:10.1080/13504622.2019.1690637

Lockshin, L., Rasmussen, M., & Cleary, F. (2000). The nature and roles of a wine brand. *Australia and New Zealand Wine Industry Journal*, *15*(4), 50–58.

Lockshin, L., & Spawton, T. (2001). Using involvement and brand equity to develop a wine tourism strategy. *International Journal of Wine Marketing*, *13*(1), 72–81. doi:10.1108/eb043371

Logan, R. J. (1994). Behavioral and emotional usability: Thomson Consumer Electronics. In M. E. Wiklund (Ed.), *Usability in practice: how companies develop user-friendly products* (pp. 59–82). Academic Press Professional Inc., Retrieved from https://dl.acm.org/doi/10.5555/180981.180984

Lohse, G. L., & Spiller, P. (1998). Electronic Shopping. *Communications of the ACM, 41*(7), 81–87. doi:10.1145/278476.278491

Lopes, B. D. C. M., & da Silva, E. P. (2020). A divulgação de acervos arquivísticos na web: potencialidades da perspectiva de User Experience aplicada ao Sistema de Informações do Arquivo Nacional. *Ciência da Informação em Revista, 7*, 70-90.

López-Pérez, M. V., Pérez-López, M. C., & Rodríguez-Ariza, L. (2011). Blended learning in higher education: Students' perceptions and their relation to outcomes. *Computers & Education, 56*(3), 818–826. doi:10.1016/j.compedu.2010.10.023

Lovejoy, K., & Saxton, G. D. (2012). Information, community, and action: How nonprofit organizations use social media*. *Journal of Computer-Mediated Communication, 17*(3), 337–353. doi:10.1111/j.1083-6101.2012.01576.x

Lu, Zhao, & Wang. (2010). From virtual community members to C2C e-commerce buyers: Trust in virtual communities and its effect on consumers' purchase intention, *Electronic Commerce Research and Applications, 9*(4), 346-360.

Luckin, R., Bligh, B., Manches, A., Ainsworth, S., Crook, C., & Noss, R. (2012). *Cambridge professional development qualifications for Teaching with Digital Technologies: Decoding Learning: The Proof, Promise and Potential of Digital Education.* Nesta.

Luhmann, N. (1979). *Trust and power.* Wiley.

Luis, C. E. M., Gutiérrez, J. M., & Marrero, A. M. G. (2014). Using mobile devices and internet technologies in problem-based learning: Design of a suitable active and collaborative learning environment in engineering education. *2014 IEEE Frontiers in Education Conference (FIE) Proceedings.* 10.1109/FIE.2014.7044184

Lutz, J. (2015). The validity of crowdsourcing data in studying anger and aggressive behavior. *Social Psychology, 47*(1), 38–51. doi:10.1027/1864-9335/a000256

Lyotard, J.-F. (1984). *The postmodern condition: A report on knowledge* (Vol. 10). U of Minnesota Press.

Machado, E., Inácio, H., Fortes, J., & Sousa, J. (1999). Projecto em Simulação Empresarial: Uma Experiência em Desenvolvimento. *Revista Estudos do ISCAA, 2*(5), 113–127.

Mackiewicz, J., & Moeller, R. (2004). Why people perceive typefaces to have different personalities. International Professional Communication Conference, 2004. IPCC 2004. Proceedings, 304–313. doi:10.1109/IPCC.2004.1375315

Madden, T. J., Hewett, K., & Roth, M. S. (2000). Managing images in different cultures: A cross-national study of color meanings and preferences. *Journal of International Marketing, 8*(4), 90–107. doi:10.1509/jimk.8.4.90.19795

Maechler, N., Neher, K., & Park, R. (2016). *From touchpoints to journeys: Seeing the world as customers do.* https://www.mckinsey.com/business-functions/marketing-and-sales/our-insights/from-touchpoints-to-journeys-seeing-the-world-as-customers-do#

Mahemoff, M. (2006). *AJAX design patterns: creating Web 2.0 sites with programming and usability patterns.* O'Reilly Media, Inc.

Mahlke, S., & Thuring, M. (2007) Studying antecedents of emotional experiences in interactive contexts. *Proceedings of the SIGCHI Conference on Human Factors in Computing Systems (CHI '07)*, 915-918. 10.1145/1240624.1240762

Mahood, C., Kalyanaraman, S., & Sundar, S. S. (2000, August). *The effects of erotica and dehumanizing pornography in an online interactive environment*. In Annual conference of the Association for Education in Journalism and Mass Communication, Phoenix, AZ.

Maia, C. L. B., & Furtado, E. S. (2016). A systematic review about user experience evaluation. In *Lecture Notes in Computer Science (including subseries Lecture Notes in Artificial Intelligence and Lecture Notes in Bioinformatics)* (Vol. 9746, pp. 445–455). Springer Verlag., doi:10.1007/978-3-319-40409-7_42.

Mainardes, E. W., Marcio de Almeida, C., & de-Oliveira, M. (2019). e-Commerce: An analysis of the factors that antecede purchase intentions in an emerging market. *Journal of International Consumer Marketing*, 31(5), 447–468. doi :10.1080/08961530.2019.1605643

Mair, J., & Reischauer, G. (2017). Capturing the dynamics of the sharing economy: Institutional research on the plural forms and practices of sharing economy organizations. *Technological Forecasting and Social Change*, 125, 11–20. doi:10.1016/j.techfore.2017.05.023

Makri, K., Papadas, K. K., & Schlegelmilch, B. B. (2019). Global-local consumer identities as drivers of global digital brand usage. *International Marketing Review*, 36(5), 708. doi:10.1108/IMR-03-2018-0104

Manisha, M. (2018). *Digitalization's Impact on Work Culture. In Radical Reorganization of Existing Work Structures Through Digitalization*. IGI Global.

Marketing Science Institute (2018). *Research Priorities 2018-2020*. Marketing Science Institute.

Martin, & Chris, J. (2016). The sharing economy: a pathway to sustainability or a nightmarish form of neoliberal capitalism? *Ecological Economics, 121*, 149-159.

Marttunen, M., & Laurinen, L. (2001). Learning of Argumentation Skills in Networked and Face-to-face environments. *Journal of Instructional Science*, 29(2), 127–153. doi:10.1023/A:1003931514884

Martyakova, E., & Gorchakova, E. (2019). *Quality Education and Digitalization of the Economy*. Paper presented at the International Conference on the Industry 4.0 model for Advanced Manufacturing. 10.1007/978-3-030-18180-2_17

Maslow, A. H. (1943). A theory of human motivation. *Psychological Review*, 50(4), 370–396. doi:10.1037/h0054346

Massa, C., & Bédé, S. (2018). A consumer value approach to a holistic understanding of the winery experience. *Qualitative Market Research*, 21(4), 530–548. doi:10.1108/QMR-01-2017-0031

Mastercard. (n.d.). *MASTERINDEX 2017 Pan-European e-commerce and new payment trends*. https://newsroom.mastercard.com/wp-content/uploads/2017/03/Masterindex-2017.pdf

Mata, L., Panisoara, G., Fat, S., Panisoara, I. O., & Lazar, I. (2019). Exploring the Adoptions by Students of Web 2.0 Tools for E-Learning in Higher Education: Web 2.0 Tools for E-Learning in Higher Education. Advanced Web Applications and Progressing E-Learning 2.0 Technologies in Higher Education, 128-149.

Matzler, K., Bailom, F., Von den Eichen, S. F., & Anschober, M. (2016). Digital Disruption. Wie Sie Ihr Unternehmen auf das digitale Zeitalter vorbereiten, Vahlen, München.

Matzler, K., Friedrich von den Eichen, S., Anschober, M., & Kohler, T. (2018). The crusade of digital disruption. *The Journal of Business Strategy*, 39(6), 13–20. doi:10.1108/JBS-12-2017-0187

Matzler, K., Veider, V., & Kathan, W. (2015). Adapting to the sharing economy. *MIT Sloan Management Review*, 56(2), 71.

Maulana, R., Opdenakker, M.-C., & Bosker, R. (2016). Teachers' instructional behaviors as important predictors of academic motivation: Changes and links across the school year. *Learning and Individual Differences*, *50*, 147–156. doi:10.1016/j.lindif.2016.07.019

Mayer, R. E. (2014). Cognitive theory of multimedia learning. In The Cambridge Handbook of multimedia learning. Cambridge University Press. doi:10.1017/CBO9781139547369.005

Mazman, S. G., & Usluel, Y. K. (2010). Modeling educational usage of Facebook. *Computers & Education*, *55*(2), 444–453. doi:10.1016/j.compedu.2010.02.008

McCabe, A., & Harris, K. (2020). Theorizing social media and activism: Where is community development? *Community Development Journal: An International Forum*, bsz024. Advance online publication. doi:10.1093/cdj/bsz024

McCarthy, M. S., & Mothersbaugh, D. L. (2002). Effects of typographic factors in advertising-based persuasion: A general model and initial empirical tests. doi:10.1002/mar.10030

McCarthy, M. S., & Mothersbaugh, D. L. (2002). Les effets de la typographie sur la persuasion publicitaire: Un modèle général et des tests empiriques préliminaires [Effects of typographic factors in advertising-based persuasion: A general model and initial empirical tests]. *Recherche et Applications en Marketing*, *17*(4), 67–89. doi:10.1177/076737010201700404

McChrystal, G. S., Collins, T., Silverman, D., & Fussell, C. (2015). *Team of teams: New rules of engagement for a complex world*. Penguin.

McClinton, D. (2019). *Global attention span is narrowing and trends don't last as long, study reveals*. https://www.theguardian.com/society/2019/apr/16/got-a-minute-global-attention-span-is-narrowing-study-reveals

McKay, J., Prananto, A., & Marshal, P. (2000). E-Business maturity: The SOG-e Model. *Proceedings of ACIS 2000*, 6-8.

McKinsey & Company. (2014). *Accélérer la mutation numérique des entreprises: un gisement de croissance et de compétitivité pour la France*. Retrieved from: https://www.mckinsey.com/fr/~/media/McKinsey/Locations/Europe%20and%20Middle%20East/France/Our%20Insights/Accelerer%20la%20mutation%20numerique%20des%20entreprises/Rapport_Accelerer_la_mutation_numerique_des_entreprises.ashx

McKnight, D. H., Choudhury, V., & Kacmar, C. (2002). Developing and validating trust measures for e-commerce: An integrative typology. *Information Systems Research*, *13*(3), 334–359. doi:10.1287/isre.13.3.334.81

McLeod, S. A. (2019, July 17). Constructivism as a theory for teaching and learning. *Simply Psychology*. Retrieved from: https://www.simplypsychology.org/constructivism.html

McLoughlin, C. E., & Alam, S. L. (2019). A case study of instructor scaffolding using Web 2.0 tools to teach social informatics. *Journal of Information Systems Education*, *25*(2), 4.

McMillan, S. J., & Hwang, J. S. (2002). Measures of perceived interactivity: An exploration of the role of direction of communication, user control, and time in shaping perceptions of interactivity. *Journal of Advertising*, *31*(3), 29–42. doi:10.1080/00913367.2002.10673674

Mechant, P. (2012). An illustrated framework for the analysis of Web2. 0 interactivity. *Contemporary Social Science*, *7*(3), 263–281. doi:10.1080/21582041.2012.716524

Meens, E. E. M., Bakx, A. W. E. A., Klimstra, T. A., & Denissen, J. J. A. (2018). The association of identity and motivation with students' academic achievement in higher education. *Learning and Individual Differences*, *64*, 54–70. doi:10.1016/j.lindif.2018.04.006

Mehta, A., Morris, N. P., Swinnerton, B., & Homer, M. (2019). The Influence of Values on E-learning Adoption. *Computers & Education*, *141*, 103617. doi:10.1016/j.compedu.2019.103617

Méndez Rodríguez, E. M., Bravo, A., & López, L. M. (2007). *Microformatos: web 2.0 para el Dublin Core*. Academic Press.

Merholz, P. (2007). *Peter in Conversation with Don Norman About UX & Innovation*. Adaptative Path.

Mesbah, A., & Van Deursen, A. (2009, May). Invariant-based automatic testing of AJAX user interfaces. In *2009 IEEE 31st International Conference on Software Engineering* (pp. 210-220). IEEE. 10.1109/ICSE.2009.5070522

Mesquita, A., Oliveira, L., & Sequeira, A. (2019). *The Future of the Digital Workforce: Current and Future Challenges for Executive and Administrative Assistants*. Academic Press.

Messick, D. M., & Kramer, R. M. (2001). *Trust as a form of shallow morality*. Russel Sage Foundation.

Meyer, C., & Schwager, A. (2007). *Understanding Customer Experience*. https://hbr.org/2007/02/understanding-customer-experience

Miller Heiman Group (2018). *The Growing Buyer-Seller Gap: Results of the 2018 Buyer Preferences Study*. https://www.csoinsights.com/wp-content/uploads/sites/5/2018/06/Growing-Buyer-Seller-Gap-White-paper_FINAL.pdf

Miller, C. (2019). *Leading Digital Transformation in Higher Education: A Toolkit for Technology Leaders. In Technology Leadership for Innovation in Higher Education*. IGI Global. doi:10.4018/978-1-5225-7769-0.ch001

Miralles, I., Dentoni, D., & Pascucci, S. (2017). Understanding the organization of sharing economy in agri-food systems: Evidence from alternative food networks in Valencia. *Agriculture and Human Values*, *34*(4), 833–854. doi:10.100710460-017-9778-8

Mistry, A., Rajan, P., & Arokia, R. (2019). Evaluation of web applications based on UX parameters. *International Journal of Electrical & Computer Engineering*, 9.

Mitchell, A. (2007). Get real! – Reviewing the design of a mobile learning game. In N. Pachler (Ed.), *Mobile learning – Towards a research agenda* (pp. 75–104). The WLE Centre.

Mitchell, K. J., Becker-Blease, K. A., & Finkelhor, D. (2005). Inventory of problematic internet experiences encountered in clinical practice. *Professional Psychology, Research and Practice*, *36*(5), 498–509. doi:10.1037/0735-7028.36.5.498

Moher, D., Liberati, A., Tetzlaff, J., & Altman, D. G. (2009). Preferred reporting items for systematic reviews and meta-analyses: The PRISMA statement. *Annals of Internal Medicine*, *151*(4), 264–269. doi:10.7326/0003-4819-151-4-200908180-00135 PMID:19622511

Möhlmann, M. (2015). Collaborative consumption: Determinants of satisfaction and the likelihood of using a sharing economy option again. *Journal of Consumer Behaviour*, *14*(3), 193–207. doi:10.1002/cb.1512

Molinillo, S., Aguilar-Illescas, R., Anaya-Sánchez, R., & Vallespín-Arán, M. (2018). Exploring the impacts of interactions, social presence and emotional engagement on active collaborative learning in a social web-based environment. *Computers & Education*, *123*, 41–52. doi:10.1016/j.compedu.2018.04.012

Monferrer, D., Moliner, M., & Estrada, M. (2019). Increasing customer loyalty through customer engagement in the retail banking industry. *Spanish Journal of Marketing*, *23*(3), 461-484.

Moon, J.-W., & Kim, Y.-G. (2001). Extending the TAM for a World-Wide-Web context. *Information & Management*, *38*(4), 217–230. doi:10.1016/S0378-7206(00)00061-6

Moon, Y., & Nass, C. (1996). How "real" are computer personalities? Psychological responses to personality types in human-computer interaction. *Communication Research, 23*(6), 651–674. doi:10.1177/009365096023006002

Moore, C. (2013, February 20). *Create an A+ site with WordPress.com Classrooms.* Retrieved from https://en.blog.wordpress.com/2013/02/20/classrooms

Moore, R., Stammerjohan, C., & Coulter, R. (2013). Banner advertiser web site congruity and color effects on attention and attitudes. *Journal of Advertising, 34*(2), 71–84. doi:10.1080/00913367.2005.10639189

Mora, H., Signes-Pont, M. T., Fuster-Guilló, A., & Pertegal-Felices, M. L. (2020). A collaborative working model for enhancing the learning process of science & engineering students. *Computers in Human Behavior, 103*, 140–150. doi:10.1016/j.chb.2019.09.008

Moreno, A., Navarro, C., Tench, R., & Zerfass, A. (2015). Does social media usage matter? An analysis of online practices and digital media perceptions of communication practitioners in Europe. *Public Relations Review, 41*(2), 242–253. doi:10.1016/j.pubrev.2014.12.006

Morgan, B. (2019). *The Customer of the Future.* HarperCollins Leadership. Edition.

Morris, K. (2018, March). *Why teachers and students should blog: 18 benefits of educational blogging.* Retrieved from http://www.kathleenamorris.com/2018/03/14/benefits-blogging

Moulard, J., Babin, B. J., & Griffin, M. (2015). How aspects of a wine's place affect consumers' authenticity perceptions and purchase intentions. *International Journal of Wine Business Research, 27*(1), 61–78. doi:10.1108/IJWBR-01-2014-0002

Muñoz, R., Fernández, M., & Salinero, Y. (2019). Assessing consumer behavior in the wine industry and its consequences for wineries: A case study of a Spanish company. *Frontiers in Psychology, 10*(2491), 1–7. PMID:31780997

Muro, A., Soler, J., Cebolla, À., & Cladellas, R. (2018). A positive psychological intervention for failing students: Does it improve academic achievement and motivation? A pilot study. *Learning and Motivation, 63*, 126–132. doi:10.1016/j.lmot.2018.04.002

Murphy, K. (2015). *Donuts makes private deal with wine-makers.* Retrieved from: http://domainincite.com/?s=.vin+.wine

Murugesan, S. (2007). Understanding Web 2.0. *IT Professional, 9*(4), 34–41. doi:10.1109/MITP.2007.78

Murugesan, S., Rossi, G., Wilbanks, L., & Djavanshir, R. (2011). The future of web apps. *IT Professional, 13*(5), 12–14. doi:10.1109/MITP.2011.89

Muslim, E., Moch, B., Wilgert, Y., Utami, F., & Indriyani, D. (2019). User interface redesign of e-commerce platform mobile application (Kudo) through user experience evaluation to increase user attraction. *IOP Conference Series. Materials Science and Engineering, 508*(1), 6. doi:10.1088/1757-899X/508/1/012113

Mustafa Kemal, T. (2020). *Competency Framework for the Fourth Industrial Revolution. In Human Capital Formation for the Fourth Industrial Revolution.* IGI Global.

Nabal-Heller, N., Raviv, S., Lidor, R., & Levianne, Z. (1999). *Guided movement activity aimed at motor development.* Reches.

Nageswarakurukkal, K., Gonçalves, P., & Moshtari, M. (2019). Improving Fundraising Efficiency in Small and Medium Sized Non-profit Organizations Using Online Solutions. *Journal of Nonprofit & Public Sector Marketing*, 1–26. doi:10.1080/10495142.2019.1589627

Naidu, S. (2006). *E-Learning: A Guidebook of Principles, Procedures and Practices* (2nd Revised Edition). CEMCA.

Nakamura, J., & Csikszentmihalyi, M. (2014). The Concept of Flow. In M. Csikszentmihalyi (Ed.), *Flow and the Foundations of Positive Psychology* (pp. 239–263). Springer Netherlands. doi:10.1007/978-94-017-9088-8_16

Nakilcioğlu, İ. H. (2013). The effects of font type choosing on visual perception and visual communication. Online Journal of Art and Design, 1(3). Retrieved from https://arastirmax.com/en/publication/online-journal-art-and-design/1/3/effects-font-type-choosing-visual-perception-and-visual-communication/arid/e1e93307-3481-44b6-a2dc-f35eed6f139f

Namecheap. (2020). *Cheval-blanc.wine Wois*. Retrieved from: https://www.namecheap.com/domains/whois/result?domain=cheval-blanc.wine

Nasdaq. (2020) *Market activitiy: GoDaddy Inc Class a Common Stock*. Retrieved from: https://www.nasdaq.com/market-activity/stocks/gddy

Nath, K., & Iswary, R. (2015). What comes after Web 3.0? Web 4.0 and the Future. In *Proceedings of the International Conference and Communication System (I3CS'15), Shillong, India* (pp. 337-341). Academic Press.

Nath, K., Dhar, S., & Basishtha, S. (2014, February). Web 1.0 to Web 3.0-Evolution of the Web and its various challenges. In *2014 International Conference on Reliability Optimization and Information Technology (ICROIT)* (pp. 86-89). IEEE. 10.1109/ICROIT.2014.6798297

Neelakandan, S., Annamalai, R., Rayen, S. J., & Arunajsmine, J. (2020). Social Media Networks Owing To Disruptions For Effective Learning. *Procedia Computer Science*, *172*, 145–151. doi:10.1016/j.procs.2020.05.022

Nelson, M. J., Voithofer, R., & Cheng, S.-L. (2019). Mediating factors that influence the technology integration practices of teacher educators. *Computers & Education*, *128*, 330–344. doi:10.1016/j.compedu.2018.09.023

Network Information Center (NIC). (2020). Retrieved from https://nic.com

Neumann, T., & Weikum, G. (2008). RDF-3X: A RISC-style engine for RDF. *Proceedings of the VLDB Endowment International Conference on Very Large Data Bases*, *1*(1), 647–659. doi:10.14778/1453856.1453927

Newbery, R., Lean, J., Moizer, J., & Haddoud, M. (2018). Entrepreneurial identity formation during the initial entrepreneurial experience: The influence of simulation feedback and existing identity. *Journal of Business Research*, *85*, 51–59. doi:10.1016/j.jbusres.2017.12.013

Nicholas, D., Rowlands, I., Clark, D., & Williams, P. (2011). Google Generation II: Web behaviour experiments with the BBC. *Aslib Proceedings*, *63*(1), 28–45. doi:10.1108/00012531111103768

Nielsen, B. B. (2004). The role of trust in collaborative relationships: A multi-dimensional approach. *M@ n@ gement*, *7*(3), 239-256.

Nielsen, J. (2000). *Designing Web Usability. New Riders Publishing*.

Nikou, S. A., & Economides, A. A. (2017). Mobile-Based Assessment: Integrating acceptance and motivational factors into a combined model of Self-Determination Theory and Technology Acceptance. *Computers in Human Behavior*, *68*, 83–95. doi:10.1016/j.chb.2016.11.020

Nilsson, T. (2006). Legibility of colored print. doi:10.1201/9780849375477.ch293

Ninan, N., Roy, J. C., & Thomas, M. R. (2019). Training the workforce for industry 4.0. *International Journal of Research in Social Sciences*, *9*(4), 782–790.

Nogueira, T. D. C., & Ferreira, D. J. (2019). Systematic Review of Visually-Impaired and Blind User Experience of Web Trends. *Revista de Sistemas e Computação-RSC*, *8*(2).

Norman, D. A. (2004). Emotional Design. New York: Academic Press.

Norman, D. (1988). *The Design of Everyday Things*. MIT Press.

Novak, T. P., Hoffman, D. L., & Yung, Y.-F. (2000). Measuring the Customer Experience in Online Environments: A Structural Modeling Approach. *Marketing Science*, *19*(1), 22–42. doi:10.1287/mksc.19.1.22.15184

Novemsky, N., Dhar, R., Schwarz, N., & Simonson, I. (2007). Preference fluency in choice. *JMR, Journal of Marketing Research*, *44*(3), 347–356. doi:10.1509/jmkr.44.3.347

Nowak, K. L., & McGloin, R. (2014). The Influence of Peer Reviews on Source Credibility and Purchase Intention in Societies. *Societies (Basel, Switzerland)*, 690.

Nunwood, K. P. M. G. (2018). *Developing empathy in customer experience design: Why this challenge is more important than you think*. https://www.nunwood.com/excellence-centre/blog/2016/developing-empathy-in-customer-experience-design-why-this-challenge-is-more-important-than-you-think/

O*NET, N. C. f. O. N. D. (2018a). *Executive Secretaries and Executive Administrative Assistants. 43-6011.00*. Retrieved from https://www.onetonline.org/link/details/43-6011.00

O*NET, N. C. f. O. N. D. (2018b). *Secretaries and Administrative Assistants, Except Legal, Medical, and Executive. 43-6014.00*. Retrieved from https://www.onetonline.org/link/details/43-6014.00

O'Reilly, T. (2012). *What is web 2.0. Design patterns and business models for the next generation of software*. Academic Press.

O'Reilly, T. (2007). What is web 2.0, design patterns and business models for the next generation of software. *Communications & Stratégies*, *65*, 17–37.

O'Reilly, T., & Battelle, J. (2009). *Web squared: Web 2.0 five years on. Special Report*. O'Reilly Media, Inc.

Oblinger, D., & Oblinger, J. L. (2005). *Educating the Net Generation*. Boulder, CO: Educause. Retrieved March 19, 208, from https://www.educause.edu/educatingthenetgen/

OECD. (2019). *Youth not in employment, education or training*. NEET.

Okano, M. T. (2017, September). IoT and industry 4.0: the industrial new revolution. In *International Conference on Management and Information System* (pp. 75-82). Academic Press.

Oliver, K. H., & Coble, R. R. (2016). *Teaching with blogs*. Vanderbilt University Center for Teaching. Retrieved from https://cft.vanderbilt.edu/teaching-with-blogs/

Oliver, K. M. (2000). Methods for developing constructivism learning on the web. *Educational Technology*, *40*(6), 5–18.

Oliver, R. L., Rust, R. T., & Varki, S. (1997). Customer delight: Foundations, findings, and managerial insight. *Journal of Retailing*, *73*(3), 311–336. doi:10.1016/S0022-4359(97)90021-X

Oravec, J. A. (2003). Weblogs as an emerging genre in higher education. *Journal of Computing in Higher Education*, *14*(2), 21–44. doi:10.1007/BF02940937

Orehovački, T., Granić, A., & Kermek, D. (2011, June). Exploring the quality in use of Web 2.0 applications: the case of mind mapping services. In *International Conference on Web Engineering* (pp. 266-277). Springer.

Ovans, A. (2015). How emotional intelligence became a key leadership skill. *Harvard Business Review*, 28.

Owens, D. C., Sadler, T. D., Barlow, A. T., & Smith-Walters, C. (2020). Student Motivation from and Resistance to Active Learning Rooted in Essential Science Practices. *Research in Science Education*, *50*(1), 253–277. doi:10.100711165-017-9688-1

Pahpy, L. (2017). *Comment rétablir la compétitivité de la viticulture française. Les propositions de l'IREF*. Etudes et Monographies, Institut de Recherches Economiques et Fiscales.

Palfrey, J. G., & Gasser, U. (2011). Born Digital: Understanding the First Generation of Digital Natives. New York: ReadHowYouWant.com.

Palloff, R. M., & Pratt, K. (2004). *Collaborating Online: Learning Together in Community* (1st ed.). Jossey-Bass.

Panisoara, G., & Panisoara, I. O. (2005). *Motivarea Eficienta. Ghid Practic*. Polirom.

Papenhausen, C. (2010). Managerial optimism and search. *Journal of Business Research*, *63*(7), 716–720. doi:10.1016/j.jbusres.2009.05.007

Pappas, C. (2013, September 26). *How to use blogs in the classroom*. Retrieved from https://elearningindustry.com/how-to-use-blogs-in-the-classroom

Pappas, C. (2014). *The 20 Best Learning Management Systems (2019 Update)*. Retrieved from https://elearningindustry.com/the-20-best-learning-management-systems

Pappas, I. (2018). User experience in personalized online shopping: A fuzzy-set analysis. *European Journal of Marketing*, *52*(7/8), 1679–1703. doi:10.1108/EJM-10-2017-0707

Park, C. H., & Kim, Y. G. (2003). Identifying key factors affecting consumer purchase behavior in an online shopping context. *International Journal of Retail & Distribution Management*, *31*(1), 16–29. doi:10.1108/09590550310457818

Park, M., & Yoo, J. (2020). Effects of perceived interactivity of augmented reality on consumer responses: A mental imagery perspective. *Journal of Retailing and Consumer Services*, *52*, 101912. doi:10.1016/j.jretconser.2019.101912

Patching, G. R., & Jordan, T. R. (2005). Assessing the role of different spatial frequencies in word perception by good and poor readers. *Memory & Cognition*, *33*(6), 961–971. doi:10.3758/BF03193205 PubMed

Patel, K. (2013). Incremental journey for World Wide Web: Introduced with Web 1.0 to recent Web 5.0–a survey paper. *International Journal of Advanced Research in Computer Science and Software Engineering*, *3*(10).

Patel, P., Ali, M. I., & Sheth, A. (2017). On using the intelligent edge for IoT analytics. *IEEE Intelligent Systems*, *32*(5), 64–69. doi:10.1109/MIS.2017.3711653

Patterson, T., Buechsenstein, J., & Comiskey, P. J. (2018). *Wine and Place: a terroir reader*. University of California Press.

Pavlou Paul, A., Liang, H., & Xue, Y. (2007). Understanding and Mitigating Uncertainty in Online Exchange Relationships: A Principal-Agent Perspective. *Management Information Systems Quarterly*, *31*(1), 105–136. doi:10.2307/25148783

Pea, R. D. (1985). Beyond amplification: Using the computer to reorganize mental functioning. *Educational Psychologist*, *20*(4), 167–182. doi:10.120715326985ep2004_2

Peer, E., Vosgerau, J., & Acquisti, A. (2014). Reputation as a sufficient condition for data quality on Amazon Mechanical Turk. *Behavior Research Methods*, *46*(4), 1023–1031. doi:10.375813428-013-0434-y PMID:24356996

Penny, K. I. (2011). Factors that Influence Student E-learning Participation in a UK Higher Education Institution. *Interdisciplinary Journal of E-Learning and Learning Objects*, *7*, 81–95. doi:10.28945/1377

Perez-Uribe, R. I., Ovalle-Mora, O. O., Ocampo-Guzman, D., & Ramirez-Salazar, M. D. P. (2020). Innovation Trends in Human Management for Competitiveness in SMEs. In *Handbook of Research on Increasing the Competitiveness of SMEs* (pp. 1–25). IGI Global. doi:10.4018/978-1-5225-9425-3.ch001

Perrault, W. D., & McCarthy, E. J. (2002). *Principios de Marketing*. LTC.

Perren, R., & Kozinets, R. V. (2018). Lateral Exchange Markets: How Social Platforms Operate in a Networked Economy. *Journal of Marketing*, *82*(1), 20–36. doi:10.1509/jm.14.0250

Perrouty, J. P., d'Hauteville, F., & Lockshin, L. (2006). The influence of wine attributes on region of origin equity: An analysis of the moderating effect of consumer's perceived expertise. *Agribusiness: An International Journal*, *22*(3), 323–341. doi:10.1002/agr.20089

Petersen, E., & Petersen, K. (2000). E-Parenting: Using the Internet and Computers to be a Better Parent. Macmillan Published Co

Pettit, P. (2008). *Trust, reliance, and the internet*. Cambridge University Press.

Pine, J. B. II, & Gilmore, J. H. (1999). *The Experience Economy: Work is theatre and every business a stage*. Harvard Business School Press.

Pinheiro, M., Sarrico, C., & Santiago, R. (2011). Competências de autodesenvolvimento e metodologias PBL num curso de contabilidade: Perspectivas de alunos, docentes, diplomados e empregadores. *Revista Lusófona de Educação*, *17*(17), 147–166.

Pirâu, M. (2008). Introducere în pedagogie. Editura Risoprint.

Pirilla, C. (2019, August 21). Education blogs UK top 10. *Vuelio*. Retrieved from https://www.vuelio.com/uk/social-media-index/top-10-uk-education-blogs/

Pitler, H., Hubbell, E., Kuhn, M., & Malenoski, K. (2007). *Using technology with classroom instruction that works*. ASCD.

Pizzutti, C., & Fernandes, D. (2010). Effect of recovery efforts on consumer trust and loyalty in e-tail: A contingency model. *International Journal of Electronic Commerce*, *14*(4), 127–160. doi:10.2753/JEC1086-4415140405

Popov. (2018). https://www.ecommercetimes.com/story/85620.html

Porter, M. (2001). Strategy and the Internet. *Harvard Business Review*, *79*(2), 63–78. PMID:11246925

Porter, M. E., & Heppelmann, J. E. (2015). How smart, connected products are transforming companies. *Harvard Business Review*, *93*(10), 96–114.

Postman, N. (1985). *Amusing ourselves to death*. Penguin Group USA.

Prahalad, C. K., & Ramaswamy, V. (2004). Co-creation experiences: The next practice in value creation. *Journal of Interactive Marketing*, *18*(3), 5–14. doi:10.1002/dir.20015

Prahalad, C. K., & Ramaswamy, V. (2004). *The future of competition: Co-creating unique value with customers*. Boston Harvard Business School Press.

Prensky, M. (2009). H. Sapiens Digital: From Digital Immigrants and Digital Natives to Digital Wisdom. *Innovate: Journal of Online Education*, *5*(3). Retrieved March 4, 2020 from https://www.learntechlib.org/p/104264/

PricewaterhouseCoopers. (2017). *IAB internet advertising revenue report: 2016 full year results*. Retrieved from https://www.iab.com/wp-content/uploads/2016/04/IAB_Internet_Advertising_Revenue_Report_FY_2016.pdf

Prichard, J. S., Stratford, R. J., & Bizo, L. A. (2006). Team-Skills Training Enhances Collaborative Learning. *Learning and Instruction, 16*(3), 256–265. doi:10.1016/j.learninstruc.2006.03.005

Pride, W. M., Ferrell, O. C., Lukas, A. B., Schembri, S., Niininen, O., & Casidy, R. (2018). *Marketing Principles.* Cengage Learning Australia.

Priporas, C., Stylos, N., & Fotiadis, A. (2017). Generation Z consumers' expectations of interactions in smart retailing: A future agenda. *Computers in Human Behavior, 77*, 374–381. doi:10.1016/j.chb.2017.01.058

Provost, F., & Fawcett, T. (2013). *Data science for business.* Academic Press.

Puškarević, I., Nedeljković, U., & Pintier, I. (2014, November 13). Visual analysis of typeface management in brand identity. Academic Press.

Pušnik, N., Podlesek, A., & Možina, K. (2016). Typeface comparison – Does the x-height of lower-case letters increased to the size of upper-case letters speed up recognition? *International Journal of Industrial Ergonomics, 54*, 164–169. doi:10.1016/j.ergon.2016.06.002

Puybaraud, M. (2012). *Digital Natives: A Tech-Savvy Generation Enters the Workplace.* WorkDesign Magazine. http://workdesign.com/2012/02/digital-natives-a-tech-savvy-generation-enters-the-workplace/

PwC. Total Retail. (2017). *Ecommerce in China – the future is already here.* https://www.pwccn.com/en/retail-and-consumer/publications/total-retail-2017-china/total-retail-survey-2017-china-cut.pdf

Qualters, D. M. (2010). Bringing the Outside in: Assessing Experiential Education. *New Directions for Teaching and Learning,* (124), 55-62. Retrieved from https://onlinelibrary.wiley.com/doi/abs/10.1002/tl.421#

RaboSearch. (2019). *Wine Quarterly, Q1-2019: Online wine is growing in Europe.* Author.

RaboSearch. (2019). *Wine Quarterly, Q1-2019: Online wine is growing in Europe.* https://en.wikipedia.org/wiki/InterNIC

Rachinger, M., Rauter, R., Müller, C., Vorraber, W., & Schirgi, E (2019). Digitalization and its influence on business model innovation. *Journal of Manufacturing Technology Management, 30*(8), 1143–1160. doi:10.1108/JMTM-01-2018-0020

Rahimi, E., van den Berg, J., & Veen, W. (2015). Facilitating student-driven constructing of learning environments using Web 2.0 personal learning environments. *Computers & Education, 81*, 235–246. doi:10.1016/j.compedu.2014.10.012

Rahwan, I., Krasnoshtan, D., Shariff, A., & Bonnefon, J.-F. (2014). Analytical reasoning task reveals limits of social learning in networks. *Journal of the Royal Society, Interface/the Royal Society, 11*(93).

Rajavi, K., Kushwaha, T., & Steenkamp, J. M. (2019). In Brands We Trust? A Multicategory, Multicountry Investigation of Sensitivity of Consumers' Trust in Brands to Marketing-Mix Activities. *The Journal of Consumer Research, 46*(4).

Ramaswamy, S. (2015). *How Micro-Moments Are Changing the Rules.* https://www.thinkwithgoogle.com/marketing-resources/micro-moments/how-micromoments-are-changing-rules/

Ramseier, E. (2001). Motivation to learn as an outcome and determining factor of learning at school. *European Journal of Psychology of Education, 16*(3), 421–439. doi:10.1007/BF03173191

Ras, E., Wild, F., Stahl, C., & Baudet, A. (2017). Bridging the skills gap of workers in Industry 4.0 by human performance augmentation tools: Challenges and roadmap. *Proceedings of the 10th International Conference on PErvasive Technologies Related to Assistive Environments.* 10.1145/3056540.3076192

Ratner, N. (2019). *The Rise of the Smartphone Ecosystem and Kodak's Fall.* https://digital.hbs.edu/platform-digit/submission/the-rise-of-the-smartphone-ecosystem-and-kodaks-fall/

ReadWriteThink. (n.d.). *Teaching with blogs*. Retrieved from http://www.readwritethink.org/professional-development/strategy-guides/teaching-with-blogs-30108.html

Reeves, B., & Nass, C. (2000). Perceptual user interfaces: Perceptual bandwidth. *Communications of the ACM, 43*(3), 65–70. doi:10.1145/330534.330542

Relojo, D. (2017). Blog psychology: Insights, benefits, and research agenda on blogs as a dynamic medium to promote the discipline of psychology and allied fields. *Psychreg Journal of Psychology, 1*(2), 70–75. doi:10.5281/zenodo.1289165

Rembach, J. (2017). *What is a Customer Empathy Map*. https://customerthink.com/what-is-a-customer-empathy-map/

Rensselaer Polytechnic Institute Lighting Research Centre. (2012). *Can't sleep? Turn off your iPad*. The Times.

Reynolds, F. (2008). Web 2.0–in your hand. *IEEE Pervasive Computing, 8*(1), 86–88. doi:10.1109/MPRV.2009.22

Rigby, B. (2008). *Mobilizing Generation 2.0: A practical guide to using Web 2.0: technologies to recruit, organize and engage youth*. John Wiley & Sons.

Rintala, N., & Suolanen, S. (2005). The implications of digitalization for job descriptions, competencies and the quality of working life. *Nordicom Review, 26*(2), 53–67. doi:10.1515/nor-2017-0258 PMID:17290637

Rioja, A. (2019, July 27). *The evolution and history of blogging*. Retrieved from https://alejandrorioja.com/blog/history-of-blogging/

Robben, H. S. J., Webley, P., Elffers, H., & Hessing, D. J. (1990). Decision frames, opportunity and tax evasion: An experimental approach. *Journal of Economic Behavior & Organization, 14*(3), 353–361.

Robert, J., Kubler, S., & Le Traon, Y. (2016, August). Micro-billing framework for IoT: Research & Technological foundations. In *2016 IEEE 4th International Conference on Future Internet of Things and Cloud (FiCloud)* (pp. 301-308). IEEE.

Robinson, S. (2002). General concepts of quality for discrete-event simulation. *European Journal of Operational Research, 138*(1), 103–117. doi:10.1016/S0377-2217(01)00127-8

Rocha, D. R. do R. (2016). *A Importância da Metodologia PBL nos Diplomados em Contabilidade: Estudo de Caso* [Dissertação de Mestrado]. Instituto Politécnico de Bragança.

Rogers-Estable, M. (2014). Web 2.0 Use in Higher Education. *European Journal of Open. Distance and E-Learning, 17*. Advance online publication. doi:10.2478/eurodl-2014-0024

Romano, J., Wallace, T. L., Helmick, I. J., Carey, L. M., & Adkins, L. (2005). Study procrastination, achievement, and academic motivation in web-based and blended distance learning. *The Internet and Higher Education, 8*(4), 299–305. doi:10.1016/j.iheduc.2005.09.003

Rosa Pulga, A., Basso, K., Viacava, K., Pacheco, N., Ladeira, W., & Dalla Corte, V. (2019). The link between social interactions and trust recovery in customer–business relationships. *Journal of Consumer Behaviour, 18*(6), 496–504. doi:10.1002/cb.1788

Rosenzweig, E. (2015). UX Thinking. In E. Rosenzweig (Ed.), *Successful User Experience: Strategies and Roadmaps* (pp. 41–67). Morgan Kaufmann. doi:10.1016/B978-0-12-800985-7.00003-X

Rotter, J. B. (1967). A new scale for the measurement of interpersonal trust. *Journal of Personality, 35*(4), 651–665. doi:10.1111/j.1467-6494.1967.tb01454.x PMID:4865583

Rovai, A. P. (2004). A constructivist approach to online college learning. *The Internet and Higher Education, 7*(2), 79–93. doi:10.1016/j.iheduc.2003.10.002

Ryan, R. M., & Deci, E. L. (2000). Intrinsic and Extrinsic Motivations: Classic Definitions and New Directions. *Contemporary Educational Psychology*, *25*(1), 54–67. doi:10.1006/ceps.1999.1020 PMID:10620381

Ryan, R. M., & Deci, E. L. (2000). Self-determination theory and the facilitation of intrinsic motivation, social development, and well-being. *The American Psychologist*, *55*(1), 68–78. doi:10.1037/0003-066X.55.1.68 PMID:11392867

Saavedra, M.-J., Rusu, C., Quiñones, D., & Roncagliolo, S. (2019). *A Set of Usability and User eXperience Heuristics for Social Networks*. Paper presented at the International Conference on Human-Computer Interaction. 10.1007/978-3-030-21902-4_10

Safran, C., Helic, D., & Gütl, C. (2007*). E-Learning practices and Web 2.0. In Proceedings of the International Conference of 'Interactive computer aided learning' ICL2007: E-Portofolio and Quality in e-Learning.* Available at: https://halshs.archives-ouvertes.fr/hal-00197260/

Salehi, F., Abdollahbeigi, B., Langroudi, A. C., & Salehi, F. (2012). The impact of website information convenience on e-commerce success of companies. *Procedia: Social and Behavioral Sciences*, *57*, 381–387. doi:10.1016/j.sbspro.2012.09.1201

Salomon, G. (1993). On the nature of pedagogic computer tools. The case of the wiring partner. In S. P. LaJoie & S. J. Derry (Eds.), *Computers as cognitive tools* (pp. 179–196). Lawrence Erlbaum Associates.

Samuel-Azran, T., & Ravid, G. (2016). Can blogging increase extroverts' satisfaction in the classroom? Lessons from multiple case studies. *Interactive Learning Environments*, *24*(6), 1097–1108. doi:10.1080/10494820.2014.961483

Sankar, K., & Bouchard, S. A. (2009). *Enterprise web 2.0 fundamentals*. Cisco Press.

Santosh, S. (2017). Adoption of Web 2.0 Applications in Academic Libraries in India. *DESIDOC Journal of Library and Information Technology*, *37*(3), 192–198. doi:10.14429/djlit.37.3.10918

Sauro, J., & Dumas, J. S. (2009). Comparison of three one-question, post-task usability questionnaires. In Conference on Human Factors in Computing Systems - Proceedings (pp. 1599–1608). ACM Press. doi:10.1145/1518701.1518946

Sawyer, S., & Tapia, A. (2005). The sociotechnical nature of mobile computing work: Evidence from a study of policing in the United States. *International Journal of Technology and Human Interaction*, *1*(3), 1–14. doi:10.4018/jthi.2005070101

Scaraboto, D. (2015). Selling, Sharing, and Everything In Between: The Hybrid Economies of Collaborative Networks. *The Journal of Consumer Research*, *42*(1), 152–176. doi:10.1093/jcr/ucv004

Scheibehenne, B., Greifeneder, R., & Todd, P.M. (2010). Can There Ever Be Too Many Options? A Meta-Analytic Review of Choice Overload. *Journal of Consumer Research*, *37*(3), 409-425.

ScheidiesN. (n.d.). *The 20 biggest benefits of blogging*. Retrieved from https://www.incomediary.com/biggest-blogging-benefits

Schlickum, M. K., Hedman, L., Enochsson, L., Kjellin, A., & Felländer-Tsai, L. (2009). Systematic video game training in surgical novices improves performance in virtual reality endoscopic surgical simulators: A prospective randomized study. *World Journal of Surgery*, *33*(11), 2360–2367. doi:10.100700268-009-0151-y PMID:19649553

Schlosser Ann, E. (2003). Experiencing Products in the Virtual World: The Role of Goal and Imagery in Influencing Attitudes Versus Purchase Intentions. *The Journal of Consumer Research*, *30*(2), 184–198. doi:10.1086/376807

Schlosser, A. E., White, T. B., & Lloyd, S. M. (2006). Converting Web Site Visitors into Buyers: How Web Site Investment Increases Consumer Trusting Beliefs and Online Purchase Intentions. *Journal of Marketing*, *70*(2), 133–148. doi:10.1509/jmkg.70.2.133

Schmitt, B. H. (1999). Experiential Marketing. *Journal of Marketing Management, 15*(1-3), 53–67. doi:10.1362/026725799784870496

Schmitt, B. H., Pan, Y., & Tavassoli, N. T. (1994). Language and consumer memory: The impact of linguistic differences between Chinese and English. *The Journal of Consumer Research, 21*(3), 419–431. doi:10.1086/209408

Schmitz, B. (2014). *Mobile games for learning: A pattern-based approach* (PhD thesis, Open University, SIKS Dissertation Series No. 2014-45, Datawyse). Retrieved from http:// dspace.ou.nl/bitstream/1820/5833/6/Thesis%20BSZ_print.pdf

Schneider, P., & Zielke, S. (2020). Searching offline and buying online – An analysis of showrooming forms and segments. *Journal of Retailing and Consumer Services, 52*, 52. doi:10.1016/j.jretconser.2019.101919

Schor, J. B., & Fitzmaurice, C. J. (2015). Collaborating and connecting: the emergence of the sharing economy. In Handbook of Research on Sustainable Consumption (pp. 410-425). Cheltenham, UK: Edward Elgar Publishing. doi:10.4337/9781783471270.00039

Schroll, R., Schnurr, B., & Grewal, D. (2018). Humanizing products with handwritten typefaces. *The Journal of Consumer Research, 45*(3), 648–672. doi:10.1093/jcr/ucy014

Schwab, K. (2016). *The Fourth Industrial Revolution: what it means, how to respond.* https://www.weforum.org/agenda/2016/01/the-fourth-industrial-revolution-what-it-means-and-how-to-respond/

Schwab, K. (2017). *The fourth industrial revolution.* Currency.

Schwartz, M. (2012). *Experiential Learning Report.* Ryerson University. Retrieved from: https://www.ryerson.ca/content/dam/lt/resources/handouts/ExperientialLearningReport.pdf

Schwarzmüller, T., Brosi, P., Duman, D., & Welpe, I. M. (2018). How Does the Digital Transformation Affect Organizations? Key Themes of Change in Work Design and Leadership. *Management Revue, 29*(2), 114-138.

Seda, M., & Yeşim, G. (2020). *The Nature of Digital Leadership in Managing Employees Through Organizational Culture. In Business Management and Communication Perspectives in Industry 4.0.* IGI Global.

Sein-Echaluce, M. L., Fidalgo-Blanco, Á., & Esteban-Escaño, J. (2019). Technological ecosystems and ontologies for an educational model based on Web 3.0. *Universal Access in the Information Society, 18*(3), 645–658. doi:10.100710209-019-00684-9

Seo, H., & Vu, H. T. (2020). Transnational Nonprofits' Social Media Use: A Survey of Communications Professionals and an Analysis of Organizational Characteristics. *Nonprofit and Voluntary Sector Quarterly, (4), 849–870. Advance online publication. doi:10.1177/0899764020908340

Sequeira, A., & Santana, C. (2016). *O Trabalho Especializado do Secretariado/Assessoria: a comunicação assertiva como competência diferenciadora.* Retrieved from https://issuu.com/anavieira34/docs/anais_cisa2016

Shackel, B. (2009). Usability – Context, framework, definition, design and evaluation. *Interacting with Computers, 21*(5–6), 339–346. doi:10.1016/j.intcom.2009.04.007

Shankar, V., & Malthouse, E. C. (2009). *A peek into the future of interactive marketing.* Academic Press.

Sharafi Farzad, F., Kolli, S., Soltani, T., & Ghanbary, S. (2019). Digital Brands and Web 3.0 Enterprises: Social Network Analysis and Thematic Analysis of User activities and Behavioral Patterns in Online Retailers. *AD-Minister, (34), 119–138.

Sheehan, D., & Katz, L. (2012). The Practical and Theoretical Implications of Flow Theory and Intrinsic Motivation in Designing and Implementing Exergaming in the School Environment. *The Journal of the Canadian Game Studies Association, 6*(9), 16.

Sheep, J. (2013). *Social Media Marketing for the Wine Industry*. Presentation at a Wine Intensive Executive MBA, Sonoma State University. Retrieved from: https://fr.slideshare.net/earthsite/social-media-for-the-wine-industry-by-joey-shepp

Sherborne, V. (2001). *Developmental movement for children*. Worth Publishing Ltd.

Shin, N. (2019). The Impact of the Web and Social Media on the Performance of Nonprofit Organizations. *Journal of International Technology and Information Management*, *27*(4), 17–35.

Shivalingaiah, D., & Naik, U. (2008). *Comparative Study of web 1.0, web 2.0 and web 3.0*. Academic Press.

Shrivastava, P. (1998). Management Education for the Digital Economy. *Academy of Management Proceedings*.

Shuen, A. (2018). *Web 2.0: A Strategy Guide: Business thinking and strategies behind successful Web 2.0 implementations*. O'Reilly Media.

Sigala, M., & Haller, C. (2018). The Impact of Social Media on the Behavior of Wine Tourists: A Typology of Power Sources. In M. Sigala & R. Robinson (Eds.), *Management and Marketing of Wine Tourism Business* (pp. 139–154). Palgrave Macmillan.

Silva, A.L. (2014). *A. N. Leontiev And The Critical To "Learning To Learn"*. School Physical Education Teaching.

Silva, P., & Bertuzi, R. (2015). The Contribution of Business Simulation to Improve Management Competencies. *EDU-LEARN 2015 - 7th International Conference on Education and New Learning Technologies*.

Silva, P., & Bertuzi, R. (2017). Students' Perception about the use of Action-Based Methodologies. *EDULEARN 2017 - 9th International Conference on Education and New Learning Technologies*.

Silva, P., & Bertuzi, R. (2019). How Business Simulation Methodologies Can Impact on the Improvement of Students' Skills. *ICERI2019 - 12th annual International Conference of Education, Research and Innovation*.

Silva, P., & Mesquita, A. (2018). The Creative Internprize International Project: Preparing Students to be Entrepreneurs. *ICERI2018 - International Conference on Education, Research and Innovation*.

Silva, M. de L., Martins, D., & Jesus, M. J. (2018). *O Projeto em Simulação Empresarial como um Novo Paradigma de Investigação/Experimentação no Ensino Superior*. XVII AECA International Meeting, Lisbon, Portugal.

Silva, P., Santos, J. F., & Vieira, I. (2014). Teaching Accounting and Management through Business Simulation: A Case Study. In E. Ariwa (Ed.), *Green Technology Applications for Enterprise and Academic Innovation* (pp. 33–47). Information Science Reference. doi:10.4018/978-1-4666-5166-1.ch003

Simpson, J. (2009). *Old World versus New World: the origins of organizational diversity in the international wine industry, 1850-1914*. Retrieved from: https://e-archivo.uc3m.es/bitstream/handle/10016/3742/wp-09-01.pdf?sequence=5

Sinclaire, J., & Vogus, C. E. (2011). Adoption of social networking sites: An exploratory adaptive structuration perspective for global organizations. *Information Technology Management*, *12*(4), 293–314. doi:10.100710799-011-0086-5

Sivarajah, U., Irani, Z., & Weerakkody, V. (2015). Evaluating the use and impact of Web 2.0 technologies in local government. *Government Information Quarterly*, *32*(4), 473–487. doi:10.1016/j.giq.2015.06.004

Skrba, A. (2019, July 15). *8 types of blogs and bloggers. What type is yours?* Retrieved from https://firstsiteguide.com/blogging-types-revealed/

Slattery, T., & Rayner, K. (2010). The influence of text legibility on eye movements during reading. *Applied Cognitive Psychology*, *24*(8), 1129–1148. doi:10.1002/acp.1623

Slemp, G. R., Field, J. G., & Cho, A. S. H. (2020). A meta-analysis of autonomous and controlled forms of teacher motivation. *Journal of Vocational Behavior*, *103459*, 103459. Advance online publication. doi:10.1016/j.jvb.2020.103459

Solomon, G., & Schrum, L. (2007). *Web 2.0: New tools, new schools. ISTE*. Interntl Soc Tech Educ.

Sonnleitner, A., Pawlowski, M., Kässer, T., & Peissner, M. (2013). Experimentally manipulating positive user experience based on the fulfilment of user needs. In Lecture Notes in Computer Science (including subseries Lecture Notes in Artificial Intelligence and Lecture Notes in Bioinformatics) (Vol. 8120 LNCS, pp. 555–562). Springer. doi:10.1007/978-3-642-40498-6_45

Souto, J. E. (2015). Business model innovation and business concept innovation as the context of incremental innovation and radical innovation. *Tourism Management*, *51*(December), 142–155. doi:10.1016/j.tourman.2015.05.017

Sparrow, B., Liu, J., & Wegner, D. M. (2011). Google effects on memory: Cognitive consequences of having information at our fingertips. *Science*, *333*(6043), 776–778. doi:10.1126cience.1207745 PMID:21764755

Squire, K. (2003). *Video Games in Education. International Journal of Intelligent Games & Simulations.* https://pdfs.semanticscholar.org/72fa/723394b80532947b19ecf9aa3039d12af5e3.pdf?_ga=2.260854669.1850271032.1583530991-573723792.1583530991

Starkey, K., & Tempest, S. (2009). The Winter of Our Discontent: The Design Challenge for Business Schools. *Academy of Management Learning & Education*, *8*, 576–586.

Statista Research Department (2019). *Number of network connected devices per person around the world from 2003 to 2020.* https://www.statista.com/statistics/678739/forecast-on-connected-devices-per-person/

Statista. (n.d.). *Retail e-commerce sales worldwide from 2014 to 2023.* https://www.statista.com/statistics/379046/worldwide-retail-e-commerce-sales/

Steenkamp, J.-B. E. M., & Geyskens, I. (2006). How Country Characteristics Affect the Perceived Value of Web Sites. *Journal of Marketing*, *70*(3), 136–150. doi:10.1509/jmkg.70.3.136

Stein, A., & Ramaseshan, B. (2016). Towards the identification of customer experience touch point elements. *Journal of Retailing and Consumer Services*, *30*, 8–19. doi:10.1016/j.jretconser.2015.12.001

Steinberg, M. (2019). *The Platform Economy: How Japan Transformed the Consumer Internet*. U of Minnesota Press.

Stewart, J., Procter, R., Williams, R., & Poschen, M. (2013). The role of academic publishers in shaping the development of Web 2.0 services for scholarly communication. *New Media & Society, 15*(3), 413-432.

Stoica, M. (2001). *Pedagogie şi Psihologie pentru Examenele de definitivare şi Grade didactice: profesori, institutori / învăţători, studenţi şi elevi ai şcolilor normale*. Editura Gheorghe Alexandru.

Stone, R. W., & Baker-Eveleth, L. (2013). Students' expectation, confirmation, and continuance intention to use electronic textbooks. *Computers in Human Behavior*, *29*(3), 984–990. doi:10.1016/j.chb.2012.12.007

Stratham, D. S., & Torell, C. R. (1996). *Computers in the classroom: The impact of technology on student learning*. Army Research Institute.

Strawbridge, F. (2010). *Is there a case for Web 2.0 in higher education? Do the benefits outweigh the risks?* Available at: http://online.education.ed.ac.uk/gallery/strawbridge_web_2.pdf

Sultan, N. (2013). Knowledge management in the age of cloud computing and Web 2.0: Experiencing the power of disruptive innovations. *International Journal of Information Management*, *33*(1), 160–165. doi:10.1016/j.ijinfomgt.2012.08.006

Summer, M., & Hosterler, D. (2002). A Comparative Study of Computer Conferencing and Face-to-face Communications in Systems Designs. *Journal of Interactive Learning Research, 13*(3), 277–291.

Sun, R., & Asencio, H. D. (2019). Using Social Media to Increase Nonprofit Organizational Capacity. *International Journal of Public Administration, 42*(5), 392–404. doi:10.1080/01900692.2018.1465955

Sun, S. (2008). An examination of disposition, motivation, and involvement in the new technology context computers in human behavior. *Computers in Human Behavior, 24*(6), 2723–2740. doi:10.1016/j.chb.2008.03.016

Susskind, R. E., & Susskind, D. (2015). *The future of the professions: How technology will transform the work of human experts*. Oxford University Press.

Szolnoki, G., Thach, L., & Kolb, D. (2016). Successful Social Media and Ecommerce Strategies in the Wine Industry. Palgrave Macmillan. doi:10.1057/9781137602985

Taimalu, M., & Luik, P. (2019). The impact of beliefs and knowledge on the integration of technology among teacher educators: A path analysis. *Teaching and Teacher Education, 79*, 101–110. doi:10.1016/j.tate.2018.12.012

Tang, Y., Wang, H., Guo, K., Xiao, Y., & Chi, T. (2018). Relevant Feedback Based Accurate and Intelligent Retrieval on Capturing User Intention for Personalized Websites. *IEEE Access : Practical Innovations, Open Solutions, 6*, 24239–24248. doi:10.1109/ACCESS.2018.2828081

Tavakoli, R., & Wijesinghe, S. N. (2019). The evolution of the web and netnography in tourism: A systematic review. *Tourism Management Perspectives, 29*, 48–55. doi:10.1016/j.tmp.2018.10.008

Tavassoli, N. (2001). Color memory and evaluations for alphabetical and logographic brand names. *Journal of Experimental Psychology. Applied, 7*(2), 104–111. doi:10.1037/1076-898X.7.2.104 PubMed

Taylor, D.C., Parboteeah, D.V., & Snipes, M. (2010). Winery websites: effectiveness explored. *Journal of Business Administration, 9*(2), 1-11.

Taylor, K. (2019). *The $225 billion pet care industry is exploding, as millennials delay marriage and babies while turning to pets to 'fill that void*. https://www.businessinsider.com/pet-care-industry-grows-as-millennials-elevate-pets-2019-5?IR=T

Taylor, D. C., Parboteeah, D. V., & Snipes, M. (2010). Winery websites: Effectiveness explored. *Journal of Business Administration Online, 9*(2), 1–11.

Teacher Toolkit. (n.d.). *About us*. Retrieved from https://www.teachertoolkit.co.uk/about

TeachThought. (2020, January 15). *52 Education blogs you should follow*. Retrieved from https://www.teachthought.com/pedagogy/52-education-blogs-you-should-follow

Technical University of Denmark (2019). *Abundance of information narrows our collective attention span*. https://www.eurekalert.org/pub_releases/2019-04/tuod-aoi041119.php

Teece, D. J. (2018). Business models and dynamic capabilities. *Long Range Planning, 51*(1), 40–49. doi:10.1016/j.lrp.2017.06.007

Teixeira, A. B., Aleixo, M. da C., & Silva, S. (2012). *Simulação Empresarial e as Novas Metodologias de Ensino: Estudo de Caso*. XV Encuentro AECA.

Teng & Huang. (2012). More Than Flow: Revisiting the Theory of Four Channels of Flow. *International Journal of Computer Games Technology*. Advance online publication. doi:10.1155/2012/724917

Teng, W., Ma, C., Pahlevansharif, S., & Turner, J. J. (2019). Graduate readiness for the employment market of the 4th industrial revolution. *Education + Training, 61*(5), 590–604. doi:10.1108/ET-07-2018-0154

Teo, H. H., Oh, L. B., Liu, C., & Wei, K. K. (2003). An empirical study of the effects of interactivity on web user attitude. *International Journal of Human-Computer Studies, 58*(3), 281–305. doi:10.1016/S1071-5819(03)00008-9

Teo, T., Sang, G., Mei, B., & Hoi, C. K. W. (2019). Investigating pre-service teachers' acceptance of Web 2.0 technologies in their future teaching: A Chinese perspective. *Interactive Learning Environments, 27*(4), 530–546. doi:10.1080/10494820.2018.1489290

Thach, L., Lease, T., & Barton, M. (2016). Exploring the Impact of Social Media Practices on Wine Sales in US Wineries. *Journal of Direct, Data and Digital Marketing Practice, 17*(4), 272–283. doi:10.1057/dddmp.2016.5

Theimer, K. (2009). *Web 2.0 tools and strategies for archives and local history collections.* Neal-Schuman Publishers, Inc.

Themeisle. (2019, June 3). *The history of blogging: From 1997 until now (with pictures).* Retrieved from https://themeisle.com/blog/history-of-blogging

Thode, S. F., & Maskulka, J. M. (1998). Place-based marketing strategies, brand equity and vineyard valuation. *Journal of Product and Brand Management, 7*(5), 379–399. doi:10.1108/10610429810237673

Thomas, H. (2010). Learning spaces, learning environments and the dis'placement' of learning. *British Journal of Educational Technology, 41*(3), 502–511. doi:10.1111/j.1467-8535.2009.00974.x

Thomson, M. (2018, April 23). *Why your students should blog: 6 powerful benefits.* Retrieved from https://www.emergingedtech.com/2018/04/why-your-students-should-blog-6-powerful-benefits

Thongpapanl, N. T., Ashraf, A. R., Lapa, L., & Venkatesh, V. (2018). Differential effects of customers' regulatory fit on trust, perceived value, and m-commerce use among developing and developed countries. *Journal of International Marketing, 26*(3), 22–44. doi:10.1509/jim.17.0129

Thorndike, E. L. (1983). *Învăţarea umană.* EDP.

Thygesen, A. (2018). *Beyond the traditional marketing funnel – a new formula for growth.* https://www.thinkwithgoogle.com/intl/en-145/perspectives/global-articles/beyond-traditional-marketing-funnel-new-formula-growth/

Ting, P.-H., Wang, S.-T., Bau, D.-Y., & Chiang, M.-L. (2013). Website evaluation of the top 100 hotels using advanced content analysis and eMICA model. *Cornell Hospitality Quarterly, 54*(3), 284–293. doi:10.1177/1938965512471892

Topcu, M. K. (2020). Competency Framework for the Fourth Industrial Revolution. In *Human Capital Formation for the Fourth Industrial Revolution* (pp. 18–43). IGI Global. doi:10.4018/978-1-5225-9810-7.ch002

Transparency International. (n.d.). *Corruption Perception Index.* https://www.transparency.org/en/cpi

TrautmanS. (2016, October). *Edublogs.* Retrieved from https://www.commonsense.org/education/website/edublogs

TrustRadius (2018). *The 2018 B2B Buying Disconnect An in-depth study on buyer preferences, vendor impact, and the persistent trust gap in B2B technology.* http://go.trustradius.com/rs/827-FOI-687/images/TrustRadius_2018_B2B_Buying_Disconnect.pdf

Tuckman, B. W. (2007). The effect of motivational scaffolding on procrastinators' distance learning outcomes. *Computers & Education, 49*(2), 414–422. doi:10.1016/j.compedu.2005.10.002

Tuominen, H., Niemivirta, M., Lonka, K., & Salmela-Aro, K. (2020). Motivation across a transition: Changes in achievement goal orientations and academic well-being from elementary to secondary school. *Learning and Individual Differences*, *79*, 101854. doi:10.1016/j.lindif.2020.101854

Tussyadiah, I. P. (2015). An exploratory study on drivers and deterrents of collaborative consumption in travel. In Information and communication technologies in tourism 2015 (pp. 817-830). Cham, Switzerland: Springer. doi:10.1007/978-3-319-14343-9_59

Tvenge, N., & Martinsen, K. (2018). Integration of digital learning in industry 4.0. *Procedia Manufacturing*, *23*, 261–266. doi:10.1016/j.promfg.2018.04.027

Ullrich, C., Borau, K., Luo, H., Tan, X., Shen, L., & Shen, R. (2008). Why Web 2.0 is Good for Learning and for Research: Principles and Prototypes. In *Proceedings of the 17th International World Wide Web Conference* (pp. 705-714). ACM. 10.1145/1367497.1367593

Ulrich, J., & Karvonen, M. (2011). Faculty instructional attitudes, interest, and intention: Predictors of Web 2.0 use in online courses. *The Internet and Higher Education*, *14*(4), 207–216. doi:10.1016/j.iheduc.2011.07.001

Ulusoy, B. (2020). Understanding Digital Congruence in Industry 4.0. In Business Management and Communication Perspectives in Industry 4.0 (pp. 17-31). IGI Global.

Urban, G. L., Amyx, C., & Lorenzon, A. (2009). Online Trust: State of the Art, New Frontiers, and Research Potential. *Journal of Interactive Marketing*, *23*(2), 179–190. doi:10.1016/j.intmar.2009.03.001

Usabilis. (2020). *Qu'est-ce que l'ergonomie?* Retrieved 15/06/2020 from https://www.usabilis.com/qu-est-ce-que-l-ergonomie/

Uzzi, B. (1997). Social structure and competition in interfirm networks: The paradox of embeddedness. *Administrative Science Quarterly*, *42*(1), 35–67. doi:10.2307/2393808

Väänänen-Vainio-Mattila, K., Wäljas, M., Ojala, J., & Segerståhl, K. (2010, April). Identifying drivers and hindrances of social user experience in web services. In *Proceedings of the SIGCHI Conference on Human Factors in Computing Systems* (pp. 2499-2502). 10.1145/1753326.1753704

van de Sand, F., Frison, A. K., Zotz, P., Riener, A., & Holl, K. (2020). The Intersection of User Experience (UX), Customer Experience (CX), and Brand Experience (BX). In *User Experience Is Brand Experience* (pp. 71–93). Springer. doi:10.1007/978-3-030-29868-5_5

Van Riel, A. C., Liljander, V., & Jurriens, P (2001). Exploring customer evaluation of e-services: A portal site. *International Journal of Service Industry Management*, *12*(4), 359–377. doi:10.1108/09564230110405280

Vandekerckhove, P., de Mul, M., Bramer, W. M., & de Bont, A. A. (2020). Generative Participatory Design Methodology to Develop Electronic Health Interventions: Systematic Literature Review. *Journal of Medical Internet Research*, *22*(4), e13780. doi:10.2196/13780 PMID:32338617

VandenBos, G., Knapp, S., & Doe, J. (2001). *Role of reference elements in the selection of resources by psychology undergraduates*. Retrieved from http://jbr.org/articles.html

Velikova, N., Wilcox, J. B., & Dood, T. H. (2011). Designing effective winery Websites: Marketing-oriented versus wine-oriented Website. *The 6th International Conference of the Academy of Wine Business Research.*

Venkatachalam, S. (2014). *Five things that make you an empowered consumer.* https://www.weforum.org/agenda/2014/11/five-things-that-make-you-an-empowered-consumer/

Venkatesh, V., Morris, M. G., Davis, G. B., & Davis, F. D. (2003). User acceptance of information technology: Toward a unified view. *Management Information Systems Quarterly, 27*(3), 425–478. doi:10.2307/30036540

Verčič, A. T., & Verčič, D. (2013). Digital natives and social media. *Public Relations Review, 39*(5), 600–602. doi:10.1016/j.pubrev.2013.08.008

Verhoef, P., Kooge, E., &Walk N., (2016). *Creating Value with Big Data Analytics: Making Smarter Marketing Decisions.* Academic Press.

Verhoef, P. C., Lemon, K. N., Parasuraman, A., Roggeveen, A., Tsiros, M., & Schlesinger, L. A. (2009). Customer Experience Creation: Determinants, Dynamics and Management Strategies. *Journal of Retailing, 85*(1), 31–41. doi:10.1016/j.jretai.2008.11.001

Verisign Domain Name Industry. (2019). *Report Q4-2019.* Retrieved from March 2020 https://www.verisign.com/en_US/domain-names/dnib/index.xhtml

Vickery, G., & Wunsch-Vincent, S. (2007). *Participative web and user-created content: Web 2.0 wikis and social networking. Organization for Economic Cooperation and Development.* OECD.

Victoria. (2016, August 24). *7 benefits of blogging in the classroom.* Retrieved from https://www.teachstarter.com/gb/blog/7-benefits-blogging-classroom-gb

Vieira, M. M., Ferreira, T., & Pappámikail, L. (2018). *Fazer o futuro no presente?* Jovens em condição NEEF e o programa Garantia Jovem.

Vilarinho, T., Floch, J., Oliveira, M., Dinant, I., Pappas, I. O., & Mora, S. (2017, November). Developing a social innovation methodology in the web 2.0 era. In *International Conference on Internet Science* (pp. 168-183). Springer.

Vin et société. (2019). *Key figures of the French wine industry.* Retrieved from: https://www.vinetsociete.fr/chiffres-cles

Viot, C., & Passebois-Ducros, J. (2010). Wine brands or branded wines? The specificity of the French market in terms of the brand. *International Journal of Wine Business Research, 22*(4), 406–422. doi:10.1108/17511061011092438

Vivence, K., & Geoff, A. G. (2020). *Human Capital Management in the Fourth Industrial Revolution. In Human Capital Formation for the Fourth Industrial Revolution.* IGI Global.

Vivian Wagner. (2019). https://www.ecommercetimes.com/story/86012.html

Vuorikari, R., Punie, Y., Gomez, S. C., & Van Den Brande, G. (2016). *DigComp 2.0: The digital competence framework for citizens. Update phase 1: The conceptual reference model.* Retrieved from.

Vygotsky, L. (1978). *Mind in society: The development of higher psychological processes.* Harvard University Press.

Wadhwani, P., & Gankar, S. (2019). *Global eLearning Market Size worth over $300bn by 2025.* Retrieved from https://www.gminsights.com/pressrelease/elearning-market

Wallagher, M. (2015, September 8). *How blogging is being used in the classroom today: Research results.* Retrieved from https://www.emergingedtech.com/2015/09/the-state-of-blogging-in-the-classroom

Walter, O., & Hen, M. (2012). Sherborne Developmental Movement (SDM) teaching model for pre service teachers. *Support for Learning, 27*(1), 20–30.

Wang, Y., & Yang, Y. (2017). How do Organizations Use Social Media to Build Dialogic Relationships? A Comparison between Nonprofit and For-profit Organizations. In B. R. Yook, Y. G. Ji & Z. F. Chen (Eds.), *Proceedings of the 20th International Public Relations Research Conference - "Looking Back, Looking Forward: 20 Years of Developing Theory & Practice"* (pp. 390-401). Academic Press.

Wang, C. L., He, J., & Barnes, B. R. (2017). Brand management and consumer experience in emerging markets: Directions for future research. *International Marketing Review, 34*(4), 458–462. doi:10.1108/IMR-01-2016-0009

Wang, C., Fang, T., & Gu, Y. (2020). Learning performance and behavioral patterns of online collaborative learning: Impact of cognitive load and affordances of different multimedia. *Computers & Education, 143*, 103683. doi:10.1016/j.compedu.2019.103683

Wang, J., Tigelaar, D. E. H., & Admiraal, W. (2019). Connecting rural schools to quality education: Rural teachers' use of digital educational resources. *Computers in Human Behavior, 101*, 68–76. doi:10.1016/j.chb.2019.07.009

Wang, Y., Minor, M., & Wei, J. (2011). Aesthetics and the online shopping environment: Understanding consumer responses. *Journal of Retailing, 87*(1), 46–58. doi:10.1016/j.jretai.2010.09.002

Wang, Y., Rod, M., Deng, Q., & Ji, S. (2020). Exploiting business networks in the age of social media: The use and integration of social media analytics in B2B marketing. *Journal of Business and Industrial Marketing*. Advance online publication. doi:10.1108/JBIM-05-2019-0173

Wang, Y., & Yang, Y. (2020). Dialogic communication on social media: How organizations use Twitter to build dialogic relationships with their publics. *Computers in Human Behavior, 104*, 106183. doi:10.1016/j.chb.2019.106183

Ward, A. F., Duke, K., Gneezy, A., & Bos, M. W. (2017). Brain Drain: The Mere Presence of One's Own Smartphone Reduces Available Cognitive Capacity. *Journal of the Association for Consumer Research, 2*(2), 140–154. doi:10.1086/691462

Warren, C. (2019). *"Soft Skills" are the Essential Skills*. Institute for Health and Human Potencial. Retrieved from https://www.ihhp.com/blog/2019/08/29/soft-skills-are-the-essential-skills/

Warren, K. (1995). The Student-Directed Classroom: A Model for Teaching Experiential Education Theory. In K. Warren (Ed.), *The Theory of Experiential Education* (pp. 249–258). Kendall/Hunt Publishing Company.

Wassim, A. (2019). *Entrepreneurship and Innovation in the Digitalization Era: Exploring Uncharted Territories. In Business Transformations in the Era of Digitalization*. IGI Global.

Waters, R. D., Burnett, E., Lamm, A., & Lucas, J. (2009). Engaging stakeholders through social networking: How nonprofit organizations are using Facebook. *Public Relations Review, 35*(2), 102–106. doi:10.1016/j.pubrev.2009.01.006

Weathers, D., Sharma, S., & Wood, S. L. (2007). Effects of Online Communication Practices on Consumer Perceptions of Performance Uncertainty for Search and Experience Goods. *Journal of Retailing, 83*(4), 393–401. doi:10.1016/j.jretai.2007.03.009

Wedel, M., & Kannan, P. K. (2016). Marketing Analytics for Data-Rich Environments. *Journal of Marketing, 80*(6), 97–121. doi:10.1509/jm.15.0413

WEF. (2018). *The Future of Jobs Report 2018*. Retrieved from Geneva: http://www3.weforum.org/docs/WEF_Future_of_Jobs_2018.pdf

Welter, F. (2012). All you need is trust? A critical review of the trust and entrepreneurship literature. *International Small Business Journal, 30*(3), 193–212. doi:10.1177/0266242612439588

Wenger, E. (1998). *Communities of practice: Learning, meaning and identity*. Cambridge University Press. doi:10.1017/CBO9780511803932

White, K. F., Gurzick, D., & Lutters, W. G. (2009). Wiki anxiety: Impediments to implementing wikis for IT support groups. *Proceedings of the 2009 Symposium on Computer Human Interaction for the Management of Information Technology*, 64. 10.1145/1641587.1641597

Wigfield, A., & Koenka, A. C. (2020). Where do we go from here in academic motivation theory and research? Some reflections and recommendations for future work. *Contemporary Educational Psychology, 101872*. Advance online publication. doi:10.1016/j.cedpsych.2020.101872

Wijaya, S., Spruit, M., Scheper, W., & Versendaal, J. (2011). Web 2.0-based webstrategies for three different types of organizations. *Computers in Human Behavior, 27*(4), 1399–1407. doi:10.1016/j.chb.2010.07.041

Wike, R., & Stokes, B. (2018). *Pew Research Center: In Advanced and Emerging Economies Alike, Worries About Job Automation*. Retrieved from https://www.pewglobal.org/2018/09/13/in-advanced-and-emerging-economies-alike-worries-about-job-automation/?fbclid=IwAR02CjIGbpQ1PNYepFmL6gQaK87w4lAm66EcNMsFDwnXb_dTLJBHRMR6uLY

Wilkinson, A., Forbes, A., Bloomfield, J., & Gee, C. F. (2004). An exploration of four webbased open and flexible learning modules in post-registration nurse education. *International Journal of Nursing Studies, 41*(4), 411–424. doi:10.1016/j.ijnurstu.2003.11.001 PMID:15050852

Williams, A. M. (2015). *Soft Skills perceived by students and employers as relevant employability skills* (Doctoral dissertation). Walden University.

Williamson, O. E. (1998). The economic institutions of capitalism. Firms, markets, relational contracting. *Social Science Electronic Publishing, 32*(4), 61–75.

Wilmer, H. H., Shermann, L. E., & Chein, J. M. (2017). Smartphones and Cognition: A Review of Research Exploring the Links between Mobile Technology Habits and Cognitive Functioning. *Frontiers in Psychology, 8*, 605. doi:10.3389/fpsyg.2017.00605 PMID:28487665

Wilson, A. (2015). *YouTube in the Classroom* (Unpublished Master thesis). The University of Toronto, Toronto, Canada.

Winge, T. M., & Embry, M. C. (2013). Fashion Design Podcast Initiative: Emerging Technologies and Fashion Design Teaching Strategies. In Increasing Student Engagement and Retention Using Mobile Applications: Smartphones, Skype and Texting Technologies. Cutting-Edge Technologies in Higher Education. Volume 6D. Emerald Group Publishing Limited. doi:10.1108/S2044-9968(2013)000006D008

Wong, S. S., & Boh, W. F. (2010). Leveraging the ties of others to build a reputation for trustworthiness among peers. *Academy of Management Journal, 53*(1), 129–148. doi:10.5465/amj.2010.48037265

Woo, A. (2018). *Understanding The Research On Millennial Shopping Behaviors*. https://www.forbes.com/sites/forbesagencycouncil/2018/06/04/understanding-the-research-on-millennial-shopping-behaviors/#82758d75f7ab

Work-Learning Research Inc. (2017). *Definition of MicroLearning*. Retrieved from https://www.worklearning.com/2017/01/13/definition-of-microlearning/

World Economic Forum. (2015). *New Vision for Education: Unlocking the Potential of Technology*. Author.

World Internet Stats. (2020). *Internet Users Distribution in the World – 2020 Q1*. Retrieved from https://www.internetworldstats.com/stats.htm

Worldwide, A. C. I. (2020). *Global eCommerce Retail Sales Up 209 Percent in April.* https://www.aciworldwide.com/news-and-events/press-releases/2020/may/global-ecommerce-retail-sales-up-209-percent-in-april-aci-worldwide-research-reveals

Wu, F., Huang, X., & Jiang, B. (2019). A Data-Driven Approach for Extracting Representative Information From Large Datasets With Mixed Attributes. IEEE Transactions on Engineering Management, 1–17. Advance online publication. doi:10.1109/TEM.2019.2934485

Wu, D. (2020). Empirical study of knowledge withholding in cyberspace: Integrating protection motivation theory and theory of reasoned behavior. *Computers in Human Behavior, 105,* 106229. doi:10.1016/j.chb.2019.106229

Wurdinger, S. D. (2005). *Using Experiential Learning in the Classroom.* ScarecrowEducation.

Xie, H. (2000). Shifts of interactive intentions and information-seeking strategies in interactive information retrieval. *Journal of the American Society for Information Science, 51*(9), 841–857. doi:10.1002/(SICI)1097-4571(2000)51:9<841::AID-ASI70>3.0.CO;2-0

Xu, Z., Fu, Y., Mao, J., & Su, D. (2006, May). Towards the semantic web: Collaborative tag suggestions. In Collaborative web tagging workshop at WWW2006, Edinburgh, UK.

Xu, C., & Zhang, Q. (2019). The dominant factor of social tags for users' decision behavior on e-commerce websites: Color or text. *Journal of the Association for Information Science and Technology, 70*(9), 943.

Yamakami, T. (2007, April). MobileWeb 2.0: Lessons from Web 2.0 and past mobile Internet development. In *2007 International Conference on Multimedia and Ubiquitous Engineering (MUE'07)* (pp. 886-890). IEEE. 10.1109/MUE.2007.155

Yang, C., Hsu, Y.-C., & Tan, S. (2010). Predicting the determinants of users' intentions for using YouTube to share video: Moderating gender effects. *Cyberpsychology, Behavior, and Social Networking, 13*(2), 141–152. doi:10.1089/cyber.2009.0105 PMID:20528269

Yasin, M., Liébana-Cabanillas, F., Porcu, L., & Kayed, R. (2020). The role of customer online brand experience in customers' intention to forward online company-generated content: The case of the Islamic online banking sector in Palestine. *Journal of Retailing and Consumer Services, 52,* 52. doi:10.1016/j.jretconser.2019.101902

Yazid, S., & Zghal, M. (2015). *L'Interactivité en Ligne: un Etat de l'Art.* Le 6ème Colloque de l'URAM (Printemps du Marketing), Hammamet.

Ye, Y., & Lau, K. H. (2018). Designing a demand chain management framework under dynamic uncertainty: An exploratory study of the Chinese fashion apparel industry. *Asia Pacific Journal of Marketing and Logistics, 30*(2), 198–234. doi:10.1108/APJML-03-2017-0042

Ye, Y., Lau, K. H., & Leon, K. Y. T. (2018). Drivers and barriers of omnichannel retailing in China. A case study of the fashion and apparel industry. *International Journal of Retail & Distribution Management, 46*(7), 657–689. doi:10.1108/IJRDM-04-2017-0062

Young, & Rubicam (2017). *The decline of trust.* Academic Press.

Young, J. A. (2017). Facebook, Twitter, and blogs: The adoption and utilization of social media in nonprofit human service organizations. *Human Service Organizations, Management, Leadership & Governance, 41*(1), 44–57. doi:10.1080/23303131.2016.1192574

Youngsoo, K., & Krishnan, R. (2015). On Product-Level Uncertainty and Online Purchase Behavior: An Empirical Analysis. *Management Science, 61*(10), 2281–2547.

Yu, T.-K., Lin, M.-L., & Liao, Y.-K. (2017). Understanding factors influencing information communication technology adoption behavior: The moderators of information literacy and digital skills. *Computers in Human Behavior, 71*, 196–208. doi:10.1016/j.chb.2017.02.005

Zaichkowsky, J. L. (2010). Strategies for distinctive brands. *Journal of Brand Management, 17*(8), 548–560. doi:10.1057/bm.2010.12

Zaltman, G. (2003). How Customers Think: Essential Insights into the Mind of the Market. Academic Press.

Zannettou, S., Sirivianos, M., Blackburn, J., & Kourtellis, N. (2019). The web of false information: Rumors, fake news, hoaxes, clickbait, and various other shenanigans. *Journal of Data and Information Quality, 11*(3), 1–37. doi:10.1145/3309699

Zeithaml, V. A., Parasuraman, A., & Malhotra, A. (2002). Service quality delivery through Web sites: A critical review of extant knowledge. *Academy of Marketing Science Journal, 30*(4), 362–375. doi:10.1177/009207002236911

Zenger, J., & Folkman, J. (2019). *The 3 Elements of Trust.* https://hbr.org/2019/02/the-3-elements-of-trust

Zephaniah, C. O., Ogba, I. E., & Izogo, E. E. (2020). Examining the effect of customers' perception of bank marketing communication on customer loyalty. *Scientific African*, e00383.

Zervas, G., Proserpio, D., & Byers, J. W. (2017). The rise of the sharing economy: Estimating the impact of Airbnb on the hotel industry. *JMR, Journal of Marketing Research, 54*(5), 687–705. doi:10.1509/jmr.15.0204

Zeynali, S., Pishghadam, R., & Hosseini Fatemi, A. (2019). Identifying the motivational and demotivational factors influencing students' academic achievements in language education. *Learning and Motivation, 68*, 101598. doi:10.1016/j.lmot.2019.101598

Zhang, Q., Oo, B. L., & Lim, B. T. H. (2019). Drivers, motivations, and barriers to the implementation of corporate social responsibility practices by construction enterprises: A review. *Journal of Cleaner Production, 210*, 563–584. doi:10.1016/j.jclepro.2018.11.050

Zhang, S., & Schmitt, B. H. (2001). Creating local brands in multilingual international markets. *JMR, Journal of Marketing Research, 38*(3), 313–325. doi:10.1509/jmkr.38.3.313.18869

Zhang, Y., Liu, L., & Ho, S. (2020). How do interruptions affect user contributions on social commerce? *Information Systems Journal, 30*(3), 535–565. doi:10.1111/isj.12266

Zhou, T., Li, H., & Liu, Y. (2010). The system effect of flow experience on mobile SNS users' loyalty. *Industrial Management & Data Systems, 110*(6), 930–946. doi:10.1108/02635571011055126

Zhu, W., Mou, J., & Benyoucef, M. (2019). Exploring purchase intention in cross-border E-commerce: A three stage model. *Journal of Retailing and Consumer Services, 51*(C), 320–330. doi:10.1016/j.jretconser.2019.07.004

Zinger, L., & Sinclair, A. (2013). Using blogs to enhance student engagement and learning in the health sciences. *Contemporary Issues in Education Research, 6*(3), 349–352. doi:10.19030/cier.v6i3.7907

Zucker, L. G. (1986). Production of trust: Institutional sources of economic structure, 1840–1920. *Research in Organizational Behavior, 8*(2), 53–111.

About the Contributors

Jean-Eric Pelet holds a PhD in Marketing, an MBA in Information Systems and a BA (Hns) in Advertising. As an assistant professor in management, he works on problems concerning consumer behaviour when using a website or other information system (e-learning, knowledge management, e-commerce platforms), and how the interface can change that behavior. His main interest lies in the variables that enhance navigation in order to help people to be more efficient with these systems. He works as a visiting professor both in France and abroad (England, Switzerland) teaching e-marketing, ergonomics, usability, and consumer behaviour at Design Schools (Nantes), Business Schools (Paris, Reims), and Universities (Paris Dauphine – Nantes). Dr. Pelet has also actively participated in a number of European Community and National research projects. His current research interests focus on, social networks, interface design, and usability.

* * *

Oryina Akputu holds a B.Sc. (Hons) in Mathematics and Computer Science from the Joseph Tarka University Nigeria, an MSc of Computer Science from the University of Nottingham UK, and a PhD in Computing from Sunway University Malaysia. He is with Ritman University where he heads the Department of Mathematics & Computer Science, and Office of Research and Innovation. Dr. Akputu's research interests span, Pattern Recognition, Signal Processing, Affective Computing, Information Systems, eLearning, and Big Data Analytics.

Kingsley Attai holds an MSc in Computer Science from University of Uyo, Nigeria and B.Sc. (Hons) in Computer Science from All Nations University College, Ghana,where he served as a Teaching Assistant. He is presently an Assistant Lecturer with the Department of Mathematics & Computer Science, Ritman University, Nigeria. His research interest is in wireless communications networks, Big Data Analytics and Information Systems.

Silvia Carter is founder and CEO of ToWebOrNotToWeb, specialized in international digital and multichannel services. With a career in global sales and marketing for technology products (electronics, smart-home, domestic appliances, DIY, etc.), Silvia has worked for both large corporations, such as Technicolor and Archos, and SMEs, such as Okidokeys and MyFOX. With an Executive MBA from HEC Paris, she has a fondness for anything tech, and, with a Master's degree in Web/Multimedia Management and Webmaster from the Digital Campus Paris, she acquired strong digital skills to assist firms in their international web strategy. As a mentor for accelerators in Europe, Silvia also helps startups grow their domestic and international sales through retailers, B2B/OEM distributors, marketplaces and ecommerce across countries and channels. Silvia is also preparing an English translation of her French book Développer son business à l'international grâce au webmarketing (Eyrolles, 2019), which is about how to export more with international web-marketing. When she's not "connected", you can find Silvia spending time with her husband hiking mountains around the world.

Ruxandra Chirca is a PhD lecturer in the field of Computer Assisted Instruction, at the Department for Teacher Training, Faculty of Psychology and Educational Sciences, University of Bucharest, Romania. Her papers published so far approach topics such as learning in the knowledge society, digital natives, new media, information and communication technology or educational platforms and software.

Reinaldo França, B.Sc. in Computer Engineering in 2014, is an Ph.D. degree candidate by Department of Semiconductors, Instruments and Photonics, Faculty of Electrical and Computer Engineering at the LCV-UNICAMP working with technological and scientific research as well as in programming and development in C / C ++, Java and .NET languages. His main topics of interest are simulation, operating systems, software engineering, wireless networks, internet of things, broadcasting, and telecommunications systems.

Coralie Haller completed an MSc in European Business Administration (Burgundy School of Business, France), an MBA and a Graduate Certificate in Higher Education (Griffith University, Australia) and a Master Research (IAE of Aix en Provence, France). After several years of professional experience within various companies and educational environments in France and Australia, she obtained a PhD from Aix-Marseille University. As an associate-professor at EM Strasbourg Business School, her research interests and teaching expertise concern information system management and entrepreneurship in wine and tourism industry. Her work has been published in several journals (Systèmes d'Information et Management, Entreprendre et Innover, International Journal of entrepreneurship and small business, International Business Review), books and academic and professional conferences. Dr Coralie HALLER is currently in charge of the Master of International Wine Management and Tourism (she has created) and the Master in Tourism Management at EM Strasbourg Business School. She is also the founder of a Corporate Chaire in "Wine and Tourism" in partnership with the Alsace Wine Council, Grands Chais de France and a bank, the Crédit Agricole Alsace Vosges. She is also president of Wine and CO^2 and member of Wine Brotherwood Confrérie Saint Etienne, Saint Urbin and Confrérie des Bienheureux du Frankstein.

Gabriel Lazar is an experienced Professor with a demonstrated history of working in the physics, education, and environment protection domains. Skilled in Thin Films, Sustainability, Physics, Engineering, and Spectroscopy. Strong education professional with a Postdoc focused in Solid State Physics from Université de Picardie Jules Verne Amiens, France. Experience as project manager in national and international projects in environmental protection, education management, and e-learning.

Iulia Lazar, PhD in Science Education, is a researcher and university teacher with high reputation through over 27 years of teaching practice in public universities from Romania. Currently, she is involved as expert and coordinator in several international projects implemented by InfoCons Association, Romania and as associate teacher, at Bucharest University, Romania. She has been graduated in Physics

(Bachelor's degree in Engineering Physics) from Bucharest University, Romania and Medicine (Master's degree in Biophysics and Cell Biotechnology) from Carol Davila University of Medicine and Pharmacy, Romania. Also, she has got the scientific habilitation in Science and Environmental Engineering as Associate Professor. This highest qualified attestation of PhD Coordinator in Environmental Engineering was obtained through the Order of the Minister of National Education no. 4104MD/05.07.2013. Obtaining a PhD in Educational Sciences at Bucharest University from Romania, she can offer her knowledge in testing of acceptance use of new digital tools in learning and teaching activities by different types of users. Her present areas of expertise are educational research methodology, statistics, environmental protection, and characterization of living matter.

Chunying Li received her Master's degree in Applied Statistics at Dongbei University of Finance and Economics, Dalian, China in 2019. She was hired by the Bank of China and is currently an audit technique secretary. Her research area is mainly focusing on the sharing economy.

Jialei Li is now a Ph.D. candidate major in Business Management at the School of Business Administration, Dongbei University of Finance and Economics, Dalian, China. His research area is mainly focusing on the sharing economy, marketing strategy, and network organizations. He writes and presents widely on issues of the model and formation mechanisms of sharing economy organizations, and published several papers around these issues.

Benjamin Louis is CEO of SPARKLING, the company manage the top level domain .alsace, a french GeoTLD. He works closely with ICANN and AFNIC to ensure the well-being of .alsace. He has previously worked for the Agence d'Attractivité d'Alsace where he managed and launched the .alsace. He also worked as a consultant for SdV Plurimedia, a French web agency, hosting center. He is a web veteran and has worked in the field since 1998. He is also board member at Afnic.

Adriana Malureanu is a graduate of the National Pedagogical College Gh. Lazăr from Cluj-Napoca, with the specialization teacher-educator and graduate of the Faculty of Sociology and Social Assistance, the Babeş-Bolyai University, the Sociology specialization, has chosen a research and development career within Ascendia, a company specialized in educational software, closely following the accomplishment of several educational projects, educational content for the computer, educational CDs, from pre-school children, to the continuous training of adults. Currently, she is an implementation expert in the project "Innovative services for publishing, publishing, consulting and managing online school textbooks", Operational Program Competitiveness 2014-2020, Priority Axis 2: Information and Communications Technology for a competitive digital economy, Action 2.2.1. Currently, she is a doctoral student at the University of Bucharest, Doctoral School of Education Sciences, with a thesis in the field of Instructional design of teaching material and motivation of learning, the textbook in the age of technology.

Cosmin Mălureanu is the founder and CEO of Ascendia S.A. (www.ascendia.ro), an eLearning solutions company listed on the Bucharest Stock Exchange, a company founded in 2007.

Tao Meng received his doctor's degree in industrial economics from Dongbei University of Finance and Economics, Dalian, China in 2008. He was hired by Dongbei University of Finance and Economics and is currently the professor of International Business College at Dongbei University of Finance and

Economics. He used to charge more than 14 national and provincial projects and grants, and published over 70 papers focused on the peer production, marketing strategy, network organizations, and sharing economy.

Anabela Mesquita is a professor at the School of Accounting and Administration of Porto / Polytechnic of Porto since 1990. She is the Vice Dean of the school since 2007. She is the President of the SPACE European network. She is also a member of the Algoritmi Research Centre (Minho University) and the Director of CICE (Research Centre for Communication and Education). She has been (and is) involved in many European and National research projects both as a researcher and as a coordinator. She has published numerous papers in various international journals and conference proceedings. She is a member of the Programme Committee and Scientific Committee of several national and International conferences, in most cases also as a referee. She serves as Member of the Editorial Board and referee for IGI Global. She also serves as Associate Editor of the Information Resources Management Journal and is co-Editor-in-Chief of the International Journal of Technology and Human Interaction. She has also been evaluator and reviewer for European Commission projects.

Ana Carolina Monteiro is a Ph.D. student at the Faculty of Electrical and Computer Engineering (FEEC) at the State University of Campinas - UNICAMP, where she develops research projects regarding health software with emphasis on the development of algorithms for the detection and counting of blood cells through processing techniques. digital images. These projects led in 2019 to a computer program registration issued by the INPI (National Institute of Industrial Property). She holds a Master's degree in Electrical Engineering from the State University of Campinas - UNICAMP (2019) and graduated in Biomedicine from the University Center Amparense - UNIFIA with a degree in Clinical Pathology - Clinical Analysis (2015). In 2019, he acquired a degree in Health Informatics. Has to experience in the areas of Molecular Biology and management with research animals. Since 2017, she has been a researcher at the FEEC/UNICAMP Visual Communications Laboratory (LCV) and has worked at the Brazilian Technology Symposium (BTSym) as a member of the Organizational and Executive Committee and as a member of the Technical Reviewers Committee. In addition, she works as a reviewer at the Health magazines of the Federal University of Santa Maria (UFSM - Brazil), Medical Technology Journal MTJ (Algeria) and Production Planning & Control (Taylor & Francis). Interested in: digital image processing, hematology, clinical analysis, cell biology, medical informatics, Matlab, and teaching.

Muhammad Zahid Nawaz has previously worked as Marketing and sales capabilities manager in the corporate sector (PepsiCo, Alain Class motors, Dunia finance, Xarasoft footwear and United bank limited). Currently he is a PH. D scholar at the School of Business Administration, Dongbei University of Finance and Economics in China. His main research interests include mobile marketing, social media marketing, consumer behavior, sharing economy, collaborative consumption, and green supply chain management. He has published academic papers in different refereed journals.

Luciana Oliveira, PhD in Communication Sciences and MSc in Multimedia. Has been developing research in the domain of social media analytics for organizational communication development and performance benchmarking as well as on the field of learning analytics. Her work falls under other core areas such as strategic/corporate communications, marketing communications, organisational communications, digital marketing and content marketing. On the domain of learning analytics, she has been working on social network analysis (SNA), sentiment analysis and on the integration of social media platforms and learning management systems.

Ion-Ovidiu Panisoara is Professor, director of the Department of Teacher Education from Faculty of Psychology and Educational Sciences. He coordinates PhDs in Education Sciences Domain at University of Bucharest, Romania. He participated as an expert at international and national seminars and conferences (as moderator, key-speaker and president). Also he is involved in research programs (as director, trainer and evaluator). He actively participates with written contributions and interviews to the academic press.

Arminda Sequeira teaches at Polytechnic of Porto – School of Business and Administration – Organizational Communication Department. PhD (ongoing project) in Strategic and Organizational Communication. Research interests: Strategic Communication, Leadership, Organizational Identity, Institutional Brand, Challenges of 4.0 technology and its social impacts on jobs. Is a member of the Portuguese Society of Communication. Has taken part on several international projects and conferences and published several articles.

Ilenia Vidili is on a mission to help businesses take advantage of the digital revolution and disrupt from within before being disrupted. She believes that delivering exceptional customer experiences is what unlocks the future of businesses. As a researcher, she became fascinated by consumer behavior and brands since her University studies in Cambridge, UK. As a marketer, she developed her knowledge throughout her extensive working experience among a number of start-ups and blue-chip companies in both B2B and B2C. Ilenia is the proud founder of The Smarter Crew (www.thesmartercrew.com), an innovative customer experience consulting company helping businesses worldwide make customer experience their competitive edge.

Index

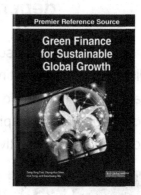

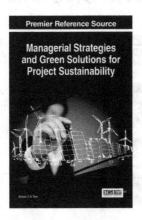

IGI Global Proudly Partners With eContent Pro International

Receive a 25% Discount on all Editorial Services

Editorial Services

IGI Global expects all final manuscripts submitted for publication to be in their final form. This means they must be reviewed, revised, and professionally copy edited prior to their final submission. Not only does this support with accelerating the publication process, but it also ensures that the highest quality scholarly work can be disseminated.

English Language Copy Editing

Let eContent Pro International's expert copy editors perform edits on your manuscript to resolve spelling, punctuaion, grammar, syntax, flow, formatting issues and more.

Scientific and Scholarly Editing

Allow colleagues in your research area to examine the content of your manuscript and provide you with valuable feedback and suggestions before submission.

Figure, Table, Chart & Equation Conversions

Do you have poor quality figures? Do you need visual elements in your manuscript created or converted? A design expert can help!

Translation

Need your documjent translated into English? eContent Pro International's expert translators are fluent in English and more than 40 different languages.

Email: customerservice@econtentpro.com   **www.igi-global.com/editorial-service-partners**